STATE PAPERS OF VERMONT

VOLUME EIGHT

GENERAL PETITIONS

1778-1787

EDWARD A. HOYT

EDITOR

HOWARD E. ARMSTRONG

SECRETARY OF STATE

MONTPELIER   VERMONT

1952

PRINTED IN THE UNITED STATES OF AMERICA
BY THE LANE PRESS, BURLINGTON, VT.

FOREWORD

This eighth volume of the *State Papers of Vermont* is the first of a series containing general petitions and covering the years 1778 through 1799. It is published at the direction of the Secretary of State under the authority vested in him by Number 259 of the Acts of 1912–1913 entitled "An Act to provide for the Publication of State Papers." This statute directs him to prepare for publication certain specified historical documents and "such other of the manuscript records of his office as in his judgement are of general public interest." These manuscript records consist of official documents covering particularly the early years of the state's history and have come to be known as the *Manuscript Vermont State Papers*.

In the preparation of this book the editor has had guidance and assistance from the following persons: Mr. Harrison J. Conant, State Librarian of Vermont; the Honorable Rawson C. Myrick, former Secretary of State; Professor Arthur W. Peach, director of the Vermont Historical Society; Professor Richard A. Newhall of Williams College, civilian consultant to the historical section of the Joint Chiefs of Staff; Mr. Karl L. Trever, editor of The American Archivist; Mr. Henry Howard Eddy, State Records Officer of Pennsylvania; Mr. H. B. Eldred, director of the Robert Hull Fleming Museum, University of Vermont; Miss Helen E. Burbank, Deputy Secretary of State; Miss Ethel Richmond, reference librarian of Williams College; Miss Ethel Knight, cataloguer of the Vermont State Library; Miss Clara E. Follette, librarian of the Vermont Historical Society; Mr. Howard Doyle of the Vermont Purchasing Department; Sergeant Kennith J. Fletcher of the Vermont Department of Public Safety; Mr. Albert J. Gravel, Mr. Proctor Page, Jr. and Mr. Eugene L. Bishop of the Lane Press, Burlington; Mrs. Nancy Hall, editorial transcriber; and Miss Lena Augustoni and Mrs. Emilio Canas, editorial assistants. To each of them grateful acknowledgment is hereby made.

Mrs. Mary G. Nye, former editor of State Papers, has been of invaluable help in many phases of the work. The high standards of her own editing as well as her vast knowledge of Vermont history have been indispensable to the task in hand. Mr. John Clement, vice-president and curator of the Vermont Historical Society, has given freely of his time and deep understanding of Vermont history and editorial technique. He has supplied generous and much needed guidance through the maze of problems, technical and otherwise, which are the essence of all attempts at systematic editing.

This project has been carried out not only at the direction of the present secretary of state, the Honorable Howard E. Armstrong, but with his active interest and support. Without that interest and support it could never have been brought to completion.

TABLE OF CONTENTS

PREFACE ix

GUIDE TO EDITORIAL APPARATUS
    1 TEXTUAL DEVICES xv
    2 ABBREVIATIONS xvi

INTRODUCTION xvii

GENERAL PETITIONS, 1778–1787 3

INDEX 405

The Honorable the Representatives of the Freemen of the State of Vermont to be Conveaned at Rutland on the Second thursday in October next —

The Petition of the Subscribers Inhabitants of of the Town of Windhall in the County of Bennington in Said State, humbly Sheweth. —

That whereas Said Town lies Cituated on the green moun-tain between Manchester & London Derry and much the greater part unsettled — one Road leading from Said London Derry to Manchester through Said Windhall which would be of great Utility to the Publick if were occupied & altered another Road from Townshend to Manchester through Said Windhall which Likewise needs repairing and must be of great Consequence, there is Likewise another Road leading from wardsborough to Manchester there is Likewise a Considerable Number of Streams which need bridging, and the Said Inhabitants being indigent and unable to Occupy and repair Said Roads which renders it almost Impracticable to pass with any kind of Carriage, and which is a great Imbarreement to a Considerable Tract of Country Relitive Transporting their necessary Supplies of Salt grain &c

Your Petitioners therefore humbly pray your Honor to take this our humbly Petition under your wise Consideration and grant relief in the Premises by Granting a Tax of Two pence on Each acre of Land in the Said Town of Windhall (Publick Lands Excepted) for the purpose of working and Repairing Roads and building Bridges in Said Town to be Collected & disposed of by Such Person or Persons as May hereafter be ap-pointed for Said Purpose and your Petitioners as in Duty bound Shall ever Pray. —

Dated at Windhall September 17th 1796 — Nath:el Brown

James Williams   Dudley Day   Ephraim Whitney
                  Joseph Ross   Ebenezer Day
Asa Beebe   Benjamin Ross   Russell Day
Ebenezer Whiting Isaac Williams John   Beriah Wheeler
Gershom Taylor   Ira Taylor   John   Brooks
Asa Beebe Moses Taylor   Adonijah
                                  Oliver Day
Ezra Bigelow   Jonathan Taylor
Moses Day   Jon Day   Benjamin Barr

Facsimile of a typical petition reduced from its original dimensions of 7¾″ x 12⅛″.
(For the printed reproduction of this document, see p. 199, *post*.)

Petition of the
Inhabitants of
Windhall
resolved
Filed 16th Oct.

To the Honoroball General Assembly now sitting
your Comity to whom was referd the Consideration
of the with ~~~~ Petition Beg Leve to report that
they ~~~~~~~~~~~~~~~ the fase being stated & the
Dedication Proved that t: ther oppinion that
the Prayer of the Petition be granted under such
restrictions as in your Wisdom think Proper
Dated Rutland 23th oct.r 1786   Eben'r Allen for the Com'e.

In General Assembly Oct.r 23d 1786
the above report read and accepted and leave given the petitioners
to bring in a bill accordingly —   attest Ros'r Hopkins Clerk

Endorsements on the reverse side.

PREFACE

THE content, organization and editorial technique of this volume require full explanation. Like any other similar work, it proposes to present a definable unit of historical material systematically arranged, properly related to other sources, and edited textually so as to be intelligible.

The title, "General Petitions, 1778–1787," is obviously not a complete definition of the contents. There are published in these pages petitions addressed to the General Assembly, to the Governor, to the Council, to combinations of these authorities, and to the Council of Censors. The broad category employed is that of petitions addressed to all possible state authorities except the Superior or Supreme Court.

Of these petitions only those not already printed in the text of some previous volume of the *State Papers of Vermont* are published herein. Many of these documents have already been printed in this series: volume V contains petitions for land; volume VI those concerned with the sequestration, confiscation and sale of Tory estates; and volume III (the Assembly journal) the complete transcription of a few miscellaneous ones. These have *not* been republished here. However, all others now located in the *Manuscript Vermont State Papers* in the office of the Secretary of State have been included. Although most of these have been found in volume XVII of that collection, several have been located in other volumes.

The documents within these pages do not, of course, comprise all those actually drawn up and presented to authority. Many were doubtless misplaced at the time of their presentation, and others have been lost since that time. Most of those addressed to the Governor and Council have been destroyed or are missing along with many of the other papers belonging to that body. As a result, the great majority of the petitions included in this volume were addressed to the General Assembly. Even these do not include all that were originally in existence. An inspection of the Assembly journal indicates that many actually presented cannot now be located, particularly those dated prior to 1785. Nevertheless, fewer are missing for the years 1785 through 1787, and those remaining for that period may be taken as representative of the whole number originally in existence.

Under the broad head of petitions there are published here not only documents so entitled but addresses, memorials, representations, and remonstrances. These terms were loosely and almost interchangeably employed in the eighteenth century. At least so it appears. In any case, all of these documents were formal requests to some authority or other for action, and they thus comprise a unity of historical material.

The items printed in these pages are arranged chronologically according to the date on which they were drawn up. When the date is not indicated, as it often is not, the petition is placed at the beginning of the month in which by its content and other evidence it appears to belong.

A general title composed by the editor is placed at the head of each petition· This is intended to give a broad idea of its contents. The student who prefers to inspect the volume page by page may thus be enabled to decide whether or not he will read the whole document. Immediately under the title are the volume and page where the manuscript petition will be found in the *Manuscript Vermont State Papers*. The originals of all the petitions printed in these pages are found in that collection.

Certain additional material is printed in this volume along with the main documents. Almost all of the original manuscripts carry or are accompanied by such material. It is often located on the reverse side, but is sometimes found on separate papers. It consists both of writings added to the petition prior to its presentation to authority and of notations of the action taken upon it thereafter. The former are ordinarily printed herein as part of the main document, while the latter when transcribed, are usually placed immediately after it between two symbols of this order: — *&* —. When, as in some cases, the manuscript contains only the text of the petition, indication of this is made by the words "No Additional Material" in brackets between the two symbols. On occasion the reverse of the manuscript contains repetitious, irrelevant and unintelligible writings. These are silently omitted from the transcription.

The notations on the manuscript of the action taken by authority on any petition are not printed in these pages when there is a substantially equivalent record of them printed in volume III (four parts) or volume IV of the *State Papers of Vermont* or in the first three volumes of the *Records of the Governor and Council*. That is to say, when the progress of a petition through the Assembly and the Council, including committee reports thereon, is recorded in any of these volumes, the notations of this progress on the petition itself are not transcribed. An ellipsis followed by an asterisk is employed to indicate their omission. This asterisk refers to other asterisks which precede entries in the subjoined note immediately following the transcribed text. These entries in turn refer to the printed equivalent of the omitted notations. Any significant differences between the record on the manuscript petition and that in the printed references are covered by footnotes. From this practice it follows, of course, that whenever the notations on the manuscript are not found in the printed volumes, they are transcribed here in full.

Following such additional material as is copied from the manuscript, there is the subjoined note. This note, printed in smaller type, is composed by the editor and is not based on the manuscript sources. It consists of entries which take note of all the items in the *State Papers of Vermont* series and the *Records of the Governor and Council* that concern the action taken on the petition or in apparent consequence of it by the Assembly or the Council. It does not include material which is descriptive or explanatory of the text. Material of that sort is covered by the usual form of footnote annotation.

The entries in the subjoined note are a resumé or brief description of the actions taken on the petition. They include the record, if any, of the passage of

legislation in response to its prayer. But they are only a resumé, and the scholar in case of need should consult the printed volumes to which reference is made. The entries in the note are taken first from the Assembly journal, next from the reports of the committees, and finally from the Council journal. Within these groups they are arranged chronologically.

As has already been noted, if the action taken is also recorded on the manuscript petition and omitted from the transcription, this is indicated by an asterisk immediately before the entry. By observing these asterisks the reader may easily fill in the substance of the material which has been left uncopied.

If the printed sources contain no record of any action, the words "No Record" in brackets comprise the subjoined note. It will be observed that many of these notes are obviously incomplete; that is, the record of certain actions is missing. In this connection it must be kept in mind that the early journals of the Assembly and of the Council are themselves incomplete, many of the actions which those bodies are known to have taken never having been recorded therein.

The usual form of annotation is employed through footnotes which are keyed to the text by means of superscript numerals. These notes concern any matter descriptive or explanatory of the text. They may refer to the peculiar condition of the original manuscript; they may simply explain one of its terms; they may refer to other related material in this volume; or they may refer to other sources, printed or in manuscript, which may throw light on the meaning of these documents. In this connection it should be noted that there are in these pages a great many footnote references to the *Manuscript Laws of Vermont* (*Ms. Laws of Vt.*). Although such references are unavoidable due to the absence of any printed alternative, they constitute a serious limitation on the value of this work. However, it is intended that at some future date these manuscript laws will be published (with the original pagination noted) as a part of the *State Papers of Vermont* series. This will, of course, make generally available an otherwise restricted source.

No purely biographical data is included in the footnotes. It would be a vast and impossible undertaking to supply such data for all the names, obscure and otherwise, included in this volume. The persons prominent in the state's history for these years are well covered biographically in the previous volumes of this series and in the *Records of the Governor and Council*. Genealogies and town histories will supply information for the more obscure.

Within the obvious limitations imposed by the transcription of handwritten manuscript into type, the original documents have been reproduced here as exactly as possible. The spelling and capitalization have been left unaltered in all cases regardless of errors and variations from modern practice, of which there are a vast number. Punctuation remains as in the original — except for the dash and superfluous periods. A single standard dash is employed to represent one or more dashes of any length in the original, and those used in the manuscript to fill in space at the end of a line are omitted entirely. Parentheses, braces and other special forms

GENERAL PETITIONS 1778–1787

of punctuation are copied from the original, while brackets are introduced in the course of the editing. Wherever reasonable doubt arises as to the spelling, capitalization, or punctuation actually intended, modern practice is followed.

Other matters in connection with the transcription require brief mention. The accidental or unnecessary repetition of words is silently omitted. The paragraphing as indicated by indenting or otherwise has been followed as closely as doubtful and peculiar cases have allowed. All words underlined in the manuscript are printed in italics. Raised letters, as in Honble and Junr, etc., are kept, although the periods and dashes which often subtend such letters are omitted due to the difficulties these present to the printer. The lines and marks which on occasion cover certain letters are likewise omitted for the same reason. The old style s (ʃ) is copied as the modern letter.

The doubtful and peculiar aspects of the text are indicated and corrected through the employment of various editorial devices and marks. Wherever the misspelling or abbreviation of a word creates serious doubt as to its meaning, its correct and full spelling is, if possible, inserted in square brackets [ ] immediately after it. The same correction is made only once, however, in the same document. If the word inserted in square brackets is itself doubtful, it is followed by a question mark within the brackets. In those instances where the absence of correct punctuation baffles an ordinary effort to understand the text, possible punctuation marks are added in square brackets.

It is obvious that the transcription of old and handwritten manuscript involves of necessity a certain amount of conjecture. When, due to the obscurity of the writing or the destruction or erasure of a small portion of the text, conjecture is demanded, the hazarded word or words are enclosed in square brackets. If the conjecture is itself doubtful, it is followed by a question mark within the brackets. This duplicate employment of the square bracket can scarcely result in confusion, since in the case mentioned in the previous paragraph the word is clearly a substitution for the word that precedes it and in this case it is a possible continuation of its predecessors.

At times, due to the destruction, inaccessibility, or illegibility of a considerable portion of the manuscript, conjecture is impossible. When one or two words cannot be conjectured, they are indicated by three suspension points in square brackets [. . .] if at the beginning or in the middle of a sentence, and by four points [. . . .] if at the end. When more than two words cannot be conjectured, the same devices are employed, and a footnote is appended to estimate the number of words missing or to explain the absence of text.

On a few occasions it was clear to the editor that some essential word or words were omitted in the original due to an error on the part of the writer. Such words are inserted in italics in square brackets. Similarly omitted numbers and parentheses are also inserted in italics in square brackets.

In some instances the words in print will appear to the reader to be possible

errors in transcription and not true representations of the original. This doubt occurs usually in cases of bizarre spelling and word usage. Wherever reasonable doubt as to the accuracy of the transcription might arise, the questionable word is followed by *sic* in italics in square brackets.

In only one circumstance are crossed out or erased words included or noted in the text. This is where such words indicate clearly that the writer or some other person acting for him changed his intention or meaning. In this case the crossed out words or those erased, if legible, are placed in angle brackets < >. If the words are doubtful, they are followed by a question mark within the angle brackets. Words which are inked out and are illegible are passed over in silence, and words which are legible and obviously inked out because of misspelling or slips of the pen are similarly treated.

For the most part insertions in the original text are simply included silently in the transcription. In the case of the petitions it is usually impossible to determine exactly when an insertion has been made, that is, whether at the time of the first writing or at some later time. Consequently an insertion need not involve a change of intent or meaning but may be simply a correction of an omission made at the time of writing. In that case it has little or no significance. Blank spaces in the midst of the writing are also passed over in silence, unless they clearly have significance in the context. In that case they are indicated by the word "Blank" in square brackets.

Only when insertions are clearly in a different hand from that of the body of the text, are they noted as such. Short of advice from handwriting experts, it is extremely difficult to be sure that another hand has been employed. The petitions are written in almost as many hands as there are documents, and acquaintance with any one hand is thus rather brief. However, in the rare cases where there is no reasonable doubt that another hand has made the insertions, the words are placed in small brackets [ ].

An attempt has been made to maintain as much as possible the original order of the names which are appended to the petitions. In many cases they are very numerous, and it is often impossible, due to the erratic location of the signatures on the manuscript to determine exactly what the order is. In most cases, however, the first ten or twelve names can be identified as such. It is these names that are of the most importance, since they are ordinarily those of the sponsors of the petition. In the handwritten original these are usually at the *right* of the page, and the remaining names are located in various other places. In this transcription the names (when there are more than ten or so) are evened off in columns and placed according to their apparent order in the regular sequence of reading by column from *left* to right. This is done in the interest of economy as well as legibility.

Certain cautions to the scholar are necessary in the matter of the names. In the first place, absolute confidence cannot be placed in the meaning of their arrangement in print. The editor's judgment as to their order may be at fault. Sec-

ondly, the presence of any name appended to a petition does not necessarily indicate that that person actually signed the document. From the originals it is clear that many names were often written in by the same hand. This was done presumably with the consent of the persons involved, but in any case it cannot be properly said that they signed the document. Consequently, whenever the order of the names or their actual signature is a vital question, the scholar should consult the original.

Similar caution is necessary in the matter of the actual composition and writing of any petition. In some cases it appears that the signer or signers of a document did not write it, and in others it is probable that they did not compose it. Whenever the actual composition or writing of the petition is an important issue, the student should, as in the case of the names, inspect the original manuscript.

GUIDE TO EDITORIAL APPARATUS

1. TEXTUAL DEVICES

[ ]   Conjectured words or correct spelling of misspelled and abbreviated words, whichever the context indicates.

[?]   Doubtful corrections or conjectures as above.

[,]   Possible punctuation inserted to clarify a difficult text.

[. . .]   One or two words missing and not conjecturable at the beginning or in the middle of a sentence.

[. . . .]   One or two words missing and not conjecturable at the end of a sentence.

[. . .]¹ [. . . .]¹   More than two words missing and not conjecturable. A footnote keyed to the superscript numeral estimates the number of words missing or explains the absence of words.

[*italics*]   Words omitted in the manuscript through error, but clearly intended.

[5] [)]   Number or parenthesis omitted similarly but clearly intended.

[*sic*]   Confirmation of the accuracy of the transcription.

< >   Words crossed out or erased in the manuscript which show a change of intent or meaning.

< ?>   Doubtful words as above.

[ ]   Words inserted in the manuscript by a hand certainly other than that of the rest of the text.

[Blank]   Significant blank spaces in the manuscript.

xvii, 35   Volume and page of the *Manuscript Vermont State Papers* where the original documents printed in this volume are located.

— & —   Symbols preceding and following the material which is in addition to the body of the petition and which concerns for the most part the action taken upon it by authority.

[No Additional Material]   No material of the sort described above found on the manuscript.

...*   An ellipsis with an asterisk indicates additional material not transcribed from the manuscript but found in the printed volumes of the *State Papers of Vermont* or the *Records of the Governor and Council.* The material in these volumes is summarized in those entries in the subjoined note which are preceded by another asterisk.

[No Record]   No record of any action taken by authority on the petition recorded in the printed volumes of the *State Papers of Vermont* or of the *Records of the Governor and Council.*

2. ABBREVIATIONS

A. J.   Assembly Journal (*S. P. of Vt.*, III, Parts I, II, III, and IV).

C. J.   Council Journal (*G. and C.*, I, II, and III).

G. and C.   Records of the Governor and Council of the State of Vermont. 8 vols. Montpelier, 1873-1880.

Ms. Laws of Vt.   A Record of the Acts and Laws of the State of Vermont in America. Binder's Title: Laws of Vermont. These volumes are the engrossed manuscript laws and are located in the office of the Secretary of State, Montpelier.

Ms. Vt. S. P.   Manuscript Vermont State Papers, located in the office of the Secretary of State, Montpelier.

Ms. Vt. S. P. — Laws   Those volumes of the above collection which contain the original acts as distinguished from the engrossed laws.

Rep. of Com.   Reports of Committees to the General Assembly . . . 1778-1801 (*S. P. of Vt.*, IV).

Slade   Vermont State Papers . . . Compiled and published by William Slade, Jun., Secretary of State. Middlebury, 1823.

S. P. of Vt.   State Papers of Vermont (printed series). 7 vols. Montpelier, 1918-1947.

Vt. Rev. Rolls   The State of Vermont: Rolls of the Soldiers in the Revolutionary War 1775 to 1783. Rutland, 1904.

INTRODUCTION

Eᴀʀʟʏ in its history Vermont, like several of the other American states, made
constitutional provision for the establishment of the right of petition. The first
constitution adopted in 1777 and copied almost verbatim after the Pennsylvania
document of the previous year declared "That the people have a right . . . to apply
to the legislature for redress of grievances, by address, petition or remonstrance."
In addition, it specifically empowered the legislature to "redress grievances."[1]

When this constitution was drawn up, the right of petition had long been
established in principle and in practice both in England and in America. It had
developed along with democratic and representative institutions. In the seventeenth
century it was on several occasions declared to be "an inherent right" of the English
subject, and the Bill of Rights adopted immediately after the Revolution of 1688
enshrined it in the English constitution. Nor was the right without exercise. Both
parliament and the colonial assemblies received and acted upon a vast number of
petitions dating from their earliest days.

The events leading up to American independence were the occasion for a
reaffirmation of this right. Petition was employed by the colonists in their con-
troversy with the mother country over the issue of taxation. First the Stamp Act
Congress and later the Continental Congress petitioned the authorities in England,
including the crown, for redress of their grievances. Their prayers were ignored.
As the Declaration of Independence put it, "In every stage of these Oppressions
We have petitioned for redress in the most humble terms. Our repeated Petitions
have been answered only by repeated injury." The failure of the British government
to give any consideration at all to the colonial petitions could only renew the
American devotion to this right when the imperial tie was broken and independence
finally maintained.

The right of petition had a new birth in the principles of the American Revolution and in the spirit which pervaded them. In substance it was the opportunity for
persons not only to seek redress of grievances but to further their rights and interests by presenting their requests to proper authority. When it is proposed
absolutely that all government derives its powers from the consent of the governed
and that all men are endowed with the unalienable rights of life, liberty and the
pursuit of happiness, the right of petition becomes absolutely indispensable. In his
"Commentaries on the Constitution of the United States" Justice Story voiced
this view in a discussion of the provision of the first amendment which secures
"the right of the people peaceably to assemble and to petition the government for
a redress of grievances." Commenting on this provision Story declared that "This

---

1. For these quotations from the Vermont constitution, see *G. and C.*, I, 95–96.

would seem unnecessary to be expressly provided for in a republican government, since it results from the very nature of its structure and institutions."[1]

The very idea of the petition was confirmed by the spirit of Reason, the rationalism of the eighteenth century, which was the essence of the American Revolution. The right to address public authority and present an argument for certain rights and interests is, as it were, the gentlest of the civil liberties. Petition is in the form of a prayer and is unaccompanied by any threat of action in case its request is refused. It rests its case on the strength of its reason. The moral and intellectual frame of reference which the Revolution created gave impetus to this form of contact between government and people.

The provision in the Vermont constitution of 1777 was thus not original but was the product of English and colonial history and of the contemporary American political environment. Vermont was settled almost exclusively from New England and like any other American community was the child of English institutions. It was likewise the child of the American Revolution — and in a double sense. It not only joined in the revolt against Great Britain but established itself as a separate state in revolt against the jurisdiction of New York. The revolutionary spirit, which was national in its scope, fathered the institutions of Vermont as surely as it fathered those of the other states.

The role of the petition as a device in the political life of the eighteenth century was largely informational. On the one hand, it was a means whereby the citizen might make his needs and desires known, and, on the other, a means whereby the government might learn of those needs and desires. The great avenues of information, such as the press, political parties and lobbies, then existed, if they existed at all, only in embryo. To a great degree petitions fulfilled their function.

In assessing the use of this device certain general factors about this period of American history must be kept in mind. In the first place, government had a more passive role at that time than it now has. It proposed to "secure" the rights and interests of the citizen but not to promote them actively. The present day departments of government with their positive responsibility for the welfare of the citizen simply did not exist. Secondly, the representative tended to act out of his own judgment rather than out of the immediate interests of his constituents. And finally, government was, in spite of the American Revolution, still to some extent viewed in the traditional way as superior to the ordinary citizen. Its favor had thus to be supplicated. With these factors in mind the use of the petition in this period becomes intelligible, and its relative absence in our own time equally so.

During the years 1778 through 1787 — the years covered by this volume — receiving and dealing with petitions took up well over half of the time of the General Assembly and the Governor and Council. The journals of those bodies make it evident that a very large share of their business comprised the reading of such

---

1. See Fifth Edition of the "Commentaries" (Boston, 1891), Sections, 1893–1894.

papers, the appointment of committees to report on them, the consideration of the reports, and the passage of legislation in response to them. Somewhere in the neighborhood of one thousand were presented to the Assembly alone during this ten year period. By the use of petition the citizen thus had a direct part in the initiation of a large share of the legislation of the time.

There was undoubtedly a standard procedure employed in dealing with these documents. Most of this procedure may be described from known facts, while the remainder must be surmised. Prior to its presentation to the Assembly — the great majority of such papers were addressed to that body — each petition had to be filed with the Secretary of State.[1] The date of this filing was ordinarily entered on the reverse side of the document. Some sort of record of each petition was kept in the Secretary of State's office, as other entries on the reverse side of the actual manuscripts themselves indicate.[2] The full text may have been transcribed, although this seems very doubtful. Certainly the date of filing and possibly the progress of the paper through the Assembly were noted in some register kept for that purpose.

Having been filed, the petition could then begin its course through the Assembly. The first step was the reading of the document. Although no conclusive evidence has been found to indicate it, there is no reason to doubt that the clerk of the Assembly rather than a member did the actual reading. If the prayer was not thereupon dismissed, it was ordinarily either granted or referred to a committee. If it was granted, leave was then given to bring in a bill in accordance with its desires. If it was referred to a committee, a report would later be submitted for the approval of the house. If this report was favorable in whole or in part and was accepted by the Assembly, leave was granted to bring in a bill accordingly. The bill when presented followed the ordinary course of legislation. Although petitions were on occasion withdrawn by the petitioners, and others were allowed "to lie on the table" or "referred to the next session", most of them usually pursued their course to dismissal or approval and legislation.

To all appearances the General Assembly welcomed petitions and placed few obstacles, technical or otherwise, in the way of their consideration. On certain occasions, indeed, specific provision was made for them to be addressed to the house. For instance, such provision was made in favor of towns doomed by the legislature[3] and in behalf of persons who had actively opposed the authority of

---

1. See the resolution passed by the Assembly 22 Oct. '79 (*S. P. of Vt.*, III (I), 87).

2. Many of the manuscripts carry on their reverse side such entries as "Recorded vol 2ᵈ page 87", "See page 79 vol 2ᵈ", or simply the word "Entered" alone. These entries appear, for the most part, to be in the same hand for all the documents. The volumes to which they refer are not now among the *Ms. Vt. S. P.*

3. Provision was made that towns doomed by the legislature — i. e. towns whose property valuation had been arbitrarily fixed by the legislature for purposes of taxation — could appeal for relief from any over-valuation. See "An Act for the purpose of procuring Provisions for the Troops, to be employed in the service of this State, for the year ensuing." (*Slade*, 407–411).

Vermont and supported New York jurisdiction in the southeastern part of the state.[1] As far as any evidence indicates, only a few petitions were refused consideration or dismissed on the ground of their being in improper form.[2] As the manuscripts themselves show, documents were received and considered which had interlineations and corrections in a hand obviously other than that of the petitioner. Others were similarly acted upon which were signed not by the persons whose names were appended but by one person in their behalf. Such irregular practices were not ordinarily allowed by legislative bodies. The deletion from the documents on occasion of slanderous remarks suggests that some limitation may have been placed on abusive language, even though this was not rigidly or consistently enforced.

Except for the period prior to October, 1782 no fees were charged for the filing of the ordinary general petition. Even during these years the fees were small and were increased only to cover the depreciation of the currency.[3] In fact, on one occasion when other fees were raised to take account of this depreciation, those for the filing of petitions were specifically excepted.[4] After October, 1782, only those petitions which concerned legal disputes "between party and party" and those for grants of land were required to pay any filing fee at all: the former eight pence and the latter one shilling.[5] Beginning in 1780, the former were also required to pay an additional fee of one pound, originally to the General Assembly and later to the Secretary of State for the use of the Treasurer.[6]

The vast majority of the petitions presented to the Assembly during these years were private in nature, as that term has been applied historically to such documents. That is to say, their object was to secure some particular benefit for the petitioner or petitioners. Accordingly they belonged to this category even though such benefit was to accrue to a town or a county and was not confined to a private person or group of persons. A few of the petitions were public, however, and sought some general advantage or the redress of broad grievances in which the petitioner had no special interest beyond that of every citizen.

The petitions for a tax on land to build roads and bridges and other public works and those for the right to sell real property to settle an estate require special consideration. The former are by far the most numerous class of petitions to be found in this volume, while the latter are very common. Peculiar circumstances occasioned them.

---

1. Encouragement was given to New York adherents to petition for pardon and reinstatement as citizens of Vermont. See *S. P. of Vt.*, III (II), 209–210.

2. For examples of such action, see *S. P. of Vt.*, III (I), 171; also *Ibid*, IV, 30(2), and p. 158, *post*. Unfortunately where a petition was simply read and dismissed without receiving further consideration, the reason for the dismissal was not ordinarily given in the Assembly journal.

3. For these fees and their increase, see *Slade*, 318, 390, 391, 401.

4. For this occasion, see *S. P. of Vt.*, III (I), 16.

5. For these fees, see *Slade*, 465.

6. For this fee, see *Slade*, 401, 465.

The necessity for the petitions for a land tax arose from the fact that under the law unimproved lands — unlike improved holdings — could not be given any valuation in the compilation of the grand list.[1] In consequence these lands were not subject to taxation by any town without the specific authorization of the legislature. The need for public works was very great and the amount of unimproved land was large. As a result an impossibly heavy prospect of taxes was faced by those who had improved their holdings — that is, the actual residents of the towns. A petition to the legislature for the power to tax *all* land or unimproved land was thus the only possible answer to the situation. In this connection it may be noted that most of the unimproved lands were owned by non-resident proprietors and consequently came to be identified with them. However, the need for special legislation did not arise out of the fact that the owners of these lands were non-residents but out of the fact that the lands were unimproved.

The petitions for the right to sell real property to settle an estate were a direct consequence of a provision of "An Act for the settlement of testate and intestate estates" passed by the legislature in February, 1779.[2] One section of this act required the administrator of an estate to obtain the permission of the General Assembly or of "the judge finding the estate insolvent" before the sale of any real property. In other words, in the administration of estates a distinction between real and personal property, which already existed in the common law, was established by statute.

This distinction, like so many other elements of the common law, had its origins in the feudal system of land tenure. Under this system land was not held in absolute ownership but by purely voluntary grant from the feudal lord in return for services and duties. On the death of the holder or tenant the land reverted to the lord, and neither a creditor nor an heir was entitled to it. Land passed to an heir not by descent but by renewed grant. It thus followed that feudal grants could not be taken for the debts of the tenant.

The break-up of the feudal system saw a change in the status of the heir in this respect but not in that of the creditor. Statute law secured the unconditional descent of lands from the ancestor to the heirs without the intervention of the lord. Yet the creditors were still not allowed to subject lands in the hands of heirs to the satisfaction of their claims against the ancestor. In brief, absolute ownership was transferred from the feudal lord to the heir. In consequence the administrator,

---

1. For this provision, see "An Act directing Listers in their office and duty" passed February, 1779 (*Slade*, 295–298). In October, 1781 the Assembly passed "An Act enabling the inhabitants of the several towns to tax the lands, within their respective towns, for certain cases therein mentioned" — that is, "for the purpose of building houses for public worship, school houses, and bridges" (*Slade*, 440). However, this act was repealed a year later 24 Oct. '82 (*Ms. Laws of Vt.*, I, 264).

2. See *Slade*, 339–346.

whose main function was to pay the creditors of an estate, had no interest in its lands.[1]

In passing the act of 1779 concerning the settlement of estates with its provision in regard to real property, the Vermont Assembly was maintaining a distinction between personal and real property which the feudal system had originated. The maintenance of this distinction long after feudal tenure ceased to exist may well be attributable to the fact that in the eighteenth century land both in England and America was still the greatest source of wealth and livelihood.

It may be noted here that the revision of the Vermont laws adopted in 1787 took this matter out of the hands of the Assembly. A new act empowered the probate court alone to authorize the sale of real property to settle an estate.[2] This change, of course, put an end to petitions of this sort to the Assembly.[3]

The documents published in these pages contain a wide variety of historical data. Those who drew them up seldom confined themselves to a simple request but often went into considerable detail about the reasons for their prayer. The reasons involved a description of the circumstances which occasioned the request, and these circumstances frequently covered a wealth of detail, some of which was only remotely related, if at all, to the object of the petition. The following are among the facts of historical interest which are found in this volume: the location of roads, bridges and interstate ferries; the amount and nature of highway traffic including the commodities carried; the wages of those who worked on the roads; the price or value of land, cattle, crops and such miscellaneous items as board and room, fire wood and candles; the details of incidents and service in the American Revolution; the manner of the pay and supply of the Vermont troops; the location of county court houses; the details of the dispossession of settlers because of land disputes; the manner of conducting elections; and so forth. In addition to the material found in the body of the documents, there were in many cases numerous names appended to them. These names are thereby located in terms of time and place.

The material in this volume will give some idea of the literacy and characteristics of the early Vermonter. As has already been noted in the *Preface*, the spelling and punctuation have been left unaltered in the transcription. This makes it possible not only to assess the general level of literacy but to note those petitions which are distinguished for their correctness of spelling and punctuation as well as for their refinement of style. By and large the spelling was naturally very poor and disclosed the crudity of a frontier community. Yet even the most ignorant com-

---

1. For a consideration of this whole problem, see J. G. Woerner, *A Treatise on the American Law of Administration (Including Wills)*, Third Edition. (Boston, 1923) vol. I, pp. 13-18.

2. For this act, see *Statutes of the State of Vermont, passed by the Legislature in February and March 1787* (Windsor, 1787), p. 57.

3. For printed samples of acts passed in response to both petitions for special settlement of an estate and those for a tax on land, see *Slade*, 460, 509.

positions possessed a peculiar dignity of style that marked them as the work of respectful and confident minds. In many cases the spellings were obviously phonetic. An excellent idea of the way words were pronounced at this period can thus be obtained from a careful perusal of these pages.

The petitions not only supply simple historical data but also yield insight into the problems of the early Vermont community. Among these problems were the following: the opening up of travel and communication, the land disputes resulting from conflicting grants and inadequate surveys, the readjustment of town and county lines to meet the demands of topography, the location of the shire or county towns, the depreciation of the currency, the administration of justice under frontier conditions, the establishment of religious organizations and educational institutions, the inclusion of certain New York towns within the boundaries of Vermont, the grant of special favors to infant industries, the relief of debtors, and the redress of public grievances against the economic, religious and political structure of the state.

The pages of this volume will bear study as well as search. Many statements within them have broad and significant historical implications, and these are of a sort which usually defy indexing. These petitions obviously were not drawn up with any thought in mind that they would be studied. They were only intended to attain some particular immediate objective. Consequently what they disclose unconsciously and non-deliberately, by the way and apart from their argument and pleading, may be accepted as historical revelation of the very first order.

Examples will serve to illustrate the point. One petitioner, in connection with her desire to settle her husband's estate after several years delay, declared by way of preface to her prayer that in the early years of settlement prior to the establishment of the Vermont government "there was no Law in force within the limits of this State."[1] Such a statement, considered with other evidence, has vast importance to the history of the early settlements on the New Hampshire Grants. In another instance, certain petitioners, seeking compensation for Revolutionary services, averred by way of conclusion that they "have ever Esteemed themselves happier on account of their being Citizens of this Free and Independent State than they could possibly have been had they been Citizens of any other of the United States."[2] The significant implications of this statement are that the petitioners, although they assumed Vermont to be a "Free and Independent State," also assumed it to be one "of the United States", and that furthermore they had no hesitation in disclosing this assumption in a document addressed to the Vermont legislature and seeking its favor. Such implications have great bearing on the question of the actual status of Vermont prior to its admission to the Union in 1791. Both these examples, like

---

1. For the full text of this petition, see p. 55, *post.*
2. For the full text of this petition, see p. 291, *post.*

others that might be given, provide historical insights which long and careful research in simple facts might never completely reveal.

In a similar way there will be found in these pages revelations of the mood and tendency of the Vermont community as a whole. Coming as they did from a great number of ordinary citizens in all parts of the state and thus having their origins, so to speak, in the grass roots, the petitions spoke the public mind from its very foundations. The broad objectives, the uncriticized assumptions, to which many of these documents appealed for sanction of what they sought in particular, thus constituted the mood and temper — the basic frame of reference — of the Vermont community.

As far as the evidence in this volume is indicative, the prevalent objective was the settlement and development of the state. It was to this frame of reference that appeal was most commonly made in justifying prayers for legislative action. On numerous occasions it was held that a proposed measure would "Incourage the Settlement of a New Country", and there were frequent references to the development of "a new and rising state." Such was the paramount aim which emerged from the great confusions and uncertainties of Vermont's early history. And such, of course, was one of the basic purposes of the whole American community.

Montpelier, Vermont   EDWARD A. HOYT
10 October 1951

GENERAL PETITIONS
1778-1787

STATE OF VERMONT
General Petitions, 1778-1787

FOR COMPENSATION FOR WAR SERVICES
xvii, 7

Damiges Sustained to Jonathan Chipman of Middeleberry by his hors being Taken to goe and express at the Time of the Fight at Shelburn[1] the hors being Detained Seven Weaks by Reason of the freshets in the Creek and other Storms it Being Empossabel to git the hors away and likewise the money Paid for Keeping the hors when Detained and the hire of the hors

Middal [sic] 27 March 1778

Hors hire 30 miles	0 . . 15 . . 0
Money Paid for Keeping the hors when Detained }	3 . . . 0 . . 0
Damages for the hors Being Detained }	3 . . . 0 . . 0

£ 6 . . 15 . . 0

Jonathan Chipman Humbley Pray that your Exelency Will be Pleased to heair and Consider the Contents of the above Bill and if in your Wisdom Can think fit To alow the Same or aney Part Theair of your Humbel Potisinor Shall Receive the Same with Grait thankfullness as I am Poor and Neady and Stand in Nead of all that is my Just Right as I subscribe my self your Humble Servant

Jonathan Chipman

Head^{qrs} Rutland Nov^{br} 4th 1778 —

This may certify that Jonathan Chipman's Horse was in Public Service and employed as above Mentioned.

Thos Sawyer Cap^{tn}

— & —

the Within account examined and approved and The Treasurer is ordered to pay the Some Which is Six pounds fifteen shillings.

Thos Chittenden

the 9th of December 1778 then Rec vd the Contents of the above Order.

Jonth Chipman

Jonathan Chipman
£6 . . 15 . . —

— & —

[No Record]

---

1. For a brief account of "the fight at Shelburn", see *G. and C.*, I, 245*n*, 528. See also the next petition.

FOR COMPENSATION FOR WAR SERVICES AND LOSSES
xvii, 8

To the honorable the Governor & Council of the State, Vermont —

These are to Shew your Honours, that I did Repair to Shelborn On the first Day of March Last In order to Enform mySelf Concerning the circomstances of the Little Armaments under the Command of Cap^{tn} Thos Sawyer who were Daily Sending & demanding Men from our Neighborhood to join them &c upon my arival there; I was enformed that A Quantity of wheat Viz 50 Bushels which I Bought the fore parte of Last Winter & pay^d for; to Peter Sevieni the Frenchman on Logan's Estate; was Sure to me, as Capt Fausete had before alowed, So Mr Smith Capt Sallisbury &c had allowed but to my Surprize In Less than Three Hours Capt Sawyer Lieut Barnum &c Concluded Thate the wheat must pay their Men their Wadges; Let Peters Deb^{T}s go where they would And that I cou^d have none there; unless I Stayed & Earned it as Wadges or bought it of the Soldiers; my Family Almost destitute of Bread; depending upon the Supply of wheat already pay^d for to French Peter — I was Constrained to try a second time to procure some Bread for my Family & some I Bot of One Nathan Griswold a soldier & engaged some of Mr. Peirson & joined the party my self — they knowing & I observeing to them that I had then a Lei^{ut}s Commission In my Pocket; Thus I was with them Eight Days; then It appeared there was no wheat for me before it was threshed; I then demanded If I might have the privilege of Buying what I could thresh in 4 or 5 Days & do my parte of the Duty in Arms — It was granted to me; Accordingly I went to threshing for 4 Days; at the End of which Time happened our bloody Fray;[1] In which I was wounded So that my Left Hand is Ruined & with another Shot I was Bruised Badly Bruised in the Back; Our Fray being Ended; Capt. Sawyer Cryd out for Some One to Run Express with Tidings to the Inhabitants for help to Secure our prisoners &c I observing a little Backwardness in Men I offered to Run with the Express; Capt Sawyer urged me to go Advanced that my going would save the time of writeing &c I came of [off] with the express about sunrise & arived at McIntoshes about 1 oclock afternoon; — & Capt Sawyer sent a Man Round upon the Ice on horse back; who arrived a Little before me and was gone again; And It appeared that Capt Sawyer & his party In as Short a time as might be after the Second Express came of; In a surprize which no one can Accounte for; Came of Leaveing the Dead Men unburied In the Spot where they were Kill^d & one of their Own Men not Quited Dead — And my wheat that I had Bot, a Second time And threshd not yet Foun^d Left to destruction which is destroy^d I left my Blanquett & Hatt I Left & they Lost In their Retreat. My dissappointment has Occassioned me the moste Extream Difficulty for provison; not A; Farthing of Wadges have I Rec^d; nor a Ration of Victuals Since the 11th of March — I am now not only unable for Labour but In Great Anguish with my broken hand —

I have now Recited my Case to your Exilency & the honourable Council — I now pray that you will grante me Such Redress as in your Wisdom & patriotism you shall find Humane honorable to the State & Equitable on all hands I am, Excelent & honourable — your moste Obedient, Humble Servt

Dated at Ferrisburgh   John Cannon
15th April 1778

1. See note for previous petition.

N.B the Anguish of my broken hand I hope may Attone for Bad Inditeing — & the Bad Ink & Ruffled paper for Bad Letters

J. Cannon

— & —

[For] his Excelency Thomas Chittenden, Esqr Governor in Chief in and Over the State of Vermont in North America
John Cannon's Petition
Voted to take the Same into consideration

— & —

> A. J.: Considered and referred to a committee, 11 June '78, S. P. of Vt., III (I), 24. C. J.: Report of committee addressed to Governor and Council recommended that a proper person investigate the matter and that petitioner have £20 from the treasury in the meantime, 12 June '78, G. and C., I, 265.

FOR RIGHT TO COLLECT TOLL ON A ROAD
xvii, 17

To the Honourable the Representatives of the Government and People of the State of Vermont Convened in General Assembly at Bennington Within the Said State in June 1778 —

The Petition of the Undernamed Subscribers Inhabitants of the Township of Pownal Within the Said State Humbly Sheweth

That Your Petitioners Residing and Inhabiting on the Albany Road so Called leading through the Said Town along by the River Commonly called Hoosack River, Have been Used and accostomed Since their first Settlement for More than Thirty Years past to have their Improvements on the Low lands by the Said River [Secur^d ?] by Swing Gates[1] Accross the Said Road — the Lands on the Said River being Subject to Great Inundations — and Floods, and not Capable of admitting a horse Unless Yearly Rebuilt Which to many of Your Petitioners Would be utterly Impracticable — And as it is Usual and Customary in all Places under Similar Sercumstances for Gates to be allowed,

Your Petitioners Humbly Pray Your Honor to take their Situation into Your Wise Consideration, and Grant that they may have the Priviledge of their Gates being Continued under Proper Regulations as they have been Used to do — And as in Duty Bound Shall Ever Pray

Dated at Pownal aforesaid ⎰
the 1 Day of June 1778 ⎱

Abiathar Angel
Joseph Bennet Junr
Nicholas Potter
Abraham Gardner
George Potter
Benja. Gardnar
Joseph potter

---

1. "Swing Gates" were apparently the means of shutting off a portion of the road and collecting toll for its use. In this case the toll was to pay for annual flood damages.

Adam fisher
his
X   Henrich [invik?]
mark
John Hans Singer

— & —

Petition to yᵉ Honorable General Assembly For Gates to be Continued As Usual on Hoosuck River in Pownal
— & —

A. J.: Considered and referred to a committee, 5 June '78, *S. P. of Vt.*, III (I), 22; act permitting gates to be erected on the Albany Road in Pownal passed, 6 June '78, *Ibid*, III (I), 22.

FOR ADVICE AND AID IN BRINGING RIOTERS TO JUSTICE
xvii, 9

State of Vermont   {   Hallifax September ye 26: 1778

Cumberland County {

    To His Exelency the Governor To his Honour the Lieut Governor to the Honourable Council and House of Representatives Greeting —
The Complaint of William Hill Most Humbly sheweth that your Complainant Did on the 24th Day of Instant September receive a Warrant from Hubbel Wells Esq to arrest the Bodys of John Kirkley and Hannah his Wife of the Town and County afore Said for asault and Battery parpetrated in the Highway on the body of David Williams in Hallifax afore sᵈ: I therefore took the Said John and Hannah persuant to the orders and Brought them Before Said Athority without any abuse. the Warrant was returned the partys Called and the Cort Opened — then there Came Thomas Clark Thomas Baker Isaac Orr Henrey Henderson Alexander Stewart Jonathan Safford Elijah Edwards Peletiah Fitch with about Sixteen Others of Said Town armed with Clubs to attempt to Resque the prisoners or to set the Court aside and in a Tumultuous Manner Rushed into the House Drew their Clubs and Shok them over the Justises Head and Swore he Should not try the Case Called him a Scoundral and that [he ?] to Shew himself Such was forgery Which he Should Answer for and Bid Defience to the State and all its authority with Many more Insults and abuses Which Stagnated the free Course of Justice. in that way overpowered the athority and Stopt the Court — all Which is against the peace of the Community Subversive of the athority of the State against the peace and Dignity of the Same your Complainant prays for your advice and assistance in this Matter that Some Method may be taken Whereby the above Said Offenders may be Brought to Justice for Such acts of Contempt of athority and for Such atrotious acts of out rage. —
this Granted and Your Complainant as in Duty Bound Shall Ever pray
                             William Hill {
                                    { Constable

— & —

[No Additional Material]

— & —

[No Record]

FOR COMPENSATION FOR WAR LOSSES
xvii, 12

State of Vermont

Cumberland County

⟨Thetford⟩ Woodstock 6th Oct. 1778

To the Honb^le the General Assembly now

Sitting at Windsor in Said State —

The petition of Moses Evens of Said Woodstock ⟨Thetford⟩ Humbly Sheweth that whereas your Petitioner haith been engaged in the Service of the State, and was Captivated Last October. and Continued in Captivity untill the 20th of the Sucseeding June. During which time your Petitioner underwent great hardship & Dificulty. and at the End purchased his Redemtion at the Risk of an Escape from the enemy upwards of Two hundred miles through the wilderness to the Inhabitants In which time your Petitioner Suffered much Hungar Cold & fatiague. The Honb^le the Council of this State have granted your Petitioner Sargant pay During the time of Captivity. & for Gun & Blankit —

and whereas your Petitioner haith Sustained Damages by Loss of the following articles (viz) one good New Coat. one Jacket. Two Shirts. one pair of Trowzers. Two pair Stockins, and Sund^y other Small articles. —

Your petitioner Humbly prays that your Honours would Consider the Case and grant Such Relief as in your wisdom you Shall think Just & Reasonable — and as in Duty bound your Petitioner Shall Ever pray

Moses Evens

— & —

Moses Evens Petition
Rec d Oct. 16, 1778
Fees Payed for Entry.

— & —

[No Record]¹

---

1. Although there is no record of any action at this time on this or any other petition of Moses Evens [Evans] either in the Assembly journals or in the records of the Governor and Council, such action was taken by both of these bodies on a new petition drawn up by Evens on 15 Oct. '78 at Windsor. Its prayer was granted. See *The State of Vermont: Rolls of the Soldiers in the Revolutionary War 1775 to 1783* (Rutland, 1904), pp. 694–695 [Hereinafter cited as *Vt. Rev. Rolls*]. Payment under this decision was apparently made in Continental currency, and Evens petitioned in June, 1782 for compensation for the depreciation in his pay for this service. For this petition, see p. 72, *post*.

FOR A NEW TRIAL IN AN ACTION OF FELONY
xvii, 10

State of {
Vermont {

To the Honorable General Assembly to Be Holden
at Windsor the 8th Day of Octr AD 1778
The Pettition of Lemuel White of Clarendon Humbly Sheweth that Whereas
James Mead of Rutland in the County of Bennington and State afor Said Gentm
before the Spetial Court for the halfe Shier of Rutland Obtained Judgment of Said
Court against your Pettitioner in an Action of Felony for Taking a Certain Watch
from the Said James Mead as appears of Record of Said Court / your Pettitioner
Knowing himselfe Inocent and Confident that he is Now able to Make it appear
So to any Court that is or that may Be appointid to hear and Determin ye Matter
and Since there is no appeal to be Obtained from our Special Courts and your
Honorable Board is the only Meanes of Redress your Pittitioner therefore Prayeth
that this honorable Assembly would take the Matter under Consideration and in
your Wisdom and Goodness grant him another hearing Before the Same or Sum
other Court that you in your Wisdom Shall appoint that So your Pititioner May
Recover his Property as well as his Carracter Which Must Greatly Suffer from
the imputation of so horid a Crime and your Pittitioner as in Duty Bound Shall
Ever Pray

Lemuel White

Clarinden Oct 7 AD 1778

— & —

Lemuel White's Petition
Rec d on file Oct 1778
Fees Paid

— & —

   A. J.: Resolved that a court be appointed and that a bill be brought in, 17 Oct.
'78, *S. P. of Vt.*, III (I), 38.

FOR SALE OF TORY LANDS TO BUILD A ROAD
xvii, 22

To <his Excellency Thos Chittenden Esqr and the Honbl General Assembly> the
Honorable the house of Representatives of the State of Vermont now Sitting in
Windsor in said State — the Memorial of the Proprietors and Others Inhabitants
of the Town of Willmington [Wilmington] and towns adjacent in the Counties of
Cumberland Bennington &c humbly Sheweth —
   That the publick Road leading from said Willmington to Bennington is
greatly out of repair, to wit, in that part of the Country lying between said Willmington & Bennington the bridges broken down and dangerous passing, that the
Whole or most of those lands between the two Towns aforesd belongs to Tories
and Other Inimical persons who have gone Over to the Enemy and Joined them.
That said road is indispensibly Necessary for the Good people of this State and
particularly So in this day of publick Calamity and war in Marching Troops,
driving droves of Cattle and Other important publick purposes, that the Memori-

alists and Others as is the [condition?] of all New Settlers, have as much as they Can do to make and repair their Own roads and Subdue and Cultivate their Own farms so as to Support their Families That as all lands are bettered by lying on Great and publick roads, So it is reasonable that the proprietors of those lands or the lands themselves should be Subject to and Obliged to Support their Own roads, your Memorialists therefore humbly pray your Honors to take this Memorial into your Equitable Consideration and appoint a wise and Judicious Comt^ee to repair the road afores^d and make the Same Feasable for the Travelling of the Good people of this and the neighboring States and also to empower Said Comt^ee to make Sale of So much of Said Inimical persons land as shall pay the Expences of repairing the road afores^d or Otherwise Grant relief as your Honors in your Wisdom Shall think fit and the Memorialists as in duty bound shall ever pray Dated at Willmington the 9th day of October 1778

> Wm Williams
> Gideon Granger
> Benja Willard
> Silas Hamilton
> David Dickinson

— & —

Will. Williams Memorial
Rec'd Oct 17th 1778
Fees Paid

— & —

A. J.: Read and granted, and resolved to bring in a bill accordingly, 17 October '78, *S. P. of Vt.*, III (I), 38; resolve passed to make a road from Wilmington to Bennington, 24 Oct. '78, *Ibid*, III (I), 48.[1]

FOR AN ORDER TO CERTAIN PROPRIETORS TO BUILD ROADS
xvii, 13

To the Honble Representatives of the Freemen of the State of Vermont in General Assembly to be holden at Bennington in Said State on the Second Thursday of February A D 1779
　　The Petition of us the Subscribers, Inhabitants of the Towns of Rockingham, Chester, and Kent in the County of Cumberland in Said State
HUMBLY SHEWETH
That in the Township of Brumley there is but Two Families Sitled, and but one Family in the Township of Winnhall, and the Publick Roads thro' said Townships have great need of Repairing, for Safty of Travelors, and Quick Dispatch of Publick Business. And as nothing will Incourage the Settlement of a New Country more than Laying out, Making, and Mending Publick Highways, And as the Inhabitants in Said Townships are so few that no rational Beings can Expect that they can or will Repair Said Roads thro' Said Two Townships

---

1. The next assembly resolved on 25 Feb. '79 to empower a committee to sell the lands of those proprietors of Readsboro and Woodford who refused to pay their assessment for the road. This would imply that the Tory lands were not sold or that the sale of such lands produced an insufficient sum for the purpose. See *S. P. of Vt.*, III (I), 62–63.

Your Petitioners therefore Humbly pray that your Honours would take this Affair into your Wise and Serious Consideration, and Resolve, and order that the Proprietors of Said Brumley And Winhall should be Desired Immediately to lay out, make and Repair, the Roads from Kent and Andover Across the Green Mountain to Manchester, and to be under the Inspection of a Committee appointed by the Hono^ble General Assembly for that Purpose; and upon the proprietors being Notified of Said Resolution, and Neglecting or Refusing to Comply therewith; That then Said Committee be Impowered to Sell so much of Said Land in Said Two Townships as shall be Soficient to make, mend, or Repair Said Roads and be Impowered to Give Good and Soficient Deeds thereof to those who shall Purchase Said Land. or Otherways Resolve Conserning Said Bond as your Honours in your Great Wisdome Shall See fit

And as in duty bound, Shall ever pray

January 4th 1779

Thos. Chandler	Isaac Stack	Robert Anderson
Jabez Sargeant	Josiah Reed	Ja^s Hopkins
Timothy Parker	Lemuel Sergants	James Patterson
Amos Sargeant	Joseph Wood	John Patterson
Wm Gillkey	Elisha Knights	Robert Mountgomery
John Smith	Silas Dutton	Andrew Patterson
Oliver Atwood	John Pulsipher	John Miller
Nicolas Smith	Tim^o Walker	Hugh Montgomery
John E. Chandler	Timothy Clark	John Woodburn
David Hutchison	Edward Aiken	[Ja^s?] MacCormick
John Chandler	Hugh Montgomery	Wm Cox
William Gillkey Junr	Wm Mack	Robt McCormick
George Earll	Henry Montgomery	Edward Aiken
Wm Simonds	James Anderson	Archibald Mack
Colburn Preston	James Miller	James Rogers Junr
Elijah Knights	Robert Miller	David Cochren
Wm Stearnes		

— & —

The Petition of the Inhabitants of the Towns of Rockingham Chester & Kent, Recd Feby 16th 1779

. . .*

— & —

A. J.: *Granted, and a committee appointed to make road at cost of proprietors and to sell their lands if they neglect paying the same, 16 Feb. '79, S. P. of Vt., III (I), 56–57.

FOR COMPENSATION FOR WAR SERVICES AND LOSSES
xvii, 15

To his Excellency the Governor, and the honourable the Council of the State of Vermont

The Petition of Abner Blanchard of Pollet [Pawlet] humbly sheweth —

That Your Petitioner engaged in the defence of this and the United States of America as a Voluntier about the latter End of June, and continued therein until the sixteenth Day of August in the Year 1777, for which he has received no Wages.

That Your Petitioner soon after this, engaged in the ranging Service under Col. Harrick. —[1] that in the Month of December in the Year afores[d] he was ordered on a Scout down the Lake, at which Time Your Petitioner had the misfortune to fall into the Lake thro' the Ice, and thereby lost his Gun-Valued at 40 Dollars, for which he has received nothing,[2]

that Your Petitioner is now in this Town with his Family on their remove to the Northward, & under necessitous Circumstances, being unable to remove any further for want of Money

Your Petitioner therefore Prays Your Excellency & Honours to take his s[d] Service, loss, and Circumstances, into Your Wise Consideration, and grant to him as to Your Wisdom, Justice, and Generosity may appertain, And Your Petitioner as in Duty bound shall ever Pray

Bennington 22[d] ⎱
Feb[y] 1779 ⎰   Abner Blanchard

— & —

Petition of Abner Blanshard
Rece-d on file 22 Feb[y] 1779
to y[e] Gov[r] & Council.

22d Febr[y] having Taken into Consideration the within petition; praying for Some reward for Service done in the Militia from the last day of June to the 16th day of August 1777 — ordered that 20 Dollars be paid out of the treasury towards his reward, and the remainder ly for further Consideration[3]

— & —

[No Record]

FOR A ROAD AND A COMMITTEE TO DIRECT ITS CONSTRUCTION
xvii, 18

State of Vermont Windsor 4th June 1779 —
To the Honb[le] the General Assembly Now Sitting at Said Windsor
The Petition of Phineas Williams John Strong and John Throop Humbly Sheweth

---

1. For record of this service, see *Vt. Rev. Rolls*, 50. For references to the activities of the regiment of Vermont Rangers under Colonel Samuel Herrick, see *G. and C.*, I, 160*n*–161*n*, 176, 185, 187.

2. For Abner Blanchard's petition for compensation for his services in this scout, see p. 73, *post*.

3. There is no indication here that this action was taken by the Governor and Council and no record of it in their journals. However, in view of the address of the petition there is no ground to doubt that the decision was taken by that body.

That whereas our Situation is Such, as makes it verry inconvenient for us to pass & Repass from Woodstock to Rutland on account of having no Road, without Travilling Sixty Miles. whereas if there was a Road Direct from Said Woodstock to Rutland through Bridgewater. and Killington. it would not be but about Twenty five Miles. where there might be a good Road made which would be of great Advantage to the Inhabitants of the ajacent Towns Eastward westward & Northward as well as to the publick in General. as it will Save a great Deal of fateague & Expence of Travil as well as time —

Your Petitioners therefore Humbly pray that the Honb^le Assembly would grant that a Road may be Laid out and made from Said Woodstock to Rutland through Bridgewater and Killington as aforesaid and that The Honb^le Assembly would appoint A Committee to Lay out Said Road & See that it be made in Such manner as the Honb^le Assembly Shall Direct and your Petitioners in Duty Bound Shall Ever pray

John Throop
John Strong
Phinehas Williams

— & —

Capt Troop^s Petition

— & —

[No Record]

FOR COMPENSATION FOR WAR SERVICES
xvii, 19

Stat of Vermont

Guilford August the 3 day 1779

to the HornoroBel the General Assembly of this State your parteshener Reseved orders from Colo° Sam^ll feletcher in March ye 9 d [day] 1779:[1] and in parsuence of the same was aBliged to Raise two men from my Compeny wich I ded By the way of Clasing [,] the Clases[2] Refuseing to provid the two men was a Blig [obliged] to hire the two men and pleging the faith of the Stat for the payment of the Saim and By advice Reseved of Ben. Carpenter Esq: from his Excellency the Governer not to Colect the money from those that was Assesed wich Casued me a journey to his Excellencys to get the money[3] wich was fore days of my self and hors for my Self and expences par day Sexten Dolors — 19-4-0-0 and for my hors fifty five miles one dolar par mile 16-10-0-0

---

1. For the resolution of the Governor and Council, 26 Feb. '79, raising, among others, twenty men from Col. Fletcher's regiment for the defense of the northern frontiers, see G. and C., I, 290. This was doubtless the occasion for the order to Captain Starr.

2. For the matter of the division of militia companies into classes, see An Act for forming and regulating the militia, passed in February, 1779 (Slade, 305–312, particularly 309–310).

3. Captain Starr was eventually allowed £105.5.0 for money paid to these men. See Vt. Rev. Rolls, 797.

and as your parteshener was and is desiurs of promoting the Comon Cause and the Good of this State shall tak it as a Grat Faver if the HonnoroBel AssemBely will Grant the aBove Sum or Sumes or so much of them as thea Shall in thear Grate Wisdom Shall think is my du as in Duty Bound Ever Pray —

Comfort Starr Capt

— & —

To Thomas Chandler Esq.
The faver of Ben. Carpenter Esq.

To his Excellency in Council for their Perusel and Adjustment

In Council Manchester 22ᵈ Octʳ 1779
    The within Account Examined and the Treasurer is Directed to Pay Twenty two Pound thirteen Shillings on the within account

Thoˢ Chittenden

To I. Allen Treasurer
Recd Date above of I. Allen Treasurer Twenty two Pounds thirteen Shillings for & in behalf of Capt. Starr

Benjamin Carpenter

— & —

[No Record]

FOR TITLE TO LANDS REGARDLESS OF MISSING DEEDS
xxi, 101

State of }   To the Honourable General Assembly of the Govᵒʳ Council
Vermont }   and House of Representives of the Freemen of the State of Vermont to be Holden at Manchester in Said State on the Second Thursday of October Next —
    The Petition of Capᵗ Benjamin Dorchester of the Town of New Haven in the State of Connecticut Humbly Sheweth that Your Honours Petitioner was Sometime in the month of November 1770 applied unto by one Simon Stevens of Charlestown in the State of New Hampshier [Hampshire] which Said Stevens then acting falsly and a hipocritical part did persuade Your Honours Petitioner by Deceitt, and Craft to Deliver to him the Said Stevens Nine Deeds of Nine original proprietors Rights in the township of Windhal [Winhall] in this State and Gave his Receipt to Your petitioner to return the Same and Your Honours petitioner unfortunately lost Said Receipt or had it Stole out of his possession whereupon Your Honours petitioner applyed to Said Stevens and obtained the following Receipt Viz
    Novʳ 1770 Receivᵈ of Capᵗ Benjamin Dorchester Deeds for Nine Rights of Land in a township callᵈ Winhall for which I then Gave a Receipt to Return the Deeds or the Sum of Ninety Dollars as Soon as Letters Pattent Should pass the Seals for Said town of Winhall which Said Dorchester Says he has Lost for his better Security I Do Now agree to return the aforesaid Deeds or Ninety Dollars as Soon as Letters Patent Shall pass the Seal for the aforesaid township &C —

As witness my Hand this Six Day of August 1772
Witness   Simon Stevens
   Nathⁿ Stone
   as p^r Said Receipt to be Seen may appear
And Now Your Petitioner would further remark to you Honours that Said Stevens
did Soon after the Dispute commenced between Great Britain and these American
States take an active part against thes American States and to avoid Suffering the
just punishment Due to his flagrant Crimes added iniquity to Sin and finally filed
up the measure of his Guilt in Going over to the Enemy and joining their Ranks
and Did also Carry with him Your pititioners Deeds —
and Your Petitioner would further remark to Your Honours that Said Stevens
Never did pay to Your petitioner any money or reward for Said Land whatsoever
but Contrary to You petitioners Expectation Carryed of [off] Said Deeds whereby
your petitioner is Left without remedy unless Your Honours will interpose —
Your petitioner would therefore pray Your Honours to inquire into the premises
and order and Decree Your petitioner to be put into full and Legal possession of
the aforesaid Nine Rights in the township of Windhall and Your petitioner as in
Duty bound will ever pray
Dated at Manchester the 30th Day of September 1779
                                                                     Benjamin Dorchester

— & —

Capt Benjamin Dorchester Petition Versus Simon Stevens
1779
Granted see report
— & —

> *A. J.*: Read and referred to a committee to join a committee from the Council,
> 16 Oct. '79, *S. P. of Vt.*, III (I), 79; report of committee declaring that peti-
> tioner has good right to lands regardless of deeds, read, and resolved that it
> be accepted, 18 Oct. '79, *Ibid*, III (I), 79. *C. J.*: Committee appointed to join
> assembly committee, 16 Oct. '79, *G. and C.*, II, 7.

FOR AUTHORITY TO BUILD COUNTY COURT HOUSE AND JAIL
xvii, 27

To his Excellency the Governor his honorable Council and General Assembly of
the State of Vermont Now Sitting at Manchester in Said State.
    The petition of the Subscribers Humbly Sheweth that Whereas it is of ab-
solute necessity that a Court house and Goal be built within the County of Bennington and especially a Goal for the better Securing Criminals and other offenders,
    And Whereas the raising of money for the Building and Defraying the Charges
of Said Buildings in Said County by way of a Rate or Tax would be Attended
with many difficulties and Disadvantages to the State in General — And whereas
there is a Subscription made by the Inhabitant of Bennington and adjacent Towns
Sufficient for the Building and Completely finishing a Court house and Goal Afforesaid for the use and Benifit of said County — Therefore Pray your honours to
pass a Resolution Granting Leve to your petitioners to Erect the Said Buildings,

and to Establish the County Court to be held Either the whole or part of the time in the said Town of Bennington and house afforesaid when Completed — under Such Regulations as your honours Wisdom Shall direct and as in duty bound your petitioners shall Ever pray

> Sam[ll] Robinson
> Moses Robinson
> Joseph [Fay?]
> Benjamin Fay
> John Burnham Junr
> Nathan Clark

— & —

Petition to Gen[l] Assembly For Building a Gaol &c
Granted —
Rec d Oct[r] 1779

In Council 22[d] October, 1779
Considered the Within Petition passed in Council, and recommended to the general Assembly for their Consideration
> Attest Joseph Fay Sec[y]

Passed the House
> attest Ros[l] Hopkins — Clerk

— & —

> *A. J.*: Resolved that prayer be granted and that a committee be appointed to bring in a bill, 23 Oct '79, *S. P. of Vt.*, III (I), 88; report of committee recommending that the buildings be built in Bennington and that county court be held there one half of the time, read, and resolved that it be accepted, 23 Oct. '79, *Ibid*, III (I), 89–90.[1] *Rep. of Com.*: Report (as above but differing in some details), 23 Oct. '79, *S. P. of Vt.*, IV, 7–8.[2]

FOR EXEMPTION FROM TAXES TO COVER WAR LOSSES
xvii, 52

To The Honorable the General Assembly of the State of Vermont now Sitting at Manchester —
The Petition of Anne Willard in behalf of herself & children, the heirs of her husband Eliakim Willard late of Manchester Deceased humbly Sheweth that in the month of August 1777 after the troops of this & the united States retreated from Ticondaroga, a Number of Troops Were Quartered in & near the house of your honors Petitioner that thro' carelessness or design of s[d] Troops the barn of

---

1. There is no record in the journal of any further action by the Assembly. Presumably this acceptance was equivalent to the passage of a resolution to the effect of the report. For a remonstrance against this decision, see p. 19, *post.*

2. For the claim that Bennington failed to fulfill its promises in this matter, see pp. 111, 346, *post.*

your honors Petitioner Filled with hay oats &c was set on fire & wholly consumed, for which your honors Petitioner has received no compensation, & your honors Petitioner would further remark that s^d troops did then up & consume about 3½ acres of Indian corn then growing & standing in her field ‹& about [Blank] of patatoes› and further she would remark to your honors that a large Number of her Cattle Sheep &c were by order of Col° Warner Command^t at Manchester driven to Bennington to prevent their falling into hand of the enemy & that 9 young neet Cattle & 32 Sheep were wholly lost to your honors Petitioner, being Supposed to be Sold at Bennington thro' mistake for the Benifit of the public, all which loss & damage was then apraised by Mrss Gidion Barber Jonathⁿ Page at the Sum of 230 £ L.M. as money then went — for all which your Honors Petitioner has never received any ‹consideration› compensation whatever — your honors Petitioner therefore prays that your Honors will take her loss into your wise consideration & order her to be restored to her damages afsd by granting her & her estate an exemption from public taxes untill Such her damages Shall be made good; or in some other way grant relief in the premises as to your honors in their great wisdom shall seem meet & your Petitioner as in duty bound Shall ever pray

Anna Willard

— & —

Widow Willers Petition —
Referred to the next Session of Assembly —
See page 162 —

— & —

A. J.: Read as referred from last session, and ordered referred to next session, 14 Mar. '80, S. P. of Vt., III (I), 111.

FOR REVIEW OF A DISPUTED ELECTION
xvii, 23

To the Honourable Assembly of Representatives of the Freemen of the State of Vermont to be Holden at Manchester in October 1779 whereas we the Potitioners do humbly Shew that on the Freemans meeting For Chooseing Govr Dep^t Govr &c. Met with Such Emberrasments and abusive Conduct which Prevented our Proceeding in the Choice of A Representative &c. therefore we Take Liberty to State the Facts as Followeth
1st the meeting being opened by the Constable a despute arose whether the Freemen had aright to Judg of the Qualifications of their own Members as their was no Selectmen that belongs to the Body of Freemen[1] and it was Put to Vote and it Past in the affirmative then Col. Wm Williams and Capt Josiah Look Presented them Selves and demanded the Freemens Oath and there was objections made

---

1. Under the Constitution of 1777 every male of twenty one and of one year's residence prior to a state election who was of "quiet and peaceable behaviour" and would take the freeman's oath, was entitled to the privileges of a freeman. Under statute law a person had to obtain the approbation of the selectmen of his town before he could be admitted to take the oath. See G. and C., I, 96 and Slade, pp. 326–327.

aganst Col. Williams and it was Put to Vote whether he Should be admited and it Past in the Negative and then there was much opposition with threatening and Shakeing thare Fists at us so that the Constable Could not keep orders and they being so violent that it was not Safe to do any business and the day being thus spent it was Adjourned to the Next day att one of the Clock

2nd Being Met according to Adjournment and the Meeting being Opened then Esq Haris being Present Made Proclimation that if there was any that had amind to take the Freemans oath to present themselves for to receive approbation of the selectmen and take the Oath then we told him that we had no selectmen that belonged to the Freeman therefore we Judged it our Right to Judge of the Qualifications of our own Members then Esq Haris said we had no business with it but said if the Selectmen Should Approbate any that he new was not Qualified he would not administer the Oath to them then we asked whether or no he would give the Oath to such as the Selectmen Should Approbate if we Could Prove that they were disqualified and he said no he should not then there was a Number Presented themselves then Esq Haris Asked us if we had any Objections Against any of them and we objected against a Number then Esq Haris turned and asked the Rest of them Concerning them that we Objected aganst and they said that they were good peaceable Inhabitants we told him that we was Ready to Prove what we had to Eledge against them then Esq Haris said he did not want to hear any of our Objections for he Preicived it Sprung from an Old Quaril and gave them the Oath and being thus foreclosed by Esq Haris which we humbly look upon unconstitution and then we withdrew from the Meeting and then they went on and made Choice of Col Wm Williams for their Representative which we look upon not A leagal Choice Would therefore Beg leave to lay our Grievance before your Honours and Pray the Same may be taken into Consideration and Grant your Humble Pititioners Such Releaf as your Honours in your Great wisdom Shall think most Expedient and as your Pititioners in duty Bound Shall Ever pray Wilmington October 11th 1779

Phinehas Smith	Freemen of
William Miller	the Town of
Eleazer Goodman	Wilmington
Elijah Alvord	in the
Medad Smithe	County of
Reuben Cumings	Cumberland
Thomas Davison	and State
Samuel Bridge	of Vermont
David Lewis	
John Rugg	

Wilmington [*October*] 12th 1779. This may certifie that the within facts are true [Test?]

[Ephraim?] Titus { moderator[1]

— & —

Petition of the Freemen of Wilmington
Not Granted. Reconsidered and a Committee appointed

---

1. Apparently moderator of this group of freemen. Presumably "Esqr Harris" was moderator of the town.

page 141

— & —

A. J.: Read and resolved that Col. Williams was a legal member of the House, 15 Oct. '79, *S. P. of Vt.*, III (I), 76–77; previous resolution reconsidered and committee appointed to go to Wilmington and investigate, Col. Williams keeping his seat in meantime, 16 Oct. '79, *Ibid*, III (I), 78; report of committee finding complaints groundless read, and resolved that Col. Williams keep his seat, 9 March '80, *Ibid*, III (I), 101–102. *Rep. of Com.:* Report (as above but differing in some particulars), 29 Feb. '80, *S. P. of Vt.*, IV, 13–14.

FOR THE INSTITUTION OF THE STATE UNIVERSITY
xvii, 24

To the honorable the general Assembly of the Representatives of the freemen of the State of Vermont conven'd at Manchester in Said State

The petition of the Subscriber humbly Sheweth

That whereas the Constitution of this State makes provision for setting up one University in it under the direction of the general Assembly. See plan or form of Government Sect 40[1]

And whereas it is of Vast importance to the new and Rising State, both for strength and ornament, to set up such and maintain a University

Your Petitioner in behalf of the State humbly prays your honours to take this Important matter into your wise and most Serious Consideration and Act there upon as Wisdom shall direct

And if your honours shall see fit to take up the matter and act upon it Your petitioner humbly prays that your Honours would Appoint Thirteen Men Within this State, as Trustees to negotiate all Affairs relative to the beginning founding and carrying on a University in this State Under direction of the General Assembly and that one of said Thirteen may be appointed by said Assembly as President and that said president and Trustees have orders to prepare a Charter for Said University for the Inspection and Approbation of said Assembly at their next Session.

And furthermore your petitioner humbly prays Your Honours would Sequestre a Tract of Land to the Value of Twenty miles square to be appropriated for the benefit of Said University and this State as your Honours in your Wisdom shall direct

And as in duty Bound Shall ever Pray

James Treadway

October 14th 1779

— & —

James Treadways Petition for a University &c or Colledge
Rec-d 22[d] Oct[r] 1779
no fees.

— & —

[No Record]

---

1. Constitution of 1777 (*G. and C.*, I, 102).

FOR ESTABLISHMENT OF CERTAIN TOWN LINES
xvii, 28

To the Honrable General Assembly of the State of Vermont now sitting at Manchester

The humble petition of Timothy Andrus Esq in behalf of the Proprietors of the Townships of Guilhall [Guildhall] & Granby respecfully Sheweth, that the aforesaid Guildhall and Granby were the first Town chartered in the uper Cohoss and that the aforesaid Guildhall was by charter to be laid thirty miles on a straight line above the Mouth of Ammanoosacks [Ammonoosuc] River emptying into Connecticut River at the Lower Cohoss in the Township of Haverhill — and that the Townships of Maidstone on the River and Ferdenand [Ferdinand] in the second tier and eight other Townships were chartered in succession by the same point of compass northerly of the aforesaid Townships of Guildhall and Granby And your Honors Petitioner begs leave to represent that the aforesaid Townships of Guild [sic] and Granby were the first chartered[1] and were the bounds from which all the adjoining Towns were to be Located and that the aforesaid Townships of Guildhall & Granby [by] reason of a mistake in the first survey were laid three miles and an half farther to the Northward than they were authorized by the aforesaid Charter which was to be 30 miles on a straight line from the mouth of Ammanoosacks River as we find by accurate surveys since made — and as great inconvenience has arisen to the aforesaid [Tows?] of Guildhall and Granby an also to several other adjoining Towns on account of the aforesaid mistaken survey your Honors Petitioner prays that a Committee may be appointed to go at the expence of the proprietors under the direction of the Surveyor Gen[ll] and Make and establish the bounds of the aforesaid Townships of Guildhall & Granby and your Petitioner as in duty bound shall ever pray —   Timothy Andrus

Dated at Manchester [October] 27th[2] 1779

— & —

Timothy Andrus Petition
Granted —
filed 1779

— & —

A. J.: Read and granted, and a committee appointed to make the necessary surveys, 26 Oct. '79, S. P. of Vt., III (I), 92–93.

FOR CENTRAL LOCATION OF COUNTY COURT HOUSE AND JAIL
xvii, 29

To the Honble General Assembly, to be holden by Adjournment, at Westminster,

---

1. For the charters of Granby and Guildhall, see *State Papers New Hampshire: The New Hampshire Grants*, vol. XXVI (Town Charters, vol. III), 192, 196.

2. This date must have been an error on the part of the petitioner, since the Assembly acted in the matter on the 26th of October. There is no reason to believe that the petition was written in September, because it refers to the Assembly as now sitting and the Assembly was not sitting in September.

on the second Wednesday of March next. The Petition & Remonstrance of us the Subscribers, Inhabitants of several Towns in ye County of Bennington humbly Sheweth: That by the Records of the House of Representatives it appears that a Bill passed the Assembly at their last Sessions constituting Bennington a County-Town;[1] & enabling the Inhabitants of Sd Town to build a Goal & Court-house for the Use of the County aforesaid, against which the Subscribers humbly beg leave to remonstrate & that for the following Reasons. 1st Because the aforesaid Town of Bennington is situated nearly in one Corner of the County, And therefore cannot on any Rational Principles be adjudged the proper Place for the Buildings aforesaid. 2ndly Because the apparent Motives, which induced the Honorable Assembly to pass the aforesaid Bill, seemed to be too insufficient to justify the Representatives of a free People in selling the Rights of their Constituents, which ought always to remain sacred and unimpaired.

The Idea of saving a triffling Expence ought to be rejected with Disdain, when it is opposed to the Interest & well-being of the Community at large. We dare assure your Honors that there is not one Town in the County which would not be willing to accept of the same offer made to the Town of Bennington, & build the aforesaid Houses at its own Cost. One minutes Reflection will convince any rational Mind that it will be nearly impossible to alter the County-Town after Those Houses are once built: And to subject us, our Children, & future Generations to the grievous Task of being obliged to go six times so far for all our County Previleges as those of our Brethren who reside in Pownal would be a Proceedure by no means reconcilable [with] the Principles of justice, and therefore we doubt not will be rejected by your Honors —

We therefore pray that the Honorable Assembly would take the aforesaid Bill into your wise Consideration; and order that the aforesaid Houses be built in the Center of the County. And your Petitioners, as in Duty bound, shall ever pray.

Rupert, 20th Decr. 1779

Moses Robison	Saml Francis Jr	Nathel Smith Jr
Tihan Noble	Danil Reed	Nehemiah Hermon Jr
Jonathan Eastman	Joseph Tower	Amos Soct [Scott?] Jr
Nehemiah Harrison	Enoch Eastman	Wm Towsley
John Nelson	Wm Smith	Ashbel Sikes
Amos Curtis	Joel Shelden	Josiah Risden
Ebenezer Hulbert	Nathl Tower	Enos Hermon
Danel Smith	Amos Hermon	Pliney Smith
Stephen Eastman	Jonth Eastman Jr	Joseph Levate
Zeperan Eastman	Amos Scott	Isral Smith
Reuben farnsworth	Hezekiah Scott	Oliver Scott
Daniel Hopkins	Abdiel Webster	Josiah Terril

— & —

Petition for Removing the Court House and Goal from Bennington
See page 185
Petition & Remonstrance

— & —

---

1. For the petition from which this bill originated, see p. 14, *ante*.

A. J.: Read and referred to a committee to join a committee from the Council, 16 March '80, *S. P. of Vt.*, III (I), 121; report of committee recommending that action of previous session be adhered to, read and accepted, 16 March '80, *Ibid*, III (I), 122.

FOR COMPENSATION FOR PUBLIC SERVICES
xvii, 31

To his Excellency Thomas Chittenton [Chittenden] Governour of the State of Vermont And to the Honourable Council of Said State — the petition of we the Subscrib^{rs} humbly Shewing — that my horse was pres^t Into the Servis of Said State — by the Sherrif of the County of Cumberland About the 24th of Last May — and Detain^d About Eight days — And Abus^d In a manner Hard fully to discribe — unfitted for much business for near three months — for which Servis I pray I may be allowed thirty Six pounds — Which Sum is not half the Damage Had he Not been abused Should not have troubld you with a Detail of the affair — I Remain as in Duty bound your Humble petitioner — Dated at Townshand [Townshend] the 9th of March A D 1780 —   Joshua Wood

— & —

Sam^{ll} Fletcher
£36 —
March 14 1780

Westminster 14th of March 1780
Sir Please to Pay Samuel Fletcher the Barrer hereof out of the Treasury of this State thirty Six pound to the Use of Dot^r Joshua Wood the within Pititioner take s^d Fletchers Resait as the Recept thereof & this order Shall Discharge You —
                                                           Thos Chittenden
To Ira Allen Esqr Treasurer —
Rec'd Westminster 14th March 1780 of Ira Allen Treasurer thirty six Pounds L money in full
                                                           Sam^{el} Fletcher
L 36 —

— & —

[No Record]

FOR PAYMENT FOR WAR SERVICES
xvii, 16

To his Excellency the Gov. his honble. Council and General Assembly of the State of Vermont now sitting at Westminster —
   The Petition of the subscribers Humbly Sheweth that Whereas the present Winter has been such and the repeated Intelligence from Canada that great apprehenssons arose in the minds of the frontier Inhabitants that the Enemy would Attempt an invasion upon Some Quarter; And as your petitioners and the In-

habitants of the Towns of Royalton & Sharon whom we have the honour to represent was frontiers and exposed to such Invasion did by the advice of one of the
members of the Board of War and others; Raise one subbaltarn and Eight privates
to reconniter the Woods — and keep Guard for their Security — and Engaged to
pay them (viz) the subbaltarn equal wages Allowed by this State, & Each private
forty Shillings per Month and Money Made Good as in the year 1774 — on Condition this State would not pay them —

And Whereas your Petitioners are of opinion that said Scout So Raised was
of public Service to this State; do therefore pray your honours to take the Matter
under Consideration and if Consistant Grant that said subbaltarn & Eight member
paid out of the Public Treasurry of this State or Such Other Relief as your honors
in your Wisdom Shall Judge Requisite and for the best Good of this State, and as
your petitioners in duty bound Shall ever pray

Westminster 12th March 1780

Elias Stevens ⎫ Representatives
Daniel Gilbert ⎬ for
⎭ Sd towns

The Guard Mentioned in said petition were in Service one Month and a half —

— & —

. . .*

— & —

A. J.: *Read and referred to Governor and Council for adjustment and payment, 16 Mar. '80, S. P. of Vt., III (I), 116.

_____

FOR POSTPONEMENT OF THE GRANT OF A TOWN ALREADY SETTLED
xxi, 185

Moretown Oct° Y^e 7th 1780 —
To the Honnourable House of Representatives of the State of Vermont, the Peti-
tion of the Ihabitants [sic] of Moretown [Mooretown][1] with in Said State most
Humbly Sheweth, that they are Inform'd that one Jonathan Mc Connel of Permont
[Piermont][2] has Petition^d for the Township of Moretown,[3] and as this Town was
Setled before Pearmont and before Said McConnel ever knew Said Town, it Ap-
pears to us A very Odd affair, as the Setlement of this Town was begun under the
Government of New Hampshire, after wards we paid dear for it to New York[4]

_____

1. Now Bradford. See S. P. of Vt., II (Vermont Charters), 325. There is no reason
to doubt that the town referred to in this petition is Mooretown (now Bradford) and not
Moretown, a town granted by New Hampshire in 1763 and now in Washington County.

2. A New Hampshire town opposite to Bradford on the Connecticut River.

3. This petition is not now among the Ms. Vt. S. P. For other similar petitions, see
S. P. of Vt., vol. V (Petitions for Land), 139-140, including notes.

4. Although the settlement of the town may have begun while it was under the
authority of New Hampshire, it never received a charter from that province. It was
patented by New York in 1770. See reference in note 1, supra. The fact that the inhabitants
held under New York title was doubtless the reason why a new grant was sought from
Vermont in disregard of the actual settlers. Bradford is now the single town in the state
which exists by virtue of a New York patent alone. All other towns in the state were
granted by New Hampshire or Vermont.

we have don the full Setlement and all Other Dutys Equal to any Town what ever, and have ben faithfull in the Amarican Cause, we are Surprise'd to think that Any Gentleman of Caractor, who is AQuainted with the Cirumstances of this Town, Should Petition for A Grant of Said Town with out AQuainting the Inhabitants of it, its true we hear there is A few of the Inhabytants Names made use of in their Petition, tho Som of them Affirm they never knew it only by hear Say, at the Sametime we are upwards of Sixty Setlers in this Town — At present we have our hands and Hearts full of cares to protect our Selves Against the Enemies of the United States and are daly called upon to do Somthing for the Publick, We Rested easey as to our Lands thinking our title Indisputable but the most Confidant may be Diseav'd, our only Prayers to you is that Any and all Petitions for this Town may be Postpond till we can have A Reasonable or conveniant time to reason together and all Duty on our part Shall be comply'd with for further Perticulars Doc^r Andros will Inform you who is Deligated by us to Treat with you in our Behalf

　　by Order of Committe　　　　　　　　　　　Benj^a Baldwin Town Clerk

— & —

Doct^r Andres Caveat, against Moretown Petition
Octr 1780

— & —

　　A. J.: Agent of inhabitants set forth views of petition, and resolved that granting of said township be referred to next session, 17 Oct. '80, *S. P. of Vt.*, III (I), 133–134.

FOR THE DETERMINATION OF CERTAIN TOWN LINES
xxi, 203

To the Honble The General Assembly of the State of Vermont —
The Petition of The Subscribers being Proprietors of The Township of Clarendon in Said State Humbly Sheweth — That the Lines between The Township of Said Clarenden [Clarendon] Wallingford and Tinmouth, are So uncertain as to occassion uneasiness and unless Some measures are Speedily taken to asertain Said Lines and the bounds of Said Town, they fear Great Dificculty will arise, they therefore Humbly pray this Honorable Assembly will Appoint a wise and Impartial Committee with a Surveyor to Ascertain Said Lines and bounds, and they as in duty bound Shall Ever pray, Bennington Octo^r 21st 1780

　　　　　　　　　　　　　　　　　　Elihu Smith
　　　　　　　　　　　　　　　　　　Silas Whitney
　　　　　　　　　　　　　　　　　　Andrew Potter
　　　　　　　　　　　　　　　　　　Joseph Smith
　　　　　　　　　　　　　　　　　　Moses Robinson

— & —

[A] Petition for asertaining the bounderry line between Clarenden, Tinmouth &.c

— & —

　　A. J.: Read, 24 Oct. '80, *S. P. of Vt.*, III (I), 142.

FOR RELIEF FROM CHARTER FEES BECAUSE OF WAR LOSSES
xvii, 36

To the Honorable General Assembly of the State of Vermont; to be convened at Windsor, on the first Wednesday of February next — The petition of the distressed inhabitents of the Town of Royalton humbly showeth —

That, whereas, by the providence of God, we your honors petitioners, who were not long since in affluant circumstances, are reduced to a state of indigence, by the depredations of a cruel and savage Enemy,[1] having our whole substances destroyed, to that degree that many of our families, who were heretofore accustomed to hold forth the liberal hand of charity, to supply the wants of the necessitous, are now reduced to the sad alternative of beging their bread, or perishing with hunger. And whereas, by the same providence, we have been prevented making payment of our Charter Fees for the grant of said Town, which, if required at our hands in our present suffering condition, must sensibly add to the miseries that we now feel.[2] And being fully sensable that your Honours are possesed of all that tenderness & compassion which are the ornaments & beauty of the Representatives of a free People, and which ever tend to promote the progress of humanity in society, and also of your readiness to support the sinking in the day of adversity. This is therefore to pray your Honors that this House would order that each of your Honor's Petitioners, sufferers in the late distruction of Royalton, may be discharged of their several dues to the State, on account of the Charter of said Town: and also that your Honors would be pleased further to manifest your charitable disposition towards us by ordering that the Charter Fees, of the non-residents, proprietors and those who were so happy as to escape the Calamity that has fallen upon us, be paid to some meet person appointed for that purpose, to be distributed among the sufferers, in proportion to the losses they have sustained & the distresses to which they are reduced —

This Petition, if granted, would effect the Public so little that the most selfish & contracted of all your Honor's constituents would [never] feel the proportion that was taken from him, while at the same time it would render the most essential service to your Petitioners in their present distressed situation, & lay them under recent obligations, as they are in duty bound, ever most cordially to pray —

Timothy Durkee	Elish Kent	Daniel Gilbert
Heman Durkee	Daniel [Rix?]	Simon Shepard
Aden Durkee	John Hibberd	Jeremeah [Trescoot?]
Timothy Durkee Jur	Joseph-Johnson Rix	Nathaniel Morse
David Fish	Medad Benton	Joseph Havens

---

1. The town of Royalton was burned 16 October 1780 in a raid by a party of Indians under the command of a British officer.

2. Royalton had been granted 16 March 1780 under a resolution of the Assembly (S. P. of Vt., III (I), 120). The record of the actions of the Governor and Council in their session with the Assembly in March 1780 is incomplete. The charter fees for Royalton under the Assembly resolution cannot thus be determined from this source. However, under resolutions of 16 March 1780 the Governor and Council charged the proprietors of Chittenden fees of five hundred and forty pounds lawful money "made Good as in the year 1774" and those of Philadelphia five hundred and eighty pounds of the same money (G. and C., II, 27-28). There seems little reason to believe that the charter fees of Royalton would have differed greatly from those of these towns.

Joseph Fish
David Bruster
Zebalon Lion
Elias Stevens
Robert Hendy
Calvin Parkhurst
James Cooper
Jo Parkhurst

Jonathan Benton
Nathan Morgan
John Billings
Benjn Day
Israel [Walton?]
[Pilleg?] Parkhurst
Phinehas Parkhurst
Jabez Parkhurst
Ebenez^r Parkhurst

Widow Sarah [Rude?]
Isaca [Isaac] Morgan
Elias Curtice
Robert Havens
Daniel Havens
John Evens
Martin Fuller
Garner [Rix?]

— & —

Petition of the Town of Royalton Cufort [Cumfort] Seaver Esqr Agant [Agent]
Granted
Report — Granted
. . .*

State of ⎱   Windsor February 13 1781
Vermont ⎰
To the Honnourable Assembly Now Convened
Your Committee appointed to Take into Consideration the Pertition of the unhappy
Sufferers of the Town of Royalton Beg Leave to Report our Opinion (Viz) that
the Prayer of the Pertition be answered [. . .] Some and that a Committee of three
Be appointed of Substantial meet Persons for the Purpose of making a Proper
averige of the Charter Fees of those that are Nott Sufferers in the Said Town
which is Due to this State and it is our Opinion that the Prisioners taken from the
Town of Royalton and Now in Captivity have a [part?] of Said money according
to the Discretion of Said Committee

By order of the Comtt.   John Powell ⎰Chair
                                                    ⎱man

— & —

A. J.: *Read and referred to a committee, 12 Feb. '81, *S. P. of Vt.*, III (I),
188; report of committee read and accepted and a committee appointed accordingly, 13 Feb. '81, *Ibid*, III (I), 189; previous resolution reconsidered,
and resolved that suffering proprietors be discharged from their granting fees
and that a committee be appointed to determine who ought to be so released,
16 Feb. '81, *Ibid*, III (I), 199; previous resolutions reconsidered and report of
committee appointed the 16th passed, 22 Feb '81, *Ibid*, III (I), 207. *C. J.:*
Resolve of Assembly postponing for five years payment of granting fees by the
proprietors who signed the petition, read and concurred, and payment by other
proprietors postponed until April next, 22 Feb. '81, *G. and C.*, II, 81.

FOR SETTING ASIDE A JUDGMENT FOR RIOT AND FOR
THE SETTLEMENT OF CONFLICTING CHARTER GRANTS
xvii, 37

To the Honorable Generial Assembly of the State of Vermont Now Sitting at
Windser [Windsor]

The Pittition of Co^ll Wm. Williams one of the Representatives For Said State in Behalfe of himselfe and Sam^ll Ely, Stephen Forbs, Nathan Foster, and Edward Foster, all of Willmington [Wilmington] Within Said State —

Humbly Sheweth that Sum Time in the month of June Last the Constable of the Town of Said Willmington Commanded your Pittitioners To assest him in the Execution of His office (viz) In Carrying one William Millin a Transhant Person out of Said Town / Who had Ben Warnd and Continued under Warning From Time to Time as by Law Directed —1 and Whareas Stephen R Bradly Esqr States attorney for the County of Cumberland in Pursuance of a Motitious [malicious?] Complaint to Him Exhibated — Cumminced an action Inbehalfe of this State against your Pittitioners for a Riot and by the undue Influance of interisted Men have obtained a Judgment in Behalfe of Said State for a Suposed Riot and your Pittioners being Greaved and Supose themSelves Greatly Ingured by Said Judgment Which Judgment if not Sett aside Will Ever be a Meanes of Detering the Good Subjects of this State from assisting the Sivel Oficers in the Execution of their office — and such actions insted of suporting the Govement Will Become an Enjoine [engine?] for its Distruction and will Be a Means of Vexation to the Inhabitants of this Common Welth if [as] soon as they assist one of the Civil officers in the Excution of his Office They Expose themselves to an action of Riot We have Further to Lay Before your honers The Pitticular Situation of Co^ll Williams Who is one of the Representatives for the Town of Willmington Who by the Judgment of S^d Court is in the Same Predicament With those Caled Rioters / and by means of Said Judgment is Diprived by Law from a Seat in this House (untill Said Judgment is) [sic] Sett a Side — and Consequently the Town of Willmington Diprived of its Shear of Representation — When by the Constitution of this State This House are to Judge of the Qualifications of there own Members.[,] Which[,] if Rioters[,] by long Custom and usage of Legislatures will be Deprived of a Seat and Whereas all the Dificalties Cummation [sic] and Contentions of the Town of Willmington are Consaqqent upon and Derive from the Dispute that Subsists Between the Differant Clamants to the Writs of Soil (and notwithstanding the Great Pains that has ben taken to Prevent your Honers from takeing Cognizeance of Said Dispute) — [your Honors' Petitioners beg?] that your honers as the Supream Court of the State — Would Interpose and Determin Said Disputes Between the Differant Clamants and Whereas the Proprietors under the Latter Charter by the Name of Draper Do utterly Decline Taking any advantage of the act of this House Pased at the Sessions in Benington in Octr Last —2 and as the Willmington Proprietors are in actual Posesion of Said Lands under a Prior Charter by the Name of Willmington[,] <and as the Draper> that they are-not under advantages to

---

1. See "An Act for ordering and disposing of transient persons" passed February, 1779 (Slade, p. 315).

2. An act entitled "An Act to impower the Superiour Court to try the validity of the Charters of Wilmington and Draper" was passed in its October session by the Assembly on 8 Nov. '80 (S. P. of Vt., III (I), 179). There is no record of the concurrence of the Council in this act or of the act itself in Ms. Laws of Vt. or Ms. Vt. S. P., Laws. Presumably it did become law, however, in view of the statement in the petition. In addition, an act entitled "An Act to prevent Trial of the Titles of Lands" was passed into law on 8 Nov. '80 and specifically declared that it should "not be construed to exclude a Trial concerning Wilmington and Draper" (Ms. Laws of Vt., I, 192).

Proseed in a Course of Law.[,]¹ as the Draper Proprietors have Purchased Lands under the Willmington Charter to Defend themselves from a Trial at Law[,] Therefore your Honers Pittitioner beg this Honorable House in Due time / And after Due Notice given the parties to Enter upon a Hearing of the Differant Clamants and Determin and Confirm the Title to Said Land as your Honner in Your Wisdom Shall Find Just and your Pittioners as in Duty Bound Shall Ever Pray
Wm Williams —

— & —

Coll Williams and Others
Petition —
. . .*

— & —

A. J.: *Petition "for a new hearing before the Superior Court &C" read and referred to a committee to join a committee from the Council, 23 Feb. '81, S. P. of Vt., III (I), 209. Rep. of Com.: Committee recommended that execution against petitioner et al. for riot be stayed and that Superior Court grant a rehearing, and further that the Assembly as a court of equity may determine the disputed grants; report read and accepted by Assembly, which resolved accordingly, 23 Feb. '81, S. P. of Vt., IV, 205–206. C. J.: *Committee appointed to join House committee, 23 Feb. '81, G. and C., II, 82.

FOR REDUCTION OF PROVISION QUOTA AND FOR
INDEPENDENT MILITIA SERVICE
xvii, 34

To the Honourable the General Assembly of the State of Vermont to Be Convened at Windsor on Wednesday the 7th Day of February A.D. 1781 The Memorial of your honours Most obediant and humble Servants Inhabitents of the Town of Shrewsbury in the County of Benington humbley Sheweth that your honours Memorialest Stand Ready and are free to exert themselves according to their Abilletys Equil With the Inhabitents of any Town in this State Both for the seport of Vermont its Goverment and the Defence of this and the United States A gainst the Common Enemy yet notwithstanding finding by Computation that the Quota in the provision act afixed to the Town of Shrewsbury² according to a Tru list of the poles and Ratable Estate of Said Town very unequil Being over Charged there fore Send to your honours our List³ and pray for Such Redress as your honours in their Wisdom Shall See Fit we would Begg Leave further to Informe your honours that the Gratest Matter of Greavance to us from which we Begg Releaf is that the Town of Clarindan [Clarendon] and Their Melitia officers Chalinge us and hold us in their Melitia Roles and Lay their Arbrateray Injunctions on us for Raiseing

---

1. The meaning of this clause is not clear. It is probable that the "they" in "they are-not under, etc." has reference to the petitioners, that is, Williams and those for whom he signed.

2. For this provision act and Shrewsbury's quota under it, see *Slade*, pp. 407–411.

3. For the method of computing the Grand List, see "An Act directing Listers in their office and duty" (*Slade*, pp. 295–298).

of the Men for the Insuing Campaign as they have heretofore Done as we think Very unEquil. as it is not More than Eighteen Months Since their has ben three families in the town. and we to a Man have Turnd out in the Larrams [alarms] the Last year and are now free to Comply with what Shall be judged our Quota in Raiseing the men for the Insuing Campaign by the Capt General or his Brigader or the field officers of the Rigment to which we Belong. unto whom proper Returns Shall Emediately be Made. if we May be freed from the Arctary [arbitrary?] Yoak of Clarindan as we Your Honours Memorialest in Duty Bound Shall Ever Pray Shrewsbury 4th of February A.D. 1781

Sum Total of the List of the
Poles and Ratable Estate of the
Town of Shrewsbury £128:10

Jeremiah Colvin
Nehemiah Smith
Lemiel White
Obadiah Green
Joseph [Rondart?]
Aaron Estey
Bennedeick Webber
William Smith
Amos Cass

— & —

the Petition & Grand List of Shrewsbury

— & —

[No Record]

FOR POSTPONEMENT OF COLLECTION OF PROVISIONS BECAUSE OF NEW YORK ADHERENTS
xvii, 32

To His Exelency Governer Chittenden together With the Honourable Council and General assembly of the Representatives of the freemen of the State of Veront [Vermont] Greeting
The petition of the Authority Melitioa Officers Selectmen and Others Inhabitants of the Town of Hallifax [Halifax] Humbly Sheweth that the Situation of your peteioners at present is Such that Renders it impracticable for us to discharge our Duty in our Respective Offices for to prosecute the orders Which we Receive from our Superiors Officers and in perticular our Raising our proportion of Provisions for the armey your peteioners therefore pray the Collection of the provision may be postponed for the preasant for the following Reasons (viz) first Because we are not able to Inforce one Single act by Reason of our Devision[1] Secondly Because at a Legal Town Meeting there were but 13 in the Town that Voted to Raise it 3^{ly} Because Many that Were friends to the State Do Declare they will revolt if they are oblig^d to pay it under the preasant administration of Goverment 4^{ly} Because the Yorkers have Invited all those who are oposed to the act to

---

1. This "devision" was, of course, the division among the inhabitants between the adherents of New York and those of Vermont.

take protection under them and Some have Gone Already and Signed their articles and we are Confident if it Must be Raisd at this time that the Inhabitants in General Will fling of [off] Goverment.

When we have Sent our under officers to warn them of a Draught the Yorkers have Confinᵈ Beat and abuseᵈ them Made them Burn their Orders and promis never to Return on Such Busines in this Manner we have Bin Treated for this Many Years without any Redress Which Renders Government a Burden to us insted of Secureing our Lives and properties under this Situation Your petitioners pray they may not be Called on for men or Money untill they have their Greavences Redressᵈ and are able to Soport Goverment

For as all Goverment ought to be Instituted and Soported for the Securety and protection of the Community as Such and to Enable the Individuals who Compose it to Enjoy the [Natural] Rights and the other Blessings Which the Great Author of Existance hath Bestowed on Man and Whenever those Great Ends of Goverment are not Obtained the people have a Right by Common Consent to Change it and Take Such Measures as to them may appear Necessary to promote their Safety and Happines and as your petetioners are friend to Goverment for the affore Said purposes and the Natural tendency a Disregard of this addrass May have in the Weakening this Riseing State We Canot But Hope and Expect that Your Exelency and Honours in Your Great Wisdom Will Redress our Greavences or those of us in Commission Must of Necessity Resign our office and Do Hearby Resign untill we see our Grevences Redressed —

This May Certifie to the Honourable assembly to Whom it is addrest that Doʳ William Hill and Mʳ Joseph Tucker Were Chosen (by a Large Number of the Inhabitants of Hallifax Conveanᵈ for Raiseing Men) to present this petition With the State of the Town to your Exelency and Honours Hallifax February ye 5ᵗʰ 1781

Hubbel Wells		Hubbel Wells Justes of peas
Israel Guile	Select	Caleb Owen Capt
John Sawtell	Men	Stephen Gates Leut
Wᵐ Hill		David Williams [Jⁿˢ]

— & —

[No Additional Material]

— & —

[No Record]¹

FOR CHARTER PRIVILEGE FOR A FERRY²
xvii, 45

To the Honourable the General Assembly of the State of Vermont to Set at Windsor on the first Wednesday of April 1781 —

---

1. For "An Act for the punishment of conspiracies against the peace, liberty, and independence of this State," passed in June, 1782, see *Slade*, p. 454. Attested copies of this act were sent to Halifax and other southeastern towns where the New York adherents were numerous and active. See *G. and C.*, II, 160*n*.

2. See note 3, p. 87, *post*.

The Petition of Amos Robinson Humbly Sheweth —
That your petitioner Did move into Hartford in Said State above nine years ago,
Settlements was then making on both Sides of Connecticut River, the Connections
of the people on both Sides of the River, Rendered it Necessary to have Correspond
[sic] with Each other, But they were put to much Difficulty by Reason of there
being no Boat to Cross the River in, within Twenty miles, So that they were
obliged to Swim Cattle horses &ᶜ across the River, and at Some Seasons of the
year at Great hazzard, Your petitioner Seeing the many Difficultys the people
Labourᵈ under upon them accounts, Did as Soon as possible build A Convenient
ferry Boat, and have given Constant attendance on the ferry for this Nine years,
Except one year your petitioners Boat was Caried away by the Ice in the Spring,
also your petitioner haith Expended Not Less than fifty Silver Dollors, in making
Landings & making & maintaining the Roads to the ferry, and as there are Some
persons that have never been at any Such Expence that frequently ferry people
when it will Sute their business, and Say they have a good Right So to Do, because
it is not Charterᵈ to any Body, which is an injury to your petitioner, and as it has
Ever been found by Experiance to be Necessary for the good of the publick to
have ferrys Regulated, —
    Therefore your Petitioner prays that your Honours would grant to him his
heirs and assigns A Charter privilidge of A ferry across Connecticut River within
the whole Limmits hereafter mentioned (viz) from the mouth of white [White]
River ‹to the Mouth of [Water?] Quechy [Ottauquechee] River› Thence Down
Connecticut River to Hartford South Line which is about four miles under Such
Restrictions and Regulations as in your wisdom Shall think proper —
and your petitioner as in Duty bound Shall Ever pray —

                                                        Amos Robinson

— & —

Amos Robinson Esqʳ
Petition for ferriage
. . .*

— & —

A. J.: *Read and referred until Wednesday next, 9 April '81, S. P. of Vt., III
(I), 219; *read again and dismissed, 10 April '81, Ibid, III (I), 221.

FOR REPRESENTATION IN THE ASSEMBLY FOR
A NEW YORK TOWN[1]
xvii, 40

To the Honble the Leagislature of the State of Vermont to be Conveaned at Windsor
on the first Wednesday of April Nixt the petition of the Subscribers Inhabetants
of Camdon [Camden] Humbly Sheweth that they are well in formed that the
Legislature of Vermont have Laid a Juresdictional Claim to all the Lands & waters
from where the Sd State now [exercises?] Jurisdiction to the Cernter of the Diepest

---

1. For an almost identically worded petition from Cambridge District, N. Y.,
see p. 36, post. For another petition with the same general purpose, see p. 33, post.

Channel of Hudson River[1] &c Where as the Government of N York have Niglected Guarding our Northern fronteers from British Invasions from the provence of Quebec & the fronteers have Much Destressd & Suffered great Losses on that Account and Such Calamitees Beeing In all Humain probility [Like?] to Continue if We Continue under the State of N Yourk and Where as it appears to us that if Vermont Extend Her Boundarees as Mentioned in Sd Claim the Whole would be abel to Raise A Compitant Number of men to Secure the Whole of her fronteers with the Assistance of her Melita [militia] in Case of Alarm it Appears By Various Accounts that there was A Goverment Ericted By the Court of Great Britain Before the presant Rivolution in Cluding the Lands that Vermont now Exercises Jurisdiction Over & A Considerable Westirn Extent over which Goverener Skeen was to have presided which in[duced?] us to acquees in the Aforesaid Claim of Vermont[;][2] that the Honr^ble the Legislature would pint out to us. Some way whereby the people in Cluded in the Said Claim might Be Represented in the Assembly Vermont as Soon as may Be & injouy Equel priviledges with the Citinsens of Said State and your petitianers as in Duty Bound Shall Ever pray

March 1781

Let [sic] John Patterson	abram Deboice	John P [Magee?]
Let [sic] James Morison	Alex^r Patterson	John Grinis
John Patterson	Jacob [. . .]	Jonas Saven
Jacob Patterson	Mical McCabe	Levi patterson
James Ramage	David [Barry?]	John Cimmons
John M^cmillan	Ezra Patterson	Tho Morison
Joseph Beitlett	James Morison Junr	James [. . .]
Elijah Scoot	Hue Martan	James Archer
Joseph Beitlet J^r	John m^cmillan	Josheph peterson
David Rice	John Nicklson	James Bolton
Bartholo Bartlet	Samuel Murdock	Thos Steel
David potison	John Murdock	John Steel
Chrisor page	Eley Murdock	

— & —

Petition of the Inhabitants of Camdon
See page 386

— & —

A. J.: House formed themselves into a Committee of the Whole with the Governor and Council to consider this and several other similar petitions, 10 April '81, S. P. of Vt., III (I), 220; report of Committee of the Whole recommending terms for admission of New York towns to representation in the assembly, read and accepted (Yeas and Nays given), 11 April '81, Ibid, III (I), 221–222. C. J.: Joined General Assembly in committee, 10 and 11 April '81, G. and C., II, 89.[3]

---

1. For the committee report and the consequent resolution of 14 Feb. '81 concerning this jurisdictional claim, see S. P. of Vt., III (I), 193–197.

2. For a discussion of Skene's alleged charter, see G. and C., II, 239n–240n.

3. For the actions of the Assembly and the Governor which joined to Vermont the New York towns north of the Massachusetts line and east of Hudson River in what was known as the Western Union, see G. and C., II, 297–308.

FOR RELIEF FROM INEQUITIES IN APPORTIONMENT
OF MILITIA SERVICE
xvii, 38

To the Honble the Legislature of the State of Vermont to be Convean^d at Windsor on the first Wednesday of April Next —
The Petition of the Town of Sunderland humbly Sheweth that your Petitioners Conseive themselves to be Called on to bear an unequal Burthen in Raising men for the Present Campaign that in giving the same Bounty that Neighbouring Towns do & Preportioning the same on the Grand List it amounts to about one third more on the Pound than such Bounty does in Neighbouring Towns which is Grievous — Your Petitioners ever willing to Contribute their Equitable Proportion of all Burthens to be Bourn by the State and unwilling to do more than their just share — [. . .] to sojest [suggest] a remedy[:] that the Legislature Pass an act in addition to the Melitia act that there shall be at Least twice a year a Return of Each Military Company of their numbers & the footing of the Grand List of such Company to the Officer Commanding the Reg^t who shall make a Regemental Return in Like manner to the Board of War[,] that the Board of War & the field Officers be Directed to have Referance to the List only in Proportioning men for the State's Service[,] that where any Reg^t Town or Company have done more than thier just Proportion that they be Equitably Considered in further military Services[,] that a Just Consideration be made to such as Turnd out in alarms this we Conseive as Esentially Necessary for the Peace & welfare of the state Who Cannot See why the giving a Bounty to raise men for the States Service is not the same in Essence as a State Tax Therefore we Cannot see why it Ought not to be Equaly Borun by the State at Large —
That for the Due Incouragement of that Patrioetick spirit of Freedom that has hitherto Defended this Country from Ruin & Imboldend her Bravest Sons to turn out in alarms much to the Prejudice of their Privat Conserns that the Board of War the feild & Other Officers of Melita be Directed to make Equitable allowances in other military services —
We submit these matters to the Consideration of the Honb^le the Legislature not Doubting but they in their Wisdom will Enact Laws that will Lighten the Burthens of their petitioners and do Equal Right throughout the State — and your Petitioners as in duty bound shall Ever Pray —

Signd p^r Order   Joseph Bradley ⎫ Moderator
of the Town   ⎬
                               Abner Hill ⎧ Town Clerk
                                          ⎩

State Vermont

Sunderland March 27 AD 1781
At a Legal Town Meeting held in Sunderland on the 27 Day of March 1781 Voted the above Petition be delivered the Representative and he be directed to Lay the Same before the General Assembly at their Next Session
Test   Abner Hill ⎫
                   ⎬ Town Clerk
                   ⎭

— & —

[No Additional Material]

— & —

A. J.: Read and referred to a committee to join a committee from the Council and if necessary to bring in a bill, 6 April '81, *S. P. of Vt.*, III (I), 216.[1]

FOR INCLUSION OF A NEW YORK TOWN IN THE GOVERNMENT OF VERMONT[2]
xvii, 39

To Thos Chittendon Esqr Capt General Gov[r] and Commander in Chief in and over the State of Vermont
this petition of the Subscribers Inhabitants of the town of Granvill [Granville] In the County of Charlottee and State afore Said humble Shoeth that your Excellency humble petitioners are fully [Sensable?] that the Extent Jurisdiction of Said State includes us and we Dearly feel the Sad Consequence of Not Being Enexed [annexed] to Said State of Vermont for Reseons [Reasons] that Ever Since the year 1777 we have been Left without any provition for Defence against the Maciless Indevations of our unnatierl Enmey and we Being a fruntier town to the Northward but ever Calld upon to Raise our Equl quotto of men year by year <and both pay and> and [who are] ever Stationed fair [far] below us —
and whareas the Right and Lawfull Juridiction of the State of Vermont Extend to the West of us We your Excullency Humble petitioners Begeth that your Excellency would Except of us as true and fathfull Subjects to the afore Said State of Vermont and adopt sum Mesher whearby we may be Better governd. Agreeable to the Ruels and Laws of the Constitution of the Afore Said State of Vermont
Your Excellency Humble petitioners Intrust your Greacious attention to this our Humble petition
As we in Duty Bound will ever pray
Granvill March 28th 1781

[Isat[r]?] Bennett	W[m] Tanner	David Aldridge
Jere. Burroughs	John Tanner	John Stuard
Asaph Cook	Jonathan Right	John Backus
Richard Crouch	Aaron Smith	John Thompson
David Skinner	John Walker	David Blakly
Thomas Grefas	Abraham Vanduzee	John Steward[,] Senor
Nath[ll] Spring	James V[n] Duzee	Solmon Baker

---

1. It is not clear from the Assembly journal whether or not any bill was brought in under this action. On 7 April '81 the Assembly, having placed the matter of the militia on its agenda, appointed a committee to consider the militia east of the Green Mountains (including the New Hampshire towns then in union with Vermont) and to bring in a bill for establishing the lines of the regiments (*S. P. of Vt.*, III (I), 217 (2). On 9 April '81 "An Act entitled 'An Act in addition to an Act for forming and regulating the Militia' was Read and Refered back to the Committee who prepared the same for alteration and amendment" (*Ibid*, III (I), 219). It seems probable that this act was reported by the committee appointed on the 7th and not by that of the 6th. In any case, although passed by the Assembly 11 April '81, it was sent back by the Council 12 April '81 and never became law (*Ibid*, III (I), 223, 225).

2. For two other petitions with the same general purpose, see p. 30, *ante*, and p.36, *post*.

Jabin Williams
Abraham Corly
Peter Grover
Isaac Moriethy
Micah Griffeth
Joseph Cook
Silas McWethey
Andrew Shory
Ebenezer Walker
Moses Sawyer
Josiah Mix
Stephan Grover
John Grover
Wm [Sumner?]
Moses Powers
Mikel Bowker
Joel Egbertson
James Hewenton
John Bateman
Rubin Mewethy
Wintrup Grayham
Jesse atwater
Eleazer Allbee
David Sawyer
Henry Watkins
Peter [Haverenton?]
Joseph [Hewenton?]
Daniel Sewerd
Natll Parker

John Spring
Eli Griffeth
Jeames Walker
Diah Sawyer
Abraham <Sawyer> foster
Richard Shapley
Wm Powers
Semeon Mcghelly
John Peyton
Gideon Allen
John Grover
Barichiah Harnden
Jonathan Harnden
Samel Harnden
John Harnden
Jeams Barns
Bejn Baker Jr
Daniel Curtice
Joseph Backus
James [. . .]
Ebenezer Gould
Charles Willson
Josiah fanswith
Zackeriah patterson
Jeremiah Browen
Jeams Barns
John Barns
Silas Child
Wintrop Graham

Samuel Colven
James Orcutt
Thos Gould
Benjn Baker Senr
Josiah farnsworth
Solm farnsworth
penawill Grover
Jeremiah Spencer
Thomas Gilberd
Timothy Baker
John Lutee
Obediah Witners
peter fullar
Isak row
Jediah Blackmer
Bennone Hoskins
Joseph Hide
Abrham Sharp
Josah Squires
Saml Chruch
Nukins Spoor
Leamaul Hide
Wm pair [. . .]
Aarnsiah Chrich
Silas Plicker
Stephen pipkin
Willis thomson
James Covel
David Warnor

108

— & —

To Thos Chittendon Esqr Capt General Govr and <commander>
Petition of the Inhabitent of Granvil
See page 386

— & —

A. J.: House formed themselves into a Committee of the Whole with the
Governor and Council to consider this and several other similar petitions, 10
April '81, S. P. of Vt., III (I), 220; report of Committee of the Whole recommending terms for admission of New York towns to representation in the
assembly, read and accepted (Yeas and Nays given), 11 April '81, Ibid, III
(I), 221–222. C. J.: Joined General Assembly in committee, 10 and 11 April
'81, G. and C., II, 89.[1]

---

1. For the actions of the Assembly and the Governor which joined to Vermont
the New York towns north of the Massachusetts line and east of Hudson River in what
was known as the Western Union, see G. and C., II, 297–308.

FOR A LOTTERY TO RELIEVE PERSONAL TROUBLES
xvii, 42

To the Honorable General Assembly of the State of Vermont Now Sitting at Windsor — The Pittition of Zebalon Case of Hartford in the County of Windsor Within Said State Humbly Sheweth that your Pettitioner is By the Providence of God Redused to the Greatest Destress for the Want of the Nesesaries of Life as Well as Wharewith to Discharge his Honest Depts Which Calamities are Brought on your Pittitioner by a Long and Continued Sean of Disteess By Sickness With Which your pettitoners Wife Irena Case is now Exersised / Ocationed by a Canser that Has ben of a Long Continuance in one of Hir Brests and has Continued untill of Late Dissected from Her Body Which will in all Provibility Continue hir yet for a Long time in a Languishing Condition if Life Should be Spared and Consequently Be a meanes of Increasing the Distreses of Your Pittitioner, therefore your Pittitoner With Humility Would Pray your Honers to take his Distressed Curcumstances into your Wise Consideration and Grant a Lotery for the Releaf of your Pittioner of the Folowing Construction and apoint Managers for the Same (viz) To Consest of 4000 Tickets at one Doler Each Which is 4000 Dolers

1 Prize of 200 Dolers is   200
2 D⁰   of 100 D⁰ — is   200
4 D⁰   of 40 D⁰ — is   160
10 D⁰   of 20 D⁰ — is   200
20 D⁰   of 10 D⁰ — is   200
1220 D⁰   of   2 D⁰ — is 2440
15 per Cent Deduction 600 is 600

————

4000

Thus in Pursuance of the advice of my Affectinat Neighbours I have Layd Before your Honers my Curcumstances and Request and Would Pray your Honners to Grant the Prayer of your Pittitioner and your Pittitioner as in Duty Bound Shall Ever Pray

Zebalon Case

— & —

Zebalon Case Pettition
Withdrawn
. . .*
In Council Windsor 6th Apl 1781
Voted John Throop Esqr to join the within committee.

Jos. Fay

— & —

A. J.: *Read and referred to a committee to join a committee from the Council, 6 April '81, S. P. of Vt., III (I), 217.

———

FOR ADDITIONAL COMPENSATION FOR WAR SERVICES
xvii, 41

To the Honble General Assembly of the State of Vermont To Set at Winsor [Windsor] April 4th 1781

The Petition of Samuel Robinson in Behalf of himSelf & officers and Soldiers To the Number of Sixtythree — Sheweth —
that your Petitioner was ordered To march To Rutland June 12th 1778 by the Captain General[1] and their Take the command of a Militia Company which orders your Petitioner obey[d] and their Staid Till July 10th then was Dismist: for which Service your Petiti[rs] was To have Proper Pay: and your Petiti[r] agreable To his orders from the Cap[t] Gen[r] — made up his Pay Role and Carried To Albany to the Paymaster their But No money in said office and So it was Repetedly Till your Peti[r] had spent more money then was Due to him on Said Role Wherefore his Excellency Some Time in the Begining of the year 1780 ordered your Pet[r] To Deliver his Role To Noah Smith Esq[r] Who was appointed Paymaster and In august Last your Peti[r] Received of him about 160 [lb?] Continental Currency amounting To Seven Dollars a Soldier But when they found out their wages would Not by them one Jill of Rum they Refused To Take it. and Desired your Piti[r] To Lay the matter before your Hon[rs] for an order of the house To his Exe[ll] & Council or the Board of war To Take the matter up: or your Hon[rs] in Some other way Grant Rilief as Honours Shall See meet and your Petitioners in Duty Bound Shall Ever Pray

Bennington April 2th 1781

Sam[ll] Robinson   { In behalf
                    { of the officers
                    { & Soldiers

N B
Col. Walbridge Can Inform Relating the Truth of facts as above

— & —

The Petition of Cap[t] Sam[ll] Robinson
. . .*

— & —

A. J.: *Read and referred until Monday next, 6 April '81, *S. P. of Vt.*, III (I), 214; *read and referred to the next session, 9 April '81, *Ibid*, III (I), 219.

FOR REPRESENTATION IN THE ASSEMBLY FOR A NEW YORK TOWN[2]
xvii, 44

To the Hon[le] the Legislature of the State of Vermont to be Convened at Windsor on the first Wednesday of April next —
The Petition of the Subscribers Inhabitants of Cambridge Destrict humbly Sheweth — That they are well Informed that the Legislature of Vermont have laid a Juris-

---

1. Presumably Capt. Robinson's orders were given to him personally, since the Governor and Council were then sitting at Bennington. There was a concentration of the militia in Rutland at this time for the defence of the frontier. See *G. and C.*, I, 265–267.

2. For an almost indentically worded petition from Camden, N. Y., see p. 30, *ante*, including notes. For another petition with the same general purpose, see p. 33, *ante*.

dictional Claim to all the Lands and waters from where Said State now Exercises Jurisdiction to the Centre of the deepest Channel of Hudsons river &c

Where as the Goverment of New York have neglected guarding our Northeren frontiers, from British Invasions from the Province of Quebec and the frontiers have been much distressed, and Suffered great Losses on that account, and Such Calamities being in all human probabillity, like to Continue, if we remain under the State of New York: — and whereas it appears to us that if Vermont Extend her Boundaries as mentioned in Said Claim the whole would be able to raise a Competant number of men to Secure the whole of her frontiers with the assistance of her malitia in Case of alarm — It appears by various accounts that there was a Goverment Erected by the Court of Great Britain before the present Revolution Including the Lands that Vermont Now Exercises Jurisdiction over and a Considerable western Extent over which Gove[r] Skeen was to have Presided; which Induces us to acquiesec in the aforsaid Claim of Vermont — That the Honor[l] Legislature would point out to us Some way whereby the people Included in Said Claim might be represented in the Assembly of Vermont as Soon as may be and enjoy equal priviledges with the Citizens of Said State and your Petitioners as in Duty bound Shall ever pray —

April 3[d] 1781

John Austin	John Selfridge	Solomon King
Solomon Hodge	John Morison Jn[r]	John Buskirk
Amos Buck	Austin Wells	Dirick Buskirk
William Skelly	W[m] Johnson	John Gibbs
Eben[r] Seely	Oliver Selfridge	Stephen Heath
Wm King	Joseph Caldwell	Thomas Foard
Sam[l] Morison	William Woodworth	Simeon Heath
Job Prince	David French	Jonathan Ward
Walter Rollo	George Duncans	David Backer
Nehemiah Earle	John Blair Jun[r]	W[m] Sharp
Josiah Cumar	Wm Edgar	Jacob Beaver
James Warner	Adin Tubbs	James Cowdin
Isaac Gibbs	Bazaleel Culver	Abel Fowler
Eneas Tubbs	Sam[l] Bell	Parvis Austin
Christ Lewis	Wm Woodworth Jn[r]	John Reynolds
Sam[l] Deming	Wm Shaaff	John Morison
Wm Burt	Joseph Dunham	Eben[r] Besse
Nathan Culver	Jacob Hoghtailior	James Cowan
John Shaaff	Thomas Jaquas	Bejuen Small
Peter Scott	Wm Gillmon	Thomas Steel
Archd Robertson	Robt Cowan	Tim[y] Heath
Daniel Wells	John Corey	Daniel Cloyd
Peter Rurner	Martinus Loop	Sam[l] Clark
Jn[o] Wier	Sam[l] Heath	Amos Weller
Henry Boice	John Money	Dan[l] Heath
James M[c]Waters	Thomas Whiteside	Oliver Selfridge Jn[r]
Jn[o] Scott	Joseph Peters	

— & —

Petition of the Inhabitants of Cambridge
See Page 386

— & —

A. J.: House formed themselves into a Committee of the Whole with the Governor and Council to consider this and several other similar petitions, 10 April '81, *S. P. of Vt.,* III (I), 220; report of Committee of the Whole recommending terms for admission of New York towns to representation in the assembly, read and accepted (Yeas and Nays given), 11 April '81, *Ibid,* III (I), 221–222. *C. J.:* Joined General Assembly in committee, 10 and 11 April '81, *G. and C.,* II, 89.[1]

FOR NEW COUNTY ELECTIONS OR SUSPENSION OF
TORY OFFICERS
xvii, 43

Rockingham Aprill y⁰ 9ᵗʰ 1781
To His Excelency The Govener and Council of the State of Vermont Now Setting at Windsor in Said State — the petition of us the Subscribers Inhabitents of the County of Windham Humbly Sheweth That Whereas the Honourable the General assembly Did at their Last Sessions appoint Times and places for County Elections[2] — Those friends to Ministerial Tiorany and Usarpation who was a Vowed Enemies to all authority Save what Derived from the Crown of Great Britton was Known Enemies to this and the United Stats of America at that Time Turnd Short about and be Came freemen of the State of Vermont and Not: onely published a Lybell in the Vermont Gazetee of anomination for County officers but privetly handed about Hand bils to friends to Ministerial power that they may be agred in the Choice — that the whol administration of Justice in the County of windham may be in the hands of the Known Enemies to this and the United States — and if there is proof wanted of this we will bring in their being active in and acserary [accessory] to the sheding the first Blood that Was shed in America to Support Brittanic Goverment: at: the Horrid and Never to be for Got Massacre Committed at Westminster Cortt House on the Night of the 13th of March 1775 O: horred Cean [scene] — And we Your Honours petitioners Cant Concive any Differance between being halled to Great Britton for Tryal or being Tryed by those Tools amongst our Selves } only we have precurd the Greatest illwill of those that Live amongst us who have Seen our Exartions In Supportt of Liberty — and as your Honours Wish well to those friends of Justice who have Sacrafised their all and Risked their Lives in the Supportt of Americain Independence and to Whoom Vermont owes its Existence — You will Ever: Do Every thing in Your power that their Liberties Should be Supported Inviolate — and With a firm Reliance on Your Wisdom: and Intigarity to Those Over whom You preside — We Humbly pray Your Honours To Take Your petioners Case into Your Wise Consideration — and move to the Honᵈ Assembly to appoint a New Election in and for the County of Windham or Suspend the Commisionating Noah Sabin Esqʳ as Judge of probate John bridgman Esqʳ Luke Knowlton Esqʳ & benjⁿ Burtt as Judges of the County Cortt } Oliver Lovell Esqʳ and Elias oliott as Justices of

---

1. For the actions of the Assembly and the Governor which joined to Vermont the New York towns north of the Massachusetts line and east of Hudson River in what was known as the Western Union, see *G. and C.,* II, 297–308.

2. See "An Act directing County Elections" passed February, 1781 (*Slade,* p. 421).

the peace — and Joneth^n Huntt as High Sheriff untill Your petitioners may Have oppertunity to Enter a proper Impeachment and prove to Your Honours that Said persons are Not onely Disquallefied for holding any public Station By their own bad Conduct: but Cannott be freemen of the State of Vermont by the Constitution thereof } or in Som other way Grant Releif: in the premisies as Your Wisdom Shall Dierect — as In Deauty bound Shall Ever Pray

Isaac Stoel	Joel Smith	William Hay
Elijah Knights	Luke Hitchcock	John Harwood
Moses marsh	⟨Elijah D^o⟩	Lemuel Bur
Charles Richards	Benjn Worcester	William Glazier
Charles Richards ^{Jr}	Timothy [Clossen?]	Nath^{ll} Davis
[Daniel?] Richards	Luke Hitchcock Jnr	Levi Davis
Tim^o Walker	Josiah White	Nathan Ware
John Rowndy	Wm Simonds	Ebenezer Pulsipher
⟨David Pulsipher⟩	Eben^{zr} Fuller	David Pulsipher
Uriah Rowndy	Gardner Simonds	Colburn [Pexston?]
Elisha Knight	John Titus	Wm Storrs
Wm Storrs J^r	Cornelius Baker	Tim^o Clark
John Pulsipher	Ebenezer [Hael?]	Joseph Parmetr
John Whitney	David Campeble	Nath^{ll} Whitcomb
Ezra Whitney J^r	Jonathan fuller	Philip Safford
Ezra Whitney	Andrer Simonds	Joseph Wood

NB the petitioners of this paper hold it sacred that it is our Right and priviledge to Chuse our own Justices in the Respective Town and them only, and We Trust that Your honours will Do Your Endevors to accomplish the Same for the futur — as Great Satisfaction will be Seen thereby —

— & —

[To?] His excelency the Governer and Honourable Counsil of the State of Vermont Now Setting at Windsor
Pitition of the Inhabitents Rockingham
Rec d in [Commit?] filed
filed 14th Ap^r 1781
refered for future Consideration

— & —

C. J.: Read and question put whether the commissions be suspended, which passed in the negative, 16 Apr '81, G. and C., II, 96.

FOR CONFIRMATION OF SQUATTERS' RIGHTS IN TOWN GRANTED BY ASSEMBLY

xxii, 25, 31

To the Honourable General Assembly Now Sitting in Bennington and in the State of Vermont —
Whareas we the Inhabetants of Farehaven [Fair Haven] which is now Your Honours Petitionars have been Grately Injured in our Persons and property by a

Number of Evil minded Persons who have a Grant of Said Fairhaven from the Honourable General Assembly in October in the Year one Thousand Seven Hundred and Seventy Nine[1] Yet we Suppose that the Grant was obtained through Some misrepresentation or Evil Design in those Persons. But through Inadvertancy in Your Honours as you was not made Sensible of our former Settlement in Said Town by any of those Persons But through their Low Cuning have Indevoured to Git a Grant of Said Land and turn of our Families into the open Clemency of the weather without Giveing of us the Least oppertunity of Securing our Selves in any Shape we being Persons who had for a Long time before Improved the Land and Ware Determined to Petition Your Honours the first Oppertunity that would Present but was Cut Short by those persons who Never Gave us the Least Oppertunity to be represented in the Petition which we think is Cruel and hard and which will tend to abridge us of our wrights and Previlidges unless Some Meathods are taken by your Honours to redress Injured Justice and prevent those Persons from Disturbing us in our Possessions as we are Persons that have Left the Southern Parts of the New England States of Amaraca and have flead to Vermont to Resume its Liberties —

And Promote it Intrest by Cultivating and Menuring its Lands and by Defending the Liberties of our Country and we find our Selves under the Necesity of Lifting up our Earnest prayers to your Honours that we may be Redressed in this Case and Quieted in our Possesions as it is the only Resort that We Can take and we flatter our Selves as your Honours are now Informed of the true State of our Situation and this unjust measurs that those persons have taken to Ruin us that we Shall find favour in your Sight and as other Persons who have ben in our Situation have Ben Quieted in their Possessions we most Earnestly Pray That this may be the Case with us and we your Petitioners as In Duty Bound Shall Ever pray

Joseph Carver
Joseph Haskin
Jonathan Hall
Benoni Halebart
John Vanduzer

— & —

Joseph Carver Petition
Filed 13th June 1781
See page 429 —
Report Recorded Vol. 2[d] page [95?]
. . .*

Whereas it appears that one Certain Joseph Carver a triantient [transient] Person said to be an Inhabitant of the State of Rodiseland [Rhode Island] — Not having the fear of God before his Eyes — with out my Consent has by a petision Signd by him Self & others made up of my Name which I avar [aver] to be With out the Least koledge [knowledge] or Concent of mine Which is Not only a gainst my will but a gainst my Intrust and Do here by Remonstrate against any act or things being Done in answer to said Petision by the Honorable General Asembly to whome said Petision is Directed as it is a Lye bill [libel] in its Nature and

---

1. For this grant, see *S. P. of Vt.*, III (I), 94–95; and for charter of Fair Haven, see *S. P. of Vt.*, II (Vermont Charters), 73–74.

attends Not only to make disturbance and doo great Evel in the Town ship of Fair haven [Fair Haven] but Will greatly impede the Settlement of Every other Grant obtaind under the Seal of Vermont —

and I further Declare that I do not hold my intrust in said town by Vertue of Possession only but by Vertue of the grant made to the Proprietors in oct[obr] 1779 who have Not Disturbd me in my improvements but otherwise have granted me the Previledge of Covering my Possestion with any Part of a Proprietors Right which Land has bin given me by Col[o] Clark to prevent any Disturbance being made to the old Possessiers — &c Given under my hand at Chester this 26th Day of May 1782

Benoni Hurlbut

in Presants of —
Ber[h] Mitchel
Eleazar Dudley

— & —

A. J.: *Read and referred to next session, 19 June '81, S. P. of Vt., III (I), 248; *read and referred to a committee, 23 Feb. '82, Ibid, III (II), 65; *report of committee recommending that petition be laid over to next session, that adverse party be notified, and that petitioners not be disturbed in possession until next session, read and ordered that a bill be brought in accordingly, 25 Feb. '82, Ibid, III (II), 76; resolved that adverse party be notified and that petitioners be quieted in possession until next session, 25 Feb. '82, Ibid, III (II), 77; *read again as referred from last session, and, petitioners being thrice publicly called and none appearing to show cause why petition should not be dismissed, said petition dismissed, 20 June '82, Ibid, III (II), 110.[1]

FOR SETTLEMENT OF THE STATE'S ACCOUNTS[2]
xvii, 46

To the Hon[ble] the Gen[l] Assembly of the State of Vermont now Convened in Bennington The Petition & address of Ira Allen Treasurer of Said State Humbly Sheweth — That he haith been from the formation of Said State annually Elected to the office of Treasurer — That he haith at several Differant Sessions of the Legislature Petitioned Either by Writing or Verbally for a Settlement Showing the Necessity of the states first Setling with the several Commissioners of Sales Sequestration &c — That he haith never been able to make one settlement & haveing a Learge Number of Receipts on file Taken in Continental money at the Varing Stages of Depretiation the State is Credited for their Respective Sums & a Number of Such Receipts are Delivered the Paymaster Who must Settle them on the Payroles by the Scale of Depretiation many other accounts are nearly in a Similar Situation

The Treasurer Therefore Earnestly requests That the Gen[l] Assembly would Take up these matters & Give him some Instructions on the subject so as to Enable

---

1. The entry on the manuscript petition includes the notation that this action was taken "On motion made by M[r] Brace in behalf of the proprietors of Fair Haven".

2. For other petitions from Ira Allen in connection with the settlement of the state's accounts, see pp. 332, 348, post.

him to do Justice to the State & himself & Keep his Books in such a Manner that the Accounts may Stand fairly Ballanced in a Day when a Council of Censures may Examin them — The Treasurer Thinks it of the utmost Consequences for the Safety Peace & Wellfare of the State that himself Together with all other Persons that have been intrusted with Public money should be setled with without Loss of Time & the more so as there is additional Territories added to this State

Your Petitioner Flatters himself that his Requests will appear so reasonable & so Intresting to the State that it will Claim the serious attention of the Legislature & that your Honers will Grant your Petitioners Requests which will Lay him under an additional obligation.

Ira Allen

Bennington 13th June 1781

— & —

Col^o Allen [Treasury?]
Petition for a Settlement
. . .*
To the Hon^l Genl Assembly now Sitting

Your com^{ee} appointed to take into Consideration the Subject matter of this petition beg Leave to Report that it is our Opinion that the commisinon [commission] appointed to auditt Publick acc^t be further Directed & Impowerd for Setling accts with the Treasuer to ajust the Same agreeable to Equity on the Case as may appear to them

Nath^{ll} S Prentice for Com.

In General Assembly June 27 1781
The above report was read & dismissed and the petition recommitted to Mr Olin Mr Powell & Mr King to join a committee from the council

Attest B Woodward clk P.T.

In Council 27th June 1781
Voted John Fassett Esqr to Join the within Committee

Attest Joseph Fay Secy.

— & —

A. J.: *Read, 18 June '81, S. P. of Vt., III (I), 246; *read and referred to a committee, 26 June '81, Ibid, III (I), 264; *report of committee [appointed 27 June '81, see supra] recommending that treasurer be directed to settle with the auditors appointed to settle public accounts as the law of this state directs, read and accepted, 27 June '81, Ibid, III (I), 265–266.

FOR SECURITY AGAINST DEBTS CONTRACTED FOR THE PUBLIC
xxi, 301

[To the Hon^{ll} the Legislature of the State of Vermont in General Assembly convened —

The Petition of Isaac Tichenor Esqr lat Com^y of P. for the States of New Hapshire [Hampshire] & Vermont Sheweth, that]

Whereas your Petitioner in the Year 1777 was Commissioned as Purchaser for the Armies of the United States in the Limits above described, under the Directions of Jacob Cuyler Esqr D C G^{ll} for the N. Department, and continued in

s^d Office untill the resignation of Jeremiah Wadsworth Eq^r C.G of P. for the U.S — s; when Congress directed each State to furnish their proper Quota of Provision for the use of the Army, & appoint their own Purchasers, & by a Resolve requested Col^n Wadsworth and his Agents to continue their Services, untill the States by their appointment & Exertions were enabled to Supply the Army with Provisions, which took Place in Sepr 1780 —

Your Petitioner has never been enabled by the Public to discharge the whole of his Contracts for the use of the Army in the Year 1779 & 1780, tho' repeated applications has been made to Congress for the purpose; and that Hon^{ll} Body by a Resolve of the 26th of Augt 1780, declared their inability to discharge the debt due to Col^n Wadsworth and his Agents; & requested each State to take proper Measures for the discharge of the Same & that Congress would Credit such State or States for Money so paid —[1] Which Resolution has been complyed with, on the part of the United States, & Col^n Wadsworth & his Agents are freed from those Debts, & the Public Creditors have the States Security in which they reside for the Payment of their Dues —

Your Petitioner in the Execution of his Office has made considerable Contracts for the Army in this State, which s^d Contracts, he has never been enabled by the Public to discharge — And as the Resolutions of Congress, respecting the purchasing Departments cannot be pleaded in this State, in Justification of the Contracts he was obliged to make upon the Faith of the States [. . .][2] Interest by the [law] of this State is [. . .] to the [payment?] [. . .],[2] & in fact is [. . .] for the [. . . .][2]

He therefore earnestly requests the Hon^{ll} House to secure to him and his Agents their Private Property entire, from answering those Debts, Contracted in & for the Public, by such ways & means as the Wisdom of the House shall direct — And your Petitioner as in Duty Bound will ever pray

Isaac Tichenor
late A.C.G^{ll} of P.[3]

Bennington June 25th 1781

— & —

The Petition of Isaac Tichenor late A. C. G of P. for the United States
. . .*
In Council June 25th 1781
Resolved that Mr Emmons & Mr Spooner be a Committee from the Council to Join the above committee

Attest Thos Tolman D. Secr^y

Report of Committee on Mr Tichenors petition
June 26th 1781
June Session 1781
To the Honorable the Generall Assembly of the State of Vermont now Setting at Bennington
The Committee Appointed to take into Consideration the Petition of Isaac Tichenor

---

1. For this resolution, see *Journals of the Continental Congress 1774–1789* (Washington, 1910), vol. XVII (1780), pp. 782–783.

2. Three or four words are lost because of the partial destruction of the manuscript.

3. Assistant Commissary General of Purchases.

Esq beg leave to Report that it appears to us by the Certificates given by Jacob Cuyler Esq late Deputy Commissary General of Purchases dated May 30th 1781. that There is due to the said Techinor & his Agents for Publick purchases made since the Year 1777 & 1778. Sixty Five thousand one hundred & Eighty Four pounds. Nine shillings & Fourpence Continental money & One Thousand Three hundred & twenty Four pounds Fourteen shillings & two pence in Specie Value besides His Wages and That he hath taken due pains to procure said Monies from the Publick but hath hitherto been wholly unable to obtain The same We also find that said Tichinor and the Agents under him have given their private Notes of hand to the Several persons of Whom they Purchas'd for the use of the Publick. and that said Tichiner & his Agents are in Danger of being entirely ruind if Actions should be bro't and Supported on the Notes before Mentiond. in order to prevent the said Tichinor and his Agents who Served the Publick from being ruind. Your Committee give it as their Opinion that all and every Action already commenced against The said Techinor or his Agents for Publick purchases by Them made Shall be Stayed until the rising of the next Session of the General Assembly in October next unless The said Tichiner shall recieve the Publick Monies Due to him as above mentioned. which may first happen and That no Action shall be Supported that may be commenced against said Techinor or his Agents for Purchases made in behalf of the Publick until the rising of the next Session of the General Assembly in October next or until the said Techinor shall Recieve the Monies due to him as before mentioned —

In behalf of the Committee
Benj. Emmons   Chairman

In General Assembly June 26. 1781. The within [report] was read & accepted, and order'd that a bill in form [be] bro't in accordingly —

Attest Beza Woodward Cl pro. tim —

— & —

A. J.: *Read and referred to a committee to join a committee from the Council, 25 June '81, *S. P. of Vt.*, III (I), 261; act to suspend prosecutions against petitioner for public purposes till rising of next session read and passed and sent to Council, 27 June '81, *Ibid*, III (I), 265.[1]

FOR THE WITHDRAWAL OR RENEWAL OF AN APPOINTMENT TO OFFICE
xvii, 47

To the Honourable the House of Representatives of the Freemen of the State of Vermont in General Assembly met in Bennington. —

The Petition of Matthew Lyne of Said State. —

Humbly Sheweth

That the Honorable House did in their Sessions in October last appoint your Petitioner Superintendant Commissary of Issues for this State, but the same being sent to the upper House, by whom it was referred to the reconsideration of the next Sessions, deeming it unnecessary, at that Juncture, that such an Appointment

---

1. For this act, see *Ms. Laws of Vt.*, I, 250–251.

should take place on acc^t of the Winter Approach and very little to do in that department, At the next Sessions it was forgot and has passed hitherto neglected.[1]

That your Petitioner in Consequence of the above determination of the Upper house and Resolves of the Lower has remained here and waited for its Accomplishment (having with a View to serve the State refused an Appointment under the United States) and in full Expectation of his being either reconsidered or finally rejected.

Your Petitioner not desirous of remaining in an Ambiguous Situation pray the Honorable House to either rescind their Resolves of October Sessions last, or renew them in this.

And your Petitioner
Shall ever pray &c

Bennington 28th June 1781   Matthew Lyne

— & —

Petition of Matthew Lyne
In General Assembly June 28th 1781
Read & Dismissed
Matthew Lynde Esqr
Petition
Dismissed — June 28th 1781

— & —

[No Record]

FOR RIGHT TO TRY TITLE TO CERTAIN LAND AND TO SELL REAL PROPERTY TO SETTLE AN ESTATE

xxi, 307

To the honorable the Representatives of the freemen of the State of Vermont to convene in Legislature at Charlestown the second Thursday in October next.

The Petition of Mary Whipple of Brattleborough [Brattleboro] in the County of Windham, Widow of Daniel Whipple Esqr late deceased Humbly sheweth,

That Atherton Chaffee late of Westminster in the said County deceased, by his Deed, dated the 23^d day of November Anno Domini 1770, for a valuable Consideration, conveyed to your Petitioner's late Husband, a Lot of Land situate in Westminster aforesaid, containing by Estimation thirty Acres. —

That when the Town of Westminster was afterwards repatented under New York, the said Chaffee was not named in the Patent, but the said Lot was conveyed by Josiah Willard Esqr (who sued out the Patent) to your Petitioner's late Husband; who, as owner of the said Lot, paid his proportion of the Expence of sueing out the new patent. —[2]

---

1. For record of this appointment, and its reconsideration and postponement 7 Nov. '80 and 8 Nov. '80, see *S. P. of Vt.*, III (I), 172, 181. No record remains of any action in the matter by the Governor and Council.

2. For the Westminster patent, granted 26 March '72, see *S. P. of Vt.*, VII (New York Land Patents covering Lands within the State of Vermont), 321–328.

That the said Daniel Whipple, by virtue of the said Deed from said Chaffee, was in Possession of the said Lott for the space of one year or upwards; and was then dispossessed by the said Atherton's entering thereon immediately upon the said Daniel's Tenant moving out; whether by collusion with the said Tenant, or otherwise, your Petitioner is unable positively to say.

That the aforementioned Daniel in his lifetime commenced a Suit against the said Atherton for recovering Possession of the said Lot, which was by the aforesaid Atherton first removed into the supreme Court of the Province of New York, and from thence into the Court of Chancery; which afforded ample Opportunity for the Intrigue of a designing crafty Attorney to protract the Suit, until the Death of your Petitioner's said late Husband, which happened in January 1775. —

That by this sorrowful Event your Petitioner was left to provide for seven Children, all of whom were unable to earn a Subsistence for themselves; and with an Estate much incumbered with Debts which carry Interest, as well as others.

That your Petitioner having hitherto been unable to settle said Estate for want of proper officers with whom to transact the Business, is fearful that from the accumulated Interest, and the necessary Expences attending the Support and Education of so large a Family of helpless Children, the whole Estate of her late husband, both real and personal, is now but barely sufficient to pay just Debts; — or perhaps will net a small Surplussage for supporting and educating the younger Children. —

Being thus circumstanced your Petitioner has no where to apply for Relief but to this honorable House the Friend of the Widow and the Fatherless

And therefore humbly prays that this honorable House will give leave to your Petitioner to bring forward a Suit for trying the Title of the said Lot of Land as speedily as possible; and grant leave to your Petitioner to sell so much of the real Estate as (including the personal Estate which by Law ought to be disposed of) will be sufficient to discharge the Debts of her said late Husband. —

And your Petitioner, as in duty bound, shall ever pray &c. — Brattleborough
24th August 1781   nary [Mary] Whipple

— & —

. . .*

— & —

A. J.: *Read and ordered to lie on the table, 13 Oct. '81, S. P. of Vt., III (II), 8; *committee appointed to consider petition, 17 Oct. '81, Ibid, III (II), 13; report of committee recommending that petitioner be empowered to sell £750 of real property to settle debts, read and accepted, and ordered that a bill be brought in accordingly, 26 Oct. '81, Ibid, III (II) 35; act read and passed the House, 27 Oct. '81, Ibid, III (II), 36. C. J.: Act read and concurred in,[1] 27 Oct. '81, G. and C., II, 126.[2]

1. For this act, see Ms. Laws of Vt., I, 265.
2. On 21 Oct '83 the petitioner presented a new petition (not now among the Ms. Vt. S. P.) seeking liberty to try the title to the land in Westminster. This was granted and an act passed accordingly. See S. P. of Vt., III (II), 206, 208; also Ms. Laws of Vt., I, 410.

FOR A NEW TRIAL IN A LAND CASE
xvii, 49, 50[1]

State of Vermont

    To the Honorable the Representatives of the Freemen of the State of Vermont, in general Assembly convened —

Humbly Shewn

Enoch & Eliphalet Bean, that the Said Enoch was Lawfully Seized in Fee Simple of a Certain Lott of Land numbered 18, in the first Range in Strafford, and The said Eliphalet was in Possession of the Land under The said Enoch as Tenant; That Some time in July last a Complaint was made against your Petitioners By John Alger of Strafford in the County of Orange for forceably Entering & Detaining the Possession of the Same Lott of Land. That on a Trial on That Complaint Before Jonathan Child and Bildad Andross Esq[r] Two of the Justices of The Peace for said County on the 23d Day of August Last, The said Enoch Bean was aquitted By a Verdict of a Jury, and the said Eliphalet found guilty, and a Judgment given against him, and he was accordingly Put out of Possession, and The Said Alger put, in By which means the said Enoch is deprived of his Freehold, of which he was Lawfully Seized in Fee-Simple, and ought now to be in full Possession — And your Petitioners Beg Leave further to Suggest, that the said Judgment was Erroneous, and illegal — Because they Say that the verdict on which said Judgment was rendered — was founded on Evidence which was not legally admissable on that trial: and that The officer who attended The Jury was not an indifferent Person, being nearly related to the Complaint — and The said officer Did Converse with The Jury on the Matter, Before them while agreeing in their Verdict, and as no Appeal lay from Said Judgment and as your Petitioners think it extremely hard, that the one Should Be Deprived of his Freehold and the other subjected to the Payment of a large Bill of Cost, which is taxed against him, They are therefore Reduced to the Disagreeable necessity of troubleing this House to grant them that Releif, which as they Conceive, they can obtain from no other authority whatever They Therefore pray that they may have Leave to Bring in a Bill to disanul The Said Judgment and granting them a new trial in the Premises — And as in duty bound shall ever pray

Enoch Bean for
himself and the said
Eliphalet Bean

Charlestown Oct[r] y[e] 16th 1781.

— & —

The Petition of Enoch and Eliphalet Bean: praying for a New Trial.

Filed 17th Oct[r] 1781

Fees p[d]

Report of Com[tee] of Oct. 20th 1781 — Read & accepted

Feb[y] 12th Read and granted.

---

    1. The manuscript on p. 49 is the original, while that on p. 50 is a copy identical as far as the body of the petition is concerned, except for punctuation. The copy contains additional material not found in the original. The printed text follows the punctuation of the original and contains additional material from both the original and the copy.

State of Vermont
To the Sheriff of the County of Orange or his Deputy or any Constable of Strafford in said County Greeting
In the Name of and by the authority of the Freemen of the State of Vermont you are hereby commanded to make known to the said Alger that he appear before the General Assembly of this State on the Second day of their next Session to shew cause if any he have why the prayer of the said petition should not be granted. Given under my hand this 19th day of Octr AD 1781

                                        Jon^a Childs Jus^t Peace
Strafford November 8th Day AD 1781
this Day [Read?] the within in the hering of John Alger By me
                                        David Chamberlin Constable
. . .*

— & —

A. J.: *Read and referred to a committee, 18 Oct. '81, S. P. of Vt., III (II) 15; *report of committee recommending that a hearing be granted at the next session, read and accepted, 20 Oct. '81, Ibid, III (II), 18; *referred to a committee, 11 Feb. '82, Ibid, III (II), 46; report of committee recommending a new trial read, and ordered that a bill be brought in accordingly, 12 Feb. '82, Ibid, III (II), 48; an act granting a new trial and annulling the previous judgment read and passed,[1] 13 Feb. '82, Ibid, III (II), 50. C. J.: Read and concurred in, 14 Feb. '82, G. and C, II, 139.

FOR ESTABLISHMENT OF NEW TOWN LINES
xxii, 41

To the Honorable the Legislature of the State of Vermont now convened
The petition of John Simonds Agent in behalf of the Proprietors of the township of Andover in the County of Windsor
Sheweth —
That in the Charter of said Township of Andover, the bounds of said town are thus laid down viz. "Beginning at the South westerly corner of Ludlow, from thence running South fifty five degrees east six miles by Ludlow to the Northwesterly corner of Flamstead, then by Flamstead about six miles to the southwesterly corner thereof, thence north sixty three degrees west six miles, thence 30^d east six miles and three quarters to the south westerly corner of Ludlow the bounds begun at" —[2] which surveys are not laid down so as to contain the true intent and meaning of the Charter; for we have since found that the last line mentioned in said bounds which is 30^d east six miles and three quarters, will carry the line east of the bounds begun at between one and two miles, and will therefore curtail your petitioners of a large quantity of land, which your petitioners judge of right belongs to them, and which is meant by the Charter, but entered through a mistake —

---

1. The Assembly journal contains an identical entry for the passage of this act on 14 Feb. '82. See S. P. of Vt., III (II), 53. The double entry was probably an error by the clerk. For the act itself, see Slade, pp. 444-445.
2. For the charter of Andover, see State Papers New Hampshire, vol. XXVI (Town Charters, vol. III), pp. 7-11.

And your petitions would further inform your Honors that the said town of Andover is bounded on Flamstead &.C. which Flamstead is since called Chester. We therefore pray your honors would order confirm and establish the lines of Andover to be as follows viz ["] beginning at the Southwesterly corner of Ludlow, from thence running South 55ᵈ east 6 miles by Ludlow to the northwesterly corner of Chester, then by Chester about 6 miles to the South westerly corner thereof, and the north easterly corner of Londonderry, then on the north line of Londonderry six miles thence North 13ᵈ east 6¾ miles to the south westerly corner of Ludlow the bounds begun at" which we humbly conceive is the true intent of the charter afore mentioned and pray your honors would take our case under consideration and grant us relief therein and we as in duty bound shall ever pray —
Charlestown Octʳ 19ᵗʰ 1781   John Simons ⎱ Agent in behalf of the
                                                 ⎰ proprietors

— & —

Capt John Simonds Agent in behalf of the Proprietors of Andover
Petition
Filed 23ᵈ Octʳ 1781
Recorded vol. 2ᵈ page 106
. . .*

— & —

> *A. J.:* *Read and referred to a committee, 25 Feb. '82, *S. P. of Vt.*, III (II), 76; *report of committee recommending that petition be granted, read and accepted, and ordered that a bill be brought in accordingly, 26 Feb. '82, *Ibid*, III (II), 84; bill establishing town's bounds read and passed, 27 Feb. '82, *Ibid*, III (II), 88; resolved that last line mentioned in the charter close at the corner where the description of the bounds begins, 28 Feb. '82, *Ibid*, III (II), 92.¹

FOR A TOWNSHIP OF LAND
xxi, 325

To His Excellency the Governor the honorable Council & general Assembly of the State of Vermont the humble Petition of the subscribers sheweth —

That being impressed with a deep sense of the Right the Inhabitants of Vermont have to be a free & independant State and having a high veneration for those brave & virtuous citizens who have not only distinguished themselves against the common Enemy of the United States but against all the clandestine Enemies to the Rights of Mankind and the State of Vermont in particular —

And having an earnest desire to be leagued with them in Interest as they ever have been in Affection and principle most humbly pray your Excellency the Honorable Council & Assembly to grant a certain tract or Township of Land in some part of the territory of Vermont And your Petitioners as in duty bound shall ever pray

Benjamin Colt	Gardiner Kellogg	Samuel Clark
John Eastman	Moses Cook	Phinehas B Clark
Moses Marsh	Ethan Pomeroy	Joshua Clark

---

1. The bill passed 27 Feb. '82 apparently never became law. Possibly the concurrence of the Council was refused, although of this there is no record. In any case the petition was granted by the resolution passed 28 Feb. '82.

Timothy Eastman
Noadiah Warner
Noah Goodman
Ithamar Goodman
Moses [Hannun?]
Elijah Lyman
Tho⁵ Gates
Jonathan Town
Thomas Smith
Ephraim Smith
Job Marsh
Joseph Marsh
Moses Kellogg
Enos Nash
Josiah Nash
Noah Cooke
Amasa Cooke
Sam¹¹ Cook
Nathaniel White

Daniel Marsh Jᵘⁿ
Caleb Lyman
Joseph Coots
William Lyman
Joseph Clarke
Joseph Lathrop
Cha⁵ Phelps
David Mitchell
Thomas [a Whit]
Eliphalet Gaylord
Martin Wait
Job Alvord
Ruggles Woodbridge
Gad Cook
Joseph Smith
Amasa Smith
Eli Smith
Enos Smith
Caleb Clark

Eleazer Clark
Stephen Goodman
James Goodman
Stephen Goodman juʳ
Moses Hubbard
David Dickinson ⎱ 6/ paid
Simeon Burt   ⎰
Sam¹¹ Hopkins
Joseph Latroop
Bulkley Olcott
John Chester Williams
Ebenezer Sparhawk
Joshua Darte
Danᵉˡ Tillotson
Benjⁿ Butterfield Junʳ
Joseph Smith 3ᵈ
Timothy Lyman
Phinehas Lyman

— & —

Petition from Benjⁿ Colt & Associates for Land
filed 7ᵗʰ Novʳ 1781 —

— & —

[No Record]1

FOR AUTHORITY TO HOLD A PROPRIETORS' MEETING AT A DISTANCE

xxii, 21

To His Excillency the Goverer and Counsel and Genneral Assembley of the State of Vermont to Be Holden at Benington [Bennington] in Sᵈ State on the Last Thursday of january Next —
the Pertition of the proprietors of Williams town [Williamstown] in Sᵈ State Humbly Sheweth that Wharas Sᵈ town Lyeth Very Remote from the gratest part of Sᵈ proprietors and as it is Nessesery that a Lawfull meeting of Sᵈ proprietors Should Be Holden and your petitioners Humbly pray that your Excillency and Honours wold take it into your Consideration and pray that in your Wisdom you may See fit to grant that a meeting may Be held in the County of Benington in Such town as your Excillency and Honours Shall See fit to apoint as the proprietors Live Chiefly in the South part of the County of Benington and in Williams town in the Common Wealth Massachusetts

---

1. The names of Benjamin Colt and many other signers of this petition appear in the charter of Brookfield granted 5 Aug. '81. However, it should be noted that this grant antedated the filing of the petition. See *S. P. of Vt.*, II (Vermont Charters), 30–31.

Sign^d in Behalf of S^d proprietors

Absalom Baker ⎰ [prop?]
⎱ Clerk

— & —

Absolom Baker's Proprietors Clerk petition —
See page 65. vol. 2^d
. . .*

— & —

A. J.: *Read and dismissed, 14 Feb. '82, S. P. of Vt., III (II), 53.

FOR COMPENSATION FOR WAR DISABILITY
xvii, 53

To the Honourable the General Assembly of the State of Vermont to be Convened
at Bennington on the Last Thursday of January A D 1782 —
The Petition of Joseph Frost of Westminster in the County of Windham and State
of Vermont
    Humbly Sheweth —
    That your Honour^s Petitioner in August 1777 was a Soldier in Capt Ferry'^s
Company and Col^n Wm Williams Rigement of Militia of this State and was Call^d
forth into Action on the 16th Day of August aforesaid in Defense of his Country
in that ever Memorable Battle of Bennington where twas the Misfortune of Your
petitioner to receive a Shott in his Left Arm which Cut the Sinews of Said Arm
and so far Shattered the Bones as rendered your petitioner unable to do any manner
of Work for Six Months —
your Honours Petitioner would further Remark that he has intirely Lost the uše
of his Thum and Little finger on Said Arm which Greatly Obstructs your Petitioner
in procuring a Surport by the Labour of his hands on which he Solely Depended
    Your petitioner would therefore pray your Honours to take his Case into
your Wise Consideration and for the Loss of Blood and Limb, which he has sustained in Defence of your Honours Sovereignty Grant him Some Reward as to
your Honours Shall Seem Just and Your petitioner as in Duty Bound Shall ever pray
                                                                    Joseph Frost

— & —

Joseph Frost Petition —
. . .*

— & —

A. J.: *Read and referred to next October session, 20 June '82, S. P. of Vt.,
III (II), 110.[1]

---

1. On 8 June '85 this or a similar petition from Joseph Frost was read and referred
to a committee. The report of this committee was brought in 10 June '85 and recommended that Frost receive £35 for his service at Bennington and for his wound. The
Assembly, having read the report, directed the Treasurer to pay him that sum. See S. P.
of Vt., III (III), 132, 137. If a new petition was drawn up in 1785, no copy of it has been
found in the Ms. Vt. S. P.

FOR COMPENSATION FOR WAR SERVICES
xvii, 78
(Incomplete)

[. . .][1] and all reasonable expenses of such recovery allowed [them] That as he was then serving in the voluntary company who had turned out for defense of inhabitants within the original limits of Vermont,[2] he conceives it reasonable that his said expenses of time & money in recovery of his wound be discharged by the said State, [and] has no where else to look for relief —

Your petitioner therefore humbly prays that this honorable assembly will be pleased to allow and grant [. . . .][1]

— & —

Charles Tilden's Petition — 1782
Feb[y] Session Refered to next Session —
. . .*3

— & —

A. J.: *Read and referred to a committee, 12 Feb. '82, S. P. of Vt., III (II), 48.

FOR THE DETERMINATION OF A DISPUTED TOWN LINE
xxii, 9

To the Honorable General Assembly of the state of VERMONT to be held at Bennington on Thursday 31st Jan[y] Instant.

The Petition of the Proprietors, and other inhabitants of Dorsett, Bennington County, humbly Sheweth.

That whereas disputes have arose between the inhabitants of Manchester, and those of Dorset, respecting the boundary line between said Towns; which disputes have been for a number of years past, and still continue to exist: and especially between those persons in each town, whose land lays Contiguous to said line — in consequence of which, many of your petitioners are involved in very unhappy circumstances; not being able to ascertain their boundary lines; and thereby wholly prevented from giving, or receiving conveyances of the land adjoining said line — beside a train of evils which arise from a supposed intrusion by the inhabitants of each town, upon each others property — which evil to prevent, Your petitioners humbly pray, that your HONORS would direct the Surveyor General, or such other person, or persons, as in wisdom your Honors shall judge most suitable, to

---

1. All but a small portion of this petition has been destroyed.

2. For record and details of this service, see Vt. Rev. Rolls, 792, 794–795; and for petitioner's other military service, Ibid, 344, 642, 644, 647.

3. Only the names of the members of the committee appear on the remnant of the petition.

traverse and establish said line agreeable to the Charters and Lines of the towns adjacent, and your petitionors will in duty pray.

Dorsett January 14th 1782

David Brydie	Henry Allen	Silas Baldwin
Isaac underhill	Isaac Farwell	Asahel Harmon
Augustin Underhill	John Farwell	John Gray
Ephraim Reynolds	Eleazr Baldwin	John manley
	Benja Baldwin	

— & —

Petition of the Inhabitants of Parts of Dorset for a Settlement of their Boundary Line. —
. . .*

— & —

> A. J.: *Read and granted, and ordered that a bill be brought in accordingly, 25 Feb. '82, S. P. of Vt., III (II), 76; act to ascertain the boundaries of the towns therein mentioned read and passed the House, 26 Feb. '82, Ibid, III (II), 81; act, having been returned by council with proposals of amendment, read and concurred in, 26 Feb. '82, Ibid, III (II), 81–82.¹ C. J.: Act read and amendment proposed "that the Surveyor General report to this Assembly in lieu of his line being conclusive", 26 Feb. '82, G. and C., II, 147.

FOR COMPENSATION FOR LOSSES IN SUIT AGAINST TORIES
xvii, 54

To the Honorable, General Assembly of the State of VERMONT, to be held at Bennington on Thursday the 31st Janry 1782.

The Petition of James Lewis of Manchester, County of Bennington humbly Sheweth,

That on or about the 10th of June 1779 your Petitioner entered a complaint to Martin Powel Esqr Justice of the peace for the County of Bennington, against Abel Castel, Jonathn Castel, David Castel, Nathan Castle and Lewis Castel of Pawlet in sd County — that as enemies to their country, they had Feloniously taken a number of Arms from those, who were in the service of the united States, and concealed the same — which said persons were brought before said Justice, and by him bound over to the Superior Court — and at the Superior Court Novemr Term 1779 said delinquents were dismissed for want of a prosecutor; and your petitioner had judgment rendered against him upon a Nonsuit, for Cost of

Prosecution Taxed £100..0..6

Sheriffs fees was   23..8..–

The whole of which is £123..8..6

Your Petitioner would humbly pray your Honors, to grant him an order upon the Treasury of this state for the aforesaid sum of £123..8..6 And your petitioner will in duty pray

James Lewis.

----

1. For this act, see Ms. Laws of Vt., I, 275. Dorset and Manchester were among the towns mentioned in the act.

Manchester 21st Jan^ry 1782.

— & —

James Lewis
Petition
. . .*
See page 65. vol. 2^d

— & —

A. J.: *Read and dismissed, 14 Feb. '82, S. P. of Vt., III (II), 53.

FOR AN ORDER TO A TOWN TO REPAIR A ROAD
xvii, 55

To the Honorable, the General Assembly, of the State of Vermont, to be Convened at Bennington on the last Thursday of January AD 1782 —
    The Petition of a number of the Inhabitants of the Town of Pownal, Sheweth,
that the Great Traveling Road through the Said Town of Pownal has been often
almost Impassable, and Still Continues greatly out of Repair, much to the Inconvenience and damage of the Publick, at a Place Called the digged way,1 and the
Inhabitants living near the Said Digged way, have for a long Time Endeavoured
to keep and maintain the Said Road at the afore Said Place in Repair, much to
their Damage and Cost, but are not able, and the Said Town of Pownal wholly
refuses to help or assist them in any wise — Wherefore Your Petitioners Pray,
that the Said Town of Pownal may be ordered by the Honorable General Assembly,
to Repair and maintain the Said Publick Road, at the afore Said Place at the Publick
Cost and Expence of Said Town, as your Petitioners ever bound in duty Pray
Dated in Pownal January 22nd AD 1782

> Charles Wright
> Michael dunning
> Nathaniel Seely
> Thos Jewett
> Caleb Reynolds
> Thomas Green
> George Parker
> Joseph Wheeler
> Josiah Wright
> Beulah Waldo

Pownal January 30th AD 1782
    Then I read the within Petition in the hearing of Thomas Jewett Wm Hendrick
& Elisha Barber the Select Men for the Town of Pownal —
        attest Na^th Wallace Constable
        attest Solomon Wright [Indepenent?] Person

---

    1. The act passed by the Assembly in response to this petition (see note) mentions
"the dug way" as "by the side of Hosack [Hoosic] River, on the great road leading to
Williamstown [Mass.]"

— & —

Petition for the Town of Pownal to keep in Repair the digged way
Recorded Vol 2ᵈ page 64
. . .*

— & —

A. J.: *Read and referred to a committee to join a committee of the Council,
13 Feb. '82, S. P. of Vt., III (II), 51; *report of committee recommending that
an act require the town to maintain the piece of road, read and ordered that a
bill be brought in accordingly, 14 Feb. '82, Ibid, III (II), 52; act passed, 26
Feb. '82, Ibid, III (II), 79.¹ C. J.: Petition read and committee appointed, 13
Feb. '82, G. and C., II, 138; act read and concurred in, 26 Feb. '82, Ibid,
II, 148.

FOR RIGHT TO SELL THE REAL PROPERTY OF AN ESTATE
xxii, 12

To the Honourable the General Assembly of the State of Vermont to be Holden
at Bennington on the last Thursday in Jannar Instint —
   Gentlemen —
The Pitition of Sarah Watkin widdow to James Watkin late of Townshend De-
cesed —
Humbly Sheweth —
that whenas there was no Law in force within the limits of this State at the Time
of the Said James Watkins Decess therefore no Settlement of Said watkins Estate
Ever made according to Law, and Your Pititioner has bin in porsesion of the Said
Estate Untill this time and paid Sᵈ Watkins Debts to the amount of twenty three
Pounds and as the Chief of the Improoved Land on Said farm is Tilled and therefore
Growing Poorer and Said Farm will now Sel at a large price, which in the Opinion
of Your Pititioner will be better for the Heirs of Said Watkins to be at Intrest then
to have the Said Farm Kept for Said Heirs Untill they are of Lawfull Eage to act
for them Selves
therefore it is the Earnest Desire of Your Pititioner that Some Sutable Person or
Persons may be appointed and Impowered to Sel Said farm with the Buildings
thereon and put the avails thereof upon Intrest for the Benifit of Said Heirs, or
other ways as Your Honours in Your Great Wisdom Shall think best — and Your
Pititioner as in Duty bound Shall Ever Pray
                                                    Sarah Watkin
Dated Townshend 25ᵗʰ of January 1782 —

— & —

Petition of Sarah Watkin for leave to sell Land in Townshend. —
. . .*

— & —

   A. J.: *Read and referred to a committee, 12 Feb. '82, S. P. of Vt., III (II),

---

1. For this act, see Ms. Laws of Vt., I, 276–277.

46;[1] report of committee recommending that petition be granted read, and ordered that a bill be brought in accordingly, 12 Feb. '82, *Ibid*, III (II), 47-48; *report of committee reconsidered, and both report and petition dismissed, 13 Feb. '82, *Ibid*, III (II), 49-50.

FOR A NEW TOWN CHARTER IN PLACE OF A LOST NEW HAMPSHIRE CHARTER[2]

xxii, 14

To the Honourible the genorol Assembley know [*sic*] Setting at Bennington, the Potition of your honours Potitioners, of the Town of Shrewsburey [Shrewsbury] humbley Sheweth, that thay are in Emanant danger and icspossed to grate Loss in there Landed intrust, on the account of the former Charter: Being Lost, and We not able to Pocuer a True and Attested Copy of the Same, Which Charter was granted by his Excellency, Bennin [Benning] Wentworth Esq[r] and by the advice of his Councel,[3] We Can asure your honour that Eavrey Measure, Possible has Ben Taken by ous the inhabetance of Said Town, to git Said Charter and to act thereon, agreeable to the Laws of this State, We therefor think our Selves not Secour under the Present Setuation of affares, as maney of our nabring Towns, are Plunged into a Scene of difficulty on the account of fols Persons, going abought With there Protended Titels, a deseving the Peopel, to Which Situation We are daley Ecsposed to, onless Some Spedy method is taken to, Exterecate ous from the Present defeculty to Which We are icsposed, We therefore Pray, that your honours Will order and direct What may be done in this Case, and order that a new Charter Shall be amediately maid out for Said Town in its former Bounds and Limmets, and We the inhabetence thereof may be Considered, and if your honours Should not judg fit to, make a grant of Said Town according, to our Request, We Pray that your honour, Would order that Some, other affectual method mite be taken, to Put a final Bar to the Before mentioned deficultes, to Which We are day icspossed, as We your honours Potitioners in duty Bound Shall Ever Pray —

Sruesburey Januarey 26th AD 1782 —

Nehemiah Smith	Jeremiah Colvin	Bennedeick webber
Lemuel Whit	Joseph Congil	Ezra Freman
Aaron Estey	John Thomson	Zibe Aldridg
Amos Cass	Elihu Grant	Ichabod Robinson
Thomas Eddy	Zebadiah Green	Jabez Weaver
David Niels	Willmor Smith	

— & —

A Potition for the Tow[n] of Srewsburey
A petition of the Proprietors of Shrewsbury —

— & —

---

1. For another petition from Sarah Watkin read on this date, see *S. P. of Vt.*, V (Petitions for Land), 309-310.
2. For a similar petition from Tunbridge, see p. 75, *post*.
3. For the text of the charter of Shrewsbury, see *State Papers New Hampshire*, vol. XXVI (Town Charters, vol. III), 427-430.

[No Record]¹

FOR SONS' PAY AS UNDERAGE SOLDIERS
xvii, 68

Lime in the State of Vermont² Janu^ry the 26th Anno Domini 1782. — To the honorable the general Assembly of the State of Vermont to be Convened at Bennington in said State on one of the last Days of January instant Anno Domini 1782. — The humble Petition of Samuel Cary and Samuel Hovey, both of Lime in the State of Vermont Sheweth. —
That whereas, Christopher Cary son to the abovesaid Samuel Cary, and Daniel Hovey, son to Samuel Hovey aforesaid, both Soldiers under Age, and now Captives in Canada; and were taken when garding the Frontiers of the State of Vermont at Corinth being sent there by the authority of said State, and were voluntiers, in the Company of Capt Charles Nelson, of Lime belonging to Colonal Waits Regiment —³ And whereas likewise, we their parents, have each of us a numerous, and chargeable Family, to take Care of being poor Men; S^d Cary has been Confined about four Months with the rheumatism, and still continues, unable to work out Doors; and said Hovey has but little help. — We therefore, Samuel Cary and Samuel Hovey your humble Petitioners do humbly pray the honorable the general Assembly of the State of Vermont now convened at Bennington in Sd State, to grant, that what is due of the wages of the aforesaid Soldiers, so far forward as to the expiaration of the time they listed for, to serve their Country, in Captain Charles Nelsons Company belonging to Colonal Waits Regiment, may be paid to us their Parents, and we your humble Petitioners as being bound in duty
    Shall ever pray & C.

Samuel Cary
Samuel Hovey

— & —

For The honorable the general assembly of the State of Vermont to be communicated
Saml Carey and Saml Hovey's petition
See page 70 Vol 2^d and 72
. . .*

— & —

A. J.: *Read and referred to a committee, 15 Feb. '82, S. P. of Vt., III (II), 56;

---

   1. On 27 Feb. '82 the Council appointed a committee to join a committee from the Assembly to consider "a petition signed by the inhabitants of Shrewsbury" (G. and C., II, 149). Although there is no record of any other petition from Shrewsbury at this session, it is impossible to determine whether the petition mentioned in the Council journal is the one printed here.
   2. Lime is, of course, now in the state of New Hampshire. At the date of this petition, however, it was joined to Vermont in what was known as the "Eastern Union."
   3. For record of this service and ultimate payment therefor, see Vt. Rev. Rolls, 343, 389, 446, 741, 752; also S. P. of Vt., III (II), 169.

*report of committee recommending that prayer be granted, read and accepted, and ordered that a bill be brought in accordingly, 16 Feb. '82, *Ibid*, III (II) 57; *report of committee reconsidered and petition dismissed, 18 Feb. '82, *Ibid*, III (II), 58.[1]

FOR ABATEMENT OF TAXES ON CERTAIN NEW SETTLERS
xvii, 56

Weathersfield Jany 28th AD 1782 —
To the Honourable Assembly for the State of Vermont to be holden at Bennington / in sd State / the 31st ins^t —
We the Subscribers beg leave to inform S^d Assembly that we moved into this town the last Spring with our families under many Disadvantages by moveing upon our farms which were then unoccupied haveing at the Same time to buy Provision for the Sustinance of our families. Some time in June the listers of S^d town Warned us to give in our lists. We told them. we thought the Propriety of taxation arose from Profit & Priviledges (agreable to Constitution of this and the other States) and we had nor Could Enjoy Either of them. Notwithstanding the [they] Put us in theire list. which being made up the Selectmen imposed the full quota of tax upon us to Defray the Charge of S^d town which arose before we Came to town to live. and our list was Sent in to the Honourable Assembly — and the State tax was leviled on us. but that which we look upon most unreasonable is the tax Demanding Provision which is Demanded of us. which apears impossible to Pay: We therefore Do humbly Petition the hon. assembly to take this our request into Consideration and Consider our Ingidant [indigent] Circumstances — and release our Case Either the Whole or in part. which to us appears both Just and Equal Doubting not but that it will be So Considered by your honours.
at the time we would inform the Venerable body that when our Circumstances will admit and we be Entiled to the Priviledge of freemen./ or inhabitants [/] of this State we Shall be willing to Pay our reasonable proportion of taxes, Submiting ourselves to the Justice & Discretion of the Affores^d hon. assembly from Whom we Expect Justice informing them that we made redress to the Selectmen but met with no relief. —

Names	Names	Names
Joshua Darte	Justus Darte	Henry Tools [Toles?]
Joseph Josulin	Ichabod yong	Clerk Tools [Toles?]
John Bennet	Edward Goodwin	Oliver Chaberlin
		Nath^{ll} Stoughton

— & —

For Weathersfield
Petition of Joshua Darte, Joseph Josulin and 8 others —
. . .*

---

1. Possibly the reason for the dismissal was the fact that the Assembly was at this time considering the dissolution of both Eastern and Western Unions, the latter including towns in New York east of the Hudson. The dissolution was voted 21 Feb. '82 (*S. P. of Vt.* III (II), 62).

See page 68 Vol 2^d

— & —

A. J.: *Read and dismissed, 15 Feb. '82, *S. P. of Vt.,* III (II), 55.

FOR COMPENSATION FOR WAR LOSSES[1]
xvii, 57

To the Honourable the General Assembly of the State of Vermont to Be Convened at Bennington January 31st 1782
The Memorial of Jonathan Rowlee and Caleb Handy of pitsford [Pittsford] in Rutland County Humbly Sheweth that your honours Memorialest Situation in pitsford Leying adjoining the Garrison Chiefly on the North Side of the Garrison Rendred it Impracticable for us Consistant with prudance to Continue on and Improve our houses and Lands we thought fit with the advise of the prinsople officers of the Garrison to Removed our famelys in to the More Interior parts of the Stat Since which time the Garrison hath Made Use of about two thousand feet of Good Boards for the Use of the Barracks which was the property of Jonathan Rowlee your Honour^s Memorialest the Biger half of Said Boards were Taken from his house the upper and under flores Being Loos and the petitions [partitions?] Sealing Board &c taken and Improved for the Barraks and a Considerable N° of Nails taken for the Same use Many of the Shingles taken off the Roof for the Sake of the Nails Likewise the State hath bin Benefited by our fields and Meddos for feeding their Cattle Horses and also for fating Cattle and all for the Benefit of the State and as your honours Memoriales Have Bin and Still are put to Grate Destress to Suport their familes we think it alltogeather Reasonable that the State Should pay us at Least what they have bin Benefited by our property if not the Damiges for Burning up our fences for fire wood and Many other Damiges your honours Memoriales would therefore Pray that the Honourable the General Assembly would appoint a Com^{tee} to Look into the afair and Examin into the Whol of the Circumstances and Make their Report to Some Board as your honours Shall think proper that your Honours Memoriales May be Considered and have justice Dun to them in the Case as your Honours Memoriales In Duty Bound Shall Every pray
Dated in Danby 29th of January 1782   Jonathan Rowlee
                                                          Caleb Handey

— & —

Jonathan Rowlee and Caleb Handy
. . .*
See vol 2^d page 60

— & —

A. J.: *Read and dismissed, 12 Feb. '82, *S. P. of Vt.,* III (II), 48.

---

1. For a petition presented 18 Oct. '86 by Caleb Handy for compensation for rental of his farm to the state, see p. 257, *post.* This petition was dismissed. For the presentation and dismissal in October, 1784 of another petition by Caleb Handy (not now among the *Ms. Vt. S. P.*), see *S. P. of Vt.,* III (III), 73, 87.

FOR A NEW TRIAL IN AN ASSESSMENT CASE
xvii, 33, 59[1]

To the Honorable the General Assembly of the State of Vermont to be holden in Bennington on the 31st day of Jany 1782

The Petition of the Subscribers, Listers for the Town of Manchester in the County of Bennington humbly Sheweth —

That in the year 1781 Your Honors Petitioners were Chosen Listers for Said Town, and in Compliance with their Duty aded fourfold[2] to the List of Capt. Silas Goodrich, on Forty acres of Land, in which Case the Said Goodrich applied to your Petitioners for Releaf but without Success, but being Dissatisfied, made application to Eliakim Stoddard Esqr and two of the Selectmen of Said Town a Leagal Court in Such Case who on the 16th of Oc^t Last Past awarded that the Said fourfold Should be taken of [off], and the Single Sum aded, which in the opinion of your Petitioners, is a violation of Law, which judgment being awarded by a Leagal Court, admits of no other Redress, Except before your Honorable Body —

Your Petitioners therefore Pray your Honors to take the Case under your wise Consideration, and grant Such Releaf as the nature of the case Requires, and your Petitioners as in duty bound Shall ever pray —

Manchester ye 30th of Jany 1781 [1782] —

Thomas Bull ⎫
Thomas Barney ⎪
Jonth Sexton ⎬ Listers
Martin Powel ⎭

— & —

Petition of the Listers of Manchester
. . .*
See page 78 Vo. [2?] —

State of Vermont ⎫
County of Bennington ⎬
To the Sherriff of Said County his Deputy or Either Constable of the Town of Manchester within Said County Greeting —

In the name and by the Authority of the Freemen of Said State you are hereby Directed to Notifie Capt Silas Goodrich of s^d Manchester within Said County to appear before the General Assembly of this State now Siting in Bennington on the 19th Instant to shew Cause why the Judgment Rendered on the 16th of October Last past by Eliakim Stoddard Esqr & two of the Select Men of S^d Manchester Should not be Reversed & Likewise Leave a Coppy of the within Petition if Requested [;] make Return according to Law —

---

1. The manuscript on p. 33 is the original, while that on p. 59 is a copy identical, as far as the body of the petition is concerned, except for spelling and punctuation. The copy contains additional material not found in the original. The printed text follows the spelling and punctuation of the original and contains additional material from both the original and the copy.

2. A fourfold was a quadruple assessment for neglect to make return of taxable estate.

Bennington y[e] 15th of Febra[ry] 1782

Tim[o] Brownson Asist

Manchester y[e] 18th of February 1782 then the within Sitation Serv[d] by a Coppy
Attest Chris[r] Robets Consto
fees £2:8:6

State of Vermont in Gen[l] }
Assembly Feb[y] 21st 1782 }
The above petition was Read and Refered to a Com[tee] of three to take the Same
under consideration and make report of their opinion with the facts to this House
— the members chosen Mr. Olin, Mr. Chandler, and Mr. Sergeant[1]
attest Ros[ll] Hopkins, Clerk

To the general Assembly &c   Feb[y] 22[d] 1782
Your Committee to whom was Referred the petition of Thomas Bull &c Listers
for the Town of Manchester Report as their Opinion, that S[d] petition ought to be
Dismist this Assembly not being a proper board to try the Same &c.
J Chandler for Committee
The above Report was read and accepted and said petition was dismissed accordingly
attest Ros[ll] Hopkins Clerk

— & —

A. J.: *Read, prayer granted, and bill ordered brought in accordingly, 14 Feb.
'82, S. P. of Vt., III (II), 51; act read and passed, 15 Feb. '82, Ibid, III (II),
54; request of Council in returning the act that adverse party be notified to
attend and show cause why act should not be passed, agreed to, 15 Feb. '82,
Ibid, III (II), 54–55;[2] dismissal reconsidered and matter referred to a committee, 26 Feb. '82, Ibid, III (II), 79; report of committee recommending that
the judgment of the court be reversed and a new trial ordered, read and accepted, and ordered that a bill be brought in accordingly, 27 Feb. '82, Ibid,
III (II), 84–85; act read and passed, 27 Feb. '82, Ibid, III (II), 87.[3]

FOR RELIEF FROM SUPPORT OF AN INVALID STRANGER
xvii, 69

To the Hon[ble] General Assembly now sitting at Bennington, The Petition of
the Selectmen of the Town of Danby humbly sheweth:
That sometime in the month of March 1780 one Sarah Farris a Refugee from
the Northward Came into the Town of Danby, being in a state of Pregnancy in

1. The exact course of action in the Assembly on this petition is obscure. Presumably Goodrich appeared as directed and failed to show cause why the judgment should
not be reversed.
2. Although the title of this act, which is all that is known of it, reads "An Act to
reverse a certain judgment therein named" and thus does not indicate specifically its
connection with this petition, there is no reasonable ground to doubt that it was the bill
ordered to be brought in on 14 Feb. '82.
3. For this act, see Ms. Laws of Vt., I, 278.

consequence of which she was soon taken sick, before her recovery from which she was seized with a Complication of Disorders which confined her to her bed for several Months. & she is not yet so far recover'd as to be able to earn her living. she being destitute of Money has been ever since a Town-charge — tho in justice she ought to have been supported at the Charge of the State, as the Town to which she properly belongs is without our Lines and her Father a Prisoner in Canada. The whole Expence of Doctors Attendance & support, which has been already paid by the Town is eighteen Pounds twelve shillings which is a burden that your Petitioners think they ought not to sustain — Wherefore they pray your Honors to take the matter into your consideration & grant them that Relief, which you shall think reasonable and as in Duty bound Shall ever pray

Eben^r Willson ⎫ Selectmen
Daniel Shearmun ⎬ of the
Edward Vail ⎭ Town of
        Danby

— & —

Ebenezer Willson and others Selectmen of the town of Danby

. . .*

See pag 72 Vol. 2^d

— & —

A. J.: *Read and dismissed, 18 Feb. '82, *S. P. of Vt.*, III (II), 58.¹

FOR TAX ON PROPRIETORS TO REPAIR A ROAD
xvii, 72

To the Hon^{bl} General Assembly of the State of Vermont in General Coart Assemble^d

The petition of Aseph White & — the Subscribers to the Clearing of the Road from myrifield [Myrifield]² to Bennington Humbly Sheweth that we inhabitants of Charlemont and myrifield in the Commonwealth of Massachusetts Did subscribe Largely to the Clearing the Road now Traviled from myrifield to Bennington which together with the generus subscriptions of people of said Bennington was the onely means opening Said Road which since has bin found usefull to the publick and Would be a good Road and abundantly Travilled if properly Repaired Which Would be greatly benefitial to the publick as well a [as] your petitioners but a [as] the Road new [now] lies it is impassable for waggons and Exstreemly Dificult for Slayes by the roughness of about ten or twelve miles onely of said Road which Turns the greattest part of the Travilers from the estward of us by Chesterfield and Gageborough which in many instances is more then thirty or forty miles round and Whareas thare is now a good waggon Road from Con-

---

1. Unless a transient person had been duly warned out of town within one year of his arrival, he was, under the law, the responsibility of the town and its selectmen. See "An Act for the ordering and disposing of transient persons" and "An Act for maintaining and supporting the Poor": *Slade*, pp., 315, 378–379.
2. Myrifield is now the town of Rowe, Massachusetts.

necticut River through Charlemont and myrifield to the State line and a good and substantial Bridge over Deerfield River in Readsboro^h <it seams that a little more cost in Comparison of What has bin all Ready Laid out> and Whareas the Building of the Bridge and makeing said Road Will be greatly to the Advantage of the proprietors of the Lands through which the Road passes in [promoting?] the Setling and Advancing the price of Said Lands which would be otherways of none or little value (Said Road runs from myrifield line about three miles on Whitingham then about Eight miles through Readsborough then about two or three miles on the line between Stanford [Stamford] and Woodford Sumtimes on one and Sometimes on the other Town then about five or six miles through the south part of Woodford; the Last part of said Road has bin Repaired by the order of the Assembly but the other parts through Stanford Readsborough and Whitingham to myrifield line lyes in the same situation as Left by your petitioners except two Bridges over the small Branches of Deerfield River) your petitioners therefore pray your Honnours to take the matter into your serious Consideration and order that sumthing may be Dun as Sun as may be to the Repairing the Road as above mentioned by laying Sumthing on the proprietors in proportion of the Advantage the Road is to them; or by granting a Lotterry or some other way as your Honnours in your Wisdom Shall Direct

As your petitioners bound in Duty shall ever pray

Asaph White p^r order

— & —

Asaph Whites Petition
. . .*

— & —

A. J.: *Read and referred to a committee, 23 Feb. '82, S. P. of Vt., III (II), 72; *report of committee read and petition referred to next session, 26 Feb. '82, Ibid, III (II), 82; *referred to next October session, 17 June '82, Ibid, III (II), 101.

FOR DIRECTIONS REGARDING THE SEIZURE OF PRIVATE PROPERTY BY THE MILITIA

xvii, 60

To the Honorable Legislature of the State of Vermont —

The Memorial of Benjamin Bartlet of Arlington Humbly Sheweth That your Honor's Memorialist was legally Elected and Commissionated a Subaltern Officer of the Company of Militia in Arlington commanded by Capt. Elijah Gelusha —

That at the Time of the Alarm in October last,[1] by Reason of the Absence of superiour Officers the Command of said Company devolved on your Honors Memorialist That consequently your Honours Memorialist received Orders Dated 16th of October aforesaid from the Ajetant of the Regiment agreeable (he says) to Orders for that Purpose from General Safford to muster said company and to march one Half thereof immediately to Castleton propertly Officered, Armed and Accutered —

---

1. For brief mention of the occasion for this alarm, see G. and C., II, 118n.

That your Memorialist immediately issued Orders and Mustered said Company detached one Half, ordered them to parade agreeable to the Orders received and appeared to march the Detachment aforesaid Accordingly —

That your Honour's Memorialist was detained by the Non appearance of some of said Detachment who excused themselves by urging that some of the civil Authority said they was Not Needed

That your Honours Memorialist received Orders from Leut. Colº Pearl for the Whole of Said Company to march without lose of Time as an Invasion of the Garrison was immediated expected, and a Line from Lt Colº Fletcher, Commandant at Fort Warrin dated 20th Octr 1781 at 6. o'clock P.M. that a large Body of the Enemy had landed and requested said Company to repair to said Fort for the Defence of the Garison without Loss of Time —

That in this Situation your Memorialist found himself under the disagreeable Necessity to impress Horses to expedite our March as no Baggage Carriages were otherwise Provided and Orders were to march with several Day Provision Whereupon your Honours Memorialist isued a Warrant for the Purpose and Ordered a Serjent of said Company with a Soldier to attend him to impress to [two] Horses belonging to William Serls of said Arlington they being Near and the Owner excused from the Tour by Reason of Bodily Infirmity —

That pursuent to said Orders said Horses were taken for the Purpose aforesaid

That said Serles made application to the Civil Authority Namely Eli Petibone Esq of said Arlington Justice of the Peace for the County of Bennington who immediately Issued a Precept in the following Words

> To the Sheriff of the County of Bennington his Deputy or either of the Constables of the Town of Arlington in said County Greeting
> In the Name and by the Authority of the Freemen of the State of Vermont — You are hereby Commanded to take the Bodies of Levi Hill and Stephen Hard both of said Arlington and also to take the Saddle and Mare and Horse wherever they may be found and deliver the said Effects unto the said Serles — and safely keep the said Hill and Hard and them safely keep so that they may be had before the County Court holden in Manchester on the fourth Tuesday of April Next then and there to answer unto the above Complaint and to be delt with as the Law directs in such Cases — which is to the Damage of the pltf as he says one Hundred Pounds L.M. and for the Recovery the Pltf brings this Suit — fail not but make due Return according to Law —
> Dated in Arlington this 21th Day October 1781
> Bond of Prosocution being given   Elihu Petibone Jus' Peace

That by Virtue of said Precept Serjt Levi Hill and Stephen Hard Private both of said Company were taken and likewise said Horses and Saddle all detained by means whereof your Honours Memorialist together with the Company under his Command were detained more than half a Day on so critical an Exegency as to appearence the Enemy were invading our Country and the said Hill and Hard were detained till your Honours Memorialist was Bail for their Appearence &c —

therefore your Honour's Memorialist prays your Honors to take the Matter of this Memorial into your Wise Consideration, and if your Memorialist has misconducted in the Premises that your Honors would be pleased to give him perticular Directions how to conduct in like Cases in Future — but if he has not misconducted — he prays that your Honors issue an Order for the Release of said Hill and Hard from their Obligation to appear as aforesaid — and further that if the Authority

aforesaid be guilty of Maleadministration he your Honors Memorialist prays that he may be delt with according to Charter and your Memorialist shall as in Duty bound ever Pray

Benjamin Bartlit

Arlington 4th February 1782

— & —

Benjⁿ Bartlets Memorial
. . .*
See page 57 Vol 2^d

— & —

A. J.: *Read and dismissed, 12 Feb. '82, S. P. of Vt., III (II), 46.

FOR DESCENT OF AN INTESTATE'S ESTATE TO HIS WIDOW
xvii, 61

To the Honble General Assembly of the State of Vermont
The Petition of Martha Syms of Hertford[1] in s^d State humbly sheweth
That your Petitioner was the late wife of Col^o William Syms of s^d Hertford deceased with whom she lived as such for many years.
That the s^d deceased died seized of an Estate worth about £200 — intestate
That said deceased left neither Son nor Daughter or any Relation to whom, by the Laws of this State,[2] his s^d Estate shall Descend.
Your Petitioner therefore Prays that your Honors would order that the Descent of said Estate — should be to your Petitioner solely after the same shall be settled according to Law by the Judge of Probate for this District.
And your Petitioner as in Duty bound shall ever Pray —

Martha Syms

Hertford 7th Feby 1782

— & —

A Petition of Martha Syms
. . .*
See page 69 Vol. 2^d

— & —

A. J.: *Read and prayer granted, and ordered that bill be brought in accordingly, 14 Feb. '82, S. P. of Vt., III (II), 51; act read and passed, 15 Feb. '82, Ibid, III (II), 56.[3]

---

1. The name Hertford was changed to Hartland by an act passed 15 June 1782 For this act, see Ms. Laws of Vt., I, 284.

2. For the law with respect to the descent of the estates of intestates, see "An Act for the settlement of testate and intestate estates" passed February, 1779: Slade, pp. 339–345.

3. For this act, see Slade, p. 445.

FOR ABATEMENT OF A PROVISION TAX
xvii, 62

To the hon^ble the Representatives of the Freemen of the State of Vermont now convened in General Assembly at Bennington in said State. —

The Petition of the Subscribers, Selectmen of Hinsdale[1] in Windham County in said State —

Humbly sheweth,

That in & by a certain act of the Legislature of this state passed October 25th 1780 entiteld "An Act for the purpose of procuring Provision for the Troops to be employed in the Service of this State for the year ensuing"[2] The said Town of Hinsdale was doomed[3] (it having then no Representation in the Legislature) to raise 3000 Flour, 1000 Beef, 500 Pork, 84 Bushels of indian Corn & 42 Bushels of Rye —

That it was declared by the said Act That any Towns aggrieved by the said assessment, might make Application to the present General Assembly at their Session in October now last past, & shew that such town was assessed higher than it ought to have been; and that it should be the Duty of the Assembly to make a proper Allowance to such Town out of their next rate. —

That the Grand List was compleated so late in October Session, that your Petitioners had not time to make an Application to the Legislature for an Abatement of their Tax.

That upon a Calculation made your Petitioners find that the Town of Hinsdale was over rated in the said Act about nineteen Pounds ¼ at the rates which the commissary received silver money in lieu of the said Tax —

Your Petitioners therefore humbly pray that Credit may be given to the said Town, for the said Sum, upon the Act passed at Charlestown in October last for the purpose of raising Provision,[4] according to the Terms of the Act first before mentioned. —

And your Petitioners as in duty bound shall ever pray &c.

Bennington 11th Febry 1782.

John Bridgemen	}	Selectmen
		for the town
Arad Hunt		of Hinsdale

— & —

Petition of the Select [sic] of the Town of Hindid [Hinsdale] in Windham County. Recorded vol 2^d page [57?]

. . .*

— & —

---

1. The name of Hinsdale was changed to Vernon by an act of the legislature passed 21 Oct. 1802 (*Acts & Laws . . . 1802* [Bennington, 1802], p. 3).

2. For this act, see *Slade*, pp. 407–411.

3. If a town failed to make a regular return of its property valuation for purposes of taxation, the legislature would doom it. That is to say, the legislature would arbitrarily fix its property valuation on the basis of such information as was at hand.

4. For this act, see *Slade*, pp. 440–442.

A. J.: *Read and referred to a committee, 12 Feb. '82, *S. P. of Vt.*, III (II), 46; *report of committee recommending that town be allowed four pounds seven shillings on the present tax as overcharge on the last tax, read and accepted and ordered that a bill be brought in accordingly, 12 Feb. '82, *Ibid*, III (II), 46; act passed, 14 Feb. '82, *Ibid*, III (II), 52.[1] *C. J.:* Act concurred in, 14 Feb. '82, *G. and C.*, II, 139.

FOR AN ORDER TO A TOWN TO BUILD A BRIDGE
xvii, 63

To the Honorable, the General Assembly of the State of Vermont, Convened at Bennington, the Petition of the Subscribers, being a Number of the Inhabitants of the Town of Pownal, Sheweth, that a Bridge aCross Hoosack River is much wanted and would be of great Advantage, and accommodate the Publick, at a Place near Seelyes Mills (so Called) in Pownal, Wherefore Your Petitioners Pray that the Inhabitants of the Town of Pownal may be ordered by the Honorable, the General Assembly, to Build Errect & maintain a Good Convenient Bridge at the afore Said Place, for the Conveniency and Benefit of Travelling, at the Publick Cost and Charge of Said Town, or that the Said Bridge be ordered to be built in Such way and manner as the General Assembly in their Wisdom Shall think best, as Your Petitioners ever bound in Duty Pray
Dated in Pownal February 11th AD 1782 —

Nathaniel Seelye	Petter Barrit	Abel Pratt
Samuel Green	David Perrigo	Abram Anderson
his	Thomas Peirce	Jonathan Reynold
Adam X fisher	Rufus Perrigo	Silos Pratt Junr
mark	George Johnson	William pratt
Jonathan Royce	Jonothon hill	Caleb Reynolds
John Perrigo	Peter [Page?]	John Hans Singer

Pownal February 11th 1782
Then I Read the Petition in hearing of Elisha Barber Wm Hendrick Jona Hunt & Thos Jewett Select men for the Town of Pownal.

attest Nath Wallace Constable

— & —

Petition to ye General Assembly for the Town of Pownal to be ordered to build a Bridge aCross Hoosack River
. . .*
Recorded Vol 2d page 65 —

— & —

A. J.: *Read and committee appointed to join a committee from the Council, 13 Feb. '82, *S. P. of Vt.*, III (II), 51; *report of committee recommending that petition be dismissed, read and accepted and so ordered, 14 Feb. '82, *Ibid*, III (II), 52. *C. J.:* *Read and committee appointed, 13 Feb. '82, *G. and C.*, II, 138.

---

1. For this act, see *Ms. Laws of Vt.*, I, 314.

FOR ABATEMENT OF A PROVISION TAX
xvii, 64

To the hon^{ble} the Representatives of the Freemen of the State of Vermont now convened in General Assembly at Bennington in Said State —
The Petition of the Subscriber, Select man of Pomfret in Winsor [Windsor] County in Said State —
Humbly Sheweth;
  That in & by a certain act of the Legislature of this State passed October 25th 1780 entitled an act for the purpose of procureing Provisions for the Throops to be employed in the Service of this State for the year ensuing,[1] The Said town of Pomfret was Doomed[2] (it haveing then no Representation in the Legislature) to raise 2400 Flour, 800 Beaf, 400 Pork, 66 Bushel Indian Corn 33 Bushel of rye, which is more than their Just Proportion of Provision according to the List of Said town about 327 flour, 109 of Beaf 54½ Pork 9 Bushel Corn, and 4½ Bushel of Rye.
Therefore your Petitioner Humbly Prays that your Honnours would take y^e matter into your wise Consideration and grant Relief, by takeing of [off] what is more than their just proportion, and give orders for Discharing [discharging] the town from the same.
and your Petitioner as in Duty Bound Shall ever Pray
Bennington 11th of Feb^r 1782

John W. Dana $\left\{ \begin{array}{l} \text{one of y}^e \\ \text{Select} \\ \text{men for} \\ \text{the town} \\ \text{of Pomfret} \end{array} \right.$

— & —

Select Men of Pomfret's petition respecting Provision tax —
Feby 13th 1782 Read and granted —
See Vol. 2^d page 60
. . .*

— & —

  A. J.: *Read and referred to a committee, 12 Feb. '82, *S. P. of Vt.*, III (II), 48; act entitled "An Act discharging the town of Pomfret from a certain part of a tax therein mentioned," read and passed, 13 Feb. '82, *Ibid*, III (II), 50.[3]

FOR AN ACT OF PARDON PRIOR TO RETURN TO THE STATE[4]
xvii, 66

To the Honourable Representatives of the Free men of the State of Vermont in General Assembly met

---

1. For this act, see *Slade*, 407–411.
2. For the meaning of the term "doomed", see footnote 3, p. 66, *ante*.
3. For this act, see *Ms. Laws of Vt.*, I, 267.
4. For a related petition see p. 71, *post*.

The Petition of Seth Smith of Brattleborough[1] in the County of Windham in said State

Humbly Sheweth

That in December last your Petitioner with Others was apprehended by a warrant for assembling to Impead the Commissary of this State in the Execution of his office; and bound over to Court, your Petitioner urges it as an Extenuation of his offence that it was the prevaling openion of the Inhabitents of Brattleborough that no part of the Provison Tax laid in 1780. could Legally be called from Said Town because the Act which laid Said Tax was passed before the Town of Brattleborough became united with and Represented in the Legislature of this State — That the Commissary General Seized and Took from your Petitioner Eight head of fat Cattle when he was Driving them to Boston in order to procure hard money to pay a Debt he had pledged his Hon[r] to Satisfy. — That your Petitioner attended at the County Court at Marlborough from Tuesday untill Saturday morning in order to Save his Bail and was then Informed that the Grand Jury of Said County had found a Bill (thro: Ignorance and Contrary to their real Intentions) which Subjected your Petitioner to be Imprisoned untill the next Superiour Court and then have a Trial for his Life; which Induced your Petitioner to fly from the State to avoid a Trial — That your Petitioner is very desirous of returning to, and becoming a good Subject of this State — and is willing to Deliver himself up to the next County Court for the County of Windham and answer unto all matters which may then be Objected against him on the part of this state (exept the matters in said Indictment) your Petitioner Truly and penitently sensible of his heinous offence Therefore humbly Prays That the Honourable the Legislature will be pleased to Pass an act pardoning his Said Crime for which the Said Bill of Indictment was found against him by the Grand Jury afore said under such Regulations as this Honourable Assembly in their Great Wisdom and Clemency Shall think Proper — and he as in Duty bound Shall ever pray &c. —

Seth Smith

Barnard [Tun?] [Bernardston, Mass.?]
Febr[y] y[e] 14th 1782 —

— & —

The Petition of Seth Smith
. . .*
Recorded vol. 2[d] page [83?]

— & —

A. J.: *Read and referred to a committee, 23 Feb. '82, S. P. of Vt., III (II), 65; *report of committee recommending that prayer be granted, read, and ordered that a bill be brought in accordingly, 23 Feb. '82, Ibid, III (II), 66; act read and passed, 23 Feb. '82, Ibid, III (II), 72; act returned by Council with an addition, which was read and ordered added to act, 26 Feb '82, Ibid, III (II), 83–84.[2] C. J.: Petition read and granted on condition that Smith take oath of allegiance to state, and act returned to house, 26 Feb. '82, G. and C., II, 147.

---

1. For brief note of the petitioner as an adherent of New York, see G. and C., II 147[n].

2. For this act, see Ms. Laws of Vt., I, 274.

FOR RELIEF FROM EXCESSIVE COSTS IN A JUDGMENT
xvii, 58, 67

To the Honorable the Representatives of the Freemen of the State of Vermont in General Assembly met.

The Petition of Lewis Walker of Clarendon, in behalf of himself, Daniel Briggs, Joshua Priest and Francis Matteson.

Humbly Sheweth,

That your Petitioners having been lately arrested by the Freemen of this State in the Superior Court, on Tryal were cast in Damages and Costs of Suit; since which a Bill of Costs has been made out ag^t them and taxed, exceeding (as they conceive) the fees usually allowed in such cases by the Laws of this State,[1] as may fully appear by Said Bill and other vouchers relative thereto now in your Petitioners hands, and ready to be exhibited to the Honble House.

Your Petitioners thus considering themselves aggrieved in the premises, and the bad tendency of so ill a precedent, have no other appeal but to the Justice of the House. Do humbly pray them to grant such redress as they in their Wisdom Shall See fit.

Bennington 15th Feb^{ry} 1782

And your Petitioners
Shall ever pray &^{e}
Lewis Walker in behalf of
himself, Danl Briggs, Joshua Priest
and Francis Matteson. —

— & —

Lewis Walker's Petition in behalf of Danl Brigs, Joshua Priest & Francis Matteson —

. . .*

See page 70 Vol 2^d

Certificate of Ab^m Ives Sheriff on Danl Briggs Execution the Sum Total of Mr Daniel Brigs Execution is Twelve Pound Eighteen Shilings and Sixpence Lawfull money and Dated 3d of october 1781

Abraham Ives Sheriff

Deposition in favour of Lewis Walker's petition &C

Elihu Allen & Jedediah Jackson of Lawfull Age testifieth and Sath that at August Session of our Superior Court sitting in Rutland County in the y^r 1781 thay were Sommonsed as Jurey men to attend Said Court and in the Coures [Course] of Said Courts Setting there was onley one Case Committed to ous for tryal Between the freemen of this State and daniel Briggs and others and further the deponants Saith that in the Tryal of Said Case We Receiv'd onley the yousal [usual] fee for trying one Case further the deponant Sath not —

January the [29?] AD 1782 Parsonely a pred [appeared] Elihu Allen & Jediah Jackson Both a greaing in the Sam Evidence and mad Oath to the Same Befour me

Elihu Smith Justis of peace

— & —

---

1. For the law presumably in force at the time of these charges, see "An Act for regulating Fees", passed October, 1780: *Slade*, 398–402.

A. J.: *Read and dismissed, 16 Feb. '82, S. P. of Vt., III (II),56.

FOR DISCHARGE FROM BAIL BOND[I]
xvii, 70

To the hon^ble the Representatives of the freemen of the State of Vermont in General Assembly met —
The Petition of Joseph Burt of Brattleborough in the County of Windham in said State
Humbly sheweth,

That in December last Seth Smith of Brattleboro aforesaid, with several others, were apprehended for assembling to impede the Commissary General of this State, in the Execution of his office; & your Petitioner was Surety in the Sum of £100 for the Appearance of the said Seth at the then next County Court to be held for Windham County. —

That the said Smith did appear at the said Court, & attended from Tuesday until Saturday Morning, when having obtained Intelligence that he was indicted for a matter which would bring his Life in Question & would be confined in close Goal for some time before he could have a Trial, he fled; & the Bond that your Petitioner had given for his Appearance, was adjudged forfeit — That your Petitioner has since, without effect, endeavored to get Security from the said Smith to indemnify him. That your Petitioner has several Children, is considerably advanced in years & the Exacting the Penalty of the said Bond would render him poor & miserable the rest of his Life —

That your Petitioner is advised that his sole Remedy is from the Lenity & compassion of this hon^ble House —
And as it appears from a Petition herewith presented that said Smith is desirous of surrendering himself & taking a Trial for any other matters than those for which the said Bill is found, —
Your Petitioner humbly prays that this hon^ble House would pass a Bill discharging him from the said Bond or grant him such other Relief in the Premises as to this honorable House shall seem meet
And your Petitioner as in Duty bound shall ever pray &c. —

Joseph Burt

Bennington Feb^ry 21st 1782 —

— & —

Petition of Joseph Burtt
. . .*
Recorded page 83 vol. 2^d

— & —

A. J.: *Read and referred to a committee, 23 Feb. '82, S. P. of Vt., III (II), 65; *report of committee recommending that prayer be granted, read, and ordered that bill be brought in accordingly, 23 Feb. '82, Ibid, III (II), 66; act read and passed, 23 Feb. '82, Ibid, III (II), 72; act returned by Council with an addition,

---

1. For a related petition, see p. 68, ante.

which was read and ordered added to act, 26 Feb. '82, *Ibid*, III, (II), 83.[1]
C. J.: Petition read and granted on condition that Burtt take oath of allegiance
to state, and act returned to house, 26 Feb. '82, *G. and C.*, II, 147.

FOR COMPENSATION FOR WAR SERVICES
xvii, 71

To the Honble General assembly of the State of Vermont Now Setting at Bennington
Humbly Sheweth that your Petitioners Did go to Pitsford [Pittsford] by orders of
the Commitees of the New Hampshire Grants at their meeting at arlington [Arling-
ton] June 29, 1776[2] at the Time when Major Brownson was out with a Number of
men; and your Petitioners have Never Received any Pay for their Time and
Expence for that Tower [tour] — Pray your Hon^{rs} To Grant them Such Relief as
your Hon^{rs} in your Great wisdom Shall See meet and your Petitioners in Duty
Bound Shall Ever pray
Bennington February 22th 1782

Seth Warner
Sam^{ll} Robinson
Azel Washborn

— & —

Seth Warner Saml Robinson and Azahel Washbourn's Petition
. . .*
Recorded vol. 2^d 108

— & —

A. J.: *Read and dismissed, 25 Feb. '82, *S. P. of Vt.*, III (II), 77; *read and
referred to a committee, 26 Feb. '82, *Ibid*, III (II), 83; report of committee
recommending that petitioners be paid wages and extra rations for their
service, read and accepted in so far as it related to Robinson and Washbourn,[3]
and ordered that a bill be brought in accordingly, 27 Feb. '82, *Ibid*, III (II),
85–86. *Rep. of Com.:* Committee recommends that petitioners be paid wages
and extra rations for their service, 27 Feb. '82, *S. P. of Vt.*, IV, 21–22.

FOR COMPENSATION FOR DEPRECIATION IN SOLDIER'S PAY
xvii, 76

To the Honourab^{le} General Assembly Now Sitting at Windsor —

---

1. For this act, see *Ms. Laws of Vt.*, I, 275.
2. For a discussion both of the Pittsford alarm and of the early conventions in the
New Hampshire Grants, see *S. P. of Vt.*, IV, 21*n*–24*n*.
3. The exception from this payment of Seth Warner, one of the early leaders of the
Vermont community and colonel of the Continental regiment raised in the state, is difficult
to explain. It may have been a consequence of a difference of opinion between Warner
and Governor Chittenden and his supporters over the issue of negotiations with the
British. At least such a difference almost resulted in an open clash between them later
in this year. See *G. and C.*, II, 153*n*–154*n*; also *Vermont Historical Society Collections*, vol.
I (1870), 460: The Natural and Political History of the State of Vermont, by Ira Allen
(1798).

the Petition of Moses Evens Humbly Sheweth that whereas your petitioner Served
as a Sarg^t in Capt Benjamins Company of Malitia in the year 1777: and your
petitioner was made prisoner & Carried to Canada and under very great hardships
by almost A years Captivity and Recv^d His pay for his Services onely in the
Nominal Sum in Continental money in the year 1778:[1] Your petitioner prays that
your Honours would take his Case under your wise Consideration and grant to
your petitioner the Depreciation Agreable to An Act of Assembly[2] as in your
Wisdom Shall think Just & Reasonable and as in Duty bound Shall Ever pray

Moses Evens

— & —

Moses Evans Petition
. . .*
See page 153 Vol. 2^d

— & —

A. J.: *Read and referred to next session ("N. B. Said Petition was given to
said Evans"), 20 June '82, S. P. of Vt., III (II), 110; *read and referred to a
committee, 14 Oct. '82, Ibid, III (II), 124; report of committee read, and
prayer granted and referred to Committee of Pay-Table for adjustment, 15 Oct.
'82, Ibid, III (II), 126.

FOR COMPENSATION FOR WAR SERVICES[3]
xvii, 74

Catelton [Castleton] 18th June 1782

Sir
    Pray do not for git my Distressed Brother and his affairs Left to your trust
I am your

Most Obedient Se^t Wm Blanchard

C^{olo} Lyon   { To the honorable General Assembly
                     { the petition of Abner Blanchard humbly sheweth
that he was one of three persons sent by Col Herrick in the year 1777 to Reconoitre
the Lake & overtaken prisoner that this State have Paid the other two persons for
their service & that your petitioner had no pay for his Service he humbly prays
your honours to Take his case into your wise Consideration and Grant him the
same kind of relief which his fellow sufferers have had & he as in duty bound will
ever pray

Abner Blanchard

Castleton ⟨Windsor⟩ June 17th 1782

---

    1. For Evens' petition for this pay and for the action taken on it, see p. 7, ante,
including note.
    2. The act referred to here was doubtless "An Act directing what money and
bills of credit shall be a legal currency in this State," which was passed in the October
Session, 1780. See Slade, 398.
    3. For a previous petition from Abner Blanchard for compensation for war services
and losses and for the light it throws on this petition, see p. 11, ante, including notes.

— & —

C^olo Lyon
Abner Blanchard petition —
. . .*

— & —

A. J.: *Read and referred to next session, 21 June '82, *S. P. of Vt.*, III (II),
115; read and referred to a committee, 18 Oct. '82, *Ibid*, III (II), 132; report
of committee recommending that petitioner receive his pay and rations for
this service, read, and ordered that committee of Pay Table make adjustments
and order Treasurer to pay the same, 18 Oct. '82, *Ibid*, III (II), 134.

FOR INTEREST ON "DUE BILLS" GIVEN FOR SOLDIERS' PAY
xvii, 73

To the Honorable the General Assembly now sitting in Windsor
    The Address and Petition of Thomas Tolman
        Humbly Sheweth —
That having had the Honor of being appointed [Pay] Master to the Troops of this
State, he has endeavoured [according to] the best of his abilities to discharge the
Duty with Faithfulness — And flatters himself that he has given as much satisfac-
tion to Individuals as the Want of Money to discharge the Dues of the Soldiery
could naturally admit —
He informs your Honors that (excepting a few soldiers) the Troops for the year
1780 are settled with in full, which was paid partly in Silver, partly in Continental
Money and the several States New Emission Money, and the remaining part in
the Paper Currency of this State, soon after it was emitted —
That for the year 1781 — in the month of August, he made a Payment to the
Battalion commanded by General (then Colonel) Fletcher, from the Commencement of their Services to the 1st of July in s^d year, and afterwards to Colonel
Wait's Battalion three Months pay — all which was made in the Paper Currency
of this State —
That by reason of the unhappy Depreciation of s^d Currency, it became not only
the Interest of the Soldiery to refuse receiving any more of it as Law^l-Money;
but it occasioned considerable Dissatisfaction at what they had already received,
(as will readyly be conceived reasonable) when they found it did not answer the
purpose & value intended —
That through the Depreciation of s^d Currency & the want of other Money to
supply its place, Colonel Walbridge's Battalion was entirely unpaid at the Close of
the Campaign, and Colonels Fletchers' and Waits' the greater part. — And, excepting some inconsiderable Payments your Petitioner has been able to make in
Money, — and the Provision your Honors have been pleased to grant in Lands,
The Troops continue unpaid to this Day —
That as your Honors at your last session in Bennington gave no Direction to the
Paymaster in what manner he should certify the Dues of the Soldiery, He did not
think himself authorized to give more than a simple Certificate that such a Sum or
Sums were due from him in Behalf of the State (which are commonly called Due
Bills) and which, from their Simplicity, bearing neither Interest nor Date of Pay-

ment, he is assured they will not any longer be received in their present Form, as satisfactory, or doing Justice to the possessors —

Therefore he requests, in Behalf of the Troops yet unpaid, and others who, upon the Faith of being paid by the State, have satisfied the Soldier & received his Order, that your Honors would take this Matter into your serious Consideration — And grant an Interest of Six per. Centum per. annum on s^d Bills, from such Date as your Honors shall think just which will raise their value to the possessor, and thereby not only encourage the possessor to wait until the State shall be enabled to discharge them, but may add such Credit to them, as in some Degree to make up the Deficiency of a present circulating Medium

And further that your Honors will give any other Directions to your Petitioner in his Office of Pay Mas^r as in your Wisdom shall seem just and equitable, and conducive to the best good of this State —

Tho. Tolman

Windsor June 18th 1782

— & —

To the Honble Thomas Porter Esquire Speaker of Assembly (present)
Thos Tolman P. Master's petition
. . .*

— & —

A. J.: *Read and referred to next session in October, 18 June '82, *S. P. of Vt.,* III (II), 102.

FOR A NEW TOWN CHARTER IN PLACE OF A LOST NEW HAMPSHIRE CHARTER[1]
xxii, 36

To the General Assembly of the State of Vermont

The Petition of the subscribers holding lands in the town of Tunbridge in said state humbly sheweth, that whereas the town of Tunbridge was incorporated by a charter from the Governor of New Hampshire,[2] and a charter of the same township bearing date, sometime in the year of Our Lord 1760 was granted to Ebenezer Fletcher the first & a number of original proprietors his associates, whose names can be ascertained to your Honours, and whereas by misfortune and [Accident, the aforesaid] charter was lost and destroyed Your Petitioners humbly pray that your Honours will direct a new Charter to be granted to the original proprietors, as a security to the said proprietors, their alieners and assigns for the rights and immunities granted by the act of Incorporation, as aforesaid — or in some other way as your honors may think best and Your petitioners shall ever pray —

Ebenezer Fletcher
John Welding
Ezra Fellows
Seth Austin

---

1. For a similar petition from Shrewsbury, see p. 56, *ante.*
2. For a copy of this charter, see *State Papers New Hampshire,* vol. XXVI (Town Charters, vol. III), 506–510.

— & —

Petition of the Proprietors of Tunbridge for a New Charter —
Filed 18th Septr 1782 —
. . .*

The Honorable the General Assembly
    Your Committee to whom is refered the consideration of the within Petition
report vizt
    That the further consideration of the s^d petition be Postponed until the next
session of this Assembly, and that the Secretary be directed to make out and forward a Citation directed to some One ‹of the Constables› indifferent person of
the Town of Tonbridge, to Serve and return directing him to Summon the present
Settlers of s^d Tunbridge to appear by themselves, their Agent, or Agents before
the Genl Assembly at their next adjourned sessions and shew cause (if any they
have) why the prayer of this petition should not be Granted, or that the original
charter be confirmed

Jonas Fay for Committee

— & —

A. J.: *Read and referred to a committee, 21 Oct. '82, S. P. of Vt., III (II),
139;[1] *report of committee read and dismissed, 22 Oct. '82, Ibid, III (II), 146;
act to secure to the proprietors of Tunbridge their rights in said town granted
by the Governor of New Hampshire read and passed the House, 23 Oct. '82,
Ibid, III (II), 147. C. J.: *Read and resolved that no committee be appointed
to join Assembly committee at this time and that petition be referred to next
session, 22 Oct. '82, G. and C., III, 10; *previous resolution reconsidered and
committee appointed to join Assembly committee, 22 Oct. '82, Ibid, III, 10;
act read and concurred in, 23 Oct. '82, Ibid, III, 12.[2]

FOR CONFIRMATION OF A COPY OF A WILL DESTROYED BY FIRE
xxii, 38

    To the honorable the General Assembly of the State of Vermont to be con-
vened at Manchester on the second Thirsday of October Inst. —
    Humbly sheweth
    The Petition of Elias Stevens of Royalton in said State That Rufus Rude
late of s^d Royalton deceast. did a few days before his death make and compleat a
certain Instrument. which he declared to be his last will and Testament and the
same was properly witnessed and finished according to law — That at the destruction of s^d Royalton in October seventeen hundred and eighty the house of your
Petitioner with his furniture and writings particularly the forementioned Will
were consumed by fire by the enemy — whereby a considerable Estate is exposed
to extraordinary expences & perhaps confusion. — That a copy or substance of
the said last will is preserved as may appear by the accompanying affidavits —
    Your Petitioner therefore prays that your honors will take this Petition and
the said Affidavits into candid consideration and pass an act establishing & con-

---

    1. This entry on the manuscript petition correctly states that this committee was
to join a committee from the Council.
    2. For this act, see Ms. Laws of Vt., I, 352–353.

firming the said Will as specified in the said Affidavits — or afford such direction in the premises as in wisdom may appear best

And your Petitioner will ever pray —

Royalton 5th Octob^r 1782 }   Elias Stevens

— & —

Petition of Elias Stevens
. . .*

— & —

> A. J.: *Read and referred to a committee to join a committee from the Council, 14 Oct. '82, *S. P. of Vt.*, III (II), 125;[1] petition returned by Council, 15 Oct. '82, *Ibid*, III (II), 125; *resolved that petition be referred to next session and that adverse party be served with a copy of the petition and the resolutions of this House thereupon, 25 Oct. '82, *Ibid*, III (II), 125; read, and, the adverse party (the deceased) not appearing, resolved that petition be granted and that a bill be brought in accordingly, 18 Feb. '83, *Ibid*, III (II), 160. *C. J.*: *Read and voted not to appoint a committee to join Assembly committee "as the adverse party had not been cited to answer the same," 14 Oct. '82, *G. and C.*, III, 5;[1] act confirming a writing purporting the last will and testament of Rufus Rude, having passed the Assembly, read and concurred in, 19 Feb. '83 *Ibid*, III, 17.[2]

FOR SUPPORT OF DECEASED TORY'S IDIOT CHILD
xvii, 77

To the Hon^l the Genl Assembly, the Petition of John Alsworth of Pownall [Pownal] Humbly Sheweth —

That in July 1780 your Petitioner married the Widow of Elijah Osburn that the s^d Widow then had a Child of between 2 & 3 Years of Age; that was then & now is, an Ideot, one that is helpless & in all probability ever will be so

Your Petitioner further declares that the Widow was possessed of an Estate at Rutland sufficient to support her & her Children, which s^d Estate was confiscated by Act of this State on acc^t of her former Husbands misconduct in this State.[3]

Your Petitioner therefore prays your Honors, that he may have a reasonable Sum allowed him for the Support of the s^d Child — And as in Duty Bound will ever pray —

                                      John Alsworth

Pownell Octr 7 1782

— & —

Petition of John Alsworth
. . .*

— & —

---

1. This entry has been crossed out on the manuscript petition.
2. For this act, see *Slade*, 469–470.
3. For record of the confiscation of Elijah Osburn's estate at Clarendon (not Rutland), see *Sequestration, Confiscation and Sale of Estates: S. P. of Vt.*, VI, 15–17.

A. J.: *Read and referred to next session, 21 Oct. '82, *S. P. of Vt.*, III (II), 142.[1]

FOR DIRECTIONS TO THE TREASURER IN REGARD TO TAX COLLECTION

xvii, 79

To the Honble the General Assembly of the State of Vermont, Conveaned at Manchester.

The Representation of Ira Allen Treasurer Humbly Sheweth

That the Legislature have in Sundry instances Remitted Taxes on the fourfolds[2] and otherwise Naming only the person and not Specifying the Sum on the Grand list of the Town Such person lives in for which Reason I Cannot Balance my Book and unless I have other directions in Case of Giving Executions against the Collectors must Give it for all the arerages including the afore Said proposed abatements and further in several Towns since Compleating the Grand list for the past year Several persons have Moved out of Such Towns therefore the Collectors Cannot Collect their proportion of Such Tax and to oblige Such Collectors to pay all Such arerages is by them thought unreasonable which they must do unless there be Some New Regulation.

There are Some arerages of the Several Taxes Heretofore granted and as there is Some disorders in Some parts of the State I wish for advice or directions as to the propriety of Giving out Executions.

There are Some Notes and Receipts in the Office Due from Individuals to the State I Expect Some direction on that Head before I proceed to take any Definite Measures for the Collecting the Same

Manchester Octr 21st 1782
To Increase Mosely Esqr
Speaker to be Communicated
To the Assembly

I am with
due Respect Your
Hum^le Servant.
Ira Allen

— & —

Representation of the Treasurer —
. . .*
To the hon^ble Genl Assembly now sitting
Your Com^ee to whom was refered the within representation beg leave to report

That the Treasurer be desired to suspend giving out Executions against the

---

1. Another petition from Alsworth [Aysworth] to the same effect was read in the Assembly 23 Oct. '86, and, after a report from a committee, was dismissed 24 Oct. '86. See *S. P. of Vt.*, VI, 98.

2. The "fourfolds" were a quadruple assessment for neglect to make return of taxable estate. See "An Act directing Listers in their office and duty," passed February, 1779 (*Slade*, 296).

delinquent Collectors until the rising of the next session of Assembly & no longer — and that the several Towns who have had an abatement made on any of their Lists by the Gen¹ Assembly be desired to send in to the next session the sum total of such abatement & on what List — That the Treasurer may collect of such Towns accordingly — And in case of any person removing out of any Town before having paid his Tax — that such Town shall pay out of the Town Treasury such Tax or arrearage —

Benj. Emmons: Chairman

— & —

A. J.: *Read and referred to a committee to join a committee from the Council, 21 Oct. '82, *S. P. of Vt.*, III (II), 142; resolved that Treasurer suspend executions and that the towns send in the total of their abatements, 23 Oct. '82, *Ibid*, III (II), 147. *C. J.:* *Committee appointed to join Assembly committee, 21 Oct. '82, *G. and C.*, III, 10.

FOR RELEASE FROM A PAST PROVISION TAX
xvii, 81

UNOT [Unto] the Hounorable the Representatives of the freemen of the State of Vermont to meet in General Assembly at winsor [Windsor] in the month of february next The petition of the select men in Name and behalf of the Inhabitants of peachum [Peacham] Humbly Sheweth

That the inhabitants of this town have allways endevoured to conform themselves to the laws of the state tho our Exposed Situation has Rendered our Circumstances as a town poor and perplexing in the year 1781 our Constable and almost all our other town officers Moved out of the town so that we were unable to take a list of our Rateable Estate in any Regular Manner in Consequence of which the assembly doomed¹ us much above our just valuation we nevertheless voluntarily colected the money tax formerly leveyed by the state according to our Doom without any Constable or other officer to Conduct in the matter altho at that time there was only seven familys in town in so much that the Raising of three men which the town were ordered to Raise that year would amount to one Dollar on Each pound of our Rateable Estate and as the Cheif of our few settlers are newly come on and Labour under great disadvantages from our situation and otherways

Might it therefor plase the Honourable house to grant your Humble petitioners a Release from the provision tax of the year 1781² as also the Money for the three men ordered to be Raised for said year which we were Not able to Raise and your

---

1. For an explanation of the term "doomed," see p. 66n, *ante*. For the action of the Assembly and for the amount the town was doomed, see *S. P. of Vt.*, III (II), 137, 146–147.

2. See "An Act for the purpose of procuring provision for the troops, to be employed in the service of this State, for the year ensuing," passed in October Session, 1781 (*Slade*, pp. 440–442).

petitioners shall for the futher Endevour to Exeart themselves in the suport of the State and your petitioners shall for Ever pray

Jonathan Elkins ⎫
Moses Bayley   ⎬ Select men
John Scales   ⎭

— & —

The petition of peachum
1783
. . .*

— & —

A. J.: *Read and referred to a committee to join a committee from the Council, 20 Feb. '83, *S. P. of Vt.*, III (II), 164; report of committee recommending that arrears of taxes (except those on land) be remitted, read and accepted, and ordered that a bill be brought in accordingly, 21 Feb. '83, *Ibid*, III (II), 167; act read and passed, 22 Feb. '83, *Ibid*, III (II), 168.[1] *Rep. of Com.:* Committee recommends that arrears of taxes (except those on land) be remitted, 20 [Feb.] '83, *S. P. of Vt.*, IV, 197.

FOR RIGHT TO SELL REAL PROPERTY TO SETTLE AN ESTATE
xxii, 77

To The Honorable Gen[ll] Assembly of the State of Vermont To Be holden By adjournment at Windsor on the Second Thursday of Febuary next in Suing — The Petition of Samuil Cambell Administrator and Esther Crippen Administratrix on the estate of Samuel Crippen late of pitsford [Pittsford] Deceased Humbly Sheweth. that whereas it appears That the Estate of the Said Deceasd is Indebted to Several Creditors To the amount of £70: lawfull money more than the value of the personal estate of the Said Deceased and therefore Humbly Request That the Legeslature of Said State. — Would Grant liberty To the Said administrators to Sel So much of the Real Estate of the Deceased as to amount to the afore Said Sum of £70: l:m: To pay Said Debts and other Incident Charges And your Petitioners shall as in Duty Bound Ever pray

Rutland 24th Jan'y 1783

Samuel Cambell ⎫ administrator
Esther Crippen ⎬ administratrix

— & —

Sam[l] Campbell Esther Crippen's Petition
The Petition of Sam[ll] Camble To the General Assembly

— & —

A. J.: Read and granted, and ordered that a bill be brought in accordingly, 19 Feb. '83, *S. P. of Vt.*, III (II), 161; act read and passed the house, 19 Feb. '83, *Ibid*, III (II), 161. *C. J.:* Act read and concurred in, 19 Feb. '83, *G. and C.*, III, 17.[2]

---

1. For this act, see *Ms. Laws of Vt.*, I, 370.
2. For this act, see *Ms. Laws of Vt.*, I, 368.

FOR ABATEMENT OF UNPAID TAXES
xvii, 82

To the Honourable the general assemble of the State of Vermont to be held at windsor [Windsor] on the second Thursday of this Instant February —
The Petition of the freeman and others Inhabitants of Ryegate Humbly Sheweth that your Petitioners being unwilling to Trouble the assembly with any Tideous Representation of our Particular case and as our [Difsetualties?] [difficulties] are the same with our Neighbouring Towns as is more Fully Represented in there Memorial we Referr the Assembley to [it] Being much the same as our own[1] we therefore Humbly Desiere and Hope that the assembley considering our Particular case will in there wisdom see meet to abet all Demands on us for baygons [bygones] to this Present we engage under your Protection for the futture to pay all Due Respect to what orders we may from time to time Receive from you in confidence of your goodness we beg Leave to subscribe our selves your Honour⁵ most obedient and very Humble Serv⁵

In Behalfe of the Town of
Ryegate —

Alex^r Sym
Andrew Brock
James Henderson

— & —

Petition of Rygate
. . .*

— & —

A. J.: *Read and referred to a committee to join a committee from the Council, 20 Feb. '83, S. P. of Vt., III (II), 164; report of committee recommending that arrears of taxes (except those on land) be remitted, read and accepted, and ordered that a bill be brought in accordingly, 21 Feb. '83, Ibid, III (II), 167; act read and passed, 22 Feb. '83, Ibid, III (II), 168.[2] Rep. of Com.: Committee recommends that arrears of taxes (except those on land) be remitted, 20 [Feb.] '83, S. P. of Vt., IV, 197.

FOR COMPENSATION FOR WAR SERVICES AND LOSSES
xvii, 80

To the Honourable the General Assembly of State of Vermont at there Resent Session at Windsor the Petetion of the Subscriber humbly Sheweth that Some Time in month of July in the year 1781 — Your Petetionour Inlisted in the Service of this State under the Command of Leiut. Ward Bailey and made a Part of his Chore [corps][3] and on the fifteenth Day of October following being out on a Scout was Surprised and Captivated by a Party of Indians and Caried by them to Canada and forwarded immeadiatly to Quebecc and there Put in Close Goal and under Such Confinement Survived a Tedious winter and on the Seventeenth of may Left

---

1. See the petition from Peacham to the same effect on p. 79, ante.
2. For this act, see Ms. Laws of Vt., I, 370.
3. For record of this enlistment, for which payment began 30 June '81, see Vt. Rev. Rolls, p. 521.

Quebecc on an Exchange of Prisoners and Returned home the fifteenth of June being a Prisoner Eight month Your Petetioners time Inlisted for Expired on the Last of November but as your Petetoner was a Soldier in the Severice and on Command at the time of his being taken flatters himself that your Hon^rs in your known Justice & Humanity will Continue his Pay till his Return and as your Petetioner was accouttered with a good gun Blanket Hatchet & Knapsack &c of which he was Stript by the Indians and being in a new setelment and under very Indigent Circumstances Prayes Your Hon^rs to take this his Petetion into your Wise Consideration and Redress his Greaviance by Paying him his monthly wages and for the Loss he has Sustained or Make him Such other allowance as your Honors Shall think Proper and your Petitioner Will Ever Pray
Brunswick Feb^r 8th 1783   David Hicks

— & —

David Hicks Petition —
. . .*

— & —

> *A. J.:* *Read and referred to a committee, 19 Feb. '83, *S. P. of Vt.*, III (II), 161; report of committee recommending that prayer be granted, read and accepted, and ordered that a bill be brought in accordingly, 20 Feb. '83, *Ibid*, III (II), 163; *resolution allowing petitioner £16 in all passed accordingly, 20 Feb. '83, *Ibid*, III (II), 164.

FOR RESTORATION OF A TOWN TO A CERTAIN COUNTY
xvii, 83

To the honorable the General Assembly now Sitting the petition of the Representatives of the Freemen of the County of Orange humbly shews that the County is small as to number of people notwithstanding which they have had the Prinpal [principal] part of Randolph taken from them[1] and Attempts has been made to take the Township of Brookfield in the same manner[2] which your petitioners Look upon as Grevous & oppresive Considering the Circumstances of the County.
    Therefore Your Petitioners would humbly pray that said Town of Randolph be restored to the County of Orange as we are in duty bound will ever pray
Windsor Feby 26th 1783   Neh^h Lovewell
                                                           Moody Freemen

---

1. At this time part of the town of Randolph was in Rutland County and part in Orange (*Ms. Laws of Vt.*, I, 386). An act entitled "An Act annexing the township of Randolph to the County of Windsor" passed the Assembly 18 Oct. '81 (*S. P. of Vt.*, III (II), 15). This act apparently never became law. There is no record of the concurrence of the Governor and Council in its passage, and it is not included in the *Ms. Laws of Vt.*

2. These attempts were frustrated. An act entitled "An Act to annex the town of Brookfield to the County of Orange" passed the Assembly 21 Feb. '83 (*S. P. of Vt.*, III (II), 167). The Governor and Council concurred therein 27 Feb. '83 (*G. and C.*, III, 20). For the act itself, see *Ms. Laws of Vt.*, I, 369. According to this act the town was originally in Rutland County.

Elijah Beeman
Noah White
Beriah Lomis

— & —

Petition of Col° Nehemiah Lovewell
Feby 26th 1783 —
. . .*

— & —

A. J.: *Read and prayer thereof granted, and ordered that a bill be brought in accordingly, 26 Feb. '83, *S. P. of Vt.*, III (II), 180. *C. J.:* *Act annexing Randolph to Orange County, having passed the General Assembly, received and read, and concurred in, 27 Feb. '83, *G. and C.*, III, 20.[1]

FOR DIVISION OF A TOWN INTO TWO RELIGIOUS SOCIETIES
xvii, 84

To the Honorable General Assembly of the State of Vermont to meet at Westminster on the second Thursday of October next — The Petition of the Inhabitants of Windsor in said State humbly sheweth —

That whereas the Town of Windsor at a legal & general Meeting of the Inhabitants of said Town holden on the ninth Day of November Anno Domini seventeen hundred and seventy eight — Did for the Benefit of said Town — mutually agree, and unanimously Vote to Divide said Town into two Distinct Societies, for the purpose of maintaining the Gospel and many other matters — And by virtue of said Vote did settle two Ministers of the Gospel — one in each Society in said Town; and did & performed many other Acts & Deeds for the benefit of said Town — which cannot be carried into Execution without the Interposition of the Legislature — And whereas some Difficulty has of late arisen by reason of Individuals refusing to comply with the necessary Requisitions of said Societies — because they were not established by a particular Vote of the Legislature — Therefore your Petitioners humbly pray your Honors to ratify & confirm the Vote of said Town above mentioned, and their Doings in Consequence thereof — and as in Duty bound shall ever pray

Windsor 8th Septr 1783 }

Thomas Cooper ⎫ Committee
Briant Brown ⎪ in Behalf
Stephen Jacob ⎬ of said Town
Reuben Deane ⎭ of Windsor

— & —

A Petition from the Town of Windsor
To the Hounourable Assembly of the State of Vermont
— & —

A. J.: Read and prayer granted, and member requested to bring in a bill ac-

---

1. For this act, see *Ms. Laws of Vt.*, I, 386.

cordingly, 14 Oct. '83, *S. P. of Vt.*, III (II), 193; bill read and recommitted, 15 Oct. '83, *Ibid*, III (II), 195; bill read, passed, and sent to Council for proposals of amendment, 15 Oct. '83, *Ibid*, III (II), 196; bill returned from Council with amendments, which were read, agreed to, and passed into law, 17 Oct. '83, *Ibid*, III (II), 200.[1]

FOR POSTPONEMENT OF A HEARING BEFORE THE ASSEMBLY
xvii, 87

To the Honorable the General Assembly for the State, of Vermont, to be holden at Westminster on the second Thursday in October Anno Domini 1783 —
Humbly Sheweth,

Joseph Kimball of Plainfield, that at the last, Session of this honorable Court held at Windsor Major Jonathan Child at Lime preferr'd a petition to this Court, praying that he might have a new trial in an action which your petitioner commenced against him,[2] and upon which he recovered a Judgment, against said Child in August AD 1781, at Keene in the then County of Washington — and your Petitioner was then cited to appear, at the present Session of this Court, to shew cause, why the said Child should not have a new trial; But as no particular day was appointed for the hearing of the same, and as it would be extremely inconvenient, for your Petitioner to attend, during the whole Session of this assembly, and as he further concieves it can be no injury to Major Child to have the matters delay'd — your Petitioner therefore prays, that, this honorable Court would defer the hearing and determination of the matters, until the next Session of the Assembly, and appoint some Day for the hearing of the Same —
And your petitioner as in Duty bound Shall Ever pray —

Joseph Kimball

— & —

Joseph Kimball's Petition —
Filed 21ˢᵗ Octʳ 1783

— & —

A. J.: Read and ordered to lie on the table, 14 Oct. '83, *S. P. of Vt.*, III (II), 194–195.[3]

FOR RIGHT TO SELL REAL PROPERTY TO SETTLE AN ESTATE
xvii, 85

Probate office } Bennington 3ᵈ October 1783
Bennington District }

---

1. For this act, see *Ms. Laws of Vt.*, I, 392.

2. This petition was read and referred to a committee, and then referred to the next session 26 Feb. '83 (*S. P. of Vt.*, III (II), 177, 179). The document itself is not among the *Ms. Vt. S. P.*

3. According to a petition presented by Jonathan Child dated 5 Oct. '84 Kimball's prayer was granted. For this petition and subsequent developments in this case, see p. 100, *post.*

This certifies that by the amounts exhibited to me this day by Isaac Matthews legally appointed sole Administrator on the Estate of Jesse Newell late of Shaftsbury in the County of Bennington and Probate District afoursaid Deceased that there appears to be wanting the Sum of twenty Seven pounds Eighteen shillings and three pence of the personal Estate of the S^d Deceased to pay the several creditors of s^d Estate their several Just dues as adjusted and allowed

£27..18..3^ee   Jonas Fay Prob^e Judge

To the Honble the Representatives of the Freemen of the State of Vermont to be convened at Westminster on the 2^d Thursday of October Instant
     The Petition of the Subscriber Sheweth
     That Twenty Seven pounds 18/3 Lawful Money is due to Several persons, creditors to the Estate of Jesse Newell late of Shaftsbury deceased over and above the ammount of the personal Estate of the s^d Deceased as appears at foot by the Certificate and examination of the above named Jonas Fay Esqr Judge of Probate which it is necessary should be paid your Petitioner Therefore prays that an order may be granted by our [your] honors for the Sale of so much of the Real Estate of the s^d Deceased as will pay the Sum of £27–18–3 and the incident charges arrising thereon, under such regulations and restrictions as your honors shall judge proper and
                    your Petitioner shall ever pray
                                        Isaac Mathews Administrator

                              — & —
Petition of Isaac Mathews
                              — & —

     A. J.: Read and prayer granted, and resolved that petitioner bring in a bill accordingly, 20 Oct. '83, *S. P. of Vt.*, III (II), 203–204; act read and passed, and sent to Council for proposals of amendment, 20 Oct. '83, *Ibid*, III (II), 204. *C. J.:* Act read and concurred in, 24 Oct. '83, *G. and C.*, III, 32.[1]

FOR A TAX ON THE LANDS OF NON-RESIDENT PROPRIETORS TO BUILD ROADS
xvii, 88

To the Honorable General Assembly of the State of Vermont now convened at Westminster.
The Petition of Isaac Lyman, in Behalf of the Inhabitants of the town of Whitingham,
     Your Petitioner, in Behalf of his Constituents, the Inhabitants of the Town of Whitingham aforesaid, begs Leave to represent,
     That at this present Time there are two public Roads laid out thro' the said Town; one of which Roads leads from the Town of Merryfield,[2] to that of Wilmington; the other from the said Town of Whitingham, communicating with the Post Road to Bennington, &c.
     That the said Inhabitants, considering the great Utility of the said Roads to

---

1. For this act, see *Ms. Laws of Vt.*, I, 399.
2. Myrifield [Merryfield] is now the town of Rowe, Massachusetts.

the Public, have already taxed themselves to the Amount of one shilling and two Pence on the Pound, on their Polls & rateable Estates, in order to compleat and make convenient the said Roads; which Sum has been expended, and found to be insufficient for the Purpose.

That the said Inhabitants, thro' the great Expence they have incurr'd, in building Bridges, Mills, &c. have greatly advanced the Value of the Lands of the non-resident Proprietors, and greatly impovorished themselves.

And as the said Roads are not yet compleated, your Petitioner prays this Honorable House would grant Liberty to the Select Men of said Town to tax the Lands of the non-resident Proprietors, in the Sum of One Penny Half Penny per Acre, for the Purpose of compleating the said Roads.

And your Petitioner, as in Duty bound, will ever pray

Isaac Lyman, in Behalf
of his Constituents

Octr 21st 1783.

— & —

the petition of Isaac Lyman in behalf of the Town of Whitingham
Filed 21st Octr 1783 —

— & —

[No Record][1]

FOR TAX ON LAND TO BUILD ROADS
xvii, 89

To the Honourable General Assembly of the State of Vermont in General Assembly met
We Your Petitioners Proprietors of Bridgewater Being legally Met at a Proprietors Meting Do Humbly Shew — That we are Informed by Maj^r Safford That A Petitions has been Presented To The Honourable Assembly by A Number of The Inhabitants in the Northern and Easterly Parts of the County of Windsor Praying That A Road may be Opened from Woodstock threw the Towns of Bridgewater and Killington To Rutland att the Expence of the Land holders and Proprietors of s^d Towns,[2] — And We Your Petitioners are Desirous of Promoting So Lawdable

---

1. The selectmen of Whitingham presented a petition (not now among the *Ms. Vt. S. P.*) on 25 Oct. '84 for the power to levy a tax of one penny on each acre of unimproved land in the town. This petition was referred to a committee and ultimately granted, an act being passed accordingly on 29 Oct. '84 (*S. P. of Vt.*, III (III), 90, 99, 108, 110; also *Ms. Laws of Vt.*, I, 464–465).

It is possible that the above petition presented by Isaac Lyman, who was the representative from the town of Whitingham at the time of its presentation (*S. P. of Vt.*, III (II), 197), was held by the Assembly to be not in proper order. Presumably only the selectmen had authority to petition in behalf of the town for such a purpose.

2. This petition (not now among the *Ms. Vt. S. P.*) was taken into consideration by the Assembly and favorably acted upon 21 Oct. '83, but no legislation was passed granting its prayer (*S. P. of Vt.*, III (II), 204, 206).

A Designe and hope it may be Effected, —
That your Petitioners are Desirous That a Land Tax be Granted, on all The Lands in The Townships of Bridgewater and Killington, Not Exeding One Penny on the Acre, for The Purpos of Looking Out (and Making) s^d Road Thr^o S^d Towns. —
    Your Petitioners in Duty Bound Will Ever Pray
Bridgewater Novr 25th 1783 —   atest Jes^e Williams Prop^s Cleark

— & —

Bridgewater Petition
1783

— & —

[No Record]¹

FOR THE RIGHT TO RUN A FERRY
xvii, 95

    To the Honble Gen^ll Assembly of the State of Vermont at their adjourned Sessions in Bennington
February [Blank] AD 1784
The Petition of David Powers Humbly Sheweth
    That your Petitioner has Served the Public in Several Capacitys During the last War² and being Desirous to be further Serviceable proposes to errect a Ferry from Mount Independence in Orwell across to Ticonderoga Therefore Humbly Prays this Honble Gen^ll Assembly to Grant Your Petitioner Liberty to Errect Said Ferry for any Limited Time Under Such Rules and Regulations as Your Honours Wisdom May Direct³ and As in Duty Bound Shall ever pray
                                                        David Powers

— & —

Leut. David Powers Petition
. . .*

— & —

    A. J.: *Read and ordered to lie on the table, 2 Mar. '84, S. P. of Vt., III (III), 32.

---

    1. No action was taken in the matter of a land tax in Bridgewater until 27 Oct. '85, when the Assembly granted a tax of one penny and half penny on the acre for the construction of roads in the town, including the road marked out as a portion of the highway from Woodstock to Rutland (Ms. Laws of Vt., I, 531).
    2. For David Power's military services, see Vt. Rev. Rolls, pp. 27, 174, 206, 333, 395, 486, 564, 634, 635, 774, 782.
    3. The town authorities were authorized to establish and regulate ferries running within the state by "An Act for the regulating Ferries and Ferriages within this State", passed in February, 1779 (Slade, 329–330). Those running to points outside the state, however, were apparently established and regulated by the legislature.

FOR RELIEF OF AN INDIGENT SUPPORTER OF THE WESTERN UNION
xvii, 96

To the Honorable General Assembly now Sitting in Bennington

The Petition of those whose Names are under writtin for and in behalf of Barnard Hyatt of Rupert in the County of Bennington humbly sheweth; That Your Petitioners influenced, not only by the unfortunate and Indegent Circumstances of him the said Barnard for whom they Petition; but by a Conviction, that they as individuals of this State and as members of this Honorable House, have in their zeal for the Promotion and inlargement of this State, had a share (tho indirectly and undesignedly) in intailing that same Indegence and Depression of Circumstances on him, for whom your Petitioners at this Time have taken the liberty to address this honorable House: Your Petitioners will beg the Indulgence of this Honorable House but a minute while they point out the Causes of that Misfortune and Indigence, which has so unsupportably heaped it-self on the Person for whom they petition, they will then [. . .] him with their warmest wishes and Desires; recommended to this Honorable House, for their Charitable Notice and Regard. — Barnard Hyatt was a man who during the Existance and Continuation of the Western Union, lived in Pitstown a Place then situate within the Jurisdiction of Vermont, and was then and there a warm and Zealous Friend to the said State and the Union aforesaid and ever since has continued to be such, and the said Barnard did then and there take an active Part in behalf of such State and Union and further to promote, inlarge and Establish the Interest and welfare of Said State and Union did then and there take upon himself or receive the office of Constable in said Town as an [executive?] officer of Said State and did faithfully carry in to execution all the Business and Duties of said office, by Reason whereof he the said Barnard rendered himself adious [odius] and obnoxious to those who in the Union aforesaid was unfriendly to its Existance yet the said Barnard [reffusing?] the ill will and adium [odium] that flowed forth and was exercised toward him only for a cincere and faithful adhereance to the state and Union aforesaid, continued steadfast and unshaken in promoting its wellfare and Establishment thereof, until the Honorable General Assembly of this state were pleased to consider that Union as Desolved and withdrew their Protection,[1] when he was Left to the mercy of his political Enimies and obliged to indure more than two months Emprisonment in the City Hall in Albany and when relieved was forced to Quit the Union aforesaid with the Loss of his possessions and all his personal Property except a little Household furniture; which loss of Property Can be evidenced to this Honorable House to be nearly one Hundred Pounds: now the said Barnard having a large expensive Family is unable (notwithstanding he is possessed of a Spirit of Industry and Econimy and exercises prudence in the Distrubution of what little he accquires) is unable (we say) to procure for himself and Household a convenient or even Decent support. — Your Petitioners therefore not only believing this Honorable House to be the Patrons of the Poor and necessitous, but a Body, who are to be esteemed and viewed as an Example and Patern, for Acts of charity and Generosity; have taken the Liberty to intercede this Honorable House;

---

1. The union between Vermont and the towns in New York State north of the Massachusetts line and east of the Hudson River — known as the Western Union — was instituted 16 June 1781 and dissolved 20 Feb. '82. See *S. P. of Vt.*, III (I), 242; *Ibid*, III (II), 62.

disiring and praying that they would grant some small Pitance or afford some small gratuity for the Relief of him and Famely of whom this Petition has frequently made mention; that this may be the Case and that the Designs of the Petition may be answered, — Your Petitioners as in Duty bound Shall ever pray

Wm Smith

Joel Sheldon   } Selectmen

Enos Harmon

Amos Curtis

Eben^r Hulburd

— & —

Selectmen of Rupert in behalf of Barnard Hyatt
Petition
. . .*

— & —

A. J.: *Read and referred to next session, 8 Mar. '84, S. P. of Vt., III (III), 58.

FOR ESTABLISHMENT OF THE LINES OF A TOWN AND A GORE
xxii, 63

To the Honorable the Legislature of the State of *Vermont* —
The Humble Petition of Elijah Dewey, in behalf of himself and Ass^{ts} — And Lyman Hitchcock Agent for more than ¾ of the proprierters of the Town of Cabot — Most Humbley Sheweth —
That in the month of November 1780, The Honorable the Legislature, did Grant unto Capt. Jesse Leavenworth and his Ass^{ts} a township of Land, known on the Map or Chart, by Number 21, *Now known by the Name of Cabot* to be Six miles Squar, bounded South on Peachum &c —[1] and also a Township to Capt Rosserter Griffen and his ass^{ts}, Six miles Square bounded South on the Town of Cabot, known by the Name of *Walden* —[2] That your Petitioner at the Time of the Granting the Said Towns — was Informed, *Col Arnold*. Had obtained a moving Grant, and on being Informed that this Town Lay Adjoining North of Those in which he had an [Agemcy?] — Waited on His Excellency — (*a Considereble Number of the Council Present*) in Company with Capt Jessee Leavenworth, Agent for one half of the Town of Cabot. To know the Truth of that *Report* — but was Informed in that official Manner That Col Arnold, had Liberty to move his Grant, East or North, on unappropriated Lands, *but by No Means* to Move South to the Injure of any other Grant — in Consequence of this assurance They keept their Grants, *and Paid for the Same* — which otherways they Should not have done —
and your Petitioner further begs Leave to observe, that from Many Curcumstence and *Col Arnold own Confession* and Maps Made by himself — *and the Survey*, by him made. on which he has Obtained his *Charter* — Previouly [previously] to

1. For this action of the Assembly, see *S. P. of Vt.*, III (I), 154, 158–159. For the charter of Cabot, see *Ibid*, II (Vermont Charters), 36–37.
2. For this action of the Assembly, see *S. P. of Vt.*, III (I), 154, 160. For the charter of Walden, see *Ibid*, II (Vermont Charters), 201–203.

the out Lines of the other Towns in that Quarter of the State *beeing Run* — and has Brought the South East Corner of his Town *Viz Linden*, [Lyndon][1] within Less then *Nine Miles* of the Northeast Corner of *Peachum* This Incroashment of three miles South on the Towns above Mentioned; which we [Concieve] to be Contrary to the True Intent and meaning of the *Legislature* when the Several Grants was made — and much to the [Injurrey] of the Proprierters of the Town of *Cabot* and the *Gore* Granted Said Dewey in Feby 1782 Laying East of Cabot —[2]

we your Petitioners in behalf of Ourselves, and ass^ts or proprierters in the Town of *Cabot* and the Gore before Mentioned — do Humbly Request the Honorable the Legislature to take this our *Petition* into their Consideration, and if they in their wisdom Shall Think fit, Grant an Order to the *Surveyour Gen^el* to Run the out Lines of the Town of *Cabot* and the *Gore* — as soon as [Conveinnt?] — agreeable to the Grant — and the True Spirit and Meaning of the *Legislature* at the Time Such Grants were obtained — without Paying any Regard to Col Arnold *Pretended* Right of Moveing his Grant *South* — This your Petitioners Humbly Concieve themselves Intitled to, in Common with their Countrymen, who [Recieved?] Simmaler Grants — *Justice* is all we ask, *Justice* is all we wish and from the Honorable the Legislature we doubt not of [*Recieving?*] it —

and your Potitioners as in duty Bound Shall Ever Pray

Bennington Feby 3th 1784

Elijah Dewey
Lyman Hitchcock

— & —

[Petition of Elijah Dewey &] Lyman Hitchcock
Fil^d 3^d March 1784
. . . *

— & —

> *A. J.:* *Read and referred to a committee, 3 March '84, *S. P. of Vt.*, III (III), 36;[3] *referred to next session for further consideration, 5 March '84, *Ibid*, III (III), 45. *C. J.:* *Read, and recommended that consideration be suspended because the proprietors of Lyndon, who were interested against the petition, had not been cited to appear to show cause why it should not be granted, 3 March '84, *Ibid*, III, 43.

FOR COMPENSATION FOR WAR SERVICES
xvii, 92

To the honorable general Assembly now sitting in Bennington; the petition of Samuel Rice of Charlemount in the County of Hamshire [Hampshire] & Com-

---

1. For the grant of Lyndon by the Assembly, see *S. P. of Vt.*, III (I), 149. For its charter, see *Ibid*, II (Vermont Charters), 129–132.

2. This gore was known as Deweysburgh and has since been annexed to Danville and Peacham. For its grant by the Assembly, see *S. P. of Vt.*, III (II), 91. For its charter and an historical note, see *Ibid*, II (Vermont Charters), 60–62, 286.

3. This entry on the manuscript petition correctly states that this committee was to join a committee from the Council.

monwealth of Massachusetts humbly sheweth that on or about the 12th day of
Jan^{ry} 1778 your petitioner until that time [. . .] in the service received orders (from
Brigadier general Starks and Col° Samuel Herrick being then in Bennington) to
take to his assistence three or four men and go upon an enterprise of reconoitring
the situation and strength of the enemy on Lake Champlain and at Fort St. Johns —
In consequence of which your petitioner; desirous of serving his Country engaged
three men and proceeded upon the enterprise <and accomplished it>[1]; which necessarily employed your petitioner with his men from the 14th of January 1778 until
the 28th June in the same year; being 166 days in service for which your petitioner
has received no pay from any quarter; and not being in the regelor Returns of the
Army is intitled to none from the paymaster — your petitioner therefore humbly
prays the honorable Assembly to take his case into consideration and grant him
pay for his services; and your petitioner as in duty bound shall ever pray —

Samuel Rice

Dated Bennington 24th February 1784 —

— & —

Petition of Samuel Rice
. . .*

— & —

A. J.: *Read and referred to a committee to join a committee from the Council,
24 Feb. '84, *S. P. of Vt.*, III (III), 14; *report of committee recommending
that petitioner receive captain's pay for time of expedition, read and accepted,
and ordered that a bill be brought in accordingly, 25 Feb. '84, *Ibid*, III (III),
17; *petition, report of committee, and bill thereon referred to next session,
8 March '84, *Ibid*, III (III), 53; *report and petition read and dismissed, 18
Oct. '84, *Ibid*, III (III), 185. *C. J.:* *Committee appointed to join a committee
from the Assembly, 24 Feb. '84, *G. and C.*, III, 38.

FOR COMPENSATION FOR SERVICES IN RESCUE OF VERMONTER
SEIZED BY YORKERS
xvii, 93

Bennington February 25 1784
To the Honourable general Assembly of the State of Vermont now Siting The
potition of the Subcribers Humbly Sheweth that on the 16th day of January Last A
band from the opposers of this government[2] assalted the Hous of Landlord Arms
in Bratelborough [Brattleboro] and after fireing Several musquit balls with buck
shot into the House they entered and in their Common desperate manner took
Ensign Oliver Waters whome they Conveyed on foot to the edg of the Masschusets
[Massachusetts] State where they put on his hands a huge weight of Ill Shaped

---

1. The Assembly journal notes that Rice was taken prisoner in the course of the
expedition (*S. P. of Vt.*, III (III), 14).

2. At this time the southeastern part of Vermont contained many persons who
actively adhered to the authority of New York. See B. H. Hall, *History of Eastern Vermont*
(New York, 1858), pp. 485–513.

Iron and delivered him into the Care of two of their party who ware ordered to Carre him to poukeepsey [Poughkeepsie] —

The nuse reached Halifax on the night of 17 by express from Leut John Noyce of Guilford when amediately your potitioners procured horses and arms — prosued and overtook them and rescued Mr. Waters at Northhamton [Northampton] — your potitioners (then in high Spirits) knowing that Timothy Phelps was then in Hadley bownd to New York and Congress with interesting papers resolved he Should retorn in the way mr. waters went out — they according went into the Hows whare he was and notwithstanding high resistance from his brother &c. took him and brought him as far as Dearfield [Deerfield] but was their unhappily over-taken by the High Sherriff of the County of Hampsheir [Hampshire] and 24 men with a warrent from a justis of the peas of that County unto whom phelpses brother had represented your potitioner as Rierters — the Sheriff utering these words when he came into the hous (whare⁸ these damn⁴ Vermonters) made your petitioners take him and his company for yorkers and Consequently fel upon him and (al-though our party was small to that of his) Should have kiled or taken them had he not Cryed out I am the High Sheriff of the County of Hampsheir upon which wee tamely submited was Carried back tried by three Justices and four of our Company was adjudged to pay in fines and Costs £21:8:0. This was done entirely through the Instrumentality of phelpses brother the High Sheriff declairing in open Court wee were good fellows and although he had received more wounds than all the rest he frankly forgave us and promised his assistence for the futer both as a gentel-man and a majistrat in proventing our people from being Carried through that visinity by the Yorkers &c Now your potitioners did all this soully out of Loielty and freindship to this government.

And although we did not carre our points In everything yet we prevented Mr. Waters from being now Confined in New york which doubtliss the Yorkers would have gloryed much in — And also obtained the favour of the offer in the Mass-chusets State before mentioned which will in all probibilety be interesting to this State. Now your potitioners in the management of the whole of this business have expended in Silver money at least £6:9:7 besides what was before mentioned — and in time horse ride &c. which Cannot be estimated at les than £21:16:4 as has been Carefully Calculated your potitioners therefore earnistly and Humbly desire that this Honourable Assembly would take their Case into their wise Considera-tion and grant unto your potitioners such releaf and in such a way as to your Honours Shall Seme Most agreable and your potitioners as in dewty bownd Shall ever pray

Joseph Tucker	Elijah philips	Samiel [Denson?]
Thomas [Hall?]	gorham [Gersham?] Noys	John Noys
Oliver Waters	Joel Sumnor	Caleb owen
Steven gates	pheleman Stacy	thomas fansworth
timothy [Woodard?]	Daniel [Wallworth?]	Nathan Witteny
David Williams	Rufus fish	

— & —

The Petition of Joseph Tucker and others
Filed 26ᵗʰ Febry 1784 —
...*

— & —

A. J.: *Read and referred to a committee, 26 Feb. '84, S. P. of Vt., III (III),

20;[1] *report of committee recommending that prayer be granted and payment of £49–13–11 be made from a confiscated Yorker estate, read and accepted, and an act passed and sent to Council for proposals of amendment, 5 March '84, *Ibid*, III (III), 46.[2] *C. J.*: *Committee appointed to join that of Assembly, 26 Feb. '84, *G. and C.*, III, 39.

FOR ANNEXATION OF A GORE TO A TOWN
xxii, 65

State of Vermont

To the Hon[ble] the Gen[ll] Assembley of the State of Vermont Now Siting at Bennington

the Petition of Nathaniel Brown of Windhall [Winhall] in the County of Bennington Agent for the proprietors of a Gore of Land Lying between Londonderry and Said Windhall Granted by the Assembly of the State of Vermont and annexed to Londonderry[3] Humbly Prayeth

that Said Gore may be annexed to Windhall and your petitioners as in Duty bound will Ever pray

Dated Bennington Feb[r] 26th 1784

Nath[n] Brown

— & —

Petition Nath[l] Brown
Filed 3[d] March 1784
. . .*

— & —

A. J.: *Read and granted, and ordered that a bill be brought in accordingly, 4 March '84, *S. P. of Vt.*, III (III), 43; bill read and referred to next session, 8 March '84, *Ibid*, III (III), 56.[4]

FOR COMPENSATION TO THE WIDOWS AND ORPHANS
OF TWO OFFICERS
xvii, 94

To the Hon[ble] the General Assembly now convened —

---

1. This entry on the manuscript petition correctly states that the committee was to join a committee from the Council.

2. The record of this action on the manuscript petition does not include the fact that an act was passed by the Assembly and sent to the Council. The act itself was never passed into law, but provision for the payment of a smaller sum was included in "An Act pardoning [*Charles Phelps*] Esq. of Marlborough . . .", passed October, 1784 (*Slade*, 494–495). On 17 June '85 the assembly by resolution made additional provision for the collection by the petitioners of funds from Phelps (*S. P. of Vt.*, III (III), 157. For a petition from Phelps in this connection, see p. 121, *post*.

3. Aikin's Gore. See *S. P. of Vt.*, II (Vermont Charters), 250.

4. For a similar petition to the same effect, see p. 283, *post*.

The petition of Benj^a Fassett & Mindwell Hopkins Administrators on the estate of Maj^r Wate [Wait] Hopkins late of Bennington deceased & Stephen Hopkins Administrator of the Estate of Capt. Benj^a Hopkins late of said town deceased —
Humbly Sheweth —
That the aforesaid Major and Captain Hopkins were in the first commencement of the war appointed into office in Col^o Seth Warners Reg^t and served as offiers [officers] therein until the first formation of his Continental Regiment raised for three years and during the war when each of them received Commissions and performed the duty of officers of said regiment until they were both killed by the Enemy, as many of your honors are well acquainted with[1] — And that during their continuance in office the Congress of the United States among many other Resolutions in behalf of the suffering offcers and soldiers raised during the war, passed a Resolution recommending to each state to give unto the widow & orphans of any officer belonging to such state that should loose his life in the service of the United States seven years half pay and charge the same to the United States and that said state should be credited therefor[2] — and as said Maj^or & Capt. Hopkins were both killed by the enemy and the widows and orphans of them are fairly intitled to the said seven years half pay agreeable to said Resolution of Congress — They therefore pray your honors (as they the said Maj^r and Capt. Hopkins were both liege subjects of this state, and were always among the first to act in its defense both before and since the formation and spent most of their interest, as well as all their time in promoting the settlement of this state and carrying on the War and as your petitioners have no other place to get any redress) — that your honors would take their case into serious consideration and grant them the said seven years half pay according to their rank when they were killed for the benefit of the said widows and orphans, or otherways as your honors in your great wisdom shall direct and they as in duty bound shall ever pray —
Bennington 27th Feby 1784

> Benj^a Fassett
> Mindwell Hopkins
> Stephen Hopkins

— & —

Petition of the Administrators of the Estate of Maj. Hopkins & Capt Hopkins Filed
. . .*
In Council date above [28 February 1784]
Resolved the Mr. Emmons join the above Committee

> Joseph Fay Sec^y

— & —

---

1. For the service of Wait Hopkins, see *Vt. Rev. Rolls*, pp. 107, 110, 623, 814, 815, 836, 837, and for that of Benjamin Hopkins, see *Ibid*, 107, 110, 623.
2. For this resolution passed 24 Aug. '80, see *Journals of the Continental Congress*, XVII (Washington, 1910), pp. 771-773. See also *Letters of Members of the Continental Congress*, edited by Edmund C. Burnet, vol. V (Washington, 1931), p. 368; and *Resolutions, Laws, and Ordinances relating to the Pay, Half Pay, Commutation of Half Pay, Bounty Lands, and other promises made by Congress to the Officers and Soldiers of the Revolution;* . . . (Washington, 1838), p. 11.

A. J.: *Read and referred to a committee to join a committee from the Council, 28 Feb. '84, S. P. of Vt., III (III), 26; *report of committee recommending that "under the present circumstances and situation of the state" the prayer "ought not to be granted at this time",[1] read and accepted, and ordered that petition be referred accordingly, 4 March '84, Ibid, III (III), 41–42.

FOR THE ENLARGEMENT OF COUNTIES
xvii, 97

To the honourable the General Assembly of the Representatives of the freemen of the State of Vermont to convene at Rutland in said State on the second Thursday of Octr next

The petition address and Remonstrance of us the subscribers freeholders and Inhabitants of ye County of Windsor in said State,

Humbly sheweth

That the general Assembly, did at a former sessions pass a Law impowering the Civil Authority of the County of Windsor afores^d to agree upon and Establish a Place to Erect a Court House and Goal on, in the Township of Windsor and to Assess the Inhabitants of s^d County in a Sum Suitable for the Purpose[2] And the Authority aforesaid by Virtue of said Law met at Windsor afores^d and by an Adjournment to the Month of May last, at which time the said Authority agreed that said Courthouse and Goal Should be Erected in East Windsor, about half a mile from Connecticut River, and also did assess the Inhabitants of said County Two pence on the pound to Carry on the building of the Goal and other Contingent Charges which Law & proceedings appears to your Petitioners very unjust and unreasonable and prejudicial to the Inhabitants of said County and the State at Large, for these Reasons, the Inhabitants of the now Windsor County when Called a Part of Cumberland County Were Assessed (with the Inhabitants of the other part of s^d County which now is Call'd Windham County) for the purpose of Erecting a Court house and Goal in the town of Westminster and payed said Assessment and the money has been Appropriated to the use designd for, and your petitioners by Dividing said County of Cumberland Loose all the priviledge of said Courthouse and Goal and the County of Windham unjustly enjoy our money or the Effects of it, therefore it is a Prejudice to the Inhabitants of the County,

2^{ly} If the Old County of Cumberland had not been Divided the County Cost wou'd not have been more than it is now in Each of the said Countys. One set of Judges one Shiriff one Grandjury &c would answer the Same purpose as Double that Number does now and perhaps better as it is Easier to find five Qualifyed Persons for Judges than Ten and so on thro' the whole officers, one Court House

---

1. The committee's reference to "the present circumstances and situation of the state" doubtless concerned the fact that the Congress had not recognized the existence of Vermont as a separate state. The Assembly could thus have no confidence that the state would be credited for any payments it might make under resolutions of the Congress.

2. No record of any such law has been found. On 21 Feb. '81 the Assembly passed "An Act for establishing the Shire or County Towns . . . ", and this act established Windsor as the county town of Windsor County. However, it contained no provision empowering the civil authority to select a place for the court house or to assess the inhabitants (Ms. Laws of Vt., I, 216–218).

and Goal would serve the same purpose &c we Conceive that it would be much Easier and much Cheaper for the Judges of the Circuit, as the Business That is to be Done in Two Counties would be performed in one County were they to be made in to One County[,] which we Conceive Ought to be the Case[;] it Appears very unjust that there should be so many Seperate bodies in this State that have power of Taxing themselves, besides the General Assembly and Towns[;] if the Counties were made as we Conceive they Ought to Comprehend Thirty six Towns and a Court house and Goal Set in the middle every Individual would be Contented Provided that a Law Should Pass your honourable Body granting Liberty for such a Set of Town to the amount of Thirty six to form into a County and the Gen¹ Assembly Grant a Tax for the Purpose of Build [sic] their Court House Goal &c we therefore are of the Opinion that Two Counties on the East Side of the Green Mountains would be Soficient for the Inhabitants thereof and very much Lessen the State Tax as well as County Taxes. At present there is but Eighteen Towns in Each of the Counties (viz) of Windham and Windsor, it appears that, that Number of Town is too small to make a Respectable County beside the Extraordinary Cost. If we View the new England States we shall find the Counties there far Exceed in bigness three of our Counties altho they are much Older Setled and if it was an Advantage to have Small Counties; their Experience purhaps [might] have induced them before this time to have altered their Large Counties, they have not Cut them up[;] therefore we Conceive that Large Counties are best they are at Least more Respectable and less Expensive and if Government ought to be instituteᵈ for the Common benefit of the People at large[,] than [then?] Particular Towns or Sets of men ought not to frustrate that Design by bringing heavy burdens on Government if multiplying Counties is beneficial we Conceive that every town ought to be a County but that Idea ought to [be] Reprobated at first view[,] and Eighteen Towns Erected into a county in this new World is so Small, they ought to be lightly Esteemed

We your honours Petetioners humbly pray that you would take this our Petition under your wise and Serious Consideration and give your Petitioners such Relief by Enlarging the Counties and Deminishing Taxation as you in your Wisdom Shall Judge most Condusive to the peace and hapiness of the good People of this County of Windsor and Windham and for the Honour and Emolument of this State at Large, your Petitioners as in Duty bound shall ever Pray.
Sepᵗ 7ᵗʰ 1784

Moses Gile Junʳ	Elijah Parker	Amos Sargeant
Micah Bowker	Ezekiel Colburn	Joseph Whitmore
Ezra Sargeant	Solomon Wilson	Ezra Ormsbee
Jabez Sargeant Jun	Wᵐ Gilkey	Thomas Chandler Jnʳ
James Robinson	John Stone	Tho Chandler
John Smith	George Earll	Joshua Church
Timᵒ Olcott	Thomas Stone	Abner Gile
Abner Wilson	William Thompson	

— ර් —

Moses Gile Junʳ and 23 others
Petition
. . .*

— ර් —

A. J.: *Read, 18 Oct. '84, S. P. of Vt., III (III), 77; *read again and dismissed, 19 Oct. '84, *Ibid*, III (III), 79.

FOR RELEASE FROM COLLECTING TAXES
xvii, 101

To the Honorable General Assembly for the State of Vermont convened at Rutland, the Petition of Moses Joy of Putney in Windham County humbly Sheweth that whereas your Petitioner was appointed first constable for said Putney for the year 1783 that in Discharge of s^d office your Petitioner has collected one /5 on the pound Tax in State Notes, and /3^d in hard money and a County Tax So far as to Settle the whole with the Sheriff of Windham County, that your Petitioner has been obleged to Pay between four & five Pounds fees to the Said Sheriff; and has also been obleged to Pay £35 out of his own Estate to make out the whole of the Said Taxes which is Still Uncollected and is the most of it Due from very Poor Persons, that your Petitioner did not recive the warrants for the collection of the s^d Taxes more then two months before the Extents were essued ag^t your Petitioner, that your Petitioner ⟨is a Seafaring man and⟩ did Previous to having any knowledge of the Present Taxes engage to take the command of a Vesel [on] a Voige to the westindies [West Indies] this full [fall]; that if your Petitioner is obleged to collect the Late Taxes agreeable to the Directions of Law he must be Wholly Desapointed in his s^d Voige which your Petitioner concieves will be greatly to his Damege that your Petitioner did not receive the warrants for the collection of the Late Taxes till more then two months after the time that Some of the money was to have been Paid into the Treasury. therefore your Petitioner Prays this Honorable Assembly would be Pleased to release their Petitioner from the collection of all the Taxes Granted by the Last Assembly and appoint the first constable of s^d Putney for the Present year or some other sutuble Person to collect the same. and make your Petitioner compensation for £4:17:0 Paid the Sheriff as fees. your Petitioner cannot but have Sanguine Expectations in the Clemency of this Honorable Assembly in granting his Prayer, when they are informed that he has not, nor never had, any Estate but what he has obtained by his own industry, and has exerted his Utmost abilities in the Servis of this State. and your Petitioner in duty bound will ever Pray

Moses Joy

NB the above Petitioner affirms that he has not taken any fees of the inhabitants as he did not Expect any would be taken of him

Moses Joy

— & —

Moses Joy Petition
fees pd —
. . .*

— & —

A. J.: *Read and dismissed, 15 Oct. '84, S. P. of Vt., III (III), 71.[1]

---

1. The editor of the Assembly journal copied Moses Joy as Moses Fay. The original manuscript makes this an understandable error. However, the manuscript of this petition leaves no ground to doubt that the name is Moses Joy.

FOR RELOCATION OF CERTAIN COUNTY BUILDINGS
xvii, 105

To the Honble Genl Assembly of the State of Vermont
Convened at Rutland on the Second Thursday of Oct^ber 1784 The Petition of
the Subscribers Inhabitants of the County of Rutland Humbly Sheweth:
That the Advantages arising to the Public from a Regular Transaction of
Bussiness are greatly promoted by the appointment of Places and Seats of Accommodation where Individuals may most commodiously attend and the concerns of
the Public transacted with Dispatch & least Expence
The Committee appointed to place the Stake for a County House were doubtless Influenced by the aforementioned Principles but through Mistake unhappily
Placed the Same where on one Side an impregnable Swamp & on the other impassable Hills are very ill adapted to aforesaid purpose besides Surrounding parts
admitt only Partial improvement very poorly calculated for the accommodation
of Assembly's Courts & Numbers of Men on Public Bussiness[1]
Your Petitioners are informed that the Honble Assembly have lessened this
county by taking of [off] one Tier of Towns North Since the last Com^tee reported
on the Subject.[2] We would further observe that the East part of Rutland is the
Most commodious Place for the communication of the East & Northerly Parts
with the western Part of the State on account of Several New Roads allready made
and to be made So that Bussiness may be done with less Trouble & Expence.
Therefore Humbly Pray that this Honble House will Set aside their former Resolutions and Establish the Seat of Public Bussiness in the Easterly Part of Rutland or
otherwise Resolve as your Honours Wisdom may direct and as in Duty Bound
Shall ever pray

Elkanah Billing	Gedion Hewt	Silas Whitney
N Lee	James Cummings	Wiliam Smith
A. Ives	David Yewes	Aaron [Eastar?]
Eb^n Pitcher	\<Gedion Hewt?\>	Elihu Grant
Whitefield Foster	Jacob Walker	Josiah Soyer
Thomas Eddey	Elias Stewart	Epriam Soyer
Jethro Jackson	Job Congdon	Benjamin Bell
Abraham Jackson Jn^r	Lemuel White	John [Sauier?]
Jedidiah Jackson	Joseph Smith	Jonathan Parker
Asahel Jackson	Abraham Salsbury	Abel Spencer
John Smith	Rheuben Pitcher	Ichobut Robenson
John Gould	Joseph Congdon	Peter Aldridge
Jonathan Read	Daniel Hill	Zibe Aldridge
Prine Sherman	John [Paul?]	Ezra Freemen
Jedediah Clark	Oliver Arnold	Benjamin Parker

---

1. For a reference to this committee and its location of a site for the Court House,
see "An Act for describing the bounds of the County of Rutland and Establishing the
Town of Rutland a County Town . . .", passed 9 March '84 (Ms. Laws of Vt., I, 444-445).
According to this act the committee "did pitch a stake" "nigh the Great Road that leads
from said town [Rutland] to Castletown, and about twenty Rods West of the House
where Mr. William Roberts now lives . . ."
2. The reduction in the size of the county was doubtless due to the new bounds
established in the act mentioned in note 1.

Daniel Plat	Joseph Randol	Daniel Briggs
Jedediah Clark Junr	Benedick Weber	Philip Briggs
(Isaac Hambelton)	Thomas Hinman	John Mack
Solomon Spafford	Nehemiah Smith	Oliver Steward
John Bordman	Joshua Webster	George Palmer
Ezra Crary	Ebenezer Howard	John [Varny?]
Nathan Crary	Thadeous Curtis	Samuel Wetherby
James Wels	Ebenezer Pitcher Jr	Ezekel Clark

— & —

Petition of the Inhabitants of Rutland County respecting Court House
Octr 1784

— & —

A. J.: Read along with two other petitions to the same effect and referred to a
committee, 19 Oct. '84, *S. P. of Vt.*, III (III), 79–80;[1] report of committee
recommending that location for buildings was inconvenient and ought to be
removed, read and accepted, 21 Oct. '84, *Ibid*, III (III), 84; resolved that
committee be appointed to fix on a place for buildings, 21 Oct. '84, *Ibid*, III
(III), 84; report of committee read and referred until Tuesday next, 23 Oct.
'84, *Ibid*, III, (III), 87; report of committee read and accepted, and leave given
to bring in a bill accordingly, 26 Oct. '84, *Ibid*, III (III), 98; bill read and
accepted and sent to Council, 28 Oct. '84, *Ibid*, III (III), 105–106; proposal
of Council to postpone bill until next session rejected, 29 Oct. '84, *Ibid*, III
(III), 110; bill read the last time and passed into law, 29 Oct. '86, *Ibid*, III
(III), 112.[2] *C. J.:* Act read and Council recommendation made that bill be
referred to next session, 29 Oct. '84, *G. and C.*, III, 61.

FOR THE RELIEF OF A TAX COLLECTOR PAID IN COUNTERFEIT BILLS
xvii, 103

To the Honorable Representatives of the freemen of the State of Vermont in
General Assembly met to be Held at Rutland
The petition of Isaac Miller J^r Collector of States Taxes in the town of Dummerston
appointed in 1781 Humbly Sheweth
that Whereas Execution have ben Sent against me for the Land tax Granted in
the year affores^d [3] & whereas I have the money on hand & by Reason of Some
Counterfit Bills which I have Rec'd in office of Collector & cannot tell who of[,] &
some that I have Sworn Back on the persons I recd them & for the want of a certain
Act (which is not to be found in this town) made & provided in Such Case I am

----

1. The two other petitions are not now among the *Ms. Vt. S. P.*
2. See "An Act establishing the place for erecting Public Buildings in the county of
Rutland" (*Ms. Laws of Vt.*, I, 473). This act directed that the county buildings "shall be
built on or as near as may be to the spot of Ground where a Stake is set by a Committee
appointed by the Assembly for that purpose — (Viz) about Two Rods north of the Road
leading from Ely Browns to Castletown and about twenty Rods West from said Brown's
dwelling House any Act or Law to the contrary hereof in any wise notwithstanding."
3. See "An Act for the purpose of emitting a sum of Money, and directing the
redemption of the same," passed April, 1781 (*Slade*, 424–426).

not able to Settle the same —;[1] but am obligd to pay the Cost of s^d Execution Which is more than I am allowed for Collecting s^d tax —; & Whereas there has ben no allowance made me for Collecting the provision tax Granted in s^d year 1781[2] & the troubles which have Subsided [subsisted?] in this part of the State has Rendered it almost imposable (in times past) to collect the same till of late. While some part of the inhabitants have Removed out of the State & other wise Disinabled from paying the Same So that I have ben Obligd not only to pay part of the Cost of the Extent But Nearly one Quarter part of s^d tax out of my Own Intrest —; this is therefore to pray your Honours to ordour that the Cost of the Extent for the provision tax & the Execution for the Land tax be Defrayed by the freemen of the State & that Some Small fees be allow'd me for collecting the provision tax, & your Honours Humble petitioner as in Duty Bound Shall Ever pray

Isaac Miller Junr

— & —

Millers Petition
. . .*

— & —

A. J.: *Read and referred to a committee, 18 Oct. '84, *S. P. of Vt.*, III (III), 77; *report of committee recommending that prayer ought not to be granted, read and accepted, 19 Oct. '84, *Ibid*, III (III), 79.

FOR A NEW TRIAL OF A SUIT OVER ARMY SUPPLIES
xvii, 99
(Partly Obliterated)[3]

To the Honble [General Assembly] to [be held] at Rutland on the second [Thursday] of October [Instant] The Petition of Jonathan [Child] of Lime in the [State of] New Hampshire humbly [sheweth]

That [. . .] Joseph [Kimball of] Plainfield in the county of [. . .] [State of New Hampshire] on the second day of October [. . .]^4 [one] thousand seven hundred & eighty [. . .]^5 against your Petioner [. . .]^5 which was purchased for the [use of the Army of these States], and the [sum] of two [. . .]^6 Petitioner to the said Joseph [. . .]^6 Receiving; & being more than the [. . .]^4 of the flour, as may fully appear from a proper [Examination] into the premises. Which action was transfered into the County Court, in the County of Washington, and Judgment

---

1. The act referred to was "An Act respecting counterfeit money", passed 15 Oct. '82 (*Ms. Laws of Vt.*, I, 303). This act set up a procedure whereby collectors of taxes might be credited by the Treasurer of the state with any such money which they might have received for taxes.

2. "An Act for the purpose of procuring provision for the troops, to be employed in the Service of this State, for the year ensuing," passed October, 1781 (*Slade*, 440–442).

3. Portions of the manuscript have been obliterated. Some of the information thus lost may be found in the entries in the Assembly journal cited in the subjoined note.

4. Three words obliterated.

5. Five words obliterated.

6. Six words obliterated.

rendered in favour of the said Joseph for the [sum of Twenty six pounds twelve] shillings & [six] pence, [damages]; and Six Pounds seventeen shillings two pence, costs of suit — at a time when it was impossible for your Petitioner to attend by himself or counsel to make a proper Defense — Being at the time of Trial Purchasing commissary for the Troops of this State & They allmost entirely destitute of Provisions — And your Petitioners Counsel being detained from court by sickness in his family — whereas your Petitioner, would have been enabled could he have made a proper Defense to have received a judgment in said Action for his cause —

And your Petitioner would further suggest that the said Joseph has since commenced an Action on the aforesaid Judgment in the County Court in the County of Windsor, by reason of which your Petitioner will be very greatly injured in his Property if proceedings therein are not stayed & he indulged by your Honors with a proper remedy —

Your Petitioner would further shew that he preferred a Petition to your Honors, at the Session of the General Assembly in February Anno Domine seventeen hundred & eighty three [which] was referred to the then next stated Sessions and [. . .] that referred, at the request of the said Joseph,[1] to the next Session of Assembly, which was supposed by your Petitioner and his Counsel to mean the present Session — by reason of which mistake your Petioner did not attend at the adjourned [Term?] of the same Session, holden at Bennington in February last, and the said Joseph procured an Order in his favour, which [forecloses?] your Petitioner from obtaining his Right in the Premises —

Wherefore your Petitioner requests your Honours again to take his Case under your Consideration, and to grant him a New Trial in the Original Action in the County Court in the County of Windsor or some other County in this State, as soon as may be convenient for the Parties — and that all farther Proceedings in the former Judgment may cease & be discontinued, that the Merits of the cause may be fairly & candidly determined: And as in duty bound shall ever pray —

Jonathan Child

State of Vermont
5ᵗʰ Octʳ AD 1784

Octʳ 9, 1784. — Then I delivered to Mrs. Kimball, wife of Joseph Kimball, at his house in Plainfield, a true and attested copy of this petition with Notice that the same would be presented to the General Assembly at their Session at Rutland in October Instant

Attest. — George Hough.

— & —

Petition of Col. Child
Filed 15ᵗʰ Octʳ 1784
. . .*

— & —

A. J.: *Read and ordered to lie on the table until Friday next, 15 Oct. '84, S. P. of Vt., III (III), 70–71; *read and resolved that it be taken up at some future session and that Windsor County Court "continue" the cause before it, 22 Oct. '84, Ibid, III (III), 85; *read and referred to a committee to join a committee from the Council, 10 June '85, Ibid, III (III), 139; *referred as

---

1. For this request, see p. 84, ante, including note.

"referred from the last session," to a committee to join a committee from the Council, 14 Oct. '85, *Ibid*, III (III), 173; *report of committee recommending that prayer be granted, read and accepted, and resolved that a new trial be held under certain conditions, 27 Oct. '85, *Ibid*, III (III), 207. *C. J.:* Committee appointed to join Assembly committee, 10 June '85, *G. and C.*, III, 71; committee appointed to join Assembly committee, 15 Oct. '85, *Ibid*, III, 80.

FOR REDRESS OF GRIEVANCES AGAINST THE LEGISLATURE
xvii, 102

To the Honourable General Assembly, of the Representatives of the Freemen of the State of Vermont; at their Session of Assembly, to be holden at Rutland, on the Second Thursday, of this Instant October.

The Petetion, of a Number of Towns, by their Deligates in County Convention Met, this Sixth Day of October A.D. 1784. at the house of Capt John Strong in Woodstock, Humbly Sheweth: That in the Course of our Enquiry, we find many Infringments on the Constitution & Rights of the People, which from an Ardent Desire that Peace and Harmony may be Restor'd; we Omit for the present, and proceed to Mention, Only Such Acts and Measures of the Legislature, as appear to us to be Extreemly Dangerous, and a Gross Revertion, of the Trust Reposed in them, by their Constituents — (Viz) —

First. An Act adopting the Common and Statute Law of England, to be a part of the Laws of this State:[1] by which the Good People of this State are Deprived of one Essential previlidge Secured to them by the Constitution, which Requires, that all Bills of a publick Nature, before they are Anacted into Laws, Shall be presented for the Consideration of the People. —[2]

2^{ly} The Opening the Law for Land trials Agreeable to the Mode pointed out by the Late act of Assembly,[3] Published for the Consideration of the People, in our Opinion is Impolitick and will Eventually be Productive of the Greatest Injustice and Confution. —

3^{ly} the not Printing the Journals of the house as pointed out by the Constitution. —[4]

4ly That Plaintiff that Bring Suit in this State that live out of the State Should be Allow'd, travalling Fees from the most Extensive part of the State and Six Shilling more for Crossing the line. —

5^{ly} That Publick Accounts are not Adjusted. —

6^{ly} That a fair Stating of the Publick Debts and where and how the Publick Money has been Applied, has not as yet been laid before the People. —

7^{ly} That the Govournours Salary Considering the Circumstances of the People is Burdensome and Ought to be Redused to a Lessor Sum. —[5]

8^{ly} That the High Sheriffs fees for Collecting the Publick Monies, is Burdensome Considering, there are Post Offices kept at the Expense of the Publick by which

---

1. See *Slade*, 450 (also 287).

2. For this provision of the Constitution of 1777, see Chapter II, Section XIV (*G. and C.*, I, 97–98).

3. *Slade*, 443–444.

4. For this provision, see Chapter II, Section XIII (*G. and C.*, I, 97).

5. On 23 October '83 the Assembly *"Resolved* that his Excellency's Salary for the year ensuing be two hundred Pounds lawful Money." (*S. P. of Vt.*, III (II), 213).

Monies might be Conveyed to the Treasury[1]

9[ly] The Act of the Legislature Impowering the Surveyor General to make a General Survey;[2] is in our Opinion unnecessary and will Burden the Good People of this State with a Needless Expence as the Old lines in General must be Established or many of the People will Suffer the Loss of their Landed property. —

10[ty] That unimproved Lands, tho' Rising in Value Bear no part of the Publick Expence. —[3]

We your Petetioners Humbly Pray your Honours to take the Above Articles of Grievence into your wise Consideration and Grant Such Redress as you in your Great Wisdom Shall think Best: As we your Humble Petetioners in Duty Bound Shall Ever pray. —

By order of Convention

Joseph Foster Chairman

Resolved that Hono[e] Benjamin Emmans Esq[r] Major Jesse Safford and M[r] William Perry be a Committee to present the Above Petetion to the General Assembly

Extract from the minutes Elijah Mason Clerk

— & —

A Petition of a Number of Towns in the County of Windsor —
Filed 18th Oct[r] 1784

See how his Paper Shakes —

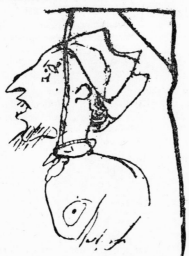

So let the man swing that signed this paper or any other person who may [signen] scandalous paper —[4]

---

1. For the Sheriff's and the collector's fees, see "An Act for the regulation of Fees", passed October, 1783 (*Slade*, 477–481).

2. See "An Act for the regulation and Establishment of Town Lines," passed 22 Oct. '82 (*Ms. Laws of Vt.*, I, 350–351).

3. See pp. xx–xxi, Introduction.

4. The manuscript itself gives no reason to doubt that this drawing and writing were done at about the time the petition was presented to the Assembly.

State of Vermont In General Assembly Octr 18th 1784

The aforesaid petition or Remonstrance was read and ordered to lie on the table until the Com^{tee} of the whole meet this day for their consideration.

attest Ros^l Hopkins Clerk

. . .*

— & —

A. J.: *Read and dismissed, 18 Oct. '84, S. P. of Vt., III (III), 74.

___

FOR RELOCATION OF A COUNTY COURT HOUSE
xvii, 104

To the Honourable General Assembly of the Representitives of the freemen of the State of Vermont, to be holden at Rutland on the 2^d Thursday of october Inst. The Petition of the Inhabitants of the Towns of Bethel Royalton Barned [Barnard] Sharon Pomfret Cavendish Reding [Reading] Wood Stock [Woodstock] And Hartland all in the County of Winsor [Windsor] by their Deligates in Convention Met at Wood Stock in S^d County on the 6th Day of October AD 1784. Humbly Sheweth — that the Appointment of the Town of Winsor, to be the Place in S^d County, for Erecting Buildings Necessary for the Public Use of S^d County,[1] is in the oppinion of your Honours Petitioners, Unjust, and grevously Burthensom, to the greatest Part of the People Inhabiting S^d County. (Viz) Because that the Town of Winsor is Sittuate at the Eastermost Sid [side] of S^d County; and the Place Pick^d upon in S^d Town for the Erecting S^d Buildings on, is at or Near the Eastermost Line of S^d Town and is More than ten Miles from the Center of S^d County on account of which all the People Inhabiting the Westward Part of S^d County, are ⟨Burdened⟩ Burthened With Extraordanery Travel, in Case of County Meetings. and Larg Bills of Cost for Travil of officers, Partys, and Witnesses in Case of tryals at Law. and farther that these Burthens are Dayly Increasing, by the Rappid Settlements of the Westward Part of S^d County. — and your Honours Petitioners, Beg Leve farther to observe that it is Become Necessary in order to Do Equal Justice to the People Inhabiting the County at Larg. and that Each Indeviduals May Injoy the Blessing of a Happy Government; that the Place for Transacting Publick Business in the County be as Near the Center of the County as Can be With Convenancy. and your Honours Petitioners, Concidering the unhappy Devisions occasioned by Dissolution of the Union,[2] Together With the Cruel and Bloody War in Which We have Been Involved, have Been Patient Several years, Waiting a More favourable oppertunity for the Removal of those Grevances; and Concidering that those Troubles are in Some Measure Removed by the Return of Peace beg Leve farther to observe that the Inhabitants of this County, Grow impatient for the Removal of the ⟨Rest of the⟩ fore Mentioned Burthans. —

and your Honours Petitioners Pray that your Honors Would tak these our Grev-

___

1. See note 2, p. 95, ante.

2. This presumably refers to the dissolution of the "Eastern Union," the union between Vermont and certain towns in the western part of New Hampshire. For a history of the dissolution of both Eastern and Western Unions, see G. and C., II, 379–384.

ances into your Wise Concideration and grant order that Deligates be appointed and sent, from Each Town in S^d County, with Powers to Fix upon a Place for S^d Buildings to be Erected on, as Near the Center of S^d County as May Best Accommodate the County at Larg or otherways grant Reliefe as you in your greate Wisdom Shall See Fit, and your Petitionours as in Duty bound Shall Ever Pray. — Sign^d By order of Convention —

[P^{er}?] Joseph Foster Cheairman

— & —

Petition of Woodstock Convention respecting Windsor County-Court-House — Filed [28th?] Octr 1784

. . .*

In Council Rutland 25th Octr 1784

Mr. Brownson is appointed to join the above Committee for the above purpose

Jonas Fay Secy P Tem.

— & —

A. J.: *Read and referred to a committee to join a committee from the Council, 25 Oct. '84, S. P. of Vt., III (III), 90; *report of committee recommending that a committee be appointed to determine the matter and that the work on county buildings be suspended, read, and resolved that a committee be appointed and work suspended, 28 Oct. '84, Ibid, III (III), 105; new member of committee appointed in substitution, 4 June '85, Ibid, III (III), 122; report of committee recommending that Woodstock be site of county buildings, read and ordered to lie on table until tomorrow morning, 9 June '85, Ibid, III (III), 135; report accepted and ordered that bill be brought in accordingly, 10 June '85, Ibid, III (III), 136–137; bill read and referred to next session, 16 June '85, Ibid, III (III), 149; *the matter referred to next session, 20 Oct. '85, Ibid, III (III), 194; ordered that matter be taken into consideration the next Thursday, 14 Oct. '86, Ibid, III (III), 221–222; referred to next Saturday, 19 Oct. '86, Ibid, III (III), 231; act referred from June session 1785, read and accepted, and sent to Governor and Council, 21 Oct. '86, Ibid, III (III), 236; read with proposals of amendment by Council and passed into law, 27 Oct. '86, Ibid, III (III), 253.[1] Rep. of Com.: Committee recommends that Woodstock be site of county buildings, 9 June '85, S. P. of Vt., IV, 31. C. J.: Act read and concurred in, 27 Oct. '86. G. and C., III, 113.

FOR A TAX ON LAND TO BUILD ROADS AND BRIDGES
xvii, 108

To the Honorable the general Assembly of the State of Vermont to be conven^d at Norwich on the month of June 1785
The petition of the Inhabitants of the Town of Rockingham in said State aforesaid Humbly Sheweth —
That wharas there is about one half of the Land in ye Town of Rockingham is owned by people Living in other states and Take Little or no Care to settle S^d

---

1. "An Act establishing the place for erecting public buildings in the county of Windsor . . ." (Acts and Laws, passed by the General Assembly of the State of Vermont, at their stated session, at Rutland, in October, 1786 [Windsor, 1786], p. 3).

Land and have Never been at any Cost or paid any Tax for said Land, the Ten Shillings p^r 100 acor Tax Excepted[1] Since the Town has been settled or began to Settle Now those Land have became vary Valuable even so Valuable that the owners will not Take under 20/ or 30/ Shillings p^r acor and those unresidents are Not Willing to Sell them Lands at any price unless thy Can have Cash. So that the great price thy ask & the unreasonable pay at this Day thy Insest on makes it almost Imposable for people to Trade With them and as Long as No Tax is Laid on Such Land there Will be No Likeliwhood of those Lands being Settled and wharas the Inhabitant think it Vary hard that there own Indesterey Must In rich and grandize people abroad That are not will [sic] to contrebute any thing to assist a poor people in Making Roads Bridges Meeting houses &cc and wharas there is a Large River Runs threw said Town that will Need a Number of Bridges in order that the people can posably attend the publick worish [worship] and a Large Number of Roads Runing threw Said Town which must be Made and Cultivated to Save the Town from being Fined[2] Which the people are Not able to accomplish —

In order to Remove said Defficalty your petitioners Humbly Bagg that your Honors Would Lay a Tax of Two pence pr acor on all the Lands in Rockingham for the purpose of Building Bridges Cutting and Mending Roads To and threw those unresedents Lands in such a manner and under such Ruls and Derecstions —

as your Honors in your Wisdom Shall think proper and as your petitioners are in Duty Bound Shall Ever pray —

At an anuael meeting the above was Voted too by the Town of Rockingham March 14th 1785   Jehiel Webb ⎰ Town Clerk

— & —

Rockingham petition
Filed [8th June?] 1785 —
. . .*

— & —

A. J.: Read and referred to a committee to join a committee from the Council, 9 June '85, S. P. of Vt., III (III), 133; *report of committee recommending that petition be laid over to next session and that non-residents be given opportunity to give reasons why petition should not be granted, read and accepted, and ordered that petitioner may bring in a bill accordingly, 9 June '85, Ibid, III (III), 134; report of committee reconsidered and petition recommitted to same committee, 10 June '85, Ibid, III (III), 136; same report and action taken as on 9 June '85, supra, 17 June '85, Ibid, III (III), 157;[3] act for levying a tax on all lands in the town for these purposes, read and accepted and sent to Council, 18 June '85, Ibid, III (III), 159. Rep. of Com.: Committee recommends the grant of a tax of one pence and a half penny on land for these purposes, 14 June '85, S. P. of Vt., IV, 25. C. J.: Committee appointed to join Assembly

---

1. For the ten shilling tax, see "An Act for the purpose of emitting a sum of Money, and directing the redemption of the same," passed April, 1781 (Slade, 424-426).

2. An indictment could be drawn under the common law against any town for not repairing its highways. See Laws of the State of Vermont; Revised . . . 1797 (Rutland, 1798), Chapter XXVI, Sec. 19, p. 359.

3. This entry in the journal was undoubtedly a clerical error. The second report made by the committee was that under date of 14 June '85 given in Rep. of Com. (S. P. of Vt., IV, 25), which provided for the immediate passage of an act.

committee, 9 June '85, *G. and C.*, III, 68; act read and concurred in, 18 June '85, *Ibid*, III, 75.[1]

FOR REPEAL OF AN ACT RESPECTING PUBLIC WORSHIP
xvii, 364

To the Honorable the Representatives of the Freemen of the State of Vermont to be convened in General Assembly at ⟨Rutland⟩ Norwich on the ⟨second⟩ first Thursday in ⟨October⟩ June A.D. 1785 —
    We the Subscribers Inhabitants of said State, beg leave to remonstrate against a certain Act of the Legislature of said State passed October y[e] 17th 1783 intitled "an Act to enable Towns and Parishes to erect proper houses for Public worship and support Ministers of the Gospel"[2] — Which Act as we apprehend is an infringment on the privileges vested in us by the third article of the Bill of Rights. —[3]
The Inhabitants of the State of Vermont had the peculiar happiness of assuming Government at a time when they had the collected wisdom of many ages to direct them in forming a Constitution, and at a time when the idea that one religious (sect as such) had any Right to control another in matters of religion had been long, exploded at least in this Country. — we accordingly find the Compilers of the Constitution have been very explicit in delivering their sentiments on this subject in the third Article of the Bill of Rights, which says "that no man ought, or of Right can be compeled to attend any religious worship, or erect or support any place of worship or maintain any Minister, contrary to the dictates of his Conscience, and that no authority can or ought to be vested in, or assumed by any power whatsoever, that shall in any case interfere with or in any manner control the rights of Conscience in the free exercise of religious Worship" —
    As the wellbeing of the State depends much on the preserving this Bill of Rights in its original purity, so it is the duty and interest of every individual member of the Community, to watch out, guard and defend it, and whenever he sees it in danger, to stand forth for its protections. Government generally becomes corrupt by small degrees, and is often greatly perverted, before the danger is perceived — but this Act we esteem to be a most glaring attack on the Constitutional Rights of the People; as it gives to the Majority of the Inhabitants of the Towns and parishes in the State, the power of Controling the Minority in matters of Religion; we therefore think it our duty as Freemen of the State of Vermont, and as Rational *Beings*, to remonstrate against, and Request the repeal of it ⌈and whatever els is Contrary to the Third Article⌉ —

Steel Smith	Nathan Eldreg	Wanton alsworth
Josiah Clark	John Eldreg	John Walis
Ebenezar Meacham	James Eldreg	John parkins
John Hewlett	Job Eldreg	Caleb Ranolds
Eliphelet Niles	Mikega Winant	Abel Gilby
John Gill	Stephen herenton	Abial Loyan

---

1. For this act, see *Ms. Laws of Vt.*, I, 496–497.
2. *Slade*, 472–473.
3. *G. and C.*, I, 93.

Jonathan Hammond
Peruda Stephens
John Mosely
William Lazell
Joseph Barrett Ju^r
Levi lazell
Eben^r Howard
Zenas Lazel
Jonah Strickland
Bezaliel Grandy
Simon Rumrill
Zebulon Chandler
Henry Rumrill
Benjamin Stone
Phin: Hemenway
Jonas Taylor
Amos Taylor
William Brown
Richard Brown
Daniel Gardner
John [prosen?]
Abither angel
Joseph Willims
Abraham Gardner
George Gardner
Joseph potter
peter parker
Thomas Jorden
John Blood
George parker
Job Burlson

Job herenton
Ezra Drew
Luke Landphir
Asahel Doubleday
Nehemiah Mack
Abel pain
Andrew Smith
James alsworth
Abel potter
Danel [Dun?]
[olaver?] hungerford
Ruben kennet
Danel Baker
Jonathan [Card?]
John alsworth
Benjamin Gardner
Eleser Lareby
Benjamin Gardner J^r
Daniel Ceard
John Nils
John Nils J^r
Benjadick Corey
Joshary Mattson
Thomas padock
philip alsworth
paul Gardner
Abel Mattson
Silas [Mattson?]
David Gardner
David Gott
Ruben Cartrite

Danil philips
Job philips
Thomas [Card?]
Blackmen Browning
Elisha [Card?]
Rufus [Wens?]
Josiah Botts
Isrel Williems
Joseph Williems
[Olaver Miles?]
Reuben Smith
Nathan Avery
Thomas Baldwin
Sam^{ll} Robinson
Elijah Dewey
Jonathan Scott
Joseph Safford
Nathan Russ
Jacob Bevons
George Samson
James Worshburn
James Harwood
Benjamen Sandres Jr
Asa Green
Ezekiel Palmer
Amasa Delano
Richard Southgate
Nathan Wood
Consider Fuller
Saml Raymond
Asa jones

— & —

Petition to ye Assembly ag^t ye Ministry Act —

— & —

A. J.: Read and ordered to lie on the table, 6 June '85, *S. P. of Vt.*, III (III), 123.[1]

FOR ESTABLISHMENT OF OLD TOWN LINES REGARDLESS OF NEW SURVEY
xxii, 87, 91

To the Honble General Asembly to be Conven^d at Norwich in the County of Windsor on the first Thirsday in June 1785 —

---

1. A revision of the act against which this petition was directed, was passed by the Assembly 7 June '85 (*S. P. of Vt.*, III (III), 127), but it apparently never became a law. There is no record of the concurrence of the Council in this revision or of the text of the act itself.

The Petition of the Inhabitants of Bethel in s^d county Sheweth —[1]
that we (in Pursuence of a Grant Obtained of S^d Bethel from the Honble Asemble
afores^d to Certain Persons Inhabitants of this & the Neighbouring States)[2] Purchased a Number of Lots Laid out & bounded by s^d Proprietors & Since have
Proceeded to make roads & Emprovements thereon in Conformaty to the old Line
& Bondaries but by a Late act of the Legislature a New Survey is made of S^d
Town[3] & the Lines Greatly altered Sundry of Our Land Cut of & Put in other
Towns & as the Case is Now Situated it renders it Empossible for us to go back
on the original Grantees as in manay [Instancees] they are Wholey unable to
make Good Damages & Consequently we must be Turned out of Posesion —
Therefore Pray that your Honours would Establish the old Lines as formaly
Survey^d or remedy our [Greviencee] in Such other way as your Honours Shall
Direct —

> Barnabas Strong } agent

— & —

Petition — Bethel Inhabetant
Filed 2^d June 1785
. . .*

— & —

> *A. J.:* Read and ordered to lie on the table, 3 June '85, *S. P. of Vt.*, III (III),
> 118; *read again and referred to a committee to join a committee from the
> Council, 9 June '85, *Ibid*, III (III), 135; report of committee recommending
> that establishment of town lines be postponed to next Assembly, read, and
> ordered that report be dismissed, 15 June '85, *Ibid*, III (III), 147–148;[4] petition
> considered by Assembly and dismissed, 15 June '85, *Ibid*, III (III), 148. *C. J.:*
> Committee appointed to join Assembly committee, 10 June '85, *G. and C.*,
> III, 70.

FOR ESTABLISHMENT OF OLD TOWN LINES REGARDLESS OF NEW SURVEY[5]
xxii, 88, 91

To the Honble General Assembly to be Convened at Norwich in the County of

---

1. For similar petitions presented to the Assembly at this time, see next petition
and pp. 114, 115, 116, 135, *post*. See also p. 164, *post*.
2. For the charter of Bethel, see *S. P. of Vt.*, II (Vermont Charters), 23–24.
3. See note 6, p. 114, *post*.
4. This entry in the journal — and thus the subsequent one — does not list this
petition as among those reported on. This was undoubtedly a clerical error, since the
other entries in both the Assembly and Council journals include it among those considered
in a group and referred to this committee.
5. For similar petitions from other towns presented to the Assembly at this time,
see p. 108, *ante*, and pp. 114, 115, 116, 135, *post*.

Windsor on the first Tuesday of June 1785 the Petition of the Inhabitants of the Town of Royalton in S^d County of Windsor Sheweth

That we the Inhabitants of the Town of Royalton in Persuance of a grant obtained of S^d Royalton from the Honble Assembly afores^d to Certain Persons Inhabitants of this & ye Neighbouring States¹ Purchased a Number of Lotts laid out & Bounded by S^d Propriators & Since have Proceeded to make Roads & other Improvements theron in Conformity to the old line and Boundaries but by a late act of the Legeslature a new Survey is made of S^d Town² & the lines greatly altered a number of our lotts of land Cut of [off] and put into other Towns and as the Case is now Cituated it Renders it impracticable to go back on the original Grantees as in many instances they are wholly unable to make good Dammages & Consequently we must be turned out of Possession therefore pray that your Honours would Establish the old lines and former Surveys or Remedy our greavances in any other way that your Honours Shall direct and your Petitioners as in Duty bound Shall Ever Pray —

Silas Williams ⎱

⎰ Agents for S^d Town

Elias Stevens ⎱

— ๛ —

Petition — Royalton inhabtants
Filed 2^d June 1785
. . .*

— ๛ —

[See subjoined note for previous petition.]

———————

FOR ONE SHIRE TOWN IN THE CENTER OF THE COUNTY
xvii, 108

To the Honorable the General Assembly of the State of Vermont, to be holden at Norwich on the Second Day of June Next.

The Memorial of the Towns of Pownal, Shaftsbury, Arlington, Sandgate, Sunderland, Dorset and Rupert; all in the County of Bennington and State Affores^d Most Humbly Sheweth,

that by a Law of this State we are Already Taxed and Still Exposed to Future Taxations (Without our Consent as a County) for the Express Purpose of Erecting and Keeping in Repair Two Court Houses and Goals in the Small County Afforesaid Which We Esteem to be unreasonable and Burthensome as well as Unconstitutional and unjust for the following Reasons (Viz.)³

1st We View it Unreasonable (and Doubt not but your Hon^rs upon Strict Atten-

———————

1. For the charter of Royalton, see *S. P. of Vt.*, II (Vermont Charters), 175–177.
2. See note 6, p. 114, *post*.
3. By an act passed 28 June '81 Bennington and Manchester were appointed half shire towns for Bennington County (*Ms. Laws of Vt.*, I, 255–256).

tion to the facts Stated in our Petition Presented in October Last[1] together with those in this Memorial will View the Matter in the Same point of Light) that those Persons Who Offered (in Time past) to Build a Court House and Goal in Bennington at Private Expence (in Case Said Bennington Might be Priveledged as a Shire Town) a Grant thereof Was Made[2] the Terms of which not being fulfilled by the Grantees (or Persons Afforesaid) our Interest has been Demanded to Respond the Delinquency of Said Grantees While they Reap all the Benefit of the Purchase Without Paying the Stipulated Price and the Said County at a Prodigious Expence Purchases a Most Prodigious Inconvenience.

2ndly We View it Burthensome to build two Court Houses and Goals in one Small County (having so lately Emerged from the Calamities of a most Distressing War) When one Court House and Goal (in our Opinion) Erected in or Near the Centre of the Inhabitants of Said County Would Accommodate them as well (and Much Better and with far less Expence) than two, So Near the Extream Parts thereof

3rdly Upon the Most Mature Consideration we View it Unconstitutional as we are Persuaded that the Law afforesaid was made and Enforced Without Due Defforence to the Fourteenth Section of the Sacred & Inviolable Rights of our Most Excellent Constitution[3] the Said Law not being of a Temporary Nature (Ought before it was put in force) to have been Published, Perused and Aprobated by the People Agreeable to the Said fourteenth Section of Said Constitution Which the Assembly has no Right to Infringe as is fully Express'd in the 8th Section thereof [4]

4thly We View it as unjust that the Law afforesaid (being Directly Repugnant to the Rights of Constitution) Should Continue in Force So Long to the great grief of the Majority of Said County for whom it was (or Ought to have Been Designed as a Benefit) & as Such ought to be Repealed

And Lastly when your Memorialists Consider as we are Persuaded your Honors do that Government is (or Ought to be) Instituted for the Common benefit of the Community and not for the Particular Emolument or Advantage of any Sect of Men who are a Part only of the Community According to the Declaration of Rights Section 6th [5] and that frequent Recurrence to Fundamental Principles and a firm Adherence to Justice, Moderation, Temperance, Industry and Frugality are absolutely Necessary to Preserve the Blessings of Liberty and that the People have a Right to Expect, or, as the Said Declaration of Rights Set. 16th Express it (Exact)[6] a Due and Constant Regard to them from their Legislatures in Making and Executing Laws &c. upon which Considerations together with Special Confidence in the Wisdom & Goodness of that August body the Legislature of the State we Conceive Ardent Hope that the Prayer of the Petition of your Present Memorialists (being a Large Majority of Said County) Prefered in October Last Past Will be granted (this Memorial being a Reminicence thereof) that Justice Peace and Tranquility the Sole Design thereof may Prove a Blessing to the State in General and to this County in Particular and your Memorialists as in Duty Bound Shall Ever Pray

---

1. This petition (not now among the *Ms. Vt. S. P.*) was considered by the Assembly and ultimately dismissed (*S. P. of Vt.*, III (III), 70, 80, 191–192).

2. For this offer in the form of a petition and the action taken on it, see p. 14, *ante*.

3. *G. and C.*, I, 97–98.

4. *Ibid*, I, 96.

5. *Ibid*, I, 94.

6. *Ibid*, I, 95.

At the Annual Town Meeting in Shaftsbury held by adjournment on the 4th Day of May 1785 the above Memorial was Read and unanimously aproved and ordered to be Prefered to the Next Session of the General Assembly.

Attest. —   Jacob Galusha Town Clerk

— & —

The Memorial of Shaftsbury & [Cc] [. . .] the Court House
filed Jun 7 1785
. . .*

— & —

> *A. J.:* *Read and referred to a committee to hear the parties and report to next session, the county taxes being suspended until the end of that session, 13 June '85, *S. P. of Vt.*, III (III), 142–143; report of committee reviewing the history of the matter and recommending that petition ought not to be granted but suggesting also a hearing at large on the matter, ordered to be considered in the afternoon, 19 Oct. '85, *Ibid*, III (III), 191–192; report considered in a committee of the whole, and resolved that petition be dismissed, 19 Oct. '85, *Ibid*, III (III), 194.

FOR A NEW TRIAL IN A LAND CASE
xxii, 83

State of ⎫ To the Honorable General Assembly to be holden at Norwich, in
Vermont ⎭ the County of Windsor, on y[e] [first Thursday in June 1785] the Potition of Daniel Marsh of Clarendon in the County of Rutland humbly sheweth that befour the County Court holden at Tinmouth in the County of Rutland on the third Tuesday of April in the year of our Lord 1782. Silas Whitney of Clarendon aforesaid brought an action of Ejectment against your Potitioner for a certain Farm of Land lying in said Clarendon containing one hundred Acres which Land had been improved & posses'd by your Potitioner for a number of years previous to the Commencement of said suit, & at the Commencement of said suit your Potitioner was absent out of the state & had no knledge [knowledge] of the Matter untill after one Adjudication of the Court against him & on a Review of the cause in november of the same year the plaintiff recovered final judgment for the possession of said Farm which was the only Court and the only opportunity your Potitioner had to Produce any proof of his title to said Land & was not then prepared with the best evedence of his title, & after judgment was entered up against him[;] agreeabely to A statute Law of this State then in force[1] he filed a Decleration in Court for his damages or pay for the improvements on said land which Action was by the Clark of said Court entered on the [Docket] & there [Continued?] And the Clerk did not bring forward said Action at the then next Court Acording to the Duty of his office by reason of which Discontinuence the said Whitney

---

1. See "An Act to enable persons who have entered and made improvements on Lands, under colour of title, who shall be driven out of possession by a legal trial at law, to recover the value of what the estate is made better by such improvements, from the rightful owner of the Land," passed October '81 (*Slade*, 442–443).

afterward applyed to said Clerk for a writ of seizon & Possession on the former Judgment which was Issued by said Clerk which Writ was immediately Executed In favour of said Whitney & your Potitioner was turned <out> of possession of said Land & that some time Afterward your Potitioner having supposed that the possession of said Land was wrongfully <taken from him> Atained from him did resume his former Possession after which the said Whitney on the 20 Day August 1785 brought an action against your potitioner on the statute Against forceable Entry & Detainer[1] which was by a Jury of free holders Determined in favour of your Potitioner from which Determination the said Whitney Appealed to the County Court which was holden on the thirde tuseday of November Last past from that terme the said Cause Lay untill the Adj'd term in January Last holden on the thirde tuesday Which Court the Cause was finally Determened against your potitioner And the said Whitney recovered his Cost taxed at £10–11–3 And your Potitioner further say he has been vexed with sundry actions of trespass by said Whitney for the farm & that by reason of the premices he has been much injured & sustained Great damage —

And prays your honours would take his Case into Consideration and apoint him a new trial for the title of Said farm & that he should be reposesd of his said Farm & that he should be intitled to the advanteges of his antient improvements on Said Land provided his title to Said Land Should not appear Legal & that he may be restor'd to all that which he hath Lost & that he may have his Cost & Damages which he has sustained by said whitney in Consequence of his having procured the writ of Seizon[s] aforesaid against your Potitioner Contry to the Design of the Law, or in any other way be relieved by your honors, as you in your wisdom may Direct & your Potitioner as in Duty bound shall ever pray —

Dated Clarendon the 9 day of May Ad 1785

Daniel Marsh

<To the Sherif of the County of Rutland his deapetie or> To either of Constables of the town of Clarendon, in y[e] County of Rutland & because such officer Cannot be had with out great Cost & Inconvenences to [Col.?] Abel Copper] An Indiferant person you are hereby required in the name & by the athority of the freemen of the State of Vermont to Notify Silas Whitney of Clarendon afore Said or his Lawful Attorney to appear If (they see Cause) befour the General assembly Menchoned in the above Potition at there Assession at Norwich on y[e] first Thursday of June to answer to the above Potition & shew Cause if any he has Why the prayer of Said Potition should not be granted fail not & return make

Dated At Clarendon on the 9 day of May Ad 1785

Elihu Smith Jus of [peace]

Clarendon May y[e] 23rd 1785

Then serv'd this Sitation by Reeding in hareing of y[e] above named Silas Whitney p[r] me

Abel Cooper Indifferent Person

— & —

---

1. For "An Act directing Proceedings against forcible entry & Detainer" passed 13 Feb. '79, and for another act with the same title passed 22 Oct. '82, see Ms. Laws of Vt., I, 35–37, 339–341.

Potition of Danial Marsh vs Silas Whitney
Filed 14th June 1785
. . .*

— & —

A. J.: *Read and referred to a committee, 16 June '85, S. P. of Vt., III (III) 149–150; *report of committee recommending that petitioner be quieted in the possession of farm until he have a trial for his betterments and that he be granted such trial, read and accepted, and ordered that a bill be brought in accordingly, 17 June '85, Ibid, III (III), 155–156;[1] bill read and accepted and sent to Council, 18 June '85, Ibid, III (III), 158; bill, having been concurred in by Council, passed into law, 18 June '85, Ibid, III (III), 159.[2] C. J.: Act read and concurred in, 18 June '85, G. and C., III, 75.

FOR ESTABLISHMENT OF OLD TOWN LINES REGARDLESS OF NEW SURVEY[3]
xxii, 79, 91

To the Honble Genl Assembly Now Seting at Norwich in the county of Windsor The Petition of Barnabas Strong Humbly. —

Sheweth —

That your Petition [sic] as agent & Sole Proprieter for & in behalf of the Proprietors of Brantree [Braintree]. Sayeth that s^d proprietors in conformity to the act of Assembly for begining the Settlement [of] new lands[4] Proceded to Survey & make one Division of Lots in S^d Town in order to fullfill the Settleing Duties agreable to Charter[5] conforming to the Lines Surveyed by other Town as understood before the New Survey[6] wich new Survey if Established will render our former Surveys in Sum measure frutless & reduce them to make new Surveys or other ways confuse the former ones (as by s^d new survey the Lines are Metearally altered to the Injury of the s^d proprietors) now your Petitioners prays that the old Lines might be Established as it in no wise is injurus to the freemen of the State nor in any respect to any Individual & your Petition as in Duty Bound shall Ever pray —

Brantree May 12th 1785 —

[B.] Strong ⎱ in behalf of s^d
           ⎰ Proprietors

— & —

Braintree — Petition — 1785 —
Filed 2^d June 1785 —
. . .*

— & —

[See subjoined note for similar petition on p. 109, ante.]

---

1. This entry on the manuscript petition includes only the text of the committee report and not the action taken upon it.

2. For this act, see Slade, 499.

3. For similar petitions from other towns presented to the Assembly at this time, see pp. 108, 109, ante, and pp. 115, 116, 135, post.

4. See "An Act declaring a time when to begin the settlement of new lands, that has been prevented by the late war between Great Britain and America", passed Oct. '83 (Slade, 475–476).

5. For the charter of Braintree, see S. P. of Vt., II (Vermont Charters), 28–30.

6. The "New Survey" was a new survey of all town lines in the state undertaken

FOR ESTABLISHMENT OF OLD TOWN LINES REGARDLESS OF NEW SURVEY[1]

xxii, 80, 91

To the Honble Genl Assembly of the State of Vermont to convene at Norwich within the County of Windsor on the first Thursday of June next —

The Petition of the Proprietors of the Township of Bethel in the County of Windsor humbly sheweth.

That in persuance of Directions from the Genl Assembly to begin the Settlement of said Town within a time limitted for that purpose;[2] they proceeded, agreable to the Instructions of the Assemblys Agent, to make Division of said Township into Lots, and to make Improvements on the same, which Lots were laid out & bounded agreable to the Survey upon which the said Town was granted —[3] And that the Assembly did grant a Tax of ten shillings on each hundred Acres of Land in said Town, which was collected on the Lands within the Limits of said Town agreable to the Ancient or first Boundaries —[4] And since the Division, settlement, & Payment of the Tax as aforesaid the Assembly have Ordered a New Survey of said Town[5] by which the Town Lines are materially altered, and consequently every Proprietor frustrated in his Lot. & every Settler disturbed in his Possession: And if adopted must totally Defeat all former Surveys, and & [sic] subject the Proprietors to every inconvenience, of new expence & shifting of settlements. Wherefore your Petitioners humbly pray for a confirmation of their former Boundaries as first expressed and understood — and that they may not at this stage of settlement & Improvement be disturbed in their Possessions, and As in Duty bound shall ever pray

12th May 1785

Dudly Chase

Barna^s Strong

} Proprietors Comit^{tt}

— & —

Petition of Bethel Proprietors
Filed 2^d June 1785
. . .*

— & —

[See subjoined note for similar petition on p. 109, *ante.*]

---

by the Surveyor-General according to law. See "An Act for the regulation and Establishment of Town Lines", passed 22 Oct. '82, and an act in addition thereto passed 29 Oct. '84 (*Ms. Laws of Vt.*, I, 350, 466).

1. For similar petitions presented to the Assembly at this time, see pp. 108, 109, 114, *ante* and pp. 116, 135, *post*. See also p. 164, *post*.

2. For the directions of the Assembly with respect to the settlement of Bethel, see *S. P. of Vt.*, III (I), 91, 93, 94–95. These directions were included in resolutions passed in October, 1779.

3. For the charter of Bethel, see *S. P. of Vt.*, II (Vermont Charters), 23–24.

4. For this tax, see "An Act for the purpose of emitting a sum of Money, and directing the redemption of the same", passed April '81 (*Slade*, 424–426).

5. See foot note 6 to previous petition.

FOR ESTABLISHMENT OF OLD TOWN LINES REGARDLESS OF NEW SURVEY[1]
xxii, 81, 91

To the Honble Genl Assembly to convene at Norwich on the first Thursday of June next —

The Petition of the Proprietors of the Township of Rochester humbly sheweth

That your Petitioners in conformity to the Act of Assembly for beginning the settlement of New Lands,[2] proceeded to survey & make one division of Lots in said Town; And to survey & Lot out the remainder with a view of fulfilling the settling Duties agreable to the true intent and meaning of said Act, predicating their Lines and surveys on those of the Town of Bethel,[3] as understood before the new Survey —[4] Which new Survey if established will make void all the surveys & Divisions of said Town and reduce the Proprietors to the necessity and Expence of new surveys — as by said new survey the Lines of the Town are materially altered — And the uncertainty in which the matter now rests renders it impossible for the Proprietors to proceed to perform settling duties with safety. As they can never know whether they are laying out expence on their own Lands or those of strangers 'till the Town Lines are firmly & permanently fixed —

Wherefore they Pray your Honours that the said Lines as originally understood and considered may be established, & they allowed to enjoy the benefit of their Labours & expences in settling a new Country without hindrance or Molestation,

And as in Duty bound shall ever pray

12th May 1785

> Dudly Chase
> Asa Whitecombe   Propri^trs
> David Currier
> Enoch Emerson   Comitt.
> Timothy Clemons

— & —

Petition of Rochester Proprietors —
Filed 2^d June 1785 —
. . .*

— & —

[See subjoined note for similar petition on p. 109, *ante.*]

FOR ONE SHIRE TOWN IN THE CENTER OF THE COUNTY
xvii, 109

To the Honorable the General Assembly of the State of Vermont —

---

1. For similar petitions from other towns presented to the Assembly at this time, see pp. 108, 109, 114, 115, *ante*, and p. 135, *post*. See also p. 163, *post*.

2. See "An Act declaring a time when to begin the settlement of new lands, that has been prevented by the late war between Great Britain and America", passed Oct. '83 (*Slade*, 475–476).

3. For the charters of Bethel and Rochester, see *S. P. of Vt.*, II (Vermont Charters), 23–24, 170–171.

4. See note 6, p. 114, *ante.*

The Petition of Sundry Inhabitants of the Towns of Wardsborough and Summerset in the County of Windham humbly Sheweth that whereas the said County of Windham is Small & it is attended with Unnecessary expence to have two Shire Towns therein[1] and in our Opinion it is best for the Inhabitants thereof that there Should be but one Shire Town in said County, And your Petitioners think that the Shire Town ought to be in the Centre of the County; And whereas New-Fane is situated nearly in the Centre of said County & it will in our Opinion be most conducive to the *Interest Lasting Peace* and *Welfare* of the Inhabitants of Said County that the Said Town of New-Fane should be made the Shire Town in said County; Therefore Pray your Honors would Take the Matter under your wise consideration and grant such relief in the Premises as you in your great wisdom Shall think best and as in duty bound shall ever Pray —

Wardsborough May 23ᵈ AD 1785

Philip Newell	Thomas simpson	Dan Warren
Joseph Dix	Abner Holbrook	Samuel Kidder
Edwad [sic] Walker	Thomas Allen	Hachaliah Whitney
Noah Sherman	Samuel Glover	Joseph Chamberlain
Hiram Newell	Samuel Chapin	Abner Perry jʳ
Oliver Willard	John Stacy	[Bezalel?] Jones
Lemuel Bryant	James Wallace	John Ganson
Samuel Davis	Asahel Woodcock	Daniel Warner
John Holbrook	Asa Fay	Simeon Meacham
John Jones	Pearley Fairbank	Nathan Ganson
John Wallie	Stephen Thayer	James Parmele
Thaddeus Wait	Joseph Fairbank	John Parmele
John Ramsdell Junr	John Ramsdell	Lemuel Braley
[David?] Blood	Nathaniel Bills	Seth Roberts
Silas [Waight?]	Ebenezer Bills	Eli Perry
jared newell	Jacob Chamberlin	Nathaniel Gould
Lewis Newell	Richard hiscock	Aaron Clark
Abner Allen	Asa Wheelock	Asa Jones

— & —

Petition from the Inhabitants Wardsborough & Somerset

— & —

[No Record][2]

---

1. By an act passed 21 Feb. '81 the towns of Westminster and Marlborough were established as half shire towns for Windham County. See "An Act for establishing the Shire or County Towns in the several counties . . ." (*Ms. Laws of Vt.*, I, 216–218).

2. This petition may never have been presented to the Assembly. This is suggested by the fact that a petition with the same object was presented by certain representatives from Windham County on 14 June '85. For this petition, see p. 133, *post*. For other petitions in the same connection, see pp. 208, 218, 219, 221, *post*.

FOR SPECIAL CONSIDERATION TO INHABITANTS IN A LAND DISPUTE
xxii, 82

State of ⎫   To the Honarable Generel Assembly, to be holden at Norwich
Vermont ⎰   in the County of Windsor on Thursday the second Day of June
one Thousand Seven hundred and Eighty five. The Petition of the inhabitants of
the Town of Clarendon, Humbly Sheweth.

That many of your Petitioner a number of Years ago, bought Land in said
Town under faith of the New Hamshier [Hampshire] Grants, and made Settlements theirupon agreeable to the Requisitions of Charter;[1] and by much Expence,
and Labour have Converted A wilderness into fruitful Fields — That many of
your Petitioners have ben so Unfortunate as to Purches of Men who had no Tittle
or Interest in said Town: and in the Confution of Past Times believed themselves
to be Invested with Proper Right of the Land so Purchersed.[2]

That of Late many Desinging Persons take unwearied pains to [divest?] your
Petitioner of the Land which heretofore they so dearly Purchesed with Interest,
Labour, and Improments their upon: Pretending to better Tittles then Your Peti-
tioners.

Others their are who have Purchesed of the Legal owener, Yet in their absence
or before they had any knoledge of any Person being appointed as a Clark by yᵉ
Proprietors to receive and Record such Surveys: Cartain Parsons who are lost to
all sence of Justice, have taken the advantage of a Cartain <vote of yᵉ proprietors?>
Statute that the oldest survey on Record should hold by which means they are
indevoring to Establish their fourtuns on the Ruin of others. And whereas yᵉ
Mettings of the Proprietors was not Legal Yours Petitioners Humbly Pray that
Your Honours take their Case into Considaration and Set aside the Votes of the
Proprietors; and that a Reasonable time may be allowed to those who have ben
Imposed on in Purchising Land; to Procuer good rights: and that no Undue ad-
vantage be taken of those who have Purchesed of yᵉ legal owener, or in any other
way be Reliev'd as your Honors in your wisdom may Direct. & your Petitioners
as in Duty bound shall ever Pray —
Datted at Clarendon this 23ʳᵈ Day of May 1785

Benj. Whitman	francis matteson	David hill
Thomas Rice	Timothy Winter	Phelp Briggs
Lewis Walker	Stephen Robinson	William Crosman
Joseph Smith	Daniel Colvin	Jerimiah Colven
John Seamans	Israel Robinson	Whitefield Foster
Peter Eddy	Lewis Colven	Benjaman Foster
Jonathan Eddy	Samuel Place	Daniel Washborn
Jonathan Wood	William Marsh	Benjamin Foster Junʳ
Squier Ide	Ezekiel Green	John Spencer
Nathaniel Chaffe	Joseph Congdon	Jeams Round
Amos Robinson	Daniel Briggs	George Round

---

1. For the charter of Clarendon, see *State Papers New Hampshire*, vol. XXVI (Town
Charters, vol. III), 99–102.

2. Presumably this refers to those who purchased land and settled under the Lydius
grant. For a discussion of this grant and the consequent disputes, see Matt B. Jones,
Vermont in the Making 1750–1777 (Cambridge, 1939), pp. 142–147, 317–320, and *passim*.

Joshua Priest	Pierce Spencer	David Warner
Henrey Deen	David Palmer	Asa Smith
Gorge Wescoot	Gideon hewit	Jeames Jinks
Amasa Brown	Nathan Rice	

— & —

Petition of Inhabitants of Clarendon.
Filed 4th June 1785
. . .*
The Honrb Assembly now Sitting at Norwich
your Committe to whom was Referd the within Pertition Beg Leave to Report as there Opinion that Sd Petition ought to be Laid Over to the next Session of ⟨this⟩ Assembly — and that the adverse Partee be Sited to Shew Cause whi the prayer of the within Petition ought not to be Granted

Gideon Ormsby for Comt

Norwich 9 of June 1785
— & —

A. J.: *Read and referred to a committee, 4 June '85 S. P. of Vt., III (III), 122.[1]

FOR RESTORATION OF A FARM SEIZED UNDER NEW YORK TITLE
xvii, 110

To the Honble the General Assembly of the State of Vermont To be Convened at Norwich in the County of Windsor on the first Thursday of June in the Year of our Lord 1785 —

The petition of Andrew Graham of Putney in the County of Windham and State of Vermont Humbly Sheweth —

That your Honours Petitioner Early in the Year 1767 contracted with Coln Josiah Willard of Winchester for a Lot of Wild Land in the Township of Putney and was to Give Said Willard One [hundred] pounds ⟨L Money?⟩ Old Tenor [tender?] Money thence Called and thereupon your petitioner being then poor and in Indigent Circumstances moved with a Small family on the 12th Day of March 1767 on to Said Lot of Land in Putney built him a Small Log-house to Shelter him by Night and there Endured all the Hardships and Calamities of bringing to a New farm in the Howling Wilderness having for Several years to bring (in Some Instances) the [provisions] for himself and his family sixteen Miles on his own back [that] your Petitioner Soon after he had begun his Settlement on said [. . .] of Land found the Same Claimed by a Number of Gentlemen at Boston under a Grant from the Massachusetts Bay[2] and was obliged and actually did agree with those Claimants and Continued in Tenable possession making Improvements for Eight years at the Expiration of which time your petitioner had got five & thirty

---

1. In October '85 the Assembly passed "An Act for settling disputes respecting landed property" (Slade, 500–503). Doubtless this petition and the situation which occasioned it were in part accountable for this legislation.

2. For a brief discussion of the "Equivalent Lands" granted by Massachusetts in what was later southeastern Vermont, see B. H. Hall, op. cit., pp. 13–14.

or forty Acres under Good Improvement and Could keep on Said farm twenty head of stock thro' the year —

Your petitioner would further remark that Sometime in the year 1774 after the Spirit of Oppression & Land Jobing had begun to rage with Violence among the Inhabitants of New York your Petitioner's farm was again Claimed by Billa Smith of New York under the title of that Province[1] and your Petitioner was Tried in an Action of Ejectment to answer the Said *Smith* in the City of New York why he Neglected to Surrender up the Peacable possession of Said Farm and Conceiving his Interest at that time inadequait to maintain an Action in the City of New York against so potent a Land Jober Suffered the Sum to Go without any appearance on his part, soon after which a Number of Persons headed by a Deputy Sheriff under New York without Ever producing any writ Came and Draged Your petitioner with his family and Effects off from Said farm and turned them Into the Naked Wilderness and put one Ben[j] *Wilson* into possession of Your petitioners house and farm to enjoy the Same on his Acting the Bully and keeping your petitioner out of Possession and notwithstanding frequent attempts and that to by the Assistance of Col[n] *Warner* Gen[ll] Allen and a Number of the heads of the Green Mountain Boys (then SoCalled) Yet So Numerous were the Advocates for that Government in this Vicinity that your petitioner was keept out of Possession of his house and farm for nine Years

Your Honour's Petitioner would further remark that the Said Ben[j] *Wilson* having So long Stiffled the Dictates of his Conscience in Withholding from his Neighbour and enjoying the Profits of a farm for nine years for which he never laboured or paid one farthing of Money Seems to have been left of God to fill up the measure of his iniquity to the full did in the Course of the winter now Last past leave his wife & family and run off with a prostitute to enjoy her in that Government which had So long Countenanced his Wickedness here by reason whereof your Petitioner's house and farm was left empty and unpossessed of any person in Consequence whereof your petitioner in April Last peacably moved into the House and took possession of the farm he had So long been unJustly Deprived of Since which one William Sergants of Putney aforesaid pretending to have purchased of the Said Benjamin molests & disturbs your petitioner and will not suffer him Quietly to enjoy said farm and has without the Least Colour of Law or right pulled Down your petitioners house & Chimney about his Ears and beaten & abused your Petitioner and family, Your petitioner would further inform your Honours that *all the redress* he can obtain by applying to the Law is to be told that if he has been keept out of possession three years if ever So Wrongfully he is intitled to no remedy by the Law —

Your petitioner therefore prays your Honours to take his Case into your Wise Consideration and Grant him that Justice which So long he has been unable to obtain by the Laws of the Land and your petitioner as in Duty bound will ever pray

Signed at Putney May 23[d] 1785   Andrew Graham —

[State] of Vermont   }   To the Sheriff of the County of Windham his Deputy or
[Windham] County   }   Either Constable of Dummerston within said County

---

1. For the confirmatory patent of Putney granted by New York in 1766, see *S. P. of Vt.*, VII (N. Y. Land Patents covering lands within the State of Vermont), pp. 60–66.

Greeting —
In the Name and by the Authority of the Freemen of the State of Vermont you are hereby Commanded to make known to William Sergants of Dummerston in said County that he be before the Honble Gen^ll Assembly to be Holden at Norwich within the County of Windsor on the Ninth Day of June Next if he Sees fit to Show reason if any he hath why Andrew Graham Should not be Quieted in the Peacable possession of the farm on which he now Lives in Putney agreeable to the foregoing Petition Hereof Fail Not Dated at Putney this 24th Day of May Anno Domini 1785

Benjamin Burt   Side Judge

Dummerston May ye 30th 1785 —
Then I Left True and attested Coppies of the within citation and the Petition to which the same is annexed in the House of the Usual Abode of the within Named William Sargents

attest   William Miller   Cons^t

fees for service 5/

— & —

Andrew Graham Petition —
Filed 13th June 1785
⟨20/ net p^d⟩
. . .*

— & —

A. J.: Resolved that petition be considered that afternoon, 14 June '85, S. P. of Vt., III (III), 145; *read and referred to a committee to join a committee from the Council, 14 June '85, Ibid, III (III), 145; *report of committee recommending that petitioner be quieted in his possession until paid for his labor, read and accepted, and ordered that petitioner may bring in a bill accordingly, 17 June '85, Ibid, III (III), 156; act granting possession read and accepted and sent to Governor and Council, 18 June '85, Ibid, III (III), 158; act, having been concurred in by Council, passed into law, 18 June '85, Ibid, III (III), 159.[1] C. J.: *Committee appointed to join the Assembly committee, 14 June '85, G. and C., III, 72; act read and concurred in, 18 June '85, Ibid, III, 74–75.

FOR REMITTANCE OF THE BALANCE OF A NOTE OWED TO THE STATE BY A PARDONED YORKER

xvii, 111

To the Honorable Legislature of the State of Vermont
The Humble Petition of Charles Phelps of N. Marlborough in the County of

---

1. For this act, see Slade, 500. For the recommendation of the Council of Censors 17 Oct. '85 that this act be repealed and for the Assembly's action thereon, see Slade, 515–516; and S. P. of Vt., III (III), 202, 210, 229, 256. No record of the repeal of the act has been found. As late as 20 Feb. '87 William Sargeants, a party to the dispute, petitioned for its repeal, but no final action was taken in the matter (S. P. of Vt., III (III), 277, 307). For this petition as well as a very similar previous one, see pp. 156, 308, post.

Windham in Sd State praying the Legislature to remit the remainder of the Sum of thirty five pounds Due to Sd State after a Deduction of Twenty two pounds Eleven Shillings and ten pence Lawfull Silver money I Gave to purchase Waters notes of Sheriff Porter of Hadley and Charles Phelps of Sd Hadley with the Intrest then Due upon Sd notes[1] Porters note amounted to 16–6–6 my Sons note amounted to 06–5–4 when I bought & Delivered them Notes of Waters & others promisors to the Secretary to be Endorsed on My afforesd note in his hand I Gave to Sd State[,] that there remaind Due to Ballance my note to the State twelve pounds Eight Shillings and two pence then and no more — And In as much as the State have had the use of my Library worth when I had it took from me & other Estate not sold for the use of Sd State Some Hundred of Silver Dollers and wold in fact have Fetched it to me If then I had them effects for my hands to Sel at the time I was Demised thereof and my Books were Exceedingly Dammisged all those I have recd of Mr Bradley and there is more than twenty Vollume Scattered abroad to me unknown and the best & most usefull of my Books that I Cant Get to this Day nor do I know where they are. but I am In formed they are Scattered about in various & verry far Distant places in the state that I Cant possibly get them but they are & near three years past have been no Doubt in use for the benefit of the officers and other Citizens of the State to my Damage alredy more than fifteen pounds Like money afforesd besides the Damnifying the books which no Sensible man I presume would Judge the Damage to be much more than the Ballance Due on sd 35 pound note I Gave the State which Sum maney others Judged were very Severe to Demand of me Considering Circumstances in my favor that were then made Evident to the Assembly I am advised by Good Citizens of the State of the best Judgment thus to petition for a remittance of the Ballance of my Sd note to the State —

£ 35– 0– 0

£ 22–11–10

————

12– 8– 2

But if for want of fuller Satisfaction of the truth of the premises It is thought best to omit Granting my Pitition at present till I address further proof hereof I pray the Direction of the Legislature to the treasurer not to put the note in Suit against me untill I may Evince y[e] facts better to the next assembly which by my poor State of helth & poverty to that Degree that I hant one bushel of any Sort of meal for bread for my family nor hant a Doller on Earth in hand nor Do I know where I Can procure one Shilling to buy any bread or meet for my Support I hant but one Cow and one riding beast Left me for my use of all my Stock when Allen Came over with his 400 troops and took of 26 head of Cattle from me and [my?] son[2] I hant ben able to raise 6 bushe of Bread Corn Ever Since I am [reduced] to Such Indigence & Distress & I having been So kind a benefactor to the State in its Infancy as Last fall was proved to their Honorable Legislature and acknowledged in their act passed of my Pardon[3] wherefor I hope for the remittance of the ballance ever remembering the Kings and princes of our Vermont Israel are Mercifull; hopeing they will verify that Illustrious & most Christian motto to me your aged Petitioner therefor Shall herein Ever beg Leave Earnestly to pray
Dated this 25th of May 1785 —   Charles Phelps

---

1. For the occasion for these deductions, see the petition of Joseph Tucker, Oliver Waters, et al., p. 91, ante.

2. Phelps was, of course, at this time a strong New York adherent. In September, 1782 Ethan Allen led a military force against the New York adherents in southeastern Vermont and succeeded in suppressing them (G. and C., III, 231–236).

3. Slade, 494–495.

N:B your petitioner prays on order of [this] assembly that all the remainder of his Book may be Immediately restored to him by Every one that has in time passed or at present the possession of them or Either thereof and if a refusal or neglect So to do I Earnestly Desire Mr Bradley be Directed by the Assembly to recover them who is the ondly man that knows where they are

per me   Charles Phelps   Dated the Day afforesd —

The truth of the foregoing facts and Allegations Errors Excepted Sworn to before me [sic]

— & —

Charles Phelps^s Petition to remit the Sum in Ballence of his 35£ note to Vermont State may 25th 1785 —
Filed 17th June 1785

— & —

[No Record][1]

FOR ANNEXATION OF A TOWN TO ANOTHER COUNTY
xvii, 112

To the Honorable the General Assembly of the State of Vermont —
The Petition of us the Subscribers Proprietors and Inhabitants of the Township of Stratton in the County of Bennington in said State humbly Sheweth: That the Said Town of Stratton is so Situated that it will be much better for the Inhabitants to Travel to the Centre of Windham County (Where it appears to us it is likely the Publick business for the County will be done) than to go to those Places in Bennington County where the Courts are now held, or even if they were held in the Centre of Said County, Therefore we your Petitioners Pray that the said Township of Stratton may be annexed to the County of Windham — and now Submiting the matter to your wise Consideration, nothing doubting that you will grant such relief in the Premises as you in your Great Wisdom Shall think best, and as we, in duty bound, Shall ever Pray:
Stratton May 27th AD 1785

> Joeel Stevens
> Tim^o Morsman
> Jonathan Phillips
> Oliever Morsman
> Edmund Gibbs
> Tesrel Stevens

— & —

Petition from Stratten
Filed 3^d June 1785

— & —

---

1. Although this petition was filed, it was apparently not read in the Assembly. It is significant that on the day it was filed the Assembly resolved that the balance due on the note might be collected by suit (S. P. of Vt., III (III), 157).

[No Record]

FOR THE FORMATION OF A NEW TOWN AND A NEW CITY[1]
xvii, 113

To His Excellency the Govenor Thomas Chittenden Esq
Commander in Chief of the State of Vermont and to the Honourable the General
Assembly ⟨Council⟩ of the Same Greeteing Whereas we your Humble Potetioners
Have Seen the Greate Disadvantage of the Inhabitants of the Toundship of Panton
By haveing Near two Thirds of their tound Cut off By Addison and as the tound
of Ferris Burgh [Ferrisburg] is Veary large and all on the Southwest Corner is
Cut off By otter Crick and So Brought to a point By the Lake and the Mouth of
Greate otter Crick then Growing wider till it Comes Square with the North side
of Panton and Panton Bordering west on Lake Champlain South on Adison Eeast
on Greate Otter Crick & North By that part of Ferris Burgh Cutt off By the Crick
aforesaid therefore we your Humble Potetioners Request the Favour of the Legislative Body of this State to Establish the Before Mentiond Corner of Ferrisburgh
and the Remainder of Panton to Be a County Town, for we believe that it is Best
for Both Toundships for this Reason the remainder of Ferris Burgh will Be Large
Enough for a Good Toundship on the East Side of Greate otter Crick and let
Panton Be Joind to the part of Ferris Burgh aforesaid takeing all on the west side
of Otter Crick and that will make a Conveniant Sosiety, therefore we humbly
Request the attention of the Legeslative Body of this state to Consider our Potetion,
For we. Both the Inhabitants of Ferris Burgh and the Inhabitants of the remainder
of panton are Joind in this Potetion and if it Should Be thought Best By the Honour-
able asembly to Grant the Same we Desire the Name of Gillaed [Gilead?] to Be
Enaxed in Sted of Panton. and we would further pray the Honourable Assembly to
Consider so that Every man may hold his Property of Land as he has here to fore.
Als [Also] your humble potetioners do Beg Leave to inform you that the Pro-
priators of Ferris Burgh has Voted a Conveniant Spot Between and adjoining Two
fine harbours Viz Buttenmold Bay on the South and that Noted Harbour Called
Bason harbour on the North also a Small Bay in the Middle Called Marquet harbour[2]
to Be Devided in a Suitable form for hous Lots with Streets Four rods wide one
way and two the other with a Marquet Eight rods one way and twenty the other
Near Marquet Harbour with Greens and What the Committee for that purpose
Shall think Best and they the Propriators to Draft Equally for their Hous Lots
Leaving to the amount of Sixty Lots for Setlers to Encourage a City in that Spot
you may Be asured that it is a Veary [Convenient] place for that purpose. Be
pleasd to take a View of the plan from the Surveyer Timothy Rogers Propriators
Clark, the Cuntery Road may lay Veary Conveniant on one Side their may Be a
Streete on the Back of S^d City or tound Ten rods wide the whole Length thereof
the Building may Frunt on three Sides on Lake Champlain Viz the North west
and south and the East sid [. . .] Broad road as a fore Said

---

1. The city projected in this petition may properly be viewed as an antecedent of
the city of Vergennes.
2. Buttenmold Bay was doubtless what is now Button Bay, and Bason Harbor what
is now Basin Harbor. Search has failed to disclose a more exact location of Marquet
Harbor than that which is suggested by the context supplied by this petition.

And as Timothy Rogers Owns one Hundred and twenty or thirty Acres or More
of Land on the North Side of Butten Bay and the Noted Point Adjoining Marquet
Harbour from whence you may have a fair prospect of Crownpoint in a fair Day[,]
which is Called Twelve milds [miles?] [,] S^d Lands laying Adjoining the Land
Voted By the Propriators which Makes up the Spot Described for a City as Before
Mentioned which you may see a small plan of if you pleas and he the above mentioned Rogers will give Fifty Hous Lots to any Man or Men that will Build a
Good Frame Stone or Brick Hous on Each Lot of Thirty Feete Square the Houses
to Be Sot Fronting the Lake or Streets in a regular form: And also Ground for a
Court hous and yard if Required and for one Meeteing Hous with a Burying yard
to the first Christian Sosiéty Setled By Disapline in that place all this the above
S^d Rogers Doth Volentaryly Give on his own Expence to promote the Settlement
of the City we the Subscribers do. Vearily Believe it to be Conveniant for its
Excellant Cituation for a trade from all the Northern part of this state Both By
Land and Water it also acommidateing the western Shore as well as this State
Good roads may be had from all parts of this State to the Same Likewise a transport
for Small Boats May be had Forty Miles up otter Crick Excepting New Haven
and Middle Berry [Middlebury] Fall which must Be Land Carriage round. Therefore we humbly request City privaledges for the Same as the Legeslative Body in
their wisdom Shall think proper Signed By us the Inhabitants of Ferris Burgh &
Panton <and others Subject to this> State.   May 27th 1785

Panton	Ferris Burgh	Freemen of the State
Peter Ferris	Timothy Rogers	Benjn Everest
Noah Ferris	Isaac gaig	Solomon Becker
Luis Ferris	Jacob win	Ezra Squier
Squire Ferris	Josep gaig	Nathaniel Squier
James Ferris	Elnathan Smith	
Hezeki Phelps	John huf	
Sam^ll ferris	David Hill	
Timothy Spaldin	Walter Bates	
James Goodrich	Calven Hill	
Charls Goodrich	Silas Bingham	
Henry Spalding	Benajah Webster	
Ira Phelps	Jeremiah Runnels	
Isaac Bristoll	R^d [Tatlock?]	
Welcam Giford	Sam^ll Roys	
Elijah Grandey	Zebulon Crittenden	
[Ebor?] Price	Daniel Vanolunder	
Phinehas Spaulding j^r	Benja Holcomb	
Joseph Holcombe		
Elisha Holcombe		

— & —

Petition of Timothy Rogers
Filed 9th June 1785 —

— & —

[No Record]

FOR RELIEF FROM A DEBT CONTRACTED FOR AN ATTEMPTED CONFIRMATION OF THE NEW HAMPSHIRE GRANTS[1]
xvii, 109

To his Excellency The Governor the Honourable Counsell and the General Assemble of the State of Vermont
The Memorial of William Marsh Humble Sheweth
Whereas your memorialist in the Behalf of the Town of Manchester on or about the 9th Day of November 1772 in Company With Thomas French (now Deceased) Did Give and Execute unto Martin Powel Esqr one Ceartain Noat of hand for the sum of fifty Nine Pounds Eight Shillings New York Courency: Which moneys Were intended to be Raised and Laid out to obtain a Confirmation of the New-hampshire Grants (now the State of Vermont)[2] A Part of Which Moneys has Been Raised and Paid as afforesaid Now the Residue being Required your Memorialist finds it not only Extreemly Difucult but Very unreasonable for him to Pay the Said Demand as your memorialist has Paid all the Moneys that the Town has Ever Paid to him for that Purpos

Moreover your Memorialist Begs Leave to Refer to Colo^l Brownson Martin Powell Esqr and Major ormsby for the Proof of the True State of the Whole affair — your memorialist Doth therefore Pray That the Honourable house Will favourabley be Pleased to appoint a Committee to Examian into the Premises and as they may find to Report to your Honourable House at Such Conveinant Time and Place as may be found Requsitalle [requisitable?] Which is humbly Submitted and as in Duty Bond Shall Ever Pray

William Marsh

Dorset 30 May 1785

— & —

Petition of Wm Marsh
Filed 2^d June 1785
. . .*

— & —

A. J.: *Read and referred to a committee to join a committee from the Council and make report to the next session, 3 June '85, S. P. of Vt., III (III), 118; *report of committee reviewing the history of the matter and recommending that power be granted to collect unpaid rates, read and referred to next session, 18 Oct. '85, Ibid, III (III), 187–188. C. J.: *Committee appointed to join Assembly committee, 6 June '85, G. and C., III, 66.

FOR ABATEMENT OF PROVISION TAXES
xvii, 117

To the Honnourable General Assembly of the State of Vermont Now Setting at

---

1. For a somewhat similar petition, see p. 266, *post*.
2. This confirmation was sought through the dispatch of agents to London for the purpose of presenting a petition to the crown. These funds were doubtless intended to help defray the cost of this mission. See Matt B. Jones, *Vermont in the Making, 1750–1777* (Cambridge, 1939), pp. 180–183.

Norwich the Petition of the Subscribers, the Select men of the town of Pomfret for years 1780. 1781 Humbly Sheweth,

That there was a Provision tax of wheat flower, rie[,] Indian Corn, Pork, & Beaf, Laid on Said town in ye year 1780,[1] and your Petitioners Did at the Desire and Request, of the Commesarys Exert themselves, and were at pains and troble to procure twenty five Bushel & half of Wheat and flower in the liew of fifty one Bushels of Indian Corn, and were to be allowed two bushel of Corn, for one of Wheat (it being much Better for Bread for Scouting &c) and Likewise, agreed to allow one pound of pork for two of Beaf and they Did Deliver out three hundred and Eighty five pound of Beaf in Lieu of 192½ lb of pork

And Some time Since the Honnourable Legeslature Saw fit to State the Value of the provision (viz) Wheat flower at 18 S pr hundred wait, Indian Corn at 4 S pr bushel, Pork at [9ᵈ?] pr pound Beaf at 4ᵈ Dr [sic] pound[2]

and altho your Petitioners had payed up the full of Said tax, yet the accounts not being Properly Settled, there was an Exstant Came against your Petitioners for the whole of Sᵈ tax, and they were Obliged to pay one Shilling on each Bushel of the Said 51 Bushels of Indian Corn paid in Wheat as above Said, as Likewise one penny on each pound of Said 192½ of Pork, which amounted to the Sum of £3:7 S: 0½ in the whole, and also the sheriff fees which was £ 1:19:9

and that your Petitioners Did Diliver out one hundred and sixty nine pound of good Wheat flower amounting to £1:9:4 for the tax for the year 1781[3] to go on to the troops, and the Receipt for the Same, Some how or other was Lost, and have had no Credit for yᵉ said flower besides other Costes by Storeage &c on both Provision Taxes Amounting to the Sum of £0:18:6½

Wherefore your Petitioners Pray your Honnours to take ye matter into your wise Consideration and grant Such Relief as in your wisdom Shall See fit

and your Petitioners as in Duty Bound Shall ever Pray

John W. Dana	Select
	men for
Mida Smith	the years
	1780 & 1781
Timothy Harding	

— & —

Select Men of Pomfret — Petition
. . .*

your Committee to whome was referd the forgoing Petition beg leave to report that they find the following facts to wit that by the Legislature Stating the prices

---

1. For the act levying this tax, see Slade, 407–411.

2. See "An Act for raising a tax of seven Pence on the Pound, to be paid in Due-Bills, Paytable Orders, Bills of Credit emitted by this State, Commissary General's Notes, or hard Money: and two Pence on the Pound in hard money; and respecting the Arrearages of Provisions", passed 15 Oct. '82 (Ms. Laws of Vt., I, 303–305). Section III of this act set the prices on provisions that were in arrears under the assessment of 1780 only. Otherwise the prices of provisions required as taxes were established by the Commissary. That officer was empowered by an act passed 28 Feb. '82 to receive hard money in lieu of any provisions "at such rates as said Provision may be procured . . ." (Ms. Laws of Vt., I, 280–281).

3. For the act levying this tax, see Slade, 440–442.

of Indian Corn Wheat beef Pork &c the Petitionars Suffred the Loss of £3:7½ as mentioned in the Petition

Therefore report as their Oppinion that the prayer ough [*sic*] to be granted So far as to allow the Petitionars £3:7:½ out of the Treasurey of this State

S Knigh for Committee

— & —

> *A. J.:* *Read and referred to a committee, 4 June '85, *S. P. of Vt.*, III (III), 122; *report of committee read and dismissed, and petition dismissed, 10 June '85, *Ibid*, III (III), 138.

FOR ABATEMENT OF TAXES
xvii, 123

To the Honble General Assembly of the State of Vermont now Convened at Norwich in the county of Windsor the Petition of Samuel Peck Constable of Bethel for 1783 —

Humbly sheweth —

That s^d Town of Bethel was doomed[1] on the Grand list for s^d year (1783) £100-15- over the s^d G^d List[,][2] that the S^d Town maid aplication to the Honourable Assembly (in March 1784) to have Said doomage taken off which request was Granted as apears from the folowing Extract from the Journals (Viz) —[3]

State of Vermont

in Geneal [*sic*] asembly March 8th 1784 —

Resolved that the Treasurer & comisary Geneal & Shiriffs be & are hereby severally directed to Credit the Town of Bethel so much of the taxes laid or which shall be Laid on s^d town on the list maid in the year (1783) or has been or shall be assessed on the sum of £100-15

Extracts from the Journals
Ros Hopkins Clerk —

---

that your petitioner did Not take out a Coppy of s^d Extracts by wich means he has been compeld by the Shiriff to pay on s^d sum of 100-15 ⟨three⟩ four Several Asesments amounting in all to 1/4 ⟨1/2⟩ on the pound wich is £6-14-3 ⟨5-17-6⟩ & 2-1-11 ⟨1-5-2⟩ of the same in hard Money therefore the prayor of your petitioner is that this Honble house would direct the Treasurer to pay out S^d Sums Severaly as Set in the aforegoing Petition & receive the S^d Extract before mentioned & your Petitioner in duty Bound Shall Ever pray —

Samuel Peck Constable

— & —

Petition —
Saml Peck —
filed 14th June 1785 —

— & —

[No Record][4]

---

1. For a definition of "doomed", see p. 66*n*, *ante*.
2. There is no record of this doomage in the Assembly or the Council journals.
3. For this entry in the journal, see *S. P. of Vt.*, III (III), 57.
4. For a similar petition presented to the Assembly 18 Oct. '85 and the action taken thereon, see p. 149, *post*.

FOR RELIEF FROM THE FORCED SALE OF LANDS
TO PAY A PROPRIETARY TAX

xxi, 283

To the honorable the general assembly of the State Vermont convened at Norwich —
The humble Pettition of Benjamin Chamberlin &c — Humbly Sheweth —
That your Pettioner Being a proprietor (in possession of three rights of Land in the Township of Thetford) with the other proprietors did in the year 1770 Vote to raise a tax of four Dollars with other taxes on each right of Land in said Thetford which your Pettioner together with the signers hereunto paid in the year 1771 as can be certified by the Collector of s^d taxes — And, whereas the Proprietors of S^d Thetford did in the year 1784 Vote to raise Seventeen Dollars & one third of a dollar on each right of Land in said Thetford for to discharge all Demands standing a gainst the Proprietory of Said township from its beginning untill that time[,] also the proprietory call on all persons who had accounts against it to exhibit them for settlement by such a time[,] or their Lands would be sold by such a day as was directed by a Law for that purpose —[1]
And Whereas your Pettioner & the undersigners presented their accounts in which was included the above mention'd Rate of four dollars on each right but it was not allowd for Altho' it was the just Identical proportion of the five pounds four Shillings tax for which the Land was advertized for sale yet the Collector proceeded to sell the Subscribers Lands & will deed said Lands to the Purchasers by the 17th July ensuing which will manifestly injure the signers of this pettition in their Interests —
Therefore your Pettitoner prays This hon^{ble} Assembly to pass a Bill that shall direct the Collector of this County to not Deed away his Lands until he & his cosigners be granted relief by having their just Claims against the proprietory allowed which could never have been refus'd to them from any other quarters than either mistake or design & your Pettitioner as in duty bound will ever pray

Benjn Chamberlin
Joel Chamberlin
Zebedee Howard
Abner Howard

— & —

Benj^a Chamberlin's Pettition
Filed 10 June 1785
. . .*

— & —

A. J.: *Read and dismissed, 10 June '85, S. P. of Vt., III (III), 138.

---

1. See "An Act regulating Proprietors Meetings", passed 24 Oct. '82, and two acts passed in addition thereto 23 Oct. '83 and 29 Oct. '84 (Ms. Laws of Vt., I, 354–357, 416, 465–466).

FOR OBSERVATIONS FROM THE COUNCIL OF CENSORS
ON AN IMPROPER CONVICTION FOR TORYISM
xvii, 115

To the Honble Council of Censors for the State of Vermont now convened at Norwich, the Petition & Remonstrance of Watts Hubbard Junr — Sheweth
  That the said Watts, without just cause was arrested by Virtue of an illegal and unconstitutional Precept, and brought before an unconstitutional Court in the Town of Windsor in the State of Vermont, on the 19th day of May 1778 — at which time he was subjected to a trial by a jury to which he was Denied the Previledge of making any Chalenge, without the Liberty of producing a single Witness to make his Inocence appear; or of defending himself by himself or Counsel — The result of which was a Judgt for Imprisonment & confiscation of Property —1 which Proceedings tho' in this Instance they affect an Individual only, in their tendency affect every Citizen of the State, and are a flagrant violation of the Constituion Wherefor your Petitioner prays for an Examination into the same & that such public observations may be made thereon by the said Council as shall be adjudged most suitable and as in Duty bound shall ever pray
Norwich 3rd June 1785   Watts Hubbard Junr

— & —

Petition Watts Hubbard Junr
Entered on file 3rd June 1785 —

— & —

[No Record]2

_____

FOR COMPENSATION FOR WAR SERVICES
xvii, 116

June 4th 1785
To the Honourable General Assembly of the State of Vermont now Setting in Norwich —
Honourable Gentlemen —
The Petition of Joel Ely of Windsor Humbly Sheweth That in February 1781 the Govenor with the Board of War Imployed me The Subscriber to go Down to Springfield after Sixty Tin Kittles3 for the use of the Solder's but when I Came There I Applyed to General Heath who had the Care of the Magazean and he Told me it was not Posable that I Could be Supplyed with them for there Had Lately bin a Movement of the Enehemy from New York to Rhod. land [Rhode

  1. For the confiscation and sale of the petitioner's property, see S. P. of Vt., VI (Sequestration, Confiscation and Sale of Estates), 215, 257.
  2. There is, of course, no mention of this petition in the journals of the Governor and Council or of the Assembly. No record of the journal of this Council of Censors, if any was kept, survives. For the resolutions adopted by the Council of Censors, 5–17 Oct. '85, see Slade, 511–516.
  3. These "Tin Kittles" were the containers in which the food for the troops was cooked.

Island] and the Milissia was Called for and he was obliged to Let all the Kittles go I then Consulted Some Gentlemen Vhat Method was best to be Taken they Told me no Dout I Could Get the Kittles at Wethersfield & I went to Wethersfield but Could not be Supplied There the Gentlemen Told me I Could get them at Midletown [Middletown] So I went to Midletown but Could not get any Kittles So I Returned Home — & Have Since applyed to the Board of War for pay for my Trouble the Govenor with the Board of War Told me it was a Good Accompt to Carry in to the Comisary I have Since Sent it to the Comisary general by Co^ll Benjamin Wait but he Refused to Answer it your Petitioner Prays your Honours to take the Matter into Consideration and order that I Shall be paid what is Reasonable The Accompt I Shall Exhibit on the Back of This Petition which I Think is Reasonable and I ought to Have my Pay in Silver Money or Something Equivalent to it with Interest for I have paid the Comisary with the Cost of an Execution which is a Great Hardship for I had the Promise of the Govenor that I Should Have the Provision in my Hands to pay me: which is the Prayer of your most Humble Servant —

Joel Ely

March 1781 The Board of War to Joel Ely D^r

To Eleaven Day Service Going to Midletown in Coneticut [Connecticut] for Kittles @ 6/o	3 –	6 –	o
To the Journey of Hay & Two Horses one Hundred Fifty Miles —	3	15	o
To Fourteen Dollar one Quater Expences —	4	5	6
To my Team one Day to Carry Flour & Corn into Town for Co^ll Brewster by order of Co^ll Childs Comisary —	o	10	o
To Carting one Load of Provision to Town by Genarall Fanswoth order for Capt Geer of Charlestown —	o	10	o
	12	6	o
Interest 50 months — 6% —	3	o	o
	15	6	o

— & —

The Petition of Joel Ely to the General Assembly
Filed 14th June 1785.
. . .*

— & —

A. J.: *Read and dismissed, 23 Oct. '86, *S. P. of Vt.*, III (III), 239.

FOR THE INTERVENTION OF THE COUNCIL OF CENSORS AGAINST CERTAIN LAWS AFFECTING PROPERTY
xvii, 118

To the honorable Council of Censors for the State of Vermont —

Humbly sheweth

The petition of a Committee of the proprietors & Inhabitants of the townships of — Royalton Bethel Randolph Brantree [Braintree] Rochester — in the County of

Windsor, appointed by said proprietors for that purpose — That there are two particular acts, or proceedures of the Assembly of this State by which the said proprietors feel themselves materially injured and aggrieved; and which they concieve to be
unconstitutional, and oppressive — Application for redress having been made to
the Assembly without relief[1] we now apply to this honorable board, as a denier-
resort [dernier resort]; and do it with the more confidence of being heard, as we
find, that one article of our grievances respects a matter expressly referred, by
the constitution, to the Council of Censors. We have reference to an act passed
Oct[er] 1782 [1783] for Levying, and collecting a tax of ten shillings on every hundred
acres in fifty townships in the state,[2] which we concieve to have been unreasonable,
and oppresive, for the following reasons — 1st. A large revenue has been raised
on said lands, for the use of the State, by the granting fees; such as never has been
paid to the State, or elsewhere on the lands held under New Hampshire Grants —
2[ndly] In consideration of the said revenue, the proprietors were by Charter, to
hold their lands on condition of settling for the term of five years, which, by implication of Law, contains an exemption from taxation for that term; because
where condition is annexed to a grant, nothing more than what is expressed in the
condition can be constitutionally required, till the expiration of the term limited
in the condition — 3rd As The said townships have been out of the line of protection, in the course of the war, and the proprietors of consequence were effectually
debarred from fulfilling any part of the conditions — So, by implication of law, no
part of the said term of five years is expired, but what has been since cessation of
hostilities. We applied for relief by a humble petition to the Assembly; but it was
not sufferd to be read: On the succeess of which petition many had depended and
by its failing were greatly damaged, their lands being sold, and consequently
wholly lost to them; because they were altogether unable to redeem them —
  The other matter of grievance is, that under sanction of an act or resolve of
the Assembly, the Surveyor-General has been altering and removing the lines,
and boundaries of said townships to different places than those intended in their
Charters,[3] and which, from the time of the original survey, have been of publick
notoriety; which we concieve to be a violation of the 13th article in the bill of
rights;[4] wherein it is declared that in matters of property, the parties have a right
to a Trial by Jury, which ought to be held sacred — By a removal of the boundaries
of the towns, property is wrested from us, under sanction of an act of the Legislature, without trial by Jury, and even without an hearing by any Judicial Court,
or any other way; and the injury is heightened, in that it is done at the expence
of those who are injured by it; and that expence augmented beyond what is necessary, and collected in such a manner, as, in the present extreme scarcity of money,
becomes very oppresive —
Your Petitioners concieve, that the Legislature have thereby assumed judicial
powers not vested in them; and deprived the Subject that inestimable privilege of

---

  1. This petition (not now among the *Ms. Vt. S. P.*) was ultimately dismissed. For
the action taken by the Assembly thereon 3 June '85 through 15 June '85, see *S. P. of
Vt.*, III (III), 118, 135, 146, 147-148.
  2. See "An Act for the purpose of levying the respective Taxes therein contained
. . .", passed 21 Oct. '83 (*Ms. Laws of Vt.*, I, 399-403).
  3. See "An Act for the regulation and Establishment of Town Lines" passed 22
Oct. '82 (*Ms. Laws of Vt.*, I, 350-351).
  4. *G. and C.*, I, 95.

trial by Jury, in matters of property guaranteed in the constitution, and particularly in the said bill of rights 13th article &c — your Petitioners therefore humbly pray your honors interposition, and that you will cause justice to be done in the premises, agreeably to the powers vested in you by the Constitution — And as in duty bound shall ever pray —

Norwich June 7th 1785   Dudley Chase } in behalf of the Committee of S[d] Inhabitants

Mich[l] Flynn
Silas Williams

— & —

Petition of Dudley Chase &c.

— & —

[No Record][1]

FOR ONE SHIRE TOWN IN THE CENTER OF THE COUNTY[2]
xvii, 119

To the Honorable the General Assembly of the State of Vermont now Convened at Norwich
The Petition of the subscribers Representatives in this Assembly from a number of Towns in the County of Windham in said State: Humbly sheweth That said County is Divided into two shires That there is but One Court House in s[d] County and that at the Extream part thereof: and that said house is not at present fit for the Court to be holden in Only in the summer season: That the finishing the Court House and Gaol now in s[d] County and building another Court House and Gaol therein will be attended with great Expence to s[d] County: That it is found by Experience to be very Inconvenient for so small a County as the County of Windham is to be divided into two shires That New Fane in said County is the Center Town and well situate for a Shire Town: That certain persons Offer to build a good and sufficient Court House and Gaol in seperate buildings on the Common near the Meeting house in s[d] New Fane and finish the same to the Acceptance of s[d] County within two years without any Expence to s[d] County Upon Condition that s[d] Town of New Fane may be the Shire Town in s[d] County when s[d] Court House and Gaol are built and finished —

---

1. The Council of Censors adopted the view of this petition with respect to the law for the establishment of town lines cited in note 3, p. 132. It recommended to the legislature that the act be repealed along with some other related statutes (Proceedings of the First Council of Censors 5–17 Oct. '85: *Slade*, 514).

There is, of course, no mention of this petition in the journals of the Governor and Council or of the Assembly. No record of the journal of this Council of Censors, if any was kept, survives.

2. For a similar petition presented by inhabitants of two Windham County towns, see p. 117, *ante*. For other petitions in the same connection, see pp. 208, 218, 219, 221, *post*.

Your Petitioners Therefore Humbly Pray that this Honorable Assembly will take the Premises under Consideration: and now Pass an Act of this Assembly making said New Fane the Shire Town in s^d County when s^d persons shall have built a good and sufficient Court House and Gaol in s^d Town free of expence as aforesaid to the acceptance of the County as aforesaid provided the same be done within two years —

and your petitioners as in Duty bound shall ever pray[1]

Norwich June 10th 1785

Luke Knowlton
William Ward
Saml Knight
William Bullock
Joseph Tyler
Leonard Spaulding
Oli^r Lovill
Edward Aiken
Sam^{ll} Fletcher

— & —

A petition of the member of the County of Windham
Petition & Report respecting County buildings in Windham County —
. . .*

— & —

A. J.: *Read and referred to a committee to join a committee from the Council, 13 June '85, S. P. of Vt., III (III), 143; *report of committee read and dismissed, and petition referred to next session, 16 June '85, Ibid, III (III), 148;[2] report of committee considered and speaker requested to bring in a bill for appointing supervisors to determine the matter, 25 Oct. '85, Ibid, III (III), 202–203; act passed and sent to Council, 27 Oct. '85, Ibid, III (III), 208; act, having been concurred in by Council, passed into law, 27 Oct. '85, Ibid, III (III), 209;[3] Council and Assembly in committee of the whole consider the report of the supervisors, 19 Oct. '86, Ibid, III (III), 231; report of Grand-committee respecting the county buildings read and accepted, 21 Oct. '86, Ibid, III (III), 236;[4] act for fixing shire town passed and sent to Council, 23 Oct. '86, Ibid, III (III), 238; act, having been concurred in by Council, passed into law, 23 Oct. '86, Ibid, III (III), 241.[5] Rep. of Com.: Committee recommends that petition be granted, June '85, S. P. of Vt., IV, 31–32. C. J.: *Committee appointed to join Assembly committee, 14 June '85, G. and C., III, 72; act directing choice of supervisors read and concurred in, 27 Oct. '85, Ibid, III, 93;

---

1. The petitioners, except Samuel Fletcher and William Ward, were representatives in the Assembly (S. P. of Vt., III (III), 66–67, 128). Fletcher was a member of the Council (Ibid, III (III), 68). William Ward of New Fane did not apparently have a seat in the Assembly until 15 Feb. '87 (Ibid, III (III), 265). William Ward of Poultney was a member at the date of this petition, but he would have had no reason to sign it.

2. The manuscript petition gives the date of the dismissal of the report as 25 Oct. '85. This appears to have been a confusion with a later action of the Assembly.

3. For this act, see Ms. Laws of Vt., I, 537–538.

4. This entry does not refer specifically to Windham County, but there is no ground to doubt that the action taken referred to the county seat for that county.

5. For this act, see Acts and Laws, passed by the General Assembly, at their stated session, at Rutland, in October, 1786 [Windsor: 1786], pp. 1–2.

request received from Assembly to join it in considering the issue of the Court House, 19 Oct. '86, *Ibid*, III, 109; act establishing New Fane as the county seat read and approved, 23 Oct. '86, *Ibid*, III, 111.

FOR ESTABLISHMENT OF OLD TOWN LINES REGARDLESS OF NEW SURVEY[1]
xxii, 92

To the Honble General asembly of the State of Vermont Convened at Norwich the Petetion of the Comittee in behalf of Randolph Proprietors
     Humbly sheweth
That your petitioners in consideration of receiving a Grant & charter of incorporation of s^d Township[2] proceeded to Locate & settle S^d Town after it had been surveyed according to Law by a county surveyor wich we ever considered Valid <according to Law> that since said survey & Location as aforesaid the Surveyor General has proceeded to Locate & Survey the Towns over again[3] by wich the Lines are metearaly altered & many of our Lots cut off & consequently many of us must be Turned out of our once Trifleing tho now Valuable Estates & Intrusts [interests] unless this Honourable hous will Interpose in our behalf & order an Establishment of the old Lines wich we ever considered as a final Establishment & consistant with principles of Law & Equity & your petitioners in Duty Bound Shall Ever pray —

                                                  ⎫ Comittee in behalf
                          William Lewis ⎬
                                                  ⎭ of S^d Proprietors

Randolph June 13th 1785 —

— & —

Randolph — Petition —
Filed 13th June 1785
. . .*

— & —

     A. J.: *Read and referred to a committee, 14 June '85, *S. P. of Vt.*, III (III), 145;[4] *report of committee recommending that establishment of town lines be postponed to next Assembly, read, and ordered that report be dismissed, 15 June '85, *Ibid*, III (III), 147–148;[5] petition considered by Assembly and dismissed, 15 June '85, *Ibid*, III (III), 148.

---

     1. For similar petitions from other towns presented to the Assembly at this time, see pp. 108, 109, 114, 115, 116, *ante*.
     2. For the charter of Randolph, see *S. P. of Vt.*, II (Vermont Charters), 162–163.
     3. For the legislation providing for this new survey, see "An Act for the regulation and Establishment of Town Lines" passed 22 Oct. '82 and an act in addition thereto passed 29 Oct. '84 (*Ms. Laws of Vt.*, I, 350, 466).
     4. For this committee, which was to join a committee from the Council, see *S. P. of Vt.*, III (III), 135. See also *G. and C.*, III, 70 for the committee appointed by the Council.
     5. Only the text of the committee report and not the action taken upon it is included in the entry on the manuscript petition.

FOR COMPENSATION FOR WAR LOSSES AND SERVICES
xvii, 121

To the Honble Genl Assembly of the State of Vermont Convened at Norwich —
The Petition of Moses Warren Humbly Sheweth, that he was engaged in the
Service of this State, as a Serjeant in Capt Charles Nelson's Company under the
Command of Col' Benjn Wait, in the year 1781 —[1] During which Time being on
a Scout, he was wounded and made Prisoner by a party of the enemy from Canaday
on the fifteenth day of October A D 1781 — and Carried to Quebec and there
Confined in Goal for the space of six Months, and was Detained as a prisoner
untill the Sixth day of June 1782 —, and while a prisoner was Striped of every
Valuable Article of Which he was then possessed to wit, his Arms and Accoutrements, Blanket & Compass which were in the whole appraised at four pounds
seven Shillings, and the wages of your Petitioner from the Time he was made
prisoner until the Time he was exchanged amounts to the Sum of Eighteen pounds
eight Shillings, for which he has received no Consideration — Wherefore your
Petitioner Humbly Prays that he may receive a Compensation for S^d Articles and
the Time he was in Captivity, in such a manner as your Honors in your Wisdom
shall Judge Just and Reasonable — And as in duty bound shall ever pray —

Moses Warren

Norwich 13th June 1785 —

— & —

The Petition of Moses Warren —
Filed 14th June 1785

— & —

[No Record][2]

FOR A TAX ON LAND TO BUILD ROADS AND BRIDGES
xvii, 122

To the Honorable General Assembly now Convened at Norwich —
The petition of Leonard Spalding of Dummerston in the County of Windham State
of Vermont Humbly Sheweth that Whereas the proprietors of s^d Town have never
paid any Tax on their Lands (except ten shillings on each 100 acres)[3] since the
Town was first settled and whereas their is a Large Tract of Land on the West
side of West River in sd Dummerston Alias Fullam that is not as Yet but very
Little of it disposed of or Cultivated by the Proprietors And whereas there is a
Publick Road leading through s^d land about six Miles which the Inhabitants have
to Cross West River to repair[,] that it is necessary their should be several Bridges
and the road repaired this Summer — Your Petitioner humbly prays that your

---

1. For the petitioner's service in 1781, see *Vt. Rev. Rolls,* 342, 389, 444, 446.
2. For a similar petition presented by Moses Warren to the Assembly at Windsor
in Oct. '85 and the action taken thereon, see p. 182, *post.*
3. For this tax, see "An Act for the purpose of emitting a sum of Money, and
directing the redemption of the same" passed April, 1781 (*Slade,* 424-426).

Honors would Grant a Tax of one penny half penny on each Acre on all the Lands in s^d Dummerston Alias Fullam Lying West of West River for the purpose of Making Bridges and repairing the road aff^{sd} under such Regulation as you shall think best and as in Duty bound shall ever pray

Norwich June 14th 1785   Leonard Spalding

— & —

Petition of Leon^d Spaulding
Filed 15th June 1785

— & —

[No Record]

FOR ABATEMENT OF TAXES
xvii, 124

To the Honble Gen^{ll} Assembly at Norwich Now Conveened
    the Petition of the Select Men of the Town of Hartford for the year 1782 Humbly Sheweth
    That the Town of Hartford was Doomed[1] on the List for the year 1782 by the Gen^{ll} Assembly the Sum of £ 189:[2] more than their Grand List as by written Documents you Pettittioners can make appear
    therefore pray you Honours to abate the town of Hartford the Sum of £ 189 on their Grand List for the year 1782 and as in Duty bound your Petitioners will ever pray
    Signed in Behalf of all the Select Men this 15th Day of June 1785
                                            Joshua Hazen { Select Man

— & —

Joshua Hazen Petition
1785

— & —

[No Record]

FOR A TAX ON LAND TO BUILD ROADS AND BRIDGES
xvii, 125

To the Honble the Gen^{ll} Assembly, Now Setting at Norwich The Humble Petition of John Nutting in behalf of the Inhabitants of the Town of Corinth Humbly Sheweth —
    That the Town of Corinth is so Situate that a Number of Publick Roads run through s^d Town Consequently a Large Number of Bridges is wanted and must

---

1. For a definition of "doomed", see p. 66n, ante.
2. For this action of the Assembly, see S. P. of Vt., III (II), 146–147.

be Erected and maintained as also there is much Swaley Land that needs Castwaying —[1] That s^d Town has had no help from the Proprietors — as they mostly belong to other States — And as the Burden of expences is very Heavy on the Inhabitants of said Town. Therefore Humbly Pray your Honours to grant Liberty to the Inhabitants of s^d Corinth to Levey a Tax of one Penny on each acre of Land in s^d Town (Except Publick Lands) under Proper Regulations which Tax shall be Appropriated to the use of Building Bridges & Repairing Roads &c

And your Petitioner as in Duty Bound will ever Pray

Norwich 16th June   Jno Nutting
AD 1785 —

— & —

John Nutting s Petition
filed 16th June 1785

— & —

[No Record]

FOR THE FORMATION OF A NEW TROOP OF HORSE IN THE MILITIA
xvii, 126

To the Hon^{bl} the General Assembly of the State of Vermont now Sitting — The petition of Abner Chamberlin Edward Bow Ezekiel Strong Ithamer Bartlet Moses Pearson James Waterman Elisha Freeman Elijah Brownson James Bliss A Burguoyne Thomas Foster Elijah Gates Samuel Hutchinson Gershom Bartlet Cornelius Gilbert Joel Benton Thomas Burnham Samuel Rogers Elijah Hammon Stephen Parsivel Thomas Belknap Joseph Thayer & Benjamin Chamberlin Humbly Sheweth — That as it is griatly for the improvement of Military Skill & knowledge (the cultivation of which will ever be of importance to this state) and tends much to inspire the soldiery with a martial spirit to have in each Regiment of Militia a Company of Horse & as there is in Colo^n Paul Brighams Regiment (to which your petitioners belong) a sufficient number of men who are able ready and willing to furnish and Equip them selves with Horses & accouterments to the number of 50 privates — and a sufficient number of officers — your petitioners pray your honours to grant liberty for a company to the number of 50 privates to be properly officered to be raised as a company of Light Dragoons to be under the command of & belong to the s^d Col^o Paul Brighams Regiment of Malitia the Soldiers to chuse their officers under the Direction of the s^d Colo^n Brigham to be commissioned upon the return made by him —

& your petitioners as in duty bound will ever pray —

Norwich 17th June 1785.

Abner Chamberlin	James Bliss	Sam^{el} Rogers
Edward Bow	A Burgoyne	Elijah Hammond
Ezekiel Strong	Thos Foster	Stephen Parsivel

---

1. "Swaley land" was, of course, a swamp. "Castwaying" was probably a misspelling of "causewaying". In any case the idea was to make a road over swampy land with timbers or other material.

Ithamer Bartlet	Elijah Gates	Tho[s] Belknap
Moses Pearson	Sam[l] Hutchinson Jun	Joseph Thayer
James Waterman	Gershom Bartlet	Benj[a] Chamberlin
Elisha Freeman	Cornelius Gilbert	Signed by order
Elijah Brownson	Joel Benton	Dan[l] Buck[1]
	Thomas Burnham	

— & —

Petition of Abner Chamberlin & others for a Troop of Horse
Filed 17th June 1785

— & —

[No Record]

FOR RELIEF FROM A FRAUDULENT SALE OF MORTGAGED PROPERTY
xxii, 93

To the Hon[ble] the General assembly of the State of Vermont to convene at Windsor on the second thursday in October next. —

The Petition of Eliza Elliot Executrix of the last Will and Testament of Samuel Elliot Jun[r] Late of Boston in the Commonwealth of Massachusetts deceased. —

Humbly Sheweth

That Mathew Martin of Brattleborough [Brattleboro] in the County of Windham Executed in due form of Law to Stephen Greenleaf of said Brattleborough one certain Bond dated the 24th July Anno Domini 1778 Conditioned for the Payment of the sum of Six hundred Sixty Six pounds thirteen Shillings and four pence New York Currency on or before the 24th day of October then next and also one other Bond of the Same date Conditioned for the Payment of fourteen hundred and forty pounds New York Currency on or before the first day of April then next.

That the said Mathew Martin for securing the Payment of the said Money by Indentures of Lease and release dated the 23[d] and 24th day of July Anno Domini 1778 mortgaged to the said Stephen all that certain Tract or Parcel of Land lying in the Township of Brattleborough containing 173 Acres and one fourth of an Acre it being the two hundred Acre Lot including the Grist and Saw Mill Standing on Whetstone Brook (excepting twenty six Acres and three fourths of an Acre belonging to Samuel Knight Esq[r]) —

That the said Stephen Greenleaf being largely indebted to the above mentioned Samuel Elliot on the 27th day of June Anno Domini 1783 in due form of Law did assign and transfer the said Bonds and mortgage to the said Samuel in his lifetime for a valuable consideration

That the said Samuel in and by his last will and Testament appointed your Petitioner sole Ex[x] thereof and is since dead. —

That the said Mathew Martin ever since the Execution of said mortgage has

---

1. All the names appended to this petition are in the same hand. Presumably they were signed by Daniel Buck at the direction of the persons involved.

been and still is in Possession of the said mortgaged Premises and some time in the summer of 1784 previous to the 16th August paid the Land Tax of ten shillings upon the hundred Acres to Richard Prouty Collector of the said tax in Brattleborough and to his full satisfaction —

That your Petitioner ever has been and still is ready and willing to repay the s^d Tax to said Martin when requested. —

That notwithstanding the said Richard Prouty had the money for said Tax upon the above mentioned Premises then in his hands — by the persuasion and thro' the Influence of the said Mathew Martin on the 16th of August 1784 in the capacity of Collector of Said Tax he sold to one Oliver Waters one Acre and a quarter of said Premises begining at a Stake and Stones the South East Corner of a Lot Mr Aaron Whitney bought of said Martin, thence running East four rods, thence South and West and North to said Whitneys Line in a square form — the same being Sold for one pound one Shilling and three pence the Tax on said Land and cost of Sale. —

That the Principal Value of said Mortgaged Premises consists in the Mills and Buildings erected thereon the soil of the Land being but indifferent. —

That the small part sold by the Collector includes one very valuable Grist Mill one Saw Mill with two Saws and one dwelling house and is of much more value than all the remainder of the mortgaged Premises

That there is a bona fide Mortgage upon the Premises for a large Sum prior to that owned by your Petitioner she must infallibly loose the whole or principal part of her demands unless this Honble House will interpose their authority to prevent so gross and atrocious a Collusion and frauds taking place. —

That from the Idea she entertains of the Legislative Body of the State of Vermont she has the most unshaken confidence that they will not be the less disposed to grant her Relief because this request comes from a Widow and a stranger and on behalf of several helpless orphan Children who without Justice being done in this matter must be reduced to the most extreme Penury.

Your Petitioner therefore most humbly prays this Honble House to grant her Relief in the Premises either by rendering null the said sale so Collusively made or by extending the time of Redemption of said Land to some future period or in such other mode as your Honors in your great Wisdom shall think proper and by that means render happy the friendless Widow and the helpless Orphan and entitle your Selves to their prayers for your Independence and Felicity.

19th July 1785   Eliza Elliot Ex^x of Saml Elliot Junr Dec'd

State of Vermont
        To Ephraim Nash — Greeting
        In the name and by the authority of the Freemen of the State of Vermont you are hereby required to cite Mathew Martin of Brattleborough and Oliver Waters of Halifax to appear before the Honorable the General assembly of the State of Vermont on the first monday in their next session to begin and be holden at Windsor in Windsor County on the Second thursday in October next, if the said Mathew and Oliver see proper then and there to Shew cause (if any they have) why the Prayer of the aforegoing Petition should not be granted. Hereof fail not and make return — Dated at Brattleborough the 21st July 1785
                Micah Townsend. Secry of the State of Vermont.

                                        Brattleboro' 23^d July 1785
Then served the aforegoing Citation by reading the same & the aforegoing Petition

in the hearing of the within named Mathew Martin & Oliver Waters & by delivering one true and attested Copy of the s^d Petition & Citation to said Martin & one other to said Waters —

Attest.   Ephraim Nash

— & —

Eliz^a Elliot Ex^x
of Sam. Elliot Junr

vs   Petition & Citation

Mathew Martin &
Oliver Waters

Filed 21st July 1785 —
. . .*

— & —

A. J.: *Read and referred to a committee, 24 Oct. '85, S. P. of Vt., III (III), 199;[1] *report of committee given verbally stating that they could not agree on a report, heard, and ordered that committee be dismissed and petition be referred to next session, 27 Oct. '85, Ibid, III (III), 207–208;[2] *read as referred from last session and referred to a committee to join a committee from the Council, 24 Oct. '86, Ibid, III (III), 242; report of committee read and accepted, and leave given to bring in a bill accordingly, 25 Oct. '86, Ibid, III (III), 245; bill entitled "an act to prolong the time of redemption to an acre and one quarter of land in Brattleboro' " read and accepted and sent to Council, 25 Oct. '86, Ibid, III (III), 246; bill, having been returned by Council, referred to next session, 27 Oct. '86, Ibid, III (III), 252; bill continued to next session "then to be taken up in the state it now is", 6 March '87, Ibid, III (III), 316; read again as referred from last session and passed into law, 15 Oct. '87, Ibid, III (IV), 17.[3] C. J.: *Committee appointed to join Assembly committee, 24 Oct. '85, G. and C., III, 89; *committee appointed to join Assembly committee, 24 Oct. '86, Ibid, III, 111; bill read and approved, 26 Oct. '86, Ibid, III, 113.

FOR EXEMPTION FROM LAND GRANT FEES
xxii, 104

To the Honble General Assembly of the State of Vermont to be convened at ⟨Norwich⟩ Windsor in the county of Windsor on the 2nd Thursday of October next — The Petition of Louis Button —
Humbly Sheweth
That your Petitioner in the Late unhapy war had the Misfortune to have her Husband Kill^d by the Savages Neer the Place where I Now Live — that Since that

---

1. This entry on the manuscript petition correctly adds that the Assembly committee was to join a committee from the Council. It also lists Mr. Shumway as a committee member in place of Mr. Safford.

2. The entry on the manuscript petition simply notes that the petition was referred to the next session.

3. For this act, see Ms. Laws of Vt., II, 190–191.

Time your Petitioner has undergone hardships Scarcely Parralled in a Christian Land — Considering her Local Situation from frinds and Neigbour having a family of Small Chidiren to Provide for by her industry amongst wich is one that has always been & Probablely will be an uncomon charge to suport — that your Petitioner with her husband went on to the Primises She Now Lives on under a then Suposed Title in Tunbridge that Since the New Lines have been run the Primises have fell into a Gore of Land Belonging to the Good People of this State. that the Legislature of Vermont was pleased at there Last Sesion to grant to me 200 acres in Said Gore[1] but your Petitioner Being Totaly unable to pay the Charter fees, has aplyed to his Excelency by herself, in Person thinking is [it] was in his power to have them Taken of but it not Being in his power to remit them your petitions Prays your Honours to Let her have her Land free from Charter fees and Expence and your Petitioner as in duty Bound shall ever pray —

Louis Button

— & —

Wid° Buttons Petition
Entered
filed Oct. 15. 1785
. . .*

— & —

A. J.: *Read and referred to a committee, 15 Oct. '85 *S. P. of Vt.*, III (III), 173–174;[2] *report of committee recommending that petition be granted read and accepted, and leave given to bring in a bill accordingly, 19 Oct. '85, *Ibid*, III (III), 191; resolved that granting fees be released to petitioner, 20 Oct. '85, *Ibid*, III (III), 195. *C. J.:* *Committee appointed to join Assembly committee, 15 Oct. '85, *G. and C.*, III, 80.

FOR INCORPORATION OF A RELIGIOUS SOCIETY
xvii, 127

To the Honourable General Assembly of the State of Vermont to be holden at Windsor on the Second Thursday of October next

The Petition of the Subscribers Inhabitents of the Town of Pawlett and their Adhearants in Said State humbly Sheweth —

that your honors Putisioners being Desirous of Settling and supporting a Minestor of the Gospel of the Congregational Order in this Town did on the 16th day of August 1785 Associate Covenant and agree to form our selves into a Religeous Society by the Name of the Congregational Society of Pawlett and that the cost which shall hereafter arise in settling and Supporting a Minestor as aforesaid shall be defrayed by a Tax made out on the Poles and Rateable Estates of the Several members of said Society as Set forth in the Constitution of Said Society herewith Exhibited your honors Petitioners theirfore Pray Your honors to take the matter under your wise consideration and incorporate them into a Society by the

---

1. For the grant of Spooner's Gore, see *S. P. of Vt.*, II (Vermont Charters), 185–186.
2. The manuscript petition correctly notes that this committee was to join a committee from the Council.

Name of the Congregational Society of Pawlett that your Petitioners may be
Enabled to carry into effect all the Matters and things expresd in the constitution
of Said Society as afore Said and your Petitioners as in Duty bound shall ever
Pray
Pawlett Sep^t 6th 1785 —

Nathan French	Jona^th Willard	Joel Harmon
Jacob Edgerton	Ebenz^r Cobb	Adonijah Montagiu
Moses Porter	Lem^ll Chipman	Jedediah Edgerton
Timothy Bruster	Simeon Edgerton	Moses Cleveland
Philip Read	George Mills	Nathan Bennet
Garshom Hail	John Cobb	David Gilimore
Garshom Hail Junr	W^m goodrich	Elkanah Cobb
Silas Reed	Stephen Pearl	Jonathan Prindle
Gideon Adams	Josiah Safford	David Lewis
Jonathan Willard Junr	Benoni Smith	Ezekiel Harmon
Joshua Cobb	Elisha Clark	Lem^ll Clark
Andrew Bell	Elisha Fitch	Seth Sheldon
Jonathan Willard	Jabez G Fitch	Abner French
George Mills Junr	Benajah Booshnal	Elisha Clark J^r
Sam^ll Willard	Sam^ll Butt	Daniel Welch
John Stark	John Thompson	Abisha bushnal
		Stephen Starkweathar

— & —

Petition of Inhabitants of Pawlet
filed Oct. 24 1785
Entered
. . .*

— & —

A. J.: *Read and referred to a committee, 22 Oct. '85, *S. P. of Vt.*, III (III),
197;[1] *report of committee recommending that prayer ought to be granted,
read and accepted, and leave given to bring in a bill accordingly, 26 Oct. '85,
Ibid, III (III), 205;[2] act read and accepted and sent to Governor and Council,
26 Oct. '85, *Ibid*, III (III), 205; act, having been concurred in by Council,
passed into law, 27 Oct. '86, *Ibid*, III (III), 209.[3] *C. J.:* Act read and concurred in, 26 Oct. '85, *G. and C.*, III, 93.

---

1. The Assembly journal does not note the names of the committee members, but
they are given on the manuscript. They were as follows: Mr. Shumway, Mr. Spalding
and Mr. Ward.
2. The date of the committee report is given on the manuscript as 24 Oct. '85. It
was signed "John Shumway for Committee."
3. For this act, see *Ms. Laws of Vt.*, I, 532–533. It gave the society the power to
tax its members to build and maintain a meeting house and to support a minister. The
collectors of such taxes were to have the powers of the regular town collectors. The
decision to levy taxes was to be taken by a majority of the members.

FOR RIGHT TO SELL REAL PROPERTY TO SETTLE AN ESTATE
xvii, 128

To the Honorable the General Assembly of the State of Vermont to be holden at Winsor [Windsor] on the Second Thursday of October 1785

The petition of Aaron Scott and Martha Douglass Administrators of the Estate of William Douglass late of Cornwall deceased humbly sheweth that the personal Estate of the said William Douglass is ensufficient by the Sum of fifty nine ⟨Sixty⟩ pounds Lawful Money to pay the debts due from said Estate

Therefore pray your Honors to empower us the said Aaron Scott and Martha Douglass to Sell so much of the real Estate of the said William Douglass as will pay the sum of fifty nine ⟨Sixty⟩ pounds L. Money together with necessary cost arrising on said sale for the purpose of paying the debts due from said Estate under such restrictions as you in your wisdom shall see fit as we in duty bound shall ever pray

Aaron Scott

Cornwall 14ᵗʰ Sept. 1785   Martha duglas

To the Honorable General Assembly of the State of Vermont. —
This may certify that the personal Estate of William Douglass late of Cornwal Deceased, is insufficient to pay the Debts due from said estate, by the Sum of Fifty nine pounds Lawful Money.

attest Elisha Clark Judge Prob.

Probate Office ⎫
Rutland District ⎬
Tinmouth August 1785 ⎭

— & —

The petition of Aaron Scott and Martha Douglas
[. . .]
Entered
filed Oct. 14. 1784 [1785]
. . .*

— & —

A. J.: *Read and prayer granted, and ordered that a bill be brought in accordingly, 14 Oct. '85, S. P. of Vt., III (III), 169–170; bill read and accepted and sent to Council, 14 Oct. '85, Ibid, III (III), 170; act, having been concurred in by Council, passed into law, 14 Oct. '85, Ibid, III (III), 173.1 C. J.: *Concurrs with Assembly in granting prayer and in ordering bill to be brought in accordingly, 14 Oct. '85, G. and C., III, 79; act read and concurred in, 14 Oct. '85, Ibid, III, 79.

FOR A NEW TRIAL IN A CASE OF CONVERSION
xvii, 129

To the Honᵇˡᵉ the Genˡˡ Assembly of the State of Vermont to be Convend at

---

1. For this act, see Ms. Laws of Vt., I, 503.

Winsor on the 2ᵈ Thursday of October Next —

The Petition of Gideon Cole of Farmington in the County of Hartford and State of Connecticut Humbly Sheweth that your Petitioner on the 14th Day of August 1783 was Sued by Sam Messer of Winsor [Windsor] in the County of Winsor [Windsor] in an Action of Trover & Conversion for Converting as, twas Said two Certain Notes which your Petitioner would Inform Your Honours never Came to his hands or possession that Said writ was Served by attaching one Horse and one Yoke of Oxen Shewn to the officer as the proper Estate of your Petitioner as by the Officers return on Said Writ appears which said Writ was made Returnable to the adjourned County Court to be Holden at Winsor on the fourth Tuesday of the Then Instant August which said Cause was Continued by sᵈ Court to the Last Tuesday of October then Next at which Term the Said Messer obtained judgment against your Petitioner by Default for the Sum of £ 52:10:3ˢ ᵈ L.M. Damage and for the Sum of £ 2:9:2 Costs of Suit & Took out Execution in Due form of Law for the Like Sums Your Petitioner would observe that he had no knowledge of the Suit but by a Letter and that during all that Time your petioner [sic] was engaged in the Service of the United States ⟨his country⟩ and was by no means Able to attend on sᵈ Cause or to obtain Leave to be So long absent from the Service —

Your petitioner would further remark that in March 1784 he Came up to See about the matter as Soon as he Could be discharged when to his Great Surprise the first notice he obtained he was taken by Said Execution and was compelled to pay the Same, your petitioner Can assure your Honours that he never had the Notes Mentioned in the Sᵈ Messers writ but that the Same your petitioner is informd is now in another persons hands and that your petitioner is Liable to pay the Same Your petitioner would therefore pray your Honours to Grant your Petitioner a New Tryal in the Premises before the County Court in Sᵈ County of Winsor by ordering the Said Messer to enter his Cause anew and further order that Justice shall be done in the premises & your Petitioner as in Duty bound Shall ever pray Dated at Winsor this 26ᵗʰ Day of Sept 1785   Gideon Cowls

— & —

Cole [Cowls] vs Messer Petition
Entered
filed Oct. 24. 1785
. . .*

— & —

A. J.: *Read and referred to a committee, 25 Oct. '85, S. P. of Vt., III (III), 201; report of committee read and recommitted, and two members added to committee, 26 Oct. '85, Ibid, III (III), 205; *report of committee recommending that the prayer be granted, read and accepted, and leave granted to bring in a bill accordingly, 27 Oct. '85, Ibid, III (III), 207; bill read and sent to Council, 27 Oct. '85, Ibid, III (III), 211; bill, having been concurred in by Council, passed into law, 27 Oct. '85, Ibid, III (III), 211.[1] C. J.: Act read and concurred in, 27 Oct. '85, G. and C., III, 95.

---

1. For this act, see Ms. Laws of Vt., I, 531.

FOR COMPENSATION FOR CARE OF A TRANSIENT PAUPER
xvii, 130, 131

To the honorable general Assembly of the state of Vermont to convene at Windsor on the Second thursday of October next.

The petition of Penuel Deming of Williamston [Williamstown] in the county of Orange & state of Vermont humbly sheweth.

That on the 28th day of December last a certain trancient person by the name of David Brownson called at your petitioners house in Williamston, as he was upon a journey from Canada to Connecticut, with his feet frozen in such a manner as he was unable to proceed on his journey any farther. Moved with compassion towards such an object of charity, (who was destitute of money or any property whatsoever) your petitioner consented to keep him in his house & nurse him at a time when there was no other house in Sd Williamston   After Sd Brownson had been at your petitioner house twelve weeks & one day, he died of the injury he had received from the frost when on his journey, tho faithfully nursed at the expence of your petitioner; & having no property nor friends to indemnify your petitioner for the expence which he was at in feeding & nursing Sd deceased, your petitioner prays this honorable court to grant him his account against sd deceased as is annexed to this petition. Resting satisfied that this honorable court will oblige no individual to be at the whole expence of boarding a trancient person who is unable to go from his house & has no property to indemnify the person who is at the expence of nursing & feeding such an object of charity more especially when he is in a town where there is but one house & no Overseers to take the charge of those who are considered as objects of charity.

Your petitioner further sheweth that his circumstances in life are indigent & he has a large family to maintain of his own, & was at considerable expence purchasing provisions & other necessaries for the support of sd deceased which he was obliged to obtain upon credit, which is not yet paid: he therefore presents his account to this honorable court to allow, as your petitioner is in duty bound to pray.

Penuel Deming

Williamston Sept 26. 1785

Williamston Sept 26th 1785

David Brownson deceased to Penuel Deming Dr

To boarding him 12 weeks & one day @ 6/ —	£3.12.9
nursing him 85 days @ 2/ —	8.10.0
watching with him 20 nights 1/6 —	1.10.0
6 <lbs> of candles used in watching —	0. 6.0
procuring <6 cords of> wood —	1.16.0
diging a grave & preparing for the funeral —	0.12.0

sum total   £16 6.9

Penuel Deming

— & —

Penuel Deming Petition
filed Oct 18. 1785
. . .*

the Committee to Whom was Refered the petition of Penuel Deming beg Leave to Report as follows that it hath bin provd to your Committee that the Sd Deming

did feed and nurse the S^d deceased as is Set forth in the Petition and that he must have bin at Considerable Expence as he had all his Provision to transport on his Back at a distance of nine miles: it is therefore the opinion of your Committee that the S^d Deming be alowed as a Compensation the Some of twelve pounds: all which is humbly Submited by

B. Emmons for Committee

In Genl Assembly Octr 26th 1785

The above report was read and accepted and ordered that a Bill be br^t in accordingly

attest Ros Hopkins Clerk

— & —

A. J.: *Read and referred to a committee to join a committee from the Council, 20 Oct. '85, *S. P. of Vt.*, III (III), 194; resolved that Treasurer be directed to pay petitioner £12 lawful money, 26 Oct. '85, *Ibid*, III (III), 205. *C. J.:* *Committee appointed to join Assembly committee, 21 Oct. '85, *G. and C.*, III, 87.

FOR A TAX ON LAND TO BUILD ROADS AND BRIDGES
xvii, 132

To the Honnorable General Assembly of the State of Vermont to be Convened on the Second Thursday of October next at Newwinzer [Windsor] in s^d State — The Petition of Abel Thompson and others of the proprietors & Inhabitants of the Town of Ferriss Burgh whose Names are annext Humbly showing the great Disadvantage that the public Labours under for want of public Roads through the S^d Town of Ferriss Burgh —
⟨The Proprietors at proprietors meeting which was held in S^d Town in June last, S^d proprietors Considering that the land in S^d Town was manely Lotted & nothing mention^d in the warning Concerning a tax for high ways: Suppos^d that it would not be legal to lay a tax at that meeting. Advised the people to petition to the Assembly for to grant a tax as they should Judge proper So of Consequense the public hath no Roads & by that means the Settlement of the town [Backen^d?]⟩ the town verry Larg with many Rapped streams through the Same which must be bridg^d. Impossible for the inhabitants To Cultivate & bridge these roads that the public Absolutely Stands In need of — Your potisioners would Humbly pray This Honerable Assembly would grant a tax of two pense P^r acre on Each Right of land in S^d Town of Ferriss Burgh Public Rights Excluded: for the purpose of Cutting & bridging S^d Roads in S^d Town that the public stands in need of at this time —
and furthermore your potitioners humbly pray that this Honorable Assembly would appoint a Committee in S^d Town, that they may Confide in: to Lay out S^d Roads in The most Convenien place for the public. & see the same Cut & Bridg^d as far as S^d tax will go Furthermore Your potitioners would humbly pray that this Honnorable Assembly would autherise the S^d Committee who is appointed To lay the S^d Roads to proseed & Collect S^d Tax in such a way and form as the Honnorable assembly Shall direct — Trusting & Releing [relying] on the Justice & Equitee of this Honnorable assembly as we are in duty bound Shall ever pray
Dated in Ferrissburgh
Sept. 26th 1785

Abel Thompson	Stephen middlebook	David Hill
Jonth Sexton	Joseph Burroughs	Emet [. . .]
Gideon Hawley	William Haight	Joseph Gaige
Absalom Tupper	Stephen middelbook Jun	Reuben Lane french
Zuriel Tupper	James Haight	Nehemiah Loring french
Timothy Rogers	Donald McIntosh	Charles french
Silas Bingham	Jere^m Runnels	[Moses?] Brush
Aron Rowley	Isaac Gage	Israel West
James Story	Zeblon [Crittenden?]	Gideon Spencer
	Benyar Webster	

— & —

Inhabitants of Ferrisburgh Petition
Entered
filed Oc^t 17. 1785
. . .*

    Your Com^{tt} to whome was refered the within Petition — Finds that the factes Set up in the Petition are true (viz) that the main road of travel will nessesarely go through Ferrisburg and that their air no roads nor bridges maid in Said town. and that the Township is Cheafly owned by non resident Proprietors who at their meeting in June Last Did refuse to help the Inhabitents to make roades buil [*sic*] Bridges &c — therefore Report that the Prair of the Petition ought to be granted so far as to Lay a Tax of two Pence on Each acre (Publick Lands Excepted) to be appropreated as Set forth in their Petition

Signed per order   Th^o Porter   Chm.

— & —

    A. J.: *Read and referred to a committee to join a committee from the Council, 17 Oct. '85, *S. P. of Vt.*, III (III), 185; *report of committee recommending that such a tax be laid on land, read and accepted, and leave given to bring in a bill accordingly, 24 Oct. '85, *Ibid*, III (III), 200; bill read and accepted and sent to Council, 25 Oct. '85, *Ibid*, III (III), 201; bill, having been concurred in by Council with an amendment, passed into law, 27 Oct. '85, *Ibid*, III (III), 209.[1] *C. J.:* *Committee appointed to join Assembly committee, 19 Oct. '85, *G. and C.*, III, 85; act concurred in with an addition, 26 Oct. '85, *Ibid*, III, 92.[2]

FOR A DUTY ON IMPORTED NAILS
xvii, 148

To the Honorable the General Assembly now Sitting at Windsor the Subscriber begs Leave to Represent, that he thinks it is possible to Supply this State with Nails of its Own Manufacture which Article is one of the Most Costly of any of

---

    1. For this act, see *Ms. Laws of Vt.*, I, 526–527.
    2. The nature of this addition or amendment is not noted in either the Council or Assembly journals. The original act, which also might show this addition, is not among those found in *Ms. Vt. S. P., Laws.*

the Importable Necessarys for which almost all the Circulating Cost is Constantly Carried out of the State, yet the building A Slitting Mill will be of such Great Cost that possibly at first Setting up the Nails may be imported Cheaper than they can be made at home (altho not so much to the Public benefit —) unless the Honorable the Legislature should think proper to Encourage the Building of a Sliting Mill — the Encouragement the Subscriber would propose is the Laying a Duty of two pence on Each pound of Nails brought into the State & that Effectual measures be taken for the Collection of Said Duty to take place as soon as Slit Iron can be had at four pence half penny per pound should such proposal be agreable to the Legislature the Subscriber would Set himself about building a Sliting Mill

M Lyon

— & —

Col Mathew Lyon for encouragt of a Slitting Mill —
filed 14 oct 1785

— & —

A. J.: Read and dismissed, 17 Oct. '85, *S. P. of Vt.*, III (III) 183.

FOR ABATEMENT OF TAXES[1]
xvii, 156

To the Honble Genl Assembly of the State of Vermont Now Siting at Windsor the Petition of the Subscriber Cunstable of Bethel for the year 1783 —
   Humbly Sheweth —
that on the Grand List for the Said year the Town was Domed[2] £ 100 –15 More than the List ⟨on the Grand List for said year⟩ was — that application was made to this Hous in Feby 1784 to have said Domage Taken off wich Prayer was Granted and a Certificate from the Clerk Taken out. But as there was four Diferent Warrants Issued on sd year the Certificate answered for only one (viz) that of /3d on the £ and your Petitioner has been Compeld by the Sheriff of Windsor County to pay into the Treasury £ 5–9–2 more then he could Possibly Colect Some of wich in hard cash (viz) £ – 16– 9 wich To gether with Some considerable Cost made thereon on account of Suposing the Treasurer would Credit Said Town of Bethel on the Several Taxes Granted on that year —
Therefore your Pititioner prays your Honours to Issue an order on the Treasurer to pay him the Sum of £ 5–9–2 as above Expressed or Grant him Relief in such other way as in your wisdom you shall Direct, and as in Duty Bound your Petitioner shall Ever pray —

Samuel Peck —

— & —

Saml Peck —
Petition
Entered
filed Oct 18. 1785

---

1. For a similar petition drawn up by Samuel Peck in June, 1785 and filed but not presented to the assembly, see p. 128, *ante*, including explanatory notes.
2. For the meaning of the term "domed" [doomed], see p. 66n, *ante*.

. . .*

To the hon^ble General Assembly now Sitting your comt^e to whom was refer^d the Petition of Samuel Peck Beg leave to report — That we find the Town of Bethel Credited for the year 1783 the sum of 100–15 Shilling on the Grand List. that the Treasurer has givin them Credit on the 3^d & 5^d Tax for the S^d year that the Constable has paid up the whole of The Tax for the 6^d & 2^d tax on the £ — Therefore your comi^t report that the prayer of the Petition ought to be granted in part Viz. that the Treasurer be Directed to pay the S^d Petitioner £ – 16 – 9 hard Money Orders & £ 2–10–4 in Treasurers State Notes

Sam^ll Williams for Com

— & —

A. J.: *Read and referred to a committee, 18 Oct. '85, *S. P. of Vt.*, III (III), 188–189; *report of committee read and accepted, 19 Oct. '85, *Ibid*, III (III), 193; resolved that Treasurer be directed to pay petitioner 16/10 hard money and £2-10-4 lawful money, 19 Oct. '85, *Ibid*, III (III), 193.

FOR ACTION AGAINST A JUSTICE OF THE PEACE FOR MALADMINISTRATION
xvii, 157, 168[1]

To the Honble The Representatives of Freemen of the State of Vermont
The ⟨Petition⟩ Complaint of Nathl Gott of Luninburg [Lunenburg] in the County of Orange & State of Vermont Physian [Physician]
Humbly Sheweth
That Abner Osgood of Guildhall Being Appointed one of the Justices of the Peace for the County of Orrang And that the said Osgood Esqr hath in the Execution of His office hath ⟨Ben arbitrary and Pertial⟩ Ben Guilty of [Several?] Breaches of Law in his Office as a Justice of the Peace, VIZ
for that the Said Osgood Esqr Did on the 30 Day of July Grant his Warrant to Aprehend the Body of David Hopkinson for Feloneasly taking one Pair of Oxen from Phillip Grapes of Maidston & Said Hopkinson was Taken & the oxen arrested out of his Custody & Said Hopkinson was Carryed Before Said Osgood Esqr and the Said David Did then & there Plead Not Guilty & Produced an Execution Granted ⟨on a Judgment⟩ By Alexander Harvey Esqr at Barnet on a Judgment Obtained By Caleb Hopkinson against Said Phillip Grapes & Said David Being Deputised & Sworn to the faithful Discharge of his Office in the Service of Said Execution & the Said Osgood Esqr was Not ignorant of the Said David, Being in that ofice for the Said Osgood Esqr Did administer an oth to the Said David Previous to the Said David Leveying Said Execution on Said Oxen: Notwithstanding the Self Evidence Proof & the Plea that the Said David then Made: the Said Osgood Esqr Did then & there Precad to Try Said David & By his Arbertery threats Did then oblige the Said David to indorse on Said Execution Satisfyed & take the Said

---

1. The manuscript on p. 157 is the original petition, while that on p. 168 is a true copy (except for spelling and punctuation) as certified thereon by the clerk of the Assembly. The copy contains material in addition to the body of the petition not found in the original. The printed text follows the spelling and punctuation of the original and contains additional material from both the original and the copy.

Phillip Grapeses Note of hand for and in the Value of Said Sum in Said Execution
Also for that David Hopkinson Being one of the Grand Jury & the Said David
Hopkinson Did then & there on the first Day of August AD 1785 Enter a Written
Complaint aginst Phillip Grapes for Profane Swaring & & threatning the Life of
Caleb Hopkinson and also of Striking Wich the Said David was then in the Execution of his office as a Grand juryman & the Said Phillip Grapes was then Present:
wich Said Osgood Esqʳ Did grant his warrant & apprehended the Said Delinquent
then Bifore him & the Said Grand jury man Did Produse a Person as [Evidend?] &
the Said Osgood Esqr Refused to Examine Said Evidence or Put Said Evidence
upon Oath But Did then & there Desmiss Said Delinquent; taking a moderate fine
of Seven Pence half Peney
Also for that the Said Abner Osgood Esqʳ having had a Complaint Exhibited &
Lodged With Said Osgood Esqʳ By Hezekiah Fuller of Maidston in Said County
against Ebenazar Torrey of Said Maidston Complaining of the Said Ebenazar for
Profaning the Lords Day or Sabath Day By frequently & Constantly Labouring on
Said Day & the Said Complainant Did then & there on the Second Day of august
Pray that a Warrant might Be granted to aprehend Said Delinquent that he might Be
Delt with as the Law Directs: and Said Plaintive Desired Sumons to Procure
Evidence to Suport his Complaint But the Said Abner Osgood Esq. Desmised Said
Complaint & Refused to Bring the Delinquent to Justice
Also for that the Said Abner Osgood Esqʳ Had a Complaint Lodged with him By
the hand of John young Esqʳ in Behalf of Ebenazar Torrey of Maidston in Said
County Said Ebenazar Torry Complaining of Sundry Persons Coming in the Night
in a Riotas manner & Braking into Said Torreys house & abusing said Torrey and
Destroying his Good & Estate & the Said abner Osgood hath Naglected to Bring
Said offenders to Justice: But Lets Said Delinquents Pas & Repas to and from his
the Said osgood house & Descourses with Said offenders locally & Not taking any
Notice of the Complain But Countenancing them in their [willainy?] [villainy]
Also for that the Said Abner Osgood Esqʳ Did on the 30 Day of August 1785
Grant a Writ of attachment to attach the goods or Estate of Nathˡ Gott of Luninburg
to the Value of fifteen Pounds and for want thereof to take the Body & the Said
atachment Being Leveyed on the Body of the Said Gott when from home on his
Buisness to Visit the Sick the Said Gott Procured Bonds for his apearance to Court
on the second Tuesday of September AD 1785 & the said Gott apeared at the
time & Plase for Tryal. Said Osgood Opened his Court and Proceaded to Try
Said Case the Sum in Demand in Said Writ was Nine Pound Eight Shillings ⟨L M⟩
the Defendant Plead an abatement on the Writ which was not granted as it Being
unlawfull to Try More than Six Pounds on a Book account in a Justice Court:
But Said Osgood Esqʳ Proceaded for Tryal Called for a Jury Empanelled them
Conterary to ye Law of this State & Brought judgment against the Said Gott & —
awarded Damages to the Plaintive the Defendant was then Denyed the Liberty of
an apeal By Said Osgood Esqʳ ⟨Where⟩ altho the Defendant offered & tendered
Bail
also the Defendant Requested a Coppy of his judgment & tendered the money to
the Said Osgood Esqʳ But the Said Osgood Esqʳ Did Refuse to give away Coppy
of his judgment as also for that the Said Abner Osgood Esqʳ Did Grant out his
Precept or Warrant against your ⟨Petitioner⟩ Complainant to aprehend him &
Bring him Before him Emediatly to answer to the Complaint of Eleezer Rosbrook
and Be Delt with as the Law Directs in that Case & the Said Abner Osgood Did
Not Set forth anny Cause of accusation in Said Warrant Nor anny annexed thereto

But the Said Gott Being taken By the officer in a Verry Sickly time to the Grate Damage of the Said Gott & also to an Excessive Damage to his Patiences [patients] that was Sick under his Care & the Said Gott was then ignorant of the Cause of his accusation & was taken & Carryed Before Said Osgood on thirtenth Day of September & there Kept in Custody of an officer from one of the clock in the afternoon till one of the clock in the Morning Not having the Cause of his accusation & Said Osgood Did then and there Procead to try Said Gott & Condemn him without giving him Liberty of Calling Evidance in his favour although the Said Gott did then & there Read the 10:11 & 12 articles of the Declaration of Rights[1] & Demanded the Privilages of a freaman of the State Liberty of Calling Evidence in his favour But the Said Osgood Esqr Did then & there in an Abetary & Perteal [partial] manner Procead to Try & Condemn the Said Gott on false and groundless Sermises and awarded Damages to the ⟨Plaintive⟩ Complainant the foregoing Being facts Being indisputable your ⟨Petitioner⟩ Complainant Considers the Said Abner Osgood Guilty of Male administration & Therefore your ⟨Petitioner⟩ Complainant in Behalf of the State Complaineth of the Said Abner Osgood Esqr as Being Guilty of Male Administration wich is against the Peace & Dignity of this State & Prayeth that the Said Abner Osgood Esqr May be Delt with as the Law appertains in that Case and as in Duty Boun will Ever Pray

Nathl Gott

— & —

Natt^l Gott's Petition
Filed Octr 20th 1785 —
. . .*
Natt^l Gott's Complaint ag^t Abner Osgood Esqr Dismissed —[2]

State of Vermont
 To the Sheriff of the County of Orange ⟨in the State of Vermont⟩ his Deputy or either of the Constables of the town of Guildhall in Said County — Greeting
 In the Name and by the authority of the Freemen of the State of Vermont you are hereby required to cite Abner Osgood Esqr of Guildhall in Said County to appear before the Honorable the General Assembly of this State at Rutland on Thursday the 19th day of October next to shew cause if any he has why he should not be impeached for Mal-Administration in his office of Justice of the peace agreeable to the within complaint — You will serve the same either by reading the within complaint in the hearing of the said Abner Osgood Esqr or leave a true and attested copy of the Same at his dwelling house at least fifteen days before the day appointed for his appearance before the Assembly — Fail not and due return make — Given under my hand (by order of the Genl Assembly at their last Session) at Bennington this 20th day of March A.D. 1786 —

Roswell Hopkins Clerk of Genl Assembly —

I herby Deputise John Rich of Gildhall to be my Lawfull Deputy to Sarve and Return the written writ of Sitaton

attest Abner Chamberlin Sheriff

---

 1. See *G. and C.*, I, 94–95.
 2. There is no record of Osgood's appearance before the Assembly. From this entry on the reverse of the copy, it seems possible that the complaint was dismissed prior to the date set for his appearance. Osgood himself petitioned for a postponement of the hearing until the next session. See p. 196, *post*.

Orange Ss } September 21th AD 1786

     Persuant to the above I have Served the above Writ by Leaving a true and atested Coppy With the Defendant of the Writ & Complant
                                     attest John Rich Deputy Sheriff
Fees for one hundred and twenty five 4 pence p^r Mile   2–1–8
for a copy   0–6–0
                              — & —

     A. J.: *Read and referred to a committee, 20 Oct. '85, *S. P. of Vt.*, III (III), 196; report of committee recommending that complaint be laid over and that Osgood be cited to appear at next session of Assembly and show cause why he should not be impeached, read and accepted, 27 Oct. '85, *Ibid*, III (III), 206; clerk of assembly directed to cite said Osgood accordingly, 27 Oct. '85, *Ibid*, III (III), 206; Treasurer directed to pay for the serving of the clerk's citation on Osgood, 25 Oct. '86, *Ibid*, III (III), 245.

FOR CONFIRMATION OF ACTION TAKEN BY PROPRIETORS IN A BOUNDARY CONFLICT
xxii, 103

To the Honorable General Assembly now Sitting at Windsor —
    The Petition of the Proprietors of the Towns of Addison and Panton humbley shewith — that at an early Period, soon after the two Charters of Addison and Panton[1] were obtained from the governor of New Hamshire [New Hampshire] many of the Proprietors of Panton made settlements and large Improvements on Land then supposed to be in the Township of Panton, but afterward on survey and settlement of the Lines of the Towns of Addison and Panton aforesaid according to Charter it was found that the Charters of the said Towns [necessarily?] interfere^d or laped [lapped] upon each other to the distance of three miles and half or their abouts, by means whereof one or the other of said Towns must be Cut short in their Quota of Land more than half unless the Proprietors of each of the said Towns should agree to share the loss between them. for this purpose, Proprietors Meetings both for Addison and Panton have been warned, and held and Committees appointed by both of said Towns to settle and adjust the Difficulty the said Committees on the 17th day of May 1774 Come to a mutual agreement or ajustment of the matter, and Committed the same to writing under their hand as Committees for said Towns, all which proceedings of the Propritors of the said Towns & their Committees your Petitioners by their agents have ready to produce to this Honorable Assembly, to geather with the Proceedings of after meetings of the said Proprietors of Addison and Panton on the Reports of their Committees and rattifying and Confirming the same as far as in them lay, but lest the doing of the said Proprietors of Addison and Panton might be found insufficient to remove and finish the Difficulty and Mischief it was suposed to prevent your Petitioners pray this Honorable Assembly to rattify and Confirm and render effectual the doing of the aforesaid Proprietors —

---

    1. For the charters of Addison and Panton, see *State Papers New Hampshire*, vol. XXVI (Town Charters, vol. III), 3–7, 327–331.

as your Petitioners in Duty bound shall ever pray

John Strong   agent for the Proprietors of Addison
Zadok Everest   agent for Panton

— & —

Petition of Addison & Panton
Entered
filed Oct. 14. 1785
. . .*

— & —

A. J.: *Granted, and leave given to bring in a bill accordingly, 15 Oct. '85, S. P. of Vt., III (III), 176–177; bill read and accepted and sent to Council, 18 Oct. '85, Ibid, III (III), 185; bill read and accepted and sent to Council, 24 Oct. '85, Ibid, III (III), 200.[1] C. J.: Act read and concurred in, 24 Oct. '85, G. and C., III, 89.[2]

FOR A NEW TRIAL IN A CASE OF SLANDER
xvii, 133

To the honorable General Assembly to be holden at Winsor [Windsor] in the State of Vermont on the Second Thirsday of Instant Octr the Petition of Benjamin Willard of Walpole in the State of New Hamshire humbly Sheweth, that Elkanah Cobb of Pawlett in the County of Rutland brought an action of Trespas on the Case against your Petitioner (for Slanderous wor^d) to the County Court, in the County of Rutland, at the State term, in Novr AD 1784 and recouved [recovered] Judgment by defaul^t against your Petitioner, for the Sum of fifty pounds Lawful money — and that, he had no knowledge of any Such Suit having been Commenced agains^t him untill Some time after the Said Judgment, was rendered against him as aforesaid, & that he had no day in Court, to vindicate himself agains^t the unjust Charge laid against him in said Suit, & that an Exe^n [execution] hath been Issued against him, on said Judgment, he prays therefore that, his Case may be taken into Consideration, & that the aforesaid Judgment & Exec^n may be Set aside, & that a new tryal of the Cause may be had, in the said County Court, at their Session in Nove^r nex^t or at Some other term as your honor may think best & he as in duty bound Shall ever pray —
Dated at Manchester this 3^d day of Octr AD 1785 —

Benj^a Willard

To either of the Constables of Pawlett, in the County of Rutland, or to any in-different person to Serve & return In the name & by the Authority of the freemen of the State of Vermont, you are Commanded, to Summon Elkanah Cobb — of said Pawlett, to appear before the Now General Assembly mention^d in the within Petition if he See Cause — to answer to said Petition, & to Shew his reason if

---

1. The record in the Assembly journal of the action taken on this bill is confused. In view of the date of the Council's action, it is probable that the latter of these duplicate entries is the correct one.

2. For this act, see Ms. Laws of Vt., I, 509–511.

any he has why the prayer of said Petition should not be granted —
Dated at Pawlett this 11th day of Octr AD 1785

Gideon Adams Jus^t Peace

Pawlett October 11th AD 1785
then Servd the with in Somons By reeding it in the hearing of the with in named Elkanah Cobb

atest Samuel Clark   Consta

Feese 1:6:0

— & —

Benjⁿ Willard's Petition
. . .*
Filed 21st October 1785

— & —

A. J.: *Read and referred to a committee, 24 Oct. '85, *S. P. of Vt.*, III (III), 199; *report of committee recommending that prayer ought not to be granted, read and accepted, and petition dismissed, 25 Oct. '85, *Ibid*, III (III), 202.[1]

FOR A TAX ON LAND TO BUILD A BRIDGE
xvii, 134

To the Honerble }

General Assembly of the State of Vermont to Set att Windsor October Instant the Petition the inhabitants of the Town of Hartland in Said State humbley Sheweth that there is a Bridge much wanted over water Queechy [Ottauquechee] river att or near where the Contental road So Called crosses Said river it Being the Established road that leads through this town to Hartford and Norwich, that the Number of Days work Laid on the list for makeing And Repairing Highways has been wholey Insuffisent to Complete the Same.
These are there-fore to pray your Honors to Grant us a land tax of that Small Sum of one peney upon the acre on all the lands In the town of Hartland Except the publick Lands and that the money that is Left Affter the aforesaid Bridge is Completed if aney there be Shall be for the Rebuilding a Bridge or Bridges acrost the dry gulley against Water Queeche fall So Called. and your petitioners in Duty bound Shall Ever Pray
October the 3 1785

Asa Taylor	Timothy Lull	Jeremiah Richardson
Eldad Alexander	Nial Rust	Zebulon Lee
Daniel Spooner	Nathan Billings	Elias Taylor
Joseph Evans	Elisha Gallup	Olr Taylor
Isaac Maine	Geo. Denison	Elias Gates
Olr Willard Jnr	Abner Brigham	William S. Ashley

---

1. The report of committee, as noted in the manuscript, declares "that the facts Set fourth in S^d Petition, are not Supported . . . ." This statement is omitted in the report as given in the Assembly journal.

Eli Willard   Daniel Sumner   Isaac Stevens
Frans Richardson   Wm Gallup   Paul Spooner
                               Ol^r Willard

— & —

Inhabitants of Hartland —
Petition
filed Oct. 24th 1785 —
referred to next session[1]

— & —

A. J.: Bill entitled "An Act for the purpose of levying a tax of one penny per acre on all the lands in the town of Hartland in the County of Windsor", read and sent to Governor and Council, 26 Oct. '85, *S. P. of Vt.*, III (III), 204; bill having been concurred in by Council, passed into law, 27 Oct. '85, *Ibid*, III (III), 209.[2] *C. J.*: Act read and concurred in, 26 Oct. '85, *G. and C.*, III, 92.[3]

FOR REPEAL OF AN ACT REVERSING COURT JUDGMENTS[4]
xxii, 94

To the Honorable the General Assembly of the State of Vermont to convene at Windsor on the 2nd Thursday in October instant
Sheweth
William Sergeant of Dummerstown in Windham County that he finds himself much injured both in his Interest and feelings by an Act Passed in the last Sessions of Assembly entitled "An Act confirming Andrew Grayham of Putney in the County of Windham in the quiet and Peaceable Possession of the farm on which he now lives in Said Putney and rendering all Judgments respecting the Possession of the Same heretofore had and rendered by any Court of Law whatsoever null and void"[5] That your Petitioner is informed that the Said Act was hurred [*sic*] thro' the House at the Close of the Session without his agent being able to obtain a hearing agt. it before the Honorable Assembly and therefore is not without hope that a new Assembly taking up the matter more deliberatley will rectify what appears to have been conducted amiss
That your Petitioner was some time ago Possessed of Lot N° 8 in Putney and Andrew & Caleb Grayham made a forcible Entry Upon his Said Possession — That your Petitioner to recover his said Possession and Punish the said Andrew and Caleb for their violating the Law of this State Proceeded before two Justices of the Peace agt. them for forcible Entry & Detainer and recovered a judgment as well for the Freemen as for him Self agt. them by the Verdict of a Jury of the

---

1. The Assembly journal contains no record of this action or of any action on the petition itself. There is, however, record of an act passed just after the petition was filed, which granted its prayer. See subjoined note. If the Assembly did refer the matter to the next session, it presumably changed its mind later.
2. For this act, see *Ms. Laws of Vt.*, I, 529.
3. For a petition to repeal this act, see p. 231, *post*.
4. For a similar petition to the same effect dated 6 Feb. '87, see p. 308, *post*.
5. For this act, see *Slade*, 500; and for the petition which occasioned it, see p. 119, *ante*.

Vicinity that the Said Andrew & Caleb appealed to the County Court of Windham County and your Petitioner after a full and fair Discussion of the cause again by the Verdict of a Jury recovered Judgment for the Possession of Said Lot & £9:2:1 costs of Suit —

That altho' your Petitioner was able and did Shew the com^e of the Legislature that the Said Andrew Grayham was not the most antient Possessor of Said Lot and that the said Caleb Grayham did not Pretend to have any Colour of right of Possession & that your Petitioner had at a Large Expence Purchased the Possession and improvements of Said Lot of the Person who has had the Peaceable Possession thereof Longer then this State has had Existence Yet the Ingenuity of the counsel Employed by the Grayhams induced the com^e to report in their favour — and the Legislature to take the very Extraordinary Step of vacating the Judgments so obtained by your Petitioner as also annulling a Judgment obtained agt the Said Andrew Grayham before the Existence of this State & contary to the Verdict of two Juries under oath confirming Andrew Grayham in the Possession of said Lot and Declareing that said act should be conclusive Evidence of the Legal Possession of Said Lot being in said Andrew Grayham —

Your Petitioner begs leave with all humility to Suggest that Said Act is Unconstitutional and therefore (if for no other reason) ought to be repealed

1st Because your Petitioner is without any compensation made therefor Deprived of his Property the Protection of which with that of the other members of the community is one of the principle reasons for Giving up certain natural rights and Entering into civil Society — and which is expressly and [Solemnly] Guarantied in the 9th article of the Bill of Rights —[1]

2nd Because it renders nugatory the 13th article of the same Diclaration of Rights which Declares that "in controversies respecting Property & in Suits betwen man & man the Parties have a right to a Tryal by Jury which ought to be held Sacred"[2]

3^d Because it assumes the Power assigned by the Constitution to the courts of Law, the Determination of a Particular Cause between Party & Party — <and here your Petitioner (if he may do it without offence) would observe in the words of the Great Judge Blackstone that "in all Tyranical govenment the Right both of making and of enforcing the Laws is Vested in one and the Same man or in one and the Same body of men & whenever these two Powers are United together there can be no Public Liberty" and in the words of the renowned Mr Lock who lays it down as the fundamental Law of all commonwealths "that the Legislative cannot assume to it self a Power to Rule by extemporary and arbitrary Decrees but is bound to Dispence Law and Justice and to Deside the rights of the subject by Promulgated Standing Laws and known Authorised Judges — And that men give up their natural independence to the Society with this *Trust* that they shall be govened by *known Laws* otherwise their Peace quiet and Property will be in the same uncertainty as in a State of nature>

4 Because this act being not a Temporary one was not agreeable to the 14th Sect. in the Frame of Government printed for the consideration of the People & this check appointed in the constitution agt hasty Determinations was totaly Disre-

---

1. This is a reference to the 9th Article as listed in the Constitution of 1777. See *G. and C.*, I, 94.

2. See *Ibid*, I, 95.

garded —[1]

Your Petitionir therfore both as a Person Greatly injured by the Passing the said Act and as a member of the community Prays the Honorable Legislature to repeal the said Act and he as in duty bound shall ever Pray —

October 3rd 1785   W[m] Sargeant

To the Sheriff of Windham County his Diputy or to Either of the Constables of Putney in Said County — Greeting —

In the Name and by the Authority of the Freemen of the State of Vermont you are required to notify Andrew and Caleb Grayham that they appear before the Honorable the General assembly (if they think fit) on the 18th day of this instant october at Windsor to Shew cause if any they have why the Prayer of the within Petition should not be granted — fail not and make Return. Dated at Putney October 3rd 1785 —

Noah Sabin Jun[r] Justice Peace

Putney October 3[d] 1785

Served the within by reading the same in the hearing of the within named Andrew Grayham

 attest David Davis Deputy Sheriff

Fees — 1/4

— & —

Petition of M[r] William Sergeant to git the Grayham act repealed filed Oct <22> 12th [1785?]

In Gen[l] Assembly Oct[r] 24th 1785 —

The above petition was dismissed on acc[t] of its not being filed as soon as the person cited was directed to appear.

 Attest Ros[l] Hopkins Clerk

— & —

A. J.: Read and dismissed, 24 Oct. '85, S. P. of Vt., III (III), 198.

FOR AUTHORITY TO AN ADMINISTRATOR TO GIVE DEEDS FOR LANDS PREVIOUSLY CONVEYED

xxii, 101

To the Hon[le] the General assembly of the State of Vermont, to be held <at Norwich> at Windsor by an adjournment on the first Thursday of Instant <June> October

The Pitition of John White, and Jabez Hawley, Both of Manchester in the County of Bennington and State aforesaid, Humbly Sheweth,

That Samuel Rose late of Manchester aforesaid Dec[d] did in his Lifetime Sell unto Jon[a] Wright 150 acres of Land, Lying in Manchester aforesaid, and to Isaac Peck 50 acres of Land in S[d] Manchester, (S[d] Tracts of Land Being part of the Governor Lot, So-Called) and took their Notes for the price of said Lands, and gave a bond,

---

1. See G. and C., I, 97-98.

Binding himself to give a Deed of Each of Said Tract of Land, on the S^d Wright, and Peck, paying up their afore Said Notes, Which not Being done in his Lifetime, But after his Death Samuel Rose Junr, Eldest Son, to the S^d Dec^t, (according to the Laws of the State of New york. under which Jurisdiction the Said Lands then lay) Became, Sole Heir, at Law, to all the Lands of his Dec^d father, and your Petitioners, having Before the formation of this State, purchased the afore Said Lands, of the Said Right and Peck, and thereby Enabled them to pay up the afore Said Notes, and the Said Samuel Rose Junr, as Sole Heir, at, Law, gave to your Pititioners Deeds of the S^d Lands, which in the State of Newyork would be Valued in Law, But your Pititioners are of opinion, that there is no Vility [validity] in their Deeds, according to the Laws of this State.

and that Joel Rose, of Said Manchester, has according to the Laws of this State, taken a Letter of Administration, on the Estate of the afore Said Samuel Rose Dec^d, and is Willing to do any thing in his Power to Confirm the title of your Pititioners Lands, and your Pititioners pray, that your honors would Make a Law, to Enable the afore Said Joel Rose, to give to your Honors Pititioners Deeds of the afore Said Lands, or Some other Way to Confirm your Pititioners in the Title of the afore Said Lands, as your Honors in your Wisdom Shall Judge Best. and your Pititioners, as in Duty Bound Shall Ever pray. —

John White

Manchester ⟨May⟩ October 3^d 1785

This Certifies that the Contents of the within Petition is true and that I am Willing to Confirm the Within Pititioners in the Title of their Lands Being Enabled thereto

Joel Rose ⎰ Adm^r on the Estate of
⎱ Saml Rose Dec^d

— & —

Petition of John White
filed Oct. 14. 1785
Entered
. . .*

— & —

A. J.: *Read and referred to a committee to join a committee from the Council, 14 Oct. '85, S. P. of Vt., III (III), 169; *report of committee recommending that petition be granted, read and accepted, and leave given to bring in a bill accordingly, 14 Oct. '85, Ibid, III (III), 172–173; bill read and accepted and sent to Council, 17 Oct. '85, Ibid, III (III), 183; bill, having been concurred in by Council, passed into law, 17 Oct. '85, Ibid, III (III), 184.1 C. J.: *Committee appointed to join Assembly committee, 14 Oct. '85, G. and C., III, 79; act read and concurred in 17 Oct. '85, Ibid, III, 82.

FOR DIVISION OF A TOWN INTO TWO SOCIETIES
xvii, 135

To the Honorable the Representatives of the Freemen of the State of Vermont in

---

1. For this act, see Ms. Laws of Vt., I, 504.

General Assembly Met —

The Petition of the Town of Dorset humbly sheweth that the Township being disadvantaged by a high and almost impassable Mountain Situate near the Middle of said Township by reason whereof the People inhabiting said Township, cannot without great Inconveniency meet and Enjoy the benefits, or transact such matters as are Necessary in Town or Society —

Therefore for the Mutual benefit of the People Inhabiting on Either side of Said Township, and for the laudable purposes of supporting and Enjoying a preched Gospel, Schools and other such benifits as flow from Civil Society we therefore pray that the said Town be divided into two different Societies: in the following Manner VIZ beginning at the Town line, at the Southwest Corner of a Lot of Land No 12 Second Division Joining the Main road at Manchester line, and running North 10 Degrees East to the Northwest Corner of a lot of Land No. 4 Second division, then running Easterly to the Height of Land, then running Easterly and Northerly on the Height of Land to Danby Line and your Petitioners shall ever pray, Dorset Octr 4th 1785

Cephas Kent Jr	Isaac Farwell	Jehiel Galpin
Moses Kent	Joseph Hobly	Joseph Sheldon
John Kent	Tim^y Brown	Charles Collins
John Manley Jur	Cephas Kent	Daniel Shaw
John Manley 3d	Thomas [Denten?]	Lidias Mapes
George Manley	John Farwell	Joshua Cousins Junr
Elijah B. Sill	Amos Feild	Samuel Soper
Titus Sikes Junr	Reuben Farnsworth	Jacob Cousins
Alexander Kent	Zadok Huggins	Samuel Barto
[Pecis?] Smith	John Manley	Ebenezer Baker
Ebenezer Moss	William Manley	Moses [Durphy?]
Joshua Cuzzins	Francis Barnam	Christopher Lake
Asahel Herman	Richard Duning	Reuben Rockwood
Dan Kent	Silvanus Sikes	Samuel [Gilberd?]
Abrahan Underhill	Israel Bostwick	John Mattison
Nathan Whealer	[Silas?] gray	John french
James Underhill	Gersham Martindale	Benjamin Mattison
John Shumway	John Gray	Stephen Martindail
Silas Holbrook	Isaac underhill	N^o of Signers 56

— & —

Dorset Pitition
entered
filed Oct 14, 1785
. . .*

— & —

A. J.: *Read and referred to a committee, 14 Oct. '85, S. P. of Vt., III (III), 172; *report of committee recommending that prayer be granted, read and accepted, and leave granted to bring in a bill accordingly, 15 Oct. '85, Ibid, III (III), 181–182; bill read and accepted and sent to Governor and Council, 18 Oct. '85, Ibid, III (III), 189; bill having been concurred in by Council, passed into law, 20 Oct. '85, Ibid, III (III), 196.1 C. J.: Act read and concurred in, 19 Oct. '85, G. and C., III, 84.

---

1. For this act, see Ms. Laws of Vt., I, 509.

FOR A LOTTERY TO BUILD A ROAD
xvii, 136, 137

To the Honourable the General Assembly for the State of Vermont —
The Petition of the Inhabitants of the Town of Stamford and Others
Humbly Sheweth
That your Petitioners having Since the Settlement of this Town untill this present
Period Laboured under the Disadvantage of having no Publick Road or Highway
by Which a Communication Can be had to the Other parts of this State Without
passing into the Commonwealth of Massachusetts being almost a Direct Contrary
Course And the Propriators of the Town being Involvd in a Contention with Re-
gard to the Two Charters of the Town Affords us but Small hopes of Relief from
that Quarter
    And the Inhabitants of the Town being in General under Low Circumstances,
unable to Bear the Cost of Opening and making Such Roads as is absolutely Necessary for the Advantage of the Publick in General and of this Town in Particular,
And as a Road from this Town (which will be about five miles) Leading into the
Main Road which Goes from Bennington to Wilmington in the most Convenient
Place Would Greatly Accommodate the Publick and be of Singular Advantage to
this Town —
    Your Petitioners therefore Humbly Pray that Liberty might be Granted them
to Raise the Sum of one Hundred Pounds by a Lottery [or sum other way as in
your wisdom shall Seem meet] to be Appropriated to the use of Laying out and
making Such a Road as is above set forth <under the Superintendance and Conduct
of Such men as the Town of Stamford Shall appoint> and your Petitioner as in
Duty bound Shall ever Pray

Stamford Oct[r] 4 1785	David Cook	⎰ Select
Signed for and in Behalf of ⎱	Resolved phitleplace	⎱ men
the Inhabitants of Stamford ⎰	Stephen Bates	

— & —

Stamford Petition for a Lottery
filed Oct[r] 14th 1785 —
. . .*
    Your Committee to whome was Referd the Petition of the Town of Stamford
State the following facts (Viz) there is at Present no Road or Highway from Said
Stamford to Pass into the other towns in this State with out Passing into the Commonwelth of the Massachusets State and it further appears that the land will admit
of a Road or Roads as Set forth in Said Petition.
    therefore Report as their oppinion that a tax of one peny on the acre by [be]
granted on all the lands in Said town of Stamford Public Rights Excepted, and the
Money appropriated to the Purpose mentioned in the Petition under the direction
of the Select men of Said town
    all which is Humbly Submitted.

Sam[el] Safford for Committee

— & —

A. J.: *Read and referred to a committee to join a committee of the Council,
14 Oct. '85, S. P. of Vt., III (III), 170; *report of committee recommending
tax of one penny an acre on land for making roads, read and accepted, and leave
given to bring in a bill accordingly, 24 Oct. '85, Ibid, III (III), 199; bill read

and sent to Governor and Council, 24 Oct. '85, *Ibid*, III (III), 200; bill, having been concurred in by Council, passed into law, 25 Oct. '85 *Ibid*, III (III), 203.[1] *C. J.*: *Committee appointed to join Assembly committee, 14 Oct. '85, *G. and C.*, III, 80;[2] act read and concurred in, 25 Oct. '85, *Ibid*, III, 90.

FOR RIGHT TO SELL REAL PROPERTY TO SETTLE AN ESTATE
xvii, 137, 138

To the Honorable General Assembly, Conven^d at Windsor on the Second Thursday of October 1785 —
The Petition of Zadock Averest [Everest] & Ezra Squire Administrators on the Estate of Odel Squire late of Ferrisburgh deceas^d humbly Sheweth
That whereas it appears by the records & Proceedings of the Judge of Probate for the County of Rutland, that the Personal Estate of the Said Odel Squire is insufficient to pay the Debts Due from said Estate by the Sum of one hundred & eleven Pounds Seventeen shillings and one penney —
therefore your Petitioners, pray the Honorable Assembly to ennable them to Sell so much of the real Estate of the said Odel Squire deceas^d as Shall be sufficient to discharge the Debts due from said Estate as aforesaid together with Part arising on said Sale
As your Petitioners in Duty bound Shall ever pray

Zadok Everest ⎫
Dated at Addison this fifth   ⎬ Administrators
Day of October 1785   Ezera Squier ⎭

Certificate to the Gen^{ll} Asemby
To the Honorable General Assembly of the State of Vermont.
This may certify that the Personal Estate of Odel Squier late of Ferrisburgh deceased, is insufficient to pay the Debts due from said [*estate*] by the Sum of one hundred and eleven pounds seventeen shillings and one penny
attest Elisha Clark Judge Prob.

Probate Office ⎫
Rutland District ⎬
June 9th 1785 ⎭

— & —

Zadock Everest, Petition —
Entered
filed Oc^t 14th 1785
. . .*

— & —

A. J.: *Read and prayer granted, and leave given to bring in a bill accordingly 14 Oct. '85, *S. P. of Vt.*, III (III), 173; bill read and accepted and sent to Governor and Council, 14 Oct. '85, *Ibid*, III (III), 173; bill, having been con-

---

1. For this act, see *Ms. Laws of Vt.*, I, 516.
2. The Council journal notes that Mr. Fletcher was appointed as a committee, while the entries on the manuscript petition for the appointment as well as for the committee report indicate that the person chosen was Mr. Safford.

curred in by Council, passed into law, 15 Oct. '85, *Ibid*, III (III), 174.¹ *C. J.*:
*Resolved that Council concur with Assembly in granting prayer and in giving leave to bring in a bill accordingly, 15 Oct. '85, *G. and C.*, III, 80; act received, read and concurred in, 15 Oct. '85, *Ibid*, III, 80.

FOR ESTABLISHMENT OF OLD TOWN LINES REGARDLESS OF NEW SURVEY²
xxii, 96

To the honorable general Assembly of Vermont —
The proprietors of the township of Rochester humbly shew —
That said township adjoins on the westward side of Bethel, and depends on it for its first boundary. —
That the late surveys made by order of the Surveyor-General have removed the lines of Bethel near one mile eastward and considerably southward of its heretofore known and established limits,³ by which means Rochester is likewise removed in the same manner to their great injury, in that it disconcerts the allotments of lands made in their township, obstructs their settlements and lays a foundation for endless suits at law and controversies with their neighbors — That a removal of the lines renders it uncertain where to find the township, and the proprietors cannot therefore go on to fulfil the conditions of the Charter in the midst of those confusions which arise from a removal of the lines —⁴
Your petitioners therefore humbly pray, that this honorable Assembly will be pleased to render the said late surveys null and void, and restore to us our former boundaries; so that we may go on with the settlement of our township agreeably to the requisitions in our charter —
And as in duty bound will ever pray &c —
Rochester 6ᵗʰ October, 1785 —

Dudley Chase   } Agent for the Proprietors of Rochester —

— & —

Petition of Rochester — Proprietors
filed Oct. 20. [1785?]

⟨and where as it apear that the Injury Sustaned as above was Ocationed by Reason of an [alteration?] of Norwich and Sharon Both N. Hampshire Grants [as?] apears by the New Survey and it apears to this asembly that the establishment of the Old

---

1. For this act, see *Ms. Laws of Vt.*, I, 503.
2. For a similar petition presented by the proprietors of Bethel at this session and considered along with this one, see next document. For a previous petition to the same effect from the proprietors of Rochester and the action taken thereon, see p. 116, *ante*.
3. For the legislation providing for these "new" surveys, see "An Act for the regulation and Establishment of Town Lines", passed 22 Oct. '82, and an act in addition thereto passed 29 Oct. '84 (*Ms. Laws of Vt.*, I, 350, 466).
4. For the charter of Rochester, see *S. P. of Vt.*, II (Vermont Charters), 170–171.

Lines which was run by order of this Assembly[1] before the first day of [Oct[r]] 1781 will Not Effect the New Survey in any of the Towns North or west of s[d] Towns of Bethel and Rochester only Such as adjoin s[d] Towns which Never laid any claim to said Disputed lands — therefore>[2]
. . .*

— & —

> *A. J.:* Read and referred to a committee, 20 Oct. '85, *S. P. of Vt.*, III (III), 195;[3] report of committee recommending that petition be granted, read and accepted, and leave given to bring in a bill accordingly, 27 Oct. '85, *Ibid*, III (III), 210; leave granted to bring in a bill agreeable to report of committee made last session, 23 Oct. '86, *Ibid*, III (III), 240; *bill read and not accepted, and petition dismissed, 26 Oct. '86, *Ibid*, III (III), 248.

FOR ESTABLISHMENT OF OLD TOWN LINES REGARDLESS OF NEW SURVEY[4]
xxii, 97

　　To the Honorable General Assembly of the State of Vermont — humbly shew —
The Proprietors of the township of Bethel in said State that your petitioners early after the establishment of this State Obtained a grant of said township and a Charter thereof[5] (being the first grants of lands made by the Legislature of the State) bounded as follows viz. Begining at a point Six miles and a half on a streight line north sixty one degrees west from the northwest-corner of Sharon thence south thirty three degrees west Six miles and sixty rods thence north sixty one degrees west Six miles thence north thirty three degrees East six miles and sixty rods thence south sixty one degrees East six miles to the point making the first bound. That your petitioners immediatly after the grant thereof took the measures provided by government for ascertaining the boundaries of their township and which they were then directed to as legal and proper, and laid out their land and roads accordingly and took measures for settlement, in doing all which they were at great expence — That they have paid taxes to goverment on all those lands contained within the limits as discribed by Charter — That in making the grant and Charter of Bethel great care was taken by Goverment that a proper extent of lands should remain for the township of Royalton and no more — Therefore when Royalton was some years after granted it was expressly bound south on Barnard east on

---

　　1. Presumably this order refers to the description of the town lines approved by the Assembly at the time of the grant and included at its request in the charter issued by the Governor and Council.
　　2. It is not certain exactly what this entry is. Apparently it was a portion of the bill which was brought in according to order and not accepted. See subjoined note.
　　3. For the membership of this committee, which was to join a committee from the Council, see *S. P. of Vt.*, III (III), 184. See also *G. and C.*, III, 83 for the appointment of the Council committee.
　　4. For a similar petition presented by the proprietors of Rochester at this session and considered along with this one, see previous document. For previous petitions to the same effect from the proprietors and inhabitants of Bethel, see pp. 108, 115, *ante*.
　　5. For the charter of Bethel, see *S. P. of Vt.*, II (Vermont Charters), 23–24.

Sharon, north on Tunbridge and west on Bethel and thereby Royalton and Bethel became joined side and side and both dependant on the s^d first boundary of Bethel viz six miles and a half from the northwest corner of Sharon —

The Legislature of this state have ever been duely careful that their grants should not interfere with any Newhampshire grant because those townships were already settled and which your petitioners therefore have been equaly studious to avoid in all their Surveys of said township — That your petitioners under those restrictions and limitations alloted the whole of said township as bounded by Charter and been at great expence thereon to fulfil the duties required by the Legislature in their grant thereof and have Settled nearly Seventy families in it. That your Petitioners feel themselves essentially injured and are aggrieved that when their boundaries have been thus once established, allotments of the whole township made conformably thereto, and such a number of families settled on those allotments, (exceeding in number those on most of the New Hampshire Grants) any measures should be taken to remove the boundaries of the township and of course disconcert the settlers. — This we find to be the opperation of a late act of the Legislature of this State for regulating the boundaries of townships[1] and which we therefore complain of as an insuportable grievance for the Surveyor appointed by the Surveyor-General in running the lines of Bethel hath not conformed to the boundaries prescribed in our Charter, and hath therefore commited egregious errors in crowding us southward near an hundred Rods on a Newhampshire grant the boundaries of which the Assembly of this state have covenanted to secure and maintain and likewise hath cut off near one mile of the westardly part of Said Bethel, through the whole extent of it from north to south which was covered by the boundaries in our Charter; by which errors we are deprived of a number of important settlements in the northerly part of Bethel and many appropriated lots in the westardly part, although they were not laid out so far west as our Charter gives us — Such a removal of boundaries throws us into great confusion and will lay a foundation for endless lawsuits among us and our neighbours — and the grievance is enhanced in that we are called on to pay the expence of those surveys, which opperate so greatly to our injury and are in a manner impracticable. —

For the foregoing consideration your petitioners most humbly pray that those surveys, made by order of the Surveyor General, may be set aside so far as they respect said township of Bethel, and that we may be secured in the peaceble possession of the land granted to us in our Charter, which we have the highest confidence the principles of Justice and humanity will influence this honorable Assembly to take effectual measures for, without any delay —

And as in duty bound shall ever pray

Bethel October 7th 1785

Dudley Chase ⎫ Committee for said
Joel Marsh ⎬ Proprietors

— & —

Petition of Proprietors of Bethel
filed Oct. 20. 1785
. . .*

— & —

1. See "An Act for the regulation and Establishment of Town Lines", passed 22 Oct. '82, and an act in addition thereto passed 29 Oct. '84 (*Ms. Laws of Vt.*, I, 350, 466).

A. J.: *Read and referred to a committee, 20 Oct. '85, *S. P. of Vt.*, III (III), 195;[1] *report of committee recommending that petition be granted, read and accepted, and leave given to bring in a bill accordingly, 27 Oct. '85, *Ibid*, III (III), 210; leave granted to bring in a bill agreeable to report of committee made last session, 23 Oct. '86, *Ibid*, III (III), 240; *bill read and not accepted, and petition dismissed, 26 Oct. '86, *Ibid*, III (III), 248.

FOR RIGHT TO SELL REAL PROPERTY TO SETTLE AN ESTATE
xvii, 139

To the Honorable the General Assembly of the State of Vermont to be holden at Winsor [Windsor] on the second Thursday of this Insᵗ Oct.

The Petition of James & Ebenezer Ambler Administrators of the Estate of John Ambler late of Brandon deceased: humbly sheweth that the personal Estate of the said deceased is insufficient to pay the debts from said Estate by the Sum of £56–17–10. L.M. Therefore pray Your Honors to Impower us the said James Ambler & Ebenezer Ambler to sell so much of the Real Estate of the said John Ambler deceased, as will pay the aforesaid sum of £ 56–17–10 L.M. together with the incidental charges arising on such Sale, as you in your wisdom shall direct, as we your Honors petitioners are in duty bound, shall ever pray

Tinmouth Oct. 8ᵗʰ 1785   James Ambler ⎱
                         ⎰ Administrators
                     Ebenʳ Ambler ⎰

Certificate from the Judge of Probates

To the Honᵇˡᵉ the General Assembly of the State of Vermont. —

This may certify that the Personal Estate of John Ambler late of Brandon in the Probate District of Rutland deceased, is insufficient to pay the Debts due from said Estate by the sum of Fifty six pounds Seventeen shillings & ten pence L.M.

                         pr   Elisha Clark Judge Prob.

Probate Office ⎱
Rutland District ⎰
Tinmouth Oct. 8ᵗʰ 1785 ⎰

— & —

James & Ebenezer Ambler's petition to the General Assembly
Entered
filed 14 ot. [October] 1785
. . .*

— & —

A. J.: *Read and prayer granted and leave given to bring in a bill accordingly, 14 Oct. '85, *S. P. of Vt.*, III (III), 171; bill read and accepted and sent to Governor and Council, 14 Oct. '85, *Ibid*, III (III), 171; bill, having been concurred in by Governor and Council, read and passed into law, 17 Oct. '85, *Ibid*, III (III), 184.[2] *C. J.*: *Resolved that Council concur with Assembly in granting prayer and in giving leave to bring in a bill accordingly, 14 Oct. '85, *G. and C.*, III, 80; act received, read and concurred in, 14 Oct. '85, *Ibid*, III, 80.

---

1. See p. 164, note 3.
2. For this act, see *Ms. Laws of Vt.*, I, 504.

FOR A TAX ON LAND TO BUILD ROADS AND BRIDGES
xvii, 140

State of Vermont —
   To the Honorable General Assembly, or House of Representatives in General
Assembly Met, at their October session in Windsor 1785 —
   The Petition of the Inhabitants of the Town of Cavendish in the County of
Windsor — Humbly sheweth — That whereas, we Petitioned the General
Assembly last year for a land Tax in the Town of Cavendish, & s^d Petition being
lost and the Tax not Granted,[1] to our Great misfortune & Dissapointment, we
now Repeat our Petition — Further shewing, That, your Petitioners have the
most of us lately settled in said Township, & do Labour under Great Difficulties
in Respect to the badness of the Roads, as there is so few Inhabitants in s^d Town,
makes it Exceeding Difficult to keep the Roads in good Repair, or to cut out those
that is highly Necessary to accommodate the Public as well as the Inhabitants of
said Town — Also, their being several streams the crossing of which in high water
or in Winter, is attended with the greatest Difficulties and Dangers — Especilly
that of Black River & Twenty mile stream — Also, their has of late, a Road been
looked out & partly cleared Leading from Chester through the south part of
Cavendish up Black River almost seven miles on the flatts, & thence almost a
straight course to Mr. Brookses in Ludlow; said Road crosses Black River once in
Cavendish & once in Ludlow — and is found by those of us who have been upon
it, to be well situated for making a good Road and will well accommodate for a
Country Road, it being a very Direct course from Rutland to the New Bridge in
Rockingham which is built over the Great River —[2] And Gentlemen — as your
Petitioners being unable of ourselves to Effect this Public Benefit as well as private
accommodations without assistance, therefore your Petitioners Humbly Pray, that
their may be a Tax of Two pence on an Acre Granted & laid on all the Taxable
Lands in the Town of Cavendish, for the purpose of building a Bridge over Black
River in said Town, as well as other Necessary Bridges & making & Repairing
Roads or otherwise, as your Honours in your great wisdom shall see fit to Relieve
your petitioners, so that we may be Enabled thereby to build s^d Bridges, to make &
Repair Roads that are absolutely Necessary for the good of the Public, the ad-
vantage of us the Inhabitants, & also, to promote the further settleing of the above
S^d Town, & other Towns who may be benefitted thereby — and your honest
Petitioners as in Duty bound Shall Ever pray — By order of the Town
                                                     Asa Wheeler Town Clerk
Cavendish October ye 8th 1785
                        — & —

Asa Wheeler town Clerk of Cavendish
Petition
Oct. 14th 1785 filed
Entered
A Petition from Cavendish

---

   1. This petition is not now among the *Ms. Vt. S. P.* For its presentation to the
Assembly 29 Oct. '84 and its reference to the next session, see *S. P. of Vt.*, III (III),
108, 111.
   2. Connecticut River.

. . . *

— & —

A. J.: *Read and referred to a committee to join a committee from the Council, 14 Oct. '85, *S. P. of Vt.*, III (III), 170; *report of committee recommending that prayer be granted, read and accepted, and leave given to bring in a bill accordingly, 18 Oct. '85, *Ibid*, III (III), 186; bill read, accepted and sent to Governor and Council, 20 Oct. '85, *Ibid*, III (III), 195; bill, having been concurred in by Council, passed into law, 24 Oct. '85, *Ibid*, III (III), 198.[1] *C. J.*: *Committee appointed to join Assembly committee, 14 Oct. '85, *G. and C.*, III, 79; act received, read and concurred in, 22 Oct. '85, *Ibid*, III, 88.

FOR DISCHARGE FROM NOTE GIVEN STATE FOR LAND GRANT FEES
xxii, 98

To the Honorable Representatives of the Freemen of the State of Vermont to meet in Gen[ll] Assembly at Windsor on the 13th day of Instant October

The Humble Pettition and Remonstrance of Reuben Rockwood of Dorset in the County of Benninton [Bennington] Humbly sheweth

that sometime in the year 1780: your petitioner being in possession of one Hundred acres of land, then suposed to be in the township of Brumley — and likewise had purchased 200 acres next adjoining the lot on which he then lived: but being apprehensive that the lands afors[d] ware realy scituate not in the township of Brumley afors[d] but in a tract then unapropreated: and after Granted by the Hono[le] Gen Assembly in the year 1780 to Cap[t] William Utley and associates: your petitioner did then send a prayer to the Hon[le] assembly that thay would Grant to your petitioner the afors[d] 300 acres of land Nevertheless the Honorable assemby Judging that it might in Effect answer the designs of your petitioner to put his name into the pittion of the s[d] Cap[t] Utly — and thareby he Obtained 300 acres in landgrove [Landgrove][2]: Subjected to a Granting fee of £11:0:0 for which sum Your pettitioner Gave his Note payable to the treasurer of the State of Vermont but could thareby Obtain but one Hundred acres only at or near the place whare his possesions ware — and the remaing part of said Right not being Saileable at present and Your pettitioner being poor and in low circumstance and having a family of Eleven to support: is unable to pay the afors[d] sum of £11:0:0 and therfore prays the Hon[bl] assembly that thay would pity his low Circumstances: and give him the afors[d] sum —

or otherwise that thay would take all the lands Granted to your Pettition as afor[d] Excepting one Hundred acres on which he has made Improvement and discharge him from the s[d] Note of £11:0:0 —

and Your pettitioner as in dute bound will Everpray

Dated Dorset October the 10th 1785   Reuben Rockwood

— & —

---

1. For this act, see *Ms. Laws of Vt.*, I, 511–512.
2. For the charter of Landgrove granted to William Utley and others, including Reuben Rockwood, see *S. P. of Vt.*, II (Vermont Charters), 122–123.

Reuben Rockwoods Petition
filed 14th Octr 1785 —
Entered
. . .*

— & —

A. J.: *Read and dismissed, 14 Oct. '85, S. P. of Vt., III (III), 172.

FOR AUTHENTICATION OF AN UNACKNOWLEDGED DEED
xxii, 99

To the Honorable the General Assembly of the State of Vermont to be Convened
at Windsor in sd State on the 13th Instant The Petition of Lucretia Houghton,
Widow of, and Administratrix upon the Estate of Edward Houghton late of Guilford
in sd State Deceased Humbly sheweth that the sd Edward Houghton purchased in
the year 1773 a tract of Land in sd Guilford of one Jonas Newton then living in
Guilford afsd that the sd Jonas Newton Did on the 16th of December 1773 sign
seal and deliver to the sd Edward Houghton a deed of sd land soon after Executing
sd deed the Grantor and one of the Witnesses Died and the other witness is moved
out of this State and is not to be found by your Petitioner. Therefore your Petitioner
Humbly prays your Honors to grant releif in the premises by Authenticating sd
deed in as full and Ample a manner as though the same had been Acknowledged
by the Grantor — And as in Duty Bound shall ever pray
Guilford October 10th 1785   Lucretia Houghton

— & —

Petition of Lucretia Houghton
filed Octr 17th 1785
Enterred
. . .*

— & —

A. J.: *Read and referred to a committee, 17 Oct. '85, S. P. of Vt., III (III),
185; *report of committee recommending that petition be granted, read and
accepted, and leave given to bring in a bill accordingly, 18 Oct. '85, Ibid, III
(III), 188; bill read and accepted and sent to Council, 19 Oct. '85, Ibid, III
(III), 191. C. J.: *Action of Assembly on report of committee concurred in,
20 Oct. '85, G. and C., III, 86; bill read and concurred in, 20 Oct. '85, Ibid,
III, 86.[1]

FOR RIGHT TO SELL REAL PROPERTY TO SETTLE AN ESTATE
xxii, 100

To the Honorabel the General Assembly of the State of vermont to be Convened
at winsor [Windsor] in Said State on the Second thirsday of october Instant: the

---

1. For this act, see Ms. Laws of Vt., I, 507–508.

Petetion of Asa Robinson of Dudley in the County of worcestor [Worcester] Humbly Sheweth that your Petetioner was appointed administrator By the Honer[ll] Judge of Probate for the Destrict of westminister [Westminster] in the State of vermont [Vermont] upon the Estate of one Joseph Chamberlain Late of Duglas [Douglas] in Said County of worcestor Decessed Said Chamberlain at the time of his Death was Seized of a Right of Land in the Town of townsend [Townshend] in the Said State of vermont which Land has bin apprised by Persons under oath and amounts to the Sum of Sixty one pounds the Said Decesseds Estate haveing bin administered upon in the County of worcestor and the whole of the Estate of the Decessed in Said County is found Insuffisunt to pay the Debts Charged against Said Estate to the amount of £10–8–2 which is Exclusive of all the Coust of Setteling Said Estate and allowances to the widow &c which Debts & Coust will amount to Near the Sum of fifty pounds your Petetioner therefore Humbly Prays that the Honerabel Assembly would Grant liberty to your Petetioner to Sell Said Right of Land under the Directtion of the s[d] Judge of Probate or So much of Said Lands as will Enabel him to pay the Debts and Coust of Setteling the Same and your Petitioner as in Duty bound shall Ever pray

Asa Robinson —

Putney october ye 10th 1785

this may Certify that I have Receved an attested accompt from the Rigestor of the Probate Courte in the County of worcestor In the Commonwelth of masusets [Massachusetts] bay that the whole of the Estate of the Said Joseph Chamberlain Decessed was Insufficant to pay the Debts Charged against Said Estate to the amount of £10–8–2 as Set fourth in the above Petition

attest   Noah Sabin — Judge of probate

— & —

Asa Robinson[s] Petition
Entered
. . .*

— & —

A. J.: *Read and granted, and leave given to bring in a bill accordingly, 18 Oct. '85, S. P. of Vt., III (III), 190; bill read and accepted and sent to Council, 20 Oct. '85, Ibid, III (III), 195; bill, having been concurred in by Council, passed into law, 20 Oct. '85, Ibid, III (III), 196.[1] C. J.: *Action of Assembly in granting petition concurred in, 20 Oct. '85, G. and C., III, 86; act read and concurred in, 20 Oct. '85, G. and C., III, 86.

FOR RIGHT TO SELL REAL PROPERTY TO SETTLE AN ESTATE
xvii, 141

To the Honourabel General assemble of the State of Vermont to be holden at Winsor [Windsor] in S[d] State on the Second thursday of instant October — the petition of Mary Hyde of poultny [Poultney] administrator to the Estate of

---

1. For this act, see Ms. Laws of Vt., I, 507.

Timothy Hyde Late of Poultney decest Humble Sheweth that the parsonal Estate
of the Said decest is insurfisant by the sum of twenty two pounds three shillins one
peney L Mo to pay the debts due from sd Estate therefor prays your Hounours to
impower Mary Hyde administrator to said Estate to sell so much of the Real
Estate of the said Timothy Hyde as will pay the aforesaid sum of £ 22–3–1 L Mo
togather with the Necessary Cost arising on said suit as your Honours in your
Wisdom Shall derect all Which is Humble Submited as your pretitioner in duty
Bound Shall Ever pray dated at poultney this 10th day of October [A D?] 1785
                                                        Mary Hyde adminstrata

        Certificate from the Court of Probate
To the Honorable General [*Assembly*] of the State of Vermont.
This may certify that the Claims of the Several Creditors to the Estate of Timothy
Hyde late of Poultney deceased (Represented Insolvent) allowed by Commissioners
Surmounts the personal Estate of the said deceased the sum of — £22–3–1
Probate Office ⎫   Attest Elisha Clark Judge Prob.
Rutland District ⎬
May 27. 1785. — ⎭

                            — & —

Wid° Mary Hyde's Petition
filed Octr 20th 1785 —
Entered
. . .*

                            — & —

        A. J.: *Read and a bill granting prayer read and accepted and sent to Governor
        and Council, 20 Oct. '85, *S. P. of Vt.*, III (III), 194; bill, having been concurred
        in by Council, passed into law 20 Oct. '85, *Ibid*, III (III), 196.[1] *C. J.:* *Resolved
        that Council concur with Assembly in granting prayer and in giving leave to
        bring in a bill accordingly, 20 Oct. '85, *G. and C.*, III, 86; act received, read
        and concurred, 20 Oct. '85, *Ibid*, III, 86.

                    _____

                FOR ABATEMENT OF TAXES
                        xvii, 142

        To the Honorable the General Assembly to be convened at Windsor on the
2^d Thursday of Octr Instant —
        The petition of the Subscribers Selectmen of the town of Stamford humbly
Sheweth
        That they were doomed[2] in the year 1784 one hundred & seventy four pounds
more than the true list of said Town —[3] and that the Treasurers warrants have
been Issued to collect the taxes of 3^d & 4^d on the pound laid last Session your
Petitioners therefore Pray that So much of Said taxes may be relinquished as is laid
in said £174 and your Petitioners as in duty bound shall ever pray

_____
    1. For this act, see *Ms. Laws of Vt.*, I, 508–509.
    2. For the definition of "Doomed", see p. 66*n*, *ante*.
    3. For this doomage, see *S. P. of Vt.*, III (III), 103.

Oct. 10th 1785

Oliver Smith ⎫
Benj^a Tupper ⎬ Selectmen
Amos Mead ⎭

— & —

Select-Men of Stamford's petition
filed Octr 18th 1785
Entered

These certify that the town of Stamford was doomed in the year 1784 nine hundred
pounds —
Octr 19th 1785 — attest Ros^{ll} Hopkins Clerk of Assembly
. . .*

Winsor Octr 19th 1785 To the Honble the General assembly now sitting Your
Committee to Whom was refer^d The within petition beg leave to report that they
find the facts stated therein to be Just and True and from the Evidence Exhibited
are of opinion that the prayer of the petition ought to be granted.

Jonathan Robinson for Committee
— & —

> A. J.: *Read and referred to a committee, 19 Oct. '85, S. P. of Vt., III (III),
> 190; *report of committee read and accepted, 19 Oct. '85, Ibid, III (III), 193;
> resolved that Treasurer be directed to credit town all taxes on the sum of £174
> on the list of 1784, 19 Oct. '85, Ibid, III (III), 193.

FOR RELIEF OF A TAX COLLECTOR PAID IN COUNTERFEIT BILLS
xvii, 142

To the Honorable the General Assembly of the State of Vermont to be convened
at Windsor in s^d state on the 13th of October Instant
The Petition of John Morse of New Fane in the County and State aforesaid —
Humbly sheweth That your Petitioner was first Constable in and for the s^d Town
of New Fane in the year 1781 That your Petitioner Received for State Taxes ten
pounds L.M ⟨of this State⟩ in bills emited by this State that are sd to be counterfit
That your Petitioner complied With the Act of Assembly Granting releif to such
Constable in the like Casses[1] That by means of a mistake made by the justice who
made out the Certificate required by law your Petitioner can have no releif in the
Premises and that their is now in the Sherriffs hands an Extant [Extent] Issued by
the Treasurer of this State against your petitioner Therefore your Petitioner Humbly
prays your honor to grant releif in the premises by ordering the Treasurer to
reserve s^d money and your petitioner as in duty bound shall ever pray

John Morse

New Fane October 10th 1785

— & —

Petition of John Morse

---

1. The act referred to here was "An Act respecting counterfeit money" passed
15 Oct. '82 (Ms. Laws of Vt., I, 303). This act set up a procedure whereby collectors of
taxes might be credited by the Treasurer of the state with any such money which they
might have received for taxes.

Entered
filed Oct. 15. 1785
. . .*
To the Honourable the General Assembly now Convend your Comm^tte to whom
was refered the Petition of John Morse Beg leave to report that they find the facts
set up in s^d Petition true and that the prayer of the petition in their oppinion ought
to be granted all which is Humbly Submited
Windsor Octr 19th 1785   p^r   Sam^el Knight for Committee

— & —

> A. J.: *Read and referred to a committee, 15 Oct. '85, S. P. of Vt., III (III),
> 174; *report of committee read and accepted, 19 Oct. '85, Ibid, III (III), 193;
> resolved that Treasurer be directed to receive £10 in counterfeit bills from
> petitioner, 19 Oct. '85, Ibid, III (III), 193.

FOR A TAX ON LAND TO BUILD A MEETING HOUSE
xvii, 143

To the Honorable General Assembly of the State of Vermont to be holden at
Windsor on the Second Thursday of October Instant; The Petition of the Inhabitants of the Town of Pomfret Humbly Sheweth; that being Legally formed
into an Eclesastical Society and being Legally Assembled together in November
Last, took into Consideration the Necessity of Regularly Setting up Establishing
and Supporting the Publick Worship of God in the Said Society and Did then agree
to Call to Settle with us the Revd Mr Elisha Hutchinson to be our Minister; and
thro' the Blessing of Heaven we Obtain'd the Ordination and Settlement of the
Said Revd Mr Hutchinson to the Pastoral Care and Charge of this Church and People
in the December Following: Through whose wise and Faithfull Instructions and
Admonitions the S^d Society Enjoy great Peace and Tranquility, and Seam Daily by
the Blessing of God to Increace in Love to God and one another. — and that for
the Settlement of our Worthy Pastor your Honours Petitioners Lay^d a tax upon
ourselves of one Shilling & three pence on the pound on the Common List of Poles
and Ratable Estate of the Said Society. And at the Same Meeting in November
Last your Honours Petitioners Did Mutually agree that it was Necessary to Erect
a Meeting house in Some Convenient Place near the Center of the Said town and
also Lay a tax of four pence on the pound to be Appli'd to that purpose. —
And being Now Legally Assembled together on this Eleventh Day of October A.D.
1785 your Honours Petitioners find it Necessary to Raise another tax of five pence
on the pound for the Support of our Worthy Pastor; And the aforesaid tax of four
pence on the pound when Collected will fall Vastly Short of a Sufficiency to Defray
the Expence of a work of Such Importance, And the Members of Said Society
are now so Numerous that there is no Dwelling house in the Town Large Enough,
Conveniently to Contain them, in time of Publick Worship, and We your Honours
Petitioners Beg leave further to Observe that a Great part of the Inhabitants of
this Town have Only Purchas'd Convenient Farms in S^d Town and are not Original
Proprietors and that the Greater part of the Land, in S^d Town are the Property of
men of Fortune, and that by the Expence of the Late War and other Necessary
Charges, and also by the Expence of Making Roads Building Bridges and keeping

the Same in Repair the Streangth of the Inhabitants of this town is Greatly Exhosted, and the price of the Lands of the Said Landholders Greatly Encreased for which they have not Laboured, and by Building a Meeting house the Value of the S^d Lands Will be Still more Increased. — and we your Honours Petitioners being Involved in the Above Mentioned Burdens which Render it very Dificult for your Honours Petitioners to Carry a Building of so great importance into Execution without Greatly Damaging the Interest of your Petitioners, we therefore Pray your Honours to take our Case into your wise Consideration and Grant for our Help a Land tax on all the Lands of the Said Town of Pomfret of three pence on the Acre. (Publick Lands Excepted) to be Applied for the Express Purpose of assisting the Said Society in [Building a] Meeting house in the Most Convenient place in Said Town of Pomfret or Otherways Grant Releif as your Honours in your Great Wisdom Shall think fit. — And we your Honours Petitioners as in Duty Bound Shal ever Pray. — Dated at Pomfret this 11th Day of October A.D. 1785

Sign'd by order of town Meeting by   Bar^{tw} Durkee { Moderator

— & —

Petition of the Town of Pomphret [Pomfret]
Entered
filed Oct. 18. 1785
. . .*
To the Honb^{le} G^l Assembly now sitting —
Your Comt^{ee} to whom was refered the within petition — Beg Leave to Report That the facts set up in s^d petition appear to be true, that in the opinion of Your Comt^{ee} the prayer be Granted. so far as to Grant liberty to tax two pence on the Acre on all Lands belonging to Persons of semilar Religious sentiments with the petitioners —
all which is humbly submitted. by

Gideon Olin for Committee

— & —

A. J.: *Read and referred to a committee, 18 Oct. '85, S. P. of Vt., III (III), 189; *report of committee read and accepted and leave given to bring in a bill accordingly, 19 Oct. '85, Ibid, III (III), 193; bill to authorize the inhabitants of Pomfret to raise a tax for the purpose of building a house of public worship, read and accepted and sent to Council, 25 Oct. '85, Ibid, III (III), 201; bill, having been concurred in by Council, passed into law, 26 Oct. '85, Ibid, III (III), 204.[1] C. J.: Act received, read and approved, 25 Oct. '85, G. and C., III, 91.

FOR RIGHT TO SELL REAL PROPERTY TO SETTLE AN ESTATE
xvii, 144, 145

To the Honorable the General Assembly of the State of Vermont to be holden at

---

1. For this act, see Ms. Laws of Vt., I, 518–519. In accordance with the recommendations of the committee the act exempted from the tax all persons who could certify that they were not "of semilar Religious sentiments with the petitioners —"

Winsor [Windsor] on the second Thursday of Oct. 1785
The Petition of Samuel Mattocks & David Spafford Administrators to the Estate
of Capt Daniel Edgerton late of Tinmouth deceased. Humbly sheweth that the
personal Estate of the said deceased is insufficient by the sum of Nine hundred &
ninety eight pounds Lawful money to pay the debts due from said estate. Therefore pray your Honors to impower David Spafford one of the said Administrators
to sell so much of the real Estate of the said Daniel Edgerton as will pay the aforesaid sum of £998 L. Money for the purpose of paying the debts due from said
Estate together with the necessary Cost arising on said Sale, as you in your Wisdom
Shall direct, which we your Honors petitioners are in duty bound shall ever pray —
Tinmouth 11th Oct. 1785.

Sam^el Mattocks ⎫
David Spafford ⎬ Administrators

Certificate from the Judge of Probate
To the Honorable the General Assembly of the State of Vermont. —
This may Certify that the personal Estate of Capt Daniel Edgerton late of Tinmouth Deceased is insufficient to pay the debts due from said Estate by the Sum
of Nine hundred & ninety eight pounds Lawful money.

Elisha Clark Judge Prob.

Probate office Tinmouth Oct. 11th 1785

— & —

The Petition of Sam^ll Mattocks & David Spafford Adm^s to the Estate of Daniel
Edgerton
Entered
Recd on file oct. 14. 1785
N. Chipman [. . .]

. . .*

— & —

A. J.: *Read and prayer granted, and leave given to bring in a bill accordingly,
14 Oct. '85, S. P. of Vt., III (III), 168–169; bill read and accepted and sent to
Governor and Council, 14 Oct. '85, Ibid, III (III), 169; bill, having been concurred in by Council, passed into law, 14 Oct. '85, Ibid, III (III), 171.[1] C. J.:
*Resolved that Council concur with Assembly in granting prayer and in
directing that bill be brought in accordingly, 14 Oct. '85, G. and C., III, 79;
act read and concurred in, 14 Oct. '85, Ibid, III, 79.[2]

FOR RELIEF OF A TAX COLLECTOR
xvii, 146

To the Honourable General Assembly of the State of Vermont to be Convened at
Windsor on the second Thursday of this Instant October
The Petition of Asa Putnam of Brattleboroug in the County of Windham

---

1. For this act, see Ms. Laws of Vt., I, 508.
2. For another petition in connection with this estate, see p. 299, post.

Humbly Sheweth. That your Petitioner was Colector of State Taxes in Brattle-borough in the year 1783. That your Petitioner received a Warrant from the Treasurer of this State requiring him to Colect the Sum of One Hundred and eighty pounds on the lists of the Polls and rateable Estate for the year. 1781. — That your Petitionar has been necessary put to great Cost and trouble in Colecting that, and other State Taxes. — That your Petitioner did Loose about Seventy pounds of said money after Colected which your Petitionar really belives to have been Stolen from him —

Your Petitionar therefore Humbly Prays this Honourable Assembly to take the Premises under Consideration and abate to your Petitionar the Said Sum of money So Loost as afore said or grant to your Petitionar Such other releaf as your Honours in your Wisdom Shall think fit and your Petitionar as in Duty bound shall ever pray

Brattlebro October ye 11:1785.   Asa Putnam

Windham County ss. Brattleborough October ye 11th 1785

Then Asa Putnam Subscriber to the forgoing Petition personally appeared and made Solom oath that he did Loose a Sum of States money as near as he can assatain Seventy pounds of the States Taxes which he really belives to have been Stolen from him at a time when he was endeavoring to Colect said Taxes —

before me   Saml Knight Justice of ye Peace

— & —

Asa Putnams Petition —
Entered
filed Oct. 15. 1785
...*

— & —

A. J.: *Read and dismissed, 15 Oct. '85, S. P. of Vt., III (III), 173.

FOR RIGHT TO SELL REAL PROPERTY TO SETTLE AN ESTATE
xvii, 147

To the Honerabel the Generel Assembly of the State of Vermont to be Conveened at Winsor [Windsor] in Said State on the Second thursday of October Instant the Petition of Joseph Blanchard of Jamecai [Jamaica] in Said State Humbly Sheweth that your Petitioner was appointed an administrator on the Estate of Amos Skinar Late of Said Jamecai Decessd and your Petitioner finds himself unabel to Settel the Same by Reason of the Debts Chageed against Said Estate Being more than the amount of the Personal Estate By the Sume of thirty five pounds as may appear By the Certificate from the Judge of Probate hereto annexed your Petitioner therefore Humbly prays that the Honerabel Assembly would Grant Liberty for the Sale of So much of the Real Estate as may Ennabel him to Discharge the Said Debts and the Coust of Setteling the Estate and your Petitioner as in Duty bound Shall Ever pray

Joseph Blanchard

This may Certify that the personal Estate of Amos Skiner Late of Jamaica Decessed is Insuffisant to pay the Debts Charged against Said Estate to the amount of thirty

five pounds as appears by the accompte upon file in the Probate offis in the Destrict of Westminster

attest Noah Sabin Judge of probat

Dated at Putney October yᵉ 12ᵗʰ 1785

— & —

The Petition of Joseph Blachard [sic] to ye Assembly
. . .*
Entered

— & —

> A. J.: *Read and granted, and leave given to bring in a bill accordingly, 19 Oct. '85, S. P. of Vt., III (III), 190–191; bill entitled "an act empowering the administrator to the estate of Samuel Skinner, late of Jamaica, deceased to sell part of the real estate of said Samuel Skinner", read, accepted, and sent to Council, 24 Oct. '85, Ibid, III (III), 198; bill, having been concurred in by Council, passed into law, 24 Oct. '85, Ibid, III (III), 198.¹ C. J.: Act received, read and concurred in, 24 Oct. '85, G. and C., III, 89.

FOR A TAX ON LAND TO BUILD ROADS AND BRIDGES
xvii, 149

To the Honᵇˡᵉ the Gen¹ Assembly of the Freemen of the State of Vermont, — Now Sitting at Windsor —

The Petition of John Hawkins in behalf of the Inhabitants of the Town of Bridgewater in the County of Windsor, Humbly Sheweth — that the Situation & Circumstances of the Inhabitants of the Said Town of Bridgewater, is such, that it Renders it almost impossible for them to make Necessary Roads in and through Said Town, for the accommodation of said Inhabitants and the Public at Large, and as the Inhabitants are but few in number and Settled in the different Parts of the Town — And as there are three large Streams running through said Town, that must have Several Bridges over them, and Nearly the Extent of fifteen Miles New Road to accommodate the Present Inhabitants — beside One Road that is Newly marked out from Woodstock to Rutland, which Shortens the Travel from sᵈ Woodstock and the ajacient Towns to Rutland and Otter Creek &c Nearly Forty miles, said Road above mentioned as it is now Marked Runs through the said Town of Bridgewater from East to West and will be of great use & benefit to the Public, as well as greatly advance the Value of the Lands of the Proprietors of said Bridgewater, which are the greatest Part of them Non-Residence living in the Neighbouring States — Therefore your Petitioner in behalf of said Inhabitants, Humbly Prays that your Honours would take their Case into your Wise Consideration, and Grant them relief by Granting a Tax of Two Pence on the Acre on all lands in the said Town of Bridgewater (Except Lands Granted for Public, Pious & Charitable Uses) for the Purposes aforesaid — And your Petitioners as in duty bound

---

1. For this act, see Ms. Laws of Vt., I, 513–514. There seems no reason to doubt that Amos Skiner and Samuel Skinner were one and the same person. The act itself notes that Joseph Blanchard was the Administrator of Samuel Skinner's estate. Possibly an error in the name as given in the petition was discovered before the bill was drawn.

Shall ever Pray —   John Hawkins ⎫ in behalf of the
Bridgewater Octr 15th 1785 —   ⎬ Inhabitants of Bridgewater —
                                                          ⎭

— & —

Petition —
Capt Jno Hawkins for the Inhabitants of Bridgewater —
Entered
filed Oct. 20 1785.
. . .*

— & —

A. J.: *Read and referred to a committee, 20 Oct. '85, S. P. of Vt., III (III), 194;[1] *report of committee recommending that tax of 1 ½d per acre be granted, read and accepted and leave given to bring in a bill accordingly, 26 Oct. '85, Ibid, III (III), 203; bill read and sent to Governor and Council, 26 Oct. '85, Ibid, III (III), 204; bill, having been concurred in by Council, passed into law, 27 Oct. '85, Ibid, III (III), 209.[2] C. J.: *Committee appointed to join Assembly committee, 21 Oct. '85, G. and C., III, 87; act received, read and approved, 26 Oct. '85, Ibid, III, 92.

FOR PARDON FOR ADHERENCE TO NEW YORK
xvii, 150

To the Honourable the General Assembly of the State of Vermont Conven'd at Windsor
     The Petition of Daniel Ashcraft of Guilford in the County of Windham — Humbly Sheweth
     That your Petitioner hath for a Long time (without any Just Cause) been opposed to the Government of this State
     That your Petitioner hath done many unjustifiable acts against the authority of this State in endeavoring to support the government of the State of New York — by means whereof your Petitioner hath Justly Incur'd the Indignation of this state; and almost ruined himself and Familey[3]
     Your Petitioner therefore truly Sensible of his Error hoping that he shall be enabled to Lead a better Life for the future, and, hereby solomly promising that he never will any more Rebel against the Government of this State —
     Humbly prays that this Honourable Assembly will Graciously take the Premises under their wise Consideration and grant to your Petitioner a free pardon of all the Offences he hath Committed against the Government of this State and your Petitioner as in Duty bound Shall ever pray
Guilford October ye 15. 1785 —

                                                          Daniel Ashcraft

— & —

The Petition of Daniel Ashcraft
Entered

---

     1. The manuscript petition correctly records the fact that this committee was to join a committee from the council.
     2. For this act, see Ms. Laws of Vt., I, 531-532.
     3. For note of Ashcraft's adherence to New York, see B. H. Hall, op. cit., p. 510n.

filed Oct 19 1785
. . .*
Windsor Oct. 20. 1785
To the Hon^rb Genr^l Assembly now Sitting
Your Committee to whom was refered the within Petition beg leave to report that
they find the within Named Daniel Ashcraft was formerly in opposition to the
government of the State in faver of New York — that he is likely to make a good
citizen of this State in Case of a pardon they therefore recomend to the Assembly
to grant the Said Ashcraft a pardon of all offences committed against this government in the aforesaid opposition on consideration of his taking the Oath of Allegiance to this State before some proper authority before the first of March next
all which is Humbly Submitted

Sam^el Fletcher for Committee

— & —

A. J.: *Read and referred to a committee to join a committee from the Council,
19 Oct. '85, S. P. of Vt., III (III), 190; *report of committee read and accepted,
and leave given to bring in a bill accordingly, 20 Oct. '85, Ibid, III (III), 195;
bill read and accepted and sent to Council, 20 Oct. '85, Ibid, III (III), 196;
bill, having been concurred in by Council, read and passed into law, 24 Oct.
'85, Ibid, III (III), 198.[1] C. J.: *Committee appointed to join Assembly committee, 19 Oct. '85, G. and C., III, 85; act received, read and concurred in,
22 Oct. '85, Ibid, III, 88.

FOR ABATEMENT OF TAXES
xvii, 151

To the Honble the General Assembly of the State of Vermont Convened at
Windsor
The Petition of Ebenezer Richmond Colector for the Town of Barnard Humbly
Sheweth that in Compliance unto Warrants Received from his Honour Ira Allin
Esqr Treasurer I have made the Rates for the three Penny and four Penny Taxes
which was Granted by the Assembly at their Sesion at Norwich in June 1785 on
the Grand List for [1784?][2] and do find that said List is not Rightly Added and
that it is but Eighteen hundred fifty and Six Pounds ten Shillings and by the above
mentioned Warrants the Sum total of sd List is Returned £1948 –o–o as by Certificate from Said Treas^r doth appear
Your Petitioner therefore Prays your Honours in your Wisdom to take into Consideration the Case of your Petitioner and Grant Abatement of Such a part of
those Taxes as are ogmented by the above said mistake
Your Petitioner as in Duty bound Shall Ever Pray

Ebenezer Richmond Colector

Barnard October 17th 1785

— & —

Eben^r Richmond's Petition —

---

1. For this act, see Ms. Laws of Vt., I, 513.
2. See "An Act for the purpose of Levying the Taxes therein contained" passed
16 June '85 (Ms. Laws of Vt., I, 479–480).

filed Octr 19th 1785
Entered
. . .*

Windsor Octr the 20th 1785

To the Hon^{le} the Genl Assembly now Seting your Committee to whom was referd the within Petition bege Leve to report, that the facts therein Set fourth are just & true and are of oppinion that the prair of the Petition ought to be granted and that the Treasurer be directed to C^r the petitioner one pound Seven Shillings and one peney half peney hard money, and one pound sixteen Shillings & Eight pence States money all which is humbly Submited

Jacob Burton for Committee

In Genl Assembly Octr 21st 1785

The above report read & accepted and ordered that the petitioners have leave to bring in a bill accordingly

attest Ros Hopkins [Cl?]

— & —

A. J.: *Read and referred to a committee, 19 Oct. '85, S. P. of Vt., III (III), 193; report read and accepted, and Treasurer directed to credit Barnard accordingly, 21 Oct. '85, Ibid, III (III), 196.

FOR THE LOCATION OF THE STATE UNIVERSITY
xvii, 152

To the Honorable General Assembly of the State of Vermont, now sitting at Windsor —
The memorial of Elijah Paine of Windsor humbly sheweth, that your Memorialist, influenced by a regard for the People, whom you represent, & sensible of the great advantages, which would arise to them from the early culture of the human mind, & a proper dissemination of literature in general thro the State, proposes to give as an encouragement to literature for the purpose of founding an University in the State, two thousand pounds lawful Money, on the conditions hereinafter mentioned, to be expended within two years in erecting a building proper for the reception of Students, under the direction of your Memorialist, with the advice & consent of any person or persons, whom your Honorable Body or any future General Assembly shall be pleased to appoint for that purpose — The conditions on which your Memorialist begs leave to give the said two thousand pounds are as follows (viz) that your Honorable Body shall be pleased to direct that a College or University be founded in such a part of Williamstown in the County of Orange & State of Vermont, as your Memorialist, with the advice of a Committee from your Honorable Body, shall think most proper for such an Institution — And that your Honorable body shall be pleased to endow said College or University with all the lands or estate, which have heretofore been given, granted or reserved within the State of Vermont for the purpose of founding or supporting a College or University — And that also Your Honorable Body shall be pleased to incorporate said College or University & endow it with all the powers & privileges, which the University in Cambridge in the Commonwealth of Massachusetts at present possesses — Your Memorialist further begs leave to observe that said Williamstown is very nearly in the center of the State — that it is pleasantly situated on the

road which leads from Windsor to Onion River, about forty five miles from the mouth of said River — that the roads from Connecticut River to said Williamstown will be equally good with the roads on Connecticut River, & that the roads leading from said Williamstown to Lake Champlain will, from information, be but little inferior in point of goodness — that the soil in said Williamstown & the Adjacent Country is so very fertile, that it will be capable of supporting a larger number of Inhabitants than will usually be found in the same extent of Country — that the water is good & the air very salubrious — from all which considerations, ⟨more particularly as he has endeavored to serve his country herein, your Memorialist⟩ the Subscriber flatters himself that his Memorial will meet with the approbation of your Honorable Body.

Elijah Paine

Octr 17. 1785 —

— & —

Mr Paines Petition
Entered
filed 14 Oct. 1785
. . .*

— & —

> A. J.: *Read and referred to a committee to join a committee from the Council, 17 Oct. '85, S. P. of Vt., III (III), 184; *report of committee recommending that a committee be appointed to view Williamstown and make report to next session of their opinion of a proper place for erecting a college, read and accepted and a committee appointed, 27 Oct. '85, Ibid, III (III), 206–207; committee directed to meet at Royalton second Tuesday of June next, 27 Oct. '85, Ibid, III (III), 211; petition, "which has been refered up",[1] referred along with a similar petition and other papers to a committee to join a committee from the Council, 15 Oct. '87, Ibid, III (IV), 16; report of committee recommending that it would be inexpedient to fix at present the location of the state university and that the resources for it are insufficient and that the matter be postponed to a future legislature, read and accepted, 20 Oct. '87, Ibid, III (IV), 37. Rep. of Com.: Committee appointed 15 Oct. '87 reports under date of 17 Oct. '87 to the effect given in Assembly journal for 20 Oct. '87, S. P. of Vt., IV, 38–39. C. J.: *Committee appointed to join Assembly committee, 17 Oct. '85, G. and C., III, 82–83; committee appointed to join Assembly committee, 15 Oct. '87, Ibid, III, 148(3).[2]

FOR COMPENSATION FOR WAR SERVICES AND LOSSES
xvii, 153

To the Honble Genl Assembly of the Freemen of the State of Vermont now Sitting

---

1. Presumably this clause indicates that the committee appointed 27 Oct. '85 referred the matter back to the Assembly.

2. Although only the petition of Cornelius Lynde and not that of Elijah Paine is mentioned in the Council journal, the identity of the Assembly committee makes it evident that Paine's petition was also under consideration here by the Council. Through a clerical error the action on Lynde's petition is recorded three times. The third entry should be taken as the correct one.

at Windsor —

The Petition of Moses Warren of Cornish in the State of New Hampshire, Humbly Sheweth[1]— That your Petitioner engaged in the Public service in said State of Vermont Under the Command of Col. Benjamin Wait, in the year 1781 — and on the fifteenth day of October 1781 — Your Petitioner being a Serjeant was ordered out with a Party toward the Lake and was Unhappily Wounded and made Prisoner by a Party of the Enemy from Canada, who barbarously Treated him and Striped him and Carried him to Montreal and then from thence to Quebeck and Confined him in Close Goal for the Space of six Month, and remaind a Prisoner from the time he was Captivated until about the fifteenth of June 1782 — being eight Months before he was Exchanged and returned home, for which said Eight months Captivity your Petitioners Wages amounted to Nineteen pounds four shillings and your Petitioners Gun and accoutrement Blanket and Compass, Taken from him when Captivated were appraised at four Pounds Seven Shillings, The Wages and Gun & Accoutrements &C amounting to Twenty three Pounds Eleven Shillings — for which Time your Petitioner was a prisoner, and for his Gun &C your Petitioner has never received anything but Hardship and Cruel Treatment from the Enemy — and your Petitioner Humbly requests your Honers to take his Case into your Wise Consideration and Grant him the above mentioned Sum, with the Interest — as in duty bound shall ever Pray —

Windsor 17th October 1785 —   Moses Warrin

— & —

The Petition of Moses Warren
filed Octr 18th 1785 —
. . .*
Entered

— & —

A. J.: *Read and referred to a committee, 18 Oct. '85, S. P. of Vt., III (III), 188; *report of committee recommending that £28-11-6 be allowed petitioner, read and accepted, 19 Oct. '85, Ibid, III (III), 191; resolved that Treasurer be directed to make payment accordingly, 19 Oct. '85, Ibid, III (III), 191.

FOR RELIEF OF A TAX COLLECTOR PAID IN COUNTERFEIT BILLS
xvii, 154

To the Honerabel the General Assembly of the State of Vermont Now Sitting at winsor [Windsor] in Said State the Petition of Samuel Wheat of Putney in Said State Humbly Sheweth that your Petitioner was a Constabel in Said Town for the year 1782 and in Colecting Said Tax he had the misfortune to take one Treasurers Note of this States Securetys of the Sume of Twenty pounds and Paid the Same to Elkanah Day Esqr Sherief of the County of windham and the Same was Paid to the Sherief in July 1784 and was Not [. . .] as bad by your Petitioner at the time of taking Nor by the Sherief at the time of Passing it to him Notwithstanding which the Said Bill has bin Returned to your Petitioner No Longer ago than the

---

1. For a similar petition drawn up by Moses Warren 13 June '85 and filed but not presented to the Assembly, see p. 136, ante, including note on his military service.

Last week and it appears that Said bill is bad Being altered from two pounds to Twenty and as the Said Note on bill has bin So long out of the hands of your Petitioner he must be obliged to Louse the Same Except the Honerabel Assembly Should See fit to Grant him Relief in the Premises which he flatters himself they will Readyly do when they Reflect upon the misurabel Sittuation that the Constabels are under who have to Collect the taxes in these Degenarate times when So Many Evil minded Persons are Endevoring to Cheat Not only private Persons but the Publick Likewise your Petitioner theirfore Humbly beggs the Honerabel Assembly would take the Same under their wise Consideration and Grant Such Relief as in their wisdom Shall See fit and your Petitioner as in Duty bound Shall ever pray   Samuel Wheat
Dated at Putney October ye 17th 1785

— & —

The Petition of Samuel Wheat filed Octr 20th 1785
Entered
. . .*

— & —

A. J.: *Read and dismissed, 20 Oct. '85, S. P. of Vt., III (III), 195.

FOR THE NULLIFICATION OF A RECORD OF A DEED
xxii, 105, 109

To the Honble Genl Assembly of the State of Vermont now sitting in Windsor. the Petition of Elijah West of said Windsor, sheweth
    That the said Elijah in the Year of our Lord seventeen hundred & seventy, five purchased the Farm on which he now lives of one Watts Hubbard of said Windsor — And being apprehensive that a certain person then connected with your Petitioner in trade had a Dishonest design of over-reaching him and taking from him the said farm by fraud your Petitioner, with the Advice of his Neighbours, procured a Deed of said Farm from the said Watts Hubbard to Benajah, David, Elisha & Mary West, Children of the said Elijah, and lodged the same in the Town Clerks office who thro' mistake recorded the same, and thereby the title vested in the said grantees who were then & still are ignorant of the said Conveyance — and from whom the said Elijah never rec^d any consideration And the said Grantees are now in different parts of the Country (if living) so that 'tis impossible for the said Elijah to obtain from them a Re-conveyance — and he is without remedy without the assistance of your Honours —
    Your Petitioner would farther represent, that he is now in the decline of Life & has a family of small Children that must be left unprovided, or dependent on the uncertain Generosity of those who by mear accidental opperation of Law & not for valuable Consideration, or according to the true Intent & meaning of the said Conveyance, have gotten possession of their Birth right —
    Wherefore your Petitioner prays that a Committee may be appointed to examine into the Nature of your Petitioners request — and that such relief may be granted in the Premises as is according to Equity & good Conscience, and as in Duty bound shall pray

Windsor 18th Oct. 1785   Elijah West

— & —

Elijah Wests' Petition
filed Octr 20^t 1785 —
Entered —
. . .*

— & —

A. J.: *Read and referred to a committee to join a committee from the Council,
20 Oct. '85, *S. P. of Vt.*, III (III), 194; *report of committee recommending
that record of deed be declared null and void, read and accepted, and leave
given to bring in a bill accordingly, 27 Oct. '85, *Ibid*, III (III), 205–206; bill
read and accepted and sent to Council, 27 Oct. '85, *Ibid*, III (III), 208; bill,
having been concurred in by Council, passed into law, 27 Oct. '85, *Ibid*, III
(III), 211.¹ *C. J.:* *Committee appointed to join Assembly committee, 20 Oct.
'85, *G. and C.*, III, 86; *Committee appointed in lieu of previous one, 26 Oct.
'85, *Ibid*, III, 92; act read and concurred in, 27 Oct. '85, *Ibid*, III, 94.

FOR ABATEMENT OF TAXES
xvii, 155

To the honerable Representatives of the freemen of the State of Vermont in General
Assembly Conveand at Windsor. Gentlemen the petition of the Selectmen of
Rockingham for the year 1780 humbly Sheweth that by Reason of there being no
grand Lis^t Colected in said Rockingham in said year before the Seting of assembly
— therefore the General Assembly did at their Sessions at Bennington in October
in said year Doom² Said Rockingham to be in Valuation the Sum of four thousand
and one hundred pounds upon the grand Lis^t and levied a provition tax thereon
accordingly —³ but when said grand Lis^t was Colected by the Listers of Said
Rockingham for said year it was but the Sum of three thousand three hundred
thirty & three pounds — but the Comissary General makes his full Demands upon
said Rockingham agreable to the Doomage of the Assembly we therefore pray
your honours to take up the matter: & take of [off] the Doomage which is in
Valuation the Sum of Seven hundred & Sixty Seven pounds for which your humble
pititioners in Duty bound Shall Ever pray
Dated at Rockingham October 18th — 1785
£ 4100

  3333   Elijah Knight ⎱ Selectmen
  ----   John Roundy ⎰
   767

— & —

pitition of the Selectmen of Rockingham

---

1. For this act, see *Ms. Laws of Vt.*, I, 527–528.
2. For a definition of "Doom", see p. 66*n, ante*.
3. No record of this doomage has been found in the Assembly journal. For the
provision tax, see *Slade*, 407–411.

(Entered)
. . .*

— & —

A. J.: *Read and referred to a committee, 24 Oct. '85, S. P. of Vt., III (III), 199; *report of committee recommending that prayer be granted, read and accepted, and leave given to bring in a bill accordingly, 24 Oct. '85, Ibid, III (III), 200; resolved that commissary general be directed to credit Rockingham accordingly, 24 Oct. '85, Ibid, III (III), 200.

FOR COMPENSATION FOR WAR SERVICES
xvii, 158

To the Honnourable the General Assembly of the State of Vermont Now Convened —
    The Petition of Asa Pratt & abel Rice of Gilford [Guilford] in said State Humbly Sheweth. that whereas your Petitioners Did in the year 1777 Inlist into the Ranging business in Capt. George aldriges Company in Mag[r] Benj[n] Whittcomb Corps in which your Petitioners Served four years[1] and whereas a Petition that was Exhibited to this assembly in the year [1780?] by your Petitioners & was Sett aside by the Influence of Colo: Thomas Lee Setting fourth that your Petitioners were Likely to Receive their wages from the State of Newhampshire[2] which your Petitioners have Never Received as the State of Newhampshire Refused to pay any Soldier not Inlisted into their Battallions & belonging out of the State.
    Your Petitioners therefore Humbly Prays that your Hon[rs] wold take the Cause of your Petitioners into your wise Consideration & Grant Some Releafe to your Petitioners as in your Great wisdom you Shall think Proper and your Petitioners as in Duty Bound Shall Ever Pray
Windsor Octo[r] 20th 1785

Abel Rice
Asa Pratt

— & —

Abel Rice & Asa Pratts Petition filed Oct[r] 21st 1785 —
. . .*
Entered

— & —

A. J.: *Read and dismissed, 21 Oct. '85, S. P. of Vt., III (III), 196.[3]

---

1. For this service, see Vt. Rev. Rolls, p. 663.
2. In 1781 (not 1780) Abel Rice and Asa Pratt and others presented two presumably similar petitions (not now among the Ms. Vt. S. P.) to the Assembly. For their presentation and dismissal, see S. P. of Vt., III (I), 188, 218 (2).
3. For other petitions covering the same service from Abel Rice, Asa Pratt and others, or their agent, see pp. 224, 272, 291, 394, post.

FOR A TAX ON LAND TO BUILD ROADS AND BRIDGES
xvii, 159

To the Honorable the General Assembly now Siting at Windsor in the State of Vermont The Petition of Hosea Miller of Dummerston alias Fullum in the County of Windham and State aforesaid —
Humbly sheweth that whereas their is a part of s^d Dummerston Alias Fullum which lieth West of West River and their is a Road leading from Brattleborough to New Fane and the Adjacent Towns West of s^d River which the Inhabitants of s^d Dummerston are Obliged to repair That there are several Bridges very much needed in order to make s^d road Convenient for the publick That almost the whole of S^d land West of s^d River is uncultivated and is Owned by persons who neglect to assist in repairing s^d road and not being Inhabitants of this State cannot be compeled thereto Unless your Honors grant releif in the premises Your Petitioner Therefore Humbly prays your Honours would grant a Tax of two pence p^r acres on all the land lying West of West river in s^d Dummerston Alias Fullum for the purpose of repairing s^d road and building Bridges in s^d road where it is necessary and your Petitioner as in Duty bound shall ever pray

Hosea Miller

Winsor Octr 21st 1785

— & —

Hosea Miller's Petition
Filed 23^d Oct^r [1785]
. . .*
Entered

— & —

A. J.: *Read and dismissed, 24 Oct. '85, S. P. of Vt., III, (III), 199.

FOR NATURALIZATION[1]
xvii, 160

To the Honble the Genl Assembly of the State of Vermont now sitting at Windsor in the County of Windsor.
The petition of Sol^n Willard humbly sheweth —
That your petitioner has a large landed property in the State of Vermont and feels for the independance and future prosperity of the said State as fully as any subject of the same — and being desirous of commencing a more firm connection with the said growing republic, humbly requests the Honble Legislature to pass an act of denization to naturalize your petitioner and make him a freeman and intitled to all the privileges of a natural born subject of the State of Vermont under such conditions as shall seem just, and your petitioner as in duty bound shall ever pray.

---

1. Ordinarily foreigners were naturalized automatically after one year's residence and without the passage of any special legislation (Constitution of 1777, Chap. II, Sec. XXXVIII: G. and C., I, 102). However, in this case the person was not a resident of the state.

Dated at Windsor this 21st day of October Anno Domini 1785

Sol^n Willard

— & —

Solomon Willard's Petition
Filed Octo. 24. 1785
Entered
...*

Sec^y of State's Office ⎱
Montpelier June 6. 1844 ⎰
Above & within is a true copy of the original petition & readings thereon

F. F. Merrill

Dep^y Sec^y State

— & —

A. J.: *Read and referred to a committee, 24 Oct. '85, *S. P. of Vt.*, III (III), 198; *report of committee recommending that prayer be granted, read and accepted, and leave given to bring in a bill accordingly, 25 Oct. '85, *Ibid*, III (III), 201; bill read and accepted and sent to Council, 26 Oct. '85, *Ibid*, III, (III), 205.[1]

FOR RIGHT TO SELL REAL PROPERTY TO SETTLE AN ESTATE
xvii, 162, 163

To the hon^e the General Assembly of the State of Vermont convend at Windsor on the second thursday of October 1785

The Petition of Paul Spooner & Jerusha Hough, Administrators on the Estate of Jedediah Fay late of Windsor deceas'd humbly sheweth

That whereas it appears by the Record & proceedings of the Judge of Probate for the District of Windsor that the Personal Estate of the S^d deceas'd is insufficient to pay the Debts due from s^d Estate by the sum of fifty two Pound eight Shillings

therefore Your Petitioners pray Your Honors to enable them to sell so much of the real Estate of the S^d deceas'd as shall be sufficient to discharge the Debts due from S^d Estate as afores^d together with the Costs arising on s'd sale

And Your Petitioners as in duty bound will ever Pray
dated at Windsor this 22^d
Day of October 1785

Paul Spooner ⎱ Administrators
Jerusha Hough ⎰

To the Honnorable General Assembly of the State of Vermont —

This may Certify that the Clames of the Several Creditors to the Estate of Doc^t Jedediah Fay Late of Windsor Deceased Represented Insolvent, allowed by the Commissioners Surmounts the Personal Estate of the said Deceased the Sum of £ 52 – 8 – 0

Probate Office
Windsor District
Octo^r 22^d 1785

attest Eben^r Curtis Judge Prob.

---

1. Although there is no record of the final passage of this act by the Assembly, it did become law. For its text, see *Ms. Laws of Vt.*, I, 519 or *G. and C.*, III, 385.

— & —

Gov. Spooner's & Jerusha Hough's petition Administrators
filed Octr 22^d 1785 —
. . .*
Entered

In Council Octr 22^d 1785
Read, & concurred with ye Gen. Assembly in Granting the Prayer of this Petition
attest Thos. Tolman
— & —

> A. J.: *Read and granted, 22 Oct. '85, S. P. of Vt., III (III), 198; bill read and
> accepted and sent to Council, 22 Oct. '85, Ibid, III (III), 198. C. J.: Act re-
> ceived, read and concurred in, 22 Oct. '85, G. and C., III, 88.[1]

FOR RIGHT TO SELL REAL PROPERTY TO SETTLE AN ESTATE
xvii, 166; xxxviii, 145

To the Honorable the General Assembly of the State of Vermont —
The Petition of Samuel Williams Administrator of the Estate of Eleazer Davis
late of Rutland deceased humbly sheweth: that the personal estate of the said
deceased is insufficient by the Sum of ⟨Eighty four pounds Eighteen Shillings &
eleven pence⟩ ninety two pounds & 3 pence L.M. to pay the Debts due from said
Estate Therefore prays your Honors to pass an Act impowering him the said
Samuel Williams to Sell so much of the Real Estate of the said Eleazer Davis decs^d
as will raise the aforesaid sum of £ 92–0–3 L.M. for the purpose of paying the
Debts due from said Estate together with the necessary Cost arising on such sale
under such restrictions as you in your Wisdom may think fit, which your Honors
Petitioner as in duty bound shall ever pray
Rutland Feb. 20th 1786   Sam^el Williams

   Certificate from the Judge Probate
To the Honorable the General Assembly of the State of Vermont.
This may Certify that the Personal Estate of Eleazer Davis late of Rutland Deceased
is insufficient to pay the Debts due from said Estate by the sum of Ninety two
pounds & three pence lawful Money.
Pr Elisha Clark Jude Prob.

— & —

Sam^el Williams Petition to the Gen. Assembly
Filed 23^d Octr 1786
. . .*
— & —

> A. J.: *Read and granted and leave given to bring in a bill accordingly, 23 Oct.
> '86, S. P. of Vt., III (III), 241; bill read and accepted, and sent to Council, 23
> Oct. '86, Ibid, III (III), 241. C. J.: Act read and approved,24 Oct. '86, G. and
> C., III, 112.[2]

---

1. For this act, see Ms. Laws of Vt., I, 514.
2. For this act, see Ms. Laws of Vt., I, 547.

FOR REFORM OF JUDICIAL PROCEDURE AND THE CURRENCY[1]
xvii, 169

To the Honourable General Assembly of the State of Vermont to be Convened at Rutland on the second thirsday of October next the Remonstrance and Petition of the freemen of the town of Rutland Humbly Sheweth that at the formation of the Constatution of this State we felt ourselves pleased in Prospect of haveing Laws that Should make us happy in the free and unmolested injoyment of our lives Libertys and property the Laws being founded on so Good a frain [frame] of Government we ware Ready to Expect that the cruel hand of oprestion could not be lade upon us nor Reach us in that Soft Retreat that we supposed we had made under the Protection of so Good a Constatution yet to our Greate Mortification we find that the loade of Laws that have been made by our former Legislaturs however well designed by them yet as they are understod and executed among us we find ourselves under Greate oppression and the Crys of those that are oppresed are continully heard among us which is the Cause of our now Looking up to you as our Political Fathers for Redress fearmly Relying on the Ready disposion of the Honourable Leguslature of this State that they will with Candor attend to our Grevinces and Give us all that Redress that they Can according to Constatution

And one Greate Source of our Comptant [complaint?] is the Present very Expensive and unjust mode of proceedure in Civile proceses at Law that the Leguslatur Should make Such Laws as to oblidge individuals to make Good their Contracts one with another is what we look upon to be Intirely Right and we hope that this Commonwelth may ever have Such Laws as may Serve every man in his property but when Laws Either through inadvertance or Design invests any body of men with Power to harrise [harass] the Community by forceing the payment of Unacssary [unnecessary?] Costs it doth appear to us that there is a falt some were [somewhere] which ought to be Redresed that this in fact is the Case we bege Liberty to Remonstrate to your Honours in the following perticulars

1st The Laws as they now stand doth admite of attornys harrising the People without being under any sort of Restrant and many of the Good people of this State are made to Suffer by them it is well known to be the Common practice of the Attornys to Procure an assortment of blanks and have them signed by the quantity by some justice of the peace the next step is to procure an Equil number of notes and accounts and they will issue their writs Emediately and let the Sums be ever so small it matters not and in order to increse costs they will put those writs into some Deputy Sheriffs hand and prehaps in some Extreem parts of the County by which means the Costs generally Exceed the Debt by the time it gits into an Execution then the Estate of the Debtor is posted for sail and bid off by the attornys sheriffs or some of their Creturs for little or nothing to the value of the thing sold and still in many instances the Debt Remains unpaid again it is plain that the attornys do prevent the Dispatch of Busness in our Courts by Running into the intrecaces of Law intimedating witnesses and indevoring to invaladat their Evidence and by these means blinding the jury so that in many Cases they make it more Deficult for a Court or Jury to Detarmin the Cause under their consideration than it was before they had said a word upon it and all this is done at the expense

---

1. For a brief discussion of the conditions in Vermont and other states which occasioned this petition, see W. H. Crockett, *Vermont: The Green Mountain State*, vol. II (New York, 1921), pp. 407–421. See also *G. and C.*, III, 357–380. For similar petitions presented at this time, see pp. 216, 225, 232, 238, 244, 248, 262, *post*.

of a large sum given them in fee by the Partys Consurned by these means the
Honest farmar and others are greatly Distresed and their property undjustly
Extorted from them furthermore it is manifist that they do all that they can to
prevent mens spaking in their own Cause before the Courts by intemadating them
and Casting Some Sort of Slur on them even tho they may be men of the best
Carictors and with Sorrow we must say the Courts we fear do not detect them as
they ought[.] now according to the present mode of proceeding in our Courts and
as the Law is understod and Executed among us it is good for that man that has a
just demand upon his naighbor and ought to have Redress by the Laws of the
State to let it drop and never try to git his Due for it will Cost so much to ingage
an attorney that unless the matter in Demand is very large the attorney Runs away
with it before he gets it of his neighbor

2^{ly} The Laws as they are now will admit of a number of Depety Sheriffs which
prove Burdensom to the Good people of this State for that writs are put into their
hands to serve in any part of the Countys that Doth inhance the Cost in many
instances four Dubble to what it would if the Constables that live in the town
were [where] the writ was served had served the Same it is so profitable a Buisness
to be a Depety Sheriff that many do seek to Git the office and having Got it it is
ushel [usual] for them to wate round the attornys office to fill their pockets with
writs and having Got them they draw four pence p^r mile upon every writ they
have for every mile they Ride[1] and the more writs they have the Better then they
live upon the spoils of their fellow subjects and people feel by this means the Cruel
hand of oppression

3^{ly} As the Laws are now our Justice Courts are only become a Costly Round about
way to bring every little petty action into our County Courts Justices Courts
insted of being an advantague to the public in Civil actions is only a means of
making Costs to no purpose for as our Laws are now every little petty action
between men can be appealed up to the County Court from the Judgment of the
Justice so that by that means there is but a very few actions that is Entered at a
justices court but the Cost will amount to twice as much as the Debt when the
Execution comes out so that it naturally brings oppresion upon the good people
of this State[2]

4^{ly} as our Laws are now when a Note of hand issued that is paid up by a Book
account yet it can not be plead in offset unless the account be liquidated which is
not often the Case and judgment is oblidged to be given in favour of the plaintiff
when he has got his pay and the Defendant must sue his account in order to git his
due which causeth the cost of two actions which if the Laws were not as they be
it is Likely there would be none again if one man Sues another to ballance Book
accounts it is often the man that is sued will not produce two account in court for
ballance but suffors judgment to go aganst him and then will turn about and sue
the plaintiff and Git judgment aganst him and Dubble Cost is created by that
means —

Now these accumulated grevences under which we have long laboured Causes
so Greate unesiness among the freemen of the town of Rutland Especially at this
day when money is so scarse that it can not be got even by those who have Greate
plenty of produce and much propety in their hands for they can not convert it

---

1. See "An Act for the regulation of Fees", passed October, 1785 (*Slade*, 477-482).
2. For the law against which this complaint was made, see "An Act defining and
limiting the Powers of the several Courts within this state," passed in June, 1782 (*Slade*,
450-454).

into money to pay their Debts and as the Law is now men do take the advantague of one another and do mischiefe one to another under the Santion of Law now Law we Conseave was never designed for a scourg to the Honest and industerus and when it dos become so it is high time to look out for Redress that so dispotism and injustice may be Stopt We therefore the freemen of the town of Rutland do humbly Petition the Honourable Legislature of the State of Vermont that you would take these our Grevinses under your wise Consideration and see if you can not agreable to our Constatution Enect the following Laws or somthing Like them Viz:

1st That there be but one attorney to each court whos Sole Province shall be to make a proper arrangment of all the civil Causes to be tried by the Courts for which service let his fees be stated and he laid under sollom Restricktion not to take a privit fee or Reward from any man to bias him in his cause

2ly that the office of Deputy Sheriff be anielated except were [where] the sheriff by sickness or any other way may be disenabled to discharge his duty in his office and that a sheriff would not be alowed to serve a justices writ and that the con-stables of Each town serve all Justices writs within their Respective towns and also any writs to be tried before the County Courts where the Defendent lives within their Respective towns

3ly that Justices Courts should be Courts of Equity to determin Causes according to Evidence and not as Courts of Record and that provision be made where the partys desire it that a small jury may be sommoned into the assistance of the justice and let smaller matters be finally determined there that so Justice may not be delayed nor Costs inhanced agreable to Exo: [Exodus] 18 26: The hard Causes they brought unto Moses but every small matter they judged themselves and now with Regard to those Small matters we do not find any direction for an appeal to Moses but they were desided without the trouble and Cost of caring [carrying] of it to him and if that was a good Law then why not now if it was practised upon

4ly That all fair accounts that may be alowed as good by the court be alowed as an offset to notes tho they may not be Liquidated and also that if a man is sued to ballance book accounts that if he Refuseth or Neglects to produse his account for ballance that he shall be foreclosed by Law for ever giting his accounts that so unnesesary Law suts [suits] may be prevented

5ly your Petitioners pray the Honourable Legislature that in their wisdom they would provide Some Medium of trade by making a Bank of paper Currincy upon some Substancial Baces and fix it that it may be a tendery on all Executions at least or Else to make a tender Act wereby Cattle Grain horses &c Shall satisfy executions that So men may be inabled to pay their Debts with such propety as they are possesed of and not to be obliged to pay that which they have not nor can not git in this Extreem time of the Sccarcity of Speshee and finally we pray the Honourable Legislature to Remember that Claus in the Constatution that when ever an office thru increase of fees or otherwise becomes so profitable as to ocation many to apply for it the profits ought to be lessoned by the Legislature and see if there is not two Greate fees Given to Some in Civil office and lesson the same that so the Common people may not be burdened beyond what is Right and that the fees or Reward of the Petty jury which are now so scanty[1] may be some way inlarged that they may not be so burdoned and that there may be a more proper equallety among the good freemen of this State now then as a free people who

---

1. See "An Act for the regulation of Fees", passed October, 1785 (Slade, 477-482).

desire that peace and harmonny may ever abound in this Commonwealth and that
the Laws of this State may be so calculated as to prevent so much unnesesary costs
and that Justice may be more spedily done and that there may not be so much
Room for men to hurt themselves and one another from corrupt motives and Idol
and designing men may be disheartened from Expecting to get their Living out of
other mens Labours by making use of our Laws as they have done for years back
and then they will be oblidged to take up some other method (and we hope [it
will be some Good] and honest calling) to git a living in the world and by that
means become wholsom and usefull members of Society with these views and with
an ardant desire that Righteous and just Laws may ever be in force and duly Executed we lay this our Remonstrance and Petition at your feet hoping and Expecting
you will take our grevinces under your wise Consideration and in your greate
wisdom do that which may be a proper Redress and we as in duty bound shall ever
pray

Rutland Septbr 5th AD 1786 ⟨at the⟩
Voted that the above Petition Be preferd to the General Assembly at their Next
Session the Vote was Unanimous
2nd that Deacon Willm Robards & Benjn Whipple Esq be Agents to prefer the
Above Petition to the Assembly

Attest   Daniel Squier Const

— & —

Petition of freeman of Rutland
No 6

— & —

A. J.: Read along with several other petitions and referred with them to a
committee, 18 Oct. '86, S. P. of Vt., III (III), 227; report of committee on
"petitions of grievance" read and nine of its articles accepted, 27 Oct. '86,
Ibid, III (III), 250–251; committee appointed to bring in a bill accordingly,
27 Oct. '86, Ibid, III (III), 251; committee appointed to prepare a bill agreeable to six articles of previous report, 27 Oct. '86, Ibid, III (III), 253. Rep. of
Com.: Committee recommends ten articles as basis of legislation for redress of
grievances, 26 Oct. '86, S. P. of Vt., IV, 220–221. C. J.: Committee appointed
to join Assembly committee, 19 Oct. '86, G. and C., III, 109.[1]

---

1. The Assembly journal and the report of committee is obscure and confusing
with respect to the action taken on the "Petitions of grievance." Immediately after nine
articles of the report were accepted, the Assembly voted down separately both the emission of paper money and a general tender act (S. P. of Vt., III (III), 251). On the other
hand, the Assembly provided for a vote by the freemen on these and related questions
by resolution passed 31 Oct. '86 (G. and C., III, 365–366). This vote likewise resulted
in the defeat of paper money and a general tender act (S. P. of Vt., III (III), 284–285).
    However, it is clear that these petitions did produce some alterations in the laws
during this session. See "An Act to make such articles a tender upon execution, to the
inhabitants of either of the United States, as are, by their respective laws, a tender upon
execution," "An Act defining and limiting the jurisdiction of Justice Courts within this
State, and directing the proceedings therein", and "An Act to compel the fulfillment of
contracts according to the intent of the parties", all passed in October, 1786 (Slade,
504–505, 506–508, 508–509). Furthermore, in the February-March session of 1787 the
Assembly passed "An Act to make certain articles of personal property a tender on
Execution in cases therein mentioned" (Statutes of the State of Vermont, passed by the Legis-

FOR A TAX ON LAND TO BUILD ROADS
xvii, 170

To the Honorable General Assembly to Convean at Rutland in October 1786

The Petition of the Inhabitants of the Town of Rupert humbly sheweth that your Petitioners from the mountaneous Situation of the Town in which they live and from the number of large Roads of Travel leading through said Town, which require uncommon Expence to keep in repair they are rendered unable to Defray the necessary Expence of repairing said Roads ‹and Building a Meeting House› and other necessary Public Expence

and as a large share of the landed property not taxable by Law in said Town is owned by Persons not yet Inhabitants in said town who are greatly Benefited by this Public Expence in the rise of their Lands

they therefore Request this Honorable House to enable them to levy a tax of two pence per Acre on all the landed property in said Town for the Purpous of Repairing Roads ‹and building a Meeting house› as afors^d as your Petitioners in duty bound Shall ever Pray —

Dated at Rupert this fifth day of Sep^{tr} 1786 —

Sam^{ll} Leavitt	Selectmen
Wm Hopkins	in behalf of
Enoch Eastmon	Said town

— & —

the Petition of the Selectmen of the town of Rupert
Filed 16th Octr 86
. . .*

To the honorable the General Assembly now Sitting Your Committee to whom was refer'd the within Petition beg leave to Report that it is their opinion that the Town of Rupert have Liberty to Levy a Tax on the Lands in said Town public Lands Excepted of one penny p^r acre for the purpose of Repairing Roads & making bridges —

M Lyon for Comtt^e

— & —

A. J.: *Read as "praying for a land tax for building meeting houses and repairing roads" and referred to a committee, 16 Oct. '86, S. P. of Vt., III (III), 224–225; *report of committee read and accepted, and leave given to bring in a bill accordingly, 17 Oct. '86, Ibid, III (III), 227; bill read and accepted and sent to Council, 20 Oct. '86, Ibid, III (III), 234; bill returned from Council with amendments, which were read and agreed to, and bill passed into law, 21 Oct. '86, Ibid, III (III), 237.[1] C. J.: Act read and approved, 21 Oct. '86, G. and C., III, 110.

---

lature in February and March 1787. [Windsor: 1787], pp. 153–154). This legislation may also be taken as a consequence of similar petitions presented at that session. For one of these, see p. 279, post.

1. For this act, see Ms. Laws of Vt., I, 541.

FOR A TAX ON LAND TO BUILD ROADS AND BRIDGES
xvii, 171

To the Honble the General Assembly of the State of Vermont to convene at Rutland on the 2^d Thursday in Octr next. —
To His Excellency Thomas Chittenden Esquire Captain General and Commander in Chief in and over the State of Vermont to the Honourable the Council and house of Representatives In General Assembly met —
The Petition of the Inhabitants of the Town of Tomlinson —
We your Petitioners having Taken into Consideration the many Inconveniences we Labour under by Reasons of our Late Settlement of [Emigration to] this Town Do in Particular find it to be Very Diffecult to make and maintain Roads through Said Town by Reason of bad Hills as well as Wet Valeys — and also a number of Considerable Streams of Water which are Exceeding Rappid and Very Diffecult to Support Bridges upon at many times of the year — We also find that the Greatest Part of Said Town is owned by Nonresident Gen^t whose Lands are made better Daily by the Improvement of our own and they bear no Part of the Publick Burden —
We therefore your Petitioners Do Humbly Pray that your Excelency and Honnours will take these matters under your wise Consideration and Impower your Petitioners to Tax all the Lands in Said Town (Publick Lands Excepted) two Pence on Each Acre for the Purpose of building Bridges and making Roads through Said Town and also Impower your Petitioners to Collect the Same & in Such a Limited time as your Exelency and Honnours Shall in your wisdom think Proper and as in Duty Bound we Shall Ever Pray —
Dated at Thomlinson September 5th 1786
By a Vote of the Town —

Stephen Hayward ⎱
Charles Perkins ⎬ Selectmen
Moses Gray   ⎰

— & —

Petition of Selectmen of Tomlinson
Filed 18th Octr 86
No. 11
Refered to Com^te —
(Accepted)

To the Honorobell Gen Assembly now Sitting Your Comity to whome was referd the Within Potition Fax [facts?] being Stated the declaration being Soported Bege leve to report as follows that a Penny tax be lade on Each acor Land in Sd Towne Publick rights Exsepted

Elisha Marsh for Comity

— & —

A. J.: Read and referred to a committee, 17 Oct. '86, S. P. of Vt., III (III), 225; report of committee read and accepted and leave given to bring in a bill accordingly, 19 Oct. '86, Ibid, III (III), 230; bill read and accepted and sent to Council, 23 Oct. '86, Ibid, III (III), 238; bill having been concurred in by Council, read and passed into law, 23 Oct. '86, Ibid, III (III), 241.[1] C. J.: Act read and approved "adding the words Vermont Gazzettee", 23 Oct. '86, G. and C., III, 111.

---

1. For this act, see Ms. Laws of Vt., I, 544.

FOR A TAX ON LAND TO BUILD ROADS
xvii, 172

To the Honorable the General Assembly to Convean at Rutland in October
1786 —
The Petition of the inhabitants of the Town of wilmington [Wilmington] Humbly
Sheweth that your Petitinors from the mountanious Situation of the town in which
they Live and from the Number of Roads of travel Leading through Said town.
which requires uncommon Expence to keep in repair they are renderd unable to
Defray the necessary Expence of repairing Said Roads and other necessiary Publick
Expence
and as a Large Share of the Landed property not taxable by Law in Said town is
owned by persons not yet inhabitants in Said town who are greatly Benefited by
the publick Expence — in the rise of their Lands —
They therefore Request this Honarable house to enable them to Levey a tax of
one penney p^r Acre on all the Landed property in Said town for the purpose of
Repairing Roads in Said town
and your Petitinors in Duty Bound Shall ever Pray —
Dated at wilmington this fifth Day of September 1786

Jesse Cook	Select men
Chipman Swift	in behalf of
Timothy Castle	Said town

— & —

Select Men of Wilmington
Petition
N° 2
Refered to Com^{te}
(Accepted)

To the Honorobell Genaral assembly now Setting your Comity who was Reeferd
the within Protiton Fax [facts] being Stated declaration Soported Begs leve to
report as follows that the Prior [prayer] of the within Protition be Granted Publick
rights Exsepted

Elisha Marsh for Comity

— & —

> *A. J.:* Read and referred to a committee, 16 Oct. '86, *S. P. of Vt.*, III (III),
> 224; report of committee not accepted and ordered recommitted, 17 Oct. '86,
> *Ibid*, III (III), 225; report of committee read and accepted, and leave given
> to bring in a bill accordingly, 19 Oct. '86, *Ibid*, III (III), 230; bill read and
> accepted and sent to Council, 23 Oct. '86, *Ibid*, III (III), 238. *C. J.:* Act read
> and approved, 24 Oct. '86, *G. and C.*, III, 112.[1]

FOR POSTPONEMENT OF A HEARING FOR MALADMINISTRATION
xvii, 173

Guildhall Septr 7th 1786
To the Honourable the Representatives of the freemen of the State of Vermont.

---

1. For this act, see *Ms. Laws of Vt.*, I, 546–547.

Now Setting at Rutland as I have Latly Been Cited to appear Before the Honourable the General Assembly of this State at Rutland on thursday the 19th Day of October Instant to Anser to the Complaint of Nath[el] Gott of Luninburg[1] Which Sets forth my Being Guilty of Sundry Breaches of Law in my office as Justice of the Peace. and Considering my Curcomstances the Length of the jorney and the Short time Sence I Saw this Gentlemans accusation against me Renders it almost imposable for me to attend at this time therefore I Pray that this Honourable House Would Continue the matter to the Next Setting of this Assembly so that I may have an opportunity to Convince the Publick that Doc[t] Gotts asertion is fals and groundless Not With Standing his Long Epistle and Pretended Evedences
　　　Which favour Will be greatfully Excepted By your Humble Servant
Abner Osgood

— & —

To the Honorable the Gen Assembly Now Seting att Rutland
Esq[r] Osgoods Excuse —
Oct[r] 19th 1786
Read

— & —

[No Record]

FOR A TAX ON LAND TO BUILD ROADS AND BRIDGES
xvii, 174

　　　To the Honorable the Gen[l] Assembly of Vermont to be convened at Rutland on the 2nd Thursday of Oct[r] next
　　　The Petition of the Subscribers Inhabitants of New-Haven in the County of Addison humbly Sheweth —
　　　That the Proprietors of New-Haven at their meeting holden in said Town in the Year 1784 voted a Tax of eight Dollars on each Right of Land in said Town for the purpose of clearing Roads, building Bridges and collecting Records of said Town —[2] That your Petitioners have been at great expence in Clearing Roads and building Bridges in sd Town And as the legality of said Vote of Proprietors is disputed your Petitioners earnestly Pray your Honors to grant a Tax of two Pence on each Acre of Land in said Town (except public Lands) to defray the charges hitherto been made, and to complete the Roads which have been laid out for the Convenience of sd Town and the Public, and that there be a Committee appointed to make a Survey of Roads &c. and also a Treasurer and Collector — And your Petitioners as in duty bound will ever Pray —
New Haven Sept[r] 14th 1786 —

Andrew Barton J[r]	W[m] Woodbridge	John Evarts
W[m] Brush	Adonij[h] Griswold	Ashbel Wheeler

---

　　　1. For this complaint, see p. 150, *ante*, including notes.
　　　2. For a consideration of the function of the proprietors as distinguished from that of the inhabitants of the early Vermont towns, see Florence May Woodard, *The Town Proprietors in Vermont*. Studies in History, Economics and Public Law: No. 418. Edited by Faculty of Political Science of Columbia University. New York, 1936.

Bez[l] Rudd	David Griswold	Truman Wheeler
Eli Roberts	John Turner	Reuben Field
Andrew Barton	Clark Stow	Reuben [Grenll?]
Dyer Barton	Timothy Turner	Ebenezer Feild
Luther Evarts	W[m] Eno	David Stebbins
Phin[s] Brown	Ebenezer Wright	Elijah Foote
Nathan Griswold	Asa Wheeler	

— & —

Petition of a N° of Inhabitants of New Haven for a tax of 2[d] per acre
No 3[d] Refered to Com[te]
(Accepted)

To the Honorobell General Assembly now Setting [the committee] to whom was
referd the within Protition fax [facts] being Stated Declaration being Sported
[supported] Bege leve to Report as follows that the Priar [prayer] of Sd Protition
be granted Publick Rights Exsepted —

Elisha Marsh for Comity

— & —

> A. J.: Read and referred to a committee, 16 Oct. '86, S. P. of Vt., III (III),
> 224; report of committee read and not accepted and recommitted, 17 Oct. '86,
> Ibid, III (III), 225; report of committee read and accepted, and leave given
> to bring in a bill accordingly, 19 Oct. '86, Ibid, III (III), 230; bill read and
> accepted and sent to Council, 23 Oct. '86, Ibid, III (III), 238. C. J.: Act read
> and approved, 24 Oct. '86, G. and C., III, 112.[1]

FOR CONFIRMATION OF A DISPUTED ELECTION
xvii, 175

To the Honorable Legislature of the State of Vermont Whom are to Convene at
Rutland the Second Thursday of October Next, A Petition or Remonstrance of
the inhabitants and freemen of the Town of Clarendon County of Rutland and
State of Vermont —
    Humbly Sheweth,
The advantage intended by certain persons respecting the Act directing the choice
of Representative, Governor and other Officers,[2] the Act directs the Constable to
warn all the Freemen to meet at Nine o'clock and what your Petitioners are Disatis-
fied with is as follows the Constable did not warn above one half of the Freemen
of the Town of Clarendon and A part that were warned was not informed neither
Time nor place But it appears [by] the conduct of the Constable and others that
it was a contrived plan to deprive the Freemen of their right intended by S[d] Act,
For they met the Day appointed for Choosing a Representative about 9 o'clock as
they say but tis Disputed and then opened the Meeting and choose Derius Chipman
Esq. to Represent them, & began to Call for Voats for a Govenor, but were not

---

1. For this act, see Ms. Laws of Vt., I, 546.
2. See "An Act for regulating the election of Governor, Deputy-Governor, Council
and Treasurer" (Slade, 325–327).

in so great haste to turn the Hatt as before.[1] By this time the Freemen began to collect as usual, and found the Constable calling for Votes For A Governor, which Proceedings the Freemen were dissattisfied with, and refused to bring in their Votes for a Governor, till they had made choice of a Representative, and insisted that the Constable Should call for Votes for a Representative which he did, And their was about 63 freemen then present, besides 23 that Voted in the first place, and made Choice of Mr Daniel Marsh, to Represent S^d Town in general Assembly and then proceeded to Give in their votes for Governor and other officers as the Law directs.

And now your Honors can Easily see that is [it] was a fair Choice of the freemen that did meet that Day, as their was but 23 that voted in the first Choice and 63 in the Second which made 86, and 56 of which voted for S^d Marsh which leaves but 30 against 56, Which your Petitioners conclude was as Unanimous a Choice of the Freemen as General is in any Town. Now the matter in dispute is whether 23 Freemen meeting at an Unusual Time of Day in this Town or any other in this State; Accrding to the best Information, Shall be Represented and 63 freemen deprived of representation that met the Day and Time usually attended to in this Town for Choosing Representative, Governor and other Officers as the Law directs. —

Your Petitioners look upon it as their Rite and doubt not but your Honors will view it in the same point of Light. And now your Petitioners look up to your Honors as our Political Fathers and Guardians of the People who are to Redress [Grievances] and grant Relief wherein it appears that their has any undue Advantage been taken. Upon these Considerations with Special Confidence in the Wisdom and goodness of that Honorable body the Legislature of Vermont, we conceive and [an] ardent hope that the Prayer of your Petitioners will be granted that Justice, Peace, and Tranquility, the Soul design thereof may Prove a Blessing, and your Petitioners Are in duty bound Shall ever Pray — These May Certify the Honnored Generall Assembly That On the 5th Day of September AD 1786 the Selectmen of this Town of Clarendon Set Up Notifications To Notify the Freemen To Meet To Geather then Voted this Potision Or Remonstrence Be [forrowed] to the Honnored Generel Assembly and also Voted that Thomas Rice Being Chosen An Agent To Carry Said Potision. this was: Voted at the Freeman Meeting at John Trains on the 18th Day of September AD 1786

Test Steph Arnold Town Clerk

Oliver Arnold	James Wells	Jonathan [horwood?]
Reuben Tullar	Nathen Places	Job Chadsey
William Crosman	William Carpenter	Richard Chadsey
Wm Steward	James [Jenks?]	James Chadsey
Moses Hinman	Wm Wheeler	Caleb Pratt
Elihu Allen	Abel Titus	Amos Robinson
Ezekiel Clark	John Bowman	Israel Robinson
Ebenezer Cooly	Rufus Bates	Daniel Colvin
James Wylie	Henry Greene	Squier Ide
Daniel Briggs	Timothy Winter	Joseph Smith
Philip Briggs	Philip Green	Oliver Westcot

---

1. Each voter placed his ballot in the hat rather than in a ballot box as now. Thus "to turn the Hatt" meant in present parlance to close the polls.

Elisha Boardman
Peirce Spencer
David Palmer
Ezekil Green
Job Congdon
Jos Congdon
Ichabod Walker
Christopher howard
James Wesscot
Elias Steward
Gideon Hewit
Ezra Carpenter
William Clark
Caleb Congdon
John Smith
Nathan Crary

Lewis Walker
Caleb Ingalls
Ezekel Westcout
Nathaniel Chaffe
Stephen Robisson
David Place
Caleb Harrington
Levi Calven
Jeremiah Colvin
James Edmunds
James Edmunds Jur
Andew [sic] [Edmunds]
Daniel Reynolds
Peleg Green
William [Sharman?]
John Spencer

George Westcoat
[Deliverance?] Eastman
Eli Eastman
Jesse Spragg
Charles Seamans
Peleg Cady
Jonathan Eadie
Caleb [howland?]
Benj. Whitman
Leonard Read
Abraham [Safford?]
James Round
[Obadiah?] Green
David Warner
Samuel Place
Osial Smith
Thoˢ Rice Jr

— & —

Petition of the Freemen of Clarendon [on?] Derius Chipman Esqʳ &ᶜ
Filed 12ᵗʰ Octʳ 1786

— & —

[No Record]¹

FOR A TAX ON LAND TO BUILD ROADS AND BRIDGES
xvii, 176

The Honorable the Representatives of the Fremen of the State of Vermont to be Conveaned at Rutland on the Second thirsday in October next —
 The Petition of the Subscribers Inhabitants of the Town of Windhall [Winhall] in the County of Bennington in Said State humbly Sheweth. —
 That whereas Said Town lies Cituated on the green mountain between Manchester & Londonderry and much the greater part unsettled — one Road leading form [from] Said London Derry to Manchester through Said Windhall which would be of great Utility to the Publick if altered & well occupied — another Road from Townshend to Manchester through Said Windhall which if properly Repaired and altered must be of great Consequence, there is Likewise another Road leading from wardsborough to Manchester there is likewise a considerable Number of Streams, which need bridging, and the Said Inhabitants being indegent and unable to Occupy and Repair Said Roads which Render it almost Impracticable to pass with any kind of Carriage, and which is a great Imbaracement to a Considerable Tract of Country Relative to Transporting their necessary Supplies of Salt Grain &c

---

1. Daniel Marsh was admitted to his seat on 17 Oct. '86. See *S. P. of Vt.*, III (III), 226.

Your Petitioners therefore humbly pray your Honors to take this our humbly Petition under your wise Consideration and grant Relief in the Premises by Granting a Tax of Two pence on each acre of Land in the Said Town of Windhall (Publick Lands Excepted) for the purpose of makeing and Repairing Roads and building Bridges in Said Town to be Collected & disposed of by such Person or Persons as may hereafter be appointed for said Purpose and your Petitioners as in Duty bound Shall ever pray. —

Dated at Windhall September 19th 1786 —

Nath^{ll} Brown	Benjaman Barret	Jesse Taylor
Ephraim Whitney	James Williams	Reuben Foot
Ephraim Day	Asa Beebie	Dudley Day
Russell Day	Ebenezer Whitney	Joseph Rose
Beriah Wheeler	Gershom Taylor Jr	Benjamin Rose
John Brooks	Asa Beebie J^r	Isaac Williams
Adonijah Foot	Ezra Bigelow	Ezra Taylor
Oliver Day	[. . .] day	Moses Taylor
Jonathan Taylor	Levi Day	

— & —

Petition of the Inhabitants of Windhall
Filed 16th Oct^r
. . .*

To the Honorobell General Assembly now Sitting your Comity to whom was referd the Consideration of the within Protition Bege Leve to report that the fax [facts] being Stated & the Decleration Proved that tis thar oppinnian that the Preyer of the Protition be granted under such restrictions as in your Wisdom think Proper

Dated Rutland 23th oct^r 1786   Ebe^r Allen for the Com^e
— & —

> *A. J.:* *Read and referred to a committee, 23 Oct. '86, *S. P. of Vt.*, III (III), 239; *report of committee read and accepted and leave given to bring in a bill accordingly, 23 Oct. '86, *Ibid*, III (III), 240. *C. J.:* Act read and approved with the amendment that the whole tax be collected at one time, 24 Oct. '86, *G. and C.*, III, 112.[1]

FOR NEW COUNTY LINES AND A SINGLE SHIRE TOWN
xvii, 177

To the Honourable the General Assembly of the state of Vermont to be convened at Rutland on the second thursday of October

The Petition of the subscribers Inhabitants of the County of Orange humbly Sheweth

That when said County was first established the west line of the same ran from the Northeast corner of Berlin about north thirtysix degrees east to the

---

1. For this act, see *Ms. Laws of Vt.*, I, 551. According to this reference it was finally passed 25 Oct. '86.

north line of the state and continued so to be untill the formation of the County of Addison.

The lines of the Said County of Addison now intersect the west line of the County of Orange and in some places extend within ten miles of Connecticut river.[1]

That the line now established is very inconvenient for the inhabitants of said County of Orange.

That a line beginning at the southeast corner of Middlesex may run north thirty six degrees east to the north line of the state without intersecting any town.

That said County is divided into two half shires and that Newbury one of the half shire towns is situated in the Most convenient place and at present furnished with the best Accommodations of any town in the County for holding Courts &c.

That Thetford the other half shire is the southeast Town in Said County and that it is productive of great trouble and expence to the people to have courts holden in such an extreme part of the County.[2]

Your Petitioners therefor humbly pray that the west line of said County may extend from the aforesaid Southeast corner of Middlesex north 36 degrees east to the north line of the state, That said Thetford may no longer be a half shire town in S^d County And that Newbury may for the time be established the only shire town in said County.

And your Petitioners as in duty bound shall ever Pray

Septr 20th 1786

Abiel Chamberlain	Hugh Gardner	William Pattee
Joshua Bayley	John Gray	Cornelius Morgan
John Bayley	James Henderson	John Gd. Bayley
William Hughs	Ephraim Bayley	Aaron Eastman
William Wallace	Jacob Kent	James Bayley
David Dunbar	Elezer Rosebrooks	Nathan Goddard
Hezekiah Fuller	Aaron Ames	Ezra Gates
Luther Fuller	Symon How	Elihu Johnson
Uriah Cross	Benoni Cutler	Samuel Johnson
Nathaniel Gold	Samuel Gates	William Johnson
Joseph Currier	Alexander Watson	Jacob Hall
James Baptison	Josiah Parker	Thomas Hazletine
David McKoy	Ezra Gibbs	Peter Sylvester
Thomas Sibbils	Samuel Page	William Bennet
Ward Bayley	Samuel How	Dudley Carleton
John Rich	John Page	Joseph Chamberlain
John Hugh	Phineas Brace	Raiment Chamberlain
Abner Osgood	Reuben How	Joseph Abbot
William Amey	Joseph Bucknam	Fry Bayley
John Rich Junr	Asa Bucknam	Nicholas Colby
John Amey	David Hopkinson	Elijah Houghton
Osamus Bayley	Zerubbabel Edgar	Joseph Holbrook

---

1. For the acts establishing the western boundaries of Orange County, see *Ms. Laws of Vt.*, I, 206–207, 216–218.

2. For the act establishing two shire towns in Orange County, see *Ms. Laws of Vt.*, I, 216–218.

Henery Rich
Jacob Schoff
Daniel Schoff
James Hugh
Abijah Larnard
Christian Millar
Jacob Schoff Jun[r]
Jonathan Smith
Ebenezar Torey
Mark Aldrich
Abner Minor
James Bayley
Sam[l] Fuller
Abijah Bayley
Jonathan Elkins
Jonathan Elkins Jun[r]
David Bryant
Daniel Frazier
James Abbot
Ruben Wilmot
Abraham Morrel
Richard Pulsifer
Benj[n] Ambrose
John Kennedy
Robert Kennedy
Thomas Hath
Patrick Kennedy
Abner Morrel
Joseph Magoon
David Wheeler
Serjant Morrel
Timothy Batchelor
Stephen Wood
Jeremiah Morrel
Eben[r] Varnam
James Kitteridge
William Kelley
James Kitteridge Jun[r]
Benjamin Norris
Mark Norris
David Norris
Hugh Matthews
David Norris Jun[r]
Peter Youngman
Elijah Glyns
Andrew Leckie
Robert Somers
Walter Brock
Joseph Bonett
John Gilkinson

Thomas Thurstin
Caleb Hopkinson
Joseph Hope
John Sanders
George Wheeler
Hains French
David Gaskill
Joseph Wait
Timothy Nash
Philip Grapes
Gidion Smith
David hiks
David Bradly
Nathaniel Wait
John Merril
Samuel Nash
William Joynes
Samuel Gott
Ephraim Martin
John Horner
Paul Rodgers
George Benfield
Abner Fowler
John S[t] Clair
Thomas Horner
Samuel Osborn
Silas Aldrich
Benjamin Martin
Philip Martin
Peletiah Bliss
Simeon Hovey
Nicholas White
Nathaniel White
Andrew Peters
John Smith
Benjamin Brown
Peter Brown
Samuel Glalkins
Ezekiel Colby
John Martin
Fredrick Calkins
James Heaton
Ephraim Moore
James M[c]Glauchlan
Nicholas Stephens
Robert Millar
Thomas Palmar
John Hinkson
John Templeton
Timothy How

Gidion Smith
Stephen Powers
Ev Chamberlain
Josiah Page
Joseph Smith
John Pattee
James Whitelaw
John Orr
Joel Blanchard
Abel Blanchard
Moody Morse
William Chamberlain
Ephraim Foster
Levi Carter
Peter Blanchard
Ruben Blanchard
Ezekiel Gilman
Benoni Thayer
Benjamin Bayley
James Bayley Jun[r]
Luther Bayley
Ashbel Martin
John Wey
David Martin
Cyrus Bayley
Israel Bayley
Jacob Goodwin
John Scales
John Davenport
Jonathan Fouler
Archibald M[c]Glaughland
Abiel Blanchard
Samuel Minor
Moses Bayley
Benjamin Baldwin
Noah White
James Moore
John Moore
Cyrus Aldrick
John Davis
Benj[n] Jenkins
Stephen Jenkins
Levi Collins
Archibald Harvey
James Calder
James Gilfillan
John Merrit
Alex[r] Harvey
John Robertson
Robert Brock

William Warden
John Shaw
Andrew Lang
James Orr
Hugh Gemmil
John Rankin
Daniel Goodwin
Aaron Weston
Robert Johnson
Jacob Trussel
James Johnson
John Johnson
William Neilson
Alexander Millar
James McKinley
Andrew Brock

David Kennedy
Elisha Lock
Moses Johnson
Charles Bayley
Ashar Chamberlain
Jacob Bayley
Samuel White
Caleb Willard
Benjamin Chamberlain
James Spear
Nathaniel Chamberlain
Jabes Bigolow
William Thompson
Isaac Bayley
Samuel Powers
Jacob B. Chamberlain

Walter Stewart
James Stewart
Samuel Aitkin
Claud Stewart
Isaac Brown
James Cross
William Stevenson
John McLeran
Enos Stevens
[Daniel?] Hall
Elijah King
James Buchanan
William Gilfillin
John Hyndman
Stephen Rider
William Rider

— & —

Petition of the Inhabitants of Orange County
accepted —
Filed 16th Octr
. . .*

— & —

A. J.: *Read and referred to a committee, 18 Oct. '86, *S. P. of Vt.*, III (III),
229;[1] bill entitled "an act fixing the shire town of Orange county" read and
accepted and sent to Council, 25 Oct. '86, *Ibid*, III (III), 244; bill, having been
concurred in by Council, passed into law, 25 Oct. '86, *Ibid*, III (III), 246.[2]
Rep. of Com.: Committee appointed 18 Oct. '86 recommends that the whole
county line be considered before any alteration is made,[3] and that Newbury
be the shire town, *S. P. of Vt.*, IV, 37; report read and accepted, and leave
given to bring in a bill accordingly, 24 Oct. '86, *Ibid*, IV, 37. *C. J.:* *Committee appointed to join Assembly committee, 18 Oct. '86, *G. and C.*, III, 108;
act read and concurred in 25 Oct. '86, *Ibid*, III, 112.

FOR RIGHT TO COLLECT TOLL ON A BRIDGE
xvii, 178

To the Honorable the Representatives of the Freemen of the State of Vermont in
Genl Assembly met, the Petition and Remonstrance of the Subscribers to Your

1. The entry on the manuscript petition correctly notes that this committee was
"to join a Committee from the Council."
2. For this act, see *Acts and Laws, passed by the General Assembly of the State of
Vermont, at their stated session, at Rutland, in October 1786* (Windsor: 1786), p. 3.
3. Presumably such consideration took place during this session. In any case, on
30 Oct. '86 the Assembly passed "An Act for ascertaining the westerly line of Orange
county, and the easterly line of Addison county" (*Ibid*, p. 5). See also *S. P. of Vt.*, III
(III), 253–254, 255; and *G. and C.*, III, 114.

Honors Humbly Sheweth

That they Did in the Year 1785 (in Consequence of Encouragement Given by the Town of Pownal to Raise and Give the Sum of £ 50 L.M. and Depending on a Liberal Subscription from many Benifited Individuals, at their Own Expence Erect and Build a Good Substantial Bridge) over the Hosick [Hoosic] River in the Town of Pownal on the Road Leading from Albany to Williamston [Williamstown] & Massachusetts Bay

And that Your Petitioners Did after Compleating Said Bridge in a Substantial and Workmanlike Manner In Conformity of a vote of the Town of Pownal Exhibit their Expences before a Committee appointed by said Town to Inspect the Same Which Committee after Examining and Inspecting their Said Acc^{ts} Allowed them in the Sum of £128 LM^y which they the Said Com^{tee} allowed to be Just and Reasonable, and the same was Reported to the Town, Who Notwithstanding their Former Encouragement Did Not see fit to allow Your Petitioners any Compensation at all, But Left them to Depend on a voluntary Subscription to Indemnify them for said [Expence] after they had Compleated said [Bridge] — Which Method Your Petitioners have Try'd and have obtain about the Sum of 50 Dollars Exclusive of some small Matters done by the Neighbours in Team work hand Labour &c —

Your Petitioners therefore Humbly Prays the Honorable Assembly that they to Enact and Empower the Said Petitioners to Make a Toll Bridge of the Same under Proper Regulations until they have Receiv'd a Compensation for Erecting & Building the Same and No Longer and as in Duty Bound Shall Pray —

Dated Pownal 25th Sept. 1786   William Hall
                                                                              John Potter
                                                                              David Goff

The whole amount of what has been Paid towards the Expence of the Bridge mentioned in our Petition to the Genl Assembly — by those that Subscribed towards the Same Either in Teem work Hand Labour. or any thing Else is by an Exact Computation to the amount of £ 48..13..0 LM which Sum ought to be taken out of the Sum allowed by the Committee who Inspected the Cost of the Bridge — and all those Persons that have Paid, ought to Pass the Bridge without paying Tools [tolls] and if the Hon^l Genl Assembly Should See fit in their wisdom to Grant Said Bridge to be Tool^d The Petitioners Desire that they may be put under Such Regulations & Restrictions as Shall be thought By their Honors to be Consistant with Justice, and Satisfactory to the Honest Juditious People in General

The Publicks Sincear friends   William Hall
                                                                              John Potter
Pownal October 10th 1786   David Goff
NB the Reason of this being Ennext to our Petition is because the matters mentioned here, was omitted in the petition, which ought to have been in it — to take Scrooples off of Peoples minds of our Intention

We whose Names are hereunto Subscribed do Certify that we are well knowing to the Matters Set forth in the Foregoing Petition, and that they are Founded on Facts, and view it highly Necessary that the Petitioners be Fully Indemnified for Building said Bridge

Abiathar Angel	Moses Barber	Michael dunning
Caleb Gibbs	Samuel Barber	Elisha Phillips
Gideon Towslee	William Barber	William Brown Ju^{nr}

William Brown
[. . .] [. . .]
Abel Matteson
George Gardnier Esqr
John Perkins
Francis Bates Juner
⟨Oliver Myers⟩
Hezekiah Myas
George Gardner Ju^r
Nathaniel Wallace
Isaiah Wallace
Nehemiah Wallace
Abraham Gardner
Benjamin Card

Richard Brown
David Stanard
Paul Gardner
Elisha Card
William mallory
David Mallery
Wm Gallop
Nathl Gallop
Asa Bowdish
Daniel Gardner
John Aylsworth
Nicholas Potter
Joseph Whitford
Stephen Card

Peter Vosbourgh
Abram Vosbourgh
Cornelius Letcher
Jacob Bovee
John Letcher
Peter Deal
Elisha Barber
[Joseph] Williams
Frederic Carter
John Blood
Ebenezer Seelye
James Ladd
Thomas Davison
Amos Potter ⎫ Select man
            ⎭

— & —

Petition of Wm Hall & others
Filed [16th?] Oct^r
. . .*

    Rutland Octr 22 Your Committe beg leave to report on the within Petition, that it ly over untill the next Session of Assembly and that the Town of Pownall be cited to shew Cause, if any they have why the Said Petition should not be granted

Jesse Cook for Com^{tt}

— & —

    A. J.: *Read and referred to a committee, 16 Oct. '86, *S. P. of Vt.*, III (III), 223; *report of committee read and accepted, and petition referred to next session accordingly, 23 Oct. '86, *Ibid*, III (III), 239.

FOR A NEW TRIAL IN A PROMISSORY NOTE CASE
xvii, 179, 180

To the hon^{ble} General Assembly of the Representatives of the Freemen of the State of Vermont to convene at Rutland in said State on the second Thursday of October next.
    The Petition of Uriah Morris of Chester
        Humbly Sheweth.
    That your honours Petitioner in the month of March in the year of our Lord 1772 purchased of Elijah Lovell of Rockingham a Yoak of Oxen for which your Petitioner was to give s^d Lovell twelve pounds five shillings and for that sum made and subscribed his promisory Note and the same delivered to s^d Lovell which Note was payable on the first day of Sep^t Ensuing the Date of said Note Your hon^s Petitioner not being Circumstances to pay s^d note or the sum Contained therein with the Intrest by the time specifyed therein Said Lovell put s^d note into the hand of John Grout to collect who was an Att^y at Law in the County of Cumberland somtime in the month of November in the same year your hon^{rs} Petitioner was

Arrested by John Lovell Brother to s^d Elijah Lovell a Deputy Sheriff of s^d County by Virtue of a Precept Indorsed by s^d Grout as an Att^y to s^d Lovell the Cause to be tryed at June Session following your Hon^rs Petition Procured Bail and at s^d June Session the Cause was Continued to the Next term and Grout s^d Lovells Att^y having in his hand the same Sum of Money (which he s^d Grout had Collect for your hon^rs Petitioner) as I owed s^d Lovell s^d Grout Agreed before Maj^or Chandler to Settle all matters then reletive to s^d note and the money he s^d Grout had in his hand as afores^d Accordingly s^d Grout and your hon^rs Petitioner past receipts s^d Grout Signing a receipt to your hon^rs Petitioner as Att^y to s^d Elijah Lovell acknowl-edging in s^d Receipt that he as Att^y to s^d Lovell had Received the full Sum of s^d note and its Intrest — S^d Grout said he could not give me the note as it was then in the hand of Crean Brush who was the clk. of s^d County of Cumberland said Grout and Brush both went over to the Brittish armey and your hon^rs Petitioner did not hear any thing of s^d note till Sometime in the year 1785 when s^d Elijah Lovell Purchased said note of one Samuel Avery of Westminster who Calls himself Administrator to the Estate of John Grout and s^d Lovell gave s^d Avery about Twelve Dollars for s^d note a short time after s^d Lovell made a Demand of the money Specifyed in s^d note of your hon^rs Petitioner although it was once Setled your hon^rs Petitioner having mislaid the afores^d receipt Could not procure it there-fore was forced Either to Submit the affair to Arbitration or be Sued at Law. your hon^rs Petitioner thought it Cheapest to submit all matters relative to s^d note to Arbitrators and in Consequence thereof s^d Lovell and your hon^rs Petitioner Mutually Agreed on Messrs Benj^a Burt Jon^th Fullar and Solomon Wright as Arbitrators to hear and Determin the matter agreeable to Law and Evidence, who accordingly Set on the 20th of Feby Last in Rockingham after hearing the Evidence &c awarded Judgment against your hon^rs Petitioner and ordered your Petitioner to pay to s^d Lovell the Sum of £9:[14?] and Cost of Arbitration although your hon^rs Peti-tioner Procured Evidence of the above mentioned Settlement and receipt signed by s^d Grout as Att^y to s^d Lovell and Evidence likewise that s^d Lovell Owned that he had received money of s^d Grout which was the property of your hon^rs Petitioner which was not Allowed to me there was but Two of the referees that Agreed to the award and your hon^rs Petitioner has good reason to believe that the above mention Judgment or Award of the Two referees was made by their misunder-standing of the Evidence relative to the before mentioned Settlement and receipt. —

Your hon^rs Petitioner being bound to abide Judment or Award of the before men-tioned Arbitration (by Confession) that he your hon^rs Petitioner was obldiged to Settle the Judgment or award of s^d Arbitrators or go to Goal as Judge Burt one of the Arbitrators ⟨and not a Justice of the Peace⟩ who took the Confession &c gave out an Excution for the Sum Contained in s^d Award or Judgment of s^d Arbitrators / ag^t your honours Petitioner, Which Execution was Put into the hand of Jon^th Fullar Deputy Sheriff for Windsor County who was one of the referees that made the award &c by Virtue of which Execution your hon^rs Petitioner was taken Prisoner and went part of the way to Prison before your hon^rs Petitioner would Settle &c —

Your hon^rs Petitioner therefore most humbly Prays your honours to set aside the before mentioned Judgment or Award of the s^d Arbitrators made as afores^d and give your hon^rs Petitioner Liberty of a Tryal by Law in the Premises or such other way to redress the greviance of your Hon^rs Petitioner as your honours n your great Wisdom shall Judge Just and reasonable

your Petitioner as in Duty Bound Shall ever pray

Uriah Morris

Chester Sep^t 27th 1786

Citation

State of Vermont   ⎱ To the Sheriff of Windham County his Deputy or to the
Windham County   ⎰ Constable of Rocking [Rockingham] in s^d County — Greeting
Whereas Uriah Morris of Chester in the County of Windsor and State of Vermont
hath Preferred a Petition to the Honble General Assembly of the State of Vermont
to Convene at Rutland in s^d State on the Second Thursday of Octr next praying
s^d Assembly to Set aside a Certain Judgment or Award of a Certain Arbitration
held at Rockingham in s^d County of Windham on the 20th day of Feby Last between Elijah Lovil of Rockingham in s^d County of Windham and Uriah Morris
and to grant said Uriah Morris Liberty of a tryal at Law in the Premises
These are therefore by the Authority of the State of Vermont to Require you to
Site the Above named Elijah Lovell of s^d Rockingham to Appear before the Honble
the General Assembly of the State of Vermont to beholden at Rutland in s^d State.
On the 18th Day of Octr next then and there to shew Cause if any he had why the
Judgment or award of s^d Arbitration should not be Set aside and s^d Morris have
Liberty of a Tryal at Law hereof fail not and Due Return make Dated at Rocking-
ham in s^d County of Windham this 28th Day of Sept A D 1786

Benjamin Burt [Judge]

Rockingham Septr 27th 1786
in obedenc [obedience?] I have Served the within Sitation by reding in the hearing
of the within named Elijah Lovell and gave the said Lovell a true and atsted [at-
tested] Coppy for £ 0–6–0   ast Jonathan Fuller Dep^t Shariff

— & —

Petition of Uriah Morris
(Dismissed)
Filed 18th Octr 1786 —
Call on Esqr Tichener [as also Judge best]
. . .*
To the Honarble the Gen^{ll} Assembly Now Seting at Rutland
Your Commite to whome was refer^d the within Petision having attended the
Buisness of our appointment beg Leave to Report that on the Most thurrow In-
vestegation find that the several Matter and things Set up in the within Petision
are Not seported and theirefore are of opinion that the Prayer of the Petision
ought Not to be Granted

Silas Goodrich for Commite

In Genl Assembly Octr 20th 1786
The above report was read & accepted and said petition dismissed —

attest R. Hopkins Clerk —

— & —

A. J.: *Read and referred to a committee, 18 Oct. '86, *S. P. of Vt.*, III, 228;
report of committee read and accepted, and petition referred to next session
accordingly, 20 Oct. '86, *Ibid*, III (III), 232.[1]

---

1. This entry in the journal was doubtless a clerical error. The entries on the reverse
of the manuscript, transcribed above, make it clear that the petition was dismissed.

FOR MAINTENANCE OF SHIRE TOWNS UNCHANGED[1]
xvii, 181

To the hon^ble General Assembly of the State of Vermont, to be holden at Rutland the 2^d thursday of Octr next —

The Petition of a number of the Inhabitants of the Town of Guilford in the County of Windham humbly sheweth That, in pursuance of an act of Assembly,[2] a Convention holden at Brattleborough, for the purpose of agreeing on the Shire Town or Towns in s^d County, did vote that New Fane should henceforth be the only Shire Town in s^d County — Yet we are convinced from indubitable evidence that s^d vote was procured by the undue influence & intrigue of some members of the s^d Convention, so that the design of the Legislature, which, we suppose, was collecting the minds of the people of the County, is like to be defeated, as we apprehend the minds of the people in general are by no means expressed in s^d vote —

Your Petitioners, therefore, being all legal voters in the Town of Guilford, humbly pray this hon^ble House that the above named vote may not be regarded; but the Shire Towns remain as they are,[3] or be fixed in such place as shall hereafter be unanimously agreed on by the Freemen, as we are full in the opinion that it will be very incommodious & disagreeable to the County to have the Courts holden at s^d New Fane —

And y^r Petitioners as in duty bound shall ever pray
Guilford Sepr 28th 1786 —
Signed —

John Shepardson	Amasa Russell	Benjamin Chase
Benjamin Carpenter	Joseph Peck	Comfort Starr
Joseph Slatar	Stephen Shepardson Juner	Comfort Starr Junior
Stephen Chase	Stephen Shepardson	Nicholas pullen
John Slatard [Slatar?]	Hezekiah Howel	James Sallisbury
Caleb Carpenter	Joseph Bullocke	Daniel Knight
Joseph Carpenter	Ithamar Goodenough	William Marsh Ju^r
Isaac Slatar	Humphry Palmer	Seth Shepardson
John Bolster	Matthew Dutten	Saml Shepardson
Benjamin Ballou	Paul Chase	John Camp
Elkanah Bullock	Dana Hide	[Zaccheos?] farnsworth
Nathan Horton	David Thurber	John Camp Junior
Edmond fisher	David Joy Esqr	Aaron franklin
Stafford Horton	Jonath Johnson Ju^n	Joseph Goodwin
Ebenezer Hayward	Joshua Lynde	Edward Houghton
George Read	Hezekiah Horton Ju^nr	James Houghton
Robert Alswoth	William Yeaw	

1. For other petitions concerning the shire towns of Windham County, see pp. 117, 133, *ante*, and pp. 218, 219, 221, *post*.

2. See "An Act directing the choice of Supervisors in the County of Windham and declaring their power and duty", passed 27 Oct. '85 (*Ms. Laws of Vt.*, I, 537–538).

3. That is, at Westminster and Marlborough. See "An Act for establishing the Shire or County Towns in the several Counties . . .", passed 21 Feb. '81 (*Ms. Laws of Vt.*, I, 216–218).

— & —

Petition of the Inhabitants of Guilford
50
Nº 2

— & —

[No Record]¹

FOR MAINTENANCE OF TWO BRIDGES BY THE COUNTY
xvii, 219

To the Honourable the General Assembly of the State of Vermont to be Convened at Rutland on the second Thursday of October AD 1786 —
The Humble Petition of the Select men of Arlington in Behalf of s^d Town Humbly Sheweth that Whereas the Situation of this Town is such that the Inhabitants thereof are burthened by Building and maintaining a Large Number of Bridges over large streams of warter in this Town and in perticular two which are one over a Stream known by the Name of the Roaring Branch & one over another Stream known by the Name of the Battenkill which last is near the House of Eli Pettibone Esqr and your Honours Petitioners conceive it a disproportinate Expence for this Town to support & maintain s^d Bridges and therefore pray that the s^d Bridges may in future be maintained & supported by the County of Bennington or that some other measure may be taken to Aleviate your Petetioners from the afores^d disproportinate Expence —
And as in duty bound your Honours Humble Petetioners shall ever Pray —

Constant Barney ⎫
Abel Aylesworth ⎬ Select men
Tyrus Hurd   ⎭

— & —

Petition of the Selectmen of Arlington in bhalf [sic] of s^d Town —
Filed 16th Oct^r
. . .*

— & —

A. J.: *Read and referred to a committee, 16 Oct. '86, S. P. of Vt., III (III), 224;² *report of committee read and not accepted and petition dismissed, 26 Oct. '86, Ibid, III (III), 247.³ C. J.: *Committee appointed to join Assembly committee, 18 Oct. '86, G. and C., III, 108.

---

1. On 23 Oct. '86 the Assembly passed an act establishing New-Fane as the shire town of Windham County (Acts and Laws, passed by the General Assembly of the State of Vermont, at their stated session, at Rutland, in October 1786 [Windsor: 1786], pp. 1-2). This action was equivalent to a dismissal of this petition, even though there is no record that the document was ever received or read in the Assembly.
2. The entry on the manuscript correctly states that this committee was to join a committee from the Council.
3. According to the entry on the manuscript the committee simply found that "the facts Set up are Supported therefore that tis there opinion that the prayer of the within pettion [sic] ought to bee Granted."

FOR SETTLEMENT OF COMMISSARY GENERAL'S ACCOUNTS
xvii, 226

To his Excellency the Governor the Honorable Council and Representatives of the Freemen of the State of Vermont Now Sitting at Rutland — The petition of Joseph Farnsworth Late Commissary Gen[l] of Purchases Humbly Sheweth
That your Petitioner being appointed Commissary Gen[l] of Purchases for this State in the year 1780[1] has since that Period to the Conclusion of the War Served the Public in that Capacity. The want of Credit in our then Circulating medium Necessitated the office of Commissary to the Disagreeable task of making Seizure on private property which of Course brought the Department under many Disadvantages and imbarrasments on account of out standing Debts. — These and the additional task of Collecting the arrearages Due on the Provision taxes assessed in the years 1780 and 1781 with the Difficulties Peculier to the Reluctance the Delinquents had in paying the Remainder of them taxes on pretext of their not being needed the war then being over together with the internal Divisions of the state which Required Considerable time of Personal attendance Waiting on the Posse furnishing the Militia with Provisions &C — The Different interfering acts of Assembly Respecting the Commissaries Department which of Course made a Derangement of all Previous Accounts and of Necessity Retarded the accomplishment of a final arrangement for the inspection of the auditors till some time in August 1785 at which time the Auditors met and proceeded to Examine and Continued by Adjournment till the whole accounts were Examined and Received approbation from the auditors so far as Respected their appointment —
It appears when the General footing of Provisions and other Articles Rec[d] and those Deliver[d] are Compared that the Deficiency on Account of Delivery is Considerable — But if Every Circumstance which attended the Reception and Delivery of those provisions be Duly Examined your Petitioner flatters himself that instead of increasing by a fair and Candid investigation of the matter it will appear but a moderate and unavoidable wastage — Instead when it is Considered in what manner the Provisions were Rec[d] by the Selectmen and by them Dilver[d] to the Commissary of Purchase and from him to the Com[n] of Issues with the Repackings after it has been Rec[d] from the Several Towns then in many instances transported 20 or 30 miles on Horseback before it Reaches the Issuing Department — Issuing Provisions in Small Quantities to Militia and Soldiers marching to Garrison and in Numerous other instances in all which the Commissary of Purchase is accountable for the first weight and Procures a Voucher only for the Last — I Should have Given my Personal Attendance on this Occasion but my Present Ill State of Health is not Permissive I find myself on the Decline as to health and by the Leave of Providence I intend trying a new Element as a Dernior [Dernier] Resort for my Recovery — I am now involved in a Lawsuit for a Contract made in behalf of this State in the State of NYork to the amount of £130 for flour and Beef which I first Seized afterwards agreed for and purchased and took a Bill of the Contract How the Cause will be Determined is uncertain but of this I am Certain that it is hard for me to pay Cost in Silver money which I dont Receive from the State — However of this I am not so anxious as for a Release from my Public Connection to the State. You have the whole of my accounts Exhibited in as Concise arrangements

---

1. For Farnsworth's appointment as commissary general 27 Oct. '81 (not '80), see *G. and C.*, II, 126.

as the Nature of the Business will admit and from whom I expect a Seasonable and final Determination it Becomes me as a Duty to myself under my Present Situation of Health to Request it and as a Duty that this Honorable Board owe to themselves and the State to Grant it — I have only one Idea more to Suggest. that is whether this Honorable House Conceive that the wages which I Rec^d for my services in State money at a Late Perion [period?] in which I Could Devise no advantages from New Lands Granted in this State which has been the General Lot of other Public Servants is adequate to the Idea and intention of the Board of War when they Stated my Wages in Silver money — However I Leave the Determination to the wisdom of this House in whose Integrity and Impartiality I have the Highest Confidence to trust that Every attending Circumstance will have its proper weight Agreeable to the Dictates of Justice and Equity — for which your Petitioner as in Duty Bound Shall Ever pray

Joseph Farnsworth

Bennington Octr 1786 }

— & —

Petition of Joseph Farnsworth —
Filed 17th Octr 86 —
. . .*

Your Commit^t to whom the within petition of the Com^y Genl was refered find the Genl wastage of his Department Amounts to 12 pCent, which under every Circumstance we conceive ought to be allowed by the Auditors — We also find the Com^y G^l Wages and that of his Clerk, to have been paid up to the Month of March 1784 — We are of Opinion that the Auditors continue his Pay & that of his Clerk <[. . .] from that period> to the first day of may 1785

Sam^{ll} Safford for Comtte

— & —

> *A. J.:* *Read and referred to a committee to join a committee from the Council and to confer with the Auditor, 17 Oct. '86, *S. P. of Vt.*, III (III), 226; *report of committee read and accepted, 30 Oct. '86, *Ibid*, III (III), 256; resolved that twelve percent wastage be allowed and that pay for commissary general and his clerk be allowed to 1 May '85, *Ibid*, III (III), 256. *C. J.:* *Committee appointed to join Assembly committee, 17 Oct. '86, *G. and C.*, III, 107.

FOR COMPENSATION FOR WAR SERVICES
xvii, 235

To the Honourable the General Assembly of the state of Vermont now sitting at Rutland

The Petition of Thomas Johnson in behalf of himself and Company humbly sheweth.

That in the year 1775 it was thought best by the Committees of the several towns to raise a company of Minute men so called in the town of Newbury whereupon your Petitioner being appointed to command S^d company inlisted the number of 52 including officers who were employed in scouting to Onion River

&ᶜ agreeable to aroll exhibited herewith,[1] for which service no pay hath been received either for service or subsistance

Your Petitioner therefore Prayeth that your Honours would take the matter under your consideration and grant him such assistance as you in your great wisdom shall see fit and your Petitioner as in duty bound shall ever pray

Thomas Johnson

— & —

Petition of Thomas Johnson
Filed 20ᵗʰ Octʳ
. . . *

Rutland Octʳ 22 — 1786 Your Committe to whom the within petition was refered — are of opinion, that the Committe of Pay Table are fully Authorized to liquidate & settle the Petitioners Account, to which Board he ought to Apply for Settlement

To the Honᵉ the Legislature   Isaac Tichenor for the Comᵗᵗᵉ

— & —

A. J.: *Read and referred to a committee to join a committee from the Council, 20 Oct. '86, S. P. of Vt., III (III), 235; *report of committee read and accepted, 23 Oct. '86, Ibid, III (III), 239. C. J.: *Committee appointed to join Assembly committee, 21 Oct. '86, G. and C., III, 111.[2]

FOR A TAX ON THE LAND OF CERTAIN NON-RESIDENT PROPRIETORS TO BUILD ROADS
xvii, 238

To the Honourable the General Assembly of the State of Vermont now sitting at Rutland

The Petition of James Whitelaw in behalf of the Inhabitants of the Township of Ryegate Humbly sheweth

That said Inhabitants have at great expence made considerable improvements in said Town but that they have been and still are much impeded therein by the badness of the roads through said town and that said inhabitants have been often complained of by the inhabitants of the Towns beyond on account of the badness of the roads and as said inhabitants are but few in number and have two public roads to make and keep in repair through said town which together makes upward of sixteen miles on which there are several large bridges which roads and bridges they are utterly unable to make and keep in repair without some assistance from the Proprietors a great part of which lives in Great Britain and as the badness of the roads through said town hinders not only the settlement thereof but the settlement of all the northern part of the state, your Petitioners therefore humbly prays that you would grant a tax of one penney on the Acre of all the nonresident Proprietors lands in said Township and your Petitioner as in duty bound shall ever pray

James Whitelaw

— & —

---

1. For this roll, see Vt. Rev. Rolls, 2–4.
2. For the ultimate action taken by the Committee of Pay Table, see Ibid, 4.

Petition
James Whitelaw in behalf of the inhabitants of Rygate
Filed 23ᵈ Octʳ 1786.
. . .*

— & —

A. J.: *Read and referred to a committee, 23 Oct. '86, *S. P. of Vt.*, III (III), 241; *report of committee read and accepted, and leave given to bring in a bill accordingly, 24 Oct. '86, *Ibid*, III (III), 242;[1] bill read and accepted and sent to Council, 25 Oct. '86, *Ibid*, III (III), 245; bill, having been concurred in by Council, passed into law, 25 Oct. '86, *Ibid*, III (III), 246.[2] *C. J.:* Act read and concurred in, 25 Oct. '86, *G. and C.*, III, 112.

FOR REPAIR AND CONSTRUCTION OF CERTAIN ROADS AT EXPENSE OF PROPRIETORS
xvii, 245

To the Honᵇˡᵉ the General Assembly of the State of Vermont to be convened at Rutland on the sencond [*sic*] Thirsday of October 1786 —
The Petition of the Subscribers Inhabitants of the Town of Cabot, and adjoining humbly sheweth that your Honʳˢ Petitions, having with great Difficulty begun a Settlement on the Frontiers of this State, in this Quarter, far removed from the seat of Government are almost entirely secluded from the lower Part of the State by the badness of the Road from Newbury to this Country, and the want of other Roads — a considerable Part of the Town Rygate being owned by non resident Proprietors, the Roads have not been repaired for many years and the Inhabitants of Peacham being but few, cannot repair the Roads in that Town so as to be passable with Teams in the Spring or Fall of the Year, and further the Lands on which your Petitioners are setled being annexed to the County of Addison, where we wish to remain, subject us and the other Inhabitants in this Quarter to much Difficulty, for want of Roads to the Lake, to remove which, to open a Channel for Trade, and to facilitate the Setlement of this Part of the State, your Petitioners humbly pray that your Honʳˢ will appoint and authorize some Person in this Quarter who is interested to have the Business executed, to repair alter and bridge where necessary the Road commonly called Hazens Road from Newbury to Black River so called in Greensborough, and to look out clear & Bridge a Road from Littleton through Cabot to dog River on Onion River — and another Road through Cabot, to Cambridge on the River Le Mile [Lamoille] at the Expence of the Proprietors of the several Towns through which the Roads shall be made or repaired, or Otherwise grant Relief as the Wisdom of your Honʳˢ shall direct and your Petitioners as in duty bound shall ever pray —

Jesse Leavenworth
Thomas Lyford

---

1. The report of the committee as given on the manuscript petition simply states that the facts in the petition are true and that it ought to be granted.

2. See "An Act empowering the selectmen of Rygate in the County of Orange to levy a tax of one penny on each acre of non-resident proprietors lands for the purpose of making and repairing roads and bridges" (*Ms. Laws of Vt.*, I, 549–550).

Benj^a Webster
David Blanched
James Bruce
James Adams
Jon^a Heath
Edmund Chapman

— & —

Petition of Jesse Leavenworth & others —
Filed 16th Oct^r
N° 8 —
. . .*

To the Honorabell General Assembly now Sitting your Comity to whom was referd the within Protition Bege leve to reporte that in thare opinion the Consideration thare of be Postepond untill the Protitioners Publish in Both the News Papers Printed in this State three wekes Succksively the Substance of said Protition with a notification to all Persons Consarnd to appear at Somday in the next Sessions of the Legislature to be thare in Menshoned if they think Proper to Shew Caus why the Prayer of the Protition Shold not be granted —

Elisha Marsh for Comity

— & —

> A. J.: *Read and referred to a committee, 16 Oct. '86, S. P. of Vt., III (III), 224; *report of committee read and accepted, and petition referred to next session accordingly, 19 Oct. '86, Ibid, III (III), 229.

FOR ANNEXATION OF PART OF A TOWN TO ANOTHER[1]
xxii, 117; xxxviii, 146

To the Honorable. the General Assembly (now siting at Rutland) the Petition of the Inhabitants of Panton and Ferisburgh [Ferrisburg] &C. humbly sheweth That by a Late Survey[2] of the Township of Addison the Boundaries of S̄d Town extend so far to the North as to contract the Township of Panton in such a Manner that S^d Township is but about Two Miles across from North to South likewise that the south part of the Township of Ferrisburgh adjoining Panton is seperated from S^d Ferrisburgh by Otter Creek in such a Manner as to render it very inconvenient to their being one Town. Your Petitioners humbly Conceive that by aexing [annexing] that Part of Ferrisburgh South of Otter Creek to Panton may render it a fine Township and be of the utmost Utillity to the Proprietors of S^d Towns and for which Your Petitioners shall ever pray —
Dated at Panton this 2nd Day of October — AD 1786

---

1. For a related petition, see p. 305, post.
2. This was presumably the "new" survey undertaken according to law rather than according to the provisions of the charters. See "An Act for the regulation and Establishment of Town Lines" passed 22 Oct. '82, and an act in addition thereto passed 29 Oct. '84 (Ms. Laws of Vt., I, 350, 466).

[Ferrisbourg Sinors]

Abel Thompson	Timothy Rogers	John Huff
Philip Matteson	John Huntly	Israel west
Jon^th Sexton	John wilde	Gideon Spencer
Alex^r Brush	Jesse graves	Donald McIntosh
		William Haight

The [Naims] of the Potitioners of the Town of Ferrisborg

Reuben L french	Silas Bingham	Richard Edgerton
Nehemiah L. french	Abner Bingham	Giden Ruger
Isaac Gage	Saml Roys	Samuel Pangborn
Ezra Squier	Nathaniel Squier	

The Naims of the Potitionors of the Town of Panton
<Samuel Pangborn>

Panton October the 2nd 1786
this may Certify that at a Legal town meating of the <freemen> of the town of
Panton Did Pas a Voat to Portition the Genrol assembly at their Session at Rutland
to annex the town of Panton and that Part of Ferrisborg which Lyeth on the South
west Side of Otter Crick [Creek] in to a town Ship and if the Honerable the Generol
assembly Saw fit to Grant owar Potition to ad to the town that the twoo Peases of
Land dothe make the Naim of Orlins or the Naim of Montgomery
    the above is a trew Coppy fron the town Record
                                        Attest Elijah Grandey   town Clark

— & —

The Petition of Panton & Ferrisburgh To the Hon^l Gen'rall Assembly
Filed 16th Oct^r
. . .*
Citation of Select men of Ferrisburgh to appear ag^t Panton Petition —
    To Mr Zebulan Crittenden indifferent person
    You are hereby required to cite the Select men of Ferrisburgh to appear to
the next adjourned session of the General Assembly to be holden at Bennington the
15th of February next and shew cause if any they have why the prayer of a petition
of a N° of the inhabitants of Panton and Ferrisburgh praying that, that part of
Ferrisburgh lying south of Otter Creek and west of Dead Creek so called, should
be annexed to Panton should not be granted — Your doings with this Citation you
are requested to return to me on or before the [15th?] day of February next —
Given under my hand this third day of February 1787
                                        Ros^l Hopkins Clerk of Genl Assembly

Ferisburgh the 3 of Fer^by 1787
then the within Citation Served by Reading the Same to tow of the Select Men of
Ferisburgh Served p^r me
                                        Zebulon Criettenden

— & —

A. J.: *Read and referred to a committee, 24 Oct. '86, S. P. of Vt., III (III),
242; *report of committee read and dismissed, petition referred to next session,
and ordered that selectmen of both towns be notified to show cause why petition
should not be granted, 24 Oct. '86, Ibid, III (III), 243; *report of committee
recommending that part of Ferrisburg be annexed to Panton, read and con-

sideration postponed to next session, 9 March '87, *Ibid*, III (III), 326;[1] *petition referred to next session, 22 Oct. '87, *Ibid*, III (III), 38; bill to annex part of Ferrisburg to Panton read and accepted and sent to Council, 24 Oct. '88, *Ibid*, III (IV), 109; bill returned from Council and by their advice referred to next session, 25 Oct. '88, *Ibid*, III (IV), 111.

FOR REFORM OF JUDICIAL PROCEDURE, THE CURRENCY AND TAXATION[2]
xvii, 182

To the Honourable, the General Assembly of the State of Vermont to be convened at Rutland on the second thursday of October instant.

The petition and remonstrance of the inhabitants of the town of Tinmouth in the county of Rutland

We the inhabitants of the town of Tinmouth legally met for that purpose beg leave humbly to represent to your honourable body, as Guardians of the rights of the citizens of this State that notwithstanding the wisdom, care, and vigilence of former legislatures, sundry laws, some of which were perhaps beneficial or at least necessary at first others introduced from the examples of other states wedded to established customs without sufficient attention to their operation are suffered to remain, in our apprehension, a real grievance to the people, and directly opposed to the true interest of the state

I. Our system of laws for administring justice renders prosecutions unreasonably tedious and expensive to the suitors — We beg leave to point out some of them for your wise consideration. — A greater jurisdiction is given to justices of the peace in civil actions than ought to be entrusted to single magistrates in general and to prevent the ill consequences of vague uncertain determinations an appeal is allowed from their decisions in all cases to the county courts — by which mean the determinations of justices of the peace are rendered altogether superfluous, and their courts instruments of great delay and unnecessary expence to the suitors. — We beg leave to suggest another evil attending the present mode of proceeding before justices of the peace — they are constituted courts of record, and obliged to attend to modes and forms with all that precision necessary in superior courts whose decisions must become a rule of property to the citizens and ascertain more than half the laws of the land. — Were they made courts of conscience for the final decision of such matters as might safely be entrusted to them, we apprehend they might become very useful to the community, and that if a rehearing on the merits be allowed in any case, it ought, for the sake of keeping the laws uniform,

---

1. The manuscript petition as well as the petition referred to in note 1, p. 214, makes it appear that this report was originally made to the Assembly on 24 Oct. '86 and not on this date. There is no record of any new committee being appointed and thus no reason to believe that there were two reports. The journal of the Assembly makes it evident that a report once dismissed was on occasion considered again as though still before the house.

2. For a more detailed understanding of the grievances set forth in this petition, see a somewhat similar one and its explanatory notes on p. 189, *ante*. For other similar or identical petitions, see pp. 225, 232, 238, 244, 248, 262, 279, *post*.

to be in the supreme court, and to prevent vexation, to be at the expence of the party who shall move for the same.

There appears to us the same objection against the present jurisdiction of the county courts. All actions exceeding the jurisdiction of a justice must be commenced in the county Court, and from thence may be appealed to the supreme Court. — With due submission, we cannot conceive that superior Courts can, in the decision of causes brought before them on appeals derive any advantage from the proceedings had in the lower courts — but that on the contrary this mode serves as a pretext for delay, creates a very unnecessary expence, both of money and time to the suitors and by repeated attendances of parties, and witnesses occasions a great loss to the community by taking off numbers of industrious citizens from their proper callings — We cannot be persuaded but that one fair and impartial trial in any cause would in general be more effectual for the promotion of justice than our present dilatory system, which opens a wide door for tampering with witnesses, packing juries, and a train of evils pernicious to the morals of the people and destructive of justice itself. — We beg leave therefore to suggest for your wise and deliberate consideration, whether it might not be for the public good to limit the jurisdiction of the county courts to such smaller matters as they shall be thought competent finally to decide — To make the supreme Court a Court of entries for all matters of consequence both civil and criminal — so to regulate proceedings as to give proper time of preparation to the parties and the judges an oppertunity of determining all matters of law that properly belong to them without such unnecessary delay as at present to parties, witnesses, and juries. — This we conceive will be a mean of lessening expences, expediting proceedings at law, and of giving stability and uniformity to the rules of property and the course of justice through the state.

II.   We farther wish that some more equitable way of making up costs, then the present, by travel and attendance might be devised. We think it not only unjust but very impolitic in many instances particularly in suits before justices of the peace. As it is a great temptation to the prosecution of petty lawsuits; which ought not to be encouraged in a community, and serves to maintain many Barrators and Pettifoggers of little knowledge and less integrity, to the great disturbance and vexation of quiet and peaceable citizens.

III.   We think that the great number of Sheriffs deputies employed in some Counties is detrimental to the public — that their number ought to be limited and fees ought to be allowed for the service of writs, only from the place of Service to the court or place of return.

IV.   We likewise sincerely wish that in the present extreme scarcity of cash your wisdom might direct some mode for the payment of debts that should prevent the final ruin of such as are honest debtors without a manifest injustice to creditors.

V.   Lastly, we beg leave to observe that the present mode of taxation appears to us a very great and real grievance — It appears to us to be manifestly unequal and impolitic — Unequal, because our taxes are mostly paid by the poor and middling class of people, while the owners of unimproved thousands are exempt from the burden — Impolitic, because taxing improved lands only, faculties, poles, and produce, is in fact no other than to tax industry skill and economy — Give us leave, therefore to hope that in future our taxes will be so regulated as to fall more equally on the citizens and that instead of being a check, they may, by proper exemptions, operate as an encouragement to industry, economy arts and manufactures. — And your petitioners, as in duty bound shall ever pray

Signed by order of the meeting
Tinmouth October 2ᵈ 1786

Samˡ Mattocks Moderator

— & —

Petition from Tinmouth
Nº 4

— & —

[See subjoined note for similar petition, p. 192, *ante*.]

_____

FOR RELOCATION OF A SHIRE TOWN[1]
xvii, 183

To the Honorable the General Assembly of the State of Vermont convened at
Rutland the second Thursday in October instant, the Petition of the inhabitants of
Dummerston in Windham County most Humbly Sheweth —
That Whereas the Honorable the Legislature at their Sessions in October last did
pass an act directing the choise of supervisors for the purpose of fixing the Shire
Town or Towns in Sᵈ County[2] And the Supervisors having met according the
directions of Sᵈ Act did Proceed to fix the Shire Town for Sᵈ County and Newfain
[Newfane] was fixed Upon by Sᵈ Supervisors for the Shire Town for Sᵈ County.
Now we your Petitioners notwithstanding the doings of the Supervisors pray
that this Honorable Assembly will be Pleased not Pass an act making Newfain
the Shire Town for Sᵈ County. For your Petitioners are fully convinced that some
undue influence hath been used by some Persons in this county to Procure the vote
of the Suprevisors as we are able to prove that some of the Supervisors Voted
Directly contary to the Vote and instruction of the Town they Repersented, your
petitioners therefor Pray that Putney may be made the Shire Town for Windham
County or that things Remain as they are at Present[3] till the minds of the People
can be better known — And your Petitioners in duty bound shall ever Pray
October 2ⁿᵈ 1786

[Ashbel] Johnson
T. Shepherd Gates
Artemus Morss
William wiman
John [Kathan]
John Kathan Jur
Ephraim Hall
Reuben Lamb
Mathew Hull

— & —

the Petition of Ashbel Johnson
Dummersten [Dummerston]
9 — Nº

— & —

_____

1. For other petitions concerning the shire town of Windham County, see pp. 117,
133, 208, *ante*, and pp. 219, 221, *post*.
2. See note 2, p. 208, *ante*.
3. See note 3, p. 208, *ante*.

[No Record]¹

_____

FOR RELOCATION OF A SHIRE TOWN[2]
xvii, 184

To the Honorable the General Assembly conveined at Rutland on the Second thirsday of October instant. The petition of the Subscribers inhabitants of the Town of Townshend in Windham County humbly praying Shewith —
That whereas the Honorable the Legislature did at their Sessions at Windsor in October last past Pass an act Directing the Choice of Supervisors for the purpose of fixing the Shire Towns or Shire Town in the County of Windham[3] And the Supervisors having met at Mr Armes as Directed by S^d Act, did proceed to fix the Shire Town. And Newfain [Newfane] was then and [there] fixed upon by the Supervisors for the Shire Town for S^d County however notwithstanding the doings of the Supervisors your petitioners pray that the Honorable House of Assemble will be Pleased not to Pass an act making Newfain a Shire Town for Windham County For your Petitioners are fully convinced that some undue influence hath been used by some designing Persons in this county to bring about the S^d Vote of the Supervisors, as we are able to prove that some of them Voted directly contary to the Vote of the Town they Represented. Your Petitioners therefore Pray that Putney may be made a Shire Town for Windham County or that things remain as they are at Present[4] till the minds of the People can be more firmly obtined. And your Petitioners in duty bound shall ever Pray —
dated at putney October 2nd 1786 —

Josiah Fish	Asher Skinner	Ebenezer Burt
John Spooner	Lemuel Ames	John mcMasters
David Watkins	Bala Rabyon	his
Joseph Rasey Junr	Amos gray	Joseph X Razey
Daniel Watkins	Samuel Wiswall	mark
Samuel Skinner	Asa Austen	Benj^a Clemons
William heartwell	Jons Gray	William Robins

— & —

the Petition of Josiah fish
Townsend [Townshend]
19
N° 3

— & —

[No Record]⁵

_____

1. See note 1, p. 209, *ante.*
2. For other petitions concerning the shire town of Windham County, see pp. 117, 133, 208, 218, *ante,* and p. 221, *post.*
3. See note 2, p. 208, *ante.*
4. See note 3, p. 208, *ante.*
5. See note 1, p. 209, *ante.*

FOR A TAX ON LANDS TO BUILD ROADS
xvii, 185

To the Honourable General Assembly of the State of Vermont to be Holden at Rutland on the second thursday of October instant —

The petition of a major part of the Inhabitants of Williamstown in the County of Orange & State of Vermont humbly sheweth: that it is necessary that three roads should be cleared & bridged, through said town in order to accomodate said inhabitants, & the inhabitants of other towns in said County — that the clearing & bridging said roads would be very expensive to the few inhabitants there are in said town — that all the land in said town except about seven hundred & fifty acres is divided into severalty, & that the clearing & bridging said roads would add much to the value of the unimproved land in said town — Wherefore your petitioners humbly pray that your honourable Body will grant a tax of one penny on an acre on all the land in said Williamstown, as in duty bound will ever pray

Williamstown Oct[r]
3rd 1786

Elijah Paine
John Smith
Moses Morse
Edmund Bacon
John Lothrup
Penuel Deming
Benj[n] Clark
Josiah Lyman
James Smith
Joseph Crane

— & —

Petition of Elijah Paine & others. —
Filed 17th Oct[r] 86 —
To tax Williamstown
N° 9 (accepted)

To the Honorobell General Assembly now Sitting your Comity to whome was refard the within Protition Faxs [facts] being stated the Dacleration beeing Soported Exsept that Part Wich Says will add to the value of unimproved Land Bege Leve to report as follows that a tax of one Peney on the acor be [lade] on all the Lands in Said Townd Publick rights Exsepted —

Elisha Marsh for S[d] Comity

— & —

A. J.: Read and referred to a committee, 17 Oct. '86, *S. P. of Vt.*, III (III), 225; report of committee read and accepted, and leave given to bring in a bill accordingly, 19 Oct. '86, *Ibid*, III (III), 230; bill read and accepted and sent to Council, 20 Oct. '86, *Ibid*, III (III), 235; bill, having been concurred in by Council, passed into law, 21 Oct. '86, *Ibid*, III (III), 237.[1] *C. J.:* Act read and concurred in, 21 Oct. '86, *G. and C.*, III, 111.

---

1. For this act, see *Ms. Laws of Vt.*, I, 541–542.

FOR MAINTENANCE OF THE SHIRE TOWNS UNCHANGED[1]
xvii, 186

To the Honorable General Assembly, of the State of Vermont to be holden at Rutland the 2^d thursday of Octr next —
The Petition of a, Number of Inhabitants of Wilmington, in the County of Windham humbly Sheweth. — that in pursuance of an act of Assembly,[2] a Convention met at Brattleboro: for the purpose of Agreeing On a Shire Town or Towns In this County. Voted that Newfane Should henceforth be the only Shire Town in this County. And whereas there has been various reports that the Vote was Obtaind, by the Influence of some Interested Persons. And wee suppose, the Designs of the Legislature is like to be defeated. in Not Collecting the minds of the People. Your Petitioners therefore being all Legal voters in the Town of Wilmington. humbly pray, that the S^d vote be not regarded. but the Shire Towns remain as they are[3] or be fixed at such places as shall be hereafter Unanimously Agreed On by the Freemen of the County And wee rather ask this because wee are decidedly of Opinion that it would be very disagreeable and inconvenient to have the courts holden at S^d Newfane. And ye Pettioners in duty bound Shall ever pray. —
Wilmington Octr 3^d 1786.

Singed [*sic*]

Chipman Swift	Levi Packard	Jabez Haws
Amos Fox	Nath^{el} Morgan	Richard Miller
Benjⁿ Morgan	Reuben Morgan	Ozias Dix
Jon^a Childs	Daniel Livermore	Judah Moore
Oliver Bailey	John Peirce	Joseph Marks
Edward Foster	Nathan Swift	Edward Foster
David Ball	Samuel Thompson	David Ball
Isaac Wheler	Moses Haskell Jr	Isaac wheler
Jeremiah [pamele?]	James Corse	[Jeremiah parmle]

— & —

Petition of Chipman Swift
Wilmington
19 — N° 5

— & —

[No Record][4]

FOR RIGHT TO SELL REAL PROPERTY TO SETTLE AN ESTATE
xvii, 187; xxxviii, 151

To the Honorable the General [*Assembly*] of the State of Vermont to be holden at Rutland on the second Thursday of this Ins^t October

---

1. For other petitions concerning the shire town of Windham County, see pp. 117, 133, 208, 218, 219, *ante*.
2. See note 2, p. 208, *ante*.
3. See note 3, p. 208, *ante*.
4. See note 1, p. 209, *ante*.

The Petition of Gidion Adams Administrator on the Estate of Elisha Leach late of Pawlet deceased. Humbly sheweth, that the personal Estate of the said Elisha Leach deceased is insufficient by the Sum of Twenty nine pounds fifteen shillings and eight pence L.M. to pay the Debts due from said Estate: — Therefore Prays. your Honors to pass an act impowering him the said Gidion Adams to sell so much of the real estate of the said Elisha Leach deceased as will raise to the afore said sum of £29–15–8 LM. for the purpose of paying the Debts due from said Estate. together with the necessary Cost arising on such sale under such restrictions as you in your Wisdom may think fit, Which your Honors Petitioner, as in duty bound shall ever pray

Gidion Adams Admi.

Pawlet Octo 4th 1786.

A Certificate from the Judge of Probate

To the Honorable the General Assembly of the State of Vermont. This may Certify that the Personal Estate of Elisha Leach late of Pawlet deceased is insufficient by the Sum of Twenty nine pounds fifteen shillings & eight pence to pay the debts due from said Estate

Elisha Clark Jud. Prob.

Probate Office
Rutland District
Tinmouth 28th Sep^t 1786

— & —

Gideon Adams^s Petition
Filed 27th Octr 86

— & —

A. J.: Read and granted, and leave given to bring in a bill accordingly, 30 Oct. '86, *S. P. of Vt.*, III (III), 256; bill read and accepted and sent to Council, 30 Oct. '86, *Ibid*, III (III), 256; bill, having been concurred in by Council, passed into law, 30 Oct. '86, *Ibid*, III (III), 256.¹ *C. J.:* Act read and concurred in, 30 Oct. '86, *G. and C.*, III, 115.

FOR AN ADDITIONAL LOTTERY TO BUILD A BRIDGE
xvii, 188

To the Honble the General Assembly of the State of Vermont to convene at Rutland on the 2^d Thursday of Octr instant —
This Petition humbly sheweth
    That the Subscribers were by the General Assembly at Bennington in [Blank] 178[Blank], appointed Managers of a Lottery for building a Bridge over West River in Brattleboro. —²
    That the Circumstances of the Country were such, (altho' the Managers early qualified themselves, & gave Security to the County Treasurer, as directed by the

---

1. For this act, see *Ms. Laws of Vt.*, I, 554.
2. For the resolution of the Assembly passed 2 March '84 establishing this lottery, see *S. P. of Vt.*, III (III), 33.

resolution of Assembly) that they did not conceive it prudent to make a Lottery until about a year past. —

That they have proceeded with good success in filling said Lottery — but as they were not at first impowered to raise a sufficiency of Money to compleat the Undertaking (the building of the Bridge being more expensive than was expected) they are unable to finish said Bridge without the further Assistance of the public. —

That the said Managers have unsuccessfully endeavoured to raise the Deficiency by Subscription, & therefore with out the leave of the legislature for making an additional Lottery, the expense already laid out must be wholly lost, & the beneficial purpose intended remain incomplete —

Wherefore your Petitioners pray leave to make another Lottery to raise such further sum (in notes) as a Committee of the Legislature shall conceive necessary for compleating their trust, with necessary Costs. — And they as in Duty bound shall ever pray &c. —

Brattleboro 4th Octr 1786

Benjn Butterfield ⎱ Managers of the
John Sargeants ⎰ Lottery for
Josiah Arms ⎱ building a
Saml Warriner ⎰ Bridge over
West River. —

We the Subscribers being Imployed by the Managers of West River Bridge Lottery as masters of the Stone and timber work of Sd Bridge Give it as our oppinion that the Plan laid by the manigers for building Said Bridge is as good a Plan as any could be laid and the money as Savingly laid out and by the best Calculation the money alredy raised will not Compleat the Sd bridge by two hundred pounds Lawfull money. Exclusive of the Expence of raising the money by Lottery

as Witness our hands
Stephen Gates
Elias Higley

— & —

Petition of the Managers of West River Bridge Lottery —
Filed Octr 14th
. . .*

To the honble Genl Assembly now sitting

Your Committee to whom was referred the within Petition beg leave to report as their Opinion that Benjn Butterfield Esqr Colo John Sargeants Mr. Josiah Arms Mr. Joseph Clarke & Micah Townsend Esqr have leave by Lottery to raise an additional sum of £ 280 for the purpose of compleating a Bridge over West River in Brattleboro' — That they give Bond to the Treasurer of <Windham County> the State in the sum of £ 2000 for the faithful Performance of their Trust — That they account with such person as shall hereafter be appointed by the Legislature for the expenditure of the said Money — & if there should be a surplussage that the same shall be disposed of as shall be hereafter directed by the Legislature — And that the State <be in no wise accountable> suffer no loss by said Lottery —

By Order
Phinehas Freeman Chairman

— & —

A. J.: *Read and referred to a committee, 16 Oct. '86, S. P. of Vt., III (III), 223; report of committee read and accepted, 16 Oct. '86, Ibid, III (III), 224; resolved according to the recommendations of the committee 16 Oct. '86, Ibid, III (III), 224.

FOR ADDITIONAL COMPENSATION FOR WAR SERVICES
BECAUSE OF CURRENCY DEPRECIATION[1]
xvii, 190

To the Hon[ll] General Asembly of the State of Vermont To Be convened at Rutland on the Second thirsday of october Instant the Petetion of Mess[rs] Sergant Abel Rice Nathaniel Carpenter Frances Akeley Asa Pratt & Jeduthan Roberts all of the Town of Guilford in the County of Windham & State of Vermont Most Humbly Sheweth that your Petetioners Served four years in the Continental Servis in Cap[t] Aldrichs Compiny under Major Benjamin Whitcomb[2] & that we your Petetioners Receved as wages But forty Shillings Per Month in Continental Paper money Dureing Said term your Petetioners therefore Humbly Pray that the Legislature of this State would Make up the Depreciation to them Agreable to the Continantal Scale or otherwise as you in your Greate Wisdom Shall think Best
& your Petetioners as in duty Bound Shall Ever Pray[3]

Abel Rice
Nathiniel Carpenter
Fraince Akeley
Asa Pratt
Jueduthan Robarts
John Martin
Michael Coffin

Guilford October
the 5th 1786

— & —

Petition of Abel Rice & others
Filed 18th Oct[r]
. . .*
To the Hon[ble] the Gen[l] Assembly now Sitting
The Committee to whom was refered the within Petition[4] Beg leave to report that in their Opinion the facts set forth in s[d] Petition are Supported and that the Committee of Pay Table be directed make up their Depreciation and Pay according to the Pay-Roll — Per Order Briant Brown
Oct[r] 26th 1786 —

— & —

> A. J.: *Read and referred to a committee, 18 Oct. '86, S. P. of Vt., III (III), 229;[5] *report of committee not accepted and petition dismissed, 26 Oct. '86, Ibid, III (III), 249.

---

1. For a previous petition to the same effect from Abel Rice and Asa Pratt, see p. 185, ante; and for a later one from five of the signers of this petition including an estate, see p. 291, post.
2. For record of this service by all the signers of this petition, see Vt. Rev. Rolls, pp. 663–664.
3. The last two signers presumably joined the others after the petition was composed. For a separate petition from John Martin, see p. 394, post.
4. Contrary to this statement on the petition and to the entries in the Assembly journal cited in the subjoined note, it appears that this petition was withdrawn on 19 Oct. '86 (S. P. of Vt., III (III), 230). According to this reference it was withdrawn in favor of a petition from Benjamin Whitcomb in behalf of all these petitioners. For Whitcomb's petition, see p. 272, post.
5. The date of the reading of the petition is given on the manuscript as 17 Oct.

FOR REFORM OF JUDICIAL PROCEDURE, THE CURRENCY AND TAXATION[1]
xvii, 191

To the Honorable the General Assembly of the State of Vermont to be convened at Rutland on the second Thursday of October instant —

N° 1

The Petition and remonstrance of the Free Men, & Inhabitants of the town of Danby in the County of Rutland. & state of Vermont Humbly Sheweth that whareas a Grate number of the Freemen & Inhabitants of Danby have by the present mode of administration Sufford in their property by what appears to this meeting Legally warnd & held in Danby at the useal place of holden Freemans meetings Thursday October the 5 [1786], to be needles Cost in Law Suits both by the present Latitude Granted to attornies at Law Sheriff Deputies and unnessesary Cost to plantif in Suites for Travil and attendenc and also by the many abatements of writs non Suit appeals and the Consequent delay of Justice therefrom arising and the Laws at present altring the Nature of the Contracts made by contracting parties by obblidging the debtor whare a Suit is Entered in Law to pay the Creditor Cash for the Sum in demand altho the Contract ware for produce or other property, and likewise by the present Very uneequal mode of Taxation your Petitioners therefore Pray —

Ist That no plantif in any civil action in any court in this State be alowed any thing in the bills of Cost in any Court for his her or their travil or Court attendance by him her or themselves or their attonies [sic] under any pretence whatsoever and that every person or persons in this State may have Liberty to prosecute their action in all Civil actions by themselves or any Such person as he she or they Shal Choose to Authorise by a power of attoney for that purpose & that thare may be a Short power of attoney worded in an act for the above said purpos —

II^{ly} That all writs and Executions granted by the Authority of this State be Servid and Returned by the Constable of the Town whare the Defendant dwels (but in Case a defendant Dwels in an [unorginerd] [unorganized?] Town then a Constable in the [Nerst?] Town adjoining[)] Excepting writs for Crimenal actions and those returned to the Superior or County Courts may be returnd by the Sherriff or any Constable in the County — and that the Service & return of all writs be paid for from the place of Service to the place of return and no more — that the Sherriffs be not alowed any Deputy in Serving writs issued in civil — actions —

III That Justice Courts be Courts of [Equity] who (with a Jury if requested by ither the parties in Suit) may try all Causses that comes before them whare the demand Doth not exsead the Sum of Six pounds if an unliquidated account or the Sum of Ten pounds if it be a note Bond or Liquidated Accounts & the Judgment of Such Court to be final and decsicive with out appeal or review to ither the parties and that the form of preceipts for Such Court be worded

---

'86, and the committee members correctly as Mr. Brown, Mr. Freemen and Mr. Aiken, the names given in the journal being crossed out.

1. For a more detailed understanding of the grievances set forth in this petition, see similar ones and explanatory notes on pp. 189, 216, *ante*. For other similar petitions, see pp. 232, 238, 244, 248, 262, 279, *post*.

in an acct for that purpose in Such mannor that there shal be no abatements of any writ[1] in any Such Courts and if ither the parties in Such Suit neglect or refuse to bring in their whole Accompts & demands on the other to be adjusted and finaly Settled by Such Court the parties So neeglecting or refusing Shal be for ever foreclosd the benefit of Collecting by Law any Such Accompt or demand.

IV.   That all Notes & Liquidated accompts that may Come before the County Courts that the Judgment of Such Court be final and decisive with out appeal or review to ither the parties and that the form of preceipts for Such Court be Such that thare may be no abatements of any writs in any Such Court and if ither the parties neglect or refuse to bring in all their demands or the other in notes or Liquidated Accompts to be adjusted and finealy settled by Such Court the parties So Neglecting or refuseing shal be for ever foreclosed the benefit of Collecting by Law any Such Accounts or Notes —

V.   That in all civil actions whare the Contracting parties did at the time of Contract agree to pay and receiv for the property bought & sold Speci [specie] produce or other property [for] payment ither by note bond or evidence of their agreement Such Specie produce or other property as Contracted for may be a tendery for payment of such Debts ither at the time agreed to for payment or at any time after the commencement of a Suit for Such Debts at the apprisal of men and such articles as Neet Cattls Hoses Sheep & Hoggs & grane shal answer in Lieu of any of the articles Contracted for, at the apprisal of men if the Defendant chuses wether to turn out any of the Last articles than the articles contracted for.

VI.   That the act intitald an act for the Appointment and regulating attoneis [attornies] be appeled [repealed?]²[2] —

VII.   That the Expence of govenment hereafter may be paid by the owners of property, Excepting articles of Nesescity such as Sheep Hogs all year old Cattle, one Cow to Each Family & the poles of all Minors and Such things as may incoridge agricultor arts Sciences & manfactories, and your Petitioners as in duty bound Shal Ever pray

Signed by order of the meeting
Edward Vail Moderator

Octr 5 [1786]   Ats^t Eben^r Tolman Clerk P.T.

— & —

[No Additional Material]

— & —

[See subjoined note for similar petition, p. 192, ante.]

---

1. In this context abatement of writs apparently meant the postponement or discontinuance of a suit. Such an abatement involved the defendant in the useless expense of appearing for trial in vain.

2. See "An Act for the appointment and regulating Attornies", passed February, 1779 (*Slade*, 330–331).

FOR THE CLOSING OF A ROAD
xvii, 192

To the Honble Genl Assembly to convene at Rutland on the second Thursday of October Instant — The Petition of Roger Enos of Hartland in the County of Windsor, humbly sheweth

That sometime since he purchased a farm in said Hartland, upon Connecticut River, on the mouth of Water-Quechee-River [Ottauquechee River]: And at the request of sundry Inhabitants of NewHampshire, caused a Ferry to be set up across Connecticut-River, at the mouth of said Quechee River, & opened a Road to the same thro' his farm at a considerable expence, upon the Assurance of said Inhabitants of NewHampshire, who are principally benefitted thereby, that he should have their Concurrence & Friendship in procuring a Grant of said Ferry, whenever their [Government] should be properly organized — [That] soon after their Constitution was formed he preferred a Petition to their Genl Court for that purpose which was rejected — and said Previledge was granted to one Joseph Kimball of NewHampshire, at the request of the same Persons who had formerly engaged their assistance to your Petitioner —[1] By reason of which he hath Lost said Previledge, and his farm is much injured by reason of said Roads, passing thro' his Meadows on such ground that a fence cannot be preserved from the floods — And as the Inhabitants of NewHampshire are the only people who can be more benefitted by said Ferrys, being maintained in that place, than at the place where the said Kimball, the present owner of the Ferry lives — The said Roger therefore prays an Act of Legislature may be passed enabling him to shut up said Road, & that the fee of said Land may revest [revert?] in him — And as in Duty bound shall ever pray

Hartland, 6th Octr 1786 Roger Enos

— & —

Patition Roger [Enos]
Fil^d^ Feby 26. 1787
. . .*

— & —

A. J.: Read and referred to a committee, 26 Feb. '87, S. P. of Vt., III (III), 294; *report of committee recommending that prayer be granted, read and accepted, and leave given to bring in a bill accordingly, 27 Feb. '87, Ibid, III (III), 296; bill read and accepted and sent to Council 27 Feb. '87, Ibid, III (III), 296; bill, having been concurred in by Council, passed into law, 27 Feb. '87, Ibid, III (III), 298.[2] C. J.: Act read and concurred in, 27 Feb. '87, G. and C., III, 129.

---

1. For the record of Roger Enos's petitions to the New Hampshire General Court, see Early State Papers of New Hampshire . . . , vol. XX (Manchester, 1891), pp. 113, 182, 221.

2. For this act, see Ms. Laws of Vt., II, 49–50.

FOR A LOTTERY TO BUILD A BRIDGE
xvii, 193

To the Honble Genl Assembly of the State of Vermont, to convene at Rutland on the second Thursday of Octr Instant the Petition of Roger Enos & others, Inhabitants of the County of Windsor — Sheweth

That the Inhabitants of that part of Hartland adjoining Connecticut-River near the Mouth of Water-Quechee-River [Ottauquechee River] are unable to keep the Roads in sufficient repair leading thro' said Town to Hartford along said River, & to erect the Bridges necessary to make the Communication between said Towns safe & convenient: That for that purpose, tis necessary there should be a bridge over Water-Quechee River near Col. Willard's Mills —1 which cannot be effected without a very considerable expence for defraying of which, they pray the Assembly to pass an Act granting <them> Liberty to [Amos Robinson, Daniel Spooner & Isaac Main] — to make a Lottery to raise the sum of £ 250 Pounds to be laid out in building said Bridge, under such regulations & restrictions as they shall judge proper — And as on Duty bound shall ever pray —
Hartland, 6th Octr 1786

> Roger Enos
> Wm Johson
> David Colburn
> Isaac Williams
> Thomas Holbrook
> Amos Robinson

— & —

Petition for Lottery to build a Bridge over Water-Quechee
Filed Feby 26. 1787
. . .*

— & —

A. J.: *Read and referred to a committee, 26 Feb. '87, S. P. of Vt., III (III), 294; *report of committee recommending that prayer be granted, read and accepted, and leave given to bring in a bill accordingly, 27 Feb. '87, Ibid, III (III), 296; resolved that liberty be so granted, provided that the three persons named post a bond in the amount of £1000, 27 Feb. '87, Ibid, III (III), 297.

FOR THE RIGHT TO OCCUPY CERTAIN LOTS OF LAND
xxii, 120

(Incomplete)2

To the Hon^ll general Asembly of [. . .]

---

1. That is to say, near the mouth of the river. See Dennis Flower, *Hartland in the Revolutionary War*, 2nd Edition (Hartland, 1914), p. 30.
2. A portion of the manuscript has been destroyed. The missing parts of the text are indicated by ellipses in square brackets without any superscript numerals. The actual number of words missing in any instance is difficult to estimate.

To be Conveaned at Rutland on the [. . .]
october instant
     The Petetion of Paul Chase [. . .]
of guilford [Guilford] in Windham County [. . .]
That your Petetioners are in p[. . .]
Lands in guilford Number — 11 [. . .]
Drawn to the Right of the pro[. . .]
And that your petetioners (some ti[. . .]
[Posesion] of one Joseph Peese w[. . .]
Lot in the year 1772 and made Co[. . .]
on the Same and that your Petetione [. . .]
Increase Said Improvements But [. . .]
Never had it So much as in Idea to in[. . .]
By purchasing said Posesson But on [. . .]
That the Legeslature of this State [. . .]
said [. . .] your Petetioners By h[. . .]
on the Same terms as to aney other the Subjects of This State
your Petetioners therefore [Humbly] pray that they may not be ousted But that
they may Still Injoy the Occupancy of said Lots of Land on Such terms And under
Such Restrictions as Shall Be Directed By This Hon^ll House
     and your petetioners as in duty Bound Shall Ever Pray
guilford October [9th?] 1786   Paul Chase
                                                          Nathan Horton

— & —

The Petition of Paul Chase and Nathan Horton
guilford
Filed 16th Oct^r
. . .*

— & —

     A. J.: *Read and referred to next session, 23 Oct. '86, S. P. of Vt., III (III),
239.

FOR A TAX ON LAND TO BUILD A BRIDGE
xvii, 195

To the Honorable the General Assembly to be convened at Rutland in the County
of Rutland on the Second Thursday of October Instant.
     The Petition of the Inhabitants of the Town of Westminster in Windham
County humbly
                                                          Sheweth.
     That the Inhabitants of said town have been put to great expence in makeing
& repairing roads & Bridges in said town. And that at a late meeting of s^d Inhabitants it was reported by a Committe for the purpose of viewing the Bridge
over Saxtons River in said town, that said Bridge was unsafe for Passengers to
pass over it, & that said Bridge was so far impaired by time & use that it was
impossible ever to repair it & that it was necessary for the public accomdation
that a Bridge should be immediatly built over s^d River. Whereupon the Town

voted to Build a Bridge over s^d River & Chose a Committe to draw a Petition to be presented to the Honorable the Legislature praying for a Land tax for the purpose of Building said Bridge — Your Petitioners therefore most Humbly pray this Honorable House that a tax of one penny half penny pr Accre might be laid on all the Lands in Said Town (Public rights excepted) for the purpose of Building said Bridge. And your Petitioners &c

Eliakim Spooner

Lot Hall   in behalf of said Inhabitants

Westminster Octr 9th 1786

— & —

The Petition of the Inhabitants of the Town of Westminster
Filed 18th Oct^r, 86 —
. . .*

To the Hon^le Gineral Assembly now Setting in Rutland your Com^tt to whom was Referred the within [Perttiten] bag Leve to repert that the facts Set up in the within [Pet^on] are true and that in our [oppenion] the Prayer of Said [Pe^tt] ought to be granted [in part & that ye Petitioners have leave to bring in a Bill for raising 1^d [p^r acre?]]

Jams Shafter for Comitte

Rutland October 18: 1786

— & —

A. J.: *Read and referred to a committee, 19 Oct. '86, S. P. of Vt., III (III), 229; *report of committee read and accepted, and leave given to bring in a bill accordingly, 19 Oct. '86, Ibid, III (III), 229; bill read and accepted, and sent to Council, 24 Oct. '86, Ibid, III (III), 242. C. J.: Act levying tax of one penny per acre in Westminster, read and concurred in, 24 Oct. '86, G. and C., III, 112.[1]

FOR A TAX ON LAND TO BUILD ROADS AND BRIDGES
xvii, 197

To the Honorable General Assembly of the State of Vermont — A Petition from the Inhabitants of the Town of Cornwall humbly sheweth — Whereas by reason of a large Swamp lying the East Side of this Town there must of Necessity be a Causey[2] of at least 160 Rods across which swamp there is a Road Already laid out to Middlebury which would much Accommodate the Public as well as the Private if it was made passable for the Chief Travel from Middlebury & Salisbury to the Lake must Necessarily cross the Swamp at this Place and also the Inhabitance of S^d Town think it of the utmost Importance that there should be a Bridge over a Stream Called Lemon Fare[3] this Stream though but small at low water will Require a Bridge of Twenty Five Rods long in the best place we can find which is on the same Road heretofore Mentioned to the Lake and for the Purpose of making some other Bridges in S^d Town and for making & mending Highways we your Peti-

---

1. For this act, see Ms. Laws of Vt., I, 547–548.
2. That is to say, a causeway.
3. Now Fair River.

tioners pray for a Land Tax of two Pence on the acre to enable the Town to do the Above S^d Services   This your Petitioners as in duty bound shall ever Humbly Pray

Dated at Cornwall   Je^r Bingham   ⎫   A Committee
this 9th Day of October   William Slade   ⎬
     AD 1786   Joel Linsly   ⎭   for s^d Town

— & —

A Petition for The Town of Cornwall
Filed 16th Octr 86
N° 5
. . .*

To the General Assembly now Sitting Your Comity who was referd the within Protition Faxs [facts] being Stated Declarations in Part Sported [supported] Bege leve to report as follows that a tax of one Penney on each acor of Land in Sd Townd be Granted Publick Rights Exsepted

Elisha Marsh for Comity
— & —

> A. J.: *Read and referred to a committee, 16 Oct. '86, S. P. of Vt., III (III), 224; report of committee read and not accepted and recommitted, 17 Oct. '86, Ibid, III (III), 225; report of committee read and accepted, and leave given to bring in a bill accordingly, 19 Oct. '86, Ibid, III (III), 230; bill read and accepted, and sent to Council, 23 Oct. '86, Ibid, III (III), 238; bill, having been concurred in by Council, passed into law, 24 Oct. '86, Ibid, III (III), 244.[1]
> C. J.: Act read and concurred in, 24 Oct. '86, G. and C., III, 112.

FOR REPEAL OF A TAX ON LAND TO BUILD A BRIDGE
xvii, 198

To the Honourable General Assembly of the State of Vermont to be held at Rutland in the County of Rutland on the Second Thirsday of Octobober [sic] Instant The petition of the Inhabitance of the Town of Hartland In said State being Legally warned and Assembled Humbly Sheweth that whereas the Honourable Assembly at their Sesion at Windsor in October 1785 did at the petition of a Few of the Inhabitance of the said Town of Hartland Grant a Tax on the Lands Contained in the Limits of said Town for the purpose of Building a Bridge over Queachy River [Ottauquechee River] which Rate or Tax was Granted with out the privity or knowledge of said Inhabitants and Contrary to the mind and will of the said In- habitants.[2] and as Your petitioners Humbly conceive could they have had Oppor- tunity therefor might have shewn reasons sufficient why said Tax Should not be granted and farther Your petitioners humbly beg leave to say the granting said tax Exparta [exparte] is an infringment on the rights of a Free people and therefore Humbly pray Your Honours to take the Matter contained in this petition into Your wise Consideration and Repeal Said act and Your petitioners, as in Duty

---

1. For this act, see Ms. Laws of Vt., I, 545–546.
2. For the petition referred to here, see p. 155, ante; and for the act granting the tax, see Ms. Laws of Vt., I, 529.

bound Shall ever Pray by order of said Inhabitants in Legal Meeting Met —
Dated Hartland October the 9ᵗʰ 1786 }   Elias Weld Town Clerk

— & —

Petition of the Town of Hartland —
Filed 16ᵗʰ Octʳ 86 —
. . .*

— & —

A. J.: *Read and referred to a committee, 16 Oct. '86, S. P. of Vt., III (III),
223; *report of committee read and accepted, and petition dismissed, 16 Oct.
'86, Ibid, III (III), 225.[1]

FOR REFORM OF JUDICIAL PROCEDURE, THE CURRENCY
AND TAXATION[2]
xvii, 199

To the Honorable the General Assembly of the State of Vermont to be convened
at Rutland on the second Thursday of October Instant.
    The Petition and remonstrance of the Inhabitants of the town of Pawlet in
the County of Rutland. —
    We the Inhabitants of the Town of Pawlet legally met for that purpose beg
leave humbly to represent to your honorable body, as Guardian of the rights of
the Citizens of this State that notwithstanding the wisdom care and Vigilance of
former Legislatures, sundry Laws some of which were perhaps beneficial or at
Least necessary at first, others introduced from the examples of other States
wedded to established customs without sufficient attention to their operation are
suffered to remain in our apprehension a real Grievance to the people and directly
opposed to the true Interest of the State —
    I Our system of Laws for administring Justice renders prosecutions un-
reasonably tidious and expensive to the Suitors — We beg leave to point out some
of them for your wise consideration. — A greater jurisdiction is given to justices
of the peace in civil actions than ought to be entrusted to single magistrates in
general, and to prevent the ill consequences of Vague uncertain Determinations an
appeal is allowed from their decisions in all cases to the County Courts, by which
mean the determinations of Justices of the peace are rendered altogether superfluous
and their courts instrumental of great Delays and unnecessary expence to the suitors.
— We beg leave to suggest another evil attending the present mode of proceeding
before justices of the peace — they are constituted courts of record, and obliged
to attend to modes and forms with all that precision necessary in supreme courts
whose decisions must become a rule of property to the Citizens and ascertain more
than half the Laws of the Land. — Were they made courts of conscience for the

────────

    1. According to the entry on the manuscript petition the committee simply re-
ported that the petition "ought not to be granted."
    2. For an identical petition from Tinmouth, see p. 216, ante. For other identical or
similar petitions, see pp. 189, 225, ante, and pp. 238, 244, 248, 262, 279, post.

final Determination of such smaller matters as might safely be entrusted to them, we apprehend they might become very useful to the community; and that if a rehearing be allowed on the merits in any case it ought for the sake of keeping the Laws uniform to be in the supreme court and to prevent Vexation to be at the expence of the party who shall move for the same.

There appears to us the same objections against the proper jurisdiction of the county courts. All actions exeeding the jurisdiction of a justice must be commenced in the County Court and from thence may be appealed to the Supreme Court. With due submission we cannot conceive that Superior courts can in the decsion [sic] of causes brought before them on appeals derive any advantage from the proceedings had in the lower courts, but that on the contrary this mode serves as a pretext for Delay creates a very unnecessary expence both of money and time to the suitors and by repeated attendances of parties and Witnesses occasions a great loss to the comunity by taking off numbers of industrious Citizens from their proper callings. We cannot be persuaded but that one fair and impartial trial in any cause would in general be more effectual for the promotion of justice than our present Dilatory sustem which opens a wide door for tampering with witnesses packing juries and a train of evils pernicious to the morals of the people and Destructive of justice itself. We beg leave to suggest for your wise and Deliberate consideration whether it might not be for the public good to limit the jurisdiction of the County courts to such smaller matter as they shall be thought competent finally to Decide. — To make the Supreme court a court of entries for all matters of consequence both civil and criminal — so to regulate proceedings as to give proper time of preparation to the parties and the judges an opportunity of determining all matters of law that properly belong to them without such unnecessary Delay as at present to parties Witnesses and jurors — This we conceive will be a mean of lessening expences expediting proceedings at Law and of giving stability and uniformity to the rules of property and the course of justice through the state

II We further wish that some more reputable mode of making up Costs than the present by travail and attendance might be Devised. We think it not only unjust but impolitic in many instances particularly in suits before justices of the peace as it is a great temptation to petty Law suits which ought not to be encouraged in a community and serves to maintain many Barritors & Pettyfoggers of little knowledge in the Law and less integrity to the great desturbance and vexation of quiet and peaceable Citizens

III We think that great number of Sheriffs Deputies employed in some Counties is detremetial to the publick — that there number ought to be limited and fees ought to be allowed for the service of Writs only from the place of service to the court or place of return

IV We likewise sincerely wish that in the present extreme scarcity of Cash your wisdom might direct some mode for the payment of Debts that should prevent the final ruin of such as are honest Debtors without a manifest injustice to Criditors —

V and Lastly — We beg leave to observe that the present mode of taxation appears to us a very great and real grievance — it appears to us to be manifestly unequal and impolitic — unequal because our taxes are mostly paid by the poor and middling class of people while the owners of unimproved thousands are exempt from the Burdens. impolitic because taxing improved lands only, faculties poles & produce is in fact no other than to tax industry, skill and Economy — Give us leave therefore to hope that in future our taxes will be so regulated as to fall more

equally on the Citizens and that instead of being a Check they may by proper exemptions operate as incouragement to industry, Economy arts and Manufactures and your petitioners as in Duty bound shall ever pray

Signed by order of the Meeting

Pawlet October

Lem¹ Chipman Moderator

9 AD 1786

— & —

Pawlet petition
N⁰ 2
Petition of Grievance

— & —

[See subjoined note for similar petition, p. 192, *ante.*]

FOR A TAX ON LAND TO BUILD ROADS AND BRIDGES
xvii, 200

To the Honnourable General Assembly of the state of Vermont to be Conven^d at Rutland in the County of Rutland on Thursday the 12th of Octr Instant the Patition of the select men of the Town of Bridport in the County of Addison Humbly Sheweth to your Honnors that your Honnours Patitioners have at Great Labour and Expence begun and still Continue to Carry on a very Considerable Settlement in s^d Town which is at Present Greatly Impeeded for want of Rodes and Bridges and as the Value of the Nonresident Proprietors Lands are greatly enhanced by S^d Settlement your Honnours Patitioners think it highly Reasonable they Should bear a part of the Expence of making roads and Building Bridges in S^d Town your Patitioners therefore pray that your Hon^r would grant a small Tax of one penney on the acre on the Land in S^d Town for the Purpuss above mentioned and your Honnours Patitioners as in Duty Bound Shall Ever Pray —

Dated at Bridport Octr 9th 1786

Nathan Manley ⎫ Select
Philip Stone ⎬ Men

— & —

A Patition of the Select men of Bridport
Filed 16th Octr 86.
N⁰ 1
. . .*

— & —

A. J.: *Read and referred to a committee, 16 Oct. '86, *S. P. of Vt.*, III (III), 224; report of committee read and not accepted, and recommitted, 17 Oct. '86, *Ibid*, III (III), 225; *report of committee read and accepted, and leave granted to bring in a bill accordingly, 19 Oct. '86, *Ibid*, III (III), 230;¹ bill read and accepted and sent to Council, 23 Oct. '86, *Ibid*, III (III), 238. *C. J.:* Act to

---

1. The report of the committee as given on the manuscript petition simply stated that the facts of the petition were true and that its prayer ought to be granted.

empower selectmen to levy a tax of one penny on each acre read and concurred in, 24 Oct. '86, *G. and C.*, III, 112.[1]

FOR COMPENSATION FOR CARE OF AN INVALID BOY
xvii, 201

To the Hon[ble] Gen[l] Assembly to convene at Rutland on the second Thursday of October Instant — The Petition of Stephen Conant of Windsor in the County of Windsor humbly sheweth

That sometime in the year 1785 one Thomas Phelps a transient Person brought to your Petitioner a Lad by the name of George Phelps son to the s[d] Thomas & desired him to take him upon trial to learn the saddlers trade, in the month of March 1785 the said George was taken sick with an ague sore, when your Petitioner applied to the said Thomas who was then a Prisoner in Windsor Goal, either to bind his said son to him, or provide for him in his sickness — He refused to bind him & was unable to provide for him. That your Petitioner than applied to the Select-men for the same purpose, who neglected & refused either to bind or provide for him in his sickness,[2] by reason of which your Petitioner was under the necessity of providing for the said George in his sickness for the Term of eight Weeks, for which he has received no compensation — That the expence to him, of Nurses, Watchers, Liquors & other necessaries supplied the said George during the said Term was not less than, three Pounds Lawful Money — That the said Phelps left the Country by flight, & your Petitioner is left entirely without Remedy for his said services — wherefore he prays your Honors to grant him an Order on the Treasurer for the said sum & as in duty bound shall ever pray —

Step[n] Conant

Windsor 10th Oct[r] 1786

— & —

Petition of Step[n] Conant for nursing Geo. Phelps
Filed 14th Oct[r]
. . .*

— & —

A. J.: *Read and dismissed, 14 Oct. '86, *S. P. of Vt.*, III (III), 220.

FOR RIGHT TO SELL REAL PROPERTY TO SETTLE THE ESTATE OF AN IDLE PERSON
xvii, 202

To the Honorable the General Assembly of the Freemen of the State of Vermont to be Conven[d] at Rutland on the 12th day of Oct[r] Instant —
the Petition of Benjamin Baldwin and Asahel Harmon Select, men of the Town of

---

1. For this act, see *Ms. Laws of Vt.*, I, 547.
2. For the authority of the selectmen over the children of the poor, see "An Act for maintaining and supporting the Poor", passed February 1779 (*Slade*, 378–379).

Dorset in the County of Bennington Humbly Sheweth, that agreeable to a Statute law of this State Intitled an Act for Relieving and ordering Idiots, Impotent, distracted, and Idle persons[1] Said Select men have taken all the Estate of Willm Lammon of Dorset afore s^d into there Care who by his mismanagement and bad husbantry mad it necessary and your Petitioners have applyed Such of S^d Estate as was in our power to dispose of for the Support of S^d Lammons numorous Family, and the payment of his Just debts and still there is debts to discharge and no propperty except Lands belonging to the S^d Lammons Estate —
Your Petitioners therefore humbly pray that this Honorable Assembly would order the Sale of So much of the s^d Lands as will raise the sum of Twenty pounds Lawfull money for the purposes above mentioned under Such direction as your honours in your wisdom shall See fit and your Petitioners as in duty bound shall every pray
Dorset Octr the 10th 1786

>   Benj^a Baldwin } Select
>   Asahel Harmon   } men

This Certifys that a Copy of an Invantary of Mr Willm Lammons Estate described in the above Petition was loged in the Town Clarks office in Dorset for Record the [21st?] day of June AD 1783
    Octr the 10th 1786

>   attest John Shumway Town Clark

— & —

Select Men of Dorsets Petition —
Filed 14th Oct^r
. . .*

— & —

> A. J.: *Read and referred to a committee, 14 Oct. '86, S. P. of Vt., III (III), 222;[2] *report of committee read and accepted, and leave given to bring in a bill accordingly,[3] 25 Oct. '86, Ibid, III (III), 245.[4]

FOR SPECIAL SETTLEMENT OF AN ESTATE
xvii, 203

To the honorable General Assembly of the State of Vermont to be holden at Rutland on the second thursday of October Instant

---

1. For this act, passed February, 1779, see Slade, 302–305.
2. The entry on the manuscript petition has the names of Mr. Marvin and Mr. Dewey crossed out and those of Mr. Sheldon and Mr. Burt substituted for them as members of the committee.
3. The committee report according to the entry on the manuscript petition simply found "the facts therein set up to be well seported and [we] are of opinion that the Prayer of the Petition ought to be Granted."
4. Although there is no record of its passage, a bill granting the petition was passed into law. See "An Act to empower the Sale of part of the real Estate of Wm Lammon", passed 27 Oct. '86 (Ms. Laws of Vt., I, 552).

The Petition of the subscribers Heirs Executors and Legatees to the Estate of William Fitch late of Pawlet in Rutland County Deceased humbly sheweth

That the personal Estate of the said William is Insolvent by the sum of £103 4/3 — that many of the Debts Due to said Estate are not payable short of two or three years which renders it impossible for the Executors of the Last Will and Testament of the said William to pay the Debts and Legacies in the mode prescribed by law without great loss to themselves as well as to the Estate — Your petitioners therefore pray your honors to enable them to make a Division of said estate real and personal agreeable to the Last Will of the said William under the Direction of the Judge of Probate for the District of Rutland upon the Legatees Heirs and Guardians giving security to the aforesaid Executors for the payment of Debts and Legacies and your Petitioners shall ever pray

Pawlet October 10th 1786

Altei Fitch
John Fitch
Philip Reed
Margret Reed
Ozias Clark
[Rachel] Clark
Leml Chipman
[Luna?] Chipman
Nathael Harmon
Abiel Harmon

— & —

Petition of Allei Fitch & others —
Filed 16th Octr 86
. . .*

— & —

A. J.: *Read and referred to a committee, 17 Oct. '86, S. P. of Vt., III (III), 225; *report of the committee read and accepted, and leave given to bring in a bill accordingly, 19 Oct. '86, Ibid, III (III), 230;[1] bill read and accepted and sent to Council, 19 Oct. '86, Ibid, III (III), 231; bill, having been concurred in by Council, passed into law, 23 Oct. '86, Ibid, III (III), 240.[2] C. J.: Act read and concurred in, 21 Oct. '86, G. and C., III, 110.

FOR ABATEMENT OF TAXES
xvii, 205

To the Honorable the General Assembly of the Freemen of the State of Vermont. to be convend at Rutland on the 12th day of Octr Instant the Petition of Isaac Farwell Constable & Collector of State Taxes for the Town of Dorset for the year 1786 Humbly Sheweth that the Return of the Grand List of the Town of Dorset for the year 1785 mad by the Listers of Sd Town to the Honorable the General Assembly at there Session at Windsor in Octr 1785 was three hundred and forty one pounds two large which obliges your petitioner to pay the Sum of four pounds

---

1. As given on the manuscript petition, the report of the committee simply declared that the facts stated in the petition were true and that it ought to be granted.

2. For this act, see Ms. Laws of Vt., I, 542–543.

five & three pence into the Treasurer of this State more the [than] he has any Authority to Collect, therefour your Petitioner humbly prays that this Honorable Assembly would order the Treasurer to Creadit your Petitioner the Sum of four pounds five shillings & three penc afore said or in aney other way Grant releif that your honours Shall See fit and your Petitioner in Duty bound Shall ever pray
Dorset Octr the 10th 1786

Isaac Farwell Cons^t

this may Certifys that we the Subscribers listers for the Town of Dorset for the year 1785 in our Return to the Honorable the General Assembly at there Session at Windsor in Octr 1785 of the Sum Totale of the Grand List of the Pole & Ratable Estate of the Inhabetence of S^d Town mad amistake in adding of three hundred & forty one pound Viz the mistake was in favour of the State against the Town —
attest. Eleaz^r Baldwin Junr ⎫ listers
Stephen Martindale ⎭

This may Certify that the Return of the Grand List of the Pols and Ratable Estate of the Inhabetance of the Town of Dorset, mad to me the Sum totale of which I Return^d to the Hon^le the Gen^ll Assembly at there Session at Windsor in Octr 1785 was Three hundred & forty one pounds two large which mistake was afterwards Rectify^d by the S^d Listers   Attest, John Shumway Town Clark
Dorset Octr the 10th 1786

— & —

[. . .]¹
Filed 14th Oct^r
. . .*

— & —

A. J.: *Read and granted, 14 Oct. '86, *S. P. of Vt.*, III (III), 222; resolved that Treasurer credit Dorset accordingly, 14 Oct. '86, *Ibid*, III (III), 222.

FOR REFORM OF JUDICIAL PROCEDURE, THE CURRENCY AND TAXATION²
xvii, 206

To the Honorabl the general Assembly of the State of Vermont to be convened at Rutland on the Second Thursday of October Instant —
the Petition and Remonstrance of the Inhabitants of the Town of Wallingford in the County of Rutland — we the Inhabitants of the town of Wallingford legally met for that purpose beg leave humbly to Represent to your Honorable body as guardians of the rights of the Citizens of this State that Notwithstanding the wisdom care and vigilence of former legislators sundry laws some of which were prehaps beneficial or at least necessary at first others Introduced from the Example of other States wedded to Established custom without sufficient attention to their operation are sufferd to remain in our apprehension a real greviance to the people

---

1. Three words or so inaccessible.
2. For an almost identical petition from Tinmouth, see p. 216, *ante*. For other identical or similar petitions, see pp. 189, 225, 232, *ante*, and pp. 244, 248, 262, 279, *post*.

& direcly opposed to the true Intrest of the State —

1   Our systam of laws for administring Justice renders prosecutions unreasonably tedious and Expensive to the Suitors. we beg leave to point out Some particulars for your wise consideration — a greater Jurisdiction is givin to Justices of the peace in civil actions than ought to be intrusted to Single Magistrates in general, and to prevent the ill Consequences of Vague uncertain determinations, an appeal is allowed from their Decisians in all cases to the county Courts by which means the determinations of Justices of the peace are Renderd altogather Superfluous and their courts Instruments of great delay and unnecessary expence to the Suitors — we beg leave to suggest another evil attending the present mode of proceeding before Justices of the peace they are constituted Courts of Record and obliged to attend to modes and forms with all that precision necessary in Superior courts whose Decision must become a rule of property to the Citizens, and ascertain more than half the laws of the land — were they regulated by the Statute Law of this State for the final decision of such Matters as might Safely be intrusted to them, we apprehend they might become very usefull to the communaty and that if a rehearing on the merits be allowed in any case it ought for the sake of keeping the laws uniform to be in the Supreme court, and to prevent vexation to beat [be at] the expence of the party who Shall move for the Same — their appears to us the Same objection against the present jurisdiction of the County Courts, all actions exceeding the Jurisdiction of a Justice must be commenced in the county courts and from thence may be appealed to the Supreme Court with submission we cannot conceive that Superior Courts can in the decision of causes brought before them or appeals derive any advantage from the proceedings had in the lower courts but that on the contrary this mode serves as a protest for great delay creates a very un-nesessary expence both of money and time to the suitor and by requiring repeated attendances of parties and witnesses occations a great loss to the communaty by taking off numbers of Industrious Citizens from their proper callings, we cannot be persuaded but that one fair and impartial tryal in any cause would in general be more effectual for the promotion of Justice than our present dilatory Systam which opens a wide door for tempering with witnesses packing Jurors and a train of wiles prenitious to the morals of the people and destructive of Justice itself —
we beg leave farther to Suggest for your wise and dileberate consideration, whether it might not be for the bublick [*sic*] good to limit the Jurisdiction of the County Courts to such Smaller matters as they shall be thought competant finally to decide to make the Supreme court a court of entries for all matters of consequence both civil and criminal — so to regulate proceedings as to give proper time of preperation to the parties and the Judges an opportunaty of deliberatily deliberating on matters of law that properly belong to them without such unnecessary delay as at present to parties witnesses & Jurors — this we conceive will be a means of lessning expences expediting proceedings at law and of giving Stability and uniformity to the rule of property and the course of Justice through the State —

2   We farther wish that some more equitable way of making up costs than the present by travil and attendance of parties might be devised — wethink it not only unjust but very impolitick in many Instances particularly in Suits before Justices of the peace as it is a great temtation to the [procecution] of petty lawsuits which ought not to be incouraged in a communaty and tens to maintain many Barrators & pettiffoggers of little knowledge in the law and less integrity to the great Dis-turbenc and vexation of quiet and peacable Citizens.

3   We think also that the great number of Sherriffs deputes [deputies] imployed

in Some Countyes is detremental to the publick, that their number ought to be limited not to exceed one in a county and fees ought to be allowed for Service of writs only from the place of Service to the court or place of return —

4 We likewise Sincerely wish that in present extreem scarcaty of cash your wisdom might direct some mode for the payment of debts that Shall prevent the final Ruin of Such as are honest debtors without manifest injustice to the Creditors —

5 ‹Lastly we beg leave to Observe that the present mode of taxation appears to us a very great and real greavance it appears to us to be manifestly unequal and impolitick — unequal because our taxes are mostly paid by the poor and midling class of people while the owners of unimprov^d Thousands are exemp'ed from the burthen Impolitick; because taxing improved lands only faculties, poles, produce, is in fact no other than to tax Skill industry and [Ecconomy?] give us leave theirfore to hope that in future our taxes may be So regulated as to fall more equally on the Citizens and that Instead of being a check they may by proper Exemtions operate as an incouragement to Industry [ecconomy?] arts and Manufactures — ›
and your petioners as in duty bound Shall Ever pray

Signed by order of the meeting
Abraham Jackson Moderator

Wallingford October 11th 1786

— & —

Wallingford Petition —
N° 8

— & —

[See subjoined note for similar petition, p. 192, ante.]

FOR ABATEMENT OF TAXES
xvii, 207

To the Honourable the General Assembly of the State of Vermont at their Sission to be holden at Rutland in said State on the Second Thursday of Octr 1786 —

The Petition of Robert Loggan of Manchester in the County of Binnington [Bennington] Humbly Sheweth —

Whare as your Petitioner in March in the year 1785 was Chosen Collector of State Taxes for the Town of Manchester and in the Month of August then Next Received from the Treasurer (by the hand of the sheriff of the County of Benington) two Warrants Commanding your Petitioner to Collect of the Inhabitance of the Town of Manchester three Pence and four Pence on the Pound on the List of all the Polls and Ratabell Estate for the year 1786 and after Receiving Said Warrants Applied to the Town Clerk Office and there Received An Attested Coppy of the Grand List for the afore said year, and found that the Listers in Making up said List had Made a Mistake and Returned to the General assembly and Clerk office About two Hundard Pound more then it Raly is — and as the Extents are Gon forth to the sheriff Against your Petitioner — your Petitioner Pray your Honours; that the said Sheriff be Ordered to Cridit your Petitioner such Sums as this Honourable Assembly Shall Find to be the Mistake (for which Purpos your Petetioner

hath hereunto Anexed a Coppy of the Grand Lists) Which your Pitetioner is in Duty Bound Shall Ever Pray —

Robert Loggan

Manchester Octr 11th 1786 —

John Austin	£ 12 : 0	Wm Drew	£ 15^x— 0
Daniel Arnold	16 : 10	Duncan Dun	10 — 0
David Anderson	40^x— 0	John Ellot	10 — 0
Dan Allen	25. 0	John Eeler	9^x— 0
Jonathan Akin	33 — 0	Waterman Eeler	26 — 10
James Anderson	3^x— 0	Rosel frances	20 — 0
Eli Brownson	20 — 0	Joseph French	41^x— 0
Andrew Blackman	24 — 0	Sam^{ll} French Senr	3 — 0
John W Bostick	11 — 0	Elijah French	36 — 0
Arthur Bostick	39^x— 0	David French	33^x— 0
Nathl Bostick	45^x— 0	Elias Gilburt	27 — 0
Nathaniel Burtin	54 — 10	Silas Goodrich	93^x— 0
Elijah Burtin	18^x— 0	Job Gidings	66 — 0
Sam^{ll} Beaman	18^x— 0	Wm Gould	31 — 10
Nath^{ll} Collins	51 — 10	Edward Henderson	15^x— 0
Elisha Church	20 — 10	Benj^m McIntier	25 — 0
Semor Crittinden	17 — 0	Timothy Bliss	20 — 0
Silas Canfield	17^x— 10	Lewis Beebe	43^x— 15
Jonathan Cory	22 — 10	David Bates	5 — 0
Daniel Cloid	9^x— 0	Thomas Bull	63^x— 10
Solomon Collen	12. 0	Thos Bull Ju^r	9 — 0
Elias Curtis	34^x— 0	Benona Bishop	9^x— 0
Amos Chipman	3 — 0	Henry & Charles Bolles	43^x— 0
Thos Barney	72. 10	[Royce] Beckwith	25 — 0
Martin Barber	9^x— 0	Joseph Baker	[40?] 10
Thomas Buck	19^x— 0	Abel Bristol	25^x 0
Nath^{ll} Boorn Jr	9^x— 0	Daniel Beckwith	62 — 0
Barned Boorn	16^x— 10	Sarah Bristol	13 — 0
Jered Boorn	10 — 0	Wm Bedel	40 — 10
Isaac Brevoot	28 — 0	Nathan Beaman	9^x— 0
Benjn Bears	11^x— 0	Abraham Collins	34^x— 10
Jonathan Brace	101 — 0	Ch^r Collins	29^x— 10
Gideon Barber	43 — 10	Shadrick Danks	29 — 0
[Eliezer] Bolden	107^x— 0	Sam^{ll} French Jr	32^x— 0
Nath^{ll} Boorn	43 — 0	Joseph Farrand	9^x— 0
Willm [Bennit?]	6^x— 0	Wm Hinds	44 — 0
Chr^t [Brackit]	21 — 0	Thad^s Harris	10 — 0
Daniel Boorn	12 — 0	Benjn Hamond	56^x— 0
Joseph Dixson	31 — 10	Daniel Johns	32 10
		Daniel Jones	79^x— 10
		Jehial Johns	17 — 0
		John Smith	60 — 0
		John Howard	[. . .]6^x— 0

[1026 — 00]   [[306?] 5]

Samuel Wheeler	£	6^x— 0
Seth Pettebones		11 — 0
David Lee Ju^r		49 — 0
Daniel Shaw		12^x— 0
Joshua Ramond		12 — 0
John Jones		12 — 0
Jonathan Allen		9^x— 0
James Lewis		21 — 0
Elias Hopkins		9^x— 0
Daniel Haws		23^x— 10
Joshua Hillard		11 — 10
Stephen Harrick		10 — 0
David Hubbel		19^x— 0
Barna Hatch		46 — 0
Alexander Haris		17^x— 0
Ebenezer Howard		30 — 0
Jabaz Halley		38^x— 0
Sam^{ll} Hitchcock		59^x— 0
Samuel Hull		17 — 0
Richard Henesey		36^x— 0
Nehemiah Hide		15 — 10
James Hide		12^x— 0
Ephriem Hide		6 — 0
George Sexton		32 — 10
Nathan Smith		44^x— 0
Sam^{ll} Sutharland		41 — 0
Reuben Smith		14 — 0
Aaron Sexton		3^x— 10
Palatiah Soper		27 — 10
Moses Sperry		37^x— 10
Jonathan Sexton		15 — 0
Printis Storis		13^x— 0
Timothy & Leonard Soper		57 — 0
Stephen Tuttill		24^x— 0
Amos Thompson		9^x— 0
Peleg Sutharland		18^x— 0
Wallis Sutharland		19 — 0
Calab Shelden		9^x— 0
Dan^{ll} Stephens		27^x— 10

Moses Soper	£	29^x— 10
George Smith		30 — 0
Josiah Shelden		19^x— 0
Stephen Smith		44^x— 15
Elijah Smith		15 — 0
Josiah Terrey		10 — 15
Benjn Vaughan		21 — 10
James Vaughan		65^x— 0
Jeremiah Wait		13 — 0
Stephen Washburn		11 — 0
Asa Waller		80 — 0
John White		37^x— 0
Wm Wheeler		6 — 0
Nicklus Wood		18^x— 0
Isaac Whelpley		6^x— 0
Jeremiah Whelpley		54 — 0
Ebenezer Woodard		16^x— 0
John Richardson		25 — 0
Andrew Richardson		23^x— 0
Nath^n & A. Richardson		62 — 10
Nathan Richardson J^r		12 — 0
Ara Rose		49^x— 0
Joel Rose		54 — 0
Joshua Rose		30 — 0
Sarah Rose		41 — 0
Abraham Rose		32^x— 0
John Roberts		18 — 0
John Roberts Ju^r		12^x— 0
Christopher Roberts		20 — 0
Philip Reynolds		10 — 10
Abel Pettibone		14 — 0
Alexander Prindel		26^x— 0
David Purdy		6 —[0]
Truman Powel		16^x— 0
Sam^{ll} Pettebone		61 — 0
Benjn Purdy		69^x— 10
Daniel Purdy		53 — 10
Ruben Purdy		45^x— 0
James Jameson		56 — 0
Wm Jameson		18^x— 10
		[109 — 0]

Wm Kyle	£ 25 — 0
Gideon Ormsby	75 — 0
Jonathan Ormsby	21^x— 0
Daniel Ormsby	9 — 0
Jacob Odel	33^x— 0
Robert Loggan	54 — 10
Sam^{ll} Lamfear	31 — 0
Josiah Lockwood	35^x— 0
Nath^{el} Newton	14 — 0
Martin Powel	54^x— 0
Stephen Keys	48 — 0
Eliakem Deming	63^x— 0
Wm Marsh	13 — 10
Richard McIntier	22 — 0
Isaac Marks	13 — 0
Timothy Mead	70 — 10
Truman Mead	16^x— 0
Aaron Mason	43 — 10
Jacob Mead	9^x— 0
Thado Munson	83^x— 0
Philip Mead	24 — 0
Timothy Mead J^r	32 — 10
Benjn Purdy J^r	55^x— 0
Aaron Beaman	6 — 0
Wm Parish	18^x— 0
Jered Munson	130 — 10
Sam^{ll} [Wrieght?]	41 — 0

	[107 : 0]
Philip Reynolds	9 — 0

The Sum Total of £ 5552 − 5 − 0—
The valuation of the Town of Manchester for the year 1784

{ The above named Philip Reynolds appears to be entered twice which be a mistake of at least £9 as their never but one Man of that name in Town }

    Samuel French
    Timothy Mead Junr } Listers
    Jonathan Aikin

These Certify that the foregoing is a true Coppy of the Original List of the Poles & Ratable Estate of the Inhabitants of the Town of Manchester for the year 1784 —
    attest Martin Powel Town Clerk
Manchester Octr 11th 1786 —

109 —
107 —
306 — 5
_____
522 — 5 ¹

— & —

Petetion of Robert Loggan
Filed 14ᵗʰ Octʳ 1786
. . .*

To the Honourable General Assembly Now Seting Your Committee to whom was
refered the within Petition beg Leave to report that the facts in the within Petition
are not Suported only in Part and therefore your Committee are of Opinion that
the within Petition be refered to the Next Seting of the General Assembly

Brewster Higley for Commetee

— & —

> A. J.: *Read and referred to a committee, 14 Oct. '86, S. P. of Vt., III (III)
> 222; *report of committee recommending that Manchester be credited all taxes
> laid on the error, which was found to have been £130–10, read and accepted,
> 24 Feb. '87, Ibid, III (III), 291; resolved that Treasurer credit Manchester
> accordingly on the 3ᵈ and 4ᵈ tax for 1784, Ibid, III (III), 291.

———————

FOR REFORM OF THE CURRENCY AND JUDICIAL PROCEDURE[2]
xvii, 208

To the Honorable the Representatives of the freemen of the State of Vermont to
be Conveaned at Rutland on the Second Thursday of October next. —

The Petition and Remonstrance of your Honors Petitioners humbly
Sheweth —

That there are Certain matters of grievance that So Senceably effect not only
your Petitioners but also the People at large, that unless your Honors will graccously
be pleased to enact Laws that will in Some measure relieve their burdens by preventing the unnecessary Costs and unreasonable delays of Justice, to which they
are Subjected, it appears to your Petitioners that the Consequences must be attended
with apparent Injustice & [eminant] danger, we Shall therefore endeavor to point
out Some matters that appear really grevious and propose ways & means of
Redress —

First that the People have been Reduced to many difficulties and much Impoverished
by the late Destressing War and the necessities of the People being much

———————

1. This sum, it will be observed, is approximately one tenth of the whole valuation
of the town.

No explanation offers itself for the presence of the raised x which follows the
pound figures for certain names.

2. For a brief discussion of the conditions in Vermont and other states which
occasioned this petition, see W. H. Crockett, Vermont: The Green Mountain State, vol.
II (New York, 1921), pp. 407–421; also G. and C., III, 357–380. For similar petitions
presented at this time, see pp. 189, 216, 225, 232, 238, ante, and pp. 248, 262, 279, post.

greater than their abilities the Country being almost entirely drained of
Cash render it imposible for the People to pay the demands of their Credittors
agreeable to their Contracts, it may be here objected that people ought not
to obligate them Selves further then they Can perform and that if they do it
is reasonable that they alone should Suffer the Consequences — it is true
People ought [Prmetually?] [mutually?] to fulfill their Contracts but as the
Performance of one most Commonly depend on the fulfilment of another, it
is morrally Impossible, when we Consider the Trifle of Specie in circulation
and that the best Charector in the State cannot be Safe in engaging any
Considerable Sum of which he is not Possessed, — under these Considerations
we beg leave to propose whether it would not be for the Common good and
emolement of the People at large to make produce Stock &c a tendry on
Executions to be appraised to the Credittor at the Real value — we expect
it will be further objected that, Credittors will be Injured, and that it is
ungenerous and unjust with Regard to those that live out of the State who
perhaps have the Principle demands on us. answer[:] it appears to your
Petitioners that it will do the most ample Justice of any method that can be
devised, our Reasons are these that if property is turned out at the appraisal
of Man, probably we are able to pay our Debts, but in Case our Estate is
taken and Sold at Publick Vendue to the highest bidder it is unlikely that
our whole estates would pay one quartor part. in which case three quarters
of our Credittors, must loose their whole demands (which being true) will
excite every Credittor to try to be the first, and it appears Rational that the
Debtor under these circumstances is induced to use every art and Intreague
in his Power to evade the force of Law which occations a numerous train of
Suits, and opens a door for the Chief of the Cash that can Possiblely be
found to Satisfy Court fees Attorneys &c — And with regard to other States
they have Set the example, which is an Inducement to us to follow — we
Consider our Selves on uneaqual ground whilst on the one hand we are
obliged to Receve any produce or other article, on which we levy at the true
value, and on the other hand Paper which is not a Currency in this State —[1]
All which circumstances appears to your Petitioners, Sufficient motive to
Justify the Passing a Law, for the Purpose before mentioned —

2[d]   there are Certain Laws, of this State that appear to your Petitioners to
opperate in a manner calculated to Multiply Law Suits and extraordinary
Costs reather than for the peace and advantage of the People. viz. the Law
Regulateing Civil actions,[2] likewise the Law, allowing and regulateing
offsetts,[3] it is natural to inquire in what respect the before cited Laws tend
to multiply Suits — answer — however the Legislature expected those Laws
would opperate certain it is, that every particular, Note order, Receipt Book
account, or other Contract Subsisting between any two parties each most

1. Presumably Vermont creditors received produce *or* paper money not currency
in the state in payment for out-of-state debts.
2. See "An Act for the directing and regulating of civil Actions", passed February,
1779 (*Slade*, 383–387) and "An Act in addition to, and alteration of, 'An Act regulating
civil Actions' ", passed February, 1784 (*Ibid*, 485).
3. See "An Act for the preventing multiplicity of Law-Suits", passed February,
1781 (*Slade*, 423–424) and "An Act for allowing and regulating Off-sets", passed
October, 1782 (*Ibid*, 457).

Commonly produces a Suit and an appeal must be granted from every Judgment (as many Construe the Law) if required, and frequently the Costs on each Suit, is double to the debt or Damage, tho: it is true that it is not neccessary, that every particular matter Should be brought Separate, yet few are brought otherwise, which is a means of numerous Suits and needless Costs, as also the Plaintiff in the Case being obliged to Send forth a Shedule or Coppy of his accounts with his Writ appears to your Petitioners to be attended with apparent Injustice, in this respect namely the furnishing the Defendant with a Coppy of the Plaintiffs account, puts it into his Power of fixing his own according to his wishes, and likely in many instances excites him to make a Charge of trifling articles in order if possible by enhancing his own account, at least to through [throw] the Cots [Costs] upon the Plaintiff, — and the additional Costs of the Schedule [Coppeing] &c is very Considerable — and with Respect to the act allowing and Regulateing Offsetts to appear to your Petitioners to be Calculated, in Such a manner as to Subject the Person who would wish to plead any matter in offsetts, to the Disagreeable necessity of applying to an Attorney, or run the Risk of Sacrificeing his Cause, for fees are able to form a plea in Several Counts (as the Case frequently Requires) with Proper Introductions agreeable to the Statute and is therefore under absolute necessity of loosing the benefit Law or throw away his Money, or that which is worse viz. give it to an attorney it appears to your Petitioners the Inconveniences before Cited might be Remedied by a Law directing that when ever Suit is brought before any Justice Court the Parties Should be obliged to exhibit all matters then due and after a fair hearing before said Court either Party being allowed the Previlidge of a Jury of Six Men if required and Judgment being rendered Should be a final barr against any future action; for any matter Cognizable by Said Court and due at or before the Commencement of Such Suit and that no appeal be allowed from any action brought on a fair Note of hand, or from a Suit brought on any other matter, where it appears evident that Justice may have taken place and that no appeal be allowed from any Court whatever when it appears evident to Said Court that it is done with a Design only to Delay Justice —

3dly There is another matter which Seems to Claim our attention viz. with Respect to the first framing the Laws of this State when the Several Courts were Appointed and Organized, ascertaining their Several Powers & Jurisdictions, first a Single Minister of Justice authorized to hear and Determine Causes to the amount of ten Pounds or under, likewise two Justices to hear and Determine Causes of Twenty Pounds or under, as also County and Supreme Courts with their particular Jurisdictions, but it appears that through Some mistake or misfortune one of Said Courts viz. (that holden by two Justices) is entirely expunged, and by what means, or for what reason is unknown to your Petitioners —1 we would not wish to treat any Charactors with Indignity, or disrespect, but are far from believing that it was done by design of the Legislature, or in any wise agreeable to the wishes of the People at

---

1. "An Act directing Justices of the Peace in their office and duty", passed February, 1779, provided for the trial by two or three justices of civil causes involving less than twenty pounds (*Slade*, 288–289). However, "An Act defining and limiting the Powers of the several Courts within this State", passed June, 1782 (*Ibid*, 450–454), which doubtless supplanted the previous statute, contained no such provision.

large, and that if those Courts were again revived the effects would prove salutary, and be a means of Saving great expence, and of a more Speedy execution of Justice, which will perhaps be better evinced, when we Consider the extraordinary Costs of attending the County Courts — were it only in Regard to the fees allowed to the Recoverers in the Several Causes, which Commonly falls into their Attourneys hands. — although two Shillings p^r day on each Cause appears trifling — yet when we Consider that it is Common for one attourney to have the Charge of near one hundred Causes in one Court and Sometimes more it amounts to a Considerable Sum, and when we add to that their Lawful and other extraordinary fees, we may with propriety Conclude that the whole amount for one Days attendance, frequently arrises to a sum that would hire a Common labourer at least Six months, and when we further Consider that it is Common for one attourney to attend the Courts in two or three County^s we find that the whole of their Perquisites soon arrises to a Prodigious Sum and Can easily perceive the reason why so much art and pains are used to delay and put actions over from one Court to another and even to Continue those that are Called out on Default, till near the Cloase of the Court, here we Consider that all the time that is Consumed in Contriveing to keep actions from a Cloase, and in disputeing what actions ought to be Continued or laid over (which (is very Consider-able) [*sic*] augments the Sum that is drawn out of the Treasury to pay the Court fees, which Influences the honest Man that never had a Cause in Court and perhaps never will, to Cry out and Say Allas, I am Injured, and that it is unreasonable & even unjustifyable that I Should be obliged to Support Law Suits and Contentions which I abhor, and which your Petitioners view grievous. —

4^thly Their is likewise another matter which we esteam eaqually Injurious with those before mentioned and Seems to Claim the attention of every friend to Justice viz. with respect to pleas & pleadings, it is held & Cultivated as a principle that all Pleas ought to be in writing, and that their Can be no proper foundation for record in Case of verbal pleading by which means the honest Man that is unacquainted with writeing Pleas is reduced to the alternative of applying to an attourney, which appears to your Petitioners entirely unreasonable and unjust, that the People Should be obliged to pay Such enormous Sums, to gratify those that are Seeking their Ruin, on a vain pretention of having their Pleas entered Regular when the Court might be as well Possessed of the Cause from the mouth of the party as from the at-tourneys plea and Justice in every respect as Impartially administered and a proper Record might be made that would answer every necessary purpose in case of Verbal Pleading —

5^thly We cannot do Justice to our Selves without turning our minds for a moment on the present unreasonable mode of abateing Writs on trifling matters, and which the Law two far Justifies as appears to your Petitioners —[1] We only wish that no writ might ever abate in any Case whatever where Process is legally Served, the Declaration fairly Containing the Action and plain to be understood —

When your Honors Petitioners Contemplate the needy oppressive circum-

---

1. In this context "abateing Writs" presumably meant the postponement or dis-continuance of suits on the sole basis of technical defects in procedure.

stances of the People, the extraordinary Costs arriseing and the numerous Debts Contracting to Satisfy Court fees Attourneys &c we are led to Conclude that Instead of enjoying the inesteamable liberties and priviledges of a free People we must unavoidably be subjected to Perpetual Slavery and Ruin unless some means of Relief can be devised — Surely a Serious Consideration of the matter will excite every true friend to Goverment to endeaver to adopt a Speedy Remedy — it will readily be granted that what is here laid down is a fact, but the grand point is how Shall we obtain Relief, is not the method of Practice on Law here, the only one known in Europe or America[,] and Shall Vermont attempt to alter or reform rules of antiquity. Certainly if thereby She Can promote the good of her Subjects, we therefore offer our feble Ideas on the Subject (hopeing Some Abler Pen will set the matter in a Clearer light) which are as follows. —

That a sufficient number of Persons noted for Wisdom and virtue be appointed annually by the Legislature to attend and assist the County and Supreme Courts at their Sessions by opening and explaining the particular Causes, and that the Plantiff in each Case be obliged to pay Such Sum or Sums as Shall be found Sufficient to Support the Law at Such time or times as the Legislature may by Law Direct, to Such Person or Persons as may be appointed Treasurers to Receive the Same — and that the affore Said Courts and their Assistants Receive their Respective fees or Salleries out of Said Treasuries in Such manner as the Legislature may order and that no person or Persons be allowed to draw any writ or appear at the Barr, in any Court in this State in the Charactor of an Attourney or under the Influence of a fee, on Penalty of forfeting the Sum of one Thousand Pounds —

That your Honors will graciously be pleased to take this our Humble Petition & Remonstrance under your wise Consideration and grant Such Relief in the Premises as in your wisdom Shall appear expedient — and your Petitioners as in duty bound Shall ever pray—

At a Town Meeting Legally warned and held by adjournment on the 5th day of Sept 1786 the foregoing Petition and Remonstrance was taken under Consideration and was unanimously voted to be laid before the General Assembly in October then next

attest Martin Powers Town Clerk

Manchester Oct[r] 11th 1786

— & —

[No Additional Material]

— & —

[See subjoined note for similar petition, p. 192, *ante*.]

FOR REFORM OF JUDICIAL PROCEDURE, THE CURRENCY AND TAXATION
xvii, 209

To the Honourable the General Assembly to be holden in Rutland on the second thursday of Octob[r] Next — the perticion of the Township of Pittsford

County of Rutland humbly sheweth[1]— that whereas a number of the good people of this State have by the present mode of administration suffered much in their property by what apears to the Inhabitance of this Town (viz) —

their apears to be needless Coast [cost] both by the present latitude granted to atornies at law sheriffs deputies and unnessary Cost to plantiffs in suits for travil & atendance — and also by the maney abatements of writs nonsuits apeals and the Consequents delay of Justice therefrom arising and the law at present altering the nature of the Contract made by Contracting parties by Obloigeing the debter where a suit is entered in law to pay the Credetors Cost for the sum in demand or the contract were for produce or other property — and likewise by the present very uneaquel mode of taxation your perticiners therefore pray —

first that no plaintiff be allowed aney Cost in aney Civil action in aney Court for his or her or their travil or Court atentance by him her or themselves or atornies under aney pertence whatever and that Every person or persons in this State may have liberty to prosecute their actions in all civil Causes by themselves or aney such person as he or they shall Chose or arthorise by a power of an atorney for the purpose —

secondly that all writs and Executions granted by aney athority in this state be served and returned by the Constable where the defn^d dwells Excepting writs in Crimanal actions and those returnable to the County and superior Corts may be served and returned by the sheriff or aney Constable within the County — and that the servace and returne of all writs be paid for from the place of servace to the place of return and no further and that the sheriff be not alowed aney deputy in serving writs issued in Civil actions

3ly that Justises Courts of Equity who with a Jury is requested by Either of the parties in the suit may try all Causes where the demands of the plantiff doth not Exceed ten pounds if the acount be liquidated or the demand is by note or bond if not liquedated the sum of six pounds onley and the Judgments of such Courts to be final and desisive without apeal or revew to Either of the parties — and that the form of precepts for such Courts to be worded in an act for that purpose in such a manner their shall be no abatement of aney writ in aney such Court and if Either of the parties in such suits neglect or refuse to bring in their whole account and demands to be ajusted and finially setled by such Courts the person so neglecting or refuseing may be forever foreclos^d the benefit of Colecting by law aney such account —

4ly that in all Civil actions where it apears that the Contracting parties did at the time of Contract agree to pay and receive for the property bought and sold spece [specie] produce or other property for payment Either by bond note or Evidance of their agreement such species produce or other property and as Contracted for may be a tenderry for the payment of such debts or dues Either at the time agreed to for payment or at aney time after the Commencement of a suit for such debts at the aprisal of men and all book debts where the plantiff Cannot prove he was to have Money for such debts may be satisfied with beaf pork butter Cheese wooll flax grane or Neat Cattle at the aprisal of men

5ly and that the Expence of goverment which at present is laid on articuls of necesity in a very uneaquel manner by which the burden of the State Expence is

---

1. For a more detailed understanding of the grievances set forth in this petition, see similar ones and their explanatory notes on pp. 189, 216, 225, 232, 238, 244, *ante*. For other similar petitions, see pp. 262, 279, *post*.

laid on the midling farmer and labouring poor man hereafter be paid by owners of property in propotion to the true value of the property protected Excepting of necessity such as sheep wooll flax and one Cow to Each famley all year old Cattle and such things as may incourage aggrecultar arts and Ciences and mannafactries with an intire Exemtion of the poles of minors —

6thly That the act Intiteled an Act Appointing and regulateing Attornies[1] be appeal^d [repealed?] —

as your Pertitsioners in Duty Bound Shall Ever pray —

Voted in Town meeting at Pittsford this 11th Day of October 1786

attest   Benj^a Coolley   T: Clark

— & —

Pittsford pertition —
N° 3

— & —

[See subjoined note for similar petition, p. 192, *ante*.]

FOR COMPENSATION FOR APPREHENDING HORSE THIEVES
xvii, 210

To the honorable General Assembly of the State of Vermont —

The petition of the subscriber humbly sheweth —

That sometime in the month of April last past a Couple of Villains came into the town of Dorset in the County of Bennington and stole two horses from them and rode them immediately to Newbury port in the State of New Hampshire[2] and that the subscriber pursued the said theives to the said Newbury port and there appehended one of them and brought him back and confined him in goal in the County of Bennington & after wards caused the other thief to be appehended [*sic*] and convicted before the supreme Court at their sitting in Manchester August last in doing all which he has been put to great trouble and expence for which the superior Court could not by Law allow him any reward — the Subscriber therefore prays the honorable Assembly to grant him a sum sufficient to pay him for his trouble & expence and he as in duty bound shall ever pray —

John Manley 3^d

Dorset 12th October 1786 —

— & —

Petition of John Manley 3^d
Filed 20th Oct^r

. . .*

Rutland october 23^d AD 1786
to the Honourable General assembly now Siting your Committee to hoom was Refered the within Petition Beg Leave to Report that we find the facts to Be true

---

1. See "An Act for the appointment and regulating Attornies", passed February, 1779 (*Slade*, 330-331).

2. No record of any Newburyport, New Hampshire has been found. There is no reason to doubt that the place was actually Newburyport, Massachusetts.

Set up in the Petition. Never the Less we think that the State ought not to Be at the Cost, and that the Petition ought to Be Dismised

Joshua Wood for Committee

— & —

A. J.: *Read and referred to a committee, 23 Oct. '86, *S. P. of Vt.*, III (III), 238; *report of committee read and accepted and petition dismissed, 23 Oct. '86, *Ibid*, III (III), 240.

FOR COMPENSATION FOR USE OF SAWMILL BY THE UNITED STATES
xvii, 212

To the Honorable the General Assembly of the State of Vermont now Siting at Rutland
The Petition of James Mead of Rutland in the County of Rutland & State of Vermont humbly sheweth: that his Saw-Mill was attached for the Use of the United States on the 28ᵗʰ Day of May 1778 and held in that Service 6 Months & 25 Days and 400 Pine Saw-Logs and 1000 feet of Pine boards were taken for the same use and also your Petitioner lent 50 weight of 8ᵈ Nails for the use of the Garrison then in Rutland —
and your Petitioner has made application to the Commissioner of accounts for the United States three times, for the pay for the use of his Saw-Mill and the other articles above mentioned — and has been refused any pay an account that the Garrison then maintained in Rutland was merely for the defence of this State, Do therefore pray your Honors to take this matter under your Wise consideration, and provide a way that your Petitioner may receive a Compensation for the Damage he has sustained as you in your Wisdom may think fit as your Honors Petitioner is in duty bound shall ever pray

James Mead

Rutland Oct. 13ᵗʰ 1786 —

— & —

Jaˢ Mead's Petition —
. . .*
To the honorable the General Assembly now Sitting your Committee appointed on the Within Petition Report their opinion that the facts are in the Petition Stated & that Col Mead ought to receive out of the Public Treasury forty pounds ten Shillings & four pence —

Eber Allen for the [Comʸ?]

Your Committee to Whom was refered the Within Petition Beg Leave to report that we find by Certificates from Majʳ Whitcomb that the Army had the Use of the Saw Mill as Set forth in the Petition and Likewise a Hundred Mill Logs which with the 50ʷᵗ of Nails & the Work he did for the Use of the Army he Ought to be paid for out of the Treasury amounting in the Whole to Thirty Pound fourteen Shillings
Rutland Octoʳ yᵉ 21. 1786   Jno Bridgeman for Committee
To the Honˡᵉ Generall Assembly now Sitting

— & —

A. J.: *Read and referred to a committee, 18 Oct. '86, *S. P. of Vt.*, III (III), 228; *report of committee read and dismissed, and petition referred to a new committee, 21 Oct. '86, *Ibid*, III, (III), 237; *report of second committee read and not accepted, and petition dismissed, 23 Oct. '86, *Ibid*, III (III), 240.

FOR COMPENSATION FOR LOSS BY FIRE OF STATE NOTES AND A DEED
xvii, 213

To the Honorable the General Assembly of the State of Vermont now siting at Rutland —

The Petition of Samuel Allen of Tinmouth in the County of Rutland and State of Vermont humbly sheweth, that the House of your Petitioner accidentally took fire on the night of the 21ˢᵗ Day of January last and was intirely consumed with allmost everything that it contained, amongst the articles that were consumed were Notes Issued by the Treasurer of this State to the value of Thirteen pounds ten shillings Lawful Money besides the Interest due on said Notes which he cannot ascertain exactly — And also a Deed executed by Col. Seth Warner now deceased [⟨to Ebʳ Allen⟩] of two Rights of Land in the Township of Eden in the County of Addison & State of Vermont (viz) the original Rights of Seth Warner and Reuben Warner. Do therefore, pray your Honors to pass an Act directing the Treasurer of this State to Issue his Notes to the said Samuel Allen for the above said sum of £ 13–10–0 together with such Interest as you in your Wisdom may think proper — And also your Petitioner prays your Honors to take under your Wise consideration his circumstances with respect to the Deed of the two Rights of Land and provide such way to secure to him his property as you in your Wisdom may think fit, Which your Honors Petitioner as in duty bound shall ever pray.

Tinmouth 13ᵗʰ Oct. 1786   Samˡ Allen

— & —

Petition of Samˡ Allen
Filed 24ᵗʰ Octʳ 86
. . .*

To the General assembly now Sitting Your Committee to Whom was Refered the Consideration of the Within petition Beg Leave to Report that the facts Set forth in the petition are True to the Satisfaction of Your Committee and that the Treasurer be Directed to Issue his Note for the Sum of thirteen pounds ten Shilng and that the petitioner Have Leave to Bring in a Bill for the Confirmation of the Title of the Land therein Described and that the prayer of the petition ought to be Granted as afore said all Which is Submitted

Dated Rutland octoʳ yᵉ 24ᵗʰ 1786

           Hubbel Wells for Comᵗᵉᵉ

To General Assembly Now Sitting your Committee to whome was Referd the Consideration of the within Peticion Beg Leave to Report that the facts Set forth in the Peticion are True to the Sattisfaction of your Committee & that the [Treasurer] Be Directed to Issue his Note for the Sum of fifteen Pounds & that the Perticiner Have Leave to Bring in a Bill for the Confermation of the Title of Land there in Describeᵈ and that the Prayer of the Perticion ought to Be Granted as a fore said all of which is Submited

Dated Benington February the 21 Day 1787

Gideon Brownson: for Committee

— & —

A. J.: *Read and referred to a committee, 24 Oct. '86, *S. P. of Vt.*, III (III), 243; *report of committee read and not accepted, petition referred to next session, and petitioner ordered to cite all persons concerned to show cause why petition ought not to be granted, 24 Oct. '86, *Ibid*, III (III), 243; *read again and referred to a new committee, 21 Feb. '87, *Ibid*, III (III), 282; report of committee read and accepted, and ordered that petitioner have leave to bring in a bill accordingly, 23 Feb. '87, *Ibid*, III (III), 285–286;[1] resolved that Treasurer pay petitioner £15 lawful money, 23 Feb. '87, *Ibid*, III (III), 286; bill to authenticate the deed therein named read and accepted and sent to Council, 23 Feb. '87, *Ibid*, III (III), 286; bill, having been concurred in by Council, passed into law, 23 Feb. '87, *Ibid*, III (III), 290.[2] *C. J.:* Act read and concurred in, 23 Feb. '87, *G. and C.*, III, 126.

FOR ANNEXATION OF PART OF A TOWN TO ANOTHER
xvii, 214; xxii, 128[3]

State of } To the Honorable General Assembly to be holden at Rutland on
Vermont } the second Thursday of this Instant October. The Memorial of ye Inhabitants of Ira and ye West part of Clarendon in ye county of Rutland and State of Vermont.

Humbly sheweth

That by an Act of ye General Assembly at their stated session in October 1784 a part of said Town of Ira was incorporated with that of Middletown[4] which leaves the remaining part of said Town so small and lying in such a form that it is inconvenient for them to carry on their publick business:

And whereas those Inhabitants in ye West part of Clarendon are seperated from ye Bulk of ye Inhabitants of s^d Clarendon by a Mountain which runs through the Town and the distance of Travil from ye extreem parts is upwards of six miles from ye usual place of doing publick business, which renders it dificult for them to meet with ye rest of the Inhabitants And whilst the setuation of both is such y^t [that] renders it inconvenient for them to remain as they are. Nature seemes to have pointed out ye mode of annexing the one to ye other. And as your Memorealest can conceive of no disadvantage ariseing theirfrom, as it will not enlarge representa-

---

1. The report of the committee as given in the journal under this date was in fact the first report presented 24 Oct. '86. That this entry was in error is indicated by the reports themselves given above and by the action of the Assembly following the second report.

2. For this act, see *Ms. Laws of Vt.*, II, 24.

3. The first reference is the original petition, while the second is a copy without the names appended. The spelling and punctuation of the original are followed in this transcription. The copy was apparently made in accordance with the order of the Assembly that the petitioners notify the selectmen of both towns of their prayer. See subjoined note. The citation and the service of citation are transcribed from the copy.

4. For this act, passed 28 Oct. '84, see *Ms. Laws of Vt.*, I, 462–463.

tion and consiquently will not make any additional cost. For which reasons and many others y^t [that] might be given your Memorealest pray that the said West part of Clarendon may be annexed to Ira, extending from a cartain beach Tree said to be ye Northwest corner of said Clarendon three miles and three quarters on the north line of said Town, thence south paralel with ye east line to ye south line of said Town, thence to ye south west corner, and from thence to ye first Mentioned bounds.

For reasons above recited, your Memorealest humbly prays y^t [that] your Honnors would take ye same into your wise consideration, and act as your wisdom may Direct: which your Memorealest as in Duty bound Shall ever pray

Dated at Clarendon this 13th Day of Octr 1786

Abel Cooper	Timothy Juel	Asahel Blanchard
Christopher howard	Stephen Robbinson	Jed^h Clark Ju^r
Lewis Walker	Reuben Blanchard	Ezekiel Porter
Benjn Foster Ju^r	Peleg Eady	Thaddeus Curtis
Zibe Westcot	Philip Green	Silas Hodges
Wm Shearman	Amos Robinson	Abraham Hatheway
Squier Ide	Purchis Brown	Jedidiah Clark
James Edmunds	Henry Greene	Ebenezer Pitcher
Peter Eddy	John Seamans jun	Darius Chipman
Rufus Bates	Charles Seamans	Elihu Smith
Joshua Priest	Caleb howland	Eli Eastman
Comfort Chaffee	Andrew Edmons	Alfred Hatheway
[Daley Gain?]	John Ward	Nathaniel Chaffee
[Levi Culain?]	Prince Shermon	Daniel Schovell
Daniel Reynolds	James Cummings	Barnard Wood
John Spenser	Jon^a Parker Junr	Henry Dean
Abial Tripp	Solomon Spafford	Increse Mosley
Caleb Pratt		

Ira Signers

Cephas Carpenter	Benjamin Allen	John Collins
Thomas Collins	Benjamin [Carver?]	Purchase Roberds
George Shearman	Benjn Baliy ju^r	Rufus Colvin
Reuben Baker	Jason Newton	Danel Adams
Nathan Lee	Nathan Collins	Nathanal Clough
Lemuel Roberts	Edward baly	Joseph Tower
Benjamin Baly	George Shearman Jn^r	John Burllinggame
Thomas Martin	Isaiah Mason	Hezekiah Carver
[Tamas?] Martin	Nathanel Mason	David Robad

— & —

Memorial of Inhabitants of Ira & part of Clarendon —
Filed 19th Octr 86.

. . .*

To the Sherif of the County of Rutland his Deputy or the Constable of the Town of Clarendon. Greeting.

In the name and by ye Authority of the freemen of ye State of Vermont you are

hereby commanded to summons and give notice to Mr Daniel Marsh one of the principle Inhabitants and one of ye Select men of said Clarendon the present Year and to ye rest of the Inhabitants of said Town: to appear (if they see cause) before ye Gen^el Assembly of ye state of Vermont to be holden at Benington by adjournment on the third Thursday of February next; then and their to shew reasons if any they have why ye prayer of the aforegoing Petition should not be Granted. And you are to deliver a True and an Attested Coppy of ye foregoing Petition and of this Sitation to ye said Daniel Marsh. Hereof fail not and of your Doings in ye Primisies due return make according to law. Dated at Clarendon this 29th day of December AD 1786

Elihu Smith   Jus of [peace]

Clarendon January 2 AD 1787
Then served the Within Sitation by Reading it and the foregoing Petition at a Publick Town Meeting and on the 25 Day of Januery Ins^t Left a true and attested Coppey of the within Sitation and the foregoing Petition with the Said Daniel Marsh

Attest   Alfred Hatheway   Cons^t

— & —

A. J.: *Read and referred to next session and ordered that petitioners notify the selectmen of both towns of their prayer, 19 Oct. '86, *S. P. of Vt.*, III (III), 231; *read and referred to a committee, 22 Feb. '87, *Ibid*, III (III), 283;[1] *report of committee recommending that the petition ought not to be granted, read and accepted, and petition dismissed, 24 Feb. '87, *Ibid*, III (III), 291.

FOR A LOTTERY TO IMPROVE A ROAD

xvii, 215

State of Vermont } To the Honble

Genl Assembly Convened at Rutland, The Petition of Nathan Stone & others Inhabitants of Windsor in s^d State of Vermont sheweth

That the Highways in the East society[2] are rendered expensive in the necessary repairs by the Number of Bridges to be maintained, there being no less than seven large ones in that Quarter of the town — which makes it Difficult for said Inhabitants to expend the necessary sums in raising the sunken grounds thro' which the River Road passes, so as to make the traveling safe & convenient in the spring & fall freshets — Tis judged that those grounds may be rendered permanently safe for passengers with about £ 300 expence which is a sum the Inhabitants are

1. A remonstrance against the prayer of this petition was referred to this committee at the same time. For this remonstrance and another drawn up at the same time, see pp. 310, 312, *post.*

2. See "An Act dividing the Town of Windsor into two distinct Societies", passed 17 Oct. '83 (*Ms. Laws of Vt.*, I, 392). It provided that the division line between the East and West societies was "the Center of the seventh range of hundred Acre Lotts, . . ."

unable to raise in addition to the other repairs they are annually obliged to make occasioned by the loss of bridges &c wherefore they pray your Honours to pass an Act giving Liberty to [Blank] to make a Lottery to raise the sum of £ 300 for that purpose under such restrictions & regulations as they judge proper & as in duty bound shall ever pray
Windsor 14th Octr 1786

Nath^n Stone	Alexander Daniels	John Curtis
Stephen Jacob	Benjn Cady	Reuben Smith
Hez^h Thomson j^r	Jonathan Hall	Watts Hubbard
Eben^r Curtis	Thomas H. Cady	Eldad Hubbard
Elijah West	Zebina Curtis	Samuel Smith
Step^n Conant	Caleb Stone	Hez^h Thomson
Joseph Barrett	Silvanus [Waters?]	Lathrop Thompson
Zedekiah Stone	Steel Smith	

— & —

Petition of Nathan Stone & others for a Lottery
Filed 18th Octr 86
. . .*

— & —

A. J.: *Read and referred to a committee, 19 Oct. '86, S. P. of Vt., III (III), 229; *report of committee read and accepted, and leave given to bring in a bill accordingly, 23 Oct. '86, Ibid, III (III), 238;[1] resolved that leave be given to conduct such a lottery under certain restrictions, 23 Oct. '86, Ibid, III (III), 241–242.

FOR RIGHT TO SELL REAL PROPERTY TO SETTLE AN ESTATE
xvii, 216, 217

To the Honorable the General Assembly of the State of Vermont now siting at Rutland
The Petition of Gershom Beach Administrator of the Estate of Noah Beach late of Rutland deceased humbly sheweth that the Personal Estate of the said deceased is insufficient by the Sum of twenty pounds Lawful Money to pay the debts due from said Estate: — Therefor prays your Honors to pass an Act impowering him the said Gershom Beach to sell so much of the Real Estate of the said Noah Beach deceased as will raise the sum of £ 20–0–0 L.M. for the purpose of paying the debts due from said Estate together with necessary cost arising on such sale, under such restrictions as you in your wisdom may think fit which your Honors petitioner as in duty bound shall ever Pray

Gershom Beach

Rutland Oct. 14th AD 1786.

---

1. The report of the committee, given on the manuscript petition, simply stated that "the facts set up in said Petition are true, and that in their opinion the Prayer of said Petition ought to be granted, . . ."

Certificate from the Judge of Probate
To the Honorable the General Assembly of the State of Vermont.
This may certify that the Personal Estate of Noah Beach late of Rutland deceased
is insufficient, by the Sum of Twenty pounds Lawful money, to pay the Debts due
from said estate

Pr Elisha Clark Judge Prob.

Tinmouth 14th oct. 1786

— & —

Gershom Beach^s Petition
Filed 26th Octr 86.
. . .*

— & —

A. J.: *Read and granted with leave to bring in a bill accordingly, 26 Oct. '86,
S. P. of Vt., III (III), 249; bill read and accepted and sent to Council, 26 Oct.
'86, Ibid, III (III), 249; bill, having been concurred in by Council, passed into
law, 27 Oct. '86, Ibid, III (III), 253.[1]

FOR COMPENSATION FOR THE RENTAL OF A FARM TO THE STATE[2]
xvii, 114, 220

To the Honourable General Assembly for the State of Vermont Now Sitting in
Rutland —
the Petition of Caleb Handy of Pittsford in the County of Rutland humbly Shewith
to your honours that Sometime in the month of March AD 1781 that your honours
Petitioner then Leased to Joseph Farsworth of Bennington then Commissary
Gen^{el} for the State of Vermont one Certain Tract of Land in Said Pittsford for
the use and benefit of the State Troops for one year for which your honors Petitioner
begs Leave to Observe to your honours that he has Never Rec^d any Reward or
Satisfaction for the Rent of Said farm altho' the Said Farnsworth was to have
given Twenty four Pounds in behalf of Said State for the youse of Said Farm your
Petitioner therefore prays that your honour will take S^d Matter under your wise
Consideration and order the aforesaid Twenty Fore pounds paid to your Petitioner
and also Such Damiges as Shall appeare Just as your Petitioner in Duty bound Shall
ever pray —
Dated at Rutland Octr the   Caleb Handy
    16 AD 1786 —

— & —

Caleb Handys Petition
Filed 17th Octr 86
. . .*
To the Honorable the General Assembly now Sitting your Committe to whom
was referd the within petition beg leave to report that they find that the matters

---

1. For this act, see Ms. Laws of Vt., I, 567.
2. For a petition presented 12 Feb. '82 by Caleb Handy and Jonathan Rowle for
compensation for war losses on their property, see p. 59, ante. This petition was dismissed. For the presentation and dismissal in Oct. '84 and June '85 of other petitions by
Caleb Handy (not now among the Ms. Vt. S. P.), see S. P. of Vt., III (III), 73, 87, 150.

in the Petition are truely Stated and it is the Opinion of Your Committe that the petitioner be paid out of the public Treasury forty pounds

Rutland Octr 20th 1786   Eb^r Allen for the Com^{te}

Pitsford [Pittsford] — May 28th Day A D 1785[1]

Then aplication Being made By mr Caleb Handee of S^d Pitsford to us Viz John Mott and Amos Cutler of Brandon To a Prise on S^d Day the Damage Done Him the S^d Handy on His Place in Time of the War By the Garrison Being arected their on S^d Place — We Liveing Near in S^d Brandon and Being in Sum measure a Quainted with the articles that was on S^d Handee Place that is Now Destroid or Gone we truely Judge the House Would Have Ben Worth at the End of S^d War ten Pound twelve and Six Pence Barn would Have Ben Six Pounds fenses fifteen Pounds: wood Lot Eleven Pounds maple Treas Saved for Sugaring five Pounds Aple Orcherding twenty two Pounds ten shillings

House	10:12:6		
Barn	6: 0:0		
fences	15: 0:0	Atest	
Wood Lot	11: 0:0		John Mott
M trees	5: 0:0		
Orcherd	22:10:0		Amos Cutler
Total	70: 2:6		

Mr Handee Prays that The Honnourable House of Representatives would Remember him Likewise in regard of his Place: the State Haveing the use of it two years He Saith he Hath had Pay But for one

        Caleb Hendee his a Count
                10:0:0
                30:0:0

    To the General Assembly and Honorable house of Representatives I would Inform you that Capt Safford of Benington [Bennington] aged [agreed?] with me the first Year for my place for the Use of the Garrison And he alowd Me twenty four pound which was Exepted By the State the Next year Squir Fansworth Comasary Genl Came to Me and told me that he Must have my place for the Use of the Garrison I told him If he had it he must alow me as much as they Did the Year Before Viz twenty four pounds which I have never had any thing as Yet which they had the use of My place for the use of the Garrison the Second Year

                                                    Caleb Hendee

                        — & —

A. J.: Read and referred to a committee, 18 Oct. '86, S. P. of Vt., III (III), 228; *report of committee read and not accepted, and petition dismissed, 20 Oct. '86, Ibid, III (III), 236.

---

    1. The statements below signed by John Mott and Amos Cutler and by Caleb Hendee do not actually belong to this petition. Presumably they were drawn up and presented to the Assembly with the petition mentioned in previous note as read and dismissed in June '85. They are printed here as material explanatory of this petition.

FOR CONFIRMATION OF AN UNACKNOWLEDGED DEED
xxii, 119

To the Honourable Generarl Assembly of the State of Vermont now Convend at Rutland the Petition of Nathenul Fisk of Brandon in the State of VVermont [*sic*] Humbly Sheweth —
that Benjamin Powers Late of Neshobe now Called Brandon in the State of vermont Executed a Deed to your Pititioner on the 8th Day of June 1775 Since which Time Said Powers has Deceesed and Died not in his Lifetime acknoledg Said Deed and wharas Said Deed Cannot be Proved according to Due form of Law by Reason that one of the witnesses Cannont be obtained therefore your Petitioner Humbly Praeys that your Honors will make Such order Respecting Said Deed as will make it Equally Good and Valid as if the Said Powers had acknoledgeed Said Deed in his Lifetime and your Petitioner will Ever Pray
Rutland October 16:1786   Nathinel Fisk

— & —

Petition of Natheniel Fisk
Filed Octr 20th 1786 —
. . .*

— & —

A. J.: Read and referred to a committee, 20 Oct. '86, *S. P. of Vt.*, III (III), 234; *report of committee read and accepted, and leave given to bring in a bill accordingly, 20 Oct. '86, *Ibid*, III (III), 235;[1] bill read and accepted and sent to Council, 21 Oct. '86, *Ibid*, III (III), 236; bill, having been concurred in by Council, passed into law, 23 Oct. '86, *Ibid*, III (III), 241.[2] *C. J.:* Act read and concurred in, 23 Oct. '86, *G. and C.*, III, 111.

FOR DISCHARGE FROM DEBTS
xvii, 218

To the Honble the General Assembly of the State of Vermont Now Sitting at Rutland in said State.
The petition of William Goodrich Humbly sheweth — That your petitioner from the strongest attachment to his Country & a Sincear wish to support the Rights of Humanity, & to Render his Services in procuring the freedom of American Independence, took an Early and active part in the Late *War*, your petitioner Experienced Great Hardship & fatigue in passing The Word from Boston to *Quebeck* when your petitioner was made prisoner at the Assalt made on that place by the ever Memorable General Montgomery; when your petitioner Suffered Great loss in property & long confinements your petitioner was Released in the year 1776 and Continued in the Service of the Country until 1779 when your petitioner found it Necessary to pursue Some employment for the Support of him-

---

1. The text of this report, given on the manuscript petition, simply declared that the facts set forth in the petition were supported and that it ought to be granted.
2. For this act, see *Ms. Laws of Vt.*, I, 543.

self & family;[1] And as there appeared the most flattering prospects in the Mercantile Branch, your petitioner Entered Largely into that business in which he continued for several years with Great Success as he Supposed but to his Great Surprise he found himself Defeated by the Distruction of the paper Medium on which your petitioner depended for the payment & Discharge of Large Sums which he justly owed, this Misfortune (which has proved the Ruin of Many of the Most Valuable Subjects in America) together with many other Losses & Misfortunes, has Rendered it impossible for your petitioner to Extricate himself from those difficulties in the full discharge of his honest Debts And Whereas Numerous Actions is Commenced at Law against your petitioner & Large bills of Cost constantly acumulating whereby your honors petitioner is Constantly Embarrassed and discouraged from Attending to any Constant Employment for the Support of himself & family, and Whereas your honors petitioner Sincearly wishes Still to Contribute to Render Service to the public as an Industerous faithful Subject & Member of Society, prays this honorable house to take his Case into their wise consideration & point out Some way to Relieve your petitioner who Stands free & willing to Deliver up Bonafida all his Estate boath Real & personal to Satisfy his said Creditors under Such Restrictions & directions as your honors in Wisdom shall direct and your petitioner in duty shall ever pray

Wm Goodrich

Rutland 16th October 1786

— & —

The Petision of Maj^r William Goodrich
Filed 16th Oct^r
. . .*

— & —

A. J.: *Read and referred to a committee, 16 Oct. '86, S. P. of Vt., III (III), 223;[2] *report of committee read and accepted, and leave given to bring in a bill accordingly, 17 Oct. '86, Ibid, III (III), 225;[3] bill "to discharge Major William Goodrich from his creditors on delivering up, bona fida all his estate", read and accepted and sent to Council, 18 Oct. '86, Ibid, III (III), 228; bill, having been returned from Council with proposals of amendment, was agreed to and passed into law, 25 Oct. '86, Ibid, III (III), 246; resolved that act be reconsidered that afternoon, 26 Oct. '86, Ibid, III (III), 247; resolved that vote on act be reconsidered and bill referred to next adjourned session, the petitioner giving notice in the press to his creditors and all suits and executions against him being continued or stayed, 26 Oct. '86, Ibid, III (III), 248; resolved that petition be referred to next session, all suits and executions against him being continued or stayed, 24 Feb. '87, Ibid, III (III), 292; bill again read and accepted and sent to Council, 20 Oct. '87, Ibid, III (IV), 30; bill, having been concurred in by Council, read and ordered to lie on the table, 20 Oct. '87, Ibid, III (IV), 37; bill read and passed into law [Yeas and Nays given], 22 Oct.

---

1. For William Goodrich's revolutionary service, see *Massachusetts Soldiers and Sailors of the Revolutionary War*, vol. VI (Boston, 1899), p. 595.
2. The entry on the manuscript petition correctly states that this committee was to join a committee from the Council.
3. According to the entry on the manuscript petition the committee simply found "that the facts set forth in said Petition are supported and that in their opinion the prayer of the Petition ought to be granted . . ."

'87, *Ibid*, III (IV), 40.[1] C. J.: *Committee appointed to join Assembly committee, 16 Oct. '86, *G. and C.*, III, 107; act read and passed with some amendments, 20 Oct. '86, *Ibid*, III, 110.[2]

FOR EXTENSION OF THE TIME REQUIRED
FOR SETTLING TWO TOWNS
xxii, 122

To the Honorable The Assembly of the Freemen of the State of Vermont
The Petition of Jacob Davis in behalf of him self & His Associates Humbly sheweth, that your Petitioners have Received from your Honours the Grant and Charters of the Townships of Calais and Salem[3] in Said State, In which Chaters [*sic*] certain settling duties are required To be performed within three years After the circumstances of the Then War would admit with safty, on penalty of the forfiture of each respective rite in said Towns — And wheras for the want of the Outloins of said Towns being run out and established by your Honous, It hath poot it Out of the Power of your Petitioners To comply with said Charter duties with any degree of certainty —
Therefore your Petitioners humbly pray your Honous to take their case into your wise consideration, and grant them the said Term of Three years to perform said Charter duties after the Outloins of said Towns are runout and established by your Honours, or Grant your Petitioners such other relief in the Premiss as you in your Great Wisdom shall think proper — And your Petitioners as in duty bound Will Ever Pray
Rutland 17th Oct[r] 1786   Jacob Davis

— & —

Petition of Caleb Davis
Filed 17th Oct[r] 86.
. . .*

— & —

A. J.: *Read and referred to a committee, 17 Oct. '86, *S. P. of Vt.*, III (III), 227; *report of committee read and accepted, and leave given to bring in a bill accordingly, 18 Oct. '86, *Ibid*, III (III), 228;[4] bill for prolonging the time in which grantees of lands granted by this state are obliged to settle the same, read and accepted and sent to Council, 19 Oct. '86, *Ibid*, III (III), 230; bill, having been concurred in by Council, passed into law, 23 Oct. '86, *Ibid*, III

---

1. See "An Act for discharging William Goodrich from his debts" (*Ms. Laws of Vt.*, II, 198–199).
2. For the amendments, see original act (*Ms. Vt. S. P., Laws, 1786–1789*, vol. 2, no pagination).
3. For the charters of Calais and Salem, see *S. P. of Vt.*, II (Vermont Charters) 37–39, 180–181. Part of Salem was annexed to Newport in 1816 and the remainder to Derby in 1881. See *Ibid*, II (Vermont Charters), 344.
4. The text of the report as given on the manuscript petition simply states that the petition ought to be granted.
The Assembly journal, like the entry on the reverse of the manuscript, mistakenly credits the petition to Caleb instead of Jacob Davis.

(III), 241.[1] *C. J.:* Act read and concurred in, 19 Oct. '86, *G. and C.,* III, 109.

FOR REFORM OF JUDICIAL PROCEDURE AND THE CURRENCY[2]
xvii, 194

To the Honble Gen^{el} Assembly —
Now Setting at Rutland in the County of Rutland
The Petetion of the Freemen of the Town of Castleton —
    Humbly Sheweth —
That whereas a Number of the Inhabitants of the County of Rutland have by the Present modes of Administration, Suffered in their Property, by what appears to us your Petetioners to be Needless Cost in Law Suites both by the Present Latitude granted to Attorneys at Law Sheriffs Deputies and unnesary Cost to Plaintiffs in Suits for travel and attendants and also by the many abatements of Writs Non-Suits Appeals and the Consequent Delay of justice therefrom arising, and the Laws at Present allowing the Nature of Contracts made by Contracting Parties by obliging the Debtor where a Suit is Entered in Law to Pay the Creditor Cash for the Demand although the Contract was for Produce or other Property, Your Petetioners therefore Pray —

1st   that no Plaintiff in any Civil action in any Court in this State may be allowed any thing in the bill of Cost in any Court for his her or their travel or Court attendance by him her or themselves or their Attorneys under any Pretence whatsoever and that any Person or Persons, in this State may have Liberty to Prosecute in all Civil actions by themselves or any Such Person as he She or they Shall Choose to Authorize by Power of Attorney for that Purpose —

2^{nly} That all Writs and Executions Granted by the Authority of this State be Served and Returned by the Constable of the Town where the Plaintiff or Defendant Dwells and that all Writs be Paid for from the Place of Service to the Place of Return and no more and that the Sheriff be allowed no Deputy

3^{ly}   That Justices Courts be Courts of Equety with a jury if Requested (by Either of the Perties) Consisting of Six Freeholders and Such Courts to have Power to try all Causes where the Demand of the Plaintiff Doth not Exceed the Sum of Ten Pounds if the account be unliquidated or the Sum of Twenty Pounds if the account be liquidated or the Demand be by Note or Bond and the Gudgment [*sic*] of Such Court be final and Decicive without appeal and that there be no Review Except it Shall appear Reasonable to the Court before whom the Cause is tryed, and that the form of Presepts for Such Courts be Worded in an act for that Purpose in Such Manner that there Shall be no abatement in any Such Court —

4^{ly}   That In all Civil actions where it appears that the Contracting Parties did at the time of Contract agree to Pay and Receive for the property bought and Sold Specie Produce or other Property for payment Either by Bond Note or

---

    1. For this act, see *Ms. Laws of Vt.,* I, 545. It provided that settlement must take place three years after the outlines of any town had been run by order of the legislature.

    2. For a more detailed understanding of the grievances set forth in this petition, see similar ones and the explanatory notes, pp. 189, 216, 225, 232, 238, 244, 248, *ante.* For another similar petition, see p. 279, *post.*

Evidence of their agreement Such Specie Produce or other Property as Contracted for may be a tendery for all Such Debts Either at the time agreed to for Payment or at any time after the Commencement of a Suite for Such Debt at the Apprisal of Men, and all Book Accompts where the Plaintiff Cannot Prove he was to Receive Specie Such Debts may be Satisfyed, with Beef Pork Butter Cheese Wool flax Grain or Neat Cattle at the apprisal of Men

As in Duty Bound your Petetioners Ever Pray

Castleton Octb^r 17th 1786   N Lee $\Big\{$ in behalf of
                                                 Adam Johnson   the Freemen of
                                                                 Castleton

— & —

A Petetion of the Freemen of the Town of Castleton
N° 7

— & —

[See subjoined note for similar petition, p. 192, *ante*.]

FOR COMPENSATION FOR WAR SERVICES
xvii, 221

To the Hon^l the Legislature of Vermont in Genl Assembly at Rutland —

The Petition of Gideon Brunson Lete a Captain in the Reg^t Commanded by Col^n Seth Warner in the Service of the United States Humbly Sheweth —[1]
That in Decr 1776 your Petitioner in Obedience to the Commond of Congress Armed and Accoutered a Number of Continental Soldiers in his Company for the Continentle Service to the Number of Thirty Two, at his own expence — Your Petitioner has applyed to Congress for the Amount of the Monies he imbursed for the above purpose[2] but cannot receive his pay by reason of a certain Resolve of that Honorable Body directing that persons in like circumstances with your Petitioner shall be paid by the State to which he belongs — Your Petitioner therefore prays your Honors to take his particular Case under your Consideration and give him such relief in the premises as your wisdom shall direct — And as in Duty your Petitioner will ever pray

Rutland Octr 17th 1786   Gideon Brunson

— & —

Petition of Gideon Brownson —
Filed 16th Oct^r
. . .*
To the General Assembly now Sitting
The Committee to whom was refered the within Petition Beg leave to report, that the Petitioner did agreeable to a Resolution of Congress in the year 1776 and 1777

---

1. For record of this service, see *Vt. Rev. Rolls*, pp. 107, 110, 623, 635, 636, 669.
2. For this application to Congress, see *Journals of the Continental Congress 1774–1789*, vol. XXVIII (Washington, 1933), pp. 471n, 477.

— Purchase Arms &C for the ⟨use of this State to the⟩ Purpose of Carrying on the War to the amount of £ 100–1–6– for which he has not rec^d any Pay — Therefore it is the Opinion of your Committee that the said Petitioner receive the said Sum of £ 100–1–6 with the Interest on the same to this Time amounting in the whole to the sum of £ 159–6–6–

Octr 18th 1786 —   Sam^el Fletcher for Committee

— & —

> A. J.: *Read and referred to a committee, 16 Oct. '86, S. P. of Vt., III (III), 224;[1] *report of committee read and accepted, and leave given for a bill to be brought in accordingly, 21 Oct., '86, Ibid, III (III), 237; resolved that Treasurer pay Brownson £159–6–6 lawful money, 23 Oct. '86, Ibid, III (III), 239. C. J.: *Committee appointed to join Assembly committee, 17 Oct. '86, G. and C., III, 107.

FOR A TAX ON LAND TO BUILD ROADS AND BRIDGES
xvii, 222

To the Hon^le the Legislature of Vermont convened at Rutland —
    The Petition of the Proprietors of Weybridge in the County of Addison —
                                Humbly Sheweth
    That the Inhabitants of the Said Town have been at great expence in making Roads for their Convenience & the Settlement of Said Town — And that the Said Roads are yet inclompleat, and many Bridges needed espesially a Bridge across the mouth of the River Lemon Fair,[2] and other necessary Bridges in Said Town, your Petitioners therefore pray, your Honors, to enable them by Law to levy a Tax of Two pence on the Acre upon all the Land in Said Town (to be Appropriated for the above purposes) and collected by the first Day of April next — And your Petitioners as in Duty Bound will ever pray

Rutland Octr 17th 1786   Th^s Jewett for and in behalf of the
                                       Proprietors

— & —

Thos Jewett in behalf of Proprietors of Weybridge
N° 7
To the General Assembly now Sitting to whom was referd the within Protition, Fax [facts] being Stated Decleration being Proved Bege leve to report as follows that a tax of two Pence Per acor be lade on all the Lands in Sd Townd Publick rights Exsepted under Such restrictions as the Honorobell General Assembly Shall in thare Wisdom think Proper —

                                 Elisha Marsh for Comity

— & —

> A. J.: Read and referred to a committee, 16 Oct. '86, S. P. of Vt., III (III), 224; report of committee read and not accepted and ordered recommitted, 17

---

    1. The entry on the manuscript petition correctly states that this committee was to join a committee from the Council.
    2. Now the Fair River.

Oct. '86, *Ibid*, III (III), 225; report of committee read and accepted, and leave given to bring in a bill accordingly, 19 Oct. '86, *Ibid*, III (III), 230; bill read and accepted and sent to Council, 20 Oct. '86, *Ibid*, III (III), 235; bill, having been returned from Council "with an amendment", agreed to and passed into law, 21 Oct. '86, *Ibid*, III (III), 236.[1] *C. J.:* Act read and concurred in "with some Amendments", 21 Oct. '86, *G. and C.*, III, 110.[2]

FOR A TAX ON LAND TO BUILD ROADS
xvii, 223

To the Honorable General Assembly of the State of Vermont now sitting —
The Petition of the Inhabitants of the Town of Benson in the County of Rutland humbly sheweth —
That your Honors Petitioner as well as y^e [Publick] labour under great difficulties and inconveniencies for want of Roads in said town — that the Inhabitants of said town are indebted the sum of forty pounds for labour already done on roads in said town and that much more expence and labour is necessary in order to make the Road good and passable for the inhabitants and the Publick — Your honors Petitioners therefore pray your honors to take the matters under your Wise consideration and grant relief in the premises by enabling the Inhabitants of said town to levy a tax of one penny half penny on the acre on all the land in said town of Benson to be appropriated to the use and purpose aforesaid under such restrictions as your honors shall think fit and your Petitioners as in Duty bound Shall ever pray —
Rutland October 17th 1786

Asahel Smith
James Nobel { Select
Simeon Goodrich } men

— & —

[Petition of] Select-men of Benson
Filed 19th Octr 1786
N° 10
To the Honorobell General Assembly now Setting your Comity to whome was refard the within Protition the Faxs [facts] being Stated the declaration being Soported bege leve to report that a tax be lade on all the Lands in Sd Town of one Peney Per acor Public Rights Exsepted

Elisha Marsh for Comity
— & —

A. J.: Read and referred to a committee, 17 Oct. '86, *S. P. of Vt.*, III (III), 225; report of committee read and accepted, and leave given to bring in a bill accordingly, 19 Oct. '86, *Ibid*, III (III), 230; bill read and accepted and sent

---

1. For this act, see *Ms. Laws of Vt.*, I, 540–541.
2. This amendment—not amendments—directed the committee appointed in the act to construct two bridges over "Leamon fair . . . one as near the mouth of Said Leamon fair as is conveniant—the other bridge to be in the most Conveniant Place to accomodate a road that Shall Lead Westerly from Midebury falls to Lake Champlain." See original act (*Ms. Vt. S. P., Laws 1786–1789*, vol. 2, no pagination).

to Council, 20 Oct. '86, *Ibid*, III (III), 235; bill, having been concurred in by Council, read and passed into law, 21 Oct. '86, *Ibid*, III (III), 237 (2).[1] *C. J.:* Act read and concurred in, 21 Oct. '86, *G. and C.*, III, 110.

FOR POWER TO COLLECT MONEY DUE FOR ATTEMPTED CONFIRMATION OF THE NEW HAMPSHIRE GRANTS
xvii, 225

To the Honourable the General Assembly of the State of Vermont Now Convened in Rutland
    the Memorial of Gershom Beach of Rutland &C &C — Humbly Sheweth — That Whereas your Memorialist Did in the month of November 1772 Give a Certain Note for the Sum of <forty> Seventy five Pounds New York money Which Sum Was a Coto [Quota?] of Moneys for the Towns of Rutland Pitsford and Castleton Intended to be Raised to Defray The Expence of Mrss Brakenridge and Hawley Going to England to obtain a Conformation of the then Newhampshire Grants at the Cort of Greatbritain —[2] Now the Said Money, being Demanded your Memorialist Thinks it unjust for him to Pay the afforesaid money, as he has Paid all the money, that he has Receved from The afforesaid Towns and as There is a Considerable Ballence Now Due from the Township of Rutland to Discharge the afforesaid Debt Therefore Prays that your memorialist or Some other Purson may be Athorised in Law to Collect and Pay the afforesaid Debts as in Duty bound Shall Ever Pray

                                                        Gershom Beach
Rutland 17 October 1786

— & —

Memorial
Gershom Beach
Filed 18th Octr 1786
. . .*
Your Committee to whome was Refered the consideration of the within Petition beg leave to Report as our opinion that the Petition ought to be Refered to the Next Session of Assembly and that the Town of Rutland be Notified to Appear and Shew cause if any they have why the Prayer of the Petition ought not to be Granted
                                                        J Smith for Comtee

To the Honorable Genll Assembly Now Seting
your Commite to whome was referd the Consideration of the within Petision haveing had the Nesecary Evidence beg leave to report theire opinion that the facts stated theirein are well suported and that the Petisinor is intitled and ought to Levie from the town of Rutland the Sum of forty Nine Pounds Eight Shillings & foure pence L:M: and that the Petisinor have leave to Bring in a Bill in favor
                                                        Saml Safford for [Committee]

---

1. For this act, see *Slade*, 509.
2. For an account of this attempt to obtain confirmation of the New Hampshire grants, see Matt B. Jones, *Vermont in the Making 1750–1777* (Cambridge, 1939), pp. 180–184). For another petition in the same connection, see p. 126, *ante*.

— & —

A. J.: *Read and referred to a committee, 19 Oct. '86, *S. P. of Vt.*, III (III), 228; *report of committee read and accepted, and petition referred to next session accordingly, 19 Oct. '86, *Ibid*, III (III), 231; *read again and referred to a committee to join a committee from the Council, 1 March '87, *Ibid*, III (III), 302–303; *report of committee read and accepted and leave given to bring in a bill accordingly, 5 March '87, *Ibid*, III (III), 314; bill read and accepted and sent to Council, 5 March '87, *Ibid*, III (III), 315; bill, having been concurred in by Council, passed into law, 8 March '87, *Ibid*, III (III), 323–324;[1] petition from Samuel Williams to repeal above act read and ordered to lie on the table, 13 Oct. '87, *Ibid*, III (IV), 10;[2] petition from Samuel Williams read again and prayer granted, and leave given to bring in a bill accordingly, 13 Oct. '87, *Ibid*, III (IV), 12; bill entitled an act to repeal "an act herein after mentioned" read and accepted and sent to Council, 15 Oct. '87, *Ibid*, III (IV), 13; bill, having been concurred in by Council, passed into law, 16 Oct. '87, *Ibid*, III (IV), 20.[3] *C. J.:* *Committee appointed to join Assembly committee, 2 March '87, *G. and C.*, III, 132; act read and concurred in, 5 March '87, *Ibid*, III, 136; act repealing above act read and concurred in, 15 Oct. '87, *Ibid*, III, 148.

FOR A TAX ON LAND TO BUILD ROADS
xvii, 227

To the honorable General Assembly of the State of Vermont —

The petition of the subscribers proprietors of the townships of Bromley & Landgrove humbly sheweth —

that the badness of the roads from Manchester thro' Bromley[4] & Landgrove to Andover and Chester renders it necessary that large sums should be expended in repairing the same, to make the said roads even tolerable — and as the inhabitants of the said Bromley & Landgrove are but very few in number — We humbly pray your honors to grant a tax upon the proprietory rights of the said townships of Bromley & Landgrove sufficient for the purpose of repairing the roads thro' the same — and your Petitioners as in duty bound shall ever pray

Stephen Keyes
Sam Stevens
W^m [Utley]
Asa [Utley]

Dated Rutland Octr 18th 1786

— & —

[. . .]⁵
Filed 21st Octr 86

. . .*

---

1. For this act, see *Ms. Laws of Vt.*, II, 93–94.
2. For this petition dated 25 Sept. '87, and Gershom Beach's request for a delay in its consideration, see pp. 358, 359, *post*.
3. For this act, see *Ms. Laws of Vt.*, II, 190.
4. Now Peru. See *S. P. of Vt.*, II (Vermont Charters), 273.
5. Three or four words inaccessible.

October — Rutland 23ᵈ 1786

Your Committee to whome was refered the within Petition Beg Leave to report that the facts in the within Petition are Suported and that in the Opinion of your Committee Two pence on the acre be Granted on Each Right in Said Towns of Brumley & Landgrove Publick Rights Excepted

Daniel Heald for Committe

— & —

A. J.: *Read and referred to a committee, 23 Oct. '86, *S. P. of Vt.*, III (III), 239; *report of committee read and accepted, and leave given to bring in a bill accordingly, 23 Oct. '86, *Ibid*, III (III), 240; bill, having been concurred in by Council, passed into law, 25 Oct. '86, *Ibid*, III (III), 246.[1] *C. J.:* Act read and concurred in with amendment "that the whole tax be collected at one Time", 24 Oct. '86, *G. and C.*, III, 112.[2]

FOR A SPECIAL DIVISION OF UNDIVIDED LANDS
xvii, 228

To the Honorobell General Assembly of the State of Vermont now Convend at Rutland in the County of Rutland the Protition of Ebenezer Allen in behalf of the Propitors of the Two Heeros [Two Heroes][3] being duly ortherised at a Propitors Meeting Legally Warnd Holden at the Dwelling hous of Colnᵒ Eberʳ Allen the 4 day of Sepʳ 1786 Whare as the Propˢ having Loted out a devition of 64 acors to Eachright and Still remans a remnant of Undivided Lands Still to be divided upwards of five acors and not Exseding Six Wich renders it Inconvennant to Lote and divid a Corden to Law as it now Stands[4] on accompt the laying a tax to Colect the Money wold Surmount more than the land Wold be worth and as the Rights are varey Small and the Propˢ wold be glad to Lay Sd lands out as neere the first divition Lot as Posobell Bege your Honners that a Spashal act be Made impouring Said Propˢ to draw for those Piches and to lay out thare lands on thare owne Costs by a Scovore [survey?] and a Comity that Shall be appinted for that Purpus[5] as your Protitioner in duty Bound Shall Ever Pray dated Rutland 18ᵗʰ day of October 1786

Singe [Signed?] —   Eberʳ Allen Propˢ Clerk in behalf of sd Propˢ

— & —

Petⁿ of Colᵒ Ebʳ Allen
Filed 19ᵗʰ Octʳ

---

1. For this act, see *Ms. Laws of Vt.*, I, 550–551.

2. For another petition in this connection, see p. 360, *post*.

3. Now North Hero, South Hero and Grand Isle. See *S. P. of Vt.*, II (Vermont Charters), 298, 321, 330, 350, 357.

4. See "An Act regulating Proprietor's Meetings", passed 23 Feb. '79 (*Ms. Laws of Vt.*, I, 102–104).

5. For a discussion of the distribution of land by town proprietors in colonial New England, see Florence May Woodard, *The Town Proprietors in Vermont: . . .* (Studies in History, Economics and Public Law, Edited by the Faculty of Political Science of Columbia University. No. 418. New York, 1936), pp. 23–27. For a consideration of Vermont practices with respect to the division of lands held in common, see *Ibid*, 120–122.

...*

— & —

A. J.: *Read and prayer granted, and leave given to bring in a bill accordingly, 23 Oct. '86, S. P. of Vt., III (III), 239; bill entitled "An Act empowering the proprietors of the Two Heroes to pitch the undivided lands in said town" read and accepted and sent to Council, 23 Oct. '86, Ibid, III (III), 240. C. J.: Act read and concurred in, 24 Oct. '86, G. and C., III, 112.[1]

FOR A TAX ON LAND TO BUILD ROADS
xvii, 229

To the Honourable General Assembly of the State of Vermont Now Sitting in Rutland —
the Pettition of the Inhabitance of the Town of Sutburey [Sudbury] In the County of Rutland humbley Showeth to your honours that your Petitioners have for a Longe time Laboured undred Maney Disadvantages on account of Rodes in Said Town of Sutburey we your Petitioner being but a Small number in the Town are not able to make and keep in Repare Rodes that are Necessary for your Petitioner as well as the Inhabitance of other Towns and the proprieters cannot give aney assistance for the aforesaid purposes and as it is further necessary on account of the Bridge which is of Late bilt over Ottercrick in Said Town and not aney Rodes Leading to or from the Same which puts other Towns under maney Disadvantages who has allready Laid out Rodes to Said Bridge now we your honours Petitioners pray your honours to Take Said Matters under your wise Consideration and in vewing our Situation as Above Mentioned order a Tax of Two pence on Each acre to be Lade on the Lands in Said Town for the purpus of Laying out Cutting and keeping in Repare Rodes in Said Town as we your honours Petitioners in Duty bound Shall Ever pray —
Dated at Rutland Octr the 19 AD 1786 —

John Hall in behalf of S^d Town

— & —

Petition from Sutburey —
Filed 20th Oct^r
...*

To the Hon^bl Assembly Now Siting
the Comitte to whome the Petition of John Hall in behalf of the town of Sudburry was Refered beg Leave to Report that in our opinion the Prayer of the Petition be in Part Granted and we Recommend to the Legislature to Pass an act to tax the Land in Sd Town one Peney Half Peney Per acre and that the Petitioners have Leave to Bring in a Bill in form for that Purpos   Abel Mariman for Comitee

— & —

A. J.: *Read and referred to a committee, 20 Oct. '86, S. P. of Vt., III (III),

---

1. See "An Act empowering the proprietors of the township of the two Heroes to pitch the undivided lands in said Town", passed 24 Oct. '86 (Ms. Laws of Vt., I, 549).

235; *report of committee read and accepted, and leave given to bring in a bill accordingly, 21 Oct. '86, *Ibid*, III (III), 237; bill read and accepted and sent to Council, 23 Oct. '86, *Ibid*, III (III), 238; bill, having been concurred in by Council, passed into law, 23 Oct. '86, *Ibid*, III (III), 241.[1] *C. J.:* Act read and concurred in "adding words Vermont Gazettee",[2] 23 Oct. '86, *G. and C.*, III, 111.

FOR A TAX ON LAND TO BUILD ROADS
xvii, 230

To the Honourable the General Assembly of the State of Vermont Now Sitting at Rutland

The petition of Alex[r] Harvey Esq[r] in Name and on behalf of the proprietors and Inhabitants of the Town of barnet [Barnet] in the County of orang [Orange] Humbly Sheweth

That at a proprietores Meeting of the proprietor of the Township of Barnet held in said Town on the 30th of Agust Last the proprietores present being a Major part of the whole proprietors of said barnet Voted to appley to the General Assembly at their Next Sessions for a tax of one penny on the acare of all the Lands in said barnet for the purpose of Making and Repairing Roads throw the Different parts of said Town and Likeways the Inhabitant of said barnet at their Legal Town Meeting held on the 5th Day of Sept[r] last Did aprove of and Concur with the above mentioned vote of the proprietors and appointed your petitioner to apply to the General Assembly for said purpose

May it therefor please your Honours to Grant a tax of one penney on Each acare of unEmproved Land in the above Mentioned Town of barnet for Making and Repairing publick Roads under such Regulations as your Honours in your wisdom shall think Meet and your petitioner as in Duty bound shall for Ever pray

Alex[r] Harvey

Rutland Oct[r] 19th 1786

— & —

Petition
Inhabitants of Barnet
Filed 23[d] Oct[r] 1786.
. . .*

— & —

A. J.: *Read and granted, and leave given to bring in a bill accordingly, 23 Oct. '86, *S. P. of Vt.*, III (III), 241; bill read and accepted and sent to Council, 25 Oct. '86, *Ibid*, III (III), 246; bill, having been concurred in by Council, passed into law, 27 Oct. '86, *Ibid*, III (III), 253.[3] *C. J.:* Act read and concurred in, 27 Oct. '86, *G. and C.*, III, 113.

---

1. For this act, see *Ms. Laws of Vt.*, I, 543–544.
2. That is, notice of the tax was to be published in this newspaper.
3. For this act, see *Ms. Laws of Vt.*, I, 551–552.

FOR RIGHT TO SELL REAL PROPERTY TO SETTLE AN ESTATE
xvii, 231; xxxviii, 146

To the Honorable the General Assembly of the State of Vermont now siting at Rutland

The Petition of Joel Linsley Administrator of the Estate of Jacob Linsley late of Cornwall deceased Humbly sheweth; that the personal Estate of the said deceased is insufficient by the Sum of Fifteen pounds and nine pence Lawful money to pay the Debts due from said estate,

Therefore, prays your Honors to pass an Act, impowering him the said Joel Linsley to sell so much of the Real Estate of the said Jacob Linsley as will raise the afore said sum of Fifteen pounds & nine pence Lawful money, for the purpose of paying the Debts due from said Estate together with the necessary Cost arising on such sale, under such restrictions as you in your Wisdom may think fit, which your Honors Petitioner as in duty bound shall ever pray.

Tinmouth Oct. 19th 1786   Joel Linsly

Certificate from the Judge of Probates

To the Honorable the General Assembly of the State of Vermont —

This may Certify that the Personal Estate of Jacob Linsley late of Cornwall deceased is insufficient by the Sum of Fifteen pounds and nine pence Lawful Mony to pay the Debts due from said Estate

Pr Elisha Clark Judge Prob.

Probate Office ⎫
Rutland District ⎬ Tinmouth 18th oct. 1786

— & —

Joel Linsley's Petition
Filed 18th Octr 1786 —
. . .*

— & —

A. J.: *Read and granted, and leave given to bring in a bill accordingly, 19 Oct. '86, S. P. of Vt., III (III), 231; bill read and accepted and sent to Council, 19 Oct. '86, Ibid, III (III), 231; bill, having been concurred in by Council, passed into law, 23 Oct. '86, Ibid, III (III), 241.[1] C. J.: Act read and concurred in, 21 Oct. '86, G. and C., III, 111.

FOR ADDITIONAL COMPENSATION FOR WAR SERVICES
BECAUSE OF CURRENCY DEPRECIATION[2]
xvii, 232

To the Honble the General Assembly now Sitting —

---

1. For this act, see Ms. Laws of Vt., I, 542.

2. This petition was presented in behalf of seven veterans who withdrew their own in favor of this one. See S. P. of Vt., III (III), 230. For their petition and its explanatory notes, see p. 224, ante. For other petitions in connection with this service, see p. 185, ante, and pp. 291, 394, post.

The petition of Benj[a] Whitcomb in behalf of Abel Rice late a Serg[t] in Capt. Aldridges Comp[y] in the troops which were under my command, Nath[l] Carpenter, Francis Ackley Asa Pratt & Jeduthan Roberts late soldiers in Said Company and John Martin & Michael Coffeen late Soldiers in my Company — Humbly Sheweth —

That the Said Rice, Carpenter, Ackley, Pratt, Roberts, Martin and Coffeen all lived in this State when they enlisted in Said Corps in the years 1776 and 1777 and in which they served four years or nearly, the principal part of which time they served in this State — and that they received in wages from the Continent but forty shillings p[r] month in Continental money, which pay was stayed the last of the year 1779 and that the time they served in 1780 & 1781 they have never received any wages — And that they have not nor cannot get any depreciation allowed them in any other state but this — Your petitioner therefore most earnestly prays that your Honors would make up their depreciation agreeable to their Continental troops which have had the same allowed by this State, and likewise order them to receive pay for the time they served in the years 1780 & 1781 Orotherwise as your honors in your wisdom shall judge best — And as in duty bound Shall ever pray —

Benj[a] Whetcomb

Rutland Oct[r] 19th 1786

— & —

Petition by Benj[n] Whitcomb
Filed 19th Oct[r] 86.
. . .*

— & —

A. J.: *Read and referred to a committee, 19 Oct. '86, S. P. of Vt., III (III), 230; report of committee read and not accepted, 26 Oct. '86, Ibid, III (III), 249;[1] *petition dismissed, 26 Oct. '86, Ibid, III (III), 249.

FOR A GRANT OF LAND TO THE FAMILY OF ONE OF THE FOUNDERS OF THE STATE
xvii, 233

To the Hon[ble] General Assembly of the State of Vermont convened at Rutland —
The petition of the Subscribers Humbly Sheweth, that your petitioners with many others in this State, Retain the Highest feelings of Gratitude to all those persons who have stood forth in Early period and in Time of utmost uncertainty & distress to assist & promote the Intrest of this State And we feel a more particular Gratitude to such persons who have Exerted themselves & pointed out a Systum to be pursued to bring this Government into Existence & who have acted from the most disintrested Motives any further then respicted Humanity & who has in consequence thereof suffered great injury in personal Charecter & Private property, We beg

---

1. For the text of this report, see petition, mentioned as withdrawn in previous note, on p. 224, ante.

leave to Reprinsent our former Worthy friend Doct[r] Thomas Young Dec[d] I as comeing completely under this discription from the decided part which he took in our favour in the most Critical moment as Respected the Existence of this State, having pointed out the System to be persued to Establish Government by a seperate jurisdiction & to whom we Stand Indebted for the very name of (Vermont) We now beg leave to Recommend, His Family who are left in Low & Indigent Circumstances [to your][2] notice & patronage & pray in their Behalf that [your honors] consider the Merits due to our Dec[d] friend & [that an] Hon[bl] Compensation be made to them by a [Grant of] Some Land in Such part of the State as shall be Vacant which after a Determination your [petitioners] will point out — your petitioners pray [that a] Committee may be appointed hereon that [the] Circumstances may be more fully Represented [& a] Report made to your honors as in Duty [bound] your petitioners ever pray —

Rutland 20 Oct 1786

Tho[s] [Chittenden]
Ethan Allen
Joseph Fay —

— & —

Petition of [Et?] Allen & J[o] Fay —
Filed 24th Oct[r] 1786
. . .*
Tho[s] Chittenden Ethan Allen & Joseph Fay Esq[rs] petition in behalf of Doct[r] Youngs Heirs —[3]

— & —

> A. J.: *Read and referred to next session, 24 Oct. '86, S. P. of Vt., III (III), 242; *read and referred to next session, 23 Oct. '87, Ibid, III (III), 41.

FOR THE INTEREST DUE ON A STATE NOTE
xvii, 236

To the Hon[ble] General assembly of the state of Vermont now Sitting at Rutland —
    The Petition of Barnabas Strong
                    Humbly Sheweth —
That in the years 1781 & 1782 he Served the State in the Line of the army in the capasity of Isuing Comisary that he advanced Sundry sums of money in procuring Nesesary Stores Transportation there of &c —
That he could Never obtain a Settlement till the 25th of August Last past that

---

1. For an understanding of Dr. Thomas Young's part in the early history of the state, see G. and C., I, 42–44, 58–59, 78, 83, 394–396.

2. The original manuscript has been partially destroyed. The words in italics in brackets have been inserted from a copy of the original doubtless made at the time of the presentation of the petition to the Assembly. The copy is also found in Ms. Vt. S. P., xvii, 233.

3. The additional material is taken both from the original and the copy mentioned in note 2, supra.

there was found a Ballance Due to him of £ 27-14-8 which was justly his Due on the first Day of Nov[r] 1782 -— that the General Assembly have passed an act alowing interest on all Debts Due from this State to any Individual that Should be found Due on or before the 13th of Feb[y] 1783[1] that the aforesaid sum due to your Petioner was paid him in Notes by the Treasurer on the Said 25th Day of August 1786 on Interest from the Said Day — by which means your Petitioner was Not only deprived of the principle of his money for several year but the Interest which he can No ways recover by virtue of the aforesaid act — therefore your Petitioner prays that your honours would Grant him Redress by Directing the Treasurer to pay him the Interest Due on Said Notes from the 13th Feb[y] 1783 amounting to £ 5-18-7-1 or in Such other way grant your Petitioner redress as your Honours in your wisdom shall direct and your petitioner as in duty bound Shall pray —
Bethel 20th Oct[r] 1786   Barnabas Strong

— & —

Petition of Barnabas Strong
Filed 20th Oct[r]
. . .*

Rutland Oct[r] 21st 1786 —
Your Committee to whoem was refered the within petition Beg Leave to report that they find the facts therein stated to be true and the prayer thereof ought to be Granted and that the Treasurer pay the said Barnabas Strong £ 5-18-7. [. . .] by giving him an order on Some of the Colectors of hard-Money Taxes Granted to pay Interest on State Notes or in Cirtifacates for the same —
                                        Beriah Green for Comittee
— & —

A. J.: *Read and referred to a committee, 20 Oct. '86, S. P. of Vt., III (III), 235; *report of committee read and accepted, 21 Oct. '86, Ibid, III (III), 237; resolved that Treasurer pay petitioner £5-18-7 by drawing orders on any hard money taxes, 21 Oct. '86, Ibid, III (III), 237.

FOR AUTHORITY TO CONFIRM THE ACTS
OF CERTAIN PROPRIETORS' MEETINGS
xvii, 237

To the Hon[ble] the General Assembly of the State of Vermont now sitting. —
The Petition of Israel Morey on behalf of the Proprietors of the Town of Fairlee in Orange County Sheweth
That the said Town was originally granted by New Hampshire[2] but before the Proprietors could hold any meetings they with the rest of the Hampshire Grants fell under the Jurisdiction of New York by the Adjudication of the King of Great-Britain in 1764. —[3]

---

1. See "An Act directing the Treasurer to issue State Notes on interest, for debts due from this State", passed February, 1783 (Slade, 468).
2. For the grant of Fairlee, see State Papers New Hampshire: The New Hampshire Grants . . . , vol. XXVI, Town Charters, vol. III (Concord, 1895), pp. 159-162.
3. For the Order-in-Council making this adjudication 20 July 1764, see Slade, 19.

That the Government of New York not having any Laws for warning Proprietors Meetings — the said Proprietors for the sake of alloting & settling said town and bringing it into a State of Cultivation, by an Agreement of a large majority of the Proprietors, held proprietors meetings as near as their circumstances would admit conformably to the Laws of New Hampshire & have from time to time laid taxes by votes of the said Meetings.

That a considerable part of said taxes have been collected & applied to the use of the propriety agreeable to their votes

That their situation rendered it absolutely necessary to lay some taxes in such meetings after the whole town had been allotted into Severalty

That some persons who are in arrears refuse paying their arrearages pretending that such meetings were not lawfully warned or held

Your Petitioners therefore pray the hon^ble the Legislature to pass an Act enabling the Land owners in said town to meet in such manner as proprietors meetings are by law held[1] & (if they shall see proper) by vote to confirm the Proceedings of the former meetings & to collect the arrearages of taxes heretofore voted by said Proprietors —

And your Petitioners as in duty bound shall ever pray &c. —

Israel Morey

Rutland 21st Octr 1786 —

— & —

Petition of Israel Morey on behalf of the Proprietors of Fairlee.
Filed 23. Octr 86.

. . .*

— & —

A. J.: *Read and granted, and leave given to bring in a bill accordingly, 23 Oct. '86, *S. P. of Vt.*, III (III), 239; bill read and accepted and sent to Council, 24 Oct. '86, *Ibid*, III (III), 243; bill, having been concurred in by Council, passed into law, 27 Oct. '86, *Ibid*, III (III), 252.[2] *C. J.:* Act read and concurred in, 26 Oct. '86, *G. and C.*, III, 113.

FOR THE CREDIT OF A COUNTY TAX TO A FORMER SHIRE TOWN
xvii, 239

To the Honorable General Assembly of the State of Vermont Now Setting, in Rutland

The petition of Phinehas Freeman, In Behalf of the Inhabitants of the town of Marlborough Sheweth

That there was A County Tax Granted by a Convention held at Westminster the year 1784 in the County of Windham, of one penny on the pound & that S^d Convention voted that the town of Marlborough Should Appropriate S^d tax for y^e

---

1. See "An Act regulating Proprietors' Meetings", passed 23 Feb. '79 (*Ms. Laws of Vt.*, I, 102–104).
2. See "An Act to enable the land owners of the town of Fairlee in Orange County to meet and transact the business therein mentioned" (*Ms. Laws of Vt.*, I, 553–554).

town of Marlborough, toward Compleating the goal then building by the Inhabitants of S^d Marlborough, on Condition that S^d goal was Compleated by the first of Decr then Next Which was Actually Completed to the Acceptence but for Certain Reasons the County Court Not Seeing fit to Grant the privelege of a Yard,

Your Petitioners have not been able to get Discharged from S^d tax And as by an Act of this Honorable house, the half shire is Removed from the town of Marlborough[1] & the Expence Laid out in S^d town for boulding a goal Is Lost to S^d town

Therefore your Petitioners Pray your Honors to grant An Order that the Treasurer of the County of Windham be directed to Credit the Town of Marlborough the above S^d tax, or grant Some Other releaf as your Honors Shall see fit And your Honors Petitioner as in Duty bound Shall Ever Pray

Phinehas Freeman

Rutland Octr 23 1786

— & —

Pet^n of Phin^s Freeman in behalf of the Inhabitants of Marlboro.
Filed 23^d Octr 86.
. . .*

— & —

> A. J.: *Read and referred to a committee, 23 Oct. '86, S. P. of Vt., III (III), 240; *report of committee read and accepted, and leave given to bring in a bill accordingly, 24 Oct. '86, Ibid, III (III), 242;[2] resolved that Treasurer of Windham County credit Marlboro the county tax of one penny on the pound granted in 1784, 24 Oct. '86, Ibid, III (III), 242.

FOR THE RIGHT TO COIN COPPER FOR AN ADDITIONAL TERM
xvii, 241

To the Honorable General Assembly of the State of Vermont now Sitting att Rutland —

The Petition of Ruben Herman J^r of Rupert in the County of Bennington humbly Sheweth — that the legislature of this State did at their Session held at Norwich in June 1785 grant him the sole Right of coining copper within this state for the term of two years —[3] that he your Petitioner has been at a very great expence in erecting works and procuring a quantity of genuine copper for that purpose — that Said Term is nearly expired — and that your petitioner, — by reason of the shortness of said Term will be unable to indemnify himself for said expences — farther your Petitioner conceives that in the present scarcity of a circulating medium the coining of coppers within this state may be very advantageous to the

---

1. See "An Act for fixing and ascertaining the Shire town of Windham County" passed 23 Oct. '86, by which Newfane was appointed the shire town (Ms. Laws of Vt., I, 544-545). It is significant that the date of this act is the date of this petition.

2. The report of the committee as given on the manuscript petition simply states that the facts set forth in the petition are true and that it ought to be granted.

3. For this act passed 15 June '85, see Ms. Laws of Vt., I, 478-479; and for an act in addition to this act passed 27 Oct. '85, see Ibid, I, 528.

Public — Your Petitioner therefore prays this Honorable assembly to grant him the priviledge of coining copper for a farther term of ten years or such other Term and under such regulations and restrictions as to your Honours in your wisdom shall seem meet —

and as in Duty bound Shall ever pray   Reuben Harmon Junr
Rutland Octr 23 — 1786 —

— & —

Petition of Reuben Harmon Junr
Filed 23^d Octr 1786.
. . .*

Rutland Octr 24 — 1786 — To the General Assembly now Sitting —
Your Committee to whom was referred the consideration of the within petition beg leave to report as their opinion that the sole preveledge of coining copper be granted to the said Ruben Harmon J^r for the Term of eight years from the expiration of the former grant under the following regulations viz — that he procure bond to the Treasurer as is provided in the former grant —¹ that the first three years the Said Ruben shall enjoy the said preveledge free that for the remaining five years he shall pay two & one half p^r cent to the State on all the coppers he shall coin and give Security for the payment — that the device be in future a head on one side with the motto "Auctoritate Vermontensium"² abridged — on the reverse a woman representing the genus of America with the Letters INDE — ET.LIB. for Independence and Liberty —³ All which is Humbly Submitted by
                                        Eben^r Walbridge for Commitee

— & —

A. J.: *Read and referred to a committee, 23 Oct. '86, S. P. of Vt., III (III), 240;⁴ *report of committee read and accepted, and leave given to bring in a bill accordingly, 24 Oct. '86, Ibid, III (III), 242; bill read and accepted and sent to Council, 24 Oct. '86, Ibid, III (III), 243–244. C. J.: *Committee appointed to join Assembly committee, 23 Oct. '86, G. and C., III, 111; act read and concurred in, 24 Oct. '86, Ibid, III, 112.⁵

FOR THE LOCATION OF A COUNTY GRAMMAR SCHOOL
xvii, 242

To the Honoroble general assembly Now Setting at Rutland —
The Petition of the Subscribers in habitants of Castelton Humbly Sheweth: that agreeable to the Constitution of this State Directing one grammer School in Each County in this State⁶ they have Erected a house for that Purpose in Said Castleton

---

1. That is, in the amount of five thousand pounds. See references in previous note.
2. "By Authority of Vermont."
3. For a discussion of Vermont coinage and for representations of coins produced under the terms of this report, see G. and C., III, 383–384.
4. The entry on the manuscript petition correctly states that the committee was to join a committee from the Council.
5. For this act, see Slade, 509–510.
6. See Section XL, Constitution of 1777 (G. and C., I, 102).

in a very Beautiful Place Near the Center of said town;[1] Said house is 21 by 40 feet on the ground which is supposed to be sufficient for that purpose Which the Subscribers offer as a presant to the County of Rutland If your honners Shall See fit to Establish that for the County Grammer School House for the said County of Rutland. the Subscribers would further inform your honners that Said house is not fully Compeated [sic] but that they are willing to be bound to Compeat said house when your honners shall Direct — and If your honners in your wisdom Shall See fit to Establish Said house for that purpose your Petitioners in Duty bound will Ever pray —

Dated at Castleton 25ᵗʰ of October 1786 —

> Isaac Clark
> Brewster Higley
> Solomon Garnsey
> Ambros Evert
> Nehemiah Hoit
> Noah Hoit
> John Whitlock
> [Forrist?] Sturdivant
> Araunah woodard
> Eli Cogsell
> Zadock Reminton
> George Foot

— & —

[. . .][2] Inhabitants of Castleton
Filᵈ Febʳ 27ᵗʰ 1787
for Grammar School
Entered
. . .*

To the Honorᵉ Genˡ Assemᵉ now sitting your Commᵗᵗ to whom was refered the consideration of the within petition beg leave to report that in their opinion the prayer of said Petition ought to be granted and that the petitioners have liberty to bring in a Bill accordingly provided the building be erected at the expence of the Inhabitants of Castleton

Lem. Chipman for Comᵗ

— & —

A. J.: *Read and referred to a committee, 13 Oct. '87, S. P. of Vt., III (IV), 12; bill read and accepted and sent to Council, 15 Oct. '87, Ibid, III (IV), 14; bill, having been concurred in by Council, passed into law, 15 Oct. '87, Ibid, III (IV), 17.[3] C. J.: Act read and concurred in, 15 Oct. '87, G. and C., III, 148.

---

1. For the location of the school, see Abby Maria Hemenway, The Vermont Historical Gazetteer, Vol. III (Claremont, N. H., 1877), p. 517. In terms of present landmarks the structure was located "a little to the west" of the village school and town hall building. The act passed in response to this petition placed it "near Doctor William Wolcott's." See note 3, post.

2. Two or three words inaccessible.

3. See "An Act for establishing a County Grammar School at Castleton in the county of Rutland" (Acts and Laws, passed by the legislature of the State of Vermont, at their session at Newbury, the second Thursday of October, 1787 [Windsor, 1787], p. 1.

FOR THE RIGHT TO SELL REAL PROPERTY TO SETTLE AN ESTATE
xvii, 163, 243

To the Hon[ble] General Assembly now sitting in Rutland
The Petition of Lemuel Buck & Phebe ⟨Susannah⟩ Bristol Admors [Administrators]
to the Estate of Gideon Bristol late of Sandgate in Bennington County dec[d]
Sheweth
That the personal Estate of the said deceased is insufficient by the sum of
£ 40 — for the Payment of the just Debts due from said Estate —
Your Petitioners therefore pray this Hon[ble] house to impower them to sell so
much of the real Estate of the said dec[d] as will raise the sum of £ 40 — & Costs
of sale under the direction of the Judge of Probate for the district of Manchester —
And your petitioners (as in duty bound) shall ever pray. —

	Lemuel Buck	Admors
Rutland 26th Oct[r] 1786	Phebe ⟨Susannah⟩ Bristol	of Gid[n] Bristol

The Honorable General Assembly of the State of Vermont to be holden at Rutland
on the Second Thursday in Oct[r] next — These Certifie that the Demands of the
Credittors to the Estate of Gideon Bristoll late of Sandgate Deceased Surmount
the Personal Estate of Said Deceased the Sum of Forty Pounds Lawful Money
Manchester Nov[r] 15th 1785

attest — Martin Powel Judge of Probate

— & —

Pet[n] of [Admors of ?] Gideon Bristol.
Filed 27th Oct[r] 1786
. . .*

— & —

> A. J.: *Read "with a certificate of the Judge of Probate" and granted, and leave
> given to bring in a bill accordingly, 30 Oct. '86, S. P. of Vt., III (III), 255–256;
> bill read and accepted and sent to Council, 30 Oct. '86, Ibid, III (III), 256;
> bill, having been concurred in by Council, passed into law, 30 Oct. '86, Ibid,
> III (III), 256.[1] C. J.: Act read and concurred in, 30 Oct. '86, G. and C., III, 114.

FOR REFORM OF JUDICIAL PROCEDURE
xvii, 244

To the Honorable General Assembly to be Convend at Bennington on the
Third Thursday of February Next —
the Prayer and Petition of the Subscribers Humbly Sheweth that your Petitioners
with others took an Early and Active part in the forming and Establishing Civil
Government in this State with the most Sanguine hopes and Expectations of Receiving from it that protection both in Person and Property that might with the
Blessing of Heaven Render the good People of this State Respectable Peaceable

---

1. For this act, see Ms. Laws of Vt., I, 554.

and Happy and Now your Petitioners beg leave to observe that we are in Some measure disappointed in our expectations that for a considerable time past the [sic] has been a great if not a general uneasiness among the good people of this State on account of the present Mode of Government Some of the causes of discontent have Already been laid before Your Honours but [still there remain some matters of grievance] which have not as yet been pointed out in any former Petition[1] and therefore beg leave to lay before your Honors some of those burthens which we Esteem to be matters of Real Grievance; and first we say that in our opinion the County Corts are a Creation wholly Useless in a free Government Pecularly Calculated for the Purpose of delaying Justice Mere Clogs in the Wheel of Government fit Tools for the Purpose of Swelling Bills of Cost ‹delaying Justice›: it Appears that but a Small matter of Business is done by them after a long Session and greater Part is generaly to be done again by the Supreame Cort and no advantage gaind by Either party from a Trial at the Cort We therefore beg leave to Sugest to your Honours that the Supreame Cort ought to be made a Cort of Entry for all Causes wherein the Matter in demand Shall Exceed the Sum of Fifty Pound and that a Single Magistrate might hear and determine all Causes under that Sum Except Criminal Causes that there be no Appeals allowed under the Sum of Ten Pounds if the Judgment be Rendered on a Specialty—[2] We further beg leave to observe that it Appears to us to be Burdensome to the people to pay the Judges of the Cort out of the Publick Moneys We likewise complain of the unjust and Arbitrary Proceedings of our Corts in Prohibiting Either Plantiffs or defendents or others Properly Authorized by them to Answer and Manage their Causes; and oblige them to hire an Attorney at an Extravagant Price or Sacrifice his Cause, another Cause of Extream uneasiness is the Wicked and Pernicious practice of Some of our Civil Authority by Signing Blank-Writs for Attorneys to fill at their own Discrission which is the Sole Cause of great may [many] unnessary Vexacious Petty Law-Suits to the great disturbance of the good People of this State —
We further beg leave to Say that we Esteem it altogether unjust and unreasonable that Attorney fees Should be Allowed in any Bill of Cost Received in any Cort whatever [. . .][3] allow to Either plantiff or defendent his Travel if at the Supream or County Cort and two Shillings only for his Attendence and Officers fees from the Place of Service to the place of Trial if within the County
We therefore Pray that Your Honors would take the matter into your Serious Consideration and Grant Relief in the Premises as your Honors Shall Judge Most Conducive of the peace and well being of this State and your Petitioners as in Duty Bound Shall Ever Pray —
Decr 10th AD 1786

Thomas Sawyer	John Daggett	John Squiea
Asa Bacon	William Kendal	David Wetherbee
John Lawson	Samuel Hinds	John Cobb
James Farr	Peter White	Abner Moor
Samuel Adam	John Smith	James Cummings

---

1. For previous petitions to the same general effect presented to the Assembly during the October '86 session, see pp. 189, 216, 225, 232, 238, 244, 248, 262, *ante*, and explanatory notes.

2. A specialty is, broadly speaking, an instrument of writing under the hand and seal of the parties.

3. Five or six words illegible.

David Fiske
Natha¹ Cook
Josua White
John Ripper
Eli Brown
Solomon Story
Joseph Woodward
Solmon Farr
Moses Knap
James Laflen
John Farnum
Jerahmeel Powers
Elias Chamberlin
Eph^m Stevens
Solomon Bigelow
William Pratt
Deane C Stevens

Thomas Tuttle Junr
Asa Fuller
Jehiel Hull J^r
Curtis Smith
Blanchard Powers
Caleb Hendee
Cyrus Abernethy
[edurham?] [. . .]
George Hill
John Tupper
Ephraim Sawyer
Elijah Houghton
Josiah Sawyer
John Bowman
Noel Potter
David Warner

Jabez Collins
Isaiah Golding
Asa Hammond
O. Cramton
Joseph Williams
John Rhoads
Joseph Congdon Ju^r
James [Fenekey?]
David Jewell
Ezebel Green
Abel Titus
John Rose
Thomas Eddy
Tilley Moor
Joel Foster
Dan¹ Washburn

— & —

A petition from the People¹
N° 1
the Con Vention is the second thursday in february at John Smith²

— & —

A. J.: Read along with other petitions and referred to a committee to join a committee from the Council, 19 Feb. '87, S. P. of Vt., III (III), 272;³ proposals from the Governor for the committee considering the petitions of grievances read, and, not being signed, resolved that a committee return the proposals to the Governor and request him to sign them in his official or private character, 27 Feb. '87, Ibid, III (III), 296; committee returned with proposals signed by Thomas Chittenden, and these again read and referred to committee on the petitions of grievances, 27 Feb. '87, Ibid, III (III), 297; report of committee on petitions of grievances read, and the first and second articles accepted, 2 March '87, Ibid, III (III), 309.⁴ C. J.: Committee appointed to join Assembly committee to consider above petitions, G. and C., III, 120–121.⁵

1. This was in fact a petition "from a number of Inhabitents from the County of Rutland." See G. and C., III, 121; also cf. S. P. of Vt., III (III), 272.

2. This notation on the reverse of the manuscript presumably refers to a county convention at Rutland which was projected at the time the petition was drawn up. No other reference to it has been found.

3. This petition is clearly the one mentioned in the journal as "signed by 66 persons dated Decr 10^t 1786." The identity of date and the absence of any place of signature make this plain, even though the document itself contains only 64 names. The other petitions are not now among the Ms. Vt. S. P.

4. The fact that the text of the report of this committee is not found in the journal or elsewhere makes it impossible to trace specifically the acts of the Assembly, if any, originating in this and the other petitions. For the general consequences on legislation of these and the similar petitions presented in the previous session, see p. 192, ante, note 1.

5. This entry in the Council journal contains an extract from the Assembly journal which numbers the petitions up to nine. However, neither of the journals specifies more than eight. See also S. P. of Vt., III (III), 272.

FOR THE APPOINTMENT OF A PARTICULAR JUSTICE OF THE PEACE
xvii, 284

To the Honourable General Assembly of the State of Vermont to be holden at Benington [Bennington] in Febuary 1787 —

The Petition of us the Subscribers Humbly Sheweth that whereas Elkanah Sprague Esqr haith Served as a Justice of the Peace in the Town of Hartford for many years, and as to any thing within the Compas of our knowlidge haith given general Satisfaction in the Execution of his office, and altho it is reported that there has been Some complaints thrown out against him, we conceive it to be more out of a private peek than any just foundation for those complaints, it would be a wonder indeed if Esqr Sprague Should have no Enemies, when the best man that ever lived on Earth had So many, (as we have it on Record in Sacred writ) We humbly conceive that the Hon^{bl} Council of Censors had no idea when they proposed the present mode of appointing the Justices of the peace yearly,[1] to Shift and make A new one every year, but we rather think it was to have the power when it Should so happen that a Justice of the peace did not conduct well (if not guilty of male administration) or another man Should appear that Should be Juge^d more suitable for that office, to make a new appointment, we think the pains Esqr Sprague has taken to inform himself, and the practice he has had in the office of Justice of the peace Renders him as Suitable a person as any in the Town of Hartford for that office and therefore pray that he may be appointed, and we beg leave to inform your Honours, that the Nomination for a Justice of the Peace that will probably be presented to the Honourable Assembly, was made by a few favorites and [politians?] [making?] Eight of the Town, and we presume a majority of the Town would not make that nomination for Cojant Reasons, your Petitioners firmly Relying in your Honours wisdom and that your Honours ever wish to do everything in your power to promote peace and tranquilety in the State in every part thereof, do not doubt but the prayer of our petition will be granted — and we as in Duty bound Shall ever pray —

John Hagar	Isaac Williams jun^r	Artemas Robinson
William Dammer	Jonathan Wright	Nathaniel Bugbee
Edy Buitch [Burtch]	Zerah Evans	Paul Clark
Benjam: Burtch	Benja Wright Ju^r	Josiah Williams
Jacob Hall	Phinehas Rn Wright	John Carpenter
Thomas Richardson	Samson How	Joseph Williams
Ephriam Burtch	Thomas Holbrook	Samuel Webster
Thomas Emerson	Hans Williams	Jabez Baldwin
Enoch Emerson	Amos Robinson	Peter Rider Jun
Andrew Powers	Mitchell Clark	Tho Moxley
Asahel Doubleday	William Burtch	Seth Moxley
James Burch	Willis Hall	Niel Rust
Joe Evans	Moses Evas	Lemuel Rust
John Slatteray	Daniel Ainsworth	Peter Rider
John Marsh	Jonathan Birtch	Phinehas Rust
Nathan dammon	Daniel Pinneo	

---

1. For this proposal by the Council of Censors, see *Slade*, 521. The proposed mode was included in the revised Constitution of 1786. See *Statutes of the State of Vermont, passed by the Legislature in February and March 1787* (Windsor, 1787), p. 10.

— & —

Hartford Petition
Feb^r 16. 1787
. . .*

— & —

    A. J.: *Read and ordered to lie on table until Governor and Council shall join
Assembly to elect officers and then to be laid before them, 16 Feb. '87, *S. P.
of Vt.,* III (III), 267.

FOR ESTABLISHMENT OF A TOWN'S BOUNDS AND THE ANNEXATION
OF A GORE THERETO
xvii, 177

To the Honerable House of the Representatives of the State of Vermont in General
Assembly Met
May it Please Your Honours We the Subscribers being Inhabitants or Propritors
of Winhall or owners of Land in the Gore Granted under the Seal of this State to
Capt Edward Aikin and his Asociates —¹
Beg leave to approach your Honerable house with this our humble Petition Praying
that of your wisdom and goodness you would Give some orders Whereby the
Bounds of the Township of Winhall according to charter may be certainly known
and Established: as the disputes Relative to Said bounds have much Retarded the
Settlement, both of Winhall: and the said Gore. Your Petitioners Likewise Pray
that you would Annex the Said Gore to the Township of Winhall² and your
Petitioners as in duty bound Shall Ever Pray —
Winhall January 1st 1787

Nath^{el} Browne	Asa Beebee	Gershom Taylor
Russell Day	Ezra Bigelow	Seth Taylor
Adonijah Foot	Ephraim Whitney	Elisha Whitney
Moses Taylor	Joseph Rose	Moses Taylor Jr
Ezra Taylor	Nathaniel Rose	Jonathan Taylor
John Brooks	Ebenezer Whitney	

— & —

Winhall Petition
Filed Feb^r 19th 1787
. . *

— & —

    A. J.: *Read and dismissed, 20 Feb. '87, *S. P. of Vt.,* III (III), 278.

---

    1. This gore was Aikin's Gore and was already annexed to Londonderry. See
S. P. of Vt., II (Vermont Charters), pp. 1–2, 250.
    2. For a previous petition to this effect, see p. 93, *ante.*

FOR A TAX ON LAND TO BUILD ROADS AND BRIDGES
xvii, 247

Unto the honourable General Assembly of the State of Vermont — to be conven^d in Bennington on the 15th of February Next —
The potetion of the Inhabetance of Monkton in the County of Addeson [Addison] Humbly Sheweth —
That your petetioners has Setled this town under the many Attending Deficalties of Setling a Wilderness, & what yet Remains meterily [materially?] unhapy in our Cituation is, that we are Distetute of pasable Roads to Mill & Merket, our Setling this Tow-Ship when it was a Remote wilderness, has Bin the Means of Inhancing the Vallue of the uncultivated Land to a Great Degree, & the properitors have Never given But Twelve Shilling on a Righ [right] Toward Claring & Bridging Them, which Semes to be very Inconsiderable in answering the Calls of Necesety, & we think the Task to hard for us to Do it as Town Habetance, & the Disadvantages we are under on the acount & Likewise the publick in general, Moves us to Implore the honourable Legeslature to Lay a Tax on all the Rateble Lands in S^d Town of as much as two pence on the Acre to Defray the Charges of Laying Cuting & Bridging the Nesesary Roads, So we hope the Honourable Legeslature will Take the Matter Represented in Consideration & grant us Releaf as Justice & humanity will Readely Dictate & your petetioners in Duty Bound Shall Every pray —
Dated Jen^r [Jan.] ye 1th 1787

John Forgason	Orrey Cronkhite	John Bishop Jn^r
Saml Barnum	James Brock	Stephen Fuller
Lemuel Hardy	Stephen Barnum	Ebenezer Barnum
Richard Barnum	David Robards	John Starns
Daniel Smith	Horrace Hervy	Ebenezer Starns
John Brock	Silas Hardy	

— & —

Petition of Inhabitants of Monkton — for tax for making & repairing roads & c. Entered on File Feb^r 16. 1787
. . .*

— & —

A. J.: *Read and referred to a committee, 16 Feb. '87, S. P. of Vt., III (III), 267–268; *report of committee recommending that a tax of one penny half penny per acre be granted, read and accepted, and leave given to bring in a bill accordingly, 17 Feb. '87, Ibid, III (III), 269; bill read and accepted and sent to Council, 21 Feb. '87, Ibid, III (III), 280; bill, having been amended by Council to one penny tax, agreed to and passed into law, 23 Feb. '87, Ibid, III (III), 287.[1] C. J.: Act read and amendment to one penny tax proposed, 21 Feb. '87, G. and C., III, 124.

---

1. For this act, see Ms. Laws of Vt., II, 24–25. In spite of the adoption of the Council's amendment the text of the act provides for a tax of one penny half penny.

FOR A TAX ON LAND TO BUILD ROADS AND BRIDGES
xvii, 248

To the Honorable Gen[ll] Assembly to be convean[d] at Bennington on the Third
Thursday of Febr[y] Next The Prayer and Petition of the Subscribers Inhabitants of
the Town of Leicester Humbly Sheweth. —
Your Petitioners are unable at Present to Cut and Clear Roads and Build Bridges
in Said Town Necessary for the Public Roads through Said Town Your Petitioners
therefore Pray that Your Honors would Grant a Tax of two Pence on Each Acre
of Land in Said Town for the purpose of Clearing Roads Building Bridges &C
under Such Regulations and Restriction as your Honors Shall Judge Reasonable
and Your Petitioners as in Duty Bound Shall ever Pray —
Lecister Jan[y] 2[d] AD 1787

Thomas Sawyer	Abel Johnson	Salmon Farr
Eph[m] Stevens	Moses [Knox?]	Asa Bacon
John Ripner	Eli Brown	Solomon Bigelow
David Fish	Joseph Woodward	William Kendall
Solomon Story	Elias Chamberlin	Joshua White
William Pratt	John Daggett	Denial Stevens
James Laflen	Nathaniel Cook	Peter White
John Farnum	Samuel [Kindel?]	Solomon Holman
James Farr	John Lawson	

— & —

Leicester Petition
Entered on file 16th Feb[r] 1787
. . .*

— & —

A. J.: *Read and referred to a committee, 16 Feb. '87, S. P. of Vt., III (III),
266; *report of committee recommending that a tax of 1½ pence per acre be
granted, read and accepted, and leave given to bring in a bill accordingly, 19
Feb. '87, Ibid, III (III), 274; bill read and accepted and sent to Council, 3
March '87, Ibid, III (III), 311; bill, having been returned from Council with
proposals of amendment, agreed to and passed into law, 8 March '87, Ibid,
III (III), 325; bill reconsidered and dismissed, 9 March '87, Ibid, III (III),
327. C. J.: Act read and returned to Assembly with proposals of amendment,
8 March '87, G. and C., III, 139.

FOR A TAX ON LAND TO BUILD ROADS AND BRIDGES
xvii, 249

To the Honorable the General Assembly of the State of Vermont, to be convened
at Bennington in February next — The Petition of the Subscribers Select-Men of
Wardsborough humbly Sheweth, that whereas there are two publick Roads through
Said Town, one of them leading from Wilmington to New-Fane, the other from
Connecticut River to Manchester, and that it would be greatly to the Interest of
the Publick, that the Road already begun, leading from Bennington through Som-
mersett [Somerset] and Wardsborough, to Connecticut-River, Should be com-

pleated, that the Inhabitants of said Wardsborough have been at great expence in Making Roads, that they are thinly Setled, in almost all parts of the Town, that it is necessary there Should be several expencive Bridges built, as well as further cost to repair & alter said Roads, in many Places — Therefore your Petitioners, (in behalf of said Town) humbly pray your Honors would grant them Relief in the Premises, by laying a tax of one penny half Penny, on the Acre, on all the Lands in S^d Town, except the Publick Rights, under Such regulations & restrictions as your Honors in your great Wisdom shall think fit — and your Petitioners as in duty bound Shall ever pray
Wardsborough January 3rd 1787

John [Ganson?]   ⎰ Select-Men
Ebenezer Sears   ⎱   of
Jacob Chamberlin ⎱ Wardsborough

— & —

Select-Men of Wardsborough to the General Assembly —
A Petition for a Land Tax —
Fil^d Feb^r 21 1787
. . .*

— & —

A. J.: *Read and referred to a committee, 21 Feb. '87, S. P. of Vt., III (III), 280; *report of committee recommending that petition be granted, read and accepted, and leave granted to bring in a bill accordingly, 23 Feb. '87, Ibid, III (III), 290; bill read and accepted and sent to Council, 23 Feb. '87, Ibid, III (III), 290; bill, having been concurred in by Council, passed into law, 27 Feb. '87, Ibid, III (III), 298.[1] C. J.: Act read and concurred in, 24 Feb. '87, G. and C., III, 126.

FOR A TAX ON LAND TO BUILD ROADS AND BRIDGES
xvii, 281

To the Honourable the General Assembly of the State of Vermont to be holden at Bennington on the Second Thursday in February next —
The Petition of the Inhabitants of Londonderry Humbly Sheweth — That they labour under great difficulty for want of Roads and bridges in Said Town Sufficient for the Accommodation of the Inhabitants or Publick —
And whereas the Inhabitants of Said Town are few in number they are therefore unable to build bridges make and keep in repair roads in Said Town as aforesaid and as your Honours Petitioners have never had any advantage of a Land Tax but have been Obliged to make and keep in repair at their own expence all the roads in Said Town ever Since the first Settlement thereof and as a Considerable part of the Land in Said Town is destitute of Inhabitants your Petitioners think it highly Reasonable and really necessary that Said Land Should help towards Making roads and building bridges as aforesid And Therefore Humbly Prays your Honours to take the premises under your wise and Serious Consideration and if your Honours

---

1. For this act, see Ms. Laws of Vt., II, 32–33.

in your wisdom Shall think it reasonable and Just that a Tax of two pence on the acre be granted on all the Land in Londonderry for the purposes abovementioned — Or if your Honours Should Judge it best to point out Some other method Whereby Justice may be done to the Inhabitants and that a Committee be appointed to have the whole Charge of the business and your Petitioners as in duty bound Shall ever Pray
Londonderry January 16th 1787

Abiel Eddey	John Hopkin	Archebald mcCormick
James Miller	Daniel Aiken	Joseph oterson
Joseph Mack	John Woodburn	John Cox
Hugh Montgomery	Patrick Taggred	Edward Cox
David Darby	Samul Taggred	William Cox
David Bryan	Samul Salsbery	Daniel Babot
James Mack	John Cole	Nathel Chese
Archibald Mack	Salmon Cole	Edward Aiken
David Cochran	[Samuel] Eyers	John Patterson
Jams Cary	[Antipos?] Howard	James Patterson
George McMurphy	James mcCormick	Samuel Thomson
Jas Hopkins		

— & —

Petition of Abiel Eddy & Alii[1]
Londonderry
Fild 27th [Feb. ?] 1787
. . .*

— & —

A. J.: *Read and referred to a committee, 27 Feb. '87, S. P. of Vt., III (III), 297; *report of committee recommending that commissioners be directed to sell 300 acres of unimproved land in the town belonging to the state[2] and lay out the money for roads and bridges, read and accepted, and leave given to bring in a bill accordingly, 3 March '87, Ibid, III (III), 311; bill read and accepted and sent to Council, 8 March '87, Ibid, III (III), 323; bill, having been concurred in by Council, passed into law, 9 March '87, Ibid, III (III), 326.[3]
C. J.: Act read and concurred in, 9 March '87, G. and C., III, 140.

FOR RELOCATION OF A COUNTY SEAT
xvii, 250

To the Honorable the General Assembly to Set at <Rutland> Bennington in Feby next the humble Petition of the Inhabitants of the Town of Benson humbly Shews

---

1. "Abiel Eddy & Others".
2. For the establishment and appointment of this commission or "committee of trust" for Londonderry, see S. P. of Vt., III (I), 121 and G. and C., II, 32. For a discussion of the peculiar situation with respect to the ownership of land in the town, see Addison E. Cudworth, The History . . . of Londonderry (Montpelier, 1936), pp. 30–33.
3. For this act, see Ms. Laws of Vt., II, 145.

that the County buildings in this County Stand too far Eastward[1] & that it is a Great Greivance for the people on the West & Norwest part of the County to Go Quite to East Side of the Inhabited part of the County to do County business We therefore pray Your honours to Order the Seat of the County to be affixed in Castleton & we as in duty bound will ever pray

Benson Jan[y] 18th 1787   By order of the Meeting   S. Goodridge
                                                                         Town Clerk

— & —

Petition of Benson [for removal of County Buildings]
. . .*

— & —

> A. J.: *Filed and referred along with three other similar petitions to next session, 5 March '87, S. P. of Vt., III (III), 314.[2]

FOR RELOCATION OF A COUNTY SEAT
xvii, 250

To the Honorable the General Assembly to Set at Bennington in Feb[y] next the Petition of the Inhabitants of the Town of Poultney humbly Sheweth that the County Buildings are in our opinion Set much too far East nearly under the Green Mountains[3] & that in our Opinion the Seat of the County Ought to be Set in Castleton we therefore pray your Honours to remove the Seat of the County to Castleton aforesaid & we as in duty bound will ever pray —

                                                        Samuel Kellogg town Clerk
Poultney Jan[y] 18[t] 1787

— & —

Poultney petition

— & —

[No Record][4]

FOR RELOCATION OF A COUNTY SEAT
xvii, 251

To the Hon[ble] the General Assembly of the State of Vermont to be conven'd at Bennington in an Adjourn'd Session on the 3[d] Thursday of February 1787 —

---

1. That is, at Rutland.
2. For other petitions to the same effect, see next two documents and pp. 292, 328, *post.*
3. That is, at Rutland.
4. Petitions to the same effect from Wells, Benson, Fair Haven and Orwell were referred 5 March '87 to the next session (S. P. of Vt., III (III), 314). For these petitions, see previous and next documents and pp. 292, 328, *post.*

The Prayer & Petition of us the Subscribers Inhabitants of Wells & Liege Subjects of the S^d State meekly sheweth —

That those your Hon^rs Petitioner who were Inhabiters in the State at the time of Establishing the Shire of Rutland[1] & Erecting the County Buildings there were of opinion that it was [an] improper [Centre?] & an Injurious Infringment on principles of Equality — altho' we can discover more Propriety in the Establishment as the County then extended than in continuing them there as it is now curtaild — And we beg leave to observe with all due defference & submission, that as we become more & more acquainted with the Local situation of the County (especially as it now extends) and with the quality of the Soil & the Natural form & Properties leading to Emigrations into the different Towns in the County Our Ideas of Injustice & impropriety are inhanced to such a Degree as to induce us in humble sincerity to join with our fellow Citizens (who [are in] our view more imediatly injur^d) to pray your Hon^rs to take the matter of our Prayer under your wise Consideration and order a [removal?] of the Shire to Castleton & that the County Buildings be Erected there (in Case it can be done by Subscription) — And we beg leave further to observe to your Hon^rs that we are sensible there are numerous & weighty Arguments in favour of our Request too lengthy to be set forth in a written Prayer; and which may be as properly urged & applied before the Honble House; and which we expect will be done by our Advocates in behalf of the Subject

Wherefore, we conclude in the full Assurance of being heard; And we your Hon^rs Memorialists as in duty bound Shall ever pray — dated Wells January 18th 1787 —

Jehiel Beerdsley	Amos Mix	Timothy Moss
Joseph Lamb	Joel Clemons	John franses
Lemuel Lathrop	Seth Blossom	Epaphras Nott
david Blossom	Isaac Hail	Simon Franses
Caleb harriman	[Tho^er?] Lathrop	Shubell Sumner
Peter Blossom	Isaac Andrews	Joshua Culver
[Jonathan] Francis	Asa Orsborn	Saml Culver
David Cole	Benjamin Giddings	Abdiel Webster
Samuel How	Samuel Martin	David Andrews
Joshua How	Gill Mallory	James Paull
Asa How	Wil Lamb	Daniel Wyman
Daniel Mckentosh	Abner Cone	Isaac Andrews

— & —

Prayer & Petition of Wells for the remove of the County Buildings
Filed 5th March 1787

— & —

A. J.: Filed and referred along with three other similar petitions to next session, 5 March '87, S. P. of Vt., III (III), 314.[2]

---

1. For the establishment of Rutland as the shire town of the county, see "An Act describing the bounds of the County of Rutland and Establishing the Town of Rutland a County Town . . ." passed 9 March '84 (Ms. Laws of Vt., I, 444–445).

2. For other petitions to the same effect, see pp. 287, 288, ante and pp. 292, 328, post.

FOR A TAX ON LAND TO BUILD ROADS AND BRIDGES
xvii, 252

To the Honourable Assembly of the State of Varmont To be Convaned at Benington on the 15 day of february next — The Petition of the inhabitants of Ferrisburgh hose names ar a next: humbly Shewing that this honourable Assembly did in october 1785 grant A tax of one peny on the aker in Sd ferrisburgh for the use of Cuting Rods and Bilding Bridges in Sd townd:[1] Appointed A Committee to See the Same Lad out as Shold Conduc most to Publick good: and Sd Committee perseded in the most Carefulest maner and have Lad out the hul of Sd tax and ar Still indeted to people for work the Sum of [Blank] and the Rods ar Still insufficient for the public and inhabitants of Sd townd: and thar Remands tow Brigdis [two bridges] to be Bilt At Lest one hundred feet in Length to be planked also a number more Rods to be Cut — and as the Rods Already Cut hath gratly incresed the prise of the propriators Land — and as finishing the Rods and Bridges will Stil Add to the Same: and Conduse much to the publick good — and Also pay those debts Stil du — tharfore your Petitioners inhabitants and propriators of Sd towns wold humbly pray that this honourable Assembly wold take our Case under thar Seras Consideration and grant ous Releaef By Laying a tax of one peny on the Aker on all the Lands in Sd Ferrisburgh publick Rits Excetped — and Apint a Committee to See the Same Lad out under Such Restrictions as the honourable Assembly Shal See fet as we ar in duty Bound Shal Ever pray

Dated in ferrisburgh this 21ᵈ of Janary 1787

Timothy Rogers	ISaac Gage	Zuriel Tupper
Wilam haight	Alexʳ Fraser	Jhon Huf
Wᵐ Utley Junᵒʳ	Gideon Spencer	Gidon hawly
Jonᵗʰ Saxton	Israel West	danil mckintosh
[Thor Brush?]	Elnathan Smith	Rosˡ Hopkins
	anthony field	

— & —

Inhabitants of Ferrisburgh
Petition for an additional tax for repairᵍ roads & c
Entered on File Febʳ 16ᵗʰ 1787
. . .*

— & —

A. J.: *Report of committee, to which the petition was referred, recommending that it ought to be granted, read and accepted, and leave given to bring in a bill accordingly, 17 Feb. '87, S. P. of Vt., III (III), 269; bill read and accepted and sent to Council, 21 Feb. '87, Ibid, III (III), 280; bill, having been concurred in by Council, passed into law, 27 Feb. '87, Ibid, III (III), 297.[2] C. J.: Act read and an amendment proposed that "the time for paying the Tax be two years from this date",[3] 21 Feb. '87, G. and C., III, 124.[4]

---

1. For this act passed 27 Oct. '85, see Ms. Laws of Vt., I, 526–527. A tax of two pence per acre was authorized by this legislation, although only one penny may have been levied. For the petition originating the act, see p. 147, ante.
2. For this act, see Ms. Laws of Vt., II, 51–52.
3. The Assembly journal takes no notice of this amendment but it is included in the law as passed. See note 2, supra.
4. For another petition in the same connection, see p. 352, post.

FOR COMPENSATION FOR WAR SERVICES
INCLUDING DEPRECIATION MONEY[1]
xvii, 253

To the Honourable the General Assembly of the State of Vermont to be convened at Bennington on the fifteenth day of February next Humbly Sheweth Abel Rice Nathaniel Carpenter Asa Prat Francis Akley and John Martain All of Guilford Except Sd Martain[2] in the County of Windham in this State; and Giles Roberts of Said Guilford Administrator on the Estate of Jeduthan Roberts Late of Said Guilford deceased — That on the Seventeenth day of February in the year of our Lord 1777 your Petitionars and the said Jeduthan Roberts Inlisted themselves Solders (for the Defence of this and the United States) Into Maj[r] Benjamin Whetcombs Core of Rangers, in which Service they continued about four years.[3] That great part of said four years Said Core Served within this State. — That after Said Rangers had Served a part of Said Term; the Honourable Congress by a Resolution Directed each State to pay the Troops raised in each respective State for their Services in the year 1780 and after that Time. and also by the Same or Some other Resolution Directed each State to pay the Troops raised in each respective State all Such money as was or should become Due to them on account of Depreciation; by means of which said Resolutions your Petitionars have never been able to obtain any pay for the last fourteen months of Said Service or any Depreciation money from any of the States in the Union, because at the Time of their Inlistments they were Inhabitents of this State — That all the Solders in Said Core of Rangers (Save only your Petitionars and the said Jeduthan Roberts) at the time of their Inlistments were Inhabitents of the State of New-Hampshire and from that State received pay for the last fourteen months of Said Service and the money due to them for Depreciation agreable to Said Resolutions of Congress — your Petitionars beg leave to mention to this Honourable Assembly that the Service of Said Core of Rangers in and near this State Contributed Considrable toward the Protection of the Inhabitents thereof — That the Service of Rangers in the wilds of this State, at the time your Petitionars Served was both Arduous and Dangerous — That your Petitionars and the Said Jeduthan with Patience and fortitude Endured Cold and [hunger] and Surmounted many Difficulties and Dangers which are easier to Conceive of then express, untill about four years of the prime of their Lives was wore away in Said Service having no other motive therfor, only to Contribute all in their power toward Establishing the freedom happiness and Independence of this and the United States — your Petitionars therefore cannot easily be made to beleive that this Honourable Assembly So much Destinguished for their Liberality and Justice after being made truly Sensible of your Petitionars Case will Suffer Such Disennination [discrimination] between them and their fellow Solders who Served in the Same Core and are not more Desarving than your Petitionars — as will necessarily take place if this Honourable Assembly Should not grant to your Petitionars pay for the last fourteen months of Said Service and also Depreciation money agreeable to the Resolutions of Congress your

---

1. For other petitions covering the same service from all or some of these petitioners or from their agent, see pp. 185, 224, 272, *ante*, including explanatory notes.

2. John Martain [Martin] did not sign the petition and was not included in the action taken upon it. For a separate petition from him in this connection, see p. 394, *post*.

3. For record of this service, see *Vt. Rev. Rolls*, 663–664.

Petitionars have ever Esteemed themselves happier on account of their being Citizens of this Free and Independent State then they could possably have been had they been Citizens of any other of the United States and Still hope that, That which they have Esteemed one of the Greatest faviours of Providence will not be the means of Depriving them of the Same Justice their fellow Solders have received who were Citizens in a Neighbouring State —

Your Petitionars Therefore Humbly and most ardently pray this Honourable Assembly to take this their Petition under their Consideration and grant to your Petitioners Such releif in the Premoses as to this Honourable Assembly shall appear Just and reasonable and your Petitionars as in Duty bound Shall ever pray

Dated at Guilford
this 22nd day of
January. 1787.

Aabel [sic] Rice
Asa Pratt
Giles Robarts
Francis Akley
Nathaniel Carpenter

— & —

Petition of Abel Rice & Others
Fild Febr 26. 1787
. . .*

— & —

A. J.: *Read and referred to a committee, 26 Feb. '87, S. P. of Vt., III (III), 295; *report of committee recommending that Committee of Pay-Table adjust petitioners' depreciation, read and accepted, and leave given to bring in a bill accordingly, 2 March '87, Ibid, III (III), 307; resolved that Committee of Pay-Table adjust depreciation for five signers of petition and draw on Treasurer for balance due, 2 March '87, Ibid, III (III), 310.

FOR RELOCATION OF A COUNTY SEAT
xvii, 254

To the honorable the General Assembly to set at Bennington by Adjournment in Feby next the first & humble Petition & Remonstrance of the Freemen & Inhabitants of the Town of Orwill [Orwell] humbly shews that County Conventions have been held for Consultation on the Affixing the place for the Seat of the County of Rutland at a time when this Town Could not be Represented therein in which Conventions this Town has been held up in the most Inconsiderable light & it was also held forth that Benson & Fairhaven Should not be considerd as a part of the County, by means of which Inssenuations the ‹double dealing› Conduct of the last Committe from the General Assembly & the undue influence the Inhabitants of Rutland had over the members of the General Assembly in the October Session 1784 the Seat of this County was Affixed at Rutland with [within?] about a Mile & a half of the Green Mountain & East of Seven Eights of the Inhabitants and at least twenty Six Miles East of the Extreme part of the Inhabitants on the West —1

---

1. The county seat was established at Rutland by an act passed 9 March '84 (Ms. Laws of Vt., I, 444–445), while the public buildings were relocated within the town by an act passed 29 Oct. '84 (Ibid, I, 473). In connection with this last act, see petition for relocation of the buildings and the action taken thereon in October session '84, p. 98, ante.

this we look upon as a Great Grievance and unequal dealing with the people of the West part of this County to oblige them to go to the Easterly Extreame of the County for County bussness because it accomodates a Number of people North & South of the said affixed place — we therefore pray your honours to Alter your determination on that head & order the Seat of the County to be affixed at Castleton, & we as in duty Bound will ever pray

Dated at Orwell January 22th 1787   Signed by order of the Meeting
                Cyrus Clark Constable
               David Leonard Town Clerk

— & —

Petition of Orwill
Filed 5th March 1787

— & —

A. J.: Filed and referred along with three other similar petitions to next session, 5 March '87, *S. P. of Vt.,* III (III), 314.[1]

FOR THE DIVISION OF A TOWN INTO TWO RELIGIOUS SOCIETIES
xvii, 255

To the Honorabl General Assembly of the State of Vermont, to be holden at Bennington, on the third thursday of February next — The Petition of the inhabitants of the East Part of Rutland humbly Sheweth. —

That whereas, your Honors Petitioners are Principly of Simelar Sentements in matters of Religion, and would wish to be under Such a Situation as to settle and Establish the Gosple Ministry in a Regular order. And whereas, the Centeral Part of the Town of Rutland for some Thousands of Acres, is barran, Unarrable Land, and Probably never will be Cultivated or improved, which would Render it very inconvenient for Public Buildings, And whereas the Town is so Situated as to Hill Rivers &C, that a Large number of its inhabitants both in the Easterly and Westerly Parts mus be put to Excessive Lengths of Travil to Convene in the Center, which must of Necessaty Debar numbers of families from meeting for Social worship with any Convenience.

And whereas the Town for years Past, and of Late, have had Several meetings to See if the Town would Unite to build a Meeting house in, or nigh the Center, and also to Sattle a Minister in a Regular manner, but never Could be so happy as to agree —

And whereas, your Honors Petitioners after Several attempts had been made for the Purposes above mentioned, and viewing it very unlikly that the Town would ever Unite, did unanamously agree and have been at very large Expence to Erect a Meeting house, for Divine Worship, in the Center of the Vicinity.[2] Therefor taking into Consideration the Local Situation of the Town, and other Circumstances. We would most Earnestly Pray your Honors to Take this our Petition under your wise and Deliberate Consideration, and Grant, and ordain, That the Town of Rutland be Divided, into two Societies, and that the Division line be as

---

1. For other petitions to the same effect, see pp. 287, 288, 289, *ante*, and p. 328, *post.*
2. That is, the center of the eastern part of the town.

follows (viz) beginning at the Center of the North line of Said Town from East, to west, thence Running Southerly Paralel with the East, and West, Lines of S^d Town, untill it Strikes Otter Creek, thence up the Creek as the Creek Runs to the South Line of Said Town, and that the Societies be made and known by the Names of the East, and West, Societies. —

And Your Honors Petitioners further Pray, that the East Part of Rutland from the line Disscribed may be incorporated into a Religious Societie, and that they may have the Same Power in Law as other incorporated Towns & Societies to Chuse a Clerk & other Necessary officers for S^d Societie to Call meetings to transact Business, To tax our Selves to build Meeting house or Meeting houses or to Settle a Minister or Ministers and to do any other business as the Law in Such Cases Made Provids.[1] and your Petitioners as in Duty Bound Shall Ever Pray

Rutland January 25th 1787

Ruben Harmon	Ebenezer Andrews	Nathan Fasset
Jehiel Andrews	Nathan Perry	Walter Colton
Roswell Post	Daniel Greene	Gershom Beech
Abel Spencer	Benjn Risley	Stephen Seward
John Brigham	John Bissell	Joseph Porter
Daniel Reed	Jeremiah Dewey	John Straten
Phinehas Kingsley	Simeon Lester	Amos Phelps
David Strong	Roger Higley	Ephraim Averell
William Barns	Ezekiel Cook	Simeon Wright
Elias Bowker	John Stevens	Libeus Johnson
William Post	Josiah Hale	John Sacket
Nathan Pratt	John Claghorn	Abner Lewis
John Andrews	John A: Graham	Ashbel Cook
Joseph Hawley	Elias Post	Jude Moultheroup
David Hawkins	Jno Ramsdel	Barzilla Dewey
Jesse Long	Obadiah Wheeler	Jeremiah Dewey
Solomon Smith	N B Graham	Clement Blakslee
Henry Strong	Erastus Nills	Thos Hale
Roam Brown	Oliver Harmon	Eleazer Wheelock
[. . .] [. . .]	James Claghorn	Moses Serjeant
[Issachus Reed?]	Daniel Perry	William Woolf
George Northway	Ezekiel Beebe	John Shaw
Miles Baldwine	Levi Long	James Stewart
Asa Hale	Benjamin Capron	Moses Hale
Fredk Cushman	Allen Beebe	Joshua Perry
Sam^el Williams	Ezekiel Beebe jun.	Joseph Kiler
Simeon Post	Gershom Beach j^ur	Micah Whitney
William Barr	Obediah Gill	Ezekiel Porter

To Either of the Constables of Rutland Greeting —

By Authority of the Freemen of ye State of Vermont, you are hereby Required, to Notify Benjn Whipple Esqr Col^o James Meed — & Mr John Johnson, one of y^e

---

1. See "An Act to enable Towns and Parishes, to erect proper Houses for public Worship, and support Ministers of the Gospel", passed October '83 (*Slade*, 472–473).

Select Men of the Town of Rutland to appear before ye Hon^le General Assembly at Bennington on the Thurd-Thursday of Feby next. if they see fit. Then & there to Shew Cause if any they have why the Prayor of the within Petition should not be granted —1 & you are hereby Commanded to leave a True and atested Copy of ye within Petition, & this Sitation at least — Twelve Day^s — before the Sitting of ye General Court Hereof fail not & due Return make According to Law — Dated at Rutland this 29th of Jen^y 1787

Elihu Smith Jus of peace

Rutland the 29th of Jany AD 1787
Then I Served the within Sitation by reading the Same in the hearing of the within Named Benjn Whipple Esqr and Co^l James Mead and Gave a true and an Attested Coppy of the within Sitation togather with the Petition to John Johnson one of the Slect Men

Attest   Daniel Squier Cons^t

Fees   9/0

Rutland Febry 16th 1787
These Certify that Maj^r John Stevens & Elihu Smith Esqr are apponted [sic] Agents to forward and Present the within Petition

Test   Roswell Post
William Barr   } Com^tee
James Claghorn

— & —

Petition of Reuben Harmon Jehiel Andrews & [others]
Fil^d Feb^r 21. 1787
. . .*

— & —

A. J.: *Read and referred to a committee, 21 Feb. '87, S. P. of Vt., III (III), 282; *report of committee recommending that petition be granted, read and ordered to lie on the table, 27 Feb. '87, Ibid, III (III), 296; *report of committee, referred from last session, read and accepted, and leave given to bring in a bill accordingly, 19 Oct. '87, Ibid, III (IV), 28; bill read and accepted and sent to Council, 20 Oct. '87, Ibid, III (IV), 37; bill, having been concurred in by Council, passed into law, 22 Oct. '87, Ibid, III (IV), 39.2 C. J.: Act read and concurred in, 22 Oct. '87, G. and C., III, 153.

FOR A LOTTERY TO BUILD ROADS
xvii, 256

To the Honorable the General Assembly of the State of Vermont. to be holden by adjournment at Bennington on the 3^d Tusday of Feby next. the Petition of the Inhabitence of Dorset Danby Timouth [Tinmouth] &C Humbly Sheweth that the

---

1. For a remonstrance against this petition by the inhabitants of the western part of Rutland, see p. 322, post.
2. For this act, see Ms. Laws of Vt., II, 195–196.

great Road through the West part of Dorset over Danby Mountain Leeding to Otter Crick [Creek] and the new Setelments above in the County of Addeson [Addison] is much the nearest road as was formerly and now is traveled through the East part of Tinmouth.[;] but the Road latly opened through the West part of Tinmouth and Danby is at lest five miles nearer then the Road through the East parts of Dorset & Cleradon [Clarendon], but the mountain Called Danby & Dorset Mountain, not afording but a Small number of Sallelable Lots, and the Inhabitance are poor and on able to Repaire the Road it being about five miles in length and needes a considerable labour and Expence to be done Immediatly more then the Inhabetence are able to perform & if the [there?] is owne [one?] done and well done the Sittuation of the Mountain is Such that with averey littel repair it will be a good road Time Emmemorable and further your Petitioners humbly Shew that the New Road through the West part of Tinmouth needes a considerable repaire & the Inhabatance are onable to do the Labour necessery with out destroying there familys and the [Utillete] of the Road is Such that your Petitioners View it amatter worthy of ye Attention of your honour, your Petitioners therefour humbly pray that your honours would be pleased to Grant them apreveledge of a Small Lottery the Prizes to be Sold for grain, to be desposed of for Labour according to the direction of Such Gentelmen as your Honours in your Wisdom Shall appoint and your Petitioners as in Duty bound Shall ever pray
Jany 27th 1787

Thomas Herinton	Rufus Greene	Richard Latten
Samson Herrington	John Clark	Titus Calven
Jonathan Herington	Ebenezer mery	Beniman Browen
Thomas Hernton Juner	Nathan Clarke	Gideon Vermon
Mora Hernton	Caleb Greene	Henerey Lues
Elisha Herngton	Darius Lobdell	Henery Herick Jur
Abraham Herngton	Darius Lobdell Jun	Ozial Herinton
Wm Brumley Juner	Jared Lobdell	Levi Thornton
Jonathan King	Dennis Canfield	Lot Herinton
Abner Blackman	Nathan Weller	

Tinmouth

Jona Sheperd	Elisha Utly	Charles Brewster
Jonathan Shepard Jur	Uri Hill	Nero Cramton
Elisha Shepard	Zephaniah White	Stephen Rice
Ralph Shepard	Eliphas Brewster	Jareb Palmer
James Livingston	Benjn Marvin	Levi Rice
Stephen Jackson	Ozias Perry	John Wheeler
Joel Baldwin	Aaron Mathews	Henry Herrick

— & —

Petition of the Inhabitants of the Towns of Danby Dorset & Tinmouth
Fild 27th Febr 1787

— & —

[No Record]

FOR ABATEMENT OF TAXES
xvii, 294

To the Honorable the Representatives of the Freemen of the State of Vermont in Gen¹ Assembly Met

The Petition of Abiathar Angel of Pownal in the County of Bennington and State afore said Humbly Sheweth —

That by the General List of the Rateable Estates Last Made up and Return'd by the Listors of the Town of Pownal to the Honorable Gen¹ Assembly at their Annual Session in Oct ͬ last Past, Your Petitioner was through Mistake or Inadvertincy Made up and Return'd £ 578 — instead of £ 116–⁸10 — which was Your Petitioners Just Rateable Estate, — And that a Majority of the Select Men of this Town being absent from the Time Your Petitioner had Knowledge of the said Error or Mistake until the List was Transmitted to the Hon ᵇˡᵉ Assembly, whereby Your Petitioner was left without Alternative of Redress, Short of Application to the Hon ᵇˡᵉ Gen¹ Assembly of the State — And however loth Your Petitioner is to Trouble the House in so Individual a Matter, Yet he Humbly Prays the Honorable Assembly to take his said Petition and Request into Consideration and Grant and order that he May Not be Subjected to Pay any higher Tax than for his Just Rateable Estate as Certified on the Back of this and as in Duty Bound shall Ever Pray —

Abiathar Angel

We the Subscribers do hereby Certify, that there was a Mistake Made in Making up the within Petitioners List

Joseph Wheeler ⎫ Listors for the
Amasa Hungerford ⎬ Town of Pownal
Benj ͫ Morgan ⎭ .

We the Subscribers do hereby Certify that there was a Mistake Made in Making up the within Petitioners List

Amos Potter ⎫ Select
Tho ˢ Jewett ⎬ Men for
⎭ Pownal

— & —

Petition of Abiathar Angel
Fil ᵈ 20 ᵗʰ Feb ͬ 1787
. . .*
578
116–10
———
469 10

— & —

A. J.: *Read and granted, 21 Feb. '87, S. P. of Vt., III (III), 279;[1] resolved that Treasurer credit Pownal all taxes on £469–10 on the list of 1786 and that collector of town taxes credit petitioner likewise, 21 Feb. '87, Ibid, III (III), 279.

1. This entry is given the date of 20 Oct. '87 on the manuscript petition. However, there is no entry to this effect in the Assembly journal under that date.

FOR COMPENSATION FOR WAR SERVICES
INCLUDING DEPRECIATION MONEY
xvii, 301

To the Honble General Assembly of the State of Vermont at their Sessions in Bennington Febr. 1787

The Petition of Doctr Jacob Ruback Humbly Sheweth: That in the beginning of the last War Viz in the Years of 1775 and 76 — your Petitioner living on the frontiers of this State was Continually called upon by officers and Soldiers of the Northern Army when took Sick on their March, or Sent Sick out of Camp for Recovery of Health part of them were troops raised within and belonging to this State. your Petitioner expended a Considerable part of his Intrest in taking care of Said Troops: and When at the Evacuation or Retreat of Ticonderoga Said Army with the Inhabitants were Dispersed,[1] Your Petitioner lost not only all his Effects by being Plundered; but allso the opportunity of Collecting his Accounts by which he was reduced to the utmost Necessity Your Petitioner was afterwards appointed Surgeon of Col. Harricks Regt and the Several Detachments of Troops raised for the Defense of this State[2] for Which Services Your Petitioner has his Exellencys Commissions to produse but by the Rapid Depreciation of the Currency which your Petitioner received as pay for his Services was Still more reduced in his Intrest, and in Consequences thereoff is now reduced to the unavoideable Necessity to go to Jail or become Insolvent, unless the Honble Assembly will please Generously to interpose their Wisdom and Clemency for the relief of your Petitioner by ordering his Accounts against the State which yet remain unadjusted to be paid — And allso to adjust his pay whilst in Service Agreable to the Rule of Depreciation by which Col Warners Regt and Captn Lee's Company have been benefited.[3] Your Petitioner trusts in the Wisdom and Generosity of this Honble Assembly and the Equity as well as Justice of his Prayer and as in Duty Bound Shall ever pray

Jacob Ruback

— & —

the Honble Genll Assembly
Petition of Doctr Jacob Ruback
⟨Feby 15th 1787⟩
Filed Febry 22d 1787
. . .*

— & —

A. J.: *Read and referred to a committee to join a committee from the Council, 22 Feb. '87, S. P. of Vt., III (III), 282–283; *report of committee recommending that part of petitioner's account to the amount of £35–9–9 be paid but that no depreciation pay be allowed him, read and accepted, 1 March '87, Ibid, III (III), 303; resolved that Treasurer be directed to make payment accordingly, 1 March '87, Ibid, III (III), 303. C. J.: *Committee appointed to join Assembly committee, 27 Feb. '87, G. and C., III, 128–129.

---

1. This was the evacuation which took place after the advance of Burgoyne's army in July, 1777.

2. For Ruback's services as surgeon in an official capacity, see Vt. Rev. Rolls, 72, 123, 130, 133, 139, 771, 790, 793; also S. P. of Vt., III (I), 11; and G. and C., II, 498–499.

3. See "An Act for the purpose of making up the Depreciation of the Continental Money to Col. Seth Warner's Regiment and Captain Lee's Company", passed 19 June '81 (Ms. Laws of Vt., I, 237–238).

FOR RIGHT TO SELL REAL PROPERTY TO SETTLE AN ESTATE
xvii, 305

To the Honorable General Assembly of the State of Vermont now Sitting at Bennington —
The Petition of Samuel Mattocks & John Spafford of Tinmouth in the County of Rutland humbly Sheweth that the Said Samuel Mattocks and David Spafford late of Tinmouth Deceased had taken out administration on the estate of Daniel Edgerton formerly of S^d Tinmouth Deceased — that the personal estate of the said Daniel was found insufficient to pay the Debts due from said estate by the Sum of £ 998 L.M. — That the general assembly at their session in Octr AD 1785 empowered the said David in his life time to sell so much of the real estate of the S^d Daniel as would raise the sum of £ 998 — L.M. for the purpose of paying the debts of the said Daniel —[1] That the said David is since deceased having sold so much of the real estate of the S^d Daniel only as raised the sum of £ 180 — L.M. and the S^d John Spafford has taken out administration on the estate of the S^d Daniel deceased — Your Petitioners therefore Pray that the Said John Spafford may be impowered to sell so much of the real estate of the Said Daniel Edgerton Deceased as will raise the remaining Sum of £ 818-0-0 LM for the Purpose of pay [sic] the debts due from the estate of the S^d Daniel under the direction of the Judge of probate for the district of Rutland —
and Your petitioners as in Duty shall Ever pray —

Saml Mattocks
John Spafford

— & —

Petition of Saml Mattocks & John Spafford
Fil^d 27. Feb^r 1787

— & —

[No Record]

FOR ABATEMENT OF TAXES
xvii, 306

To the Honnorable the General Assembly of the State of Vermont now Siting in Bennington —
The Petetion of Thaddeus Munson first Constable for the Town of Manchester humbly Sheweth —
Whereas the Listers for the Town of Manchester affore Said in making out the List for the year 1786 made a mistake in casting the same to the amount of about nine Hundred Pounds by which means the Sum Total of S^d List was Returned to the General Assembly in October last to the amount of the affore Said Sum of £ 900 larger than the Real amounts of Said List by which meanes your Petitioner will be obliged to pay into the Treasury about Twenty Two Pounds more than the Law will enable him to Collect —

---

1. For this act, see *Ms. Laws of Vt.*, I, 508. For the petition of Samuel Mattocks and David Spafford in this connection, see p. 175, *ante.*

Your Petitioner therefore prays your Honors to take the matter under your wise Consideration and grant Releaf by ordering the Treasurer to Credit your S⁴ Petitioner Such Sums as the Law will Oblige him to Collect in Consequence of the affore Said mistake, — or grant Releaf in Such way as in your wisdom Shall appear equitable — and your Pititioner as in duty bound Shall ever pray —

Thadˢ Munson   Collector —

— & —

Thadˢ Munson
Petition to the General Assembly
Fil⁴ Feb^r 27. 1787
. . .*

To the Honor^ble the General Assembly now Siting the Report of your Com^tt to whom the Prayer of the within Potision was Refered beg Leve to Report that in their Oppinion the Prayer ought to be granted and that the Said Monson Ought to be Cred^t on the List of the year 1786 Nine Hundred and Sixty Pounds on all Taxes Granted & to be granted on Said List and that the Potisiner have Leve to Bring in a bill in form accordingly
March 3⁴ 1787   M Lyon for Com^tte

— & —

A. J.: *Read and referred to a committee, 2 March '87 S. P. of Vt., III (III),
307; resolved that Treasurer be directed to credit town with all taxes laid on
£960 on the list of 1786, 3 March '87, Ibid, III (III), 311.

FOR A TAX ON LAND TO BUILD ROADS AND BRIDGES
xvii, 307

To the Hon^le Gen^el Assembly Now Seting
    The Petition of Gamaliel Painter in behalf of the Proprietors of the towns of Middlebury and Salisbury Humbley Sheweth
    That it is the desire of the Inhabitants of the towns above Mentioned (which will appear by the Votes of Each town) to have your Honours Lay a Land tax of two pence on the Acre for the Purpose of Paying the Expence of Bulding Bridges Across Middlebury River and other Small Streems as well the expence of Surveying Clearing and Casswaying¹ Roads in S⁴ Towns — Said tax to be Managed in Such away and by Such Persons as you in your Wisdom may Direct and your Petitioner as in duty bound shall ever Pray —

Gam¹ Painter for Proprietors

— & —

Petition of the Towns of Middlebury & Salisbury for a Land Tax
Fil⁴ Feb^r 27th 1787
. . .*

— & —

---

1. That is, causewaying or filling in portions of the road with timbers or stones.

A. J.: *Read and granted, and leave given to bring in a bill accordingly, 1 March '87, *S. P. of Vt.*, III (III) 302; bill read and accepted and sent to Council, 1 March '87, *Ibid*, III (III), 304; bill withdrawn at request of petitioner, and leave given to bring in a bill taxing land two pence per acre in Middlebury only, 2 March '87, *Ibid*, III (III), 308; new bill read and accepted and sent to Council, 2 March '87, *Ibid*, III (III), 308; bill, having been concurred in by Council, passed into law, 3 March '87, *Ibid*, III (III), 310.[1] *C. J.:* Act laying two pence tax on Middlebury and Salisbury read, and amendment proposed that Salisbury be omitted because the quantity of land there was not known, 1 March '87, *G. and C.*, III, 131; act levying two pence tax on Middlebury read and concurred in, 2 March '87, *Ibid*, III, 132.

FOR ABATEMENT OF TAXES
xvii, 257

To the honourable Assembly of the State of Vermont to be holden at Bennington on the 3rd Thursday of Febuary 1787 the petition of the Subscriber in behalf of the Town of Townshand [Townshend] humbly Shewing that the grand List for S^d Town in the year 1786 was £ 2030 — 15 — 0 but through Som mistake the grand list with the Tresurer is £ 2117 — and the town Rated accordingly your petitioner therefore prays that the matter may be taken under your wise Consideration and Such Releaf made as you in your wisdom Shall think proper —
And your petitioner as in duty Bound Shall Ever pray
Dated at Townshand Febreary: 2nd 1787

2117   Joshua Wood
2030 — 15
———————

76 — 5 [2]

— & —

The petition of Joshua Wood
Fil^d Feb^r 20. 1787
. . .*

— & —

A. J.: *Read and referred to a committee, 20 Feb. '87, *S. P. of Vt.*, III (III), 277; *report of committee recommending that petition be granted, read and accepted, 21 Feb. '87, *Ibid*, III (III), 280–281; resolved that Treasurer be directed to credit town for taxes laid on £86–5^s in 1786, *Ibid*, III (III), 281.

FOR A TAX ON LAND TO BUILD ROADS
xvii, 258

To the Honourable General Assembly Setting at Bennington by adjournment in

---

1. For this act, see *Ms. Laws of Vt.*, II, 61–62.
2. The figure should read 86–5. This error on an error was corrected by the Assembly. See the subjoined note.

Feby Ins^t The Petition of the Inhabitants of the Town of Orwel [Orwell] — humbly sheweth That whereas the Said Inhabitants are but few in Number: and are very much scatterd In their settlements in S^d Town —, also in an Infant State — but by reason of the Inhabitants being Setled in Every different quarter of The Town: which renders it nessesary to Occupy as many Roads almost as ever will be Nessary: in Said Town — and also one Long Publick Road which leads through the Stat goes through the said Town — and your Petitioners being Unable to make mend and Support the Said roads without assistance — Therefore Pray The Genl Assembly will take thise our Circumstances into their wise Consideration and Grant us the favor of raising a Land Tax in Said Town of One peny half peny upon The Acre for the Sole purpose of making mending and Supporting the roads in S^d Town of Orwel — and your Petitioners In Duty bound Shall ever Pray — Orwel 2nd Feby 1787

Eben^r Willson ⎫
Amos Spafford ⎬ Select
Wm Smith ⎭ men

— & —

[Petition] of the Select-men of Orwell.
Entered on File Feb^r 16 1787
. . .*

— & —

A. J.: *Read and referred to a committee, 16 Feb. '87, S. P. of Vt., III (III), 266; *report of committee recommending that petition be granted, read and accepted, and leave given to bring in a bill accordingly, 19 Feb. '87, Ibid, III (III), 274; bill, having been returned by Council with tax amended to one penny, agreed to and passed into law, 27 Feb. '87, Ibid, III (III), 297–298.[1] C. J.: Act read and amendment of tax to one penny proposed, 21 Feb. '87, G. and C., III, 124.

FOR RELIEF AS DELINQUENTS ON A LAND TAX LEVIED TO BUILD A CHURCH
xvii, 259

To the Honble Genl Assembly to convene at Bennington on the 15th of Feby Instant

The Petition of John Williams, William Deane & others whose Names are hereto subscribed, Freeholders in the Town of Weathersfield —

Humbly sheweth —

That in the summer of 1785 the Genl Assembly granted a Tax upon the Lands in said Weathersfield, for the Purpose of building a Congregational Meeting-house in said Town, with a Proviso that no persons Lands Should be included in said Tax, who should, within the Term of three Months, enter in the Town Clerks Office a Certificate of his belonging to a Different Denomination of Christians[2] — Your Petitioners not getting proper Intelligence of the Tenor of S^d Act within the

---

1. For this act, see Ms. Laws of Vt., II, 52–53.
2. For this act, see Ms. Laws of Vt., I, 482–483.

said Term, tho' they complied with the Act seasonably, previous to the time of selling Delinquents Lands, for the Collector to be informed of it, & also gave him Notice — Yet he has proceeded to sell your Petitioners Lands, to defray the expence of a Building, from which we shall reap no benefit, being of Different Religious Principles — As we are ever willing to contribute our Proportion in any expence that can be for the Mutual benefit of the whole of the Proprietors & Land-Owners in said Town, we think it an unreasonable hardship to have our Lands sold, barely because we have not persued the Letter of the Law, when we conceive we fully complied with the Intent of the Act, which we suppose to be that the Collector should have sufficient Notice before the time of sale — wherefore we pray your Honours to direct that the Collector pay the Redemtion Money for our Lands, before the time of Redemtion expires, out of the avails of said Tax — And as in Duty bound shall ever pray —[1]

Weathersfield 3r^d Feby 1787 —

Timothy Hatch	Levi Hicks	Nathan Deane
Isaac Allen	Jonathan Parkhurst	Saml Holley
John Burllingame	Ezra Tuttle	John Ash
Stuard Boynton	Asa Marsh	Benj^a Bridge
Aaron Blakeslee	Samuel Marsh	Thomas Prentiss
Abel Nutting	Amos Snow	David Allen
Daniel Elmer	Samuel Dike	John Lawrance
John Hatch	Jacob Gitchel	Joseph Web
T Sterne	Perly Perkhurst	Joseph Dickey
L Hardey	Silas Rice	Thos Huchings
Joseph Norton	Daniel Graves	Wm Upham
Asa Sterne	Benj^a [Warner J^r?]	

— & —

Petition of John Williams William Dean & alii[2]
Filed Feb^r 20. 1787
. . .*

To the Honorable Gen^al Assembly Now Siting
your Commite to whome was Refer^d the Consideration of the within Petition being Moved and Stimolated by Contiantious Motives of Right and Rong and founded on the third artical in the Bill of Rights or Constitution of this State[3] wherein all Men have a Natural and unalienable right to worship Almighty God according to the Dictates of theire own Consciences as in theire opinion shall be regulated by the word of God or that No man Can or of right ought to be Compelled to Erect or Seport any place of worship: &C: beg Leave to report theire opinion that the facts Stated theirein being fully Seported and that the petisinors have Leave to Bring in a Bill in form

Calvin Parkhurst for [Commt?]

— & —

A. J.: *Read and referred to a committee, 20 Feb. '87, S. P. of Vt., III (III), 277–278; report of committee read and not accepted, and petition dismissed, 21 Feb. '87, Ibid, III (III), 281.

---

1. Possibly due to the destruction of a portion of the manuscript the names of John Williams and William Dean are not found among the signers.
2. "And others".
3. For this article of the Constitution of 1777, see G. and C., I, 93–94.

FOR THE APPOINTMENT OF A PARTICULAR JUSTICE OF THE PEACE
xvii, 260

To his Excellency the Governor and Council of the State of Vermont
The Petition of part of the Inhabitants of the Town of Newhaven here unto Subscribed Humbly Sheweth We the Subscribers liveing in the Easterly part of New-
haven Beg leave to lay before your Honours this our Humble Request beseeching
you to take this our Petition into Consideration and Appoint Elijah Foot Justice of
the Peace for the year insuing if it Appears consistant for the Wellfare and Peace
of the State there is acosiderable [a considerable] Number of Inhabitants in this
Easterly part of the Town that Labour under the Necessity of going Nine or ten
Miles to get the least matter of Business done Necessary to be done by A Justice
of the Peace.
The Inhabitants of the Town of Pocock¹ do Request to Join with us in our Petition
that they may have the Previledge to come to Newhaven to get Business done
Necessary to be done by A Justice of the Peace.
We do Humbly Request that his Excellency the Governor and Council take the
matter into Cosideration in order to our Situation and Grant us ajustice of the
Peace if you in your Wisdom Shall judge best
    And your Petitioners as in Duty Bound Beg leave to Subscribe them Selves
your Honours Humble Servants
Newhaven February 5th A.D. 1787

Martin Duning	John Everts	Ebenezer Write
William Eno	Asa Wheeler	Ebenezer Field
Reubin Grinnell	Truman Wheeler	Rubin Field
Ashbel Wheeler	Ezra Loomis	Josepeh Field
David Stebbens	Simeon Field	Michael Field
	Enos Peck	

These are the Names of the Inhabetants of Pocock
Samel Stewart
Eden Johnson
Aaron Ives
Bangamin Griswell

— & —

New Haven petition for a Justice of peace
Feby 16th 1787 Read & ordered to lie on the table —²

— & —

[No Record]³

---

1. Now Bristol. See *S. P. of Vt.*, II (Vermont Charters), 336.
2. Presumably this action was taken by the Governor and Council to whom the
petition was addressed.
3. On 20 Feb. '87 the Assembly set a time for a report by the members from
Addison County on "a nomination of a justice of the peace for said County in the town
of N-Haven" (*S. P. of Vt.*, III (III), 275). On 26 Feb. '87 these members nominated the
justices of the peace for the county, including Elijah Foot of New Haven, and they were
accordingly appointed (*Ibid*, III (III), 294). Under the Constitution as revised in 1786
justices of the peace were elected by the Assembly "in conjunction with the Council."
See *Statutes of the State of Vermont, passed by the Legislature in February and March 1787*
(Windsor, 1787), p. 10.

FOR ANNEXATION OF PART OF A TOWN TO ANOTHER[1]
xvii, 261

Ferrisborgue [Ferrisburg] February the 5th 1787
To the Honoreble the General Assembly of the State of Vermont Now Siting at Beningtown [Bennington] We your Humble Petitionars beg Leav to represent that as your Humblee Petitionars being Desireous to be adjoined to the town of Panton (or Ratherest be Incorporated in to a township with a Naim your Honers will giv) & the Naim of Panton and the Lands your Humble Petitionors Beg to be maid a town & have the Naim your Honors Se fit to Giv — the Reasons for why we would be Sot off from Ferrisborgue are as follows[2]

1 [st] that we Look upon our Selvs bettor Situated to be inhabitents with the inhabitents of Panton then Ferrisborgue acording to a report of a Committee to your Honnors at your Sesion in october Last[3]

2 [ly] the Grait Difficalty of Crosing otter [Otter] Creek at Porticolor Seasons of the year to attend Publick buisenes Espetially March meeting

3 [ly] that Ferrisborgue Contains a Number of acres Superor to the towns in General on the Lake after the Proposeed Division is made

4 [ly] as Panton is Mutilated by the Late Survoy of the Survoyer General and is too Small with out our being annext there to as your Honors will See by the Plans of Each town which will Coirfully be Prodused to your Honors

5 [ly] and becaus that we live at So Grait a Distecne from the Pleice whair Publick bisones is Dun most of your Petitionars Liv at Least Seven or Eight miles from the Pleice whair town meetings are holden in Feresborgue on the accompt their Can be no Settlements Near Otter Creek — and we your Humble Petitionars Pray that in your Grait Wisdom would take our Case into your wise Consideration and if Consistant with your worthy Honours wisdom would grant our Humble Petition as in Duty bound Shall Ever Pray

> Isaac Gage
> Benajah Welstor [Webster]
> Ezra Squire
> Nathonal Squire
> Richard Gage
> Joseph Gage
> Silas Bingham
> Samuel Boyce
> Daniel [Vandorlendar?]
> Zebolon Crittendon
> Richard Edgeton
> Joseph Chilson

— & —

Petition of Isaac Gage & Others
Fil[d] Feb[r] 27. 1787

---

1. For a related petition, see p. 214, *ante.*

2. The meaning of portions of this paragraph is confused. The substance of it seems to be that the petitioners sought to have a portion of Ferrisburg joined to Panton, thereby forming a town under that name or some other name, preferably the latter.

3. This report is entered in the Assembly journal under date of 9 March '87, although it was originally presented 24 Oct. '86. See *S. P. of Vt.*, III (III), 243, and *Ibid*, III (III), 326. See also note 1, p. 216, *ante.*

— & —

[No Record][1]

FOR A TAX ON LAND TO BUILD ROADS
xvii, 262

To the Honorable the general Assembly to be holden at Benington [Bennington] in February instant — your Petitioners beg leave to inform your Honours that the Town of Reading is Scituate nigh the center of the county of Windsor and we have found it nesesary for publick travel to lay out and maintain four roads throw the Town (Viz) two from Windsor to Saltash[2] and two from Cavendish to Woodstock. — also there is two considerable streams of water that head in the Town one is Mill Brook So called & the other is black river [Black River] branch. — We have already built on S^d Streams thirteen bridges & Six more are wanted beside a number of long Slows[3] and three other Streams head in the Town and want bridging & caucying.[4] and as the Settlements are new We finde our Selves unable to make and maintain S^d roads So as to be comfortable for Publick or private use. and as there is Sundry nonresident Gentlemen who own considerable tracts of land in the Town Whos intrest is increasing by the Setlers labor. and as we have never petitioned your Honours for a land tax before. With raised expectation we now pray your Honours to grant a tax of two pence on the acre on all Lands in the Town of Reading (except Publick rights) to be paid in labor at 4^s– 6^d pr day in wheet at five Shillings p^r bushell or in hard money. at or before the first day of october Next to be improved for the use of making and mending highways in all parts of the above S^d Town — as your petitioners in duty bound do pray

Reading February 5th 1787   John Weld   ⎫ Select

                                   Aaron Kimball ⎬ Men

                                     Solomon Keyes ⎭

At a Town meting legally wan^d and held in Reading on the 7th day of February 1787 the above petition being read and considered the meting unanimosly voted to Send S^d petition to the Honourable assembly by their representative

                                  Attest John Weld   Town Clerk

— & —

Reading petition for a Land tax
Entered on File Feb^r 16. 1787.
. . .*

— & —

---

    1. That this petition was not even read in the Assembly was probably due to the fact that the petition mentioned in note 1, p. 305, was still before that body, having been referred from the previous session.

    2. Now Plymouth. See *S. P. of Vt.*, II (Vermont Charters), 345.

    3. Slows as used here is apparently a variant of sloughs: muddy, miry pieces of road.

    4. Caucying should read causewaying, filling in a slough with timber or earth and stone.

A. J.: *Read and referred to a committee, 16 Feb. '87, *S. P. of Vt.*, III (III), 266; *report of committee recommending that petition be granted to the extent of a one penny half penny tax per acre, read and accepted, and leave given to bring in a bill accordingly, 19 Feb. '87, *Ibid*, III (III), 274; bill read and accepted and sent to Council, 9 March '87, *Ibid*, III (III), 326; bill, having been concurred in by Council, passed into law, 9 March '87, *Ibid*, III (III), 326.[1]
C. J.: Act read and concurred in, 9 March '87, *G. and C.*, III, 140.

FOR A TAX ON LAND TO BUILD ROADS
xvii, 263

To the Honourable General Assembly of the State of Vermont to be Conveaned at Bennington on the 15th of February Instant the Petition of a Number of the Inhabitance of Jamaica in Windham County Humbly Sheweth That your Petitioners Ever Since they have Resided in S^d Town have Suffered great Inconveniances on Account of the bad ness of the Roads in S^d Town and as your Petitioners are but few in Number and as Nature hath formed S^d Town So uneven in Some parts of it as to Render it Very Difficult and Costly makeing Roads Where as they are Absolutely Nesessary not onley for the benifit of the inhabitence of S^d Town but also for Travilers Whose Business Calls them throw Said Town and as Great part of S^d Town is owned by Nonresidents the Value of Whose land is Daly increasing by the industry of Your petitioners Therefore to the intent that the Nonresicents [sic] Lands may for the Futer do a Proportionable part To makeing and Repairing Highways & Roads in S^d Town Your petitioners Earnestly Request that a Tax of Two Pence on the acre may be Granted on all the wild Land in Said Town for the purpose of makeing and Repairing Highways, Roads and Bridges in S^d Town S^d Tax to be Collected and Laid out in Such way and manner as Your Honours Shall see Cause to Direct and your petitioners in Duty Bound Shall Ever Pray Jamaica February the 6th 1787

Proprieters of Jamaica
Belonging to Dumner
Arad Holten
Jabes Butler
Vesp^n Miller
Marsal Miller
John M. Butler
Isaac Miller J^r

Caleb Hayward
Calvin Hayward
John B Hinds
Paul Hayward
Nathan Hayward
Wm Hayward
Ezra Livermore
Reuben Wellmon
Joseph [Blanden?]
Joseph Rodes
Ezra King
John Earden
Silas Hayward
John Howe

— & —

Petition of Jamaica Proprietors

---

1. For this act, see *Ms. Laws of Vt.*, II, 145–146.

Fil^d 20th Feb^r 1787
...*

— & —

A. J.: *Read and referred to a committee, 20 Feb. '87, *S. P. of Vt.*, III (III), 278; *report of committee recommending that petition be granted to the extent of a one penny half penny tax on each acre of land, read and accepted, and leave given to bring in a bill accordingly, 21 Feb. '87, *Ibid*, III (III), 281;[1] bill read and sent to Council, 9 March '87, *Ibid*, III (III), 326; bill, having been concurred in by Council, passed into law, 9 March '87, *Ibid*, III (III), 327.[2] *C. J.:* Act read and returned with proposal that tax be only one penny, 9 March '87, *G. and C.*, III, 141.[3]

FOR REPEAL OF AN ACT REVERSING CERTAIN COURT JUDGMENTS[4]
xvii, 264

To the Honorable the General Assembly of the State of Vermont to convene at Bennington on the 15th day of Feby Instant.
Sheweth
     William Sargeant of Dummerston in Windham County. That he finds him Self greatly injured both in his Interest and feelings, by an Act Passed in the Sessions of Assembly at Norwich in June 1785, entitled "an Act Confirming Andrew Grayham of Putney in S^d County, in the quiet & Peaceble Possession of a Farm or Lot of Land on which the said Andrew then lived and rendering all Judgements Respecting the Possession of the same; heretofore had and Rendered by any Court of Law whatsoever null and void"[5] That your Petitioner is informed that the Said Act was hurried thro' the House at the Close of the Session without his agent being able to obtain a hearing agt. it before the House of Assembly; and therefore is not without hope, that the Honorable Assembly will now take up the matter more deliberately, and Rectify what appears to have been conducted amiss. —
That your Petitioner was Sometime before the Passing the Said Act possessed of Lot N° 8 in Putney and Andrew Graham & Caleb Graham made a Forcible Entry upon his Said Possession That your Petitioner to recover his S^d Possession and to Punish the said Andrew and Caleb for their Breach of the Peace proceeded before a Justice of the peace agt. them for forcible Entry and Detainer & recovered a Judgment agt. them by Verdict of a Jury of the vinicity [vicinity]. That the S^d Andrew and Caleb appealed to the County Court of Windham County and your

---

     1. The petition prayed for a tax on "wild land", that is, unimproved land. The report, however, recommended a tax on "each acre", that is, improved as well as unimproved.
     2. For this act, see *Ms. Laws of Vt.*, II, 146-147. The act provided for a tax of one penny per acre on all land.
     3. The Assembly journal, it will be observed, has no record of this proposed amendment. However, the final act followed the bill as amended by the Council. See note 2, *supra*.
     4. For a very similar petition to the same effect presented to the Assembly in Oct. '85 and dismissed as improperly filed, see p. 156, *ante*.
     5. For this act, see *Slade*, 500. For the petition of Andrew Graham, of which this legislation was the consequence, see p. 119, *ante*, including notes.

Petitioner after a full and fair [discussion] of the Cause again by the Verdict of a Jury recovered Judgement for the Possession of the said Lot & £9:2:1 for his costs by him your Petitioner expended about the S^d Suits. That your Petitioner was able and did Shew to the Committee of the Legislature that the said Andrew was not the most antient Possessor of the S^d Lot and that the said Caleb Graham did not predent [pretend] to have any colour of Right And that your Petitioner had at large expence purchased the possession and improvement of the S^d Lot of the Person who has had the peaceable Possession of S^d Lot longer then this State has had Existence — Yet the Counsel Imployed by the Grahams by their Ingenuity Craft and Intrigue induced the Com^e to report in their favour. And the Legislature to take the very extraordinary Step of Vacating the Judements so obtained by your petitioner as also annulling a Judement obtained agt. said Andrew Graham before the Existence of this State and contrary to the verdict of two Juries under oath Confirming Andrew Graham in the Possession of Said Lot and Declaring that said Act Should be conclusive Evidence of the Legal Possession of S^d Lot being in Said Andrew Graham —

Your Petitioner begs leave with all humility to Suggest that Said Act is unconstitutional and Subversive of the Rights of the citizens of this commonweath (and if for no other reason) ought to be Repeald

1st Because your Petitioner is without any compensation made therefor Deprived of his Property the Protection of which with that of the other members of the community is one of the Principal reasons for giving up certain Natural rights and entering into civil Society — and which is expressly and Solemnly Guaranted [Guaranteed] in the 9th Article of the Bill of Rights —[1]

2nd Because it assumes the Power Assigned by the Constitution to the Courts of Law; the Determination of a particular cause between party & party. And here your petitioner (if he may do it without offence) would observe in the words of the Selebrated Judge Blackstone that "in all tyrannical Govemments the right both of making & inforcing the Laws is Vested in one and the same man or one and the same body of men and whenever these two pours [powers] are United together there can be no public Liberty" And Mr Locke on Govemment Lays it down as the fundamental Law of all Commonwealths "that the Legislative cannot assume to itself a Power to rule by extemporary & arbitrary Deecres [decrees] but is bound to dispence Law and Justice and to decide the Rights of the Subjects by Promulgated Standing Laws and *Known* Authorised Judges — And that men Give up there natural independence to the society with this *Trust* that they shall be governed by *Known* Laws otherwise their Peace quiet and Property will be in the Same Uncertainty as in a State of nature —

Your Petitioner would Suggest other Reasons but calling to mind that the [Honorable] Council of Censors have Recommended a repeal of the S^d act and have asigned much better reasons than your Petitioner is capable of giving —[2] Your petitioner much Regrets that a Repeal of the S^d Act has hitherto been evaded, to the great injury of your Petitioner and as your Petitioner thinks

---

1. This is a reference to the 9th Article as listed in the Constitution of 1777. See *G. and C.*, I, 94.

2. For the recommendation of the Council of Censors 17 Oct. '85 that the act be repealed and for the Assembly's action thereon, see *Slade*, 515–516; and *S. P. of Vt.*, III (III), 202, 210, 229, 256. No record of its repeal has been found.

much to the hurt of the good Name of this Commonwealth Your Petitioner is however fully convinced of the good intentions of this Honorable Assembly, and that whatever has heretofore been done Respecting the S^d Act has been in consequence of the Unfair and miss Representations of certain Persons influenced by large fees and other Sinister Views —

Your Petitioner therefore both as a Person Greatly Injured by the Passing the Said Act & as a member of the community prays the Honorable Legislature to Repeal the said Act, and he as in duty bound shall ever Pray &c

Dummerston Feby 6th 1787   Wm Sargeant

To the Sheriff of Windham County his Deputy or to Either of the Constabls of Dummerston in S^d County Greeting
by the Authority of the State of Vermont you are commanded to Notify Andrew Graham that he appear before the Honorable General Assembly of this State on the 19th day of this instant Feby at Bennington if he thinks fit to shew cause if any he has why the Prayer of the above Petition Should not be granted fail not & make return pr Alex^r Kathan Justice peace
Dated at Dummerston Feby 6th 1787

Dummerston ye 7th of February 1787 there Notified the Within Named Andrew Graham of this Petition by Delivering to him a true & an attested Coppy of the same —   attest Barzillai Rice   Sheriffs Dp^t —
Fees £ 0:6:0

— & —

⟨Wm Sargeant Petition⟩
Filed 19th ⟨17th⟩ Febry 1787
. . .*

— & —

A. J.: *Read and referred to a committee to join a committee from the Council, 20 Feb. '87, *S. P. of Vt.*, III (III), 277; *referred by consent of the parties to next session, 1 March '87, *Ibid*, III (III), 307. *C. J.:* *Committee appointed to join Assembly committee, 20 Feb. '87, *G. and C.*, III, 123.

FOR THE MAINTENANCE OF A TOWN UNDIVIDED[1]
xvii, 265

To the honrable genral Assembly to be holden at Bennington on the third thirsday of Instant February A petition of us the Subscribers inhabetents of the town of Clarendon and County of Rutland and State of Vermont humbly Sheweth that your Petitioners have Been Sighted to Shew Cause if any they have why the prayer of the petition of Sum part of the inhabitents of Clarendon And Ira Should Not be granted praying to be Set of [off] or Annext To the District of Ira Complaining Likewise of an Extreem Bad Mountain that Lays them under A grait Disadvantate [sic] to Meet with the inhabetents of the East part of Clarendon to Do publick

---

1. This petition had precisely the same object as the one immediately following it in this volume. Many of the same names are found in both documents.

buisness[1] which Complaint we Look upon to be Verry frivolus and intirely ground-less as the mountain or hill so much Complaind of is verry passable with horses or Carriages of any kind as there is A Number of publick Roads up and Down S⁴ Hill which are Verry good to pass or Repass from the West to the East part of this town. their Complaints is Likewise as groundless in Regard to thear beeing All ways Abliged to meet in the Etreem part of S⁴ town as we have and are Still willing to Meet with them on What they Call the mountain one half the time to Do town busness but We Conclude the Chief Deficulty with them is in Regard to town Cost for Should thear Request be granted it would Leave but A Small number of in-habitents in the East part of S⁴ town to build and Repair Not Less then Eight Verry Costly Bridges Across otter [Otter] Creek and other Verry Rapped Streems and Numbers of Which are Liable to be Destroyed or Carryed of [off] by the floods yearly which unavoidably Must Bee Repairt <by> at the County or States Cost Besides A Large Town Rate to be paid yearly in order to maintain our town poor and Defray other Nesesary Charges Now your humble petitioners beg that you Gentlemen would Take the Afair into your wise Consideration And Establish us the inhabetents of S⁴ town under our present Scituation as we your Most hum-ble petitioners as in Duty Bound Shall Ever pray
Dated at Clarendon February the 6th Day 1787

Daniel Briggs	Elisha Boardman	Reuben Tuller
Moses hinman	Perce Spencer	Joseph Williams
Elihu Allen	Ezra Crary	Ezekiel Salsbury
Ebenezer Carly	David Palmer	Abraham Salsbury
Nathan Place	Nathan Crary	Benjamin Gould
Ezekiel Clark	John Smith	Benjamin Gould Jr
Jeames Wills	Coollidge White	Leonard Read
Samuel Place	Philip Briggs	Abner Williams
Ezekiel [Green]	Samuel Withrell	Levi Hicks
David Jewill	John Vary	James Round
Ichabod Walker	James Wylie	William Round
William Ray	Gideon Hewit	Nathan Round
George Congdon	Elias Steward	Gardener Salsbury
John Congdon	Jos Congdon	Jesse Spragg
Job Congdon	Oliver Westcot	Job Westcot
William Carpenter	Caleb Congdon	Benj. Whitman
Jos^e Plumb	Asa Smith	Jn° Whitman
Thomas Arms	William Clark	Thos [Hutchinson]
Nathan Rice	John Bowman	Joshua Goodrich
James Palmer	Jonathan Partridge	Eph^m Sawyer
Oliver Steward	Jabez Wever	John Squire
David Warner	Benj Bexter	Benjamin Bell
Willm Steward	Jemes Eady	

— & —

Remonstrance ag^t *Clarendon* and Ira petition

— & —

---

1. For this petition and the consequent citation, see pp. 253, 254, *ante*.

A. J.: Read along with the petition from Clarendon and Ira referred from last session, and referred therewith to a committee, 22 Feb. '87, *S. P. of Vt.*, III (III), 283; report of committee recommending that original petition not be granted, read and accepted, and that petition dismissed,[1] 24 Feb. '87, *Ibid*, III (III), 291.[2]

FOR MAINTENANCE OF A TOWN UNDIVIDED[3]
xxii, 130

To the Honourabl Legislature of the Sate [*sic*] of Vermont who are to convene at Bennington the third <wednesday> [this day] instant February A petition of the inhabitants of Clarendon county of Rutland and State of Vermont Humbly Sheweth

That your Petitioners are cited to give reasons whi the Town should not be divided. Your Petitioners think it unjust for the following reasons. First it takes a privilage from them which the Charter gives them without their consent.   Secondly. it Subjects them to the great disadvantage of having the poor of the Town and Eight large Bridges to maintain and many of which are exposed to be disstroyed by Fluds, which will leave so great a cost on so small a Settlement that they will not be able to maintain them so the publick must Suffer or they must repair the bridges. They say that Ira is so small that it is dificult doing their publick business. and that Clarendon is too large and would fain Smooth that over by saying that there is a large Mountain running through said Town we acknowledg there is a Hill that is Somthing Seap [steep] in many places and in others very good for our cuntry where we have several publick roads and the worst is not so bad but that a small Horse did draw fourteen Bushiels of grain ut [up] it on a heavy Sled at one Load They dont ask for a Small part of the Town to be anexed to Ira but it is the biggest half which will leave Clarendon in as bad Sircumstances as Ira is in now so we think it is not just nor politics to cut a good Town in pieces to patch up a bad one and doubt not but your honours will view it in the same point of light upon these considerations with special confidence in that honourable body the Legislature of Vermont we consceive and ardent hope that the prayer of your Petitioners will be granted and the Town not divided and your Petitioners as in duty bound shall ever pray

Dated at Clarendon this 6 of february AD 1787

William Crosman	Ezra Crary	Jeamis [Wylie]
Benjamin Hazzen	Joseph Conden	Elias Steward
Oliver Whitney	Joseph Congdon	oliver Westcot
Benjamin Foster	John Congdon	Caleb Congdon
Whitfield Foster	William Ray	Asa Smith

---

1. This action was equivalent to granting the above remonstrance, since its object was the dismissal of the original petition.

2. It is impossible to determine from the journal or from the additional material on the manuscripts whether this remonstrance or the petition immediately following it in this volume was the document read and referred to the committee.

3. See preceding petition and its footnotes.

Thomas Rice
Oliver Arnold
Amos Spring
Olney Rice
John Cowee
Silvanus Smith
Abraham Spragg
Sam^{ll} Smith
Silas Page
Lemuel Hawley
Benj^a Bell
John Cook
Thaddeus Curtis
Philo Curtis
Josiah Sawyer
John Cobb
Stephen Arnold
Samuel Place
David Warner
Ruben Tullar
Benjⁿ Parker
Benjamin Foster Junr
Reuben Blanchard
Jonathan Powers
Jams Jenks
Stephan Arnold
Ichabod Randol
Ned^h Angell
David Jewel

David Palmer
Jobe Congdon
Wil^m Steward
Gedion Hewit
Daniel Briggs
Ezekil Grean
Jeames Palmer
Oliver Steward
Joseph Plumb
Philip Briggs
John Hill
Samuel Wetherell
Elisha Boardman
Nathan Rice
Coollidg White
Thomas Arms
Moses Hinman
Elihu Allen
Ebenezer Carly
Nathan Place
Ezekel Clark
Jeamis Wells
Samuel Place
William Carpender
⟨David Warner⟩
Perce Spencer
Nathan Crary
John Smith
John Vary

William Clark
John Bowman
Jonathan Patridg
Jabez Weaver
Ben^m Bexter
Jeames Eaddy
⟨Ruben Tuller⟩
Joseph Williams
Ezekiel Salsbury
Abraham Salsbury
Benjⁿ Gould
Benjⁿ Gould juner
Lennard Read
Abner Williams
Levi Hicks
Jeames Round
William Round
Nathan Round
Gardner Salsbury
Jesse Spragg
Jobe Westcot
Benj. Whitman
Jonathan Whitman
Thomas [Hutchiston?]
Joshua Goodrich
Eph^m Sawyer
John Squire
Ichabod Walker
total 100

— & —

William Crossman Benjⁿ Hazen^s Petition
Fil^d Feb^r 22^d 1787
[. . .] for filing [. . .]
William Hazen[1]

— & —

[See subjoined note for preceding petition.]

FOR RELIEF OF A TAX COLLECTOR
xvii, 267

To the Honourable General Assembly of the State of Vermont to Sit at Bennington

---

1. This name is located on the reverse of the manuscript. It was doubtless intended as a signing of the petition. The total number of names at the end of the document (excluding two crossed out) is 99, while the total claimed is 100.

on the third thirsday of Instant Feb^y — A petition of Stephen Clark Constable for
the Township of Wallingford humbly Sheweth that your honours petitioner received a warrant from the Treasurer of this State to Collect three rates of the
Inhabitants of S^d Wallingford (Viz) one tax of Eight pence on the pound one of
Seven pence and one of Six pence on the list of the year AD 1781 which he was to
Collect and Settle with the treasurer, S^d taxes being Granted by the assembly of
this State at their Sessions and whereas the grand list for S^d town was not returned
to the assembly according to law S^d town was doomed 1200 pound¹ and the Grand
list of S^d town not being but 1090 pounds for S^d year 1781 your honours petitioner
has no way to Collect the overplus which is £3:13:9 for the Eight penny tax and
£3:[42?] for the Sevenpenny and £2:15:0 for the Six penny tax in the whole
£9:12:6 which your honours petitioner must loose unless your honours Can relieve
him — likewise your honours petitioner hat [had?] at one time Collected about ten
pounds of S^d tax and returning home had the misfortune to loose his Pocketbook
and S^d £10 pounds with it which he has never found Suposed to loose it in a river
that he had to Cross, your honours petitioner had never thoughts of Coming to the
honourable Assembly with the latter but he has had the misfortune to have his
house with much of his provision and all of his household furniture Consumed by
fire of late these are therefore to pray your honours to take the matter into your
wise Consideration grant him relief by ordering the treasurer to Credit your
honours petitioner the above S^d Sum or Sums or in Some other way grant relief as
you in your wisdom Shall See fit and your honours petitioner as in duty bound Shall
ever pray
Dated at Wallingford this   Stephen Clark
7th day of Feby AD 1787

— & —

Petition of Stephen Clark
Entered on File Feb^r 16th 1787
. . .*

— & —

> *A. J.*: *Read and referred to a committee, 17 Feb. '87, *S. P. of Vt.*, III (III),
> 271; *report of committee recommending that petition be granted, read and
> accepted, 2 March '87, *Ibid*, III (III), 307; resolved that Treasurer be directed
> to pay petitioner £19–12–6 accordingly, *Ibid*, III (III), 307.

FOR ABATEMENT OF TAXES
xvii, 268

To the Hon^r General Assembly of the State of Vermont to be holden at
Bennington by Adjornment on the third thursday of February Instant The Petition
of the Subscribers humbly Sheweth — That the List Returnd by the Listers in
Said town for the year 1786 Ammounted to £1100 and that the Precepts from
the tresurer Derected to the Constable Requires him to Colect Six Pence on the

---

1. That the town was doomed simply meant that its property valuation had been
fixed according to the discretion of the legislature rather than on the basis of its own
returns.

Pound: on £1180 which is £80 more than the List Returned: wherefor your Petitioners humbly Pray that your hon^rs would Order that the Constable may be Credited for the above said Six Pence on £80 or in Some other way grant Reliff and your Petitioners as in Dutty Bound Shall Ever Pray

Datted Londonderry   John Cox   ⎫ Selectmen
february 8: 1787   Edward Aiken ⎬

— & —

Petition from Londonderry
Entered on File Feb^r 19th 1787
. . .*

— & —

A. J.: *Read and referred to a committee, 19 Feb. '87, S. P. of Vt., III (III), 273; *report of committee recommending that prayer be granted, read and accepted, 20 Feb. '87, Ibid, III (III), 275; resolved that Treasurer credit Londonderry accordingly, 20 Feb. '87, Ibid, III (III), 275–276.

FOR RIGHT TO SELL REAL PROPERTY TO SETTLE AN ESTATE
xvii, 266, 270

To the Honourable General Assembly of the State of Vermont to be Holden at Benington [Bennington] on the Third Thirsday of February 1787 the Petition of Ame Hickok of Castleton Administratrix on the Estate of Justus Hickok Late of Said Castleton Deceased Humbly Sheweth that the Personal Estate of the Said Deceased is Insufficint by the Sum of Ninty Two Pounds Eighteen Shillings Lawfull Money to Pay the Debts Due from Said Estate — Therefore Prays your Honours to Impower Eli Cogswell Esqr one of the Administrators to Said Estate to Sell So much of the real Estate of the Said Justus Hickok as will Pay the afore Said Sum of £92:18:0 Lawfull money for the Purpose of Paying the Debts Due from Said Estate together with the Nesesary Cost arising on Said Sale as you in your Wisdom Shall Direct which is Humbly Submited as your Honours Petitinors in Duty Bound Shall Ever Pray —

Castleton February 9th A.D 1787   Ame Hickok

Certificate from the Court of Probate
To the Honble the General Assembly
of the State of Vermont —

This may certify that the Personal Estate of Justus Hickock late of Castleton deceased, is insufficient by the Sum of Ninety two pounds eighteen shillings L.M. to pay the debts due from said Estate, £ 92–18–0

Pr Elisha Clark Judge Prob.

Probate Office   ⎫ Tinmouth 7th Feb. 1787
Rutland District ⎭

— & —

Ame Hickok Petition
. . .*

— & —

A. J.: *Read and granted, 19 Feb. '87, *S. P. of Vt.*, III (III), 272–273; bill read and accepted and sent to Council, 19 Feb. '87, *Ibid*, III (III), 273; bill, having been concurred in by Council, passed into law, 27 Feb. '87, *Ibid*, III (III), 297.[1] *C. J.:* Act read and concurred in, 19 Feb. '87, *G. and C.*, III, 121.

FOR ABATEMENT OF TAXES
xvii, 271

To the Honnourable House of Representatives in General Assembly met —
The Petition of Miles Putnam and Samuel Spring
Gentleman Whereas the General Assembly of this State Granted Several Taxes on the Inhabitants of Thomblinson [Thomlinson][2] in the year 1781 Setting their Grand List at 200£ when there were no more then Eleven Polls in Said Town and Some of that Number were Possest of no Rateble Estate and all of them in Very Low Circumstances and also Some of the above Number Soon after absconded and Left the Town which makes it Exceeding Difficult for the Small Remainder to Pay the above Taxes —
We therefore your Petitioners Humbly Pray that your Honnours will take the Same under your wise Consideration and abate the above Taxes or Some Part of them as it must be Very Distressing for us to Pay the Same and as in Duty Bound we Shall Ever Pray
Thomblinson February 9th 1787

Miles Putnam	Selectmen and
Samll Spring	Listers for
	Said Town 1781

— & —

A Petition —
Select men of Tomilson
Entered on File 19th Febr 1787
. . .*

— & —

A. J.: *Read and dismissed, 19 Feb. '87, *S. P. of Vt.*, III (III), 273.

FOR THE INCORPORATION OF A RELIGIOUS SOCIETY[3]
xvii, 272

To the Honorable General Assembly of the State of Vermont to be held at Bennington by Adjournment on the Third Thursday of February next — The Petition of the Subscribers Inhabitants of the Town of Cornwall in the County of Addison humbly Sheweth —
That your Honors Petitioners on the 29th day of January 1787 did mutually Associate covenant and agree to and with each other to form ourselves into a Religious

---

1. For this act, see *Ms. Laws of Vt.*, II, 52.
2. Now Grafton. See *S. P. of Vt.*, II (Vermont Charters), 355.
3. Incorporation enabled a religious society to levy taxes. See p. 143, *ante*, note 3

Society by the Name of the first Congregational Society in Cornwall for the purpose of maintaining and Supporting the worship of Almighty God agreeable to the dictates of our own Consciences and in proportion to a List of our Several Polls and Rateable Estates —We therefore pray your Honors to take our case under your wise and prudent consideration and Incorporate us into a Religious Society as afore^{sd} and your Petitioners as in duty bound shall ever pray —
Cornwall February 9th 1787

Roger Avery	Hiland Hall	Frederic Ford
William Samson	John Rockwell	Nathan Foot Junr
Sam^{el} Benton	Daniel Foot	Jesse Chipman
Jer Bingham	Stephen Tambling	Daniel Samson
William Slade	Richard Minor	Aaron Scott
Joel Linsly	Enos Ives	Cary Mead
Abiel Linsly Junr	John Holly	Eliphalet Samson
Jared Abernethy	Thomas Hall	Sam^{el} Smith
Nathl Blanchard	Jabez Watrous	Jedidiah Durfey
David Parkhill	Jeremiah Ozgood	Sardius Blogget
Erastus Hatheway	Nathan Foot	Thos Bentley
Eldad Andrus	Jared Ives	Shadrach Norton
Ethan Andrus	Enos Ives Junr	Thaddeus Palmer
Roswell Post	Nath Coggswell	

— & —

A Petition of the Inhabitants of the Town of Cornwall
Entered on File Feb^r 16th 1787
. . .*

— & —

A. J.: *Read and granted, 17 Feb. '87, *S. P. of Vt.*, III (III), 268; leave given petitioners to bring in a bill accordingly, 17 Feb. '87, *Ibid*, III (III), 268.

FOR ADDITIONAL COMPENSATION FOR WAR SERVICES BECAUSE OF THE DEPRECIATION OF THE CURRENCY
xvii, 273

To the Hon. the Genl Assembly of the State of Vermont to be conveened at Benington [Bennington] on the 3rd thirsday of Instant February the Petition of Phillip Smith Junr Humbly Sheweth —

That your Petitioner Inlisted in the month of August AD 1777 into the Service of Said State under the Command of Capt Elisha Burton as did also your Petitioners Brother Stephen Smith[1] That your Petitioner & his said Brother Stephen ware both taken Prisoners at a Place called Ticonderoga Landing in the month of Septr Following — that your Potetioners Brother Stephen Smith died in a Short time after he was made a Prissionr of a wound he unfortunately Rec^d in the ever memoreable action at that place under the Command of that worthy and

---

1. For record of this service, see *Vt. Rev. Rolls*, 51.

Brave officer Colⁿ Brown — that your Petitioner Suffered many hardships in his Captivety that he continued Prissioner about 13 months & that your Petitioner has Never Rec^d but Forty four Pounds Continantal money for his Services & his Brothers Stephens thier Guns Blankets & accoutraments & as may be Seen by the Papers herewith Transmitted — the Prayer of this Petition is that your Honours would Examine into the facts as here Stated and grant Such Relief as your Hon^{rs} in your wisdom Shall think Just & Equitable And your Petitioner as in duty bound Shall ever pray

Dated Norwich this 10th day of February

AD 1787 —   Phillip Smith J^{ur}

— & —

Phillip Smith [Jur] Petition
Enter^d on File Feb^r 19. 1787
. . .*

— & —

A. J.: *Read and referred to a committee, 19 Feb. '87, S. P. of Vt., III (III), 271–272; *report of committee recommending that petitioner be paid £22-17, read and accepted, 3 March '87, Ibid, III (III), 312; resolved that Treasurer make payment accordingly, 3 March '87, Ibid, III (III), 312.

FOR A TAX ON A COUNTY
xvii, 274

To the Honble the General Assembly to be Holden at Bennington, by Adjournment, on the third Thursday of February Instant —
    The Petition of the County Court of Windsor County, humbly Sheweth —
That Whereas, the said County Court have Examined the Debts & Demands against said County — and find they amount to the Sum of Two Hundred and Twenty Nine Pounds fourteen Shillings —
These are therefore to Pray your Honours to Levy a Tax on the Inhabitants of said County to raise the said Sum of Two hundred & Twenty Nine Pounds fourteen Shillings, to discharge said demands In such a way as your Honors shall direct — And your Petitioners as in duty bound shall ever Pray

Signed — Briant Brown, Clerk
In behalf — & by Order of — said

Windsor Feb^y ⎱   County Court —
12th 1787 — ⎰

— & —

The Petition of Windsor County Court —
Filed 6th March 1787

— & —

A. J.: Read and ordered to lie on the table, 6 March '87, S. P. of Vt., III (III), 318.[1]

---

1. "An Act for granting a tax of one penny on the pound on the list of the County of Windsor for satisfying the debts due from said County" was passed 25 Oct. '88 (S. P. of Vt., III (IV), 109, 112). For this act, see Ms. Laws of Vt., II, 285–286.

FOR INCORPORATION OF A RELIGIOUS SOCIETY[1]
xvii, 275

Poultney Feb[ry] 12th 1787

To the Honarable General Assembly of the State of Vermont Setting at Bennington on the third Thursday of Feb[y] Instant

Whereas a number of the Inhabitants of the Town of Poultney being of Semilar sentiments did Some time in the year one Thousand Seven Hundred & Eighty three form into a Society for the sake of Religious Previliges that they might worship Allmighty God According to the Dictates of their own Consciencies and have from that time to the date hereof kept up Religious Worship Accordingly and are Desirous of being Established so as to Enjoy the Priviliges of the laws of this State

Therefore we your Deutiful Subjects to the Number of Fifty Lawful Voters being of Semilar sentiments humbly Petition that we might be Established According to the Laws of this State so as to be known in Law by the Name of Congregational Society of the Standing order As we your Humble Petitioners are in deuty ever bound to pray

Attest Sam[el] Lee Societies Clark
Attest Sam[l] Kellogg Town Clerk

— & —

Petition of Inhab[t] of Poultney
Fil[d] Feb[r] 23. 1787

— & —

[No Record]

FOR A TAX ON LAND TO BUILD ROADS
xvii, 276

To the Honourable General Assembly of the State of Vermont to be conveined at Benington [Bennington] on the third thirsday of Instant Feb[y] Comes the Inhabitance of the Township of Wallingford and a Certain Gore of Land that Lyeth East and adjoining Said Wallingford and humbly Sheweth to your Honourable Body as gardians of the Rights of the Citisons of this State. That whereas theire is a Large part of this Town and the afores[d] Joining Gore of Land yet uninhabited and un-Settled by reason of the afores[d] lands Lying on the East Side of the Greanmountains and remote from aney Publick Roads of travil or aney Inhabitance[,] whereby they cand git Support untill they can Ocupy the land and raise the Same without Transporting all theire Goods and Provisions and Hey about fourteen or fifteen Moilds[,] which renders the Settlement theire of verey Difficul and Disadvantagous both to the Settlemen and Populateing this Town and State and where as theire is a verey conveinant Place to make a road a crost the Greanmountain in this Town From Ottercrick [Otter Creek] to the afore S[d] Lands which would Save half the distance of travil and Transportation of the Support for the Inhabitance of that Place and Save as much travil for all travilors whoo would goe from aney Town fron [sic] this side of Grean-Mountain which is to the south of this town to the

---

1. Incorporation enabled a religious society to levy taxes. See p. 143, *ante*, note 3.

North Part of this State that Lyeth on the East Side of the S^d Grean-Mountain[;] Which Greaveanceis to remoove That theire May be a tax layed of one Penney on each acre of Land that is in S^d Gore and on three Quarters of this Town and on the East and uninhabited Part theire of and Some meet Person or Persons who now Live on the afore S^d Gore may be appointed to Collect the Same and Dispose of it for the Makeing roads and Bridges for the fore mentioned purpose For which your humble Pertisioner as are in duty bound we humbly Prey

Signed at Wallingford this 12th day of Feby AD 1787 —

Abraham Jackson Juⁿ	Abraham Jackson	William Burlingim
David Speary	Benoni Kinne	William Dick
Joseph Benson	Joseph Randall	Thos Henderson
Noah Torrey J^r	Jethro Jackson	Phileetus Swift
Noah Torey	John Randall	Salathial Bumpus
Asahel Jackson	Perey. G. Dawley	Nathanel Ives
Ebenezer Lyon	Rowland Benson	Lnt [Lent?] Ives
Andrew Daveson	Elijah Benson	Ezekiel Mighell
Joseph Jackson	Jonah Ives	Ebenezer Lamb
David Hall	Ichabod G. Clark	Chaney Clark
Solomon Miller Junr	Hezekiah Rodes	Samual Swift
Calvin Miller		

— & —

A [Protision] of the Inhabitants of Wallingford and Jacksons Gore
Filed Feb^r 19 1787
. . .*

— & —

A. J.: *Read and referred to a committee, 19 Feb. '87, S. P. of Vt., III (III), 274; *report of committee recommending that prayer be granted, read and accepted, and leave given to bring in a bill accordingly, 20 Feb. '87, Ibid, III (III), 278; bill for laying a tax of one penny on each acre in Jackson's Gore and part of Wallingford, read and sent to Council, 21 Feb. '87, Ibid, III (III), 279; bill, having been concurred in by Council, passed into law, 23 Feb. '87, Ibid, III (III), 287.[1] C. J.: Act read and concurred in, 21 Feb. '87, G. and C., III, 123.

FOR ABATEMENT OF TAXES
xvii, 277

To the Honnourable House of Representatives In General Assembly met —
The Petition of Stephen Hayward and Others We your Petitioners Do find upon a Strict Examination that there is a Considerable Mistake which we have made in our Grand List of 73£ for the year 1786 —
We therefore Pray that your Honnours will take the Same under your wise Consideration and make an abatement on our Grand List of 73£ or Give Credit for So much or Grant your Petitioners Relief in any other way as you in your Wisdom

---

1. For this act, see Ms. Laws of Vt., II, 23. The part of the town to which the tax applied was the three quarters lying on the east side of the mountains.

Shall think Proper and as in Duty Bound we Shall Ever Pray
Tomlinson [Thomlinson]¹ February 12th 1787

Stephen Hayward	Select men
Charles Perkins	and Listers
Moses Gray	for Said Town

— & —

A Petition from the Town of Tomilson
Entered on File Feb^r 16th 1787
...*

— & —

A. J.: *Read and referred to a committee to join a committee from the Council,
17 Feb. '87, *S. P. of Vt.*, III (III), 268; *report of committee recommending
that prayer be granted, read and accepted, 21 Feb. '87, *Ibid*, III (III), 280;
resolved that Treasurer credit town with taxes laid on £73 of the list of 1786,
21 Feb. '87, *Ibid*, III (III), 280. *C. J.:* *Committee appointed to join Assembly
committee, 17 Feb. '87, *G. and C.*, III, 119.²

FOR RELIEF OF A TAX COLLECTOR
xvii, 165

To the Honorable General Assembly of the State of Vermont Who are to Convene
at <Rutland> Bennington on the 3^d Thursday of february Next The Petition of
John Barns Constable of Pittsford Humbly Sheweth —
That Sometime in the month of may Last past I was so Unfortunate as to have
my House and principal Effects Consum^d By fire. Your Humble Petitioner would
inform Your Honors that I also had four pounds ten shilling Hard money Orders
burnt; which I had Collected for the Publick — Your petitioner therefore prays he
might be made good the same by an allowance and Grant of your Honors and Your
petitioner as in Duty Bound Shall Ever pray

John Barns

Pittsford Feb 13th 1786 [1787]³

Pittsford Feby 16th 1787
This may certify that Mr Jno Barns Constable of this Town had his house
Consum^d By fire some time in May Last

Attest	Noah Hopkins	Selectmen
	Benj^a Cooley	

— & —

Petition of Jno Barns
Fil^d Feb 17th 1787

---

1. Now Grafton. See *S. P. of Vt.*, II (Vermont Charters), 355.
2. This entry on the manuscript lists Mr. Fletcher in addition to Mr. Walbridge
as appointed to the committee.
3. All the other evidence leaves no doubt that this petition was drawn up in 1787.
See certificate and subjoined note. There was no session of the legislature in February,
1786.

. . .*

— & —

A. J.: Read and referred to a committee to join a committee from the Council, 19 Feb. '87, *S. P. of Vt.*, III (III), 272; committee discharged, 7 March '87, *Ibid*, III (III), 319; *petition referred to next session, 7 March '87, *Ibid*, III (III), 319; read and granted, and Treasurer ordered to pay petitioner accordingly, 16 Oct. '87, *Ibid*, III (IV), 19. *C. J.:* Committee appointed to join Assembly committee, 20 Feb. '87, *G. and C.*, III, 122.

FOR THE MAINTENANCE OF ONLY ONE RELIGIOUS SOCIETY IN A TOWN[1]
xvii, 278

To the Honorable General Assembly of the State of Vermount [Vermont] to be holden at Benington [Bennington] on the third Thursday of Feb^ry Ins^t On a Citation of the east Part of Rutland for the west part of said Rutland, to shew cause if any they have before your Honours, why said Town should Not be divided into two societies For Religious worship[;] with Regard to sentiments the standing church In Rutland is composed of Members on each side of the Town and no Objection is made in that Respect, we Look upon the preaching of the gospel the greatest Blessing Heaven Bestows, if the Devision of the Town taks place we must unvoidably be deprived of it, within a short Distance of Center of the Town where we formerly mett for Publick worship is a Convenient place for a meeting house — to Accomodate the Majority of the Town — No place is so Convenient as the place above mention^d — the petitioners Complaint of the Town Not Agreeing to build a Meetinghouse Nigh the Center is on their own part — for this has been a Voite past at a Leagal Town Meeting Formerly to build a Meetinghouse Near the Center and Likewise about Two hundred Pounds subscribed on the west side of the Town for the same Purpose — we humbly Conceive your Honours will view the Inconsistantsy of the Petition that it is not founded on a good will to the whole our Prayer is that the Petition be not granted and we as In Duty bound shall Ever pray

Rutland Feb^ry 13th AD 1787

John Johnson ⎫
Tim° Boardman ⎬ Committee
Andrew Crocker ⎭

— & —

Remonstrance of John Johnson & Alii[2]
Fil^d Feb^r 27th 1787

— & —

[No Record][3]

1. For the petition against which this remonstrance was directed, see p. 293, *ante.*
2. "And others."
3. This remonstrance was in substance dismissed, since the petition against which it was directed was granted. See note 1, *supra.*

FOR THE LOCATION OF A COUNTY GRAMMAR SCHOOL
xvii, 279

To the Honoureble General Assembly of the State of Vermont to be Conveind at
Benington [Bennington] on the 15th day of February instant the pettition of the
Town of putney [Putney] in the county of Windham Humbly Sheweth —
that whereas the constitution of this State Hath made provision that there Shall be
one Grammar School kept in Each County in this State[1] and whereas a Number of
Gentlemen in Said Town Have appeared to Build an house in said putney for that
purpose Free from any Expence to said County as By their bond to be Presented
to the Honourable Assembly may appear — your petetioners therefore being
Impresed with the Idea of the Great Importance of Good Littereture pray that the
Honourable Assembly would take the same under their wise Considration and if
they Should think fit pass an act this present session Directing the Grammar School
for Sad County to be kept in the Said Town of putney and your petitioners in duty
bound Shall Ever pray

Signed by order of the Town

Dated at putney ye 13 day   Daniel Sabin Town Clerk
of February AD 1787

— & —

Petition of the Town of Putney
Fild Febr 27. 1787
. . .*

— & —

A. J.: *Read and ordered to lie on the table, 27 Feb. '87, S. P. of Vt., III (III),
296; *referred to next session, 3 March '87, Ibid, III (III), 310.

FOR ABATEMENT OF TAXES
xvii, 279

To the Honorable Genl Asseml of the State of Vermont to be holden at Bennington
by adjournment on the 3d Thursday of Febr Instant
The petition of the Subscribers Select-men of the Town of Pawlet in said State
Humbly sheweth —
That by a miscast the Grand list of the Town of Pawlet for the year AD 1786 was
returnd to the Asseml in October last at £ 4745 whereas the sum Total of said
List was but £ 4301 by reason of which miscast the Inhabitants of said Town are
liable to pay more than Equal proportion of publick Taxes. Your honour petitioners
therefore pray your honors to take their case under your wise consideration and
grant relief in the premises and your [petitioners] as in Duty bound shall ever pray

Jonathan Willard
Moses porter   Select-
Ezekiel Harmon   men

Pawlet Febr 14th 1787

— & —

---

1. For this provision, see Section XL, Constitution of 1777 (G. and C., I, 102).

Petition of Select-men of Pawlet
Entered on File Feb[r] 19th 1787
. . .*
4745-0
4301-5
_____
0443:15

— & —

A. J.: Read and referred to a committee, 19 Feb. '87, *S. P. of Vt.*, III (III),
272; *report of committee recommending that town be credited for taxes laid
on £443-15, read and accepted, 23 Feb. '87, *Ibid*, III (III), 286; resolved that
Treasurer credit Pawlet all taxes on £443-15 on list of 1786, 23 Feb. '87,
Ibid, III (III), 286.

FOR RELIEF FROM A TAX LEVIED TO PAY FOR A NEW SURVEY OF A TOWN'S LINES
xvii, 280

To the Honourable General Assembly of the state of Vermont the potition of the
proprietors and Land owners of the town of Vershire humbly sheweth that the
Tax of £ 27-7-9[s][d] which we are Cald upon to pay by the survayor General is oppressive and unconstitutional[1] and we Doubt not but your Honours Will view it
so when the following facts are taken under your wise consideration. Your Honourable body Did see Good at Your Last session to take off the Tax (as Asist [Assessed]
by the Governor and Councill) from those towns which ware Granted by Hampshire[2] and [we] honour your Judgments as we know that the Cost must be paid
and Cant see why we should not be set on the same Footing With those towns
that ware Granted by hampshire as our Town is bounded on those towns (viz)
our Chartor bounds us on the S W Corner of Corinth. the N W Corner of Fairlee
the N E Cornor of Strafford and the N W Cornor of Strafford and when those
Towns have their astablished bounds that Gives us our bounds with out paying
the surveyor General £27:7-9[s][d][;] it is to be observed that the New survey made
Considerable alteration in our supposed Lines Yet thay are not astablished to us
for instance the new Lines Runs into Fairlee almost half A mile through the East
end of the Town which Land is Claimd by the proprietors of Fairlee. for which
we Look upon it unconstitutional and unjust for us to pay for Running A Line We
Would beg Your Honours to observ that we are on it very Differant sitiation from
those other towns which ware Granted by the State of Vermont. and we Your
[potitionors] under the Consideration of the above facts Do Refuse to pay the

_____

1. This amount was determined by the Governor and Council on the basis of accounts rendered by the Surveyor-General for the cost of the survey of town lines. See
"An Act for the regulation and Establishment of Town Lines" passed 22 Oct. '82, and
an act in addition thereto passed 29 Oct. '84 (*Ms. Laws of Vt.*, I, 350, 466).

2. For the passage of a resolution to this effect 30 Oct. '86 and for its general import,
see *S. P. of Vt.*, III (III), 255(2) and *Ibid*, IV, 34-36.

above sd tax knowing that if the surveyor General is suffered to sell our Lands to pay sd tax by the Laws and athority of this State the same Athority can with Equel Justice take all our Intrest from us under any pretence what ever —

Your potitioners theirfore humbly pray that Your Honours Would be pleasd to cause that the above sd Tax be paid by the state that Your potitioners might be on an Equel Footing with the Rest of their fellow citysons and as in Duty bound shall Ever pray

Dated
Vershire February ye 14th AD 1787

Thos porter
Ebenezer West } Committee
Joel Walker

— & —

Petition of the [Propretors] of Vershire
Fi^l 20. 1787
. . .*

— & —

A. J.: *Read and referred to a committee to join a committee from the Council, 20 Feb. '87, *S. P. of Vt.*, III (III), 278; *report of committee recommending that town be exempted from paying more than their proportion with other towns, read and accepted, 23 Feb. '87, *Ibid*, III (III), 290; resolved that charges of Surveyor General for running the lines of Vershire be paid by the state as in the case of the New Hampshire grant towns, 23 Feb. '87, *Ibid*, III (III), 290. *C. J.:* Committee appointed to join Assembly committee, 20 Feb. '87, *G. and C.*, III, 122; *new member appointed to join committee, 22 Feb. '87, *Ibid*, III, 125.

FOR RIGHT TO SELL REAL PROPERTY TO SETTLE AN ESTATE
xvii, 106, 281

To the Honorable Gen^{ll} Assembly Now Seting in Bennington your Petisinors being appointed Administrators on the Estate of Ara Rose Late of Manchester Deses^d in the Settlement of which Estate your Petisinors find by a Statement of the Debts and Credits that the Parsoale [personal] Property is insoficant to ansure the Accounts Alredy Exeiteded [executed?] the Sum of Sixty Pounds teen Shillings and Seven Pence Lawfull Money as Certefied by the Honorable Judge of Probate for the District of Manchester for the raising Which Sum your Petisinors wish for liberty to Sel so much Lands of the said Ara Rose as will be soficant for that Purpose and as in Duty Bound shall ever Pray

Silas Goodrich } Admini^r
Tim^o Meadd Junr

Manchester February 15th 1787
To the Honerable Gen^{ll} Assembly now Sitting in Bennington in the State of Vermont it doth appear by the Inventorey which is taken of the Personal Estate of Arra Rose Late of Manchester Deceased and Exhibited by Capt Silas Goodrich Administrator on Said Estate and Stands Recorded in the Probate office in the Probate District of Manchester in the County of Bennington to pay the Demands of the Creditors to Said Estate and the Said Administrator wishes to obtain an

order from the Honorable Assembly to Dispose of So much of the Lands of the
Said Deceased as will pay the Sum of Sixty Six Pounds ten Shillings and Seven
Pence Lawfull money which is the Sum that appear to be due more than the amount
of the Said Inventorey after the widows thirds being Deducted in Such a way &
manner as the Assembly shall think most Proper

Enoch Woodbridge Probate Judge

— & —

Petition of Admors [Administrators] of Ara Rose
Filed 9th March
. . .*

— & —

> *A. J.:* *Read and granted, and a bill passed accordingly and sent to Council,
> 9 March '87, *S. P. of Vt.*, III (III), 327–328; act, having been concurred in
> by Council, passed into law, 10 March '87, *Ibid*, III (III), 330.[1] *C. J.:* Act
> read and concurred in, 10 March '87, *G. and C.*, III, 142.

FOR A TAX ON LAND TO BUILD ROADS AND BRIDGES
xvii, 262, 283

To the Honorable the General Assembly now Sitting
The petition of Calvin Parkhurst in behalf of the Inhabitants of Royalton Humbly
Sheweth,
     That the Inhabitants have been at great cost and expence in building several
large bridges in said town making and repairing roads &c — and that the General
Assembly did grant a lottery to raise the Sum of £ 140 to build a bridge over
White River in said town[2] which bridge has been compleated and has cost about
£ 300 Your Petitioner therefore prays that a tax of two pence on each acre of Land
in said town (except Public Lands) may be granted for the purpose of defraying
the cost of said bridge and if any money should remain to be laid out in making and
repairing roads and bridges in said town —
Bennington Feby 16th 1787   Calvin Parkhurst

     Royalton Vote for land Tax —
At a Leggal Town meeting of the Inhabitents of Royalton Voted To Petition the
Gen^{ll} Assembely For Them to Levy A Land Tax of two Pence on the Acre of
All the Land in S^d Town Publick Rights Excepted —
a true Copy the Vote   Attest Comfort Sever Town Clerk
Royalton Feby 5th 1787

— & —

Maj^r Parkhursts petition for a tax of 2^d on each acre of Land in Royalton —
Entered [on] file Feb^r 16 1787

---

     1. For this act, see *Ms. Laws of Vt.*, II, 188.
     2. For the resolution of the Assembly establishing this lottery passed 2 March, '84
see *S. P. of Vt.*, III (III), 32–33.

. . .*

— & —

A. J.: Read and referred to a committee, 16 Feb. '87, *S. P. of Vt.*, III (III), 267–268; *report of committee recommending that prayer be granted, read and accepted, and leave given to bring in a bill accordingly, 17 Feb. '87, *Ibid*, III (III), 270; bill read and accepted and sent to Council, 21 Feb. '87, *Ibid*, III (III), 280; bill, having been concurred in by Council, passed into law, 27 Feb. '87, *Ibid*, III (III), 297.[1] *C. J.:* Act read and concurred in, 21 Feb. '87, *G. and C.*, III, 123.

FOR A TAX ON LAND TO BUILD ROADS AND BRIDGES
xvii, 282

To the Honorable General Assembly Now Sitting
The petition of Roswell Hopkins in behalf of a number of the Inhabitants of the town of Charlottee in the County of Addison — Humbly Sheweth
That the proprietors of said township have divided the whole of said township into severalty and have disolved their proprietorship and have never done any thing towards making and repairing public roads — and their being but a few Inhabitants in said town which makes the keeping said roads passable, very hard on them — And by their settlements &c. they have raised the price of lands in said town, He therefore prays in behalf of the inhabitants of said town that a tax of two pence on each acre of land might be granted public rights excepted, for the purpose of making and repairing public roads and bridges in said town — and he as in duty bound shall ever pray —
Bennington Feby 16th 1787   Ros^l Hopkins

— & —

Petition of Roswell Hopkins in behalf of Inhabitants of Charlotte for a tax of 2^d p^r acre for roads & bridges —
Entered on File 16th Feb^r 1787.
. . .*

— & —

A. J.: Read and referred to a committee, 16 Feb. '87, *S. P. of Vt.*, III (III), 267–268; *report of committee recommending that petition be granted to the extent of a one penny half penny tax, read and accepted, and leave given to bring in a bill accordingly, 17 Feb. '87, *Ibid*, III (III), 269; bill read and accepted and sent to Council, 21 Feb. '87, *Ibid*, III (III), 280; bill, having been returned from Council with a proposed amendment, agreed to and passed into law, 27 Feb. '87, *Ibid*, III (III), 298–299.[2] *C. J.:* Read and amendment proposed that tax be only one penny, 21 Feb. '87, *G. and C.*, III, 123.

---

1. For this act, see *Ms. Laws of Vt.*, II, 50.
2. For this act, see *Ms. Laws of Vt.*, II, 50–51.

FOR A TAX ON LAND TO BUILD ROADS
xvii, 285

To the Honourable Assembly of the State of Vermont to be Holden at Benington
[Bennington] the third thursday of February Instant
The petition of the Select Men of the Town of Halifax Humbly Sheweth —
That Whereas said Town has Several Large Streams that Run through the Town
over Which it is Necessary that Bridges should be Built and Maintained for the
Benefit of the publick and the Land in S^d Town Naturally Very wet & Springey so
that Notwithstanding all the Work by way of a Highway Rate agreable to the
Law as it Now Stands is insoficient to Make the Roads Comfortable and Safe to
pass in & Several of S^d Rivers over Which Roads are Laid have no Bridges to this
Day —
And Whereas there is about five Thousand Acres of Non Residents land in the
Town Who have Never bin Called upon by way of a Tax to assist the Town in
Mending their Roads or other publick Uses the Town has Built a Meeting House
and Settled a Minister Besides Working on the Roads Near twenty years all Which
has Greatly Increased the Real Value of all the Lands in S^d Town
and Whereas the people are so publick spirit^d as to be willing Still to Do more on
the high ways accordingly have Voted to Request a land Tax of one penny on the
acre of all the land in S^d Town publick Rights Excepted for the Sole Use of Mending the Highways in S^d Town   These are therefore Humbly to Request your
Honours to Take there Case into Your Wise Consideration and Grant the Contents
of this petition as your petitioner in Duty Bound Shall Ever pray
Halifax February ye 17th 1787

Hubbel Wells   ⎫
Benjamin Henry ⎬ Select
Nathan Fish   ⎭ Men

— & —

Petition of the Select-men of Hallifax
Fil^d Feb^r 20. 1787
. . .*

— & —

A. J.: *Read and granted, 20 Feb. '87, S. P. of Vt., III (III), 276; leave given
to bring in a bill accordingly, 20 Feb. '87, Ibid, III (III), 276; bill read and
accepted and sent to Council, 10 March '87, Ibid, III (III), 330; bill, having
been concurred in by Council, passed into law, 10 March '87, Ibid, III (III),
330.[1] C. J.: Act read and concurred in, 10 March '87, G. and C., III, 142.

FOR RELOCATION OF A COUNTY SEAT
xvii, 286

To the Honorable the General Assembly to set at Bennington by Adjournment in Feby next the Humble petition & Remonstrance of the Inhabitants of the

---

1. For this act, see Ms. Laws of Vt., II, 188-189.

Town of Fairhaven [Fair Haven] Legally met humbly Shews that When this Town the Towns of Orwill [Orwell] Hubbartown [Hubbardton] & Benson were just beginning a Settlement that County Conventions were held for the purpose of Affixing the place for the Seat of the County in which it was held up that this Town & Benson should not be considered as a part of the County & at any so inconsiderable as well as the Towns of Orwill & Hubbarton that no Great Attention Ought to be paid to them in affixing the Seat of the County, that by means of the Insinuations of the Inhabitants of the Town of Rutland the Conduct of the last Committee sent on the Matter & some other Reasons Unknown & Unaccountable to us the General Assembly did at their Sessions in Octr 1784 affix the place for the County buildings in the East part of Rutland on the Easterly Extreme of the Inhabited part of the County[1] & twenty three Miles due East from the West Side of the County which twenty three Miles is all Habitable & Good Land & Mostly Settled with Good Inhabitants friends to Order & Goverment these premised Matters being fact Which we are ready to make known to your honours — your honours will see We Labour under A Great Greivance to have the Seat of the County Continued at that Extreame not only as it carries us to so great a distance from our homes when we have Occasion to sue or be sued there but when we are Called on to Support Goverment as has been the case of late,[2] the distance was so great it seamed like a long Journey but we leave to our Superior Officers to say what we have done[;] will say this for our selves that Should the Seat of the County be carried even one Mile further East even on the Height of the Green Mountain we would Attempt to Climb it if it was Necessary for the Support of Government & when we returned we would as we do now Most earnestly Entreat our political Fathers to Redress our Grievance by Affixing the Seat of the County in Castleton for which as we in duty bound will ever pray

    Signed by order of the Meeting

                                               Michael Merrit

Fairhaven Feby 18th 1787   Town Clerk

— & —

Petition of Fairhaven
Filed 5th March 1787

— & —

    A. J.: Filed and referred along with three other similar petitions to next session, 5 March '87, *S. P. of Vt.*, III (III), 314.[3]

---

1. The county seat was established at Rutland by an act passed 9 March '84 (*Ms. Laws of Vt.*, I, 444–445), while the public buildings were relocated within the town by an act passed 29 Oct. '84 (*Ibid*, I, 473). In connection with this last act, see the petition for the relocation of the buildings and action taken thereon in the October session '84, p. 98, *ante.*

2. The case here referred to was the support given by the militia to the county authorities in the suppression of the riots in Rutland in November '86. See *G. and C.*, III, 367–369.

3. For other petitions to the same effect, see pp. 287, 288, 289, 292, *ante.*

FOR A NEW TRIAL IN A CRIMINAL CASE
xvii, 289

To the Honourable General Assembly of the State of Vermont now convened at Bennington in the County of Bennington the Petition of Silas Whitney & Jabez Carpenter both of Clarendon in the County of Rutland Humbly Sheweth to your Honours that at the Session of the County Court holden at Bennington within & for the County of Bennington in Sep[t] last they were Indicted and found Guilty of assisting one Samuel Andrews to make his escape from Bennington Goal & as your Honours Petitioners were conscious that they were not guilty they moved for an appeal to the next Session of the Supreme Court to be holden in S[d] County of Bennington but as your Honours Petitioners were at a great distance from their homes & friends & families they were not able to procure bail for prosecution of their appeal by which means their appeal could not be entered by which means final judgment was entered against them your Honours Petitioners would further observe that they did not think or know that any evidence would be [admitted?] against them so that they had not any advantage of procuring counter evidence wherefore your Honours Petitioners pray that your Honours would take the matter into your wise consideration and grant them a new trial in the same court or order that upon giving suficient bonds an appeal might now be entered and the cause heard in the next Supreme Court in this County the same as it would have been had the bonds been entered in proper time and your Honours Petitioners as in duty bound Shall ever pray
Dated at Bennington this 19th day of Feb[r] AD 1787

Silas Whitney
Jabez Carpenter

— & —

the Petition of Silas Whiney & Jabez Carpenter
Filed Feb[r] 20. 1787
. . .*

— & —

> A. J.: *Read and granted, and leave given to bring in a bill accordingly, 20 Feb. '87, S. P. of Vt., III (III), 277; bill directing an appeal to be entered read and accepted and sent to Council, 21 Feb. '87, Ibid, III (III), 282; bill, having been concurred in by Council, passed into law, 23 Feb. '87, Ibid, III (III), 288.[1] C. J.: Act read and concurred in, 22 Feb. '87, G. and C., III, 124.

FOR A TAX ON LAND TO BUILD ROADS AND BRIDGES
xvii, 293

To the Honorable the General Assembly of the State of Vermont now Sitting —
    The petition of Peter Ferris in behalf of the Inhabitants of Panton — Humbly prays
        That all the Lands in said town may be taxed one penny on each acre except

---

1. For this act, see Ms. Laws of Vt., II, 23–24.

public rights, for the purpose of making and repairing public roads and bridges in said town — And your petitioner as in duty bound Shall ever pray —

Peter Ferris

Bennington 19th Feby 1787

— & —

Peter Ferris Petition for Taxing Lands in Panton —
File^d Feb^r 20th 1787
. . .*

— & —

> A. J.: *Read and referred to a committee, 20 Feb. '87, S. P. of Vt., III (III), 276; *report of committee recommending that "by the best information we can get" the petition ought not to be granted, read and accepted, and petition dismissed, 22 Feb. '87, Ibid, III (III), 283.

FOR CONFIRMATION OF AN UNACKNOWLEDGED DEED
xxii, 135

To the Honorable the General Assembly of the State of Vermont now Conveaned at Bennington

The Pitition of Filix Powel James Murdoc & Gidion Ormsby humbly Sheweth. that on the 22^d day of October — AD 1774 Samuel Aierill [Averill] of Kent, in the County of Litchfield and State of Connecticut Executed a Deed of one Right of Land in the Town of Burlington (now within the County of Addison) unto Felix Powel, (the Said Samuel being the Original Proprietor of Said Right)[1] — and on the 19th day of August 1778 the Said Felix Executed a Deed of the Same Right of Land to James Murdock — and on the 22^d day of December 1783 the Said James Conveyed the Same Right of Land to Gideon Ormsby and that the time of the Said Averills Executing Said Deed was long before any Authority existed in this State — and of Consequence S^d Deed Could not be acknowledged in Burlington where it was given — and the Said Avirill is Since Dead and the witnesses to Said Deed are out of this State and not to be found, by which means your Petitioners are unable to get S^d Deed acknowledged and Recorded therefore Humbly pray your Honors to Pass an act enabling the Town Clerk of Said Burlington to Record Said Deed and that it may be Considered a Sufficient Title in Law — And your Honors Petitioners as in Duty bound Shall ever pray —
Manchester Feby 19th 1787 —

Felix Powel
James Murdock
Giedon Ormsby

— & —

Felix Powel &cc Petition
Fil^d Feb^r 23. 1787
. . .*

---

1. For the charter of Burlington and the list of its original proprietors, see State Papers New Hampshire, vol. XXVI (Town Charters, vol. III), 75–79.

— & —

A. J.: *Read and referred to a committee, 23 Feb. '87, *S. P. of Vt.*, III (III), 287; *report of committee recommending that petition be granted, read and accepted, and leave given to bring in a bill accordingly, 23 Feb. '87, *Ibid,* III (III), 289; bill read and accepted and sent to Council, 23 Feb. '87, *Ibid,* III (III), 289; bill, having been concurred in by Council, passed into law, 23 Feb. '87, *Ibid,* III (III), 290.[1] *C. J.:* Act read and concurred in, 23 Feb. '87, *G. and C.,* III, 126.

FOR ABATEMENT OF TAXES
xvii, 295

To the Honorable the General Assambely Now Seting att Bennington the Petition of the Subscriber — Humbely Sheweth —
that where as the Grand Lest Sent in by the Lesters of the town of Dummerston Last October was 3427 pounds as may be maid to appeare and the treasure of this state has Sent his warrant for 4427 which must be a mistake of 1000 — these are therefore to pray your honers to grant Such Releaff as you in your wisdom Shall think Proper and your petitionor as in duty Bound Shall Ever pray —
Bennington febuary the 20th 1787
                    Leonard Spaulding in behalf S[d] town of Dummerston

— & —

Leonard Spalding Petition
File[d] Feb[r] 20 1787
. . .*

— & —

A. J.: *Read and referred to committee appointed last session to doom the several towns, 20 Feb. '87, *S. P. of Vt.*, III (III), 276;[2] *report of committee recommending that petition be granted, read and accepted, 20 Feb. '87, *Ibid,* III (III), 277; resolved that Treasurer credit town on all taxes laid on £1000 on the list of 1786, 20 Feb. '87, *Ibid,* III (III), 277.

FOR SPECIAL CONSIDERATION IN THE SETTLEMENT OF THE TREASURER'S ACCOUNTS BECAUSE OF ILLNESS AND DISASTER[3]
xvii, 296

To His Excellency the Governor the Honorable the Council & Representatives of

---

1. For this act, see *Ms. Laws of Vt.,* II, 25.
2. For the appointment of this committee 14 Oct. '86, see *S. P. of Vt.,* III (III), 221. That a town was "doomed" simply meant that its property valuation was fixed by the legislature rather than in accordance with its own returns.
3. For differing views of Ira Allen's conduct of the office of Treasurer, see James B. Wilbur, *Ira Allen* (2 vols., Cambridge, 1928), *passim,* and Chilton Williamson, *Vermont in Quandary 1763–1825* (Montpelier, 1949), pp. 172–173.

the State of Vermont Conveaned in Bennington — The Representation of Ira Allen Humbly Sheweth that immediately after the Rising of the Legislature in October last I gave the Necessary Instructions to my Clerk to settle Coppy and Prepare the Treasurers Accounts for a Transfer in Persuance to an Act of the Legislature[1] I then went to Onion River in Order to Contract with Proper Persons to Surply my mills with Loggs & Men to tend them during the winter & to arange some matters of surplies for Workmen &c then Expected to Return to Sunderland & attend to the Settlement of Public accounts &c But on my Arival to Onion River found my Sister & Housekeeper Unwell after implying Phisitions found her Disorder to be a Malignant or Long feavour & that of the Sevearest Kind — Several young Men that had been at work for me were then unwell & Choose to set out for home one of Which taking Cold Dyed by the way in nine days after Notwithstanding the assistance of Phisitions &c sent him from Onion River, in the mean time Every exertion was made to Procure Phisitions medison &c for Mrs Allen & her young famaly who were three of them sick with the same feavour and two other Persons which made six Sick with the same feavour amongst which was the fatherless & the Widow who had none under GOD but me to look too to Cumfort & Provide for them in the Sovearest Tryals when Life was not Expected from day to day & Given over by thier Phisitions in this Situation In a New Country where the Necessary medison & Assistance were heard [hard?] to be had my attention to Provide & do for the sick in the Different Roomes of my House was such that I did not take off my Close to sleep for about fifty days nor did I attend to my own Business But in the Time of the Sickness of Mr Hawley who Conducted my business in my Absence I imployed Mr Spafford to see to the Complesion of my mill & Stables although they were in a few Rods of my House after Sixty eight days Sickness Mrs Allen dyed Two of her young Children Remained yet sick

about the Second of January last by an Uncommon flood Accompanyed with Verry thick & heavy Cakes of Ice my mill floors & Part of the Dam about fifty feet wide & about five feet Deep on the North Side of Onion River was Carryed away this at wonce Silenced my New Saw mill & Imbarrissed Both mills on the South Side of S'd River this misfortune was Supposed by the best Judges that all the mills & Dams would be Exposed if the Breach was not Repared before the water arose in the Spring Mr Buck haveing by Written Contract agreeed [sic] to Compleat & Warrant S'd Dam &c this work not being Compleated but Carried away by the flood made it Proper for me to Call on Mr Buck to Repare his work the Children before mentioned not being well yet some better I set out for Sunderland in Order to get Mr Buck to Repare S'd Mill Dam & floors & to see to the Settlement of Public Accounts on my arival to Sunderland in Consequence of a bad Cold setling in my Eyes was not able for some days to do or attend to Examin Writings Mr Bucks Son being Dangerously Sick & Since dead forbid his going to Onion River to Repare S'd Work in Consequence of this Aditional misfortune & to see to the Children that I Left unwell I Repared to Onion River the Children I found better than I Expected from Information the Security of my Mill, &c was my next object this took up my attention untill Saturday last — as to the Truth of the Preseeding facts have to Refer the Honorable house to Judge Lane Capt.

---

1. See "An Act for transfering the papers of the Treasury of the State from the former to the present Treasurer", passed 31 Oct. '86 (*Ms. Laws of Vt.*, I, 565–566). Among other things this act provided for a final settlement and transfer of accounts by 1 Feb. '87.

Butterfield & Mr Spafford Members your Honorable body who are Neighbours to me & acquainted with most of the Preseeding matters for Information

I should not have been so Proticular had not the Preseeding Part of this Stating when Verbally made been Rejected by members of the Honorable House as being altogether in Adiquate to the [Exegincies] of the Case viz. the Settlement of Public accounts a Worthy member observed that I was not a Phisition nor Nurs that some other Person might have taken care of the sick as well as me that he Read in an Old Book Let the Dead Bury their Dead. These observations from a Gentleman Born & Educated in a Christian Land Reprobating my Conduct for Paying my utmost Attention to the Widow & fatherless in an hour of Distress I must Confess Gave me some Disagreable feeling   Nevertheless when I Consider my Conduct to one of the Best of Women in her Last Sickness & to her young & Distressed famaly I have that satisfaction that the world Could not otherwise give nor Can they take it away In this Case Equal to any in my life think I have Complyed with the Golden Rule do as you would be done by — an other Worthy Member observed that he did not think I ever Intended to Settle Public Accounts there would alwas [always] be Some Unavoidable Accident or Procrastination that my Repeated Applications to the Legislature for settlement was a Reason to him that I never Intended to Settle Therefore Some sovear [severe] Acts ought to be made &c &c this I must Confess is a Strange way of Arguing when you Consider my Early Repeated & Proticular Applications for Settlement for more than seven years Past[1] I Should have Supposed were two Resently Published to be missunderstood or forgot and that the assembly at thier Last Session did adopt the same measures for settlement of Public Accounts that I have for many years Petitioned for In case the State could not be Conclusive on thier Part — Had these measures been seasonably Adopted they might Probably have Pravented most of these Disputes — Nevertheless I feel a Willingness to Comply with any Honorable & Reasonable measures to Accomidate Business at the Present Session to Settle & Transfer the Public Accounts out of my Hands — With Due Respect I have the Honer to be your Excellincies & Honours

most Obedient
Hum^{ble} Servt

Bennington Feby 21st 1787   Ira Allen

— & —

Ira Allen Esqr
Execuse for not Settl^{ng} Treas^{rs} accounts —
. . .*

— & —

A. J.: *Read and voted to take no order on it, 22 Feb. '87, S. P. of Vt., III (III), 283. C. J.: *Read and ordered to be sent to Assembly, 22 Feb. '87, G. and C., III, 124.

---

1. For previous petitions or representations from Ira Allen in connection with the settlement of the State's accounts, see p. 41, ante, and S. P. of Vt., III (III), 143–144. For a request that the state purchase account books for use in such a settlement, see p. 348, post.

FOR RIGHT TO CONVEY REAL PROPERTY TO SETTLE AN ESTATE
xvii, 297

To the Honorable General Assembly of the State of Vermont now Sitting —
    The humble Petition of Jacob Galusha of Shaftsbury Sheweth — That your
Petitioner being appointed & Legally Authorized as an Administrator to the Estate
of Capt Elijah Galusha Late of Arlington Deceased finding himself incapable of
Settling all Accompts Respecting Said Estate for the following reason (viz) That
the said Deceased Some few days before his Death Sold a Right of Land in the
Township of Vershire in this State to Mr Noah Chittenden late of S^d Arlington,
but now of Cambridge in this State and actually Received pay for the same & being
soon after Snatched suddenly out of time, had not convey'd S^d Right of Land by
Deed to the purchaser in order therefore to do Justice between the parties your
Petitioner prays the Legislature to Authorize him to Convey the said Right of
Land to the Said Noah Chittenden the Said Deceased being the Original Grantee of
the same
    And Your Petitioner as in Duty bound shall ever pray
Dated Shaftsbury February   Jacob Galusha administrator
21st AD 1787

— & —

Petition
Jacob Galusha to the Genl Assembly
Fil^d Feb^r 27 1787
. . .*
To the Honble the Genl Assembly now sitting —
Your Committee to whom was refered the within Petition, Report that the facts
set up in s^d Petition are true, and that in our Opinion the Prayer of said Petition
ought to be Granted — and that the Petitioner have leave to bring in a Bill in form
accordingly
                                              B. Brown, for Comm^ttee

Bennington   ⎫
March 2^d 1787 ⎬
              ⎭
                      — & —

> A. J.: *Read and referred to a committee, 2 March '87, *S. P. of Vt.*, III (III),
> 310; report of committee read and accepted, 3 March '87, *Ibid*, III (III), 310;
> bill read and accepted and sent to Council, 3 March '87, *Ibid*, III (III), 311;
> bill, having been concurred in by Council, passed into law, 8 March '87, *Ibid*,
> III (III), 323.[1] C. J.: Act read and concurred in, 3 March '87, *G. and C.*, III,
> 134.

FOR A TAX ON LAND TO BUILD A TOWN HOUSE
xvii, 298

To the Honble the General Assembly Now Setting at Benington The Petition of the
Select men and other inhabetants of the Town of Chester in behalfe of them Selves

---

1. For this act, see *Ms. Laws of Vt.*, II, 96.

and inhabetants of Said Town Humbly Shewith

That there is many Large Strems Running through Said Town over Which We are oblidged to Buld many Large Bridges Which are vary Berdinsome to the Present Inhabentants of S^d Town and as their is much of Said Town owned by Pesens [persons] Living out of S^d Town and as we are Destute of any House to Hold Town meetting or to Do any Publick Buisness in we therefore Pray your Honours to Grant a Tax of one Pannay to be Laid on Each acer of Land in Said Town of Chester Publick Lands Excepted for the Purpos of Building a Town house in Said Town in Such way as your Honners may Think Proper as your Petitioners in Duty Bound Shall Ever Pray

Chester Feb^ry 21: 1787

Jabez Sargants Junr ⎫ Select
Willm Hosmer   ⎬ men
John Smith   ⎪ of
                     ⎭ Chester

Nath^el Gowing   Amos Hosmer   Waitst^ll Ranney
William Gilkey Junr   Daniel Ranney   Nathaniel Ston
Moses Gile   James White   Wm Atwood
Amos Gile   Joshua [Hatten?]   Abner Gile
Thos Warren   David M^cllen

— & —

The Pertition of the Select men and other Inhabetant of Chester —
Fil^d Feb^r 27. 1787
. . .*

— & —

A. J.: Read and referred to a committee, 27 Feb. '87, *S. P. of Vt.*, III (III), 297; *report of committee recommending that prayer be granted, read and accepted, 1 March '87, *Ibid*, III (III), 304; bill read and accepted and sent to Council, 1 March '87, *Ibid*, III (III), 304; bill, having been concurred in by Council, passed into law, 8 March '87, *Ibid*, III (III), 323.¹ *C. J.:* Act read and concurred in, 3 March '87, *G. and C.*, III, 134.

FOR COMPENSATION FOR WAR SERVICES
xvii, 299

[Bennington] Februar 21 AD 1787 To The Honoreble General Assembly now setting A petition of Daniel Marsh of Clarendon County of Rutland State of Vermont Humbly sheweth that your Petiner was Cald upon By Col Oliver Potter of said town of Clarendon to Go with his Hay and horses to Montreal for the purpos of transportting the Bagage of part of his Company² your Petiner Complied with the request and was sixten Days in said Servis wich your petitinor has not had any pay for. your Petitinor prays that your Honers will take the mater in to

---

1. For this act, see *Ms. Laws of Vt.*, II, 97–98. For a petition for the repeal of this act, see p. 349, *post*.

2. For the service of Capt. Oliver Potter's company, Col. Seth Warner's regiment, in the expedition to Canada in 1775, see *Vt. Rev. Rolls*, 4.

your wise Consideration and Derect the treashur to pay to your peti[r] the sum
that [Shall] Be Judged Just or in Sum other way releave your peti[r] as you in your
wisdom shal be Judged Just and your peti[r] as in Duty bound shall Ever pray

Daniel Marsh

— & —

Dan[l] Marsh Petition
Fil[d] Feb 21st 1787.
. . .*

— & —

> A. J.: *Read and referred to a committee, 21 Feb. '87, S. P. of Vt., III (III),
> 282; *report of committee recommending that petitioner be allowed £9–12
> hard money, read and accepted, and leave given to bring in a bill accordingly,
> 27 Feb. '87, Ibid, III (III), 297; resolved that Treasurer immediately pay peti-
> tioner accordingly, 28 Feb. '87, Ibid, III (III), 299.

FOR A LOTTERY TO BUILD A BRIDGE
xvii, 300

To the Hon[ble] General Assembly of the State of Vermont Now Setting at Bennington.

The petition of the Subscribers Inhabitents of the State of N. York Humbly
Sheweth — that in the month of ‹August last› Jan[y] 1786 in the very extraordinary
flood which happened at that Time, the Bridge which Croses Hoosaac River in
Scoitacook [Schaghticoke] was Caried off & Tottally Distroyed, which Renders the
passing to New City[I][,] Albany & other ports adjacent very inconvenient, to the
Great Detriment of Many of the Inhabitents of Vermont, as well as the Inhabitents
Living Near that place, who Improve that Road to Transport their Articles of
Produce to Market & in Return Obtain Such Necessary[s] as they Require for their
families Use — And Whereas the Erecting of a New Bridge (in which your petitioners consider themselves Deeply Interested) will be Attended with Great
Expence, And Whereas your petitioners by Enquiry find Numbers of people who
would be willimg to Encourage the building the Same by a Lottery, we are therefore encouraged to Pray your Honors Indulgence, & Grant, of a Lottery for the
aforesaid purpose, & beg Leave to Lay before your honors the Scheme proposed,
with the persons names who agree to Serve as Managers, with Sufficient Bonds to
Endemnify the State, to be Conducted under Such Restrictions & Regulations as
your honors in your Wisdom Shall Direct, & as in duty bound your petitioners
shall Ever pray   W[m] Chase
Bennington 21st Feb[y] 1787 —   Artemes Ross

— & —

Petition for a Lottery for Hoosick Bridge.
. . .*

— & —

---

1. That is, Lansingburgh, N. Y. (S. P. of Vt., III (I), 251). It is now a part of Troy,
N. Y.

A. J.: *Read and referred to a committee, 22 Feb. '87, *S. P. of Vt.*, III (III), 283;[1] *report of committee recommending that petition be granted so far as to raise £450 by lottery, read and accepted, and leave given to bring in a bill accordingly, 24 Feb. '87, *Ibid*, III (III), 290-291; resolved that petitioners have liberty to make a lottery accordingly, giving security to Treasurer of Bennington County and involving no risk to the state, 26 Feb. '87, *Ibid*, III (III), 294-295. *C. J.:* *Committee appointed to join Assembly committee, 22 Feb. '87, *G. and C.*, III, 124.

FOR A TAX ON LAND TO BUILD ROADS AND BRIDGES
xvii, 167

To the Honor^e General Assembly of the State of Vermont now Setting in Bennington
    The petition of Samuel Robinson Humbly Sheweth —
that the Inhabitants of the town of Summerset have for a year or two past been greatly desireous to have a Road Cut from that town through the township of Glastenbury to Bennington — your petitioner with others have Viewd & marked out Said Road, and your Petitioner is fully of the opinion that Provided it were Properly Cut out and Bridges made it would be of Great Service to the Publick and also Promote the Setlement of the lands in Said Glastenbury and the Ajacent Country. Your Petitioner being a large Proprietor in S^d Glastenbury therefore prays that the Honorable Assembly wou^d Grant a tax of one penny halfpenny on Each acre of Land in Said town of Glastenbury to be appropriated to the above Said use of Clearing and making said Road under the Direction of Capt John Warner, Moses Rice, & Jonathan Robinson a Committee to oversee the Labourers on Said Road which Committee Shall be accountable to the County Court in the County of Bennington
Bennington Feby 24th 1786 [1787][2]   Sam^ll Robinson

— & —

S. Robinson's Petition
Fil^d Feb^r 27. 1787
. . .*

— & —

A. J.: *Read and referred to a committee, 8 March '87, *S. P. of Vt.*, III (III), 324; *report of committee recommending that a tax of one penny be granted, read and accepted, and leave given to bring in a bill accordingly, 8 March '87, *Ibid*, III (III), 325; bill read and accepted and sent to Council, 9 March '87, *Ibid*, III (III), 326; bill having been concurred in by Council, read and passed into law, 9 March '87, *Ibid*, III (III), 327.[3] *C. J.:* *Act read and concurred in, 9 March '87, *G. and C.*, III, 141.

---

1. This committee was to join a committee from the Council. See *G. and C.*, III, 124.
2. All the other evidence indicates that this petition was drawn up in 1787. See subjoined note. There was no session of the legislature in February, 1786 and thus none could have been then "setting".
3. For this act, see *Ms. Laws of Vt.*, II, 145.

FOR VERMONT'S NEUTRALITY IN SOCIAL DISTURBANCES IN OTHER STATES[1]

xvii, 303

To the Honourable the Genl Assembly of Vermont now Conven'd at Bennington —
 the Petition of a Number of the Inhabitants of the Town of Sunderland Humbly sheweth —
 that whereas the Late Disturbances in the state of the Massachusets [Massachusetts] Bay, has Caused a Number of those unhappy people who Stil'd themselves Regulators to take Refuge in this State and whereas we are inform'd that on a Request made by Authority from the Massachusets — Your Honours have Pass'd a Resolve Directing or advising His Excelency the Govr to Issue his Proclamation Directing the Authority to Apprehend Several Persons that they may be Return'd to the S^d State from whence they came —
 Your Petitioners having a tender feeling for the peace Happiness & welfare of this State and fearing the unhappy Consequences that may arise, if this State (which is not in Confederation with the United States) shall intermeddle in that Quarrel Beg Leave to address Your Honour on the subject Requesting that Your Honours will reconsider the S^d Resolve and not intermeddle in the Affair least by taking an active part in the matter or take up the Quarrel Amongst ourselves which in our Opinion will bring this State into Confusion and Destress — we Your Honours Petitioners placing the greatest Confidence in your wisdom and understanding and believing that you will Act for the best good of the State Pray Your Honours to take this our petition into your wise Consideration and Dismiss the Petition from the Massachusets Bay —
 Your Petitioners as in Duty Bound shall ever Pray —
Dated at Sunderland this 25th Day of
Feb^y — 1787 —

Joseph Bradley	Ezra Whipple	Jacob Sherwin
Daniel Comstock	Robert Whitcomb	Saml Bartlet
Jon^a Hoit	Elijah Stoddard	John Bradly
Charles Everts	Miles Bradley	Judah Everts
Edward Giffin	Levi Comstock	Azariah Darbe
Gilbert Bradley	Benjn Griffis	Elisha Bartlet
Lem^l Bishop	Nathl Wallas	Abiather Walden
Edward Everts	Elijah Stoddard Ju^n	John Porter
Lem^l Bradley	Matthew Lewis	Benjn Lewis
Abraham Merrifield	Isaac Phelps	Peter Comstock
Saml Mills	Stephen Bradley	Azariah Lee
Jesse Averill	David Hoit	Timothy Baker
Jeremiah Center	James Carncross	Fisk Bartlet
Abner Hill	Amos Catlin	Jason Comstock
Ensign Catlin	Ebenezer Preston	Amos Chipman
Chandler Sherwin	Roswell Catlin	Timothy Bradley

---

1. This petition was, of course, occasioned by Shays' rebellion in Western Massachusetts and the flight of some of its leaders to Vermont. For the records and documents pertaining to Vermont's actions in the matter, see *G. and C.*, III, 375–380; also *S. P. of Vt.*, III (III), 270–305, *passim*.

— & —

The Petition of a Numb [Number] of the Inhabitants of Sunderland —
to the Gen¹ Assembly
Fil^d Feb^r 26. 1787

— & —

[No Record]¹

FOR A NEW TRIAL IN A CASE OF TROVER
xvii, 302

To the Honble General Assembly of the State of Vermont now sitting at Bennington. —
The Petition of Ebenezer Burges of Thomlinson² in Windham County. — Shew-
eth/
    That your Petitioner was Constable of s^d Thomlinson in the year 1785 &
by virtue of an Execution to him legally directed & delivered in the Suit Abel
Gibson against Mathew Lane levied on Goods & Chattles of s^d Lane shewn to
your Petitioner as his Property by the Pl^t Gibson & after duly posting said Goods
sold them by virtue of said Execution according to Law & caused the avails thereof
to be indorsed by the Plaintiff on the said Execution. —
    That the said Lane since the last Session of Assembly has brought an Action
of Trover ag^t your Petitioner for taking & selling said Goods before Benjn Burt
Esqr a Justice of the Peace for Windham County & recovered against your petitioner about the sum of £ 4:0:0 Damages & about £ 0:18:0 Costs of Suit because
your petitioner had not indorsed upon the Execution the particular Articles by him
taken & sold altho your petitioner was & is able satisfactorily to prove his applying
the Avails of the said Property to discharging the Execution. —
    That the Act defining the power of Justice of the Peace not allowing an Appeal
from the said Judgm^t or a Writ of Error your Petitioner has no other remedy than
by Application to this hon^ble house for a new trial of the said cause —³
    Wherefore your Petitioner prays this hon^ble house to grant him a new trial in
the said cause & that Execution upon the said Judgm^t may be suspended until the
rising of the next Session of the Legislature that your petitioner may have time
legally to notify the said Lane to appear at the next Session of Assembly & shew
cause why a new trial should not be granted — And your Petitioner as in Duty
bound shall ever pray &c   Ebenezer Burges
26th Febry 1787 Bennington

— & —

Petition of Ebenezer Burges for a new trial

---

    1. On 1 March '87 the Assembly by a vote of 33 to 30 refused to reconsider its
resolution requesting the Governor to issue a proclamation (*S. P. of Vt.*, III (III), 304–
305). This action was equivalent to a dismissal of this petition.
    2. Now Grafton. See *S. P. of Vt.*, II (Vermont Charters), 355.
    3. For "An Act defining and limiting the jurisdiction of Justice Courts within this
State, and directing the proceedings therein", passed October '86, see *Slade*, 506–508.

Entered
Filed 26th Febry 1787
. . .*

— & —

A. J.: *Read and referred to a committee, 26 Feb. '87, S. P. of Vt., III (III),
294; *report of committee recommending that execution be suspended until
next session and that plaintiff be notified to show cause at next session why
new trial should not be had, read and accepted, and leave given to bring in a
bill accordingly, 3 March '87, Ibid, III (III), 311; bill suspending execution
read and accepted and sent to Council, 8 March '87, Ibid, III (III), 322;[1]
*read again and granted, and leave given to bring in a bill accordingly, 16 Oct.
'87, Ibid, III (IV), 21; bill granting a new trial read and accepted and sent
to Council, 25 Oct. '87, Ibid, III (IV), 48; bill, having been concurred in by
Council, passed into law, 25 Oct. '87, Ibid, III (IV), 49.[2] C. J.: Act read and
concurred in, 25 Oct. '87, G. and C., III, 154.

FOR COMPENSATION FOR SERVICES AGAINST NEW YORK
AND IN THE WAR
xvii, 304

To the Honorable General Assembly Now Sitting in Bennington in and for the
State of Vermont
  The Petition of Peleg Sunderland of Manchester Humbly Sheweth,
  That Whereas there was a Committee appointed by the Grand Convention
Holden at Manchester on the third day of Feby in the year of our Lord 1775[3] to
Take into Consideration and Examine the Accounts of Seth Warner Gideon Warren
Robert Cochran Elnathan Hubbell and Also the Account of your Petitioner for
the Many hard and Disagreeable Services perform^d by them and your Petitioner
in Supporting & Defending against the N York Claimers the Little few Inhabitants
that was at that Time but Just able to Support themselves and their families, and
your Petitioner further begs Leave to Inform your honors that the State of N York
Was Wicked Enough in Addition to the then Present Dificulties and Troubles of
your Petitioner, on the 9th Day of March 1774 to pass an Act of Out Lawry[4]
against him and a Number of Other Worthy Gentleman Who had from an Early
Period to the Present Time Taken a Most Intresing and Active Part in Defending
the N Hampshire Settlers which Pernicious and Wicked Act Caused & Oblidged
your Petitioner to Support with Arms Not only his own family but to Give his
Aid and Utmost Assistance in Supporting & Definding his fellow Sufferers at the
Risque of his Life & forfiture of Property for upward^s of Two Years, Whereupon

---

  1. Although there is no record of the concurrence of the Council in this bill or of
its final passage by the Assembly, it did become law. See "An Act to suspend an Execution in a cause between Mathew Lane and Ebenezer Burgess", passed 8 March '87 (Ms.
Laws of Vt., II, 95).
  2. For this act, see Ms. Laws of Vt., II, 207–208.
  3. For a discussion of this convention, see S. P. of Vt., IV, 41n–44n. The reference
to Governor and Council given therein should read volume II, pp. 489–497.
  4. For this act, see Laws of the Colony of New York, passed in the Years 1774 and 1775
(Albany, 1888), 38–43.

the Said Committee after Duly Examining the Account of your Petitioner Made the following Report (Viz) That the Towns of Rutland Pittsford Neshobee[1] Addison Panton Bridport and Middlebury pay to your Petitioner the Sum of Twenty Pounds and one penny half Penny Lawfull Money to be paid by them to your Petitioner as Soon as May be for the Doing and Performing of the above Specified Services, which Report of Said Committee Was Examined & Accepted by the Said Grand Convention as by the Records[2] Doth fully appear and your Petitioner begs Leave to Inform the Honorable Assembly that he has Never Rec[d] any Part of the Said Sum Excepting about fifteen Shillings and that it has Not been in his Power to Collect the Same of said Towns Neither is it Now in his Power to Collect the Same by any Law, and your Petitioner Views himself Remidiless Without Some Assistance from the Honorable Assembly, And your Petitioner further begs Leave to Inform your honors that your Petitioner Some Time in the month of March 1775 was Call[d] upon and Requested by the Grand Committee at Bennington to go into Canada as a Pilot to Maj[r] John Brown who was Sent by the Provential Congress as a Delegate to Treat with the Indians in that Province Respecting the then approaching War which Service your Petitioner perform[d] at his own Expense & Charge and was out on Said Service Twenty Nine Days and has Never Rec[d] any Compensation therefor, and has No Place to Look too for Redress Except it be to your honors

Your Petitioner therefore pray[s] your honors to Take his Case into your Wise Consideration and Grant him Such Redress and Relief as your honors in your Wisdom Shall think Just and Equitable — and your Petitioners in Duty Bound Shall Ever Pray —

Dated at Bennington this 26th Day
of Feb[y] 1787 —   Peleg Sunderland

— & —

[No Additional Material]

— & —

A. J.: Read and referred to a committee to join a committee from the Council, 2 March '87, S. P. of Vt., III (III), 307; report of committee read and accepted, and leave given to bring in a bill accordingly, 7 March '87, Ibid, III (III), 319; resolved that Treasurer be directed to pay petitioner £8–14 hard money for his services to the United States in March 1775, 8 March '87, Ibid, III (III), 324. Rep. of Com: Committee recommends that towns listed in petition be cited to show cause why it should not be granted, and that petitioner be paid £8–14 for his services in piloting Maj[r] Brown, 6 March '87, S. P. of Vt., IV, 39–44. C. J.: Read and referred to a committee, 3 March '87, G. and C., III, 134.

FOR TITLE TO LAND CONVEYED BY A LOST AND UNRECORDED DEED
xxii, 138, 147

To the Hon[rbl] General Assemby of the State of Vermont Now Setting at Bennington

---

1. Now Brandon. See S. P. of Vt., II (Vermont Charters), 327.
2. The journal of the proceedings of the Convention is not now known to exist, although it was in existence at the time of this petition (S. P. of Vt., IV, 39–40).

the Petition of Benjamin Warner of New Milford in the State of Conecticutt Humbly Sheweth that your Petitioner Did Received a Deed of Ephreaim Cowen of Cambridge in the State of New york [York] of Ten Rights of Land in Sangate [Sandgate] in the County of Bennington Dated the Seventh Day of November AD 1764 the Said Deed being Lost, of the Above Said Rights Before Said deed was Recorded your Petitioner prays that he may be Intitled To Said Lands as fully and Amply by an act of this State as though he had Not Lost Said Deed As Said Cowen hath Ben Deseased for a Long Time your Petitioner having a Coppy of Said Deed, and Evidence to Support he had Paid full Sastisfaction to Said Cowen for Said Lands which he is Ready to Veryfy and your Petitioner in Duty Bound Shall Ever Pray
Bennington Febuary 27th 1787

Benjamin Warner

The Testimony of Doct[r] Benj[n] Warner of New Milford of lawful age is as follows (Viz) That on the 7th day of Nov[r] in the Year of our Lord 1764 — I Rec[d] a Deed of Ephraim Cowen of Cambridge in Albany County and then province but now State of New York of ten Rights of land in the Town of Sandgate now in Bennington County and State of Vermont, which deed I afterwards gave to my son Co[ll] Seth Warner late of Woodbury Deceas[d] — in Order that he Might git it upon Record And take Benefit of Said [Rights]. himself

Benj[a] Warner

State of Connecticut,
Litchfield County, ss, New Milford Aug[t] 29th 1787.

Personally appear[d] Doct[r] Benjamin Warner, the above deponent, and made Solemn Oath to the truth of the above deposition by him Subscribed

Coram   Dan[ll] Everitt [Ju[s] Pea[e]]

— & —

Cap[t] Benj[a] warner[s] Petition
Fil[d] Feb[r] 27. 1787
. . .*

To the Hon[ble] the Gen[l] Assembly now sitting —
Your Committee to whom was refered the within Petition Report, that in their opinion, the Petition be laid over to the next Session of Assembly, and that the Petitioner be directed to serve the Heirs or Administrators of the said Ep[m] Cowan with a Copy of this Petition and a Citation to appear at the next Session of Assembly to Shew Cause why the Prayer of said Petition Should not be Granted —

Tho[s] Porter Chm

— & —

A. J.: *Read and referred to a committee to join a committee from the Council, 2 March '87, *S. P. of Vt.*, III (III), 307; *petition referred to next session, 7 March '87, *Ibid*, III (III), 319. *C. J.:* *Petition read and committee appointed to join Assembly committee, 2 March '87, *G. and C.*, III, 133.

FOR RIGHT TO SELL REAL PROPERTY TO SETTLE AN ESTATE
xxxviii, 139

Probate Office ⎱
Bennington District ⎰   Bennington Febr[y] 28th 1787

This Certifies that by the returns of the Commissioners appointed to receive and examine the Claims of the Several Creditors of the Estate of Benjamin Fay Esq[r] late of S[d] Bennington Deceased that their remains due to said Creditors the Sum of One hundred and two pounds 12/10 over and above what the Personal Estate of S[d] Estate will pay.

Extract from the Records }   Jonas Fay Judge Prob[te]

To the Hon[ble] the General Assembly of the State of Vermont now convened

The Petition of the Subscriber Sheweth that it is found on examination that there remains due to the Several Creditors of the Estate of Benjamin Fay Esq[r] Deceased the Sum of One hundred and two pounds 12/10 over and Above what the personal Estate will pay, Your Petitioner therefore prays Your Honors to Grant her, Licence to make Sale of So much of the real Estate of S[d] Deceaseds Estate as will pay the Aforesaid Sum of £102.12.1D and Incidental Charges of Sale, and Your Petitioner as in Duty bound will ever pray

Bennington February 28th 1787.

             Sarah Fay } Administratrx

— & —

Sarah Fay Ad[x] to the estate of Benj[a] Fay Esq[r] petition/ —

— & —

A. J.: Read and granted, 10 March '87, *S. P. of Vt.*, III (III), 329; bill read and accepted and sent to Council, 10 March '87, *Ibid*, III (III), 329; bill, having been concurred in by Council, passed into law, 10 March '87, *Ibid*, III (III), 330.[1] *C. J.:* Act read and concurred in, 10 March '87, *G. and C.*, III, 141.

FOR POST RIDERS THROUGH A COUNTY
xvii, 308

To the Hon. General Assembly of the State of Vermont, now sitting at Bennington

The petition of the subscribers Representatives of the inhabitants of the county of Addison, humbly sheweth, that whereas they have suffered great inconvenience by reason of the laws not being duly promulgated in said county, and other public matters being within the compass of a post riders duty to perform, which advantages are enjoyed by the other counties in the State, and it being in their estimation, a matter of public utility, that regular post riders Should pass through every part of the state;

Your petitioners, therefore, humbly pray this honorable house, to pass an Act for extending the circuit of the post rider from Bennington to Rutland, in the County of Rutland, thro' such towns in the County of Addison as may best serve

---

1. For this act, see *Ms. Laws of Vt.*, II, 188.

the interest of said county,[1] and that the Post Master General be directed to see said business put into a regular channel as soon after the rising of this assembly as may be. — And your petitioners, as in duty bound shall ever pray. —

Dated at Bennington 28ᵗʰ of February 1787. —

John Strong
Rosˡ Hopkins
Phineas Brown
Hiland Hall
Gamˡ Painter
T. P. [Loid?]
Peter Ferris
Samᵉˡ Lane
Jedediah Lane

— & —

A Petition of the Representatives of the County of Addison
Filᵈ Febʳ 28ᵗʰ 1787
. . .*

— & —

A. J.: *Read and granted, and leave given to bring in a bill accordingly, 2 March '87, S. P. of Vt., III (III), 307; bill read and accepted and sent to Council, 3 March '87, Ibid, III (III), 311; bill, having been returned by Council with proposal of amendment, agreed to and passed into law, 3 March '87, Ibid, III (III), 311.[2]

FOR ERECTION AND MAINTENANCE OF A COUNTY'S BUILDINGS BY THE SHIRE TOWNS
xvii, 309

To the Honourable General Assembly of the State of Vermont now sitting at Bennington within said State

The Memorial of a Number of the Inhabitants of the Towns of Shaftsbury and Sunderland in the County of Bennington & State aforesaid, in behalf of themselves and the Inhabitants of the Said Towns in General [Assembly] humbly Sheweth, That your Memorialists Esteem it unreasonable and unjust for them or the

---

1. For the post offices in existence in the state at the time of this petition, see "An Act for establishing Post-Offices within this State", passed February, 1784 (Slade, 489–490). For a discussion of the establishment of post offices in Vermont, see G. and C., III, 392–395.

2. In spite of this entry in the Assembly journal it appears that this bill was not passed into law as a separate act, but was added to "An Act for establishing Post Offices within this State", passed 9 March '87 as part of the general revision of the statutes then in process. See Statutes of the State of Vermont, passed by the Legislature in February and March 1787 (Windsor, 1787), pp. 116–117. That it was to be so added may have been the intention of the Council amendment, which cannot be otherwise identified. The original act itself (Ms. Vt. S. P., vol. II, Laws, 1786–1789, no pagination) has attached to it on a separate sheet the section dealing with Addison County.

County at large to pay the present county Tax as it now stands for the following reasons (Viz[t])

That the Town of Bennington have heretofore not only offerd, but pledg'd their Faith to Build a Court House and Goal in said Town without Expence to the County if they might be privileg'd with having the Courts held there[1] but Alas they have come so far short of our Expectations that they have atcually broken their Faith Pledg'd in the most solemn manner to this Honorable House and to the Great grief of the Said County which now stands Tax'd in a considerable sum, and still larger sums threaten to usher themselves by the same Door in future time which makes us suspect that they wish to reap a very great advantage at the expence of others and to make use of their want of Faith to draw large sums of Cash from your Memorialists altogether unjustly   That the People of the Town of Shaftsbury offerd the committee (Selected to enquire into the matter in question by the Honorable the General Assembly) to provide sufficient surety to Erect and keep in repair a Goal and Court House in the Town of Shaftsbury with out Expence to the County if the Honorable House would order but one in the County & Give them the privilege thereof   That we are well assured that the said committee in their report to the Honorable House took special care that all stipulations relative to the premises should be adhered strictly to, yet notwithstanding Extents have actually issued from the county Treasurer one whereof has actually been levied on the Body of the Collector of the Town of Shaftsbury & he confined in Jail for not performing that which we esteem not to be his duty considering the minds of People in the present time   That your Memorialists are not only willing but are determind to make the utmost Dispatch in paying the said Tax excepting that part thereof which relates to building Goals &c which when deducted out we are ready to pay our Quota of the remainder of said Tax, and as your Memorialists ever have perused the matter by legal measures they ever mean to do the same so long as there may be the most distant hope of redress and as your Memorialists have none other to look to under God pray the Legislature to take our cause under your wise consideration & order the shire Towns of Bennington & Manchester to Erect & keep the court House & Goals in Repair without Expence to the Other Towns in the county or Grant such other relief as Wisdom Shall Direct   And Nothing but Flagrant injustice & oppression as Stated herein would have Induced your Memorialists to have troubled your Honors at this critical time[2] together with the Regard we ever had & still retain for the peace and Dignity of this State in General & the Honist Citizens thereof in particular so far are we from the most Distant Idea of taking advantage of the time that the preservation of order is the prime motive of your Memorialists in this proceedure — and your Memorialists in duty bound ever pray

Dated March 2nd 1787

John Taylor	James Clark	Moses Doolittel
Fisk Bartlet	Amos Huntington	Jonas Galusha
Stephen Bradley	Ichabod Cross	Ebenezer Dwinell

---

1. For the petition from Bennington in this connection and the action of the Assembly thereon, see p. 14, *ante*.

2. This was a reference to the recent civil disturbances, Shays' rebellion in western Massachusetts and the riots in Rutland and Windsor counties. See *G. and C.*, III, 357–380.

Robart Averill
Bej^m Bradley
Saml Hoit
Chadler Sherwin
Timothy Bradley
Abner Hill
Jeremiah Center
Wiman averill
Benja^m Lewis
Saml Bartlet
Jacob Sherwin
Joseph Bradley
Benj^m Griffis
Lem^l Bradley
Amaziah Everts
John Bradley
Azariah Lee
Edward Everts
mils Braley
Matthew Lewis
Abner Everts
Elijah Stoddard
Gilbert Bradly
Isaac Phelps
Peter Hawley
Samuel Philleps
Jestin Olin
Parker Cole
Joshua Munro
Isaac Matthews
Henry Dyre
George Briggs
Benj Cory Junr
William Darby
Asa Burnham
Benj^a Dyre

Masha Martain
John Olin
John Edgburt
Simeon Martain
Isaac Spencer
Elijah L Botons
Nathan Leonard
Bliss Willoughby
Jacob Galusha
David Galusha
Dan^el Bacon
Wheeler Martin
Roger Darbe
Thomas King
Samuel Huntington
Elijah Fuller
Hosea Fuller
James Sweet
Joshua Briggs
Timothy Barnum
Solomon Fuller
Simeon Prentice
Peter Lawrence
Jonathan House
Jeremiah Huntington
Nathan Huntington
Nathan Wheeler
Elijah Blodgett
Hail Mason
Charles Spencer
John Millington
Nicoles wever
Elazer Ston
Peter Mateson
Abiather Wald
Bethuel Cole

Gideon Orton
Ebenezer Willoughby
Silas Squier
Uriah Stone
Ichabod Orton
Amos Galusha
Thomas Warren
Peleg Matteson
Nehemiah Richardson
Thomas Andrew
Judah Warden
Francis Matteson
Samuel Whaley
David mateson
Henry Mattson
Nathan Stone
John Holley
Ephraim Willmarth
James Thornton
Theophilus [Herrinton]
Sinake Spink
Cyperan Downes
Timothy Carpenter
Daniel Smith
Richard Matteson
Ebenezer Smith
John Lewis
Ruben Ellis
William Herinton
Samuel Mateson
John Buck Jr
Ebenezer Harris
Bigelow Lawrence
Peter Wright
Wm Ward

— & —

Memorial of John Taylor & 113 others in Shaftsbury & Sunderland.
Filed 6th March 1787 —
. . .*

— & —

A. J.: *Read and referred to a committee to join a committee from the Council, 6 March '87, S. P. of Vt., III (III), 318. C. J.: *Committee appointed to join Assembly committee, 6 March '87, G. and C., III, 136.

FOR STATE PURCHASE OF ACCOUNT BOOKS IN SETTLEMENT OF TREASURER'S ACCOUNTS
xvii, 310

To the Honorable the General Assembly of the State of Vermont Conveaned in Bennington

The Representation & Request of Ira Allen Humbly Sheweth. That Notwithstanding the Misfourtunes of Sickness &c Since the Rising of the Assembly in October last as mentioned in my address of Feby 21st 1 Mr Knickerbaccor in Addition to Discharging the Duties of the office In Persuance to a Resolution of the Honorable House in Octr last,[2] has made Verry Considerable Progress towards Copying & footing Accounts for a Settlement, But the mode dopted is attended with Uncommon Trouble as the State on thier Part are not Ready for a final Settlement as they have not Closed accounts with Commissaries &c —

Therefore in Order for a Settlement for the Security of the Public & myself Duplicate Books &c must be made out, Copying the Books Papers &c in the Office must Require time & attention, Such Books being for the Immediate use of the State & Probably not to be had Short of Albany ought to be Purchased by the State, have therefore to Request that the State would furnish Books or Cash to Purchas Books for the aforesaid Purposes, Could this Small Request be Complyed with, In one month after the Receipt of Such Books Duplicates might be made of Books &c sufficient to Inable Judge Mattox [Mattocks] to Discharge the Duties of the office,[3] & in one month more a Settlement might be Compleated & State thereof Published for the Purusal of the Good People of the State, Such a Measure might Prove Verry usefull to the State at this Time & I wish some Honorable measures might be adopted to Accomplish So Desirable an End, & the more so as I am about to dispose of my seat at Sunderland & move all my Effects to Onion River, & wish not to have the Charge of any Books or Papers that In safty to the Public & myself Can be Transfered to such Person or Persons as have or may be appointed to Receive them —

with due respect

I have the Honer

to be your Honers

most obedient

Hum^ble Servt

Ira Allen

Bennington March 3^d 1787

— & —

Representation of Ira Allen Esqr

— & —

A. J.: Read and consideration thereof postponed until opening of House in afternoon, 8 March '87, *S. P. of Vt.,* III (III), 322.

---

1. For this representation, see p. 332, *ante.*

2. Presumably this is a reference to the act passed 31 Oct. '86 for transfer of the Treasurer's papers from Ira Allen to the new treasurer (*Ms. Laws of Vt.,* I, 565–566).

3. Samuel Mattocks was elected treasurer to succeed Ira Allen 13 Oct. '86 (*S. P. of Vt.,* III (III), 220).

FOR A TAX ON LAND TO BUILD ROADS AND BRIDGES
xvii, 311

To the Honourable the General Assembly of the State of Vermont Whom are to convene at Newbury in Sᵈ State on the second Thursday of October 1787
The Prayer and Petition of Amos Woodard Stephen Holt and George Martin of Pittsfield in the County of Rutland Humbly Sheweth — Whereas the Proprietors and inhabitants of the Township of Chittenden and County aforesaid through their Neglect and Delay have omitted making a Convenient Road or Roads in and through Sᵈ Town; as the Road Leading from Rutland to Orange County and the Northerly Part of Windsor County Passes over the mountain by way of white [White] River; also another Leading from the northerly Part of Pittsford Which falls into the Road aforesaid on the mountain or near the Height of Land in Sᵈ Chittenden. The roads in Sᵈ Town Require Great labour and fatigue; which if completed must be attended with much cost and Difficulty — We therefore earnestly Request and Pray the Honourable Assembly to Grant a Tax of One Penny on each acre of Land in Sᵈ Chittenden for the Purpose of Building Bridges and making Roads as Your Honours — in Wisdom may think fit, and we as in Duty bound shall ever Pray

Amos Woodard	The Proprietors Committee
Stephen Holt	For the townships of Pittsfield &
George Martin	Hancock to inspect the Roads and Lands

P.S The Settlers about White River are under Necessity of Going to Rutland across the mountain for many Necessarys which is attended with much Danger

— & —

The Prayer and Petition of
Amos Woodard
Stephen Holt
George Martin
Entered
Filed 15ᵗʰ August 1787 —
. . . *

— & —

A. J.: *Read and dismissed 15 Oct. '87, S. P. of Vt., III (IV), 17:[1]

FOR EXEMPTION FROM A TAX FOR BUILDING A HOUSE OF WORSHIP
xvii, 312

To the honᵇˡᵉ General Assembly of the State of Vermont to convene at Newbury in Sᵈ State on the second Thursday of Octʳ next.
The petition of the subscribers Inhabitants of the Township of Chester in

---

1. For a petition presented at this session by the inhabitants and proprietors of Chittenden seeking a similar tax, see p. 363, post. This petition was granted.

S^d State formed into a regular Baptist Society

Humbly Sheweth.

That your petitioners have been formed into a regular Baptist Society for near a Year past have setled a Gospel Minister in said Society and have agreed to erect a house for divine worship in said Chester   We your hon^{rs} Petitioners consider Ourselves not holden by Law to erect any Place of Public Worship in s^d Chester except for ourselves and for those that may Join with us in Religious Worship.

Your Petitioners consider the late Act of Assembly pased at Bennington February last (Impowering Jabez Sargeant Junr Amos Gile & Daniel Ranney to lay a Tax of One penny on Each Acre of Lands in said Chester except public rights &c. for the purpose of Erecting a building in said Chester by the name of a Town house altho' designed for Public or Social Worship.)[1] a Violation of the third Article of the bill of Rights of our happy Constitution[2] and an Infringment on our Religious Sentiments, we mean to worship Deity according to the dictates of our own Consciences Regulated by the word of God, said Tax is to be rais'd for the purpose of Erecting a house of Worship for a Different denomination of Christians to Worship in and [Cost?] a Minor part of the Township of Chester

Your Petitioners therefore humbly prays, that your honours would take our Case and Situation under your wise and serious Consideration and pass an Act or Law to Abrogate said Act for levying said Tax so far as it respects the persons or Property of your Petitioners, or such other way grant relief to your Petitioners in the premises as your honours in your great Wisdom shall Judge just and Constitutional and your honours Petitioners as in Duty bound shall ever pray

Chester August 31^t 1787

Signed by order and in behalf
of said Society —

65 Male persons freeholders

Tho. Chandler ⎫ Select
Neh. Field   ⎬ men of
Elias Watkins ⎭ Chester
Thos Chandler Moderator
Neh. Field — Clerk —
to said Society

— & —

Petition of the Baptist Society in Chester
Filed 13th Oct^r [1787]
. . .*

— & —

A. J.: *Read and referred to next session, petitioners being given leave to bring in a bill suspending the tax and being directed to serve the committee levying the tax with a copy of this petition, 13 Oct. '87, *S. P. of Vt.,* III (IV), 9; bill suspending tax read and accepted and sent to Council, 16 Oct. '87, *Ibid,* III (IV), 19; bill, having been concurred in by Council, passed into law, 17 Oct. '87, *Ibid,* III (IV), 23;[3] petition read as referred from last session, and referred to next session, 15 Oct. '88, *Ibid,* III (IV), 81.[4] *C. J.:* Act repealing act levying

---

1. For the petition requesting this tax and the action taken thereon, see p. 335, *ante,* including note.

2. See *G. and C.,* I, 93–94.

3. For this act, see *Ms. Laws of Vt.,* II, 192. It suspended the collection of the tax "until the rising of the Assembly at their Session in October next."

4. In view of the terms of the act of suspension (note 3, *supra*) this action reimposed the tax and was tantamount to a dismissal of the petition.

a tax on Chester read and concurred in, *G. and C.*, III, 149.[1]

FOR A TAX ON LAND TO BUILD ROADS AND BRIDGES
xvii, 338

To the Honourable General Assembly of the State of Vermont, to be holden at Newberry [Newbury] in Said State on the Second Thursday of October AD 1787 —

The petition of the Inhabitants of the Township of Hubbarton [Hubbardton] Humbly Sheweth —

That the Said Inhabitants of Hobouton Notwith Standing Most of them Have Newly Encountered the Difficulties of Setling a New Country, in Which their Time and Tallants are Wanted to Procure the Common Necessaries of Life for themselves and Families — have Exerted themselves to the utmost Stretch of their abilities to Make and Clear Roads through this Mountainous Township —

That they Still labour under Insurmountable Difficulties and Inbarrasments through their Badness —

That they are few in Number and Thinly Setled which Augments their Distress, and that unless They Can Draw Some assistance from the Gentlemen who are Nonresident Proprietors They Fear their Difficulties will Increase —

To Which we Concieve those Gentlemen will not Object as they have never been Called on for any Proprietors Tax, and as the Worth of their Lands will Rise in Proportion to the Encouragement for Settlement —

They Beg therefore that Your Hon^{rs} will Grant a Tax of Two pence p^r Acre on all Lands in this Township Not Exempt by Law for making & repairing Roads & Bridges in said Township Or Otherwise Grant Relief as You in Your Wisdom Shall See fit —

And your petitioners as in Duty Bound Shall Ever Pray —

John Selleck	⎰ Proprietors	David Hickok	Elisha Walker
James Church	⎬	Benjamin Hickok	John Rumsey
Nathan Rumsey	⎱ Commite	Uriah Hickok	Jeremiah Rumsey
		Abner Ashley	Ja^s Whelpley
		William Spaulding	Nathan Hoit

— & —

Inhabitants of [Hubbarton] Petition
Filed 12th Octr 1787
. . .*

— & —

A. J.: *Read and referred to a committee, 12 Oct. '87,[2] *S. P. of Vt.*, III (IV),

---

1. The Council record is inaccurate here. The act suspended the tax but did not repeal the law providing for it. See notes 3 and 4, p. 350, *ante*.

2. The Assembly journal includes no record of this Hubbardton petition under this date. However, it does list a similar one from Castleton. This entry was doubtless a clerical error, since there is no further record of any such petition from Castleton at this session. The entry on the manuscript petition has the document referred to the committee named in the journal as considering the Castleton petition. Furthermore, other petitions of this sort are referred to this committee as "appointed on Hubbardton petition". The word Castleton in the journal should therefore read Hubbardton.

8; *report of committee recommending that petition be granted provided that a new road be made through the west part of the town, read and accepted, and leave given to bring in a bill accordingly, 15 Oct. '87, *Ibid*, III (IV), 14; bill read and accepted and sent to Council, 17 Oct. '87, *Ibid*, III (IV), 21; bill, having been concurred in by Council passed into law, 17 Oct. '87, *Ibid*, III (IV), 23.[1] *C. J.*: Act read and concurred in, 17 Oct. '87, *G. and C.*, III, 150.

FOR A LOTTERY TO BUILD A BRIDGE
xvii, 313

To the Honorable the General Assembly to be convened at New bury [Newbury] in Oct[r] next —

The petition of Abel Thompson and Gideon Spencer of Ferrisburgh [Ferrisburg] in the County of Addison Humbly Sheweth —

That the Honorable Legislature saw fit Some time since to lay a Tax of one penny on each [*acre*] of land in Said Ferrisburgh to build one half of a bridge over Otter Creek at New Haven falls[2] that the petitioners undertook for the tax to build said bridge that they accordingly undertook and nearly compleated said bridge that before it could be possibly compleated it was carried away by an uncommon flood & that as they agreed to build and compleate the bridge for the tax, and a number of the proprietors think the petitioners holden to compleate the bridge — And as it is of the utmost consequence Not only to the Inhabitants but the State at large that Said bridge Should be built — they therefore Most Humbly pray that your Honors would grant the petitioners leave to raise the Sum of £ 120 Lawful money by a lottery, to rebuild Such part of Said bridge as was carried away by the flood and we as in duty bound Shall ever pray —

Abel Thompson
Gideon Spencer

Ferrisburgh Sept[r] 20th 1787

— & —

Abel Thompson Gid[n] Spencers Petition for a Lottery —
Entered
Filed 15th Oct[r] 1787 —
. . .*

— & —

A. J.: *Read and granted, and leave given to bring in a bill accordingly, 15 Oct. '87, *S. P. of Vt.*, III (IV), 13; resolved that petitioners be empowered to raise £120 by lottery accordingly, giving bonds for the performance of their trust, and that the state be in no wise accountable for the lottery, 15 Oct. '87, *Ibid*, III (IV), 17.

---

1. For this act, see *Ms. Laws of Vt.*, II, 191-192.
2. For the act authorizing this tax and for the petition which occasioned it, see p. 290, *ante*, including notes.

FOR RELEASE FROM DEBTS
xvii, 314

To the Hon¹ the Gen¹ Assembly of the State of Vermont to be convened at Nebury [Newbury] the Second Thursday of Octr 1787 —
 The Petition of Jonathan Child of Essex in the County of Addison humbly Sheweth —
 That in consequence of his having Served the United States during the late War in the Capacity of Purchising Commis^{er} & this State two years in the same Capacity — & by reason of the depreciation of the paper Currency of this & the United States he has been obliged out of his private Interest, to discharge those Debts, which were contracted for the Benefit of the [public] & by this means is unfortunately ⟨unable to pay his Debts⟩ rendered insolvent & brought to poverty & indigence — And is in his Advanced Age obliged to flee from his family & home to avoid the demands of his Creditors, & a loathsome Goal — your Petitioner therefor humbly prays, your honors to take his Case under your consideration and point out Some way to releive your Petitioner, who stands free & willing to deliver up Bona fide, all his Estate both real & personal to satisfy his Creditors, under such Restrictions & directions as your honors in your Wisdom shall direct & your Petitioner will ever pray —
Essex Sepr 20th 1787   Jon^a Child

— & —

Petition of Jon^a Child
Fild Octr 25th 1787
. . .*

— & —

 A. J.: *Read and referred to a committee to join a committee from the Council, 25 Oct. '87, *S. P. of Vt.*, III (IV), 48; *report of committee recommending that petitioner have two years and one month to settle his business and that he be granted protection from his creditors for that term, read and accepted, and leave given to bring in a bill accordingly, 25 Oct. '87, *Ibid*, III (IV), 50; bill brought in according to leave, read and dismissed, 26 Oct. '87, *Ibid*, III (IV), 51.¹ *C. J.:* *Committee appointed to join Assembly committee, 25 Oct. '87, *G. and C.*, III, 155.

FOR A TAX ON LAND TO BUILD A BRIDGE AND REPAIR ROADS
xvii, 315

To the Honourable the General Assembly of the State of Vermont — The petition of a number of the inhabitants of the Town of Norwich humbly sheweth that the Traveling back and forth from the Counties Windsor and Orange is much impeeded & at Certain Seasons of the year rendered quite impracticable within the State for want of a bridge across the River called Ompompanoosick [Ompompanoosuc] near the house of Capt Hezekiah Johnson in S^d Norwich & that the building a

---

 1. For a new petition from Jonathan Child presented to the Assembly 13 Oct. '89 and the action taken thereon, see *S. P. of Vt.*, III (IV), 130.

bridge across S^d River at or near S^d place would be of very great publick utilety in accommodating the Supreme Court & their attendants when riding the Circuits & other officers of State and also great numbers of the good subjects of S^d State who necessarily travel up & down Connecticut River & who now for the want of a bridge at S^d place are at Certain Seasons of the year Obliged to go out of the State Cross Connecticut River and travel a number of miles round to transact their business —

your petitioners therefore pray your honours that a tax may be Granted of two pence on Each acre of land in the town of Norwich except Public Rights and the Same Committed to the management of the Selectmen of S^d town or Such other persons as your honours Shall appoint to be apropriated to the use of Building S^d Bridge and making Rods And your petitioners as in Duty bound Shall ever pray Dated Sep^t 21st 1787

Hezekiah Goodrich	Cornelius Gilbert	Elisha Waterman
David Goodrich	James Crary	Humfry Ball
Jer^h Hedges	Josiah Goodrich J^{ur}	Exp^r Freeman
Hez^h Johnson	Gorshon Bartlett	Seth Morse
Paul Brigham	Elliott Bartlett	David Hebbard
Samuel Brown	Moses Bartlett	Elihu Baxter
Nath^{el} Levey	Jonathan Bartlett	Saml Hutcherson
Daniel Waterman	John Goodrich	Timothy Bush
Samuel Waterman	Peter Thacher	Timothy Smith
Elijah Burnam	Christopher Huntington	Josiah Goodrich
John Slafter	Elijah waterman	Francis Smalley
Moses Pearson	John waterman	Silvenes Owen
Joseph Wood	John Burnap	Seth Johnson

— & —

Petition of the Inhabitants of Norwich
Entered
Filed 13th Octr 1787
. . .*

to the honourable General Assembly Now Sitting Your Committee to whom was Refered the consideration of the within petition Report it as their oppinion that 2 pence on the acre of the lands in Norwich be granted for the purpose of build bridges and Repairing Roads under the Care of the Select men of Norwich
Th^{os} Jewett for Commit

— & —

A. J.: *Read and referred to a committee, 13 Oct. '87, S. P. of Vt., III (IV), 9-10; report of committee recommending that petition be granted, read and accepted, and leave given to bring in a bill accordingly, 19 Oct. '87, Ibid, III (IV), 30; bill read and accepted and sent to Council, 24 Oct. '87, Ibid, III (IV), 43; bill, having been concurred in by the Council, passed into law, 25 Oct. '87, Ibid, III (IV), 51.[1] C. J.: Act read and concurred in, 24 Oct. '87, G. and C., III, 154.

---

1. For this act, see Ms. Laws of Vt., II, 203-204.

FOR A TAX ON LAND TO BUILD ROADS AND BRIDGES
xvii, 316

To the honourable the general assembly of the State of Vermont to be Convened att NewBurry [Newbury] on the Second thursday of October next —

Your petitioners Beg Leave to Shew that the Scituation of the Town of Saltash[1] at present is Exstreamly Deficult for want of Roads bilt for traviling and as thare is two Roads that pass through Said Town from the East to the west Side of the Green mounting [mountain] of Verrey Considerable use to the public which wants Large Sums of money Expended on them to make them fit for public use and the Town is but newly Settled and its inhabitants are but few at presents and not four handed which Renders it not posable for them to make and keep Said Roads in Repaire and maintain other nessarrary Roads and Bridges in Said Town —

Tharefore your petteioners Hombly pray the Honourable General assembly to take your peticioners Destressed Surcomstances under your wese Consideration and grant them Releaf by granting a tax of two pence on the acres on all the Lands in Said Town Except public Rights or grant them Releaf Som other way as your honours in your Wisdom Shall See Best and your peticioners as in Duty Bound Shall Ever pray

Saltash Sep^t ye 24 Day 1787

Signed in behalf of Said Town

Jacob Wilder
Gotham Wilder
Ephraim Moor
R. Wheeler Wilder
Paul Sawyer
Asa Wheeler
Jacob Sawyer
John Hewitt
John Coolidge
Nathan Jones Jun
Nathan Jones

John Mudge
George Hewitt
Henery Hudgeskins
Samuel Page
James Priest
Moses Priest
Adam Brown
James Otis Prentice
John Taylor
James Priest Ju^r
Nathanel Priest

Saltash Octr 8th 1787

Att a Meeting held in S^d Town Voted Jacob Wilder Collector John Hewitt Henry Hodgkins & R Whelar Wilder a Committee for Laying out S^d Roads

John Hewitt Moderator of S^d Meeting

— & —

Saltash Petition for Land Tax
[Filed] Octr 13th 1787
Octr 13th 1787 Read & Granted

Attest Ros^l Hopkins Clerk[2]

— & —

A. J.: Bill empowering persons therein named to levy a tax of 2^d on each acre in Saltash, read and accepted, and sent to Council, 25 Oct. '87, S. P. of Vt., III (IV) 48; bill, having been concurred in by Council, passed into law, 25 Oct.

---

1. Now Plymouth. See S. P. of Vt., II (Vermont Charters), 345.
2. This action was, of course, taken by the Assembly, although there is no record of it in the journal. Roswell Hopkins was clerk of that body.

'87, *Ibid*, III (IV), 51.[1] *C. J.*: Act read and concurred in, 25 Oct. '87, *G. and C.*, III, 155.

FOR THE DIVISION OF A TOWN
xvii, 317, 318 [2]

To the Honorable the General Assembly of the State of Vermont to be Conven:d at Newbury on thursday the Eleventh Day of October Next A Petition of the inhabitants of Wardsborough [Wardsboro] in Windham County Humbly Sheweth Where as the Town of Wardsborough is near Nine miles in Length & Six miles in Bredth & a mountain Near the Center of S^d Town that makes it inconvenient for us to meate togather to Act on any mater that Conserns the Town We their Fore pray your Honours to Take our matter under your Wise Consideration & make an Equel Division in S^d Town that We may Not Remain in So an inconvenient Situation & as your petitioners in Duty Bound Shall Ever pray —

Sign:d

Wardsborough Septembar 25th 1787

Reuben Chittenden &
Nathan Cobb   106, others

At a leagal Town meeting Holden in Wardsborough [for the perpus of Deviding S^d Town] on the 25th of September 1787 — after Makeing Choyce of Aaron Hudson Esqr as Moderator by a large Majority of Persons at Said meeting Voted to divide the Town of Wardsborough Exactly in the Senter from North to South by leangth of Chains. —
A True Coppy, Test — Paul Davis, Town Clerk
[of Wardsborough]

⟨The Honourable the General Assembly of⟩ the State of Vermont to be holden at Newbury on thirsday the eleventh day of October next. The Petitionars of the inhabitants of Wardsborough Humbly Sheweth, whereas the Situation of the Town is Such as makes it inconveniant for us to assemble for Publick business, or Sotial warship, we theirfore pray your Honours to make Such Decisions as you in your wisdom shall see fit as will appear by a Plan Shown to your Honours and as your Petitionors as in duty bound Shall ever Pray

Ethan A K Allen	John Ramsdil	Ebenezer Bartlet
Elijah Baldwin	Asa Fay	Philip Jurden
Silas Wright	Joseph Fairbanks	Joseph Briggs
Paul Davis	Daniel Tidd	Gamaliel Ellis
Lemuel Johnson	Elijah Fairbank	Wm Parkhurst J^r
James Slade	Aaron Draper	Roger Birchard
Philip [Newel?]	Robert Ramsdell	Joseph Chamberlain

1. For this act, see *Ms. Laws of Vt.*, II, 204.
2. Although there are two separate documents pertaining to the prayer of Wardsboro for division of the town, it appears that they constitute substantially only one petition. The one hundred and five names signed to the second document were doubtless the one hundred and six referred to in the first, the difference being due to a miscount.

Ebenezer Allen
Lemuel Brayley
John Wallis
James Blashfield
John Stacy
John Evarts
Edwd Hathiewary
Daniel Warner
Samuel Davis
Shubil Baldwin
Asahel Woodcock
Jonathan Warner
[Steven] Worrin
Jacob Slade
Gid^n Roy
Thomas Jewett
Uzziel Putnam
Elijah Stearns
Hinsdel Hammon
Pearley Fairbank
Noah Sherman
Abner Slade
Nathan Ganson
William Sears
Aaron Thompson
Ebenezer Sears
John Holbrook
Joseph Twitchel

John Ramsdell, J^{nr}
Thomas Woodward
Stephen Perry
Simeon Hammon
Jesse Chapin
Daniel Chapin
Hiram Newell
Levie Newell
Judah Moffat
Thomas Simpson
Barna^{bs} Thurber
Samuel [Lezieur?]
[. . .] [. . .]
[. . .] [. . .]
Aaron [Clark?]
Abner Holbrook
Nathaniel [Lutts?]
David Crowninshield
Elkanah Woodcock
[Paul] Sherman
James Wallace
Joseph Porter
Richard Crowninshield
John Rice
Silas Holbrook
William Stanclift
Elijah Strickland
Dudley Wood

Richard Laten
Nathein Wood
Joab Johnson
Constant Johnson
Barnard Convis
Thomas M C Daniels
Lemuel Blackmer
Solomon Blackmer
Luther Johnson
William Dodge
Daniel Baldwin
Benjamin Nichols
Wm Strickland
Edward [badger?]
James Westurn
Daniel Mathews
Ephraim Averill
Reuben Ned
Joseph Rider
Wm Parkhurst
Thos Nichols
Amos Parkhurst
James Peirce
Jonathan Nichols
John Hamilton
James Nims
Seth Forster
Seth Johson

— & —

Wardsboro Petition for dividing the town —
. . .*

To the Honorable General Assembly Now Sitting your Com^{tt} to whoom was refered the Consideration of the Petition, of the Inhabitants of the town of Wardsboro beg Leave to report, that on Enquiry, we find the facts set up in S^d Petition to be true, & that the prayer of the Petition ought So far to be granted, as to Divide S^d town of Wardsborough into two Distinct Destricts, Each to have, & retain all the Priveleges of Incorporated towns as by Law Established, Except, that both Destricts Shall have the privelege of one representative only. & that the Petitioners have Liberty to bring in A bill Accordingly
Newbury Octr 19th 1787   Phinehas Freeman for Com^{tt}
In General Assembly Oct. [15 1788]
    The within report was read & accepted & leave given for a bill to be bro^t in accordingly

attest Ros Hopkins Sec^y

— & —

A. J.: *Read and referred to a committee, 17 Oct. '87, S. P. of Vt., III (IV), 22; *report of committee read and referred to next session for consideration, 22 Oct. '87, Ibid, III (IV), 38–39; bill dividing the town into two distinct

districts read and accepted and sent to Council, 15 Oct. '88, *Ibid*, III (IV), 80; bill, having been concurred in by Council, passed into law, 18 Oct. '88, *Ibid*, III (IV), 89.[1] *C. J.*: Act read and concurred in, 15 Oct. '88, *G. and C.*, III, 170.

FOR REPEAL OF AN ACT REQUIRING A PAYMENT FROM A TOWN
xvii, 319

To the Honourable General Assembly of the State of Vermont to be Conened at Newbury on the second Thirsday of October next the Pitition and Remonstrance of the Town of Rutland in the County of Rutland Humbly Sheweth to your Honours that they consider themselves greatly Injured by a certain Act of the General Assembly passed at Bennington in Feb[r] last past Intitled an act <directing the Select men of the Town of Rutland to levy a Tax for the purpose therein contained> to enable Gershom Beach of Rutland in the County of Rutland to Receve the sum of forty nine pounds eight shillings & four pence L.M. from the Treasurer of S[d] Rutland[2]

in the first place we say that the Town as a Town never contracted or made any agreement whatsoever with the S[d] Gersham Beach for the service for which the S[d] Tax is directed by S[d] Act to be Levied on the Town of Rutland but that the contract was made by a few Individuals whom we suppose paid nearly the whole sum that was due to the S[d] Gersham & that the present Inhabitants view it very unreasonable oppresive & unjust that they as a Town should be obliged to make good the contracts of those Individuals as they have not many of them ever been in the least benefitted by the S[d] Gershams services & we humbly conceive the Assembly might with as much propriety oblige the Town to make good the private contracts of those or other individuals with others with whom they have or may contract as well as the one made with S[d] Beach 2nd we concive it to be an unconstitutional proceeding in the assembly to judge and determine in causes which are properly cognisable before Courts of Law as most certainly the Demands of M[r] Beach were & if he has a Demand on the Town of Rutland we rather chuse to contest the matter before those courts pointed out by the constitution to determine the Rights of individuals than esewhere [elsewhere] Wherefore we would Humbly implore your Honours to take our case into your wise consideration & repeal the S[d] Act and your Honours petitioners as in duty bound Shall ever pray
Dated at Rutland this 25th day of Sep[t] AD 1787

Sam[el] Williams Agent for the town of
Rutland

To the Sheriff of Rutland County his Deputy or either of the Constables of Rutland in the County of Rutland Greeting — By the Authority of the State of Vermont you are hereby Commanded to Summon the within Named Gersham Beach to appear before the General Assembly to be conven[d] at Newbury on the second Thirsday of Oc[t] next Then & There to Shew cause if any he hath why the prayer

---

1. For this act, see *Acts and Laws, passed by the Legislature of Vermont, at their session at Manchester, the second Thursday of October, 1788*, (Windsor, 1788), 3–4.

2. For the petition of Gershom Beach dated 17 Oct. '86 and the action taken thereon, see p. 266, *ante*, including notes.

of the foregoing Petition Should not be granted Hereof fail not but make return according to Law Dated at Rutland this 25th day of Sep^t AD 1787

Elihue Smith Ju^s [peace?]

Sep^t 28th 1787 then Read the within Sitation in the hearing of the within Named Garsham Beach

Stephen Williams Cons^t

Rutland October the 2 [AD?] 1787 —

Honored Si^r

I was on the 28th of September Last past Served with a Copy of a Petition Prefered by the Town of Rutland to the General Assembly of this State in there October Session [AD?] 1787 at Newbury or About to be Prefered in that thay pray the act to be repealed Inabling me to Recover of Said Town about Fifty pounds, lawful Mony passed at Bennington in Febr^y last past and my Circumstances being Such that it puts it our [out] of my power to procure Such necessary Evidence as will be wanted on my part, I therefore pray Said matter to [be] layed over untill another Session of assembly at which Time I will be able to attend with my witnesses but cannot at this Session my notice being so short and the Distance to my Evidance so grate I am with Esteme Dear S^r your Humble Se^t

Garsham Beach

To the Speaker of the
Honourable General
Assembly of the State of
Vermont. —

— & —

the Petition of the Town of Rutland to repeal Gershom Beach's Act —
Filed 13th Octr 1787 —
Entered
. . .*

— & —

> *A. J.:* Read and ordered to lie on table, 13 Oct. '87, *S. P. of Vt.,* III (IV), 10; *read again and prayer granted, and leave given to bring in a bill accordingly, 13 Oct. '87, *Ibid,* III (IV), 12; bill entitled an act to repeal "an act herein mentioned" read and accepted and sent to Council, 15 Oct. '87 *Ibid,* III (IV), 13; bill, having been concurred in by Council, passed into law, 16 Oct. '87, *Ibid,* III (IV), 20.[1] *C. J.:* Act read and concurred in, 15 Oct. '87, *G. and C.,* III, 148.

FOR AN ACT OF INSOLVENCY
xvii, 320

To the Honourable General Assembly of the State of Vermont to be Conveaned at Newbury on the Second Tuesday of October Next the Petition of Asaph Nichols of Wells in the County of Rutland and State of Vermont Humbly Sheweth to your Honours that your Honours Petitioner Soon after the Commincement of the

---

1. For this act, see *Ms. Laws of Vt.,* II, 190.

late war being willing at that areley [early] Period of life to betake himself to
Some kind of Business that might Render his Services yousefull to himself and
Sociaty and the Marcantill business at that time promising grate Advantages to all
that might be Conserned therein Indused your Honours Petitioner to Enter largely
in the business in pursuing of which your Honours Petitioner was Ablige to make
large Contracts and Verery Considerable Debts with no other Vew at the Time
of Making but punctually and honistley to Discharge the Same but your Petitioner
being one of those unhappy members of Society that has felt the Effects of the
Depresiation of the Several kinds of Paper Currency together with Many other
unavoidable and unhappy Disasters has put it out of the power of your Honours
Petitioner to Discharge his honist Contracts your Honours Petitioner therefore
pray your Honours to Take under Consideration the Case of your Petitioner and
by an act of Legislation order and Determine that your Honours Petitioner Shall
be forever Exonarated and Discharged from all Debts due from him untill this Time
on Delivering up all the Estate of your Petitioner both Real and Personal to the
Youse [use] and benefit of his Creditors in Such away as your honours Shall order
and Direct as your Honour Petitioner thinks that in this way he may again be of
Service to himself famely and Society and as your honours Petitioner In Duty
bound Shall Ever pray
Dated at Wells Sep^t the 27 AD 1787   Asaph Nichols

— & —

the Petition of Asaph Nichols
Entered
Filed 15th Octr 87 —
...*

— & —

A. J.: *Read and dismissed, 15 Oct. '87, *S. P. of Vt.*, III (IV), 14.

FOR A NEW COMMITTEE TO BUILD ROADS
xvii, 321

To the Honor^ble Genl Assembly of the State of Vermont to sett at Newbury on
the 2^d thursday of October Next
The pittition and Remonstrance of the subscribers Humbly Sheweth that
Whareas the honorable Genl Assembly at ther sessions at Rutland in October last
past; —
on a Pittition of the Inhabitant of Brumley¹ & Landgrove did lay a tax of Two
pence on Each Acre in sad townships for the purpose of making and Repairing
Roads in the towns: and did appoint Timothy Lovel Stephen Keys and Asa Utley
a Committee to collect and lay out s^d Tax for the purpose afors^d —²
and whereas the said Committee have for the whole space of a year last past have
neglected the Business of their appointment and the Inhabitants of said Townships,
and such pasingers as have had [Occation] to pass s^d Road have suffered and Busness

---

1. Now Peru. See *S. P. of Vt.*, II (Vermont Charters), p. 273.
2. For this act, see *Ms. Laws of Vt.*, I, 550-551. For the petition which occasioned
it, see p. 267, *ante*.

has ben Impedeed &ccc

your pettitioners therefore pray (for the speedy Effecting said Busness: that Stephen Keys & Asa Utley afor^d be discharged from the afor^d Committe and Capt Jonathan Akins of Manchester and Mr Aaron Dewey of s^d Brumley be appointed to act with Mr Lovel; in the spedy performance of the afor^d purpose and your Pettitioner as in duty bound shall Ever pray &c
Brumley Sep^t the 29th 1787

David Lee Junr	Jonathan [Banadick?]	Thomas Kidder
Aaron Sexton	[Elisha?] Woodard	Thomas Kidder Junr
Andrew Richardson	[George?] Saeton	Benjamin Kidder
Edward Henderson	moses Peray	Clark hide
Stephen Washburn	David Andanson	James Hide
Price Bardslee	Robard Andanson	Amos Alen
John Cole	[Anday?] Andanson	John Lovel
Jacob Odel	John [Boland?]	James [Lock?]
Amos Richardson	James Gillman	Benjamin [Tyler?]
Nathan Richardson Ju^r	James Dewey	John Simons Junr
Nathan Richardson	James Boland	Sam^el Heywood
Wells Richardson	William Bololand	Eben^r Bullard
Dan^el Burriett	Tabor Washburn	Jesse Carlton
Edmond Burritt	Benjamin Vaughan	Artemas Rogers
Simeon Hurd	Richard [Macintire]	Fred. Rogers
Levi Hill	Thomas Bull jun^r	Sam^el Whiting
Joseph Murry	Phelix Menter	Bunker Clark
Sherman Boardman	Ebenezer Hurlbut	Amos Gile
Daniel Coy	John Byrns	Isaac Whitney
Reuben Webb	John Gilbert	Soloman Whitney
Micah judson	Aaron Dewey Junr	John Wit
Gideon Ormsby	Silas Reynolds	James Henson
Nathan [Eastman?]	Benjn Connill	Peter Bruer
Benj [Wintir?]	Josiah Cutis	[Wiles Lues?]
Timothy Mead	Luas Curtis	obediah Crook
Truman Mead	Ephram Reynolds	John Laken
Job Giddings	[Zacheus?] Hurlbut	Benjamin Hudson
James holt	Zachriah Curtis	Elijah Lovell
Nathan Smith	Ephraim Reynolds Junior	Oliver Lovel

— & —

Pet^n of David Lee &c
Filed 15th Octr 1787 —
. . .*

The Honb^le Genl Assembly Now Siting
Your Committee to whom was Refer'd the Consideration of the Petition of David Lee & others Beg leave to Report as follows Viz. that the Facts therein Sit up are Supported & that in the Opinion of your Committee the Former Committee Mentioned in S^d petision ought to be Dismissed & a New one Chosen for the Same purpose

John Shumway for Com^t

Newbury Octr the 17th 1787

— & —

A. J.: *Read and referred to a committee, 15 Oct. '87, *S. P. of Vt.*, III (IV), 16–17; report of committee read and accepted, and leave given to bring in a bill accordingly, 17 Oct. '87, *Ibid*, III (IV), 22–23; bill read and accepted and sent to Council, 26 Oct. '87, *Ibid*, III (IV), 55; bill, having been concurred in by Council, passed into law, 26 Oct. '87, *Ibid*, III (IV), 56.[1] *C. J.:* Act read and concurred in, 26 Oct. '87, *G. and C.*, III, 158.

FOR A TAX ON LAND TO BUILD ROADS AND BRIDGES
xvii, 322

To the Honorable, the General Assembly of the State of Vermont, to be Convened at Newbury on the Second Thursday of October next

The Petition of the Inhabitants of the Town of Hinesburg Sheweth —

That it is necessary much Cost and labour Should be laid out on the public roads and to erect bridges over the Streams in Said town in order to render the roads Passable with any tolerable degree of Safety and Convenience; — much more than the inhabitants are able and under Circumstances to expend, and Support them Selves and families —

Your Petitioners therefore Pray that the General Assembly would lay a tax of two pence on the acre on all the lands in Said Hinesburg, Public rights excepted to be Collected in Such way and manner as the General Assembly in their Wisedom Shall think proper, and to be expended by Said Inhabitants, in making roads and erecting bridges in Said township, as Your Petitioners ever bound in duty pray

Hinesburg September 29th AD 1787

Josiah Steele	Hezekiah Tuttle	Jonathan Marshell
Isaac Lawrance	Jacob mecham	Thomas Butler
Elisha Barber	George McEuen	Nathan [Leavenwoth?]
Elisha Meech	David Hill	Cornelius Holbut
Eliphos Steele	Zolmon Wheeler	

— & —

Hinesburg Petition for a Land Tax
Entered
Filed 12th Oct[r] 1787
. . .*

— & —

A. J.: *Read and referred to a committee, 12 Oct. '87, *S. P. of Vt.*, III (IV), 8; *report of committee recommending that prayer be granted read and accepted, and leave given to bring in a bill accordingly, 15 Oct. '87, *Ibid*, III (IV), 14; bill read and accepted and sent to Council, 22 Oct. '87, *Ibid*, III (IV), 39; *bill, having been returned from Council with amendment that tax be one penny half penny, agreed to and passed into law, 24 Oct. '87, *Ibid*, III (IV), 44.[2] *C. J.:* Act read and returned to Assembly with proposals of amendment, 22 Oct. '87, *G. and C.*, III, 153.

---

1. For this act, see *Ms. Laws of Vt.*, II, 222.
2. For this act, see *Ms. Laws of Vt.*, II, 200.

FOR THE RIGHT TO GIVE A DEED TO LAND PREVIOUSLY PURCHASED FROM AN ESTATE
xxii, 152

To the Honourable Assembly of the State of Vermont the Petition of your Petitioner Humbly Sheweth. that your Petitioner is Administrator on the Estate of Ebenezar Rice Late of Lunenburgh [Lunenburg] Deceas^d and that Said Rice Did on the Eleventh of May one thousand Seven hundred and Eighty three. give to Mr Richard Averit a Bond of one hundred Silver Dollars. for a Deed of one hundred acres of Land in the third Devision of Lots in the town of Lunenburgh. which Said Rice Sold to Said. Richard Averit as your Petitioner Does Declare and Testafy to this Honourable assembly. and that as Mr Richard Averit has not had any Deed of Said Lot of Land your Petitioner would Earnestly Desire and Request that this Honourable Assembly would Grant your Petitioner Permition to give Said averit a Sufficient Deed of Said lot of Land. as is Mentioned in the bond given by Said Rice as is hear Set forth —
And Your Petitioner will Ever Pray —
Lancaster, State Newhamshire [New Hampshire]   Samuel Johnson
Septr 29 — 1787   Administrator on the Estate of
                                                       Ebenzar Rice   Deces^d
the Honourable Assembly
State of Vermont

— & —

Samuel Johnson's Petition
Fild 17th Octr 1787
Entered
The Honourable Assembly of the State of Vermont
. . .*

— & —

A. J.: *Read and referred to a committee, 17 Oct. '87, S. P. of Vt., III (IV), 23; *report of committee recommending that petition be granted, read and accepted, and leave given to bring in a bill accordingly, 18 Oct. '87, Ibid, III (IV), 26; bill read and accepted and sent to Council, 18 Oct. '87, Ibid, III (IV), 26; bill, having been concurred in by Council passed into law, 19 Oct. '87, Ibid, III (IV), 27.[1] C. J.: Act read and concurred in, 18 Oct. '87, G. and C., III, 151.

FOR A TAX ON LAND TO BUILD ROADS AND BRIDGES[2]
xvii, 335

To the Honourable the General Assembly of the State of Vermont Whom are to Convene at Newbury in S^d State on the second thursday of October 1787
The Prayer and Petition Of the Inhabitants Resident and Non Resident proprietors of the Township of Chittenden in the County of Rutland and state aforesaid Humbly

---

1. For this act, see Ms. Laws of Vt., II, 194.
2. For a previous petition to the same effect, see p. 349, ante.

Sheweth Whereas the few inhabitants of the S^d Chittenden being unable to make a Convenient and passable Road through S^d Township are under Necessity of taking this method for the Public utility and advantage[,] as we have the Highest sense of the Legislative Power and authority and their wishes and Desires for the Progress Rise and Growth of this uncultivated Land we therefore take this very Legal and approved way for the Completing and finishing the necessary Roads in S^d Town The Road that Leads from Rutland to the County of Orange and Northerly Part of Windsor County is through S^d Chittenden which is Eight or Nine miles in Length also another Leading from the Northerly part of Pittsford through S^d Town to White River which Requires great Labour and Service; we Therefore Earnestly Request the Honourable Assembly to Grant a Tax of one Penny on each acre (public rights excepted) for the Purpose of Building Bridges and making Convenient Roads as in Your wisdom may appear Consistent and Lawful with your Warrant Directed to the Collector Mr Nathl Ladd in S^d Chittenden by our faithful Agent Mr Danl Marsh and We the Subscribers as in Duty Bound shall Ever pray

Nath^{el} Ladd	Reuben Cooley	Andrew Barnard
Jonathan Dike	Gideon Dike	John Bancroft
Jabez Edgerton	Jabez Olmsted	Dan Barnard
Gideon Cooley	Moses Bartlett	Abel Russell
Solomon Taylor .	Jeffery Amherst Booge	Thomas Keeler
Nathan Nelson	Gershom Beach	Sam^{el} Harrison
Noah Brown		

— & —

Petition of Inhabit^s & Proprietors of Chittenden —
Entered
Filed 12th Octr 1787.
. . .*

— & —

> A. J.: *Read and referred to a committee, 13 Oct. '87, S. P. of Vt., III (IV), 8; *report of committee recommending that petition be granted, read and accepted, and leave given to bring in a bill accordingly, 15 Oct. '87, Ibid, III (IV), 13–14; bill read and accepted and sent to Council, 25 Oct. '87, Ibid, III (IV), 49; bill, having been concurred in by Council, passed into law, 26 Oct. '87, Ibid, III (IV), 53.[1] C. J.: Act read and concurred in, 26 Oct. '87, G. and C., III, 157.

FOR A TAX ON LAND TO BUILD ROADS AND BRIDGES
xvii, 343

To the Honourable the General Assembly of the State of Vermont who are to convene at Newbury in Said State on the second thursday of October 1787 —
The Prayer and petition of Joseph Crary of Pittsford in the County of Rutland and State of Vermont

---

1. For this act, see Ms. Laws of Vt., II, 225–226.

Humbly Sheweth

Whereas the few inhabitans of the Township of Philadelphia[1] being unable to make convenient and Passable Roads in S^d town; Therefore your Honors humble petitioner being directed and Requested (by many of the Non resident Proprietors of Philadelphia together with several of the inhabitants on White River Viz Stockbridge Pittsfield Rochester &c) to make application to the Honorable Assembly for a Tax of one penny half penny to be granted on each acre of land for the purpose of Building Bridges Clearing and making Roads &c — Your Honors petitioner begs leave to inform that there is one Road in a particular manner wanting which would be of Essential service to travellers, and would have a tendency to much increase the advancement and settlement of the Country (Viz) it would begin in the southerly part of Leicester or Northerly part of Brandon, and passing over the Height of Land through Philadelphia would fall into the Road in Rochester on White River, which leads from Windsor to Kingston[2] There is also a number of cross Roads Wanting to accommodate the inhabitants and settlers on Otter Creek which would fall into the One first mentioned. —

And would be of great service and advantage for those whom have Occasion to Pass or Repass from Connecticut River to the Lake — Your honors Petitioner having Represented the matter agreeable to the direction from S^d Propriety — Therefore humbly Requests your Honors (to take the foregoing into your wise and prudent Consideration and for) concurrence and approbation as in Duty bound

　　　　　　　　　Shall ever pray

　　　　　　　　　　　　　　　　　{　in behalf of The Proprietors
　　　　　　　　Joseph Crary　{　　　　of Philadelphia

NB

　　　The Road which is Required from Brandon to Rochester Would be 9 or 10 miles in Length and the other cross Roads Which are wanting would amount to the same Distance, beside a number of Bridges in the S^d Philadelphia is the Reason of the Request for a penny half penny on an acre —

— & —

To The Honourable Genl Assembly State Vermont
Petition of Joseph Crary of Pittsford
Filed 15th Octr 1787 —
Entered
...*

— & —

A. J.: *Read and dismissed, 15 Oct. '87, S. P. of Vt., III (IV), 17.

FOR A TAX ON LAND TO BUILD BRIDGES
xvii, 346

To the honorable Genl Assembly of the State of Vermont now sitting at Newbury in said State

---

1. Now part of Chittenden. See S. P. of Vt., II (Vermont Charters), 334.
2. Now Granville. See S. P. of Vt., II (Vermont Charters), 299.

The Petition of the Subscribers on behalf of the inhabitants of the Town of Wells in the County of Rutland humbly sheweth that the Inhabitants of said Town labour under many inconveniences for want ⟨of public roads &⟩ bridges in said Town which they are unable to make without the assistance of the Legislature — your Petitioner therefore prays your honors to Grant a tax of one penny on each acre of land in said town (Publick lands excepted[)] to be applied to the purposes aforesaid under such restrictions as your honors shall think proper and your petitioner as in Duty bound shall ever pray

    Signed in behalf of said town

Samuel Lathop
Joseph Button   Select men
Abna Cone

— & —

Petⁿ of Wells for a Land tax —
Filed 16th Octr 1787 —
Entered
. . .*

— & —

A. J.: *Read and referred to a committee, 16 Oct. '87, S. P. of Vt., III (IV), 19; *report of committee recommending that petition be granted, read and accepted, and leave given to bring in a bill accordingly, 19 Oct. '87, Ibid, III (IV), 30; bill read and accepted and sent to Council, 25 Oct. '87, Ibid, III (IV), 49; bill, having been concurred in by Council, passed into law, 25 Oct. '87, Ibid, III (IV), 51.[1] C. J.: Act read and concurred in, 25 Oct. '87, G. and C., III, 155.

FOR A TAX ON LAND TO BUILD ROADS AND MILLS
xvii, 352

To the General Assembly of the State of Vermont convened at Newbury in said State.

    The Petition of the Subscriber, agent for the Proprietors of the Township of Ludlow, humbly sheweth, that the said proprietors did between two & three years ago grant or vote a tax on each Original Right in said Ludlow, (publick Rights excepted) which tax has been collected & expended in clearing out a Road through said Township & in erecting of Bridges, agreable to the design in voting said tax; to the great benefit of the publick, as it opened a better & more direct Course to Otter Creek, so called; which doubtless many Gentlemen in this Assembly can testify. It has greatly promoted the settlement of said Ludlow which went on very slowly previous to the clearing out of the said Road.

And whereas there is great necessity of repairing & mending the said Road, & the laying out of other Roads in Said Township, of erecting Mills, of running Sundry lines, &c. And whereas there are a considerable number of Residents in said Ludlow, & others who expect soon to become settlers therein, & who are not proprietors, but are willing to assist in bearing the charge of the aforesaid purposes:

---

1. For this act, see Ms. Laws of Vt., II, 207.

Therefore, as Agent of the aforesaid proprietors, in their behalf, & agreable to their vote, Your petitioner humbly prays that this Honorable Assembly would, take the premises under their Serious consideration & grant a tax of one penny per acre on all the taxable land in said Township of Ludlow for the purposes as herein before mentioned, And as in duty bound your petitioner shall ever pray

Asaph Fletcher

— & —

Asaph Fletcher's Pet[n]
Entered
Filed 17th Oct[r] 1787
. . *

to the honourable General assembly Now Sitting Your Committee to whom was Referd the within Petition Report as their oppinion that the prayer of the petition be Granted So far as to Grant one peny on Each acre for the sole purpose of Clearing Repairing and laying out [. . .][1] township of ludlow under the direction of Salmon dutton asaph fletcher and Jesse Gilbert

Tho[s] Jewett for Committee

— & —

> *A. J.:* *Read and referred to a committee, 17 Oct. '87, *S. P. of Vt.*, III (IV), 23; report of committee recommending that petition be granted, read and accepted, and leave given to bring in a bill accordingly, 19 Oct. '87, *Ibid*, III (IV), 30; bill for laying a one penny tax to build roads and bridges read and accepted and sent to Council, 24 Oct. '87, *Ibid*, III (IV), 44; bill, having been concurred in by Council, passed into law, 25 Oct. '87, *Ibid*, III (IV), 51.[2]
> *C. J.:* Act read and concurred in, 25 Oct. '87, *G. and C.*, III, 155.

FOR THE LOCATION OF TWO TOWNS ACCORDING TO CHARTER
xvii, 359

To the [Hon[ble]] General Assembly of the State of Vermont
    The Petition & Remonstrance of the Proprietors of Enosburgh [Enosburg] & Berkshire Humbly set forth, that they have been long prevented from making settlement not being able to asertain the bounds of said Town by reason of the Interference of Hungerford[3] Smithfield[4] and Fairfield, and as we understand your honors are Determined to alter their bounds and lay them in proper form & that a Committee has made report of their opinion,[5] and Diliverd in a plan by which

---

1. Probably three words illegible. The intention of the report appears to have been the limitation of the expenditure of the tax to building roads and bridges. This limitation excluded the use of the funds for erecting mills or running lines.
    2. For this act, See *Ms. Laws of Vt.*, II, 205–206.
    3. Now Sheldon. See *S. P. of Vt.*, II (Vermont Charters), 347.
    4. Now part of Bakersfield and Fairfield. See *Ibid*, II, 349.
    5. For a report of a committee on the report of the Surveyor General, presented to the Assembly 20 Oct. '87, see *S. P. of Vt.*, III (IV), 35–37; also *S. P. of Vt.*, IV (*Rep. of Com.*), 46–47. For a similar report presented in Oct. '86, see *Ibid*, IV, 33–34. For a petition which was presented to this session and was also concerned with the shape of these towns, see p. 371, *post*.

we find the Township of Hungerford to extend so far as to remove Berkshire and Enosburgh about Twenty nine miles from the Lake Champlain, Whereas by charter they were to be laid about Twelve miles from said Lake, Your petitioners beg leaiv [leave] to Remonstrate against said Report, as it very Greatly effects their Intret [interest] & will Totally Defeat their Intention of Settlement, we therefore pray your Honors to Establish the aforesaid Towns of Hungerford, Smithfield & Fairfield in such square form as to admit the Towns of Berkshire & Enosburgh affead [sic] Said to remain according to their Grant of Charters, as your Hum^le Petitioners will ever pray.   Roger Enos ⎫ Agents

                                                              Joseph Fay ⎭

— & —

Petition of the Proprietors of Berkshire & Enosburgh
filed Octr 22^d 1787
. . .*

— & —

A. J.: *Read and referred to committee on Surveyor General's report, 22 Oct. '87, *S. P. of Vt.*, III (IV), 39; *report of committee agreeing on the lines of Smithfield, Hungerford and Fairfield read, and resolved accordingly, 26 Oct. '86, *Ibid*, III (IV), 54–55.[1]

FOR EXTENSION OF THE TERM OF OFFICE OF A SHERIFF
xvii, 361

To the honourable General Assembly now Sitting the Petition of Abner Chamberlain late Sherif of the county of orange [Orange] humbly Sheweth that your petitioner in the Execution of his office as Sherif did on the 30th of October last take the bodys fredrick Smith oliver hamlin and Caleb martin by Virtue of Executions ag^t them in favour of Nathan Fisk Esqr of westminster and did keep them in Costody til the 2^d day of November then next at which time by my deputy was Receiv^d a bond in Common form to the Sherif of orange county for the liberties of the prison to the Said prisoners they having mad their Escape previous to any order to your Petitioner to deliver Costody of the prison and prisoners to the present Sherif wherby your petitioner is disabled from prosecuting the bond ag^t the persons bound for the prisoners on account of a Resolve of the honourable assembly then Sitting wherby it was declared that the power of my office as Sherif Should cease on the 1st of Nov^r [2] your petitioner therefore prays that an order of this house may be passed declaring your petitioner to have been the legal Sherif of the county of orange til the 4th day of Novr last past and your petitioner as in duty bound Shall Ever pray

                                                  Abner Chamberlin

— & —

---

1. The full text of the report and resolution are not given on the manuscript petition.
2. For this act, see "An Act limiting the time of holding county offices", passed 24 Oct. '86 (*Acts and Laws, passed by the General Assembly of the State of Vermont, at their stated session, at Rutland, in October, 1786* [Windsor, 1786], 2).

Petition of Abner Chamberlain —
Filed 24th [*October*] 1787 —
. . .*

The Honb^{le} Assembly now sitting —
Your Comt^{ee} to whom was referred the within petition beg leave to Report that
the facts as set up in said petition are true — therefore it is Recommended to this
Honb^{le} Assembly that an act pass this House that no advantages shall be taken
against S^d Chamberlin by Shubal Cross, Caleb Martin, Oliver Hamlin or Fredrick
Smith who signed a bond to said Chamberlin as Sheriff for the liberties of the
prison Dated 2^d day of November 1786. in Consequence of S^d Chamberlin expiring
in office previous to the Date of those bonds — by a special statute of this State
passed Octr 24th 1786 — all which is humbly submitted by Beriah Loomis for
Comt^{ee}

    Oct. 25th 1787
read & dismissed
    attest Ros^l Hopkins Clk

— & —

    A. J.: *Read and referred to a committee, 24 Oct. '87, *S. P. of Vt.*, III (IV),
47.

FOR PROTECTION FROM ARREST FOR DEBT
xvii, 362

To the Honorable Genl Assembly of Vermont now Sitting at Newbury
    The Petition of Jesse Leavenworth of Cabot in the County of Orange humbly
Sheweth that your Petitioner in the Year 1773 by reason of Sundry Misfortunes
failed in Trade in which he had been very largely concerned, and after paying his
Creditors to the utmost extent of his Property he was Still largely in Debt —
During the War your Pet^r again gathered Strength and paid Some part of his old
Debts, and thought himself in a fair way to discharge the Whole when in the Year
1780 your Pet^r lost at Sea eight Sail of Vessels out of Nine in which he was con-
cerned — This Event so far left him without Property, that he was able to pay the
granting fees on not half the Town of Cabot which was granted to him in the
Same Year. — He has been Since that Time improving his New Lands with Such
Success as he thinks insures him the Means of paying all within a Short Time
    But as all his Debts if Sued for must be paid in Money, and as lands in Such
Situation as his will raise very little it is in the Power of any considerable Creditor
to injure the Property of the others and ruin your Pet^r therefore he prays your
Honors to direct Some method to notify his Creditors to Shew Cause at the next
Session of the Assembly why his Person and Property should not be protected
from Arrests for Debts during Such Period as Shall Seem right to ye Hon^{rs} and that
his Person and Property be protected in the Mean time from arrests for Debts due
before the year 1785 or otherwise grant Relief and your Petitioner as in duty
bound shall ever pray —
                            Jesse Leavenworth

— & —

Petition
Jesse Leavenworth
Octr 1787 —
Filed Octr 24th
. . .*

Newbury Octr 24. 1787

Your Com^{ee} having examined the Facts stated in s^d Petition are of opinion they are fully Supported and beg leave to report that it is our Opinion that it is best for the Public, the Pit^r and his Creditors that the Person and Property of the Pet^r should be Exempted from Arests for Debts due for five Years,

All which is submitted
by order of Comm^t

Lem. Chipman

Newbury Octr 25 1787

To the Honorable Genl Assem^l now sitting

Your Committee to whom was recommitted the consideration of the within petition beg leave to report that the matters set forth in said petition are true and that in the Opinion of your Committee [two or more Commissioners be appointed who may have authority to prevent the Embezzelment of the Property of the Petitioner & that] all suits <not already> which may be hereafter Commenced against the said petitioner be barred till the sitting of the Assem^l in October next And that he be directed to notify his Creditors to appear at said session and shew cause if any they have why a Letter of License should not be granted to the Petitioner by the Legislature

Lem Chipman for Comm^t

— & —

A. J.: *Read and referred to a committee, 24 Oct. '87, S. P. of Vt., III (IV), 46; report of committee read and recommitted, and new members added to committee 25 Oct. '87, Ibid, III (IV), 50; *report of committee recommending that petitioner be exempted from arrest for five years, read and accepted (yeas and nays given), and leave given for a bill to be brought in accordingly, 26 Oct. '87, Ibid, III (IV), 52;[1] bill read and accepted and sent to Council, 27 Oct. '87, Ibid, III (IV), 60; bill, having been concurred in by Council, passed into law, 27 Oct. '87, Ibid, III (IV), 60.[2] C. J.: Act granting a letter of license to petitioner for one year read and concurred in, 26 Oct. '86, G. and C., III, 159.[3]

---

1. The report of committee as given in the journal on 26 Oct. '87 was actually that dated 24 Oct. '87 and presented and recommitted on 25 Oct. '87. The texts of both reports are included in the additional material above. The bill passed into law was, of course, based on the report dated 25 Oct. '87 and actually presented on 26 Oct. '87.

2. For this act, see Ms. Laws of Vt., II, 228–229. It was entitled "An Act to suspend prosecutions against Jesse Levensworth and for other purposes therein mentioned." It provided that the real estate of the petitioner could only be sold with the consent of other persons until the rising of the next session, that his creditors show cause why his prayer for exemption from arrest should not be granted, and that his person and property should be free from arrest for debt until the rising of the next session.

3. Either the date of this entry in the Council journal or the date of the first passage of the bill by the Assembly is in error.

FOR NEW TOWN LINES
xxii, 153

To the Honorable the General Assembly of the State of Vermont to be convened at Newbury in Oct[r] Instant —

The petition of the proprietors of Hungerford Humbly Sheweth —

That by reason of the lake towns lying in an irregular form, the town of fairfield [Fairfield] lies in a triangular manner which makes Smithfield[1] and Hungerford[2] lie also in a very bad shape —[3] we therefore pray your honors to take our case under consideration and reduce said town of Fairfield, Smithfield and Hungerford to a convenient form and if your Honors should not think proper to reduce the two first mentioned towns to their proper shape we pray that Your Honors would take our case under consideration and order that the lines of Hungerford May be established as follows viz beginning at the southeast corner of Highgate and running northerly in the east line of Highgate to the North Easterly corner thereof then carrying that breadth back so far about South 80[d] East as will include the contents of six miles square — we would also inform your Honors that we have subdivided the town into lots for immediate settlement in which the aforesaid bounds will include them — And by reducing the last mentioned town to this shape the towns lying East may be surveyed immediately — We would also inform your Honors that we are willing to give up our Newhampshire Charter[4] and take a Charter under this State, we therefore pray your Honors to grant this our petition and we as in duty bound shall ever pray

by order of the proprietors

Ferrisburgh Oct 1st 1787 — Timothy Rogers Agent

— & —

Petition of Tim[o] Roger in behalf of Proprietors of Hungerford —
Filed Oct[r] 20th 1787
Entered
. . .*

— & —

A. J.: *Read and ordered to lie on the table, 20 Oct. '87, *S. P. of Vt.*, III (IV), 38.[5]

FOR COMPENSATION FOR WAR SERVICES
xvii, 324

To the Honorable the General Assembly of the State of Vermont to be holden at

---

1. Now part of Bakersfield and Fairfield. See *S. P. of Vt.*, II (Vermont Charters), 349.

2. Now Sheldon. See *Ibid*, II, 347.

3. For a petition which was presented to this session and was also concerned with the shape of these towns, see p. 367, *ante*, and notes.

4. For this charter, see *State Papers New Hampshire*, vol. XXVI (Town Charters, vol. III), 414–418.

5. For the establishment of the town lines of Hungerford, see resolution passed 26 Oct. '87 (*S. P. of Vt.*, III (IV), 54–55).

Newbury on the second Thursday of Ins^t October

The Petition of John Pearl of Tinmouth in the County of Rutland and State of Vermont — humbly sheweth that your petitioner did at Clarendon in said County (from motives of humanity and a firm and steady attachment to the interest of America) receive into his house, board and Nurse, sundry such Soldiers belonging to the American Army in the year 1775 and 1776 a particular account of which, is herewith Transmited properly attested, together with other evidence to support the same, for which your petitioner has received no pay — Therefor pay^s [sic] your Honors to take this his petition under your wise consideration, and provide that he may receive a reasonable compensation in such manner as you in your Wisdom may think fit which your Honors petitioner as in Duty bound shall every pray —

John Pearl

Tinmouth Oct^o 2^d 1787

— & —

The Petition of Mr John Pearl —
Filed 12th Octr 1787 —
. . .*

— & —

A. J.: *Read and referred to a committee, 12 Oct. '87, S. P. of Vt., III (IV), 8; *report of committee recommending that petitioner receive £19–10 for his services, read and accepted, 15 Oct. '87, Ibid, III (IV), 17;[1] resolved to reconsider report and to dismiss petition, 16 Oct. '87, Ibid, III (IV), 19.

FOR AN ACT OF PARDON FOR RIOT
xvii, 325

The Honourable the Generable Assembly of the State of Vermont to be Conven^d at Newbury on the 2 Thirsday of Oc^t Ins^t —

The Petition of James Mead Thos Lee & Benjamin Johnson of Rutland Humbly Sheweth that your Petitioners are of the Number of those persons who without any Just Cause or provocation Rose up in Riotous and Tumultous Maner and we Acknowledge that we Did Interrupt the County Cort at there Session in the County of Rutland in November last[2] and when we Reflect on our Conduct we feele Guilty and Condemn our Selves and are Determined in future at the Expence of Life and fortune to Defend Goverment and Sivel Law and as we feele our Selves to be Guilty we Know not how Soon we May Be Arested Put to Grate Cost and Prehaps oblidgd to pay heavi fines and this State but little benefitted thereby —

Therefore your Petitionours humbly pray your Honours to pass an Act of Pardon for your Petitioners and as they In duty Bound Shall Ever pray
Rutland 2 of Oc^t 1787

James Mead
Thos Lee
Benj. Johnson

---

1. The entry on the manuscript petition includes the text of the report but not the fact that it was read and accepted.

2. For an account of the civil disorders in Rutland in November, 1786, see G. and C., III, 367–369.

— & —

The Petition of James Mead Thos Lee & Benj. Johnson
Entered
Filed 17th Octr 1787 —
. . .*

— & —

A. J.: *Read and dismissed, 17 Oct. '87, S. P. of Vt., III (IV), 21.

FOR A TAX ON LAND TO BUILD ROADS AND BRIDGES
xvii, 326

To the Honourable General Assembly of the State of Vermont. The Petition of
the Inhabitants and Proprietors of Readsborough [Readsboro] humbly Sheweth.
That at this time there is a Considerable Number of Inhabitants in S^d Readsborough
(in ye County of Bennington) Who have Incountered many hardships by making
Settlments in an Uncultivated wilderness, by Cuting and Clearing Roads, Building
Bridges &c: in S^d Town: By which we find ourselves Impoverished, and unable to
Repare ye Publick Roads which if not mended will be grately to the Damage of
the Publick, Therefore we your honours Petitioner Pray that your Honours will
take our Case under your wise Consideration and Grant a tax of Two Pence on
Each Acre of Land in S^d Readsborough Publick Rights Excepted and that your
Honours will appoint Aron Hudson, Esq and Mrss Isaac Lyman, and Daniel
Davison, to be a Committee to Issue their warrant to Capt Samuel Thompson of
Wilmington as Collector of S^d tax and that S^d Committee be accountable to the
County Cort of Bennington [Bennington] County for the Expendeture of the money
when Collected, as your Petitioners are in Duty Bound will Ever Pray
Readsborough Oct
ye 4th AD 1787

Aseph Wright	Siman Thayr	Ebenezer Fuller
Aron Hudson	David [Stone?]	Eliphelet Cuting
Sam^{el} Robinson	James Hayward	Wm Chapman
Daniel Davison	Siman Myre	Ebinezer Cotton
Peter Stone	Ichabod Stockwell	Elijah Town
Throop Chapman	Andrew Carnigee	Philip Jurden
	Eli Town	

— & —

Petition of Inhabitants of Readsboro'
Entered
Filed 19th Octr 1787
. . .*

— & —

A. J.: *Read and referred to a committee, 19 Oct. '87, S. P. of Vt., III (IV),
27; *report of committee recommending that petition be granted, read and
accepted, and leave given to bring in a bill accordingly, 20 Oct. '87, Ibid, III
(IV), 37; bill read and accepted and sent to Council, 24 Oct. '87, Ibid, III

(IV), 46; bill, having been concurred in by Council, passed into law, 25 Oct. '87, *Ibid*, III (IV), 48.[1] *C. J.*: Act read and concurred in, 25 Oct. '87, *G. and C.*, III, 155.

FOR LOCATION OF A COUNTY GRAMMAR SCHOOL
xvii, 327

To the Hon[le] the General Assembly of the State of Vermont to be holden at Newbury on the second thursday of October Anno Domini 1787 the petition of the Inhabitants of the Southwest district in the town of Brookfield in the County of Orange humble Sheweth,

That by law there is to be one County Grammer School to be keep & supported in said County —[2] And the particular place being not yet appointed, the petitioners humbly pray that the said Shcool [*sic*] may be established in said district, & the said Petitioners hereby engage that they will make & build a good & convenient house for the purpose of keeping said [*school*] in, finish the same completely by the expiration of one year from the date hereof on the Great Road leading from Windsor to Onion River & the said building shall be 30 feet in length & 22 feet in Breadth & finished in a good workman like manner with two good stacks of chimney in the same. as your petitioners in duty bound shall ever pray.

Brookfield Oct[r] 4th 1787

> Philip Ingram ⎫ Commitee
> Timothy Cowles ⎪ for the
> Samuel harris ⎬ above Purpose
> Abel Lymon ⎭

— & —

Petition for Grammar School Orange County in Brookfield
Filed Oct[r] 24th 1787

— & —

[No Record]

FOR A SURVEY OF A TOWN'S LINES TO SETTLE DISPUTES
xvii, 323, 329

To the Honorable Gen[ll] Assembly of the State of Vermont to be Convean[d] at Newbury in Said State on the Second Tuesday of Oct[r] Instant

the Prayer and Petition of the Subscribers Inhabitants of the Towns of Lecester and Salisbury in Said State Humbly Sheweth — that the Proprieters of Salisbury and Leicester lay claim and are making Settlement on one and the same pice of Land by reason of the towns Caping one on the other. the town of Salisbury has been Surveyed according to Charter by order of the Surveyor Gen[ll] the town of Leicester has been Surveyed only by the Proprioters Committee. the Proprioters

---

1. For this act, see *Ms. Laws of Vt.*, II, 209.
2. See Section XL, Constitution of 1777 (*G. and C.*, I, 102).

of Leicester pleads Priority by Charter,[1] the Proprioters of Salisbury Pleads Santion of the State by Survey &c, which throws us into the Greatest confusion — We your petitioners humbly beg leave to Shew that the despust [dispute] has become Serious and Destresing. allmost every day somthing of it on the carpit, Each party contending for what he thinks is his right trying to obtain possession &c threatning to a high handed degree even to the Sheding of blood if one interfears with the other

Lawsuits Commenced for trespass riots &c <we your Petitioners have a Sence of our destresed and Diagreeable [sic] Situation which Gives us courage to and we hereby> In which Situation we cannot ascertain our Juresdition consequently cannot raise money to defray our Public or Privat charges Militia afairs under the same Perdikerment Childeren with out Schools, and Highways unrepared &c, We your Petitioner have a Since [sense] of our Destressed and diagreeable Situation, which Gives us courage to, and we hereby humbly Pray that your Honours will take under consideration the Matter in despuit and give Orders to the Surveyor Gen^ll to run Such lines that is Necessary to find the true Bounds of Leicester According to Charter (which in our oppinion is the only way to Settle the despuit) Or Such other way as you in your Wisdom Shall think will be Valued when tryed by a rule of property and we your Petitionors as in duty Bound Shall ever Pray — 5th Octr 1787

Gam^l Painter } for the town of Salisbury
Thomas Sawyer } for the town of Leicester

We the Subscribers being appointed as Committees for the towns of Salisbury and Licester to Petition the Hon^le Gen^ll Assembly of the State of Vermont at their Session in Instant Oc^t Praying them to Give Directions to the Surveyor Gen^ll to run Such Lines that is Necessasary to find the true bounds of Licester According to Charter. By Vartue of which we Said Committee do hereby appoint Gamaliel Painter Esqr and Capt Thomas Sawer as a Subcommittee to Draw said Petition and refer it to the Hon^le Gen^ll Assembly —
Salisbury 1st Octr 1787

Gam^l Painter } Committees
James Waterous } for Salisbury
Eleazer Claghorn }
James Nichols } Committees
Benj^a Garfield } for Licester
[Jerathon?] Powers }

— & —

the Petition from the towns of Salisbury and Leicester to have Leicester Surveyed Entered
Filed 13th Octr 1787
. . .*

— & —

A. J.: *Read and referred to a committee to join a committee from the Council,

---

1. For the charters of Leicester and Salisbury, see *State Papers New Hampshire: The New Hampshire Grants*, vol. XXVI (*Town Charters*, vol. III), 240, 394.

13 Oct. '87, *S. P. of Vt.*, III (IV), 11; *report of committee recommending that petition not be granted and suggesting that petitioners agree among themselves on the town lines, read and accepted, and petition dismissed, 16 Oct. '87, *Ibid*, III (IV), 18.[1] *C. J.*: Committee appointed to join Assembly committee, 13 Oct. '87, *G. and C.*, III, 147.

FOR A TAX ON LAND TO BUILD ROADS AND BRIDGES
xvii, 328

To the Honorable Gen[l] Assembly of the State of Vermont to Convean in New-bury in Oct[r] ins[t] —

The Petition of the subscribers Inhabitants & Landowners in Milton Humbly Sheweth that the Proprietors have not Levied any Taxes for Roads that the other Towns Contiguous to Lake have Laid Taxes & Roads are Cuting which Roads will be imbarrised if Roads are not made through Milton That there is but Little Done on Roads in S[d] Town — Your Petitioners Therefore Pray that your Honers would Pass an Act Leveing a tax of Two Pence on Each acre of Land in S[d] Town (Except Public Rights) for the Purpose of Cuting Roads & Bridging the Same in S[d] Town

Your Petitioners as in duty Bound will Ever Pray —
Oct[r] 5th 1787

> Ira Allen
> Caleb Hendrson
> Tho[s] [Butterfild]
> Fradrack Saxton
> John owen
> Abeleson Falter
> Thades owen

— & —

Pet[n] of Milton —
Filed 19th Oct[r] 87 —
Entered
. . .*

— & —

A. J.: *Read and referred to a committee, 19 Oct. '87, *S. P. of Vt.*, III (IV), 28; *report of committee recommending that petition be granted, read and accepted, and leave given to bring in a bill accordingly, 20 Oct. '87, *Ibid*, III (IV), 37; bill read and accepted and sent to Council, 25 Oct. '87, *Ibid*, III (IV), 48; bill, having been concurred in by Council, passed into law, 25 Oct. '87, *Ibid*, III (IV), 49.[2] *C. J.*: Act read and concurred in, 25 Oct. '87, *G. and C.*, III, 155.

---

1. The entry on the manuscript petition includes the text of the report but not the facts that it was read and accepted and the petition dismissed.
2. For this act, see *Ms. Laws of Vt.*, II, 208.

FOR RIGHT TO SELL LAND TO SUPPORT AN INVALID WIDOW
xvii, 330

The Honorable General assembly of the State of Vermont to be Holden on the
Second thursday of oct^r in this present year 1787 a Petition of the Select Men of
the Town of Pitsford Humbley Sheweth that in or about the year 1775 one Joseph
Wright maid a purchst [purchase] of a Tract of Land in the Town of Pitsford and
Bult a Hous on S^d Land and maid Sum Smarle [small] inprovement on the Same
but Before he had bin an inhabitant in S^d Town Two years he was Taken away by
Death and Left a Widow and two Smarle Children but she Being an Industras
Woman Seported hur Self and Children through the Late war with out aney Cost
to the Estate Left by hur Husband but Never the less throug the Furtanges [for-
tunes?] and heardshipps She has gone through She Lost hur helth and is Now an
actiaule [actual] Charg to S^d Town of Pitsford and What Smarle Inprovements
ware maid by the s^d Joseph Desest [deceased] are Run up to Brush and Briers So
that the afoursaid Lands are valued onley as other wild Lands and so Can afford
no Releif for the the Seport of the S^d widow and at the Request of the S^d widow
and allso the Inhabitants of S^d Town of Pitsford that we the S^d Select Men of S^d
Town Should prefur a petition to the Honorable assembly praying that the S^d
Widows Equial part of S^d Lands might be Sold and the money Lodged in the hands
of Sum Proper Persons for the Seport and Benefit of the S^d Widow and allso Releef
of the S^d Town : We therefore pray that you would Take the matter under your
wise Considration and grant Such Releef as you in your Wisdom Shall See fit as
we in duty Bound Shall Ever Pray
Dated in Pitsford 5 Day of October 1787

Benj^a Cooley
Colburn Preston } Select Men
Caleb Cooley

— & —

A Petition in Behalf of the Widow Wright
Select Men of Pittsford petition
Filed [Oct^r] 1787
. . .*
Your Commity to whom was referd the Considerration of the with in petition
report that the Matters Containd in S^d Petition are in our oppinnion [not?] Supported. and beg leave to Report that in our oppinnion the prair of S^d Petition out
[ought] not to be granted All which is submitted

Daniel Marsh for Committe

— & —

A. J.: *Read and referred to a committee, 20 Oct. '87, S. P. of Vt., III (IV),
37; *report of committee read and accepted, and petition dismissed, 25 Oct.
'87, Ibid, III (IV), 50.

FOR RELIEF OF A TAX COLLECTOR FROM LOSS THROUGH FIRE
xvii, 331

To the Honourable the General Assembly of the State of Vermont Who are to convene at Newbury in S^d State on the second thursday of October 1787 —
The Prayer and petition of John Barns of Pittsford in the County of Rutland Humbly sheweth —
Whereas Your Honours petitioner being the Collector in Pittsford aforesaid in the Year 1785 was chosen to collect the State Taxes in S^d Town, and in the month of May 1786 unfortunately my Dwelling House took fire and was consumed; Your petitioner begs leave to inform Your Honors he also had a hard money order to the amount of £ 4:10:0 which he had not been return^d to the Treasurers office, was Likewise consumed; which Remain^d due to the Publick — Your Honors Petitioner hereby earnestly Requests and prays a discharge from the aforesaid Order as his sufferings were very Considerable in the Loss of his effects and furniture. Therefore prays your Honors to take the preceeding disaster into your wise consideration and grant the Relief as above Required; and Your very humble Servant as in Duty bound shall ever pray
Pitford Octr ye 5th 1787   John Barns Collector

      Rutland County
Pitsford [Pittsford] October the 8 Day 1787 Personally appered the within Petitinor John Barns and Maid oath that in May 1786 he had aheard [a hard] Money order Contents of which order was Four Pounds ten Shillengs and the Same was Burnt up in his then Dwelling Hous
Sworne Befor me   Eben^r Drury Jus^t peace

— & —

Petition of John Barns of Pittsford
Filed 16th Octr 87 —
Entered
. . .*

— & —

> A. J.: *Read and granted, 16 Oct. '87, S. P. of Vt., III (IV), 19; resolved that
> Treasurer be directed to pay petitioner £4–10 in hard money orders, 16 Oct.
> '87, Ibid, III (IV), 19.

FOR A TAX ON LAND TO BUILD ROADS AND BRIDGES
xvii, 332

To the Honourable General Assembly for the State of Vermont —
      The Petition of the Inhabitants of the Town of Midway [Medway]¹ — in the County of Rutland
      To Your Honours Humbly Shewith —
      Whereas their has been large sum^s of Money and great expenditures, laid out, by your Petitioners — for to make roads & Bridges, so that the Publick, might

---

1. Now Mendon. See *S. P. of Vt.*, II (Vermont Charters), 320.

pass & repass through said Town over the Green Mountain, as it can be made very convenient, with a little more cost — to accomidate, the Publick to cross the Mountain — And as your Petitioners have not Money, nor wherewith to go throught [sic] S^d business, of making Roads Bridges &c pray your Honours to take the same into your wise Consideration — and lay a Tax, of ⟨one penney⟩ Two pence₁ on each Acre of land in S^d Town for the purpose of making Roads & Bridges, in S^d Town — if consistant with your Honour^s will & pleasure — And as in Duty bound Your Petitioners will ever Pray —

Dated at Midway this 6th Day of Octr 1787 —

Daniel D. Bryant
Jonathan Emerson

— & —

The Petition of the Inhabitants of Midway —
Entered
Filed 15th Octr 1787 —
. . .*

— & —

A. J.: *Read and referred to a committee, 15 Oct. '87, S. P. of Vt., III (IV), 16;¹ *report of committee recommending that petition be granted, read and accepted, and leave given to bring in a bill accordingly, 19 Oct. '87, Ibid, III (IV), 29; bill read and accepted and sent to Council, 24 Oct. '87, Ibid, III (IV), 44; bill, having been concurred in by Council, passed into law, 25 Oct. '87, Ibid, III (IV), 48.² C. J.: Act read and concurred in, 25 Oct. '87, G. and C., III, 155.

FOR REFUND OF LOSSES INCURRED BY SUIT OF A TORY
xvii, 333

To the Honourable the General Assembly of the State of Vermont Who are to Convene at Newbury in S^d State on the second thursday of October 1787 — The prayer and petition of Thomas Sawyer of Leicester in the County of Addison Humbly Sheweth

Your Honours petitioner takes this method to Remind the Honourable House of his Services Rendered this State in the Year 1778 particularly in an expedition in the month of March in S^d Year to Shelburne as may be made to appear by a number of Orders Records &c —³ And Your Honours petitioner has not obtain^d the Wages due to him as an Officer Yet which he esteems unjust for him to lay out of — The soldiery under my Command were paid out of the Effects taken from one Peter Sevence of S^d Shelburne who was at that time esteemed inimical to the common Cause we were then engaged in —

in march Last past I was Sued before the County Court in and for the County of

---

1. The journal does not include the names of the members of the committee. The entry on the manuscript petition lists the members as "Messrs Jewet, Marvin, Spafford, Hunt, Emmons & Johnston."

2. For this act, see Ms. Laws of Vt., II, 210–211.

3. For a brief account of Sawyer's part in this expedition, see G. and C., I, 245n, 528.

Addison and judgment was obtaind against me by the S^d Sevence for the aforesaid
Effects to the amount of Eighty Eight pounds L.M. with Cost of suit —
Your Honors petitioner therefore earnestly Requests that the aforesaid sum may be
Refunded to him from the State in Consequence of his Loss by Legal process —
Therefore prays the Honourable house to comply with the foregoing Requisition
as your petitionor thinks in Justice it ought to be Granted — concludes and Reposes
special confidence in Your Honors in obtaining his Right and as in Duty bound
shall ever pray

Thomas Sawyer

Leicester Octr 8th ⎱
   1787   ⎰

— & —

Petition of Thomas Sawyer of Leicester
Entered
Filed 13th Octr 1787 —
...*

— & —

> A. J.: *Read and referred to a committee to join a committee from the Council,
> 13 Oct. '87, *Ibid*, III (IV), 10; *report of committee finding that petitioner
> had suffered the losses alleged and that he had received no compensation
> therefor, read and accepted, 17 Oct. '87, *Ibid*, III (IV), 23-24;[1] resolved that
> Treasurer be directed to pay petitioner £88 lawful money accordingly, 17
> Oct. '87, *Ibid*, III (IV), 24. C. J.: Committee appointed to join Assembly
> committee, 13 Oct. '87, *G. and C.*, III, 147.

FOR A TAX ON LAND TO BUILD ROADS AND BRIDGES
xvii, 334

To the Honourable Genr[1] Assembly of the State of Vermont. to be holden att
Newbury on the Second thursday of October Instant. The petition of the In-
habitants of the Town of Woodstock Sheweth. that there is large tracts of Land in
said Town owned by nonresidents that never have as yet ben Charged with any
Expence of making roads in said Town, that there is two publick roads through
said Town one from Dartmouth College and placees Ajasent. Across the Green
Mountain to Rutland Claraden [Clarenden] &c Another from Windsor to the new
Granted [...] [White] River Onion River &c Which road Crosses Water Quechee
[Ottauquechee] River in Woodstock which River att some seasons [is] Impractable
to Cross without a bridge which Inconveniance is Detremental to Travelors as
well as Veary Troublesome to the Inhabitants of the Town. that the Inhabitants of
said Woodstock have ben att Great Labour and Expence in makeing roads through
many parts of the Town by which means together with the Industry of your Honours
petitioners the Estates of nonresident Land owners in said town is greatly Ogmented And Also that the said Town of Woodstock is in futer time Appointed by

---

1. The entry on the manuscript petition includes the report of the committee but
not the fact that it was read and accepted.

the Honrb^e Assembly to be the place of holding the Supreme and County Courts in and for the County of Windsor. it therefore becomes Nesasery that roads and bridges be maid and repaird in said Town for the benefit of publick as well as private travel. therefore the Inhabitants of Woodstock in Town meeting met on the fourth day of Septr Last Unanimously Voted to petition this Honourable Assembly for Liberty to raise a tax of two pence p^r Acre on all the Lands in said Town —
Wee therefore pray your honours to take the matter into your wise Consideration and grant Liberty to the Selectmen of said Woodstock to Levy a tax of two pence p^r Acree on all the Lands in the said Town publick Lands Excepted for the purpose of building Bridges and Repairing highways &c In said Woodstock
And your Honours petitioners as in Duty bound Shall ever pray

Woodstock Octr ye 8th 1787

Joel Matthews   ⎫ Committee
Jesse Safford   ⎬ for
Oliver Williams ⎭ S^d Woodstock

— & —

Woodstock Petition
Entered
Filed 13th Octr 1787 —
. . .*

— & —

A. J.: *Read and granted, and leave given to bring in a bill accordingly, 15 Oct. '87, S. P. of Vt., III (IV), 13; bill read and accepted and sent to Council, 18 Oct. '87, Ibid, III (IV), 26; bill, having been concurred in by Council, passed into law, 19 Oct. '87, Ibid, III (IV), 28.[1] C. J.: Act read and concurred in, 18 Oct. '87, G. and C., III, 151.

FOR RELIEF FROM TAXES ON AN UNREPRESENTED GORE
xvii, 336

To the honorable General Assem^l now siting at Newbury in the State of Vermont —
The Petition of the Subscribers Inhabitants of Jacksens [Jackson's] Gore in the County of Rutland humbly sheweth that your honors Petitioners have undergone many hardships in removing into and Settling on said Gore — That they have never been represented Or Organized — notwithstanding they have by a Law of this State been directed to give in a list of their Polls and rateable Estate to the Lister in the town of Wallingford — which your petitioners Considar unjust and oppressive therefore pray your honors to take their case under your wise consideration and grant relief in the premises and your Petitioners as in Duty bound shall ever pray

Jacksons Gore Oct
12. 1787

Jethro jacson
Jonah Ives
Rowling Benson
Amos Ives
Icabod G Clark

1. For this act, see Ms. Laws of Vt., II, 195–196.

John Clark
Pedigren Doley
William Burlingham
Jacob Willcocks
Ebenezer Lyon
John Randol

— & —

Petⁿ of Jethro Jackson & others. —
Filed 19 Octr 1787 —
. . .*

Your Com^e to whom was referd the Consideration of with in Petition report. that S^d Petition is not supported and the praer of S^d Petition out [ought] not to be granted

Daniel Marsh for Com

— & —

> A. J.: *Read and referred to a committee, 15 Oct. '87, S. P. of Vt., III (IV),
> 16; *report of committee read and accepted, and petition dismissed, 25 Oct.
> '87, Ibid, III (IV), 50.

FOR A PENSION FOR WAR DISABILITY
xvii, 337

To the Honourable the General Assembly of the State of Vermont — The petition of Daniel Buck of Norwich in the County of Windsor humbly sheweth —

That on the 16th of August 1777 your petitioner in opposing the common enemy in the battle at Wollumseck near Bennington had the misfortune to receive a Wound in his left arm which three years after terminated in the final loss of it —[1] That Soon after the receipt of his wound & before the final loss he was pentioned in the Commonwealth of the Massachusetts [Massachusetts] at Twenty Shillings p^r month That sum being then supposed (as your petitioner had not at that time finally lost his arm) to correspond with the degree of his disability compaired with a person wholly disabled and on account of the great distance which your petitioner lived from the capitol when in the Massachusetts & the great trouble & expence in negotiateing business of that kind your petitioner never made application for the enlargement of his pention after he had suffered the loss of his arm & was thereby wholly disabled from supporting himself by Labour but continued to draw his pention of Twenty Shillings p^r month untill the 17th of March 1786 at which period a Resolve was passed in the General Assembly of the Commonwealth of the Massachusetts[2] in consequence of a Resolve of the United States in Congress assembled June 7th 1785[3] excluding all those who had moved & gone out of the

---

1. For Buck's military service in Massachusetts, see *Massachusetts Soldiers and Sailors of the War of the Revolution*, vol. II (Boston, 1896), 743.

2. For this resolve, see *Acts and Resolves of Massachusetts*, 1784–85 (Boston, 1884), 908–910.

3. For this resolve, see *Journals of the Continental Congress 1774–1789*, vol. XXVIII (Washington, 1933), 435.

S^d Commonwealth from any longer drawing their pentions there & as your petitioner had previous to the passing S^d Resolve removed in to this State he was
consequently cut off from his pention in that Commonwealth —
Wherefore your petitioner prays that his case may be taken into your wise consideration And as the S^d Resolve of Congress of the 7th of June 1785 Recommends
to the Several States to make provision for the officers Soldiers or Seamen resident
in their respective States who have served in the Army or Navy of the United
States or in the Malitia in the Service &c and as by S^d Resolve your petitioner
considers himself intitled to a pention of Five Dollers p^r month he prays he may
be put upon a pention by this State under the regulations of S^d Resolve from the
17th March 1786 — & that the Treasurer may be directed to pay to your petitioner
the arearage of his S^d pention from that time up to the present or that your honours
would otherwise make provision for him as your wisdom shall direct — & as in
duty bound Shall ever pray
Norwich 12th October 1787   Daniel Buck

— & —

Daniel Buck — petition —
Filed 16th Octr 1787
Entered
. . .*

— & —

A. J.: *Read and referred to a committee to join a committee from the Council,
16 Oct. '87, *S. P. of Vt.*, III (IV), 19; *report of committee recommending that
petition ought not to be granted read and accepted, and petition dismissed, 19
Oct. '87, *Ibid*, III (IV), 30. *C. J.*: Committee appointed to join Assembly
committee, 16 Oct. '87, *G. and C.*, III, 149.

FOR ABATEMENT OF TAXES
xvii, 351

To the Honorable General Assembly of the State of Vermont now Sitting — The
petition of the Constable of Addison Humbly Sheweth
        that the grand list of said town for the year 1786 is £ 1040 –15– 0 that the
Treasurers warrant for the collection of the taxes granted last Octr is £ 1300 on
Said list — and that the Treas^r extents have been issued and the tax collected on
£ 1300 Your petitioner, therefore pray that your Honors would grant relief in
the premises by ordering the Treasurer to pay back the amount of the taxes raised
on the Sum of £ 259–5 and the cost and your petitioner, as in duty bound will
ever pray
Octr 12th 1787 —   David Vallance Constable

— & —

Petition of David Vallance Constable of Addison —
Entered
Filed 15th Octr 1787 —
. . .*
To the Honorable the Genl Assembly now Seting your Committee to whome was

Referd the Consideration of the within Petition bege leve to Report that the facts set up in S^d petition are Supported, and that the prayer of the Petition Ought to be Granted So far as that the Treasurer of this State be directed to pay to your Petitioner the Sume of three pounds four Shillings and nine pence three farthings in hard money, or hard money Orders, and three pounds four shillings & nine pence three farthings in States money it being the Sume Collected on the Sume of 259:5 above the true List of the Town of Addison for the year 1786
Newbury Octr ye 17th 1787   John Shumway for Com^te

— & —

A. J.: *Read and referred to a committee, 15 Oct. '87, S. P. of Vt., III (IV), 17; report of committee recommending that prayer be granted, read and accepted, 17 Oct. '87, Ibid, III (IV), 23; resolved that Treasurer credit the town all taxes on £259–5 on the list of 1786, 17 Oct. '87, Ibid, III (IV), 23.

FOR A TAX ON LAND TO BUILD ROADS AND BRIDGES
xvii, 339, 340

To the hon^ble General Assembly of the State of Vermont now sitting in Newbury. —
The Petition of Seth Austin Agent for the Proprietors & Inhabitants of the town of Tunbridge in Orange County. —
Sheweth/
That the said Town is newly & but thinly settled, That many roads & bridges are wanted in said Town for the public convenience, & to promote the Settlement of that & other Towns which the Inhabitants of Tunbridge are unable of themselves to compleat. —
That the Inhabitants & a Com^e of the Proprietors of said Tunbridge have jointly agreed that a tax of two Pence per Acre be laid on all the Land in said Tunbridge (public rights excepted) & have appointed your Petitioner their Agent to sollicit the Grant of a tax for that sum & purpose from the Honble the Legislature —
Your Petitioner therefore humbly prays this hon^ble house to grant a tax of two pence per Acre on all the lands in said Tunbridge, public rights excepted, for the purpose of making & repairing Roads & building Bridges in said Town. —
And your Petitioner as in duty bound shall ever pray &c.   Seth Austin
Newbury 13th Octr 1787 —

Att a Legal meting of the Town of Tunbridge held att the House of Elijah Pray in S^d Town on the Second Tuesday of merch 1787 voted to potision to the general assembly in october next for a tax of three pence on the aca for the purpuse of maiking roads and bilding bridges &c voted that the Selectmen Confer with the proprietors att thare next meting to se If thay wil Joine With the Town In the potision

Test Alex^r Stedman   Town Clark

This may Sartefy that C^pt Seth Austen was apointed by the Inhabetence of the Town of Tunbridge att thare Legal meting on the first tusday of September 1787 to have the Care of a potision voted by the Inhabtance In march last and also by the proprietors of S^d Town on S^d day

Tunbrid [Tunbridge] October 8th 1787

> Elijah Tracy
> Hezekiah Hutchinson } Selectmen
> Alex^r Stedman
>
> Alex^r Stedman   Proprietors
> Hezekiah Hutchinson } Prudential Committee

At a legal Meting of the Proprietors of Tunbridge in the County of Orange & State of Vermont held September 4th 1787 Voted the Prudential Committee Join with this Town in Petitioning the General Assembly to levy a Tax of three pence on each acre of Land through this Town Public Rights excepted for the Purpose of Making Roads and Bridges

A true Copy Test   Elias Curtis P. Clerk

Tunbridge Octob^r 9th 1787

— & —

Petition of Proprietors & Inhabitants of Tunbridge
Filed 13th Octr 1787
Entered
. . .*

— & —

> A. J.: *Read and granted, and leave given to bring in a bill accordingly, 13 Oct. '87, S. P. of Vt., III (IV), 9; bill read and accepted and sent to Council, 19 Oct. '87, Ibid, III (IV), 28; bill, having been concurred in by Council, passed into law, 19 Oct. '87, Ibid, III (IV), 29.[1] C. J.: Act read and concurred in, 19 Oct. '87, G. and C., III, 151.

FOR A LOTTERY TO COMPLETE A BRIDGE
xvii, 341

To the hon^{ble} the General Assembly of the State of Vermont now convened at Newbury. —
Sheweth/
The Petition of Samuel Williams, James Ewing, Reuben Tuller, Jon^a Carpenter, & Benj^a Garfield — That your Petitioners were in Octr 1784 appointed by the Legislature Managers of a Lottery granted for the purpose of building two Bridges one over Otter Creek near Brown's Camp, the other over Leicester River. —[2] That your Petitioners undertook said Business solely with the view of serving the public & after a considerable sale of the Tickets employed Workmen upon their own Credit to finish said Bridges. — That unfortunately when the Bridge over Otter Creek was in great forwardness it was carried off by an extraordinary Freshet. — That the Lottery also lost very considerably by tickets left on hand unsold — By which means your Petitioners were rendered unable to compleat the

---

1. For this act, see Ms. Laws of Vt., II, 196.
2. For the presentation of the original petition for this lottery (not now among the Ms. Vt. S. P.) and the action taken thereon in Oct. '84, see S. P. of Vt., III (III), 79, 91–92.

beneficial Purposes of their Appointment unless at their private Expence — That in order to compleat the said Bridges & defray the necessary Expences it is absolutely necessary that the further sum of £ 125 — be raised —

Your Petitioners therefore humbly pray this hon^ble house to grant them leave to raise by Lottery a further sum of £ 125 for the purposes af^d

And they as in Duty bound shall ever pray &c.

Newbury 13th Octr 1787

Sam^ll Williams
Jon^a Carpenter
Reuben Tuller
James Ewing
Benj. Garfield

— & —

Petition of ye Managers of ye Lottery for building bridges over Otter Creek &C. Filed 13th Octr 1787 —
...*

— & —

> *A. J.:* *Read and referred to a committee, 15 Oct. '87, *S. P. of Vt.*, III (IV), 15; *report of committee read and accepted, 25 Oct. '87, *Ibid*, III (IV), 48;[1] resolved that managers have liberty to raise £125 by lottery for completing bridge, the state not being accountable therefor, 25 Oct. '87, *Ibid*, III (IV), 48.

FOR A TAX ON LAND TO BUILD ROADS AND BRIDGES
xvii, 342

To the Honb^le Assembly Now sitting at Newbury

The petition of the Inhabitants of the Town of Thetford Humbly sheweth, that Your petitioners have for a long time been under the disadvantages & particular Embarrassments of forming settlements in a New & uncultivated Country that our situation as to Roads & Bridges is peculiarly disagreeable — as we have many important Roads that need repairing as also many Bridges to be made & supported, that no less than seven large bridges are now built in S^d Town, but still there remains Great Necessity of a bridge to be built over the River Onpompynoocock [Ompompanoosuc] on the most direct Road from S^d Thetford to Norwich, which being done will have the principal Travil as a publick Road on the west side of the River Connecticut and as there is a Large proportion of the Lands in S^d Thetford belonging Non residents which have been & still will be materially advantaged by the makeing of such Roads & Bridges. which Lands have never been taxed by the publick for such purposes — Therefore we your Honours Petitioners Humbly pray your Honours to Grant a Tax on all Lands in S^d Thetford publick Lands excepted of /2^d pr Acre for the purpose of building S^d Bridge & repairing Roads in S^d Town, under such restrictions as your [Honours] in Great wisdom shall direct

---

1. The report of the committee as given on the manuscript petition simply declares that the prayer "ought to be granted, and that the petitioner have liberty to bring in a bill accordingly."

Your petitioners as in duty bound Ever pray —
Dated 13th of Octr 1787

Beriah Loomis	Joshua Tyler	Amos Wheler
Abner Chamberlain	Robert Baker	Amos Chamberlin
Phinnas [Annes]	Daniel Blanchard	Samuel Bell
Jonathan Nichols	John Bliss Jr	Moses Cadwell Jr
Thomis Evet	Abel Wright	James Sawyer Junr
Joseph Thayer	John Wright	Elijah Howard
Richard Wallace	John Frissell	Simon Newcomb
Moses Tyler	Joel Chamberlin	Wm Heaton
William Moor Jr	Walter Abbot	Elias Chamberlin
William Moor	Abraham Page	Ezekiel Strong
Asa English	Adolphus Fellows	Simon Gillet

— & —

Petn of Thetford
Entered
Filed 17th Octr 1787 —
...*

to the General Assembly Now Sitting
    Your Committee to whom was Referd the within petition Report it as their oppinion that the Prayer of the petition be granted and the monies laid out under the inspection of the Select men or a committee of Thetford for the Sole purpose of making bridges and repairing Roads

Thos Jewett for Committe

— & —

A. J.: *Read and referred to land tax committee, 17 Oct. '87, S. P. of Vt., III (IV), 21; *report of committee recommending that prayer be granted, read and accepted, and leave given to bring in a bill accordingly, 19 Oct. '87, Ibid, III (IV), 30; bill read and accepted and sent to Council, 24 Oct. '87, Ibid, III (IV), 47; bill, having been concurred in by Council, passed into law, 25 Oct. '87, Ibid, III (IV), 49.[1] C. J.: Act read and concurred in, 25 Oct. '87, G. and C., III, 155.

FOR A TAX ON LAND TO BUILD ROADS AND BRIDGES
xvii, 344

To the Honble General Assembly of Vermont
Now Convened at Newbury
The Petition of the Subscribers Humbly Sheweth
That the Inhabitants of the Town of Corinth in Said State Have been at Great Expence in making Roads and Building Bridges in Said Town; That the Inhabitants of Said Town have been at the Whole Expence of Making and Repairing Sd Highways & Bridges without any Assistance from the Non Resident Propretors and Land owners in Said Town —
That Large Sums are Still wanting to Compleat Said Roads, & Render them Con-

---

1. For this act, see Ms. Laws of Vt., II, 206–207.

venient for the Inhabitants and the Publick in general —

Your Petitioners therefore Pray that your Honours Would Grant a Tax of Two Pence per Acre on all Lands in the Town of Corinth — Publick Rights Excepted for the Purpose of making & Repairing Said Highways and Bridges under Such Regulations as your Honourable body Shall Direct — and your Petitioners as in Duty Bound Shall Ever Pray &c

Newbury October 15th 1787

Reuben Foster   ⎫

Nehemiah Lovewell ⎬ Selectmen

— & —

Petition of the Select men of Corinth
Filed Octr 15th 1787
. . .*

— & —

A. J.: *Read and referred to a committee, 16 Oct. '87, S. P. of Vt., III (IV), 20; *report of committee recommending that tax of 2d on each acre be laid under direction of a committee, read and accepted, and leave given to bring in a bill accordingly, 19 Oct. '87, Ibid, III (IV), 28; bill read and accepted and sent to Council, 25 Oct. '87, Ibid, III (IV), 49; bill, having been concurred in by Council, passed into law, 26 Oct. '87, Ibid, III (IV), 53.[1] C. J.: Act read and concurred in, 26 Oct. '87, G. and C., III, 156.

FOR A SPECIAL ELECTION FOR TOWN REPRESENTATIVE
xvii, 345

To the General Assembly of the State of Vermont convened at Newbury in said State.

The petition of the Subscribers Select Men of the Town of Cavendish humbly sheweth; that whereas at the late Annual Meeting for the election of Representatives in this State a person was made choice of, without any ill design, to represent this Town in the General Assembly, who has not been a resident in this State a Sufficient term of time to answer the requirement of our Constitution of Government;[2] And Whereas We are creditably informed that this Honorable Assembly has heretofore, in sundry instances, given orders for the choice of Representatives on other days than that for their annual election. And as there are matters of Great importance to this Town which may come before this Honorable Assembly in the present Year that will make Our *representation* expedient if not necessary; Your petitioners (holding themselves to be under great obligation to regeard the good of this Town) therefore pray that this Honorable Assembly would take the premises under their most serious consideration; & if they find it consistant to their former practice & the Constitution of this State would give or grant a Speedy Order enabling this Town to make another choice of a member to represent them in this

---

1. For this act, see Ms. Laws of Vt., II, 227–228.

2. The person elected was Samuel White. The assembly voted 12 Oct. '87 that he was not qualified to take his seat. See S. P. of Vt. III (IV), 6.

Assembly for the present year ensuing & as in duty bound your petitioners shall ever pray. —

Cavendish Octob^r 15. 1787

Leonard Wade
Samuel White   } Selectmen of
Asa Wheeler   Cavendish

— & —

Cavendish Petition
Filed 17th Octr 1787
Entered
. . .*

— & —

A. J.: *Read and granted, 17 Oct. '87, S. P. of Vt., III (IV), 23; resolved that Selectmen of town appoint a time for such election, 18 Oct. '87, Ibid, III (IV), 26.

FOR ANNEXATION OF A TOWN TO A DIFFERENT COUNTY
xvii, 313, 349

to the Hon^le Gen^ll Assembley now Siting

The petition of Daniel King for the Inhabitants of the town of Kingston[1] humbly Sheweth that Said town is now included in the County of Oring [Orange] which is disagreeable to the inhabitants of said town on account of there Cituation it is much nearer and more conveniant for the Inhabitants of said town to attend the Courts in Addison County then in the County of Oringe therefore your Petitioner humbley Pray that your Honours will anex Said town to the County of Addison and your Petitioners as in duty Bound Shall ever Pray

16th Octr 1787   Daniel King

Kingston Sep^t 11th 1787
att a meeting of the priproetors of Kingston Chose Daniel King agent to atend the Ginerel assembley to see if their honers will Relinquish the General Survey Bill[2] & to see if S^d Kingston may Be anext to the Countey of Arteson [Addison]

Joseph Patrick [Ptor?] Clark

— & —

Petition of Danl King
Filed 16th Octr 1787 —
Entered

---

1. Now Granville. See S. P. of Vt., II (Vermont Charters), 299.
2. In this context the reference to "the General Survey Bill" is obscure. A general survey of all town lines had been in progress since 1782 (Ms. Laws of Vt., I, 350, 466). It may have been that the proprietors were seeking an end of this survey as well as the annexation of the town to Addison County. On the other hand, it may have been that "the General Survey Bill" referred to the act establishing county lines in the state passed 27 Feb. '87 (Statutes of the State of Vermont, passed by the Legislature in February and March 1787 [Windsor, 1787], 41–42). The assembly would "relinquish" this act and the county lines it established by annexing Kingston to Addison County.

...*

— & —

A. J.: *Read and referred to a committee, 16 Oct. '87, *S. P. of Vt.*, III (IV), 19-20; *report of committee recommending that petition be granted, read and accepted, and leave given to bring in a bill accordingly, 16 Oct. '87, *Ibid*, III (IV), 21;[1] bill read and accepted and sent to Council, 17 Oct. '87, *Ibid*, III (IV), 23; bill, having been concurred in by Council, passed into law, 19 Oct. '87, *Ibid*, III (IV), 28.[2] *C. J.:* Act read and concurred in, 17 Oct. '87, *G. and C.*, III, 150.

FOR RELIEF OF A TAX COLLECTOR PAID IN COUNTERFEIT BILLS
xvii, 347

To the Honourable the General Assembly of the State of Vermont Now Sitting the petition of Abner Chamberlin of Thetford humbly sheweth That in 1783 he was appointed & sworn to the office of Sheriff for the County of Orange & served in that capacity untill the year 1786 That soon after his appointment he had committed to him to collect two provision Taxes granted in 1780 & 1781 & a Land Tax of 10/p^r 100 acres laid on several Towns in S^d County which taxes your petitioner collected principally in State Notes —[3] That as your petitioner had never heard of S^d Notes being any ways altered or counterfeit (nor was it then known that they were) in the first of his collection he received S^d Notes without scruple & did not take an account of the persons he received them of nevertheless he was careful to keep what he collected intire by it self & never mixed it with other money or notes nor did he dispose of any in any way whatsoever except in making change to those who payed notes but carefully transmitted the same money collected to the Treasurer who received & receipted the same — That since the Treasurer has discovered that one of those notes which your petitioner collected & paid into the treasury had been altered from £ 3 to £ 30 — which was so curiously done that it was not discoverable only by compairing it with its stump & another of the sum of £ 15 which your petitioner likewise collected & gave in change to a person who came to pay his Tax has since proved to be counterfeit & is returned back upon your petitioner and as your petitioner among the multiplicity of persons of whom he collected rates cannot determine of what particular persons he received those notes he is under the necessity of loosing S^d Sums amounting to £ 45.0 unless your Honours will please to grant him relief Wherefore he prays your honours to take his case into your wise consideration & direct the Treasurer to allow S^d Sum as in similer instances your petitioner is informed your honours have in much Justice done[4] & as in duty bound will ever pray &c —
Newbury 16th October 1787

Abner Chamberlin

---

1. The entry on the manuscript petition only includes the text of the report and not the action taken upon it.

2. For this act, see *Acts and Laws passed by the Legislature of the State of Vermont, at their session at Newbury, the second Thursday of October, 1787* (Windsor, 1787), 3.

3. For the acts imposing these taxes, see *Slade*, 407, 424, 440.

4. For similar petitions and the actions taken by the Assembly thereon, see pp. 99, 172, 182, *ante*.

— & —

Abner Chamberlin petition —
Filed 18th of Octr 1787
Entered
. . .*

— & —

A. J.: *Read and referred to a committee, 18 Oct. '87, S. P. of Vt., III (IV), 26; *report of committee recommending that petition not be granted, read and accepted, and petition dismissed, 19 Oct. '87, Ibid, III (IV), 27.[1]

FOR INCORPORATION OF A RELIGIOUS SOCIETY
xvii, 349

To the Honourable the General Assembly of the State of Vermont now Siting —
The petition of John Sessions in behalf of the Town of Westminster Humbly Sheweth — that at a Legal Meeting Said Town of Westminster Voted to Divide or otherwise Set of [off] a certain part of Said Town as a parrish or Society — These are therefore to petition your Honours to Incorporate Saidd Society the Limits of which I herewith transmit as agreed on by the Town — that they may be Invested with all necesary privilages proper for a Society[2] and as your petitioner in Duty bound Shall ever prey
Newbeury 16th Octob^r 1787   John Sessions

— & —

The Petition of John Sessions in behalf of the Town of Westminster —
Entered
. . .*

— & —

A. J.: *Read and granted, and leave given to bring in a bill accordingly, 17 Oct. '87, S. P. of Vt., III (IV), 21; bill to divide Westminster into two parishes read and accepted and sent to Council, 18 Oct. '87, Ibid, III (IV), 27; bill, having been concurred in by Council, passed into law, 19 Oct. '87, Ibid, III (IV), 28.[3] C. J.: Act read and concurred in, 18 Oct. '87, G. and C., III, 151.

FOR A TAX ON LAND TO BUILD ROADS AND BRIDGES
xvii, 353

To the Honb^{le} the General Assembly of the State of Vermont Convened at Newbury —
The Humble Petition of Col^o William Williams & Associates —

---

1. The entry on the manuscript petition includes in the report of the committee the statement that "the facts set up in said Petition are Not fully Supported . . ."
2. Incorporation enabled a religious society to levy taxes. See p. 143, ante, note 3.
3. For this act, see Ms. Laws of Vt., II, 194–195.

Humbly Sheweth that your Petitioners being Owners and Proprietors of the Township of Wildersburgh[1] in the County of Orange and the said Township at present being destitute of Roads to accommodate the same by which means it retards the Settlement, Your Petitioners humbly hopes the Honb^le House would take the same into their wise Consideration and grant an Act may be passed to raise One penny upon each Acre of Land in said Township for the purpose of making Roads, Building Bridges &^e thro' said Town, and also appoint proper Persons to raise and levy the same in such amanner as in said Act may be expressed, Your Petitioners being sensible the Honb^le House will do every thing in their Power to encourage matters of such Importance to the Interest of the State and Individuals conceives they need not enlarge upon the Subject as they are sensible of the great Advantage arising from the same and also for the public good and as in Duty bound Your Petitioners shall Ever Pray. —
Newbury 17th October 1787 — Wm Williams

— & —

Col° Williams & Associats
Entered
Filed 19th Octr 1787
. . .*
<Newborough Octr 19th 1787
the Committee appointed to take the within petition into Consideration report as their opinion the prayer of the petition Ought to be granted Provided that there be provition made in the Bill inform [in form] for Each proprietor or Land owner to pay his proportion of the tax in wheat, pork, beef, Butter, Cheese or [flower] or in Labour on Said highways as agreed on by S^d petitioner.
I. Clark for Committee>[2]

— & —

A. J.: *Read and referred to a committee, 19 Oct. '87, S. P. of Vt., III (IV), 27; *report of committee recommending that tax of one penny per acre be laid on "the two first division of lots" of 100 acres each, read and accepted, and leave given to bring in a bill accordingly, 20 Oct. '87, Ibid, III (IV), 37.

FOR EXCLUSIVE RIGHT TO PERFORM STATE PRINTING FOR SEVEN YEARS[3]
xvii, 354

To the Honorable General Assembly of the State of Vermont, now sitting.
The Representation and Petition of George Hough & Alden Spooner, Printers to said State — Humbly Sheweth:

---

1. Now Barre. See S. P. of Vt., II (Vermont Charters), 264.
2. It is impossible to determine whether this report actually belonged to another petition and was written in on this one through an error, or whether it represented the original decision of the committee for which the report submitted to the Assembly was substituted.
3. For a brief history of printing in Vermont prior to 1800, see Elizabeth F. Cooley, Vermont Imprints before 1800 (Montpelier, 1937), ix–xxx.

That the Honorable General Assembly, at their session at Windsor, in February seventeen hundred and eighty-three, appointed a Committee of five, viz. Thomas Moredock, Isaac Tichenor, Abel Curtis, Samuel Mattocks, and Ebenezer Curtis, Esquires, to agree with some person or persons, to carry on the Printing Business within and for said State: And *Resolved*, that such person or persons, so engaging with said Committee, or a major part of them, to carry on said business as aforesaid, should have the sole and exclusive right of performing the *whole* printing for said State, for the term of *five years*.[1]

Your petitioners therefore contracted with a major part of said Committee, viz. Thomas Moredock, Abel Curtis, and Eben^r Curtis, Esquires, to carry on Said Printing Business as aforesaid. And as your petitioners left other valuable employments, on the application of said Committee, and the encouragement they were empowered to give, to Serve this State as State Printers — being conscious of having faithfully discharged the duty assigned them — (and the time for which they are engaged in the capacity aforesaid will expire in April next) — and not meeting with so great employments by the State as they expected at the time of their engagements with said Committee; they find the profits arising from said Business, have but barely compensated for the disadvantages they suffered in removing from their former employments, and entering into the Service of this State.

Your Petitioners therefore pray, that your Honours will give them a further grant of the exclusive right of performing the whole printing for this State, for the term of seven years.

And as in duty bound will ever pray, —

George Hough
Alden Spooner

Dated at Newbury ⎫
Octr 17th 1787 ⎭

— & —

Hough & Spooners Petition
Filed 18th Octr 1787
Entered
. . .*

— & —

A. J.: *Read and referred to a committee to join a committee from the Council, 18 Oct. '87, *S. P. of Vt.*, III (IV), 25–26; *report of committee recommending that exclusive right of doing state's printing be granted petitioners for three years from rising of this session, read and accepted, 22 Oct. '87, *Ibid*, III (IV), 38;[2] bill read and accepted and sent to Council, 22 Oct. '87, *Ibid*, III (IV), 38; bill, having been returned by Council, passed into law, 24 Oct. '87, *Ibid*, III (IV), 46.[3] C. J.: *Committee appointed to join Assembly committee, 19 Oct. '87, *G. and C.*, III, 151; act read and returned to Assembly with pro-

---

1. For the action of the Assembly in this matter, see *S. P. of Vt.*, III (II), 132, 137, 181.

2. The entry on the manuscript petition includes only the text of the report and not the action taken on it. As originally drawn the report granted the exclusive right for three years "from the fifth day of May next — ."

3. For this act, see *Acts and Laws passed by the Legislature of the State of Vermont, at their session at Newbury, the second Thursday of October, 1787* (Windsor, 1787), 5.

posals of amendment, 22 Oct. '87, *Ibid*, III, 153.[1]

FOR COMPENSATION FOR WAR SERVICES INCLUDING DEPRECIATION MONEY
xvii, 355

State of Vermont October 18th 1787

To the Honorable General Assembly of said State now seting at Newbury in said State

Humbly sheweth John Martin of Moortown [Mooretown][2] in said State, —

That your Petitioner Inlisted into the service of the United States on the eighth of Novr 1776, that by reason of Your Petitioner living in the said State of Vermont he has not been paid for his service in the Year 1780,[3] by reason that each State, were Directed by Congress, to pay their own Soldears, That he has never ben able to git any Depreciation according to Resolve of Congress

Therefore Your Petitioner pray Your Honors to take his case under your wise & serious consideration, & grant him pay for the year 1780 and his Depreciation, as Soldiers in other States have been paid, or otherwise as may apear Just and Your Petitioner will ever pray —

John Martin

— & —

John Martin's Petition
. . .*

— & —

A. J.: *Read and dismissed, 24 Oct. '87, *S. P. of Vt.*, III (IV), 46.

FOR COMPENSATION FOR ATTENDANCE AT NEW YORK PROVINCIAL CONGRESS[4]
xvii, 350

To the Honble the General Assembly of the State of Vermont now Convened at Newbury —

The Humble Petition of Colo William Williams —

Humbly Sheweth that your Petitioner in the Month of May 1775 was Chosen a Representative to meet the Provincial Congress then sitting at the City of New

---

1. The entry for this action as recorded on the original act indicates that the Council concurred in the Assembly bill. However, as a proviso, the clause "& perform the Business of this State punctually & for a reasonable price. — " was added at the end of the act in a different hand. See *Ms. Vt. S. P., Laws, 1786–1789*, vol. II, no pagination.

2. Now Bradford. See *S. P. of Vt.*, II (Vermont Charters), 325.

3. For this service, see *Vt. Rev. Rolls*, 664. For previous petitions to the same effect on which the name of John Martin [Martain] appears, see pp. 224, 272, 291, *ante*.

4. For a similar petition from Paul Spooner and John Sessions, see next document.

York as Member for the then County of Cumberland, now County of Windham,[1] for which Service your Petitioner has never received any Pay, and to which Petition the Honble Assembly receives his Account for the Time of his Service in attending upon the same[;] Hopes the Honble House will take the same into their wise Consideration and grant him such relief in the Premises as in their Wisdom may seem most meet

> and as in Duty bound
> your Petitioner shall ever pray

Newbury
17th Octr 1787 —   Wm Williams

The County of Cumberland ⟨The State of Vermont⟩
            to William Williams — Dr
1775 & 1776

			£	S	d
To 157 days Attendance on the Provincial Congress at New York to represent the County of Cumberland at 12/ per day			94	4	0
Interest 10 years			56	5	0
		£	150	9	0
Cr			2	0	0
Interest on d°			1	4	0
		£	3	4 :	0
	Ball due	£	147	5	0

                                                                Wm Williams

Your Petitioner at this time would beg leave further to Observe to this Honorable Assembly That the Inhabitants of this State have been Greatly benefited by his attendance in Convention in New York at that time, for he contracted ⟨procured⟩ for a very Considerable quantity of Amunition from the Convention which actually arived and was made use of by the inhabitants of this State which was of great use to them being an article much wanted, and which they could not do without —

Your Petitioner would beg leave further to Observe to this Honorable Assembly That he has been sued for part of his expences while in New York Attending the Convention And is now Obliged to raise the money to pay it, which is extreemly difficult for him to do, As he has met with various delays and great disappointments in Collecting debts due to him — That your Petitioner cannot with any prospect of Success apply to the State of New York — And That your Petitioner Conceives it would be a great Hardship and very unjust that he should Spend his own time and money at the appointment of others and for their benefit and receive no Consideration therefor

Your Petitioner would further Observe that he is now makeing and bringing forward a new setlement in the northerly part of the State which will be greatly retarded if not intirely Stopped if he can have no Relief in the Case —

Your Petitioner therefore Humbly Prays that this Honorable Assembly would grant Relief
Westminster October 19th
    1789   William Williams

---

1. For a record and discussion of this service, see *G. and C.*, I, 341–343.

— & —

Col° Williams Petition
Filed 19th Octr 1787

— & —

[No Record]

FOR COMPENSATION FOR ATTENDANCE AT NEW YORK PROVINCIAL CONGRESS[1]
xvii, 356

To the hon^e the Legislature of the State of Vermont now sitting at Newbury,
    The Petition of the Subscribers hereto humbly sheweth
    That either in the Year of our Lord 1775 or '76 Your Petitioners were severally elected by the then legal electors of the then County of Cumberland under the Jurisdiction of New York, to represent them in a provincial Congress at the City of New York,[2]
    That in consequence of such election Your Petitioners did actually attend S^d Provincial Congress, altho much to the damage of their particular Interests relying on the Usual protection & support of the then powers of Government to ensure them a competent reward for their services,
    That before time proper to collect such reward for such services the territory now known by the State of Vermont including the then County of Cumberland, claim'd & began to exercise a seperate Jurisdiction, by which Your Petitioners have not been able to collect such sums as Justice & their expectations entitle them to, as a reward for S^d Services.
    Your Petitioners therefore pray Your honors to take their Cause under consideration and grant them such relief in a grant of land or otherwise as in your wisdom shall seem just & meet
    Your Petitioners in full confidence of the Justness of their cause & Your patronage have herewith exhibited their several Accounts as stated on the back of this petition

Newbury 19th October   Paul Spooner
    1787   John Sessions

October 19th 1787

The County of Cumberland to Paul Spooner D^r
to service done for them at the City of New York in the Year 1775
at 12/ p^r Day including a term of six weeks reckoning from his first
going from his home to his return finding his own horse & bearing
his own expence   £ 25 : 4: 0
to service done in the Year 1776 place of service & term the same —   25 : 4: 0
Interest on the above Sums —   37 : 7: 6

                         total   87 :15: 6

    Errors excepted p^r Paul Spooner

---

1. For a similar petition from Colonel William Williams, see previous document.
2. For these elections, see G. and C., I, 341, 342, 346.

The County of Cumberland to John Sessions Dr
to services done for them in the Year 1776 as p^r Account — £ 72 :14: 9
Interest — 40 : 0: 0
John Sessions

Being Elected one of the Deligate to Represent the County of Cumberland at the
provential Congress of the State of New York and according to S^d Election &
appointment attended 189 Days at 12/ pr day £ 111 —
[Crea^t?] by Lone to the County &c 38–6–3
remains Due £ 72:14:9
Intrest at 6/ pr C^t — £40
Octr 19 1787 John Sessions

— & —

Petition of Paul Spooner & John Sessions
Entered
Filed 19th Octr 1787
. . .*

— & —

A. J.: *Read and dismissed, 19 Oct. '87, S. P. of Vt., III (IV), 27.

FOR A TAX ON LAND TO BUILD ROADS AND BRIDGES
xvii, 357

To the hon^{ble} the General Assembly of the State of Vermont now sitting.
The Petition of Nathaniel Throop on behalf of the Inhabitants of Bethel his
Constituents —
Humbly sheweth /
     That said Town is new — but thinly inhabited is in want of a number of
Bridges — & has never had the benefit of any tax whatever — That the Inhabitants
of said town are not able of themselves to build the Bridges necessary in said
Town & repair the Highways. —
     Your Petitioner therefore prays this hon^{ble} house to grant a tax of 2^d per
Acre on all the Land in said Town (except public rights) to be expended in building
Bridges & repairing highways in said Town under the Direction of the Selectmen
thereof. —
     And your Petitioner as in duty bound shall ever pray &c.
Newbury 20th Octr 1787 Nath^{el} Throop
Elisha Barton

— & —

Nathl Troop's Pet^n
Entered
Filed 20th Octr 1787 —
. . .*

— & —

A. J.: *Read and referred to a committee, 20 Oct. '87, S. P. of Vt., III (IV),
37; *report of committee recommending that petition be granted, read and
accepted, and leave given to bring in a bill accordingly, 22 Oct. '87, Ibid, III

(IV), 38; bill read and accepted and sent to Council, 24 Oct. '87, *Ibid*, III (IV), 44; bill, having been concurred in by Council, passed into law, 25 Oct. '87, *Ibid*, III (IV), 51.[1] *C. J.*: Act read and concurred in, 25 Oct. '87, *G. and C.*, III, 155.

FOR A TAX ON LAND TO BUILD ROADS AND BRIDGES
xvii, 358

To the honorable the General Assembly of the State of Vermont now setting at Newbury the Petition of the subscribers Selectmen of the Town of Newbury in the County of Orange
  Humbly Sheweth
    That some years since a road was surveyed from the Court house in said Newbury through the western part of said Town to Onion River that if the said Road was compleated it would be much more convenient for the public than the one now traveled as well on Account of the situation of the Country as the distance
    Your Petitioners therefore pray Your honors to grant a tax of two pence on each acre of land in said Newbury public rights excepted for the purpose of cutting & clearing the aforesaid Road & making bridges upon the same and mending other public Roads in said Town and your Petitioners as in duty bound shall ever pray
Newbury Oct[r] 22nd 1787   Jacob Bayley in
                                                             behalf of the Select
                                                             Men of S[d] town

— & —

Select men of Newbury Petition
Filed Oct[r] 23[d] 1787
. . .*

— & —

A. J.: *Read and granted and leave given to bring in a bill accordingly, 25 Oct. '87, *S. P. of Vt.*, III (IV), 49; bill read and accepted and sent to Council, 26 Oct. '87, *Ibid*, III (IV), 53, 55.[2] *C. J.*: Act read and concurred in, 26 Oct. '87, *G. and C.*, III, 157.

FOR THE ENCOURAGEMENT OF LINEN, WOOLEN AND OTHER CLOTH MANUFACTURES
xvii, 240

To the Hon[ble] The General Assembly of the State of Vermont.
  The Petition of John Scott of Newbury humbly sheweth.
  Whereas it appears unto your Petitioner, That, considering the local and political

---

1. For this act, see *Ms. Laws of Vt.*, II, 204–205.
2. The second of these entries in the journal was doubtless a clerical error. The bill should have been noted as concurred in by the Council and passed into law. For the act itself, see *Ms. Laws of Vt.*, II, 223.

situation of this State, now as it were in its Infancy, entirely destitute of Sea-ports, and exposed to the jealousy and Caprice of its more potent Neighbours, for most of its Imports, especially of those Articles, which, although properly the luxuries, are by the Generality of Mankind, deemed the necessaries of Life; Consequently the Course of Exchange at This rate must be always against us and the Circulating Medium of Cash constantly low — And that the most feasible way of obviating these difficulties would be to Give the Greatest encouragement to Home Manufactures — To which end The following Hints are offered, with the Greatest deference and submission, to be adopted either wholly or in part — or entirely new modelled, as to the wisdom of the Honble House shall seem most expedient.
1st That a premium shall be Granted to the Person, or Persons, who shall raise and dress, the Greatest Quantity of Good Merchantable Flax, on the single Acre of land, within the State. —
2. That an adequate Premium might be allowed to Those who Manufactured and Brought to Market, within this State, the Largest Quantity of Linen or Woolen Cloth — The Gratuity to be so much PCent or upon the Yard, according to the value of the Cloth. —
3^d That a suitable encouragement be Given — and by such ways and Means, as to the Honble Legislature shall appear the most effectual, to the Person, or Persons, who shall attempt, and Bring to tolerable perfection any thing new, or hitherto unattempted within the state, in the Linnen, Woolen, Silk, or Cotton Manufactures — and more particularly Fine Linens, Muslins, Lawns, Gauses, Diapers &c. — such undertakings being attended with considerable expence, and scarce practicable to a private Individual, without the interposition and assistance of Those in power — But the utility and expediency of which will be very obvious to those acquainted with Modern History, from this — That the States of Switzerland, by a well regulated internal Police, and constant attention and encouragement Given to the Linen and Lace Manufactures, 'tho' lying in a Mountainous and Barren Clime, & Centre of the most potent States of Europe, Have had a constant Command of Cash, — and Lived happy and independent for Hundreds of Years.

The above is submitted to the judgment of the Honble House, Hoping it will in some degree operate to the End designed — and your Petitioner as in duty bound shall ever pray &C. —
Newbury 23 October 1787 —   John Scott

— & —

Petition of John Scott
. . .*

— & —

A. J.: *Read and referred to next session, 26 Oct. '87, S. P. of Vt., III (IV), 54; *read as "entered on file 26th of Octr 1787" and referred to a committee, 13 Oct. '89, Ibid, III (IV), 129;[1] report of committee read and "ordered to lie on the table till to-morrow morning", 19 Oct. '89, Ibid, III (IV), 146; *petition ordered referred to next session, 29 Oct. '89, Ibid, III (IV), 175. Rep. of Com.: Report recommending bounties on hemp, woolen and linen manufactures, read and ordered to lie on table, 19 Oct. '89, S. P. of Vt., IV, 53–54. C. J.: *Committee appointed to join Assembly committee, 13 Oct. '89, G. and C.,

---

1. The entry on the manuscript correctly notes that this committee was to join a committee from the Council.

III, 189.[1]

FOR A TAX ON LAND TO BUILD ROADS AND BRIDGES
xvii, 360

To the Honble General Assembly of the State of Vermont Now Convened at Newbury

The Peticion of the Inhabitence of the town of Brookfield Humbly Sheweth that the S^d town is in Low Surcumstances and are not able to Make and Repare the Rodes and Buld Bridges in Said town so as to make the Rodes Conveniant for the Inhabitince to transact there Common privit Bisness with out grate Difficulty and Likewise the Publick Suffers much at Sum Certain times of the year and it is not in the power of your perticinors to repair the S^d Rodes without grate Damage to your perticinors without Sum assistance frome your Honors — Your Porticinors therefore Pray that your Honours Would grant a Tax of one peney pe^r acre on all Lands in the town of Brookfield Publick Rights Excepted for the purpose of making and repairing Highwais and Bridges under such Restricktions as your Honourable body Shall Direct —

And your Perticinors as in Duty Bound Shall Ever Pray

⟨Brookfield Octo^r 14th 1787⟩

Newbury Octr 23^d 1787

Timothy Cowles } in behalf of S^d town

— & —

The Perticion of the Inhabitance of Brookfield
Filed 24th Octr 1787 —
. . .*

— & —

A. J.: *Read and granted, and leave given to bring in a bill accordingly,"24 Oct. '87, S. P. of Vt., III (IV), 44; bill read and accepted and sent to Council, 24 Oct. '87, Ibid, III (IV), 46; bill, having been concurred in by Council, passed into law, 25 Oct. '87, Ibid, III (IV), 48, 51.[2] C. J.: Act read and concurred in, 24 Oct. '87, G. and C., III, 154.

FOR A TAX ON A COUNTY TO PAY ITS DEBTS
xvii, 363

To the Honorable General Assembly of the State of Vermont, convened at New-

---

1. Section V of "An Act directing Listers in their office and duty", passed 26 Oct. '87, was intended "to encourage the raising of sheep, and manufacturing of linen in this State." It provided for deductions from the lists of those who raised wool and made linen cloth. See Acts and Laws, passed by the Legislature of the State of Vermont, at their session at Newbury, the second Thursday of October, 1787 (Windsor, 1787), 12.

2. The second entry in the journal was doubtless a clerical error. For this act, see Ms. Laws of Vt., II, 200–201.

bury

The Representation and Petition of George Hough, Treasurer of the County of Windsor, humbly sheweth —

That the county of Windsor have been at considerable expence in erecting a Goal in said county; and are likewise in debt to a number of the inhabitants of said county for services in various capacities: — and whereas a Committee of three become obligated in behalf of the county, for the expence of erecting the Goal, who are now under an attachment for the Same. And as the Constitution nor Laws make no provision for levying County taxes:

Your Petitioner therefore prays, in behalf of the county, that your Honors would pass a special act, impowering the Judges of the County Court for the county of Windsor, to levy a tax to discharge the debts against the county.

And as in duty bound will ever pray —

George Hough, Treasurer of Windsor County }

Dated at Newbury,
    Octr 26th 1787.

— & —

Petition of Geo^g Hough Treas. of Windsor County —
. . .*

— & —

A. J.: *Read and granted, and leave given to bring in a bill accordingly, 26 Oct. '87, S. P. of Vt., III (IV), 55; bill read and accepted and sent to Council, 26 Oct. '87, Ibid, III (IV), 56; bill, having been concurred in by Council, passed into law, 27 Oct. '87, Ibid, III (IV), 61.[1] C. J.: Act read and concurred in, G. and C., III, 159.

---

1. For this act, see Ms. Laws of Vt., II, 213–214.

INDEX

INDEX

A

Abbot, James..................202
  Joseph....................201
  Walter....................387
Abernethy, Cyrus..............281
  Jared.....................317
Accounts, State
  settlement of....41–42, 332–34, 348
  See also Finances, State
Ackley (Akeley, Akley)
  Francis......224, 272, 291, 292
Actions at law, *see* Crimes; Torts
Adams (Adam)
  Daniel....................254
  Gideon..........143, 155, 222
  James.....................214
  Samuel....................280
Addison.........124, 162, 214, 342
  tax abatement............383–84
  town lines settled........153–54
Addison County 201, 213, 296, 304, 379
  county town...............124
  lines, new................389–90
  post riders...............344–45
Agriculture, *see* Farming
Aierill, *see* Averill
Aiken (Aikin, Akin, Akins)
  ————....................225
  Daniel....................287
  Edward......10, 134, 283, 287, 315
  Jonathan............241, 243, 361
Aikin's Gore
  annexation of (also proposed) 93, 283
Ainsworth, Daniel.............282
Aitkin, Samuel................203
Akeley (Akley), *see* Ackley
Akin (Akins), *see* Aiken
Albany, N. Y......36, 88, 204, 337, 348
Aldrich (Aldrick, Aldridg,
  Aldridge, Aldrige)
  ———— [Captain].............272
  Cyrus.....................202
  David......................33
  George....................185
  Mark......................202
  Peter......................98
  Silas.....................202
  Zibe...................56, 98

Alen, *see* Allen
Alexander, Eldad..............155
Alger, John................47, 48
Allbee, Eleazer................34
Allen (Alen, Allin)
  ———— [General]............120
  ———— [Mrs.]..............333
  Abner.....................117
  Amos......................361
  Benjamin..................254
  Dan.......................241
  David.....................303
  Ebenezer....200, 252, 258, 268, 357
  Eber......................251
  Elihu.........70, 198, 311, 313
  Ethan................122, 273
  Ethan A. K................356
  Gideon.....................34
  Henry......................53
  Ira....13, 21, 41, 42, 78, 179, 332,
          333, 334, 348, 376
  Isaac.....................303
  Jonathan..................242
  Samuel....................252
  Thomas....................117
Alsworth (Alswoth, Aysworth)
  James.....................108
  John...............77, 78, 108
  Philip....................108
  Robert....................208
  Wanton....................107
Alvord, Elijah.................17
  Job........................50
Ambler, Ebenezer..............166
  James.....................166
  John......................166
Ambrose, Benjamin.............202
Ames, Aaron...................201
  Lemuel....................219
Amey, John....................201
  William...................201
Ammonoosuc River...............19
Anderson (Andanson)
  Abram......................67
  Anday.....................361
  David................241, 361
  James.................10, 241
  Robert................10, 361

Andover
  roads.....................10, 267
  town lines..................48–49
Andres, *see* Andrus
Andrews (Andrew)
  David.......................289
  Ebenezer....................294
  Isaac.......................289
  Jehiel..................294, 295
  John........................294
  Samuel......................330
  Thomas......................347
Andrus (Andres, Andros, Andross)
  ——— [Doctor]...............23
  Bildad.. 47
  Eldad.......................317
  Ethan.......................317
  Timothy.....................19
Angell (Angel)
  Abiathar..........5, 108, 204, 297
  Nedebijah...................313
Annes, Phinnas.................387
Arbitration and Award..........206
Archer, James...................31
Arlington..................110, 335
  bridges.....................209
  convention at...............72
  militia...................63–65
Arms (Armes)
  ———.....................219
  ——— [Landlord]............91
  Josiah......................223
  Thomas..................311, 313
Arnold, ——— [Colonel]......89, 90
  Daniel......................241
  Oliver.............98, 198, 313
  Stephen............198, 313
Ash, John.....................303
Ashcraft, Daniel..........178, 179
Ashley, Abner.................351
  William S...................155
Atwater, Jesse.................34
Atwood, Oliver................10
  William.....................336
Austin (Austen)
  Asa.........................219
  John....................37, 241
  Parvis......................37
  Seth....................75, 384
Averest, *see* Everest

Averill (Aierill, Averell, Avirill)
  Ephraim.................294, 357
  Jesse.......................339
  Robert......................347
  Samuel......................331
  Wiman.......................347
Averit, *see* Everitt
Avery, Nathan.................108
  Roger.......................317
  Samuel......................206
Aylsworth (Aylesworth)
  Abel........................209
  John........................205
Aysworth, *see* Alsworth

B

Babot, Daniel.................287
Backer, David..................37
Backus, John...................33
  Joseph......................34
Bacon, Asa...............280, 285
  Daniel......................347
  Edmund......................220
Badger, Edward................357
Bail Bond
  discharge from............71–72
Bailey (Baliy, Baly, Bayley)
  Abijah......................202
  Benjamin................202, 254
  Benjamin, Jr................254
  Charles.....................203
  Cyrus.......................202
  Edward......................254
  Ephraim.....................201
  Fry.........................201
  Isaac.......................203
  Israel......................202
  Jacob...................203, 398
  James...................201, 202
  James, Jr...................202
  John........................201
  John Gd.....................201
  Joshua......................201
  Luther......................202
  Moses...................80, 202
  Oliver......................221
  Osamus......................201
  Ward....................81, 201
Baker, Absalom.................51
  Benjamin, Sr................34

Baker (*cont.*)
Benjamin, Jr. 34
Cornelius. 39
Daniel. 108
Ebenezer. 160
Joseph. 241
Reuben. 254
Robert. 387
Solomon. 33
Thomas. 6
Timothy. 34, 339
Bakersfield. 367, 371
Baldwin (Baldwine)
Benjamin. 23, 53, 202, 235, 236
Daniel. 357
Eleazer. 53
Eleazer, Jr. 238
Elijah. 356
Jabez. 282
Joel. 296
Miles. 294
Shubil. 357
Silas. 53
Thomas. 108
Baliy, *see* Bailey
Ball, David. 221
Humphry. 354
Ballou, Benjamin. 208
Baly, *see* Bailey
Banadick, Jonathan. 361
Bancroft, John. 364
Baptison, James. 201
Baptist Churches. 349–50
Barber, Elisha. 54, 67, 205, 362
Gideon. 16, 241
Martin. 241
Moses. 204
Samuel. 204
William. 204
Bardslee, Price. 361
Barnam, *see* Barnum
Barnard, Andrew. 364
Dan. 364
Barnard. 104, 164
tax abatement. 179–80
Barnet. 150
roads. 270
Barney, Constant. 209
Thomas. 60, 241
Barns, James. 34

Barns (*cont.*)
John. 34, 321, 378
William. 294
Barnum (Barnam)
———— [Lieutenant] 4
Ebenezer. 284
Francis. 160
Richard. 284
Samuel. 284
Stephen. 284
Timothy. 347
Barr, William. 294, 295
Barre, *see* Wildersburgh
Barrett (Barret, Barrit)
Benjamin. 200
Joseph. 256
Joseph, Jr. 108
Peter. 67
Barry, David. 31
Bartlett (Bartlet, Bartlit)
Bartholo. 31
Benjamin. 63, 65
Ebenezer. 356
Elisha. 339
Elliott. 354
Fisk. 339, 346
Gershom. 138, 139, 354
Ithamar. 138, 139
Jonathan. 354
Moses. 354, 364
Samuel. 339, 347
Barto, Samuel. 160
Barton, Andrew. 197
Andrew, Jr. 196
Dyer. 197
Elisha. 397
Basin Harbor. 124
Batchelor, Timothy. 202
Bateman, John. 34
Bates, David. 241
Francis, Jr. 205
Rufus. 198, 254
Stephen. 161
Walter. 125
Battenkill River. 209
Baxter (Bexter)
Benjamin. 311, 313
Elihu. 354
Bayley, *see* Bailey

Beach (Beech)
    Gershom...256, 257, 266, 267, 294,
                   358, 359, 364
    Gershom, Jr..................294
    Noah...............256, 257
Beaman (Beeman)
    Aaron.....................243
    Elijah......................83
    Nathan.....................241
    Samuel.....................241
Bean, Eliphalet.................47
    Enoch......................47
Bears, Benjamin.................241
Beaver, Jacob...................37
Becker, Solomon................125
Beckwith, Daniel...............241
    Royce......................241
Bedel, William.................241
Beebe (Beebee, Beebie)
    Allen......................294
    Asa...................200, 283
    Asa, Jr....................200
    Ezekiel....................294
    Ezekiel, Jr................294
    Lewis......................241
Beech, *see* Beach
Beeman, *see* Beaman
Beerdsley, Jehiel..............289
Beitlet, Joseph, Jr.............31
Beitlett, Joseph................31
Belknap, Thomas...........138, 139
Bell, Andrew...................143
    Benjamin...........98, 311, 313
    Samuel.................37, 387
Benfield, George...............202
Benjamin, —— [Captain].......73
Bennett (Bennet, Bennit)
    Isat^r....................33
    John.......................58
    Joseph, Jr..................5
    Nathan...................143
    William...............201, 241
Bennington....11, 16, 23, 36, 42, 43,
    45, 66, 68, 70, 71, 72, 84, 90,
    93, 94, 211, 257, 258, 326, 327,
    330, 331, 332, 334, 337, 340,
          343, 344, 345, 348
    county town..14-15, 19-20, 110-11,
                  346
    "Grand Committee" at.........342

Bennington (*cont.*)
    post rider...................344
    roads....8, 62-63, 85, 161, 285-86,
                   338
    troops at....................91
Bennington Battle...........51, 382
Bennington County...8, 50, 53, 60, 64,
           240, 250, 330, 373
    bridges.....................209
    county court house.........345-47
    county town, location of.....14-15,
           19-20, 110-11, 346
    lines.....................123-24
    taxes.....................345-46
Benson, Elijah..................320
    Joseph.....................320
    Rowland....................320
    Rowling....................381
Benson...........287, 288, 292, 329
    roads....................265-66
Bentley, Thomas................317
Benton, Joel..............138, 139
    Jonathan....................25
    Medad......................24
    Samuel.....................317
Berkshire
    location of...............367-68
Berlin.........................200
Bernardston, Mass...............69
Besse, Ebenezer.................37
Bethel.........104, 116, 131, 274
    population.................165
    roads and bridges.........397-98
    tax abatement.........128, 149-50
    town lines...............163-64
    town lines, maintenance of....108-9,
           115, 164-66
Bevons, Jacob..................108
Bexter, *see* Baxter
Biblical references.......191, 282, 334
Bigelow (Bigolow)
    Ezra.................200, 283
    Jabez.....................203
    Solomon...............281, 285
Billings (Billing)
    Elkanah.....................98
    John.......................25
    Nathan....................155
Bills, Ebenezer................117
    Nathaniel..................117

Bingham, Abner................215
  Je^r....................231
  Jeremiah..................317
  Silas..........125, 148, 215, 305
Birchard, Roger................356
Birtch, *see* Burtch
Bishop, Benona................241
  John, Jr....................284
  Lemuel....................339
Bissell, John....................294
Blachard, *see* Blanchard
Black River...........167, 213, 306
Blackman, Abner................296
  Andrew....................241
Blackmer, Jediah................34
  Lemuel....................357
  Solomon....................357
Blackstone, William [English
  Jurist]................157, 309
Blair, John, Jr..................37
Blakeslee (Blakly, Blakslee)
  Aaron....................303
  Clement....................294
  David....................33
Blanchard (Blachard, Blanched,
  Blanshard)
  Abel....................202
  Abiel....................202
  Abner............10, 11, 73, 74
  Asahel....................254
  Daniel....................387
  David....................214
  Joel....................202
  Joseph............176, 177
  Nathaniel....................317
  Peter....................202
  Reuben..........202, 254, 313
  William....................73
Blanden, Joseph................307
Blanshard, *see* Blanchard
Blashfield, James................357
Bliss, James....................138
  John, Jr....................387
  Peletiah....................202
  Timothy....................241
Blodgett (Blogget)
  Elijah....................347
  Sardius....................317
Blood, David....................117
  John................108, 205

Blossom, David................289
  Peter....................289
  Seth....................289
Board of War............32, 130–31
Boardman (Bordman)
  Elisha..............199, 311, 313
  John....................99
  Sherman....................361
  Timothy....................322
Boice, *see* Boyce
Boland (Bololand)
  James....................361
  John....................361
  William....................361
Bolden, Eleazer................241
Bolles, Charles................241
  Henry....................241
Bololand, *see* Boland
Bolster, John....................208
Bolton, James....................31
Bonett, Joseph................202
Booge, Jeffery Amherst..........364
Boorn, Barned................241
  Daniel....................241
  Jered....................241
  Nathaniel....................241
  Nathaniel, Jr................241
Booshnal, *see* Bushnal
Bordman, *see* Boardman
Bostwick (Bostick)
  Arthur....................241
  Israel....................160
  John W....................241
  Nathaniel....................241
Boston, Mass........69, 119, 139, 259
Botons, Elijah L................347
Botts, Josiah................108
Bounties
  for certain produce and manu-
    factures....................399
Bovee, Jacob....................205
Bow, Edward....................138
Bowdish, Asa....................205
Bowker, Elias................294
  Micah....................96
  Michael....................34
Bowman, John......198, 281, 311, 313
Boyce (Boice)
  Henry....................37
  Samuel....................305

Boynton, Stuard................303
Brace, ———.................41
  Jonathan...................241
  Phineas...................201
Brackit, Christopher...........241
Bradford, *see* Mooretown
Bradley (Bradly)
  ———................122, 123
  Benjamin..................347
  David.....................202
  Gilbert................339, 347
  John...................339, 347
  Joseph.............32, 339, 347
  Lemuel................339, 347
  Miles.....................339
  Stephen...............339, 346
  Stephen R..................26
  Timothy...............339, 347
Braintree.....................131
  town lines, maintenance of.....114
Brakenridge, ———...........266
Braley (Brayley)
  Lemuel.................117, 357
  Miles.....................347
Brandon............166, 258, 259
  roads......................365
  See also Neshobee
Brevoot, Isaac.................241
Brattleboro.............45, 46, 71
  bridge lottery.............222–23
  convention at............208, 221
  land case................139–41
  mills....................139–40
  New York adherents in.........69
  roads......................186
  tax collection............175–76
  Vermonter kidnapped at......91–92
Brewster (Bruster)
  ——— [Colonel].............131
  Charles...................296
  David......................25
  Eliphaz...................296
  Timothy...................143
Bridge, Benjamin...............303
  Samuel.....................17
Bridgewater
  roads and bridges..12, 86–87, 177–78
Bridgman (Bridgeman, Bridgemen)
  John................38, 66, 251

Bridport.....................342
  roads and bridges.........234–35
Briggs (Brigs)
  Daniel....70, 99, 118, 198, 311, 313
  George....................347
  Joseph....................356
  Joshua....................347
  Phelp.....................118
  Philip...........99, 198, 311, 313
Brigham, Abner................155
  John......................294
  Paul..................138, 354
Brigs, *see* Briggs
Bristol (Bristoll)
  Abel......................241
  Gideon....................279
  Isaac.....................125
  Phebe <Susannah>..........279
  Sarah.....................241
Bristol, *see* Pocock
Brock, Andrew.............81, 203
  James.....................284
  John......................284
  Robert....................202
  Walter....................202
Bromley, *see* Brumley
Brookfield....................50
  county change (opposed)........82
  county grammar school.......374
  roads and bridges...........400
Brooks, John............200, 283
Brookses.....................167
Brown (Browen, Browne)
  ——— [Colonel].............318
  Adam.....................355
  Amasa....................119
  B........................335
  Benjamin.............202, 296
  Briant.........83, 224, 225, 318
  Eli..............99, 281, 285
  Isaac.....................203
  Jeremiah...................34
  John......................342
  Nathaniel.........93, 200, 283
  Noah.....................364
  Peter.....................202
  Phineas.............197, 345
  Purchis...................254
  Richard..............108, 205
  Roam.....................294

Brown (Browen, Browne) (*cont.*)
Samuel...................354
Timothy.................160
William............108, 205
William, Jr.............204
Brown's Camp.............385
Browning, Blackmen.......108
Brownson (Brunson)
———....................105
——— [Colonel]..........126
——— [Major]............72
David...................146
Eli.....................241
Elijah.............138, 139
Gideon.........253, 263, 264
Timothy.................61
Bruce, James............214
Bruer, Peter............361
Brumley, William, Jr....296
Brumley.................168
population..............9
roads........9–10, 267–68, 360–62
Brunson, *see* Brownson
Brunswick...............82
Brush, Alexander........215
Crean...................206
Moses...................148
Thor....................290
William.................196
Bruster, *see* Brewster
Bryan, David............287
Bryant, Daniel D........379
David...................202
Lemuel..................117
Brydie, David...........53
Buchanan, James.........203
Buck, ———..............333
Amos....................37
Daniel.........139, 382, 383
John, Jr................347
Lemuel..................279
Thomas..................241
Bucknam, Asa............201
Joseph..................201
Bugbee, Nathaniel.......282
Buitch, *see* Burtch
Bull, Thomas........60, 61, 241
Thomas, Jr..........241, 361
Bullard, Ebenezer.......361

Bullock (Bullocke)
Elkanah.................208
Joseph..................208
William.................134
Bumpus, Salathial.......320
Bur, Lemuel.............39
Burch, *see* Burtch
Burgess (Burges)
Ebenezer...........340, 341
Burgoyne (Burguoyne)
———....................298
A.......................138
Burlington..............331
Burllingame (Burlingham,
Burlingim, Burllinggame)
John...............254, 303
William............320, 382
Burlson, Job............108
Burnam, *see* Burnham
Burnap, John............354
Burnham (Burnam)
Asa.....................347
Elijah..................354
John, Jr................15
Thomas.............138, 139
Burriett, Daniel........361
Burritt, Edmond.........361
Burroughs, Jeremiah.....33
Joseph..................148
Burt (Burtt)
———....................236
Benjamin.....38, 121, 206, 207, 340
Ebenezer................219
Joseph..............71, 72
Simeon..................50
William.................37
Burtch (Birtch, Buitch, Burch)
Benjamin................282
Edy.....................282
Ephraim.................282
James...................282
Jonathan................282
William.................282
Burton (Burtin)
Elijah..................241
Elisha..................317
Jacob...................180
Nathaniel...............241
Burtt, *see* Burt
Bush, Timothy...........354

Buskirk, Dirick................37
  John......................37
Bushnal (Booshnal)
  Abisha....................143
  Benajah...................143
Butler, Jabez...............307
  John M....................307
  Thomas....................362
Butt, Samuel................143
Buttenmold Bay..............124
Butterfield (Butterfild)
  ——— [Captain]............334
  Benjamin..................223
  Benjamin, Jr..............50
  Thomas....................376
Button, Joseph..............366
  Louis [widow]........141, 142
Byrns, John.................361

C

Cabot.......................369
  lines uncertain........89–90
  roads.....................213
Cadwell, Moses, Jr..........387
Cady, Benjamin..............256
  Thomas H..................256
  Peleg.....................199
Calais
  settling requirements..261–62
Calder, James...............202
Caldwell, Joseph............37
Calkins, Fredrick...........202
Calven, Levi................199
  Titus.....................296
Cambell, see Campbell
Camble, see Campbell
Cambridge...................335
  roads.....................213
Cambridge, N. Y.............343
  seeks union with Vermont....36–37
Camden, N. Y.
  seeks union with Vermont....30–31
Camp, John..................208
  John, Jr..................208
Campbell (Cambell, Camble,
    Campeble)
  David.....................39
  Samuel....................80
Canada
  American prisoners in....7, 57, 62
    73, 81–82, 136, 182, 259

Canfield, Dennis............296
  Silas.....................241
Cannon, John.............4, 5
Capron, Benjamin............294
Card, Benjamin..............205
  Elisha.............108, 205
  Jonathan..................108
  Stephen...................205
  Thomas....................108
Carleton (Carlton)
  Dudley....................201
  Jesse.....................361
Carly, Ebenezer.........311, 313
Carncross, James............339
Carnigee, Andrew............373
Carpenter (Carpender)
  Benjamin.........12, 13, 208
  Caleb.....................208
  Cephas....................254
  Ezra......................199
  Jabez.....................330
  John......................282
  Jonathan...........385, 386
  Joseph....................208
  Nathaniel.....224, 272, 291, 292
  Timothy...................347
  William.......198, 311, 313
Carter, Frederic............205
  Levi......................202
Cartrite, Reuben............108
Carver, Benjamin............254
  Hezekiah..................254
  Joseph....................40
Carey (Cary)
  Christopher...............57
  James.....................287
  Samuel....................57
Case, Irena.................35
  Zebulun...................35
Cases, land, see Land cases
Cass, Amos..............28, 56
Castel (Castle)
  Abel......................53
  David.....................53
  Lewis.....................53
  Nathan....................53
  Timothy...................195
Castleton............73, 315, 351
  county grammar school....277–78
  county town (proposed)...288, 289,
    293, 329

Castleton (*cont.*)
  grievances.................262–63
  militia ordered to..............63
  New Hampshire Grants expense. 266
  roads.....................98, 99
Catlin, Amos..................339
  Ensign......................339
  Roswell......................339
Cavendish......................104
  election, special............388–89
  roads and bridges.......167–68, 306
Ceard, Daniel..................108
Center, Jeremiah............339, 347
Chaberlin, *see* Chamberlain
Chadsey, James.................198
  Job..........................198
  Richard......................198
Chaffee (Chaffe)
  Atherton..................45, 46
  Comfort......................254
  Nathaniel............118, 199, 254
Chamberlain (Chaberlin,
    Chamberlin)
  Abiel........................201
  Abner..138, 139, 152, 368, 369, 387,
                              390, 391
  Amos.........................387
  Ashur........................203
  Benjamin............129, 138, 139
  David..........................48
  Elias...............281, 285, 387
  Ev...........................202
  Jacob....................117, 286
  Jacob B......................203
  Joel.....................129, 387
  Joseph.........117, 170, 201, 356
  Nathaniel....................203
  Oliver.........................58
  Raiment......................201
  William......................202
Champlain, Lake...11, 73, 91, 124–25,
    181, 213, 230, 305, 365, 368, 376
Chandler, ——— [Major].......206
  J............................61
  John.........................10
  John E.......................10
  Thomas........10, 13, 96, 350
  Thomas, Jr....................96
  Zebulun......................108
Chapin, Daniel................357
  Jesse........................357

Chapin (*cont.*)
  Samuel.......................117
Chapman, Edmund..............214
  Throop.......................373
  William......................373
Charlemont, Mass......62–63, 90–91
Charlestown, N. H.........13, 47, 49
Charlotte
  roads and bridges............327
Charter fees
  relief from...24–25, 141–42, 168–69
Charters
  city, new..................124–25
  exchange of.................371
  lost.................56–57, 75–76
  settling requirements........261–62
  town, new....................124
Chase, Benjamin.................208
  Dudley [Dudly] 115, 116, 133, 163,
                              165
  Paul....................208, 229
  Stephen......................208
  William......................337
Chese, Nathaniel................287
Chester........9, 41, 48, 49, 205, 207
  bridges and meeting house....335–36
  churches...................349–51
  roads....................167, 267
Chesterfield, N. H..............62
Childs (Child)
  ——— [Colonel].............131
  Jonathan 47, 48, 84, 100, 101, 221, 353
  Silas.........................34
Chilson, Joseph.................305
Chipman, Amos............241, 339
  Darius [Derius]..........199, 254
  Jesse........................317
  Jonathan......................3
  Lemuel.....143, 234, 237, 278, 370
  Luna.........................237
Chittenden, Noah................335
  Reuben.......................356
  Thomas......3, 13, 21, 72, 273, 281
Chittenden......................365
  roads and bridges.......349, 363–64
Chrich, Aarnsiah................34
Chruch, Samuel..................34
Church, Elisha.................241
  James........................351
  Joshua........................96

Church and State
  relations of 83–84, 107–8, 142–43,
    173–174, 293–95, 302–3, 316–
    17, 319, 322, 328, 349–51, 391
Churches
  Baptist....................349–50
  Chester..........335–36, 349–51
  Congregational......293–95, 302–3,
                316–17, 319
  Cornwall..................316–17
  Halifax.....................328
  Pawlet...................142–43
  Pomfret..................173–74
  Poultney.............. 319
  Rutland.............293–95, 322
  Weathersfield..............302–3
  Westminster.................391
  Windsor..................83–84
Cimmons, *see* Simons
City, new.................124–25
Civil wrongs, *see* Torts
Claghorn, Eleazer................375
  James.................294, 295
  John......................294
Clarendon........8, 70, 330, 336, 372
  election dispute............197–99
  land case..................112–14
  land disputes..............118–19
  Loyalist estate at..............77
  militia....................27–28
  part to Ira (proposed).......253–55
  part to Ira (opposed).310–12, 312–13
  poor, care of.............311, 312
  roads and bridges.296, 311, 312, 380
  town lines uncertain.............23
Clark (Clarke)
  —— [Colonel]..............41
  Aaron..................117, 357
  Benjamin....................220
  Bunker....................361
  Caleb.....................50
  Chaney....................320
  Cyrus.....................293
  Eleazer.....................50
  Elisha 143, 144, 162, 166, 171, 175,
       188, 222, 257, 271, 315
  Elisha, Jr....................143
  Ezekiel..........99, 198, 311, 313
  I........................392
  Ichabod G............320, 381

Clark (Clarke) *(cont.)*
  Isaac.......................278
  James......................346
  Jedediah.................98, 254
  Jedediah, Jr...............99, 254
  John...................296, 382
  Joseph..................50, 223
  Joshua......................49
  Josiah.....................107
  Lemuel....................143
  Mitchell...................282
  Nathan.................15, 296
  Ozias.....................237
  Paul......................282
  Phinehas B...................49
  Rachel....................237
  Samuel............37, 49, 155
  Stephen...................314
  Thomas......................6
  Timothy.................10, 39
  William...........199, 311, 313
Clemons, Benjamin...............219
  Joel......................289
  Timothy...................116
Cleveland, Moses.................143
Cloid, Daniel...................241
Clossen, Timothy.................39
Clough, Nathaniel................254
Cloyd, Daniel...................37
Cobb, Ebenezer..................143
  Elkanah...........143, 154, 155
  John.............143, 280, 313
  Joshua....................143
  Nathan....................356
Cochran (Cochren)
  David..................10, 287
  Robert....................341
Coffin (Coffeen)
  Michael................224, 272
Cogswell (Coggswell, Cogsell)
  Eli...................278, 315
  Nath.....................317
Coins
  right to make.............276–77
  devices on..................277
Colburn, David..................228
  Ezekiel.....................96
  Pexston....................39
Colby, Ezekiel..................202
  Nicholas...................201

Cole, Bethuel................347
  David.....................289
  John......................361
  Parker....................347
  Salmon....................287
  See also Cowles
Collins (Collen)
  Abraham...................241
  Charles...................160
  Ch^r......................241
  Jabez.....................281
  John......................254
  Levi......................202
  Nathan....................254
  Nathaniel.................241
  Solomon...................241
  Thomas....................254
Colt, Benjamin............49, 50
Colton, Walter............294
Colvin (Colven)
  Daniel...........118, 198
  Jeremiah.....28, 56, 118, 199
  Lewis.....................118
  Rufus.....................254
  Samuel.....................34
Commissary General...42–44, 69, 71,
    127, 128, 131, 257, 258
  settlement of accounts......210–11
Commissary of Issues.....44–45, 210,
    273–74
Commissioner of Purchasing.......353
Commissioners of Sequestration
  and Sales..................41
Committee, "Grand".............342
Comstock, Daniel..............339
  Jason.....................339
  Levi......................339
  Peter.....................339
Conant, Stephen..........235, 256
Conden, Joseph...............312
Cone, Abner............289, 366
Congdon, Caleb.......199, 311, 312
  George....................311
  Job..........98, 199, 311, 313
  John..................311, 312
  Joseph.....98, 118, 199, 311, 312
  Joseph, Jr.................281
Congil, Joseph................56
Congregational Churches 293, 302–3,
    316–17, 319

Connecticut River 19, 30, 62–63, 95,
  167, 181, 201, 227, 228, 285–86,
    354, 365, 386
Connill, Benjamin..............361
Constitution (Vermont)
  cited 18, 26, 102, 107, 111, 130
    132–33, 152, 157–58, 191, 303,
    309, 323, 350, 358, 374, 388,
  origins of...................273
Conventions
  New Hampshire grants...72, 341–42
  Rutland County.......281, 292, 329
  Windham County 208, 218, 219, 221,
    275–76
  Windsor County......102–3, 104–5
Convis, Bernard...............357
Cook (Cooke)
  Amasa......................50
  Asaph......................33
  Ashbel....................294
  David.....................161
  Ezekiel...................294
  Gad........................50
  Jesse.................195, 205
  John......................313
  Joseph.....................34
  Moses......................49
  Nathaniel.............281, 285
  Noah.......................50
  Samuel.....................50
Cooley (Coolley, Cooly)
  Benjamin..........250, 321, 377
  Caleb.....................377
  Ebenezer..................198
  Gideon....................364
  Reuben....................364
Coolidge, John...............355
Coolley (Cooly), *see* Cooley
Cooper (Copper)
  Abel..................113, 254
  James......................25
  Thomas.....................83
Coots, Joseph.................50
Copper, *see* Cooper
Copper, *see* Coins
Corey, *see* Cory
Corinth.....................324
  guard at....................57
  roads and bridges....137–38, 387–88
Corly, Abraham................34

Cornish, N. H. 182
Cornwall. 144, 271
    churches. 316–17
    roads and bridges. 230–31
Corse, James. 221
Cory (Corey)
    Benjadick. 108
    Benjamin, Jr. 347
    John. 37
    Jonathan. 241
Costs, *see* Prices and Values
Cotton, Ebenezer. 373
Council of Censors. . . 42, 130, 131–33,
                              282, 309
Counterfeiting. 99–100, 172–73,
                              182–83, 390–91
Counties
    enlargement of. 95
County court houses
    erection and maintenance. . . . 345–47
    location of. 98–99
    See also County towns, location of
County elections, *see* Elections,
    county
County grammar schools
    Orange County. 374
    Rutland county. 277–78
    Windham County. 323
County lines
    changes in. 82, 123–24, 200–3,
                              389–90
County taxes. 97, 275–76, 318,
                              345–46, 400–1
County towns
    location of. 14–15, 19–20, 95–96,
        104–5, 110–11, 116–17, 124
        133–35, 200–3, 208–9, 218–19,
        219, 221, 287–89, 292–93, 328–
                              29, 346
Courts
    conduct of trials. 47
    costs. 53, 101, 309, 340
    fees of, excessive. 70–71
    grievances against. . . . 102–3, 189–91,
        216–17, 232–33, 239, 245–48,
                              280
    maladministration. . . 150–52, 195–96
    reforms (proposed). 191, 225–26,
                              249, 262, 280
    supervision of expenditures. 373

Courts (*cont.*)
    tax levy by. 401
    See also Arbitration and Award;
        New trials
Cousins (Cuzzins)
    Jacob. 160
    Joshua. 160
    Joshua, Jr. 160
Covel, James. 34
Cowan (Cowen)
    Ephraim. 343
    James. 37
    Robert. 37
Cowdin, James. 37
Cowee, John. 313
Cowen, *see* Cowan
Cowles (Cole, Cowls)
    Gideon. 145
    Timothy. 374, 400
Cox, Edward. 287
    John. 287, 315
    William. 10, 287
Coy, Daniel. 361
Cramton, Nero. 296
    O. 281
Crane, Joseph. 220
Crary, Ezra. 99, 311, 312
    James. 354
    Joseph. 364, 365
    Nathan. 99, 199, 311, 313
Criettenden, *see* Crittenden
Crimes
    aiding jail break. 330
    assault. 6, 151
    breaking and entering. 151
    horse stealing. 250–51
    kidnapping. 91–92
    riot, *see* Riots
    sabbath breaking. 151
    theft. 8, 53, 150
    unlawful assembly. 69, 71
Crippen, Esther. 80
    Samuel. 80
Crittenden (Criettenden,
        Crittendon, Crittinden)
    Semor. 241
    Zebulun. 125, 148, 215, 305
Crocker, Andrew. 322
Cronkhite, Orrey. 284
Crook, Obadiah. 361

Crosman, *see* Crossman
Cross, Ichabod................346
  James....................203
  Shubal...................369
  Uriah....................201
Crossman (Crosman)
  William........118, 198, 312, 313
Crouch, Richard...............33
Crown Point, N. Y.............125
Crowninshield, David..........357
  Richard..................357
Culain, Levi..................254
Culver, Bezaleel..............37
  Joshua...................289
  Nathan...................37
  Samuel...................289
Cumar, Josiah.................37
Cumberland County.8, 21, 26, 205, 206
  county town, location of.....95
  represented in New York pro-
    vincial congress...394–95, 396–97
Cummings (Cumings)
  James..............98, 254, 280
  Reuben...................17
Currency
  depreciation of......36, 41, 74, 210,
            260, 298, 353,360
  New York, use of.....126, 139, 266
  produce and/or labor as..4, 296, 306,
                     392
  See also Currency, reforms (pro-
    posed)
  reforms (proposed)...191, 226, 245,
              249,262–63
  scarcity of....75, 132, 190–91, 217,
      233, 240, 244–45, 276–77, 399
  See also Coins; Counterfeiting
Currier, David................116
  Joseph...................201
Curtis (Curtice, Cutis)
  Abel.....................393
  Amos.................20, 89
  Daniel...................34
  Ebenezer..........187, 256, 393
  Elias.............25, 241, 385
  John.....................256
  Josiah...................361
  Luas.....................361
  Philo....................313
  Thaddeus..........99, 254, 313

Curtis (Curtice, Cutis) (*cont.*)
  Zachariah................361
  Zebina...................256
Cushman, Frederick............294
Cuting, Eliphalet.............373
Cutis, *see* Curtis
Cutler, Amos.................258
  Benoni...................201
Cuyler, Jacob.............42, 44
Cuzzins, *see* Cousins

D

Daggett, John............280, 285
Dammer, William..............282
Dammon, Nathan...............282
Dams.........................333
Dana, John W.............68, 127
Danby....................59, 160
  grievances...............225–26
  roads....................295–96
  transient, care of...........61–62
Daniels, Alexander............256
  Thomas M. C..............357
Danks, Shadrick..............241
Danville.....................90
Darby (Darbe)
  Azariah..................339
  David....................287
  Roger....................347
  William..................347
Darte, Joshua.............50, 58
  Justus...................58
Dartmouth College............380
Davenport, John..............202
Daveson, *see* Davison
Davis, Caleb.................261
  David....................158
  Eleazer..................188
  Jacob....................261
  John.....................202
  Levi.....................39
  Nathaniel................39
  Paul.....................356
  Samuel...............117, 357
Davison (Daveson)
  Andrew...................320
  Daniel...................373
  Thomas...............17, 205
Dawley, Perey G..............320

Day, ———..................200
  Benjamin.....................25
  Dudley.....................200
  Elkanah......................182
  Ephraim.....................200
  Levi........................200
  Oliver......................200
  Russell.................200, 283
Dead Creek...................215
Deal, Peter...................205
Dean (Deane, Deen)
  Henry................119, 254
  Nathan.....................303
  Reuben......................83
  William................302, 303
Deboice, Abram................31
Debts
  estate, *see* Estates
  lottery to pay.................35
  protection from arrest for....369–70
  reforms in payment of (proposed) 191,
      226, 244–45, 249, 262–63
  relief from 43, 126, 259–61, 353,
      359–60
Debts, State
  interest on..........74–75, 273–74
Declaration of Independence
  language employed..............29
Deeds
  authentication of..............169
  confirmation of..259, 331–32, 342–43
  loss by fire.................252–53
  missing....................13–14
  nullification of............183–84
  transfer of, special..158–59, 335, 363
Deen, *see* Dean
Deerfield, Mass.
  Vermonters seized at...........92
Deerfield River...................63
Delano, Amasa.................108
Deming, Eliakim................243
  Penuel..............146, 147, 220
  Samuel......................37
Denison (Denson)
  George.....................155
  Samuel......................92
Denten, Thomas................160
Depreciation of Currency, *see* Currency, depreciation of
Derby........................261

Dewey, ———..................236
  Aaron......................361
  Aaron, Jr...................361
  Barzilla....................294
  Elijah...............89, 90, 108
  James......................361
  Jeremiah....................294
Deweysburg
  lines uncertain................90
Dick, William.................320
Dickey, Joseph................303
Dickinson, David.............9, 50
Dike, Gideon..................364
  Jonathan...................364
  Samuel.....................303
Diseases
  abnormality.................142
  ague sore...................235
  cancer......................35
  complications with pregnancy..61–62
  idiocy......................77
  "long fever".................333
  rheumatism...................57
Disputes, land, *see* Land disputes
Dix, Joseph...................117
  Ozias......................221
Dixson, Joseph................241
Doctor
  use of title 21, 23, 29, 196, 273, 278,
      298
Doctors, *see* Physicians
Dodge, William................357
Dog River....................213
Doley, Pedigren...............382
Doolittel, Moses..............346
Doomage
  Bethel..................128, 149
  Hartford...................137
  Hinsdale....................66
  Peacham.....................79
  Pomfret.....................68
  Rockingham.................184
  Stamford.................171–72
  Wallingford.................314
Dorchester, Benjamin.........13, 14
Dorset...............110, 126, 168
  care of idle person's estate...235–36
  division of.................159–60
  horses stolen...............250–51
  roads.....................295–96

Dorset (*cont.*)
    tax abatement.............237–38
    town lines uncertain.........52–53
Doubleday, Asahel.........108, 282
Douglas, Mass...................170
Douglas (Douglass, Duglas)
    Martha.....................144
    William....................144
Downes, Cyperan...............347
Draper, Aaron.................356
Draper
    charter conflict.............26–27
    See also Wilmington
Drew, Ezra....................108
    William....................241
Drury, Ebenezer...............378
Dudley, Eleazar................41
Dudley, Mass..................170
Duglas, *see* Douglas
Dummerston 120–21, 156, 218, 308, 310
    roads and bridges.......136–37, 186
    tax abatement................332
    tax collection.............99–100
Dun, Daniel....................108
    Duncan.....................241
Dunbar, David..................201
Duncans, George................37
Dunham, Joseph.................37
Dunning (Duning)
    Martin.....................304
    Michael..................54, 204
    Richard....................160
Durfey (Durphy)
    Jedidiah....................317
    Moses.....................160
Durkee, Aden...................24
    Bartholomew................174
    Heman......................24
    Timothy....................24
    Timothy, Jr.................24
Durphy, *see* Durfey
Duties, import
    on nails..................148–49
Dutton (Dutten)
    Matthew....................208
    Salmon.....................367
    Silas.......................10
Dwinell, Ebenezer.............346
Dyre, Benjamin................347
    Henry......................347

E

Eaddey (Eaddy, Eadie, Eady), *see*
    Eddy
Earden, John...................307
Earle (Earll)
    George....................10, 96
    Nehemiah....................37
East Windsor, *see* Windsor
Eastar, Aaron...................98
"Eastern Union".................104
Eastman (Eastmon)
    Aaron......................201
    Deliverance.................199
    Eli......................199, 254
    Enoch....................20, 193
    John........................49
    Jonathan....................20
    Jonathan, Jr................20
    Nathan.....................361
    Stephen....................20
    Timothy....................50
    Zeperan....................20
Eddy (Eaddey, Eaddy, Eadie, Eady)
    Abiel......................287
    James...................311, 313
    Jonathan.................118, 199
    Peleg......................254
    Peter...................118, 254
    Thomas............56, 98, 281
Eden..........................252
Edgar, William.................37
    Zerubbabel.................201
Edgburt, John.................347
Edgerton, Daniel..........175, 299
    Jabez.....................364
    Jacob......................143
    Jedediah...................143
    Richard....................215
    Simeon.....................143
Edgeton, Richard..............305
Edmunds (Edmons)
    Andrew..................199, 254
    James...................199, 254
    James, Jr...................199
Education
    county grammar schools.....277–78,
                        323, 374
    state university.........18, 180–81
Edwards, Elijah.................6

Eeler, John...................241
  Waterman..................241
Egbertson, Joel................34
Eldreg, James.................107
  Job.......................107
  John......................107
  Nathan....................107
Elections
  county 38–39, 208, 218, 219, 221,
      275–76, 292, 329
  disputes............16–17, 197–99
  special..................388–89
Elkins, Jonathan.............80, 202
  Jonathan, Jr................202
Elliot, Eliza..........139, 140, 141
  Samuel, Jr..........139, 140, 141
Ellis, Gamaliel...............356
  Reuben....................347
Ellot, John..................241
Elmer, Daniel................303
Ely, Joel...............130, 131
  Samuel....................26
Emerson, Enoch............116, 282
  Jonathan..................379
  Thomas....................282
Emmons (Emmans)
  ———................94, 379
  B.........................147
  Benjamin.........43, 44, 79, 103
English, Asa.................387
Eno, William............197, 304
Enos, Roger.........227, 228, 368
Enosburg
  location of...............367–68
"Equivalent lands"............119
Essex.......................353
Estates
  public care of idle person's...235–36
  sale of land for widow........377
  settlement of xx–xxi, 45–46, 55–56,
    65, 76–77, 80, 84–85, 144, 158–
    59, 162–63, 166, 169–71, 174–
    75, 176–77, 187–88, 221–22,
    236–37, 256–57, 271, 279, 299,
    315–16, 325–26, 335, 343–44,
    363
Estey, Aaron................28, 56
Evans (Evas, Evens)
  Joe.......................282
  John......................25

Evans (Evas, Evens) (cont.)
  Joseph....................155
  Moses..............7, 73, 282
Evarts, John............196, 357
  Luther....................197
Evens (Evas), see Evans
Everest (Averest)
  Benjamin..................125
  Zadok................154, 162
Everitt (Averit)
  Daniel....................343
  Richard...................363
Everts (Evert)
  Abner.....................347
  Amaziah...................347
  Ambrose...................278
  Charles...................339
  Edward...............339, 347
  John......................304
  Judah.....................339
Evet, Thomas.................387
Ewing, James...........385, 386
Eyers, Samuel................287

F

Fair Haven.............292, 329
  land disputes............39–41
Fair River.............230, 264
Fairbanks (Fairbank)
  Elijah....................356
  Joseph...............117, 356
  Pearley..............117, 357
Fairfield
  new lines (proposed)....367–68, 371
Fairlee
  proprietors' taxes.........274–75
  town lines................324
Falter, Abeleson.............376
Fanswith, Josiah..............34
Farming
  acreage...................120
  cattle............16, 120, 122
  crops......................16
  house and fields............59
  rental and value of property..257–58
Farmington, Conn.............145
Farnsworth (Fansworth, Fanswoth,
  Farsworth)
  ——— [General]............131
  Joseph.........210, 211, 257, 258

Farnsworth (Fansworth, Fanswoth,
     Farsworth) (*cont.*)
  Josiah.........................34
  Reuben.....................20, 160
  Solomon.......................34
  Thomas.......................92
  Zaccheus....................208
Farnum, John..............281, 285
Farr, James................280, 285
  Salmon...................281, 285
Farrand, Joseph...............241
Farris, *see* Ferris
Farsworth, *see* Farnsworth
Farwell, Isaac.......53, 160, 237, 238
  John.....................53, 160
Fassett (Fasset, Fausete)
  ——— [Captain]...............4
  Benjamin.....................94
  John.........................42
  Nathan......................294
Fay, Asa..................117, 356
  Benjamin.................15, 344
  Jedediah....................187
  Jonas..........76, 85, 105, 344
  Joseph......15, 35, 42, 94, 273, 368
  Moses........................97
  Sarah.......................344
Fees xx, 50, 53, 61, 70, 121, 127, 153,
     155, 158, 190, 191, 207, 295, 310
Feild, *see* Field
Feletcher, *see* Fletcher
Fellows, Adolphus...............387
  Ezra.........................75
Fenekey, James.................281
Ferdinand......................19
Ferries
  Connecticut River at Hartford. 29–30
  Connecticut River at Hartland. . .227
  Orwell to Ticonderoga, N. Y.....87
Ferris (Farris)
  James........................125
  Luis.........................125
  Noah.........................125
  Peter..........125, 330, 331, 345
  Samuel.......................125
  Sarah........................61
  Squire.......................125
Ferrisburg..............4, 162, 371
  city in (proposed)............124

Ferrisburg (*cont.*)
  part to Panton (proposed)......124,
               214–16, 305–6
  roads and/or bridges 147–48, 290, 352
Ferry, ——— [Captain]..........51
Field (Feild)
  Amos........................160
  Anthony.....................290
  Ebenezer.................197, 304
  Joseph......................304
  Michael.....................304
  Nehemiah....................350
  Reuben...................197, 304
  Simeon......................304
Finances, State 41–42, 74–75, 78–79,
               102, 273–74
  See also Accounts, State
Fires
  Pittsford.................321, 378
  Tinmouth....................252
  Wallingford.................314
Fish, David.................24, 285
  Joseph.......................25
  Josiah......................219
  Nathan......................328
  Rufus........................92
Fisher, Adam................6, 67
  Edmund......................208
Fisk (Fiske)
  David.......................281
  Nathan......................368
  Nathaniel...................259
Fitch, Altei [Allei].............237
  Elisha......................143
  Jabez G.....................143
  John........................237
  Peletiah......................6
  William.....................237
Flamstead, *see* Chester
Fletcher (Feletcher)
  ———....................162, 321
  ——— [Colonel]..............74
  ——— [Lieutenant Colonel].....64
  Asaph.......................367
  Ebenezer.....................75
  Samuel.......12, 21, 134, 179, 264
Floods 3, 5, 311, 312, 333, 337, 352, 385
Flynn, Michael.................133
Foard, *see* Ford

Foot (Foote)
  Adonijah...............200, 283
  Daniel 317
  Elijah..............197, 304
  George....................278
  Nathan....................317
  Nathan, Jr................317
  Reuben....................200
Forbs, Stephen.................26
Ford (Foard)
  Frederic..................317
  Thomas.....................37
Forgason, John................284
Foster (Forster)
  Abraham....................34
  Benjamin.............118, 312
  Benjamin, Jr.......118, 254, 313
  Edward.................26, 221
  Ephraim...................202
  Joel......................281
  Joseph...............103, 105
  Nathan.....................26
  Reuben....................388
  Seth......................357
  Thomas....................138
  Whitefield [Whitfield]..98, 118, 312
Fowler (Fouler)
  Abel.......................37
  Abner.....................202
  Jonathan..................202
Fox, Amos.....................221
Francis (Frances, Franses)
  John......................289
  Jonathan..................289
  Rosel.....................241
  Samuel, Jr.................20
  Simon.....................289
Franklin, Aaron...............208
Franses, see Francis
Frazier (Fraser)
  Alexander.................290
  Daniel....................202
Freeman (Freemen, Freman)
  ————......................225
  Elisha...............138, 139
  Experience................354
  Ezra...................56, 98
  Moody......................82
  Phinehas......223, 275, 276, 357

Freemen
  qualification of.........16–17
French, Abner.................143
  Charles...................148
  David..................37, 241
  Elijah....................241
  Hains.....................202
  John......................160
  Joseph....................241
  Nathan....................143
  Nehemiah L. [Loring].....148, 215
  Reuben L. [Lane].........148, 215
  Samuel, Sr.............241, 243
  Samuel, Jr................241
  Thomas....................126
Frissell, John................387
Frost, Joseph..................51
Fullam, see Dummerston
Fuller (Fullar)
  Asa.......................281
  Consider..................108
  Ebenezer...............39, 373
  Elijah....................347
  Hezekiah.............151, 201
  Hosea.....................347
  Jonathan.........39, 206, 207
  Luther....................201
  Martin.....................25
  Peter......................34
  Samuel....................202
  Solomon...................347
  Stephen...................284

G

Gage (Gaig, Gaige)
  Isaac.......125, 148, 215, 290, 305
  Joseph..........125, 148, 305
  Richard...................305
Gageborough, [N. H.?]..........62
Gain, Daley...................254
Gallup (Gallop)
  Elisha....................155
  Nathaniel.................205
  William..............156, 205
Galpin, Jehiel................160
Galusha (Gelusha)
  Amos......................347
  David.....................347
  Elijah.................63, 335
  Jacob............112, 335, 347

Galusha (Gelusha) (*cont.*)
Jonas........................346
Ganson, John...............117, 286
Nathan..................117, 357
Gardner (Gardnar, Gardnier)
Abraham..............5, 108, 205
Benjamin................5, 108
Benjamin, Jr..............108
Daniel..................108, 205
David....................108
George.................108, 205
George, Jr................205
Hugh....................201
Paul...................108, 205
Garfield, Benjamin.....375, 385, 386
Garnsey, Solomon..............278
Gaskill, David.................202
Gates, Elias...................155
Elijah...............138, 139
Ezra......................201
Samuel...................201
Stephen.............29, 92, 223
T. Shepherd................218
Thomas....................50
Gaylord, Eliphalet..............50
Geer, ——— [Captain]..........131
Gelusha, *see* Galusha
Gemmil, Hugh..................203
Gibbs, Caleb..................204
Edmund...................123
Ezra......................201
Isaac 37
John 37
Gibson, Abel 340
Giddings (Gidings)
Benjamin..................289
Job 241, 361
Giffin, Edward................339
Giford, Welcam...............125
Gilbert (Gilberd, Gilburt)
Cornelius 138, 139, 354
Daniel..................22, 24
Elias.....................241
Jesse 367
John......................361
Samuel...................160
Thomas....................34
Gilby, Abel 107
Gile (Guile)
Abner.................96, 336

Gile (Guile) (*cont.*)
Amos..............336, 350, 361
Israel......................29
Moses.....................336
Moses, Jr..................96
Gilead.....................124
Gilfillan (Gilfillin)
James......................202
William....................203
Gilimore, David...............143
Gilkey (Gillkey)
William................10, 96
William, Jr............10, 336
Gilkinson, John...............202
Gill, John...................107
Obadiah...................294
Gillet, Simon 387
Gillkey, *see* Gilkey
Gilman (Gillman, Gillmon)
Ezekiel 202
James.....................361
William....................37
Gitchel, Jacob...............303
Glalkins, Samuel..............202
Glastenbury
roads.....................338
Glazier, William..............39
Glover, Samuel...............117
Glyns, Elijah................202
Goddard, Nathan..............201
Goff, David..................204
Gold, *see* Gould
Golding, Isaiah...............281
Goodenough, Ithamar..........208
Goodman, Eleazer..............17
Ithamar...................50
James.....................50
Noah......................50
Stephen...................50
Stephen, Jr................50
Goodrich (Goodridge)
Charles...................125
David.....................354
Hezekiah..................354
James.....................125
John......................354
Joshua................311, 313
Josiah....................354
Josiah, Jr.................354
S.........................288

Goodrich (Goodridge) (*cont.*)
   Silas............60, 207, 241, 325
   Simeon.......................265
   William............143, 259, 260
Goodwin, Daniel................203
   Edward......................58
   Jacob......................202
   Joseph.....................208
Gores
   annexation of.............93, 283
   lines, establishment of.......89–90
   tax relief.....................381
Gott, David....................108
   Nathaniel.......150, 151, 152, 196
   Samuel.....................202
Gould (Gold)
   Benjamin.................311, 313
   Benjamin, Jr.............311, 313
   Ebenezer....................34
   John.......................98
   Nathaniel...............117, 201
   Thomas......................34
   William....................241
Governor 12, 28, 36, 102, 130–31, 142,
                    298, 339
Governor's lot
   Manchester..................158
Gowing, Nathaniel..............336
Grafton, *see* Thomlinson
Graham (Grayham)
   Andrew 119, 120, 121, 156, 157, 158,
              308, 309, 310
   Caleb......156, 157, 158, 308, 309
   John A.....................294
   N. B.......................294
   Winthrop....................34
Grammar schools, *see* Education
Granby
   town lines mistaken............19
Grand Isle....................268
"Grand List"
   Manchester...............241–43
Grandey (Grandy)
   Bezaleel....................108
   Elijah.................125, 215
Granger, Gideon.................9
Grant, Elihu...............56, 98
Granville, *see* Kingston
Granville, N. Y.
   seeks union with Vermont... 33–34

Grapes, Philip.........150, 151, 202
Graves, Daniel.................303
   Jesse 215
Gray, Amos....................219
   John 53, 160, 201
   Jons.......................219
   Moses..................194, 321
   Silas.....................160
Grayham, *see* Graham
Great Britain..............212, 266
Green (Grean, Greene)
   Asa........................108
   Beriah.....................274
   Caleb......................296
   Daniel.....................294
   Ezebel.....................281
   Ezekiel.........118, 199, 311, 313
   Henry..................198, 254
   Obadiah................28, 199
   Peleg......................199
   Philip.................198, 254
   Rufus......................296
   Samuel......................67
   Thomas......................54
   Zebadiah....................56
Greensboro
   roads......................213
Grefas, Thomas.................33
Greenleaf, Stephen.............139
Grenll, *see* Grinnell
Grievances 102–4, 189–92, 216–18,
     225–26, 232–34, 238–40, 244–48,
      248–50, 262–63, 279–81
Griffen, Rosserter..............89
Griffeth, Eli..................34
   Micah......................34
Griffis, Benjamin..........339, 347
Grinis, John...................31
Grinnell (Grenll)
   Reuben.................197, 304
Griswold (Griswell)
   Adonijah...................196
   Benjamin...................304
   David......................197
   Nathan...................4, 197
Grout, John...............205, 206
Grover, John...................34
   Penawill....................34
   Peter......................34
   Stephen.....................34

Guildhall........................195
    justice of peace.............150–53
    town lines mistaken............19
Guile, *see* Gile.
Guilford 12, 92, 169, 185, 208–9, 224,
                    229, 291, 292
    New York adherent at.......178–79

H

Hadley, Mass.
    New York adherent seized at.....92
Hael, *see* Hale
Hagar, John....................282
Haight, James..................148
    William...........148, 215, 290
Hale (Hael, Hail)
    Asa.........................294
    Ebenezer....................39
    Gershom....................143
    Gershom, Jr.................143
    Isaac......................289
    Josiah.....................294
    Moses......................294
    Thomas.....................294
Halebart, *see* Hurlbut
Halifax........................140
    churches...................328
    New York adherents in.....6, 28–29
    posse formed at.............92
    roads and bridges...........328
    tax postponement (proposed)..28–29
Hall, Daniel...................203
    David......................320
    Ephraim....................218
    Hiland................317, 345
    Jacob.................201, 282
    John.......................269
    Jonathan..............40, 256
    Lot........................230
    Thomas...............92, 317
    William..............204, 205
    Willis.....................282
Halley, *see* Hawley
Hamilton (Hambelton)
    Isaac.......................99
    John.......................357
    Silas.......................9
Hamlin, Oliver............368, 369
Hammond (Hammon, Hamond)
    Asa........................281

Hammond (Hammon, Hamond) (*cont.*)
    Benjamin...................241
    Elijah.....................138
    Hinsdel....................357
    Jonathan...................108
    Simeon.....................357
Hampshire County, Mass..........92
Hancock........................349
Handy (Handee, Handey, Hendee,
    Hendy)
    Caleb...........59, 257, 258, 281
    Robert......................25
Hannun, Moses...................50
Hard, Stephen...................64
Hardey, *see* Hardy
Harding, Timothy...............127
Hardy (Hardey)
    L..........................303
    Lemuel.....................284
    Silas......................284
Haris, *see* Harris
Harmon (Herman, Hermon)
    Abiel......................237
    Amos.......................20
    Asahel..........53, 160, 235, 236
    Enos....................20, 89
    Ezekiel.............143, 323
    Joel.......................143
    Nathaniel..................237
    Nehemiah, Jr................20
    Oliver.....................294
    Reuben...............294, 295
    Reuben, Jr...........276, 277
Harnden, Barachiah..............34
    John.......................34
    Jonathan...................34
    Samuel.....................34
Harrick, *see* Herrick
Harriman, Caleb................289
Harrington (Herenton, Herington,
    Herinton, Herngton, Hernton,
    Herrington, Herrinton)
    Abraham....................296
    Caleb......................199
    Elisha.....................296
    Job........................108
    Jonathan...................296
    Lot........................296
    Mora.......................296
    Ozial......................296

Harrington (Herenton, Herington, Herinton, Herngton, Hernton, Herrington, Herrinton) (*cont.*)
Samson......................296
Stephen......................107
Theophilus....................347
Thomas......................296
Thomas, Jr..................296
William......................347
Harris (Haris)
——....................17
Alexander..................242
Ebenezer....................347
Samuel......................374
Thaddeus..................241
Harrison, Nehemiah..............20
Samuel......................364
Hartford......................35
ferry......................30
justice of the peace........282–83
roads..................155, 228
tax abatement..............137
Hartland..................65, 104
bridge lottery..................228
ferry......................227
land tax (opposed)..........231–32
roads and/or bridges...155–56, 227, 228
Harvard University..............180
Harvey, Alexander......150, 202, 270
Archibald....................202
Harwood (Horwood)
James......................108
John......................39
Jonathan....................198
Haskell, Moses, Jr..............221
Haskin, Joseph..................40
Hatch, Barna..................242
John......................303
Timothy....................303
Hath, Thomas..................202
Hatheway (Hathiewary)
Abraham....................254
Alfred..................254, 255
Edward......................357
Erastus....................317
Hatten, Joshua..................336
Havens, Daniel..................25
Joseph......................24
Robert......................25

Haverenton, Peter..............34
Haverhill, N. H..................19
Hawkins, David..................294
John..................177, 178
Hawley (Halley, Hawly)
——..................266, 333
Gideon..................148, 290
Jabez..................158, 242
Joseph......................294
Lemuel......................313
Peter......................347
Haws, Daniel..................242
Jabez......................221
Hay, William..................39
Hayward (Heywood)
Caleb......................307
Calvin......................307
Ebenezer....................208
James......................373
Nathan......................307
Samuel......................361
Silas......................307
Stephen..........194, 320, 321
William......................307
Hazen (Hazzen)
Benjamin..............312, 313
Joshua......................137
Hazen's Road..................213
Hazletine, Thomas..............201
Hazzen, *see* Hazen
Heald, Daniel..................268
Heartwell, William..............219
Heath, Daniel..................37
Jonathan....................214
Samuel......................37
Simeon......................37
Stephen......................37
Timothy......................37
Heaton, James..................202
William......................387
Hebbard, David..................354
Hedges, Jeremiah................354
Hemenway, Phinehas............108
Hendee, *see* Handy
Henderson (Hendrson)
Caleb......................376
Edward..................241, 361
Henry......................6
James..................81, 201
Thomas......................320

Hendrick, William 54, 67
Hendrson, see Henderson
Hendy, see Handy
Henesey, Richard 242
Henry, Benjamin 328
Henson, James 361
Herenton, see Harrington
Herick, see Herrick
Herington (Herinton), see Harring-
    ton
Herman (Hermon), see Harmon
Herngton (Hernton), see Harring-
    ton
Herrick (Harrick, Herick)
——— [Colonel] 73, 298
    Henry 296
    Henry, Jr. 296
    Samuel 11, 91
    Stephen 242
Herrington (Herrinton), see
    Harrington
Hertford, see Hartland
Hervy, Horrace 284
Hewenton, James 34
    Joseph 34
Hewitt (Hewit, Hewt)
    George 355
    Gideon 98, 119, 199, 311, 313
    John 355
Hewlett, John 107
Hewt, see Hewitt
Heywood, see Hayward
Hibberd, John 24
Hickock (Hickok)
    Ame 315
    Benjamin 351
    David 351
    Justus 315
    Uriah 351
Hicks (Hiks)
    David 82, 202
    Levi 303, 311, 313
Hide, see Hyde
Highgate 371
Higley, Brewster 244, 278
    Elias 223
    Roger 294
Hiks, see Hicks
Hill, Abner 32, 339, 347
    Calvin 125

Hill (cont.)
    Daniel 98
    David 118, 125, 148, 362
    George 281
    John 313
    Jonathan 67
    Levi 64, 361
    Uri 296
    William 6, 29
Hillard, Joshua 242
Hinds, John B. 307
    Samuel 280
    William 241
Hinesburg
    roads and bridges 362
Hinkson, John 202
Hinman (Hyndman)
    John 203
    Moses 198, 311, 313
    Thomas 99
Hinsdale
    tax abatement 66–67
Hiscock, Richard 117
Hitchcock, Elijah 39
    Luke 39
    Luke, Jr. 39
    Lyman 89, 90
    Samuel 242
Hobly, Joseph 160
Hodges (Hodge)
    Silas 254
    Solomon 37
Hodgkins (Hudgeskins)
    Henry 355
Hoghtailior, Jacob 37
Hoit, David 339
    Jonathan 339
    Nathan 351
    Nehemiah 278
    Noah 278
    Samuel 347
Holbrook, Abner 117, 357
    John 117, 357
    Joseph 201
    Silas 160, 357
    Thomas 228, 282
Holbut, see Hurlbut
Holcomb (Holcombe)
    Benjamin 125
    Elisha 125

Holcomb (Holcombe) (*cont.*)
Joseph......................125
Holley (Holly)
John................317, 347
Samuel....................303
Holman, Solomon.............285
Holt, James.................361
Stephen....................349
Holten, Arad................307
Hoosic River.........5, 67, 204, 337
Hope, Joseph................202
Hopkins (Hopkin)
Benjamin...................94
Daniel.....................20
Elias......................242
James.................10, 287
John.......................287
Mindwell...................94
Noah.......................321
Roswell 15, 61, 104, 128, 147, 152,
     158, 172, 180, 207, 215, 290, 327,
                    345, 355, 357, 369
Samuel.....................50
Stephen....................94
Wate [Wait]................94
William....................193
Hopkinson, Caleb......150, 151, 202
David.............150, 151, 201
Horner, John................202
Thomas.....................202
Horton, Hezekiah, Jr.........208
Nathan................208, 229
Stafford...................208
Horwood, *see* Harwood
Hoskins, Benoni.............34
Hosmer, Amos...............336
William....................336
Hough, George.....101, 392, 393, 401
Jerusha................187, 188
Houghton, Edward.........169, 208
Elijah................201, 281
James......................208
Lucretia...................169
House, Jonathan.............347
Hovey, Daniel...............57
Samuel.....................57
Simeon.....................202
Howe (How)
Asa........................289
John.......................307

Howe (How) (*cont.*)
Joshua.....................289
Reuben.....................201
Samson.....................282
Samuel................201, 289
Simon......................201
Timothy....................202
Howard, Abner...............129
Antipos....................287
Christopher...........199, 254
Ebenezer.........99, 108, 242
Elijah.....................387
John.......................241
Zebedee....................129
Howel, Hezekiah.............208
Howland, Caleb........199, 254
Hubbard, Eldad..............256
Moses......................50
Watts.................183, 256
Watts, Jr..................130
Hubbardton..................329
roads...................351–52
Hubbell (Hubbel)
David......................242
Elnathan...................341
Huchings, Thomas............303
Hudgeskins, *see* Hodgkins
Hudson, Aaron..........356, 373
Benjamin...................361
Hudson River.............31, 37
Huff (Huf)
John..............125, 215, 290
Huggins, Zadok..............160
Hughs (Hugh)
James......................202
John.......................201
William....................201
Hulbert (Hulburd), *see* Hurlbut
Hull, Jehiel, Jr............281
Matthew....................218
Samuel.....................242
Hungerford, Amasa...........297
Oliver.....................108
Hungerford
new lines (proposed)....367–68, 371
Hunt (Huntt)
———......................379
Arad.......................66
Jonathan................39, 67

Huntington, Amos............346
   Christopher..............354
   Jeremiah................347
   Nathan.................347
   Samuel.................347
Huntly, John................215
Huntt, *see* Hunt
Hurd, Simeon...............361
   Tyrus..................209
Hurlbut (Halebart, Holbut, Hul-
   bert, Hulburd)
   Benoni................40, 41
   Cornelius...............362
   Ebenezer..........20, 89, 361
   Zacheus................361
Hutchinson (Hutcherson, Hutchi-
   son, Hutchiston)
   David..................10
   Elisha.................173
   Hezekiah...............385
   Samuel.................354
   Samuel, Jr...........138, 139
   Thomas..............311, 313
Hyatt, Barnard............88, 89
Hyde (Hide)
   Clark..................361
   Dana..................208
   Ephriam................242
   James...............242, 361
   Joseph.................34
   Lemuel.................34
   Mary................170, 171
   Nehemiah...............242
   Timothy................171
Hyndman, *see* Hinman

I

Ide, Squier..........118, 198, 254
Immigrants
   abatement of taxes for......58–59
Immigration
   Rutland County............289
   from southern New England....40
Indians..........24, 81–82, 141, 342
Ingalls, Caleb...............199
Ingram, Philip..............374
Interest rates 75, 131, 264, 274, 395,
                          396–97
Invik, Henrich...............6

Ira
   part of Clarendon to
     (proposed)............253–55
   part of Clarendon to (opposed)
           310–12, 312–13
Ives, A...................98
   Aaron..................304
   Abraham.................70
   Amos..................381
   Enos...................317
   Enos, Jr................317
   Jared..................317
   Jonah...............320, 381
   Lnt [Lent]..............320
   Nathaniel...............320

J

Jackson (Jacson)
   Abraham.............240, 320
   Abraham, Jr...........98, 320
   Asahel..............98, 320
   Jedediah [Jediah]........70, 98
   Jethro........98, 320, 381, 382
   Joseph.................320
   Stephen................296
Jackson's Gore
   roads.................319–20
   tax relief (proposed).......381–82
Jacob, Stephen...........83, 256
Jacson, *see* Jackson
Jails, *see* County court houses;
   County towns
Jamaica...................176
   roads and bridges.........307–8
Jameson, James..............242
   William................242
Jaquas, Thomas..............37
Jenkins, Benjamin............202
   Stephen................202
Jenks (Jinks)
   James...........119, 198, 313
Jewell (Jewel, Jewill, Juel)
   David............281, 311, 313
   Timothy................254
Jewett (Jewet)
   ———...............379
   Thomas 54, 67, 264, 297, 354, 357,
                   367, 387
Jewill, *see* Jewell
Jinks, *see* Jenks

Johns, Daniel..................241
 Jehiel......................241
Johnson (Johson)
 Abel.......................285
 Adam......................263
 Ashbel....................218
 Benjamin..............372, 373
 Constant..................357
 Eden......................304
 Elihu.....................201
 George.....................67
 Hezekiah.............353, 354
 James.....................203
 Joab......................357
 John..........203, 294, 295, 322
 Jonathan, Jr..............208
 Lemuel....................356
 Libeus....................294
 Luther....................357
 Moses.....................203
 Robert....................203
 Samuel................201, 363
 Seth..................354, 357
 Thomas...............211, 212
 William............37, 201, 228
Johnston, ———...............379
Johson, see Johnson
Jones, Asa.............108, 117
 Bezalel...................117
 Daniel....................241
 John..................117, 242
 Nathan....................355
 Nathan, Jr................355
Jorden (Jurden)
 Philip................356, 373
 Thomas....................108
Josulin, Joseph.............58
Joy, David.................208
 Moses......................97
Joynes, William............202
Judicial procedure, see Courts
Judicial reforms, see Courts, re-
 forms (proposed)
Judson, Micah..............361
Juel, see Jewell
Jurden, see Jorden
Justices of the Peace
 appointment of (also proposed)
         282–83, 304
 maladministration....150–52, 195–96

K

Kathan, Alexander...........310
 John......................218
 John, Jr..................218
Keeler, Thomas.............364
Keene, N. H................84
Kellogg, Gardiner..........49
 Moses......................50
 Samuel...............288, 319
Kelley, William............202
Kendall (Kendal, Kindel)
 Samuel....................285
 William..............280, 285
Kennedy, David.............203
 John......................202
 Patrick...................202
 Robert....................202
Kennet, Reuben.............108
Kent, Alexander............160
 Cephas....................160
 Cephas, Jr................160
 Dan.......................160
 Elisha.....................24
 Jacob.....................201
 John......................160
 Moses.....................160
Kent
 roads....................9–10
 See also Londonderry
Kent, Conn................331
Keyes (Keys)
 Solomon...................306
 Stephen......243, 267, 360, 361
Kidder, Benjamin...........361
 Samuel....................117
 Thomas....................361
 Thomas, Jr................361
Kiler, Joseph..............294
Killington
 roads...............12, 86–87
Kimball, Aaron.............306
 Joseph...........84, 100, 227
 Mrs. Joseph...............101
Kindel, see Kendall
King, ———...................42
 Daniel....................389
 Elijah....................203
 Ezra......................307
 Jonathan..................296

King (*cont.*)
  Solomon 37
  Thomas....................347
  William.....................37
Kingsley, Phinehas..............294
Kingston
  county change.............389–90
  roads 365
Kinne, Benoni...................320
Kirkley, Hannah 6
  John..........................6
Kitteridge, James..............202
  James, Jr. 202
Knap, Moses 281
Knickerbaccor, ——— 348
Knight (Knigh, Knights)
  Daniel......................208
  Elijah.................10, 39, 184
  Elisha 10, 39
  S............................128
  Samuel.........134, 139, 173, 176
Knowlton, Luke.............38, 134
Knox, Moses...................285
Kyle, William.................243

L

Ladd, James...................205
  Nathaniel...................364
Laflen, James............281, 285
Lake, Christopher.............160
Laken, John...................361
Lamb, Ebenezer...............320
  Joseph......................289
  Reuben......................218
  Wil.........................289
Lamfear (Landphir)
  Luke.......................108
  Samuel.....................243
Lammon, William.............236
Lamoille River...............213
Lancaster, N. H..............363
Land cases 45–46, 47–48, 102, 112–14,
    119–21, 139–41, 156–58, 308–10
Land disputes 22–23, 26–27, 39–41,
    56–57, 118–19, 228–29
Land grants.................49–50
  officeholders receive.........211
  special..................272–73

Land taxes xx–xxi, 10, 63, 85–87,
    105–6, 132, 136–37, 137–38,
    147–48, 155–56, 161–62, 167–68,
    173–74, 177–78, 186, 193–95,
    196–97, 199–200, 212–214, 220,
    229–32, 234–35, 264–66, 267–68,
    269–70, 284–87, 290, 300–1,
    301–3, 306–8, 319–20, 326–28,
    330–31, 335–36, 338, 351–52,
    353–56, 362, 363–67, 373–74,
    376, 378–79, 380–81, 384–85,
    386–88, 391–92, 397–98, 400
Landgrove
  land grant in.................168
  roads............267–68, 360–62
Landphir, *see* Lamfear
Lane, ——— [Judge] 333
  Jedediah......................345
  Matthew.................340, 341
  Samuel.......................345
Lang, Andrew...................203
Lansingburgh, N. Y.............337
Lareby, Eleazer................108
Larnard, Abijah................202
Laten, *see* Latten
Lathrop (Lathop), *see* Lothrup
Latroop, Joseph.................50
Latten (Laten)
  Richard.................296, 357
Lawrence (Lawrance)
  Bigelow......................347
  Isaac.......................362
  John........................303
  Peter.......................347
Lawson, John.............280, 285
Lawyers
  grievances against..189–90, 217, 233,
            239, 247–48, 280
  regulation of (proposed)....191, 248
Lazell (Lazel)
  Levi.......................108
  William....................108
  Zenas......................108
Leach, Elisha.................222
Leavenworth (Leavenwoth,
    Levensworth)
  Jesse........89, 213, 214, 369, 370
  Nathan.....................362
Leavitt (Levate)
  Joseph.....................20

Leavitt (Levate) (*cont.*)
  Samuel........................193
Leckie, Andrew................202
Lee, —— [Captain]...........298
  Azariah.................339, 347
  David, Jr...............242, 361
  N.......................98, 263
  Nathan...................254
  Samuel...................319
  Thomas...........185, 372, 373
  Zebulun..................155
Legislature
  grievances against.......102–4, 111,
        189–91, 216, 232, 238–39,
  judicial function.....26–27, 132–33,
        157–58, 309–10
  See also New trials
  qualification of members.....26, 388
Leicester...................379, 380
  disputes over lines..........374–76
  roads and/or bridges.......285, 365
Leicester River..................385
Leonard, David.................293
  Nathan......................347
Lester, Simeon..................294
Letcher, Cornelius..............205
  John........................205
Levate, *see* Leavitt
Levensworth, *see* Leavenworth
Levey, Nathaniel................354
Lewis (Lues)
  Abner.......................294
  Benjamin................339, 347
  Christ.......................37
  David....................17, 143
  Henry.......................296
  James.............53, 54, 242
  John........................347
  Matthew.................339, 347
  Wiles.......................361
  William.....................135
Lezieur, Samuel.................357
Library
  private....................122–23
Lime, N. H..............57, 84, 100
Linsley (Linsly)
  Abiel, Jr...................317
  Jacob.......................271
  Joel.............231, 271, 317
Lion, *see* Lyon

Littleton, N. H.................213
Livermore, Daniel...............221
  Ezra........................307
Livingston, James...............296
Lobdell, Darius.................296
  Darius, Jr..................296
  Jared.......................296
Lock, Elisha....................203
  James.......................361
Locke, John [English Philosopher]
                       157, 309
Lockwood, Josiah................243
Logan's Estate....................4
Loggan, Robert.....240, 241, 243, 244
Loid, T. P......................345
Lomis, *see* Loomis
London, England.................126
Londonderry......................49
  gore annexed.................93
  roads and/or bridges....199, 286–87
  tax abatement.............314–15
  See also Kent
Long, Jesse.....................294
  Levi........................294
Look, Josiah.....................16
Loomis (Lomis)
  Beriah..............83, 369, 387
  Ezra........................304
Loop, Martinus...................37
Lothrup (Lathop, Lathrop)
  John........................220
  Joseph.......................50
  Lemuel......................289
  Samuel......................366
  Thoᵉʳ.......................289
Lotteries
  bridges...222–23, 228, 326, 337–38,
                      352, 385–86
  personal.....................35
  roads......63, 161, 255–56, 295–96
Lovell (Lovel, Lovil, Lovill)
  Elijah..........205, 206, 207, 361
  John...................206, 361
  Oliver............38, 134, 361
  Timothy................360, 361
Lovewell, Nehemiah.......82, 83, 388
Lovil (Lovill), *see* Lovell
Lower Cohoss.....................19
Loyalists...................14, 206
  case against dismissed.......53–54

Loyalists (*cont.*)
    court judgment for......... 379–80
    estate confiscated.............. 77
    landholdings................. 8–9
    trial of...................... 130
    voters and officeholders....... 38–39
Loyan, *see* Lyon
Ludlow..................... 48, 49
    roads and/or mills...... 167, 366–67
Lues, *see* Lewis
Lull, Timothy................. 155
Lunenburg.......... 150–51, 196, 363
Lutee, John.................... 34
Lutts, Nathaniel.............. 357
Lydius grant................... 118
Lyford, Thomas................ 213
Lyman (Lymon)
    Abel....................... 374
    Caleb....................... 50
    Elijah...................... 50
    Isaac.................. 85, 86, 373
    Josiah..................... 220
    Phinehas................... 50
    Timothy.................... 50
    William.................... 50
Lynde (Lyne)
    Cornelius.................. 181
    Joshua..................... 208
    Matthew.................. 44, 45
Lyndon
    location of................. 90
Lyon (Lion, Loyan)
    ——— [Colonel]........... 73, 74
    Abiel...................... 107
    Ebenezer.............. 320, 382
    M.................... 193, 300
    Matthew................... 149
    Zebulun.................... 25

M

McCabe, Michael.............. 31
McCllen, David............... 336
McConnel, Jonathan........... 22
MacCormick (McCormick)
    Archibald.................. 287
    James.................. 10, 287
    Robert..................... 10
McEuen, George.............. 362
McGhelly, Simeon............. 34
McGlauchlan, James........... 202

McGlaughland, Archibald........ 202
McIntire (McIntier)
    Benjamin................... 241
    Richard............... 243, 361
McIntosh (McKentosh, McKintosh)
    Daniel................ 289, 290
    Donald................ 148, 215
McIntoshes.................... 4
Mack, Archibald............ 10, 287
    James..................... 287
    John....................... 99
    Joseph.................... 287
    Nehemiah.................. 108
    William.................... 10
McKinley, James.............. 203
McKoy, David................. 201
McLeran, John................ 203
McMasters, John.............. 219
McMillan, John............... 31
McMurphy, George............ 287
McWaters, James.............. 37
McWethey (McWethy)
    Reuben..................... 34
    Silas...................... 34
Magee, John P................ 31
Magoon, Joseph............... 202
Maidstone.............. 19, 150–51
Maine (Main)
    Isaac................. 155, 228
Mallory (Mallery)
    David..................... 205
    Gill...................... 289
    William................... 205
Manchester 10, 14, 19, 53, 54, 64, 78, 126,
      154, 160, 250, 279, 325, 331, 361
    assessment dispute........... 60–61
    county town............ 110, 346
    governor's lot............. 158–59
    "Grand Convention" at........ 341
    "Grand List".............. 241–43
    grievances................. 244–48
    roads.............. 199, 267, 285
    tax abatement...... 240–44, 299–300
    town lines uncertain......... 52–53
    troops at................. 15–16
Manley, George............... 160
    John.................. 53, 160
    John, Jr................... 160
    John, 3ᵈ.............. 160, 250
    William................... 160

Manufactures
 encouragement of linen, woolen
  and other...............398–400
 nails.....................148–49
Mapes, Lidias...................160
Mariman, Abel.................269
Marks, Isaac...................243
 Joseph....................221
Marlboro...............69, 93, 117
 county tax relief...........275–76
 county town..........208, 275–76
 New York adherent at......121–22
Marquet Harbor..............124–25
Marsh, Asa....................303
 Daniel 112, 113, 114, 198, 199, 255,
    336, 337, 364, 377, 382
 Daniel, Jr....................50
 Elisha 194, 195, 197, 214, 220, 231,
     264, 265
 Job..........................50
 Joel........................165
 John........................282
 Joseph.......................50
 Moses.....................39, 49
 Samuel......................303
 William.............118, 126, 243
 William, Jr..................208
Marshell, Jonathan...............362
Martin (Martain, Martan)
 Ashbel......................202
 Benjamin....................202
 Caleb...................368, 369
 David.......................202
 Ephraim.....................202
 George......................349
 Hugh.........................31
 John.......202, 224, 272, 291, 394
 Masha.......................347
 Matthew...........139, 140, 141
 Philip......................202
 Samuel......................289
 Simeon......................347
 Tamas.......................254
 Thomas......................254
 Wheeler.....................347
Martindale (Martindail)
 Gershom.....................160
 Stephen................160, 238
Marvin, ———............236, 379
 Benjamin....................296

Mason, Aaron..................243
 Elijah......................103
 Hail........................347
 Isaiah......................254
 Nathaniel...................254
Massachusetts grants............119
Massachusetts-Vermont relations
 Shays' rebellion refugees.......339
Mateson (Matteson), see Mattson
Matthews (Mathews)
 Aaron.......................296
 Daniel......................357
 Hugh........................202
 Isaac....................85, 347
 Joel........................381
Mattison, see Mattson
Mattocks (Mattox)
 Samuel......175, 218, 299, 348, 393
Mattson (Mateson, Matteson,
 Mattison)
 Abel...................108, 205
 Benjamin....................160
 David.......................347
 Francis...............70, 118, 347
 Henry.......................347
 John........................160
 Joshary.....................108
 Peleg.......................347
 Peter.......................347
 Philip......................215
 Richard.....................347
 Samuel......................347
 Silas.......................108
Meacham (Mecham)
 Ebenezer....................107
 Jacob.......................362
 Simeon......................117
Mead (Meadd, Meed)
 Amos........................172
 Cary........................317
 Jacob.......................243
 James 8, 251, 294, 295, 372, 373
 Philip......................243
 Timothy.................243, 361
 Timothy, Jr.............243, 325
 Truman.................243, 361
Mecham, see Meacham
Medway
 roads and bridges..........378–79
Meech, Elisha..................362

Meed, *see* Mead
Meetinghouse.................335–36
Mendon, *see* Medway
Menter, Felix...................361
Merrifield, Abraham............339
Merrill (Merril)
   F. F.......................187
   John......................202
Merrit, John...................202
   Michael...................329
Mery, Ebenezer................296
Messer, Samuel................145
Middlebook (Middelbook)
   Stephen...................148
   Stephen, Jr................148
Middlebury............3, 125, 342
   roads and/or bridges.....230, 300–1
Middlebury River..............300
Middlesex.....................201
Middletown, Conn.............131
Middletown Springs
   incorporation.............253
Mighell, Ezekiel...............320
Miles, Oliver..................108
Militia...12, 27–28, 32, 63–65, 138–39
Mill Brook....................306
Mills 86, 139–40, 149, 228, 251, 333,
                  366–67
Miller (Millar)
   Alexander.................203
   Calvin....................320
   Christian..................202
   Hosea.....................186
   Isaac, Jr............99, 100, 307
   James.................10, 287
   John......................10
   Marshal...................307
   Richard...................221
   Robert................10, 202
   Solomon, Jr...............320
   Vespalian.................307
   William................17, 121
Millin, William................26
Millington, John...............347
Mills, George..................143
   George, Jr.................143
   Samuel...................339
Milton
   roads and bridges...........376

Minor, Abner..................202
   Richard...................317
   Samuel...................202
"Minute Men"
   Newbury................211–12
Mitchell (Mitchel)
   Berʰ......................4
   David.....................50
Mix, Amos....................289
   Josiah.....................34
Moffat, Judah.................357
Money, John...................37
Money, *see* Currency
Monkton
   roads and bridges...........284
Montagiu, Adonijah............143
Montgomery (Mountgomery)
   Henry.....................10
   Hugh..................10, 287
   Richard [American general]....259
   Robert....................10
Montgomery....................215
Montreal, P. Q.............182, 336
Moore (Moor)
   Abner....................280
   Ephraim...............202, 355
   James.....................202
   John......................202
   Judah.....................221
   Tilley.....................281
   William...................387
   William, Jr................387
Mooretown....................394
   grant of opposed by settlers....22–23
   population.................23
Moredock, *see* Murdock
Moretown.....................22
Morey, Israel.............274, 275
Morgan, Benjamin.........221, 297
   Cornelius.................201
   Isaca [Isaac]..............25
   Nathan...................25
   Nathaniel.................221
   Reuben...................221
Moriethy, Isaac...............34
Morison, James...............31
   James, Jr..................31
   John......................37
   John, Jr...................37
   Samuel...................37

Morison (*cont.*)
  Thomas....................31
Morrel, Abner.................202
  Abraham....................202
  Jeremiah...................202
  Serjant....................202
Morris, Uriah............205, 207
Morse (Morss)
  Artemas....................218
  John..................172, 173
  Moody......................202
  Moses......................220
  Nathaniel...................24
  Seth.......................354
Morsman, Oliver...............123
  Timothy....................123
Morss, *see* Morse
Mosely (Mosley)
  Increase...............78, 254
  John.......................108
Moss, Ebenezer................160
  Timothy....................289
Mott, John....................258
Moultheroup, Jude.............294
Mount Indepence................87
Mountgomery, *see* Montgomery.
Moxley, Seth..................282
  Thomas.....................282
Mudge, John...................355
Munro, Joshua.................347
Munson, Jered.................243
  Thaddeus..............299, 300
  Thado......................243
Murdock (Moredock, Murdoc)
  Eli.........................31
  James......................331
  John........................31
  Samuel......................31
  Thomas.....................393
Murry, Joseph.................361
Myas, Hezekiah................205
Myers (Myre)
  Oliver.....................205
  Simon......................373
Myrifield, Mass., *see* Rowe, Mass.

              N

Nash, Enos.....................50
  Ephraim...............140, 141
  Josiah.....................50

Nash (*cont.*)
  Samuel.....................202
  Timothy....................202
Naturalization............186–87
Ned, Reuben...................357
Neilson, William..............203
Nelson, Charles...........57, 136
  John........................20
  Nathan.....................364
Neshobee......................342
  See also Brandon
"New City," *see* Lansingburgh,
  N. Y.
New Hampshire
  ferries to.........29–30, 227
  union of certain towns with
    Vermont..................104
New Hampshire Grants
  confirmation sought....126, 266
  debt............126, 266, 358
  proprietors meet under N. H.
    law....................274–75
  represented in New York pro-
    vincial congress...394–96, 396–97
  See also several entries under
    New York
New Haven.....................125
  justice of the peace.......304
  roads and bridges......196–97
New Haven, Conn................13
New Haven Falls...............352
New Milford, Conn.............343
New trials 8, 47–48, 60–61, 84, 100–1,
    112–14, 144–45, 154–55, 205–7,
                        330, 340–41
New York
  adherents
    Brattleboro.......69, 91–92
    Halifax..........6, 28–29
    Marlboro.........121–22
    pardon of.........178–79
    Putney............120
  currency in New Hampshire
    grants.........126, 139, 266
  ferry to....................87
  jurisdiction in New Hampshire
    Grants........46, 120, 159
  laws inapplicable in N. H.
    grants.................274–75

New York (*cont.*)
  New Hampshire Grants dispute
                45–46, 120, 341–42
  provincial congress...394–96, 396–97
  union with Vt. sought by certain
      towns of.....30–31, 33–34, 36–37
  Vermont adherent in Pittstown....88
  Vermont relations: roads.....337–38
New York, N. Y.....120, 394–95, 396
Newbury 384, 386, 390, 391, 392, 393,
      395, 396, 397, 398, 399, 400, 401
  county town................201–3
  "Minute Men"..............211–12
  roads and/or bridges.......213, 398
Newburyport, [Mass.]...........250
Newcomb, Simon................387
Newfane
  county town (also proposed) 116–17,
      133–35, 208–9, 218–19, 219, 221
  counterfeit bills at.........172–73
  roads....................186, 285
Newell (Newel)
  Hiram...................117, 357
  Jared.......................117
  Jesse........................85
  Levi.......................357
  Lewis.......................117
  Philip..................117, 356
Newport......................261
Newton, Jason................254
  Jonas.......................169
  Nathaniel...................243
Nichols, Asaph............359, 360
  Benjamin...................357
  James......................375
  Jonathan...............357, 387
  Thomas.....................357
Nicklson, John................31
Niels, David..................56
Niles (Nills, Nils)
  Eliphalet...................107
  Erastus.....................294
  John........................108
  John, Jr....................108
Nims, James..................357
Noble (Nobel)
  James......................265
  Tihan.......................20
Norris, Benjamin..............202
  David......................202

Norris (*cont.*)
  David, Jr...................202
  Mark.......................202
North Hero...................268
Northampton, Mass.
  Vermonter rescued at.........92
Northway, George.............294
Norton, Joseph...............303
  Shadrach...................317
Norwich 130, 134, 136, 138, 163, 318,
                    382, 383, 388
  roads and/or bridges 155, 353–54, 386
Nott, Epaphras...............289
Noyce (Noys)
  Gorham [Gersham]............92
  John........................92
Nutting, Abel................303
  John...................137, 138

O

Odel, Jacob..............243, 361
Olcott, Bulkley...............50
  Timothy....................96
Olin, ———...............42, 61
  Gideon.....................174
  Jestin.....................347
  John.......................347
Oliott, Elias.................38
Olmsted, Jabez...............364
Ompompanoosuc River.......353, 386
Onion River 181, 211, 213, 333, 348,
                    380, 398
Orange County............48, 390
  county town...............200–3
  grammar school.............374
  justice of peace...........150–53
  lines and new lines....82–83, 200–3,
                    389–90
  roads...................349, 364
  sheriff....................368–69
Orcutt, James.................34
Orlins......................215
Ormsby (Ormsbee)
  ——— [Major]..............126
  Daniel.....................243
  Ezra.......................96
  Gideon.........119, 243, 331, 361
  Jonathan...................243
Orr, Isaac....................6
  James......................203

Orr (*cont.*)
John............................202
Orsborn, *see* Osborn
Orton, Gideon..................347
   Ichabod.......................347
Orwell................292, 293, 329
   ferry...........................87
   roads........................301–2
Osborn (Orsborn, Osburn)
   Asa...........................289
   Elijah..........................77
   Samuel........................202
Osgood (Ozgood)
   Abner..150, 151, 152, 153, 196, 201
   Jeremiah......................317
Oterson, Joseph.................287
Ottauquechee River..30, 155, 227, 228,
                231, 380
Otter Creek 124, 177, 214, 215, 269,
    294, 296, 305, 311, 319, 352,
              365, 366, 385
Owen, Caleb..................29, 92
   John..........................376
   Silvenes......................354
   Thades.......................376
Ozgood, *see* Osgood

P

Packard, Levi...................221
Padock, Thomas.................108
Page, Abraham..................387
   Chrisor........................31
   Jonathan.......................16
   John..........................201
   Josiah........................202
   Peter..........................67
   Samuel...................201, 355
   Silas.........................313
Paine (Pain)
   Abel..........................108
   Elijah..............180, 181, 220
Painter, Gamaliel......300, 345, 375
[Pair . . .], William.............34
Palmer (Palmar)
   David..........119, 199, 311, 313
   Ezekiel.......................108
   George.........................99
   Humphry......................208
   James....................311, 313
   Jareb........................296

Palmer (Palmar) (*cont.*)
   Thaddeus......................317
   Thomas.......................202
Pamele, *see* Parmele
Pangborn, Samuel................215
Panton........................342
   part of Ferrisburg to (pro-
     posed)........124, 214–16, 305–6
   roads and bridges..........330–31
   town lines fixed............153–54
Pardons.............68–69, 372–73
Parish, William..................243
Parker, Benjamin............98, 313
   Elijah.........................96
   George....................54, 108
   Jonathan.......................98
   Jonathan, Jr...................254
   Josiah........................201
   Nathaniel......................34
   Peter.........................108
   Timothy.......................10
Parkhill, David..................317
Parkhurst (Perkhurst)
   Amos.........................357
   Calvin....................25, 326
   Ebenezer......................25
   Jabez.........................25
   Jonathan......................303
   Joseph........................25
   Perly.........................303
   Phinehas......................25
   Pilleg.........................25
   William.......................357
   William, Jr....................356
Parkins, *see* Perkins
Parmele (Pamele, Parmle)
   James.........................117
   Jeremiah......................221
   John..........................117
Parmetr, Joseph..................39
Parmle, *see* Parmele
Parsivel, Stephen................138
Partridge (Patridg)
   Jonathan.................311, 313
Patrick, Joseph..................389
Pattee, John....................202
   William.......................201
Patterson (Potison)
   Alexander......................31
   Andrew........................10

Patterson (Potison) (*cont.*)
David...........................31
Ezra...........................31
Jacob...........................31
James.....................10, 287
John.................10, 31, 287
Levi...........................31
Zachariah......................34
Paul (Paull)
James..........................289
John...........................98
Pawlet..........10, 154–55, 222, 237
churches....................142–43
grievances..................232–34
loyalists at...................53
tax abatement..............323–24
Pay, *see* Wages
Paymaster..................36, 74–75
Peacham.....................89–90
population.....................79
roads.........................213
tax abatement................79–80
Pearl, ——— [Lt. Colonel].......64
John..........................372
Stephen.......................143
Pearson (Peirson)
———...........................4
Moses.............138, 139, 354
Peck, Enos....................304
Isaac....................158, 159
Joseph........................208
Samuel..........128, 149, 150
Peese, Joseph.................229
Peirce, James.................357
John..........................221
Thomas........................67
Peirson, *see* Pearson
Peray, Moses..................361
Perkhurst, *see* Parkhurst
Perkins (Parkins)
Charles..................194, 321
John....................107, 205
Perrigo, David................67
John..........................67
Rufus.........................67
Perry, Abner, Jr.............117
Daniel........................294
Eli..........................117
Joshua........................294
Nathan........................294

Perry (*cont.*)
Ozias.........................296
Stephen.......................357
William.......................103
Peru, *see* Brumley
Peters, Andrew................202
Joseph........................37
Peterson, Joseph..............31
Pettibone (Petibone, Pettebone,
    Pettebones)
Abel..........................242
Eli...........................209
Elihu.........................64
Samuel........................242
Seth..........................242
Peyton, John..................34
Phelps, Amos..................294
Charles.....50, 93, 121, 122, 123
George........................235
Hezeki........................125
Ira...........................125
Isaac...................339, 347
Thomas........................235
Timothy.......................92
Philadelphia
roads and bridges..........364–65
Phillips (Philips, Phelleps)
Daniel........................108
Elijah........................92
Elisha........................204
Job...........................108
Jonathan......................123
Samuel........................347
Phitleplace, Resolved.........161
Physicians.........150–52, 298, 333
See also Doctors, use of title
Piermont, N. H................22
Pinneo, Daniel................282
Pipkin, Stephen...............34
Pitcher, Ebⁿ........98
Ebenezer......................254
Ebenezer, Jr..................99
Reuben........................98
Pittsfield....................365
Pittsford...........80, 342, 364, 365
farm rental and value......257–58
fire at..................321, 378
garrison at...........59, 257–58
grievances.................248–50
New Hampshire Grants expense.266

Pittsford (*cont.*)
poor, care of.................377
roads...............349, 364
troops at...............72
Pittstown, N. Y.
Vermont adherent in...........88
Place (Places)
David...................199
Nathan............198, 311, 313
Samuel.........118, 199, 311, 313
Plainfield, N. H...........84, 100-1
Plat, Daniel.................99
Plicker, Silas................34
Plumb, Joseph............311, 313
Plymouth, *see* Saltash
Pocock
justice of the peace...........304
Pomeroy, Ethan...............49
Pomfret....................10
churches...............173-74
provisions supplied by.........127
tax abatement.........68, 126-28
Poor
care of 26, 61-62, 146-47, 235, 235-
36, 311, 312, 377
Population
Bethel...................165
Brumley....................9
Mooretown................23
Shrewsbury................28
Thomlinson................316
Winhall....................9
Porter, ——— [Sheriff].........122
Ezekiel...............254, 294
John....................339
Joseph.................294, 357
Moses.................143, 323
Thomas........75, 148, 325, 343
Post, Elias.................294
Roswell...........294, 295, 317
Simeon...................294
William...................294
Post riders
Addison county..........344-45
Bennington to Rutland.........344
Postmaster General............345
Potison, *see* Patterson
Potter, Abel.................108
Amos................205, 297

Potter (*cont.*)
Andrew....................23
George.....................5
John....................204
Joseph.................5, 108
Nicholas..............5, 205
Noel....................281
Oliver...................336
Poughkeepsie, N. Y..............92
Poultney............170, 171, 288
church...................319
Powell (Powel)
———...................42
Felix....................331
John.....................25
Martin........53, 60, 126, 243, 279
Truman...................242
Powers, Andrew................282
Benjamin.................259
Blanchard..................281
David....................87
Jerahmeel.................281
Jerathon..................375
Jonathan..................313
Martin...................248
Moses.....................34
Samuel...................203
Stephen...................202
William....................34
Pownal...............20, 77, 110
roads and/or bridges...5, 54-55, 67,
203-5
tax abatement................297
Pratt (Prat)
Abel.....................67
Asa........185, 224, 272, 291, 292
Caleb................198, 254
Nathan...................294
Silas.....................67
William............67, 281, 285
Pray, Elijah.................384
Prentice (Prentiss)
James Otis.................355
Nathaniel S.................42
Simeon...................347
Thomas...................303
Preston, Colburn............10, 377
Ebenezer.................339
Price, Ebor.................125

Prices and Values
    apple orchard 258
    barn 258
    board and room 146
    candles 146
    care of sick 62, 146, 235
    carting 131
    farm house 258
    farm rent 257–58
    fences 258
    ferry maintenance 30
    funeral 146
    gun 11
    horse hire and keep 3, 21
    iron, slitting 149
    land 55, 106, 363
    maple trees 258
    per diem and mileage 12, 131
    provisions for troops 127
    soldier's equipment . 136, 182, 263–64
    wheat 306
    wood 146
    wood lot 258
Priest, James 355
    James, Jr. 355
    Joshua 70, 119, 254
    Moses 355
    Nathaniel 355
Prince, Job 37
Prindle (Prindel)
    Alexander 242
    Jonathan 143
Printing, state
    right to do 392–94
Promotion schemes
    for a town and a city 124–25
Proprietors
    absentee 86, 105–6, 138, 148, 177,
        186, 193, 194, 195, 212, 213, 234,
        306, 307, 328, 336, 351, 363–64,
        365, 380, 386, 387
    confirmation of acts of 274–75
    dissolution of 327
    division of undivided lands . . . 268–69
    grievances: survey and tax 132
    meetings 50–51, 118, 147
    "men of fortune" 173
    promotion schemes 124–25
    rights, sale of 13–14

Proprietors (cont.)
    settling requirements 261–62
    taxes on lands of 10, 63
      See also Land taxes
    taxes voted by . . . 129, 196, 270, 284,
                    366, 384–85
    towns' lines agreement 153–54
Prosen, John 108
Prostitute 120
Prouty, Richard 140
Provision taxes, see Taxes
Pullen, Nicholas 208
Pulsifer (Pulsipher)
    David 39
    Ebenezer 39
    John 10, 39
    Richard 202
Purdy, Benjamin 242
    Benjamin, Jr 243
    Daniel 242
    David 242
    Reuben 242
Putnam, Asa 175, 176
    Miles 316
    Uzziel 357
Putney 170, 177
    counterfeit bill at 182–83
    county grammar school (pro-
        posed) 323
    county town (proposed) . 218–29, 219
    land case 119–21, 156–58, 308–10
    tax collection 97

Q

Quebec, P. Q 81–82, 136, 182, 259

R

Rabyon, Bala 219
Ramage, James 31
Ramsdell (Ramsdel, Ramsdil)
    John 117, 294, 356
    John, Jr 117, 357
    Robert 356
Ramond, see Raymond
Randall (Randol)
    Ichabod 313
    John 320, 382
    Joseph 99, 320

Randolph.......................131
  county change..............82–83
  town lines, maintenance of.....135
Rankin, John...................203
Ranney, Daniel............336, 350
  Waitstill....................336
Ranolds, see Reynolds
Rasey, Joseph, Jr................219
Ray, William..............311, 312
Raymond (Ramond)
  Joshua.......................242
  Samuel.......................108
Razey, Joseph...................219
Read (Reed)
  Daniel....................20, 294
  George.......................208
  Issachus.....................294
  Jonathan 98
  Josiah.........................10
  Leonard...........199, 311, 313
  Margaret.....................237
  Philip..................143, 237
  Silas........................143
Reading........................104
  roads and bridges..........306–7
Readsboro
  roads and/or bridges.....63, 373–74
  vendues authorized.............9
Rebellions, see New York, ad-
    herents; Riots
Reforms (proposed)....102–4, 189–92,
    216–18, 225–26, 232–34, 238–40,
    244–48, 248–50, 262–63, 279–81
Religious liberty, see Church and
    state
Religious societies, see Churches
Reminton, Zadock..............278
Representatives
  qualification of............26, 388
Revolutionary War
  ammunition procurement.......395
  cost of equipping troops.....263–64
  cost of supplies..............44
  engagements 3, 4, 51, 81, 136, 182,
                317–18, 382
  equipment......7, 82, 130, 136, 182
  Indian raids 24, 141
  invasion.....................64
  invasion feared.............21–22
  medical care 298

Revolutionary War (cont.)
  "Minute Men".............211–12
  payment of troops 74–75
  pension 382–83
  provision procurement...43–44, 127,
                100–1, 210–11
  rangers corps..........11, 185, 291
  "scorched earth" policy ..15–16
  seizure of private property...64, 210
  services and/or losses in 3, 4, 7, 10–11,
    12–13, 15–16, 21–22, 24–25, 35–
    36, 51, 52, 57–58, 59, 72, 72–73,
    73–74, 81–82, 90–91, 93–94,
    130–31, 136, 181–82, 185, 211–
    12, 224, 251–52, 257–58, 259,
    263–64, 271–72, 291–92, 298,
    317–18, 336–37, 342, 371–72,
            379–80, 382–83, 394
Reynolds (Ranolds, Reynold)
  Caleb..............54, 67, 107
  Daniel.................199, 254
  Ephraim................53, 361
  Ephraim, Jr...............361
  John......................37
  Jonathan..................67
  Philip................242, 243
  Silas....................361
Rhoads (Rodes)
  Hezekiah..................320
  John.....................281
  Joseph...................307
Rhode Island................40
Rice, Abel.....185, 224, 272, 291, 292
  Barzillai..................310
  David......................31
  Ebenezer..................363
  John.....................357
  Levi......................296
  Moses 338
  Nathan...........119, 311, 313
  Olney....................313
  Samuel.................90, 91
  Silas....................303
  Stephen..................296
  Thomas..........118, 198, 313
  Thomas, Jr.. 199
Rich, Henry.................202
  John..........152, 153, 201
  John, Jr...................201

Richards, Charles.................39
   Charles, Jr....................39
   Daniel........................39
Richardson, A..................242
   Amos.........................361
   Andrew...............242, 361
   Frans........................156
   Jeremiah.....................155
   John.........................242
   Nathan...............242, 361
   Nathan, Jr...........242, 361
   Nehemiah.....................347
   Thomas.......................282
   Wells........................361
Richmond, Ebenezer.............179
Rider, Joseph..................357
   Peter........................282
   Peter, Jr....................282
   Stephen......................203
   William......................203
Right, *see* Wright
Riots
   Brattleboro, etc...........91–92
   Halifax........................6
   Leicester....................375
   Rutland......................372
   Rutland County...............329
   Salisbury....................375
   Wilmington 26
Ripner, John...................285
Ripper, John...................281
Risden, Josiah..................20
Risley, Benjamin...............294
Rix, Daniel.....................24
   Garner........................25
   Joseph-Johnson................24
Roads
   Albany, N. Y. to Williamstown,
     Mass......................204
   [Bennington?] to Albany, N. Y...337
   Bennington to Connecticut
     River..................285–86
   Bennington to Wilmington....8, 161
   Brattleboro to Newfane........186
   Cabot to Cambridge............213
   Cavendish to Woodstock........306
   Chester to Ludlow.............167
   Dartmouth College to Rutland
     and Clarendon.............380
   Dorset to Addison County......296

Roads (*cont.*)
   Dorset to Clarendon...........296
   Hartland to Hartford..........228
   Hartland to Norwich...........155
   Kent and Andover to Manchester. 10
   Leicester or Brandon to
     Rochester.................365
   Littleton, N. H. to Onion River..213
   Londonderry to Manchester.....199
   Ludlow to Otter Creek.........366
   Manchester to Chester.........267
   Manchester to Connecticut River 285
   Myrifield [Rowe], Mass. to
     Bennington..............62–63
   Myrifield [Rowe], Mass. to
     Wilmington. 85–86
   Newbury to Cabot..............213
   Newbury to Greensboro.........213
   Newbury to Onion River........398
   Pittsford to Chittenden.......349
   Pittsford to White River......364
   Pownal to Albany, N. Y..........5
   Pownal to Williamstown, Mass... 54
   Rutland to Castleton........98, 99
   Rutland to Orange County. . 349, 364
   Rutland to Rockingham.........167
   Salisbury, Middlebury and
     Cornwall to Lake Champlain. . 230
   Saltash across Green Mountains.. 355
   Somerset to Bennington........338
   Stamford to Bennington......161–62
   Thetford to Norwich...........386
   Townshend to Manchester......199
   Wardsboro to Manchester.......199
   Whitingham to Bennington....85–86
   Williamstown to Connecticut
     River..................181–82
   Williamstown to Lake
     Champlain.................181
   Wilmington to Newfane.........285
   Windsor to Kingston...........365
   Windsor to Onion River...181, 374
   Windsor to Saltash............306
   Windsor to White River and
     Onion River...............380
   Windsor County to Orange
     County....................353
   Woodstock to Rutland 12, 86–87, 177
   See also entries under the several
     towns

Roaring Branch................209
Robbinson (Robenson), *see*
    Robinson
Roberts (Robad, Robards, Robarts,
    Roberds, Robets)
    Christopher.............61, 242
    David.................254, 284
    Eli........................197
    Giles..................291, 292
    Jeduthan..........224, 272, 291
    John.......................242
    John, Jr....................242
    Lemuel.....................254
    Purchase...................254
    Seth.......................117
    William.................98, 192
Robertson, Archd...............37
    John.......................202
Robins, William................219
Robinson (Robbinson, Robenson,
    Robisson)
    Amos....30, 118, 198, 228, 254, 282
    Artemas....................282
    Asa........................170
    Ichabod.................56, 98
    Israel..................118, 198
    James......................96
    Jonathan...............172, 338
    Moses................15, 20, 23
    Samuel.....15, 36, 72, 108, 338, 373
    Stephen...........118, 199, 254
Rochester..................131, 365
    roads......................365
    town lines, maintenance of 116, 163–64
Rockingham............9, 38, 205–7
    roads and/or bridges.....105–6, 167
    tax abatement...........184–85
Rockwell, John.................317
Rockwood, Reuben......160, 168, 169
Rodes, *see* Rhoads
Rogers (Rodgers, Ruger)
    Artemas....................361
    Frederick..................361
    Gideon.....................215
    James, Jr...................10
    Paul.......................202
    Samuel.....................138
    Timothy 124, 125, 148, 215, 290, 371
Rollo, Walter...................37
Rondart, Joseph.................28

Rosbrook, *see* Rosebrooks
Rose, Abraham..................242
    Ara.............242, 325, 326
    Benjamin...................200
    Joel...................159, 242
    John.......................281
    Joseph.................200, 283
    Joshua.....................242
    Nathaniel..................283
    Samuel.................158, 159
    Samuel, Jr.................159
    Sarah......................242
Rosebrooks (Rosbrook)
    Eleazer................151, 201
Ross, Artemas..................337
Round, George.................118
    James.........118, 199, 311, 313
    Nathan.................311, 313
    William................311, 313
Roundy (Rowndy)
    John...................39, 184
    Uriah......................39
Row, Isaac.....................34
Rowe, Mass.............62–63, 85
Rowley (Rowle, Rowlee)
    Aaron......................148
    Jonathan................59, 257
Rowndy, *see* Roundy
Roy, Gideon....................357
Royalton..........104, 131, 164, 165
    bridge lottery.............326
    burning of.............24, 76
    roads and bridges.........326–27
    scouting party raised...........22
    town lines, maintenance of...109–10
Royce (Roys)
    Jonathan...................67
    Samuel.................125, 215
Ruback, Jacob..................298
Rudd (Rude)
    Bezaleel...................197
    Rufus..................76, 77
    Sarah......................25
Ruger, *see* Rogers
Rugg, John.....................17
Rumrill, Henry.................108
    Simon......................108
Rumsey, Jeremiah...............351
    John.......................351
    Nathan.....................351

Runnels, Jeremiah 125, 148
Rupert 20, 88–89, 110, 276
   roads 193
Rurner, Peter 37
Russ, Nathan 108
Russell, Abel 364
   Amasa 208
Rust, Lemuel 282
   Nial 155, 282
   Phinehas 282
Rutland 3, 8, 77, 80, 162, 171, 188,
   237, 256, 257, 259, 260, 261,
   263, 264, 265, 267, 268, 269,
   270, 272, 273, 275, 276, 277,
                  279, 342
   churches 293–95, 322
   county town 98–99, 288, 289, 292–93,
                       329
   division into two societies (also
     opposed) 293–95, 322
   grievances 189–92
   militia company at 36
   New Hampshire Grants
     debt 266–67, 358–59
   post rider 344
   riots 372
   roads 12, 86, 98, 99, 167, 177, 349,
                   364, 380
   saw mill 251–52
   topography 98, 293
Rutland County 70, 112–13, 154, 162,
              254, 358, 372
   conventions 281, 292, 329
   county town, location of 287–88, 288,
           288–89, 292–93, 328–29
   court house, location of 98–99
   grammar school 277–78
   grievances 279–81
   immigration 289
   lines 82
   riots 329
Ryegate
   roads and/or bridges 212, 212–13
   tax abatement 81

S

Sabin, Daniel 323
   Noah 38, 170, 177
   Noah, Jr. 158
Sacket, John 294

Saeton, George 361
Safford, ——— 141, 162
   ——— [Captain] 258
   ——— [General] 63
   ——— [Major] 86
   Abraham 199
   Jesse 103, 381
   Jonathan 6
   Joseph 108
   Josiah 143
   Philip 39
   Samuel 161, 211, 266
St. Clair, John 202
St. Johns, Fort 91
Salem
   settling requirements 261–62
Salisbury
   disputes over lines 374–76
   roads and/or bridges 230, 300–1
Sallisbury (Salsbery, Salsbury)
   ——— [Captain] 4
   Abraham 98, 311, 313
   Ezekiel 311, 313
   Gardner 311, 313
   James 208
   Samuel 287
Saltash
   roads and/or bridges 306, 355–56
Samson, Daniel 317
   Eliphalet 317
   George 108
   William 317
Sanders, John 202
Sandgate 110, 279, 343
Sandres, Benjamin, Jr. 108
Sargeant (Sargants, Sargeants,
    Sargents, Sergants, Sergeant,
    Serjeant)
   ——— 61
   Amos 10, 96
   Ezra 96
   Jabez 10
   Jabez, Jr. 96, 336, 350
   John 223
   Lemuel 10
   Moses 294
   William 120, 121, 156, 158, 308, 310
Sauier, *see* Sawyer
Saven, Jonas 31
Sawer, *see* Sawyer

Sawtell, John.................29
Sawyer (Sauier, Sawer, Soyer)
  Abraham....................34
  David......................34
  Diah.......................34
  Ephraim.........98, 281, 311, 313
  Jacob......................355
  John........................98
  Josiah...........98, 281, 313
  Moses......................34
  Paul.......................355
  Thomas 3, 4, 280, 285, 375, 379, 380
  Thomas, Jr.................387
Saxton (Sexton)
  Aaron..............242, 361
  Frederick..................376
  George.....................242
  Jonathan......60, 148, 215, 242, 290
Saxtons River..................229
Scales, John..............80, 202
Schaghticoke, N. Y.............337
Schoff, Daniel................202
  Jacob......................202
  Jacob, Jr..................202
Schools, see Education
Schovell, Daniel..............254
Scoot, Elijah..................31
Scott (Soct)
  Aaron................144, 317
  Amos.......................20
  Amos, Jr...................20
  Hezekiah...................20
  Jnº........................37
  John.................398, 399
  Jonathan...................108
  Oliver.....................20
  Peter......................37
Seamans, Charles........199, 254
  John.......................118
  John, Jr...................254
Sears, Ebenezer.........286, 357
  William....................357
Seaver (Sever)
  Comfort...............25, 326
Seely (Seelye)
  Ebenezer..............37, 205
  Nathaniel.............54, 67
Seelyes Mills..................67
Selfridge, John................37
  Oliver.....................37
  Oliver, Jr.................37

Selleck, John..................351
Sergeant (Sergants, Serjeant), see
  Sargeant
Serles (Serls)
  William....................64
Sessions, John......391, 394, 396, 397
Sevence, Peter...........379, 380
Sever, see Seaver
Sevieni, Peter..................4
Seward (Sewerd)
  Daniel.....................34
  Stephen....................294
Sexton, see Saxton
Shaaff, John...................37
  William....................37
Shafter, James................230
Shaftsbury......85, 110, 112, 335, 345
  county town (proposed).......346
Shapley, Richard...............34
Sharman, see Sherman
Sharon...........104, 163, 164, 165
  scouting party raised........22
Sharp, Abraham.................34
  William....................37
Shaw, Daniel............160, 242
  John................203, 294
Shays' Rebellion
  refugees in Vermont..........339
Shearman (Shearmun), see Sherman
Shelburne
  engagement at..............3, 4
  Loyalist at.................379
Sheldon (Shelden)
  ————....................236
  Caleb......................242
  Joel..................20, 89
  Joseph.....................160
  Josiah.....................242
  Seth.......................143
Sheldon, see Hungerford
Shepard (Sheperd)
  Elisha.....................296
  Jonathan...................296
  Jonathan, Jr...............296
  Ralph......................296
  Simon......................24
Shepardson, John..............208
  Samuel.....................208
  Seth.......................208
  Stephen....................208
  Stephen, Jr................208

Sheriffs
  extension of term..........368–69
  grievances against 189–90, 217, 233, 239–40
  regulation of (proposed) 191, 225–26, 249, 262
Sherman (Sharman, Shearman, Shearmun, Shermon)
  Daniel........................62
  George.......................254
  George, Jr...................254
  Noah...................117, 357
  Paul.........................357
  Prince.......................254
  Prine........................98
  William................199, 254
Sherwin, Chandler..........339, 347
  Jacob..................339, 347
Shire towns, *see* County towns
Shory, Andrew..................34
Shrewsbury
  charter lost...............56–57
  militia....................27–28
  polls and rateable estates........28
  population.....................28
  provision quota................27
Shumway, ————...............141
  John 143, 160, 236, 238, 361, 384
Sibbils, Thomas..................201
Sikes, Ashbel...................20
  Silvanus......................160
  Titus, Jr.....................160
Sill, Elijah B..................160
Simons (Cimmons, Simonds)
  Andrew........................39
  Gardner.......................39
  John..................31, 48, 49
  John, Jr......................361
  William....................10, 39
Simpson, Thomas..........117, 357
Singer, John Hans.............6, 67
Skelly, William................37
Skene (Skeen)
  Philip [Prominent Land Holder and Tory]...............31, 37
Skinner (Skinar, Skiner)
  Amos..................176, 177
  Asher.......................219
  David.........................33
  Samuel.................177, 219

Slade, Abner...................357
  Jacob.......................357
  James.......................356
  William................231, 317
Slafter, John..................354
Slatar (Slatard)
  Isaac.......................208
  John........................208
  Joseph......................208
Slatteray, John................282
Small, Bejuen..................37
Smalley, Francis...............354
Smith (Smithe)
  ————..........................4
  Aaron........................33
  Amasa........................50
  Andrew......................108
  Asa.............119, 311, 312
  Asahel......................265
  Benoni......................143
  Billa.......................120
  Curtis......................281
  Daniel...........20, 284, 347
  Ebenezer....................347
  Eli..........................50
  Elihu 23, 70, 113, 254, 255, 295, 359
  Elijah......................242
  Elnathan...............125, 290
  Enos.........................50
  Ephraim......................50
  Frederick..............368, 369
  George......................242
  Gideon......................202
  Israel.......................20
  J...........................266
  James.......................220
  Joel.........................39
  John 10, 96, 98, 199, 202, 220, 241, 280, 281, 311, 313, 336
  Jonathan....................202
  Joseph.....23, 50, 98, 118, 198, 202
  Joseph, 3rd..................50
  Medad........................17
  Mida........................127
  Nathan.................242, 361
  Nathaniel, Jr................20
  Nehemiah..............28, 56, 99
  Nicolas......................10
  Noah.........................36
  Oliver......................172
  Osial.......................199

Smith (Smithe) (*cont.*)
Pecis.......................160
Phillip, Jr...............317, 318
Phinehas...................17
Pliny......................20
Reuben............108, 242, 256
Samuel............256, 313, 317
Seth.....................69, 71
Silvanus..................313
Solomon...................294
Steel...............107, 256
Stephen.........242, 317, 318
Thomas.....................50
Timothy...................354
William.......20, 28, 89, 98, 302
Willmor....................56
Smithfield
new lines (proposed)....367–68, 371
Snow, Amos.................303
Soct, *see* Scott
Soldiers' Wages, *see* Wages
Somers, Robert.............202
Somerset...................117
roads.............285–86, 338
Soper, Leonard.............242
Moses.....................242
Palatiah..................242
Samuel....................160
Timothy...................242
South Hero.................268
Southgate, Richard.........108
Soyer, *see* Sawyer
Spafford, ———......333, 334, 379
Amos......................302
David................175, 299
John......................299
Solomon...............99, 254
Spalding (Spaldin), *see* Spaulding
Sparhawk, Ebenezer..........50
Spaulding (Spaldin, Spalding)
———......................143
Henry.....................125
Leonard........134, 136, 137, 332
Phinehas, Jr..............125
Timothy...................125
William...................351
Speary, *see* Sperry
Spencer (Spenser)
Abel.................98, 294
Charles...................347

Spencer (Spenser) (*cont.*)
Gideon..........148, 215, 290, 352
Isaac.....................347
Jeremiah...................34
John...............118, 199, 254
Pierce.........119, 199, 311, 313
Sperry (Speary)
David.....................320
Moses.....................242
Spink, Sinake.............347
Spooner, ———...............43
Alden................392, 393
Daniel...............155, 228
Eliakim...................230
John......................219
Paul....156, 187, 188, 394, 396, 397
Spooner's Gore
land grant in.............142
Spoor, Nukins..............34
Sprague (Spragg)
Abraham...................313
Elkanah...................282
Jesse............199, 311, 313
Spring, Amos...............313
John......................34
Nathaniel..................33
Samuel....................316
Springfield, Mass..........130
Squire (Squiea, Squier, Squires)
Daniel...............192, 295
Ezra.........125, 162, 215, 305
John.............280, 311, 313
Josiah.....................34
Nathaniel........125, 215, 305
Odel......................162
Silas.....................347
Stack, Isaac...............10
Stacy, John............117, 357
Philemon...................92
Stamford
roads.............63, 161–62
tax abatement.........171–72
Stanard, David.............205
Stanclift, William.........357
Stark (Starks)
John [American General].....91
John......................143
Starkweathar, Stephen.......143
Starns, *see* Stearns

Starr, Comfort............12, 13, 208
   Comfort, Jr...................208
Stearns (Starns, Stearnes, Sterne)
   Asa.......................303
   Ebenezer...................284
   Elijah.....................357
   John.......................284
   T..........................303
   William....................10
Stebbins (Stebbens)
   David 197, 304
Stedman, Alexander.........384, 385
Steel (Steele)
   Eliphos 362
   John.......................31
   Josiah.....................362
   Thomas..................31, 37
Stephens, see Stevens
Sterne, see Stearns
Stevens (Stephens)
   Daniel..................242, 285
   Deane C....................281
   Elias...........22, 25, 76, 77, 109
   Enos.......................203
   Ephraim.................281, 285
   Isaac......................156
   Joel.......................123
   John....................294, 295
   Nicholas...................202
   Peruda.....................108
   Samuel.....................267
   Simon...................13, 14
   Tesrel.....................123
Stevenson, William...........203
Stewart (Steward, Stuard)
   Alexander....................6
   Claude.....................203
   Elias............98, 199, 311, 312
   James..................203, 294
   John.......................33
   John, Sr...................33
   Oliver..............99, 311, 313
   Samuel.....................304
   Walter.....................203
   William...........198, 311, 313
Stockbridge....................365
Stockwell, Ichabod.............373
Stoddard, Eliakim...............60
   Elijah..................339, 347
   Elijah, Jr.................339

Stoel, Isaac....................39
Stone (Ston)
   Benjamin...................108
   Caleb......................256
   David......................373
   Eleazer....................347
   John.......................96
   Nathan............255, 256, 347
   Nathaniel..................336
   Nathⁿ......................14
   Peter......................373
   Philip.....................234
   Thomas.....................96
   Uriah......................347
   Zedekiah...................256
Storis, Printis................242
Storrs, William.................39
   William, Jr................39
Story, James...................148
   Solomon................281, 285
Stoughton, Nathaniel............58
Stow, Clark....................197
Strafford......................324
   land case................47-48
Straten, John..................294
Stratton
   county change (proposed)....123-24
Strickland, Elijah.............357
   Jonah......................108
   William....................357
Strong, Barnabas 109, 114, 115, 273, 274
   David......................294
   Ezekiel................138, 387
   Henry......................294
   John.........11, 12, 102, 154, 345
Stuard, see Stewart
Sturdivant, Forrist............278
Sudbury
   roads and bridges.........269-70
Sumner (Sumnor)
   Daniel.....................156
   Joel.......................92
   Shubell....................289
   William....................34
Sunderland (Sutharland)
   Peleg.............242, 341, 342
   Samuel.....................242
   Wallis.....................242
Sunderland 110, 333, 339, 340, 345, 348
   militia....................32

Supreme Court 53, 69, 70, 217, 233,
        239, 250, 280, 330, 354, 381
    legislature as...............26–27
Surgeons, *see* Physicians
Surveys
    new 103, 109, 110, 114, 115, 116,
        132, 135, 142, 163–64, 164–65,
            214, 305, 324, 374–76
Sweet, James...................347
Swift, Chipman............195, 221
    Nathan......................221
    Philetus.....................320
    Samuel......................320
"Swing Gates"...................5
Switzerland....................399
Sylvester, Peter................201
Syms (Sym)
    Alexander....................81
    Martha......................65
    William......................65

T

Taggred, Patrick...............287
    Samuel......................287
Tambling, Stephen..............317
Tanner, John....................33
    William......................33
Tariffs, *see* Duties, import
Tatlock, R^d...................125
Taxes
    abatement of 27–28, 58–59, 66–67,
        68, 79–80, 81, 126–28, 128, 137,
        149–50, 171–72, 179–80, 184–85,
        237–38, 240–44, 297, 299–300,
        301, 313–14, 314–15, 316, 320–
            21, 323–24, 332, 383–84
    collection of 78–79, 97, 99–100,
            175–76, 210, 321–22
    collection lost by fire......321, 378
    county........275–76, 318, 400–1
    exemption from................16
    fourfold imposed..............60
    grievances against 103, 132, 217,
                233–34, 240
    multiplication................96
    opposition to collection of.......69
    payment in produce and labor
        (proposed)................392
    postponement of............28–29
    reforms (proposed).....226, 249–50

Taxes (*cont.*)
    relief from................381–82
    surveying.................324–25
    See also Duties, import; Land
        taxes
Taylor, Amos..................108
    Asa........................155
    Elias.......................155
    Ezra....................200, 283
    Gershom....................283
    Gershom, Jr.................200
    Jesse.......................200
    John.............346, 347, 355
    Jonas.......................108
    Jonathan................200, 283
    Moses...................200, 283
    Moses, Jr...................283
    Oliver......................155
    Seth........................283
    Solomon....................364
Techinor, *see* Tichenor
Templeton, John................202
Terril, Josiah...................20
Terry, Josiah...................242
Thacher, Peter.................354
Thayer (Thayr)
    Benoni.....................202
    Joseph............138, 139, 387
    Simon......................373
    Stephen....................117
Thetford......................7
    counterfeit bills at........390–91
    half-shire town............201–3
    proprietors' taxes............129
    roads and bridges.........386–87
Thomlinson...................340
    population.................316
    roads and bridges...........194
    tax abatement.........316, 320–21
Thompson (Thomson)
    Aaron......................357
    Abel...........147, 148, 215, 352
    Amos.......................242
    Hezekiah...................256
    Hezekiah, Jr................256
    John.............33, 56, 143
    Lathrop....................256
    Samuel............221, 287, 373
    William................96, 203
    Willis......................34

Thornton, James. 347
  Levi. 296
Throop, see Troop
Thurber, Barnabas. 357
  David. 208
Thurstin, Thomas. 202
Tichenor (Techinor, Tichener,
  Tichiner, Tichinor)
———. 207
  Isaac. 42, 43, 44, 212, 393
Ticonderoga, Fort
  retreat from. 87, 298
Ticonderoga Landing. 317
Ticonderoga, N. Y.
  ferry to. .87
Tidd, Daniel. 356
Tilden, Charles. 52
Tillotson, Daniel. 50
Tinmouth 112, 144, 166, 175, 222, 257,
            271, 299, 315, 372
  fire at. .252
  grievances. 216–18
  roads. 295–96
  town lines uncertain. 23
Titus, Abel. 198, 281
  Ephraim. 17
  John. 39
Toles, see Tools
Toll bridges. 203–5
Toll Roads. 5
Tolman, Ebenezer. 226
  Thomas. 43, 74, 75, 188
Tools (Toles)
  Clerk. 58
  Henry. 58
Tories, see Loyalists
Torrey (Torey, Torry)
  Ebenezer. 151, 202
  Noah. 320
  Noah, Jr. 320
Torts
  conversion. 145, 340
  detainer. 64
  forcible entry. . .47, 113, 156–57, 308
  fraudulent sale. 139–40
  slander. 154
  trespass. 46, 113
Tower, Joseph. 20, 254
  Nathaniel. 20

Town, Eli. 373
  Elijah. 373
  Jonathan. 50
Town lines
  disputes over. 374–76
  establishment of 19, 23, 48–49, 52–53,
                     89–90, 283
  maintenance of 108–9, 109–10, 114,
      115, 116, 135, 163–64, 164–66
  new. 367–68, 371
Towns
  annexations 124, 214–16, 253–55,
      283, 305–6, 310–12, 312–13
  division of 83–84, 159–60, 293–95,
                   322, 356–58, 391
  location of. 367–68
  settling requirements. 261–62
Townsend, Micah. 140, 223
Townshend. 21, 55, 170, 219
  roads. 199
  tax abatement. 301
Towsley (Towslee)
  Gideon. 204
  William. .20
Tracy, Elijah. 385
Trades
  saddler. 235
Train, John. 198
Transportation, see Ferries; Roads
Treadway, James. 18
Treasurer 3, 13, 21, 128, 149–50, 171,
      172, 176, 179–80, 223, 235, 240,
      252, 274, 277, 300, 301, 314,
                 332, 337, 383–84, 390
  collection of taxes. 78–79
  settlement of accounts. 41–42,
                            332–34, 348
Trescoot, Jeremiah. 24
Trials, new, see New trials
Tripp, Abiel. 254
Troop (Throop)
  John. 11, 12, 35
  Nathaniel. 397
Troy, N. Y. 337
Trussel, Jacob. 203
Tubbs, Adin. 37
  Eneas. 37
Tucker, Joseph. 29, 92, 122
Tuller (Tullar)
  Reuben. 198, 311, 313, 385, 386

Tunbridge...................165
   charter lost..............75–76
   lines, change of..............142
   roads and bridges..........384–85
Tupper, Absalom..............148
   Benjamin.................172
   John....................281
   Zuriel.................148, 290
Turner, John.................197
   Timothy..................197
Tuttle (Tuttill)
   Ezra....................303
   Hezekiah.................362
   Stephen..................242
   Thomas, Jr...............281
Twentymile Stream............167
Twitchel, Joseph 357
Two Heroes
   division of undivided lands .268–69
Tyler, Benjamin................361
   Joseph 134
   Joshua 387
   Moses 387

U

Underhill, Abraham.............160
   Augustin..................53
   Isaac 53, 160
   James...................160
University of Vermont, see Education, state university
Upham, William 303
Upper Cohoss...................19
Utley (Utly)
   Asa.............267, 360, 361
   Elisha...................296
   William.............168, 267
   William, Jr................290

V

Vail, Edward.............62, 226
Vallance, David................383
Values, see Prices and Values
Vandorlendar, see Vanolunder
Vanduzee (Vⁿ Duzee)
   Abraham..................33
   James...................33
Vanduzer, John................40
Vanolunder (Vandorlendar)
   Daniel.............125, 305

Varnum, Ebenezer..............202
Varny, John....................99
Vary, John.............311, 313
Vaughan, Benjamin.........242, 361
   James...................242
Vendues.....................303
   relief from sought............129
Vergennes
   antecedent of............124–25
Vermon, Gideon................296
Vermont
   origins of name..............273
Vernon, see Hinsdale
Vershire.....................335
   surveying tax............324–25
   town lines................324
Vosbourgh, Abram.............205
   Peter....................205
Voting, see Elections, disputes

W

Wade, Leonard.................389
Wadsworth, Jeremiah. 43
Wages
   labor on roads..............306
   legislators............395, 396–97
   soldiers'......22, 136, 182, 224, 272
   soldiers' paid in wheat...........4
Wait (Waight)
   ——— [Colonel]...........57, 74
   Benjamin 131, 136, 182
   Jeremiah 242
   Joseph 202
   Martin...................50
   Nathaniel 202
   Silas...................117
   Thaddeus 117
Walbridge, ———...............321
   ——— [Colonel]...........36, 74
   Ebenezer.................277
Walden (Wald)
   Abiather.............339, 347
Walden 89
Waldo, Beulah 54
Walis, see Wallace
Walker, Ebenezer..............34
   Edward..................117
   Elisha...................351
   Ichabod............199, 311, 313
   Jacob....................98

Walker (*cont.*)
James........................34
Joel........................325
John........................33
Lewis...........70, 118, 199, 254
Timothy..................10, 39
Wallace (Walis, Wallas, Wallie,
    Wallis)
Isaiah.......................205
James..................117, 357
John............107, 117, 357
Na^th 54
Nathaniel...........67, 205, 339
Nehemiah....................205
Richard.....................387
William.....................201
Waller, Asa..................242
Wallie (Wallis), *see* Wallace
Wallingford...................381
  fire........................314
  grievances................238-40
  roads.....................319-20
  tax abatement...........313-14
  town lines uncertain........23
Walloomsac, N. Y..............382
Wallworth, Daniel.............92
Walpole, N. H...............154
Walton, Israel................25
Ward, ———.................143
  John........................254
  Jonathan 37
  William...............134, 347
Warden, Judah................347
  William....................203
Wardsboro....................117
  division of.............356-58
  roads and/or bridges....199, 285-86
Ware, Nathan..................39
Warner (Warnor)
  ——— [Colonel]..........16, 120
  Benjamin...................343
  Benjamin, Jr...............303
  Daniel...............117, 357
  David....34, 119, 199, 281, 311, 313
  James. 37
  John........................338
  Jonathan..................357
  Noadiah....................50
  Reuben 252
  Seth 72, 94, 252, 263, 298, 336, 341, 343

Warren, Fort 64
Warren (Warrin, Worrin)
  Dan 117
  Gideon 341
  Moses..................136, 182
  Stephen...................357
  Thomas...............336, 347
Warriner, Samuel..............223
Washburn (Washborn, Wash-
    bourn, Worshburn)
  Azahel [Azel].............72
  Daniel...............118, 281
  James.....................108
  Stephen...............242, 361
  Tabor.....................361
Washington County, N. H. ...100
Waterman, Daniel..............354
  Elijah....................354
  Elisha....................354
  James..................138, 139
  John........................354
  Samuel....................354
Waterous (Watrous)
  Jabez......................317
  James......................375
Waters, Oliver...91, 92, 122, 140, 141
  Silvanus...................256
Watkins (Watkin)
  Daniel....................219
  David.....................219
  Elias.....................350
  Henry.....................34
  James.....................55
  Sarah...................55, 56
Watrous, *see* Waterous
Watson, Alexander.............201
Weathersfield
  churches..................302-3
  taxes on new settlers.......58-59
Weaver (Wever)
  Jabez..............56, 311, 313
  Nicholas..................347
Webb (Web)
  Jehiel....................106
  Joseph....................303
  Reuben....................361
Webber (Weber)
  Bennedeick [Benedick]....28, 56, 99
Webster (Welstor)
  Abdiel..................20, 289

Webster (Welstor) (*cont.*)
   Benajah.................125, 305
   Benjamin....................214
   Benyar......................148
   Joshua.......................99
   Samuel......................282
Welch, Daniel..................143
Weld, Elias....................232
   John........................306
Welding, John...................75
Weller, Amos....................37
   Nathan.....................296
Wellmon, Reuben................307
Wells (Wels, Wills)
   Austin.......................37
   Daniel.......................37
   Hubbel............6, 29, 252, 328
   James.........99, 198, 311, 313
Wells................289, 359, 360
   bridges...................365–66
Welstor, *see* Webster
Wens, Rufus....................108
Wentworth, Benning [Colonial
   governor of New Hampshire]...56
Wescoot (Wesscot), *see* Westcot
West, Benajah..................183
   David.......................183
   Ebenezer....................325
   Elijah...............183, 184, 256
   Elisha......................183
   Israel.............148, 215, 290
   Mary........................183
West Indies.....................97
West River.......136, 186, 222, 223
Westcot (Wescoot, Wesscot,
   Westcoat, Westcout)
   Ezekiel.....................199
   George..................119, 199
   James.......................199
   Job.....................311, 313
   Oliver..............198, 311, 312
   Zibe........................254
"Western Union" 30–31, 33–34, 36–37,
                  88–89
Weston (Westurn)
   Aaron.......................203
   James.......................357
Westminster 21, 22, 51, 117, 170, 177,
           206, 368, 395
   bridge...................229–30

Westminster (*cont.*)
   church......................391
   county convention.......275–76
   county town.............95, 208
   land case................45–46
Westminster Massacre.........38
Wetherbee (Wetherby)
   David.......................280
   Samuel.......................99
Wetherell (Withrell)
   Samuel................311, 313
Wethersfield, Conn.............131
Wever, *see* Weaver
Wey, John.....................202
Weybridge
   roads and bridges...........264
Whaley, Samuel................347
Whealer, *see* Wheeler
Wheat, Samuel.............182, 183
Wheeler (Whealer, Wheler)
   Amos.......................387
   Asa........167, 197, 304, 355, 389
   Ashbel.................196, 304
   Beriah......................200
   David.......................202
   George......................202
   Isaac.......................221
   John........................296
   Joseph..................54, 297
   Nathan..................160, 347
   Obadiah.....................294
   Samuel......................242
   Truman..................197, 304
   William.................198, 242
   Zolmon......................362
Wheelock, Asa..................117
   Eleazer.....................294
Wheler, *see* Wheeler
Whelpley, Isaac................242
   James.......................351
   Jeremiah....................242
Whetcomb, *see* Whitcomb
Whetstone Brook................139
Whiney, *see* Whitney
Whipple, Benjamin......192, 294, 295
   Daniel...................45, 46
   Ezra........................339
   Mary.....................45, 46

Whitcomb (Whetcomb,
　　Whitecombe, Whittcomb)
　—— [Major]...............251
Asa........................116
Benjamin 185, 224, 272, 291
Nathaniel...................39
Robert.....................339
White (Whit)
Asaph...................62, 63
Coollidge.............311, 313
James......................336
John...............158, 159, 242
Joshua...............281, 285
Josiah......................39
Lemuel........8, 28, 56, 98
Nathaniel.............50, 202
Nicholas...................202
Noah................83, 202
Peter................280, 285
Samuel..........203, 388, 389
Thomas A...................50
Zephaniah..................296
White River 30, 326, 349, 364, 365, 380
Whitecombe, see Whitcomb
Whitelaw, James........202, 212, 213
Whiteside, Thomas..............37
Whitford, Joseph.............205
Whiting, Samuel.............361
Whitingham
roads..............63, 85–86
Whitlock, John...............278
Whitman, Benjamin. 118, 199, 311, 313
Jnᵒ.......................311
Jonathan...................313
Whitmore, Joseph 96
Whitney (Whiney, Witteny)
Aaron......................140
Ebenezer..............200, 283
Elisha....................283
Ephraim 200, 283
Ezra........................39
Ezra, Jr....................39
Hachaliah..................117
Isaac 361
John.......................39
Micah 294
Nathan 92
Oliver.....................312
Silas......23, 98, 112, 113, 114, 330
Solomon 361

Whittcomb, see Whitcomb
Wier, Jnᵒ......................37
Wilde, John..................215
Wilder, Gotham 355
Jacob......................355
R. Wheeler.................355
Wildersburgh
roads and bridges..........391–92
Willard (Willer)
—— [Colonel].............228
Anna [Anne] 15, 16
Benjamin 9, 154, 155
Caleb......................203
Eli........................156
Eliakim....................15
Jonathan..............143, 323
Jonathan, Jr...............143
Josiah 45, 119
Oliver..............117, 156
Oliver, Jr.................155
Samuel.....................143
Solomon 186, 187
Willcocks, Jacob 382
Williams, Abner 311, 313
David 6, 92
David, Jr...................29
Hans 282
Isaac 200, 228
Isaac, Jr..................282
Jabin 34
James......................200
Jesse 87
John..................302, 303
John Chester................50
Joseph 205, 281, 282, 311, 313
Josiah.....................282
Oliver.....................381
Phinehas [Phineas] 11, 12
Samuel 150, 188, 267, 294, 358, 385,
　　　　　　　　　　　　386
Silas..................109, 133
Stephen 359
William 9, 16, 17, 18, 26, 27, 51, 391,
　　　　392, 394, 395, 396
See also Williems; Willims
Williamstown
care of transient at..........146–47
proprietors' meeting..........50–51
roads and/or bridges.......181, 220
university site (proposed as)..180–81

Williamstown, Mass....... 50, 54, 204
Williems, Israel................. 108
　Joseph...................... 108
Willims, Joseph................ 108
Willmarth, Ephraim 347
Willoughby, Bliss 347
　Ebenezer.................... 347
Wills, see Wells
Willson, see Wilson
Wilmington................. 9, 221
　charter conflict............. 26–27
　election dispute............. 16–17
　roads.......... 8, 85, 161, 195, 285
　riot...................... 25–26
Wilmot, Reuben.............. 202
Wilson (Willson)
　Abner...................... 96
　Benjamin................... 120
　Charles..................... 34
　Ebenezer................. 62, 302
　Solomon.................... 96
Wiman, see Wyman
Win, Jacob.................. 125
Winant, Mikega.............. 107
Winchester, N. H............. 119
Windham County 69, 71, 95–96, 120,
　　157–58, 207, 223, 308, 310, 340
　conventions 208, 218, 219, 221, 275–76
　county town, location of.... 116–17,
　　133–35, 208–9, 218–19, 219, 221
　elections.................. 38–39
　grammar school 323
　lines..................... 123–24
　taxes 97, 275–76
　See also Cumberland County
Windsor 11, 75, 82, 180, 182, 185, 186,
　　　　　　　　187, 318
　churches 83–84
　county town.............. 95, 104
　division into two societies..... 83–84
　land, peculiar conveyance of.. 182–83
　Loyalist trial at............. 130
　poor, care of................ 235
　roads and/or bridges 181, 255–56,
　　　　　　306, 365, 380
　tort case.................. 145
Windsor County.. 86, 101, 149, 206–7,
　　　　　　　228, 381
　conventions......... 102–3, 104–5
　county town, location of...... 95–96

Windsor County (cont.)
　grievances................. 102–3
　roads.................. 349, 364
　taxes (also proposed)...... 318, 401
Winhall
　annexation of gore to (pro-
　　posed)................. 93, 283
　population.................... 9
　proprietors' rights.......... 13–14
　roads and/or bridges.. 9–10, 199–200
　town lines uncertain........... 283
Winter (Wintir)
　Benjamin................... 361
　Timothy............... 118, 198
Wiswall, Samuel............. 219
Wit, John.................. 361
Withrell, see Wetherell
Witners, Obadiah.............. 34
Witteny, see Whitney
Wolcott, William............. 278
Wood, Barnard............... 254
　Dudley... 357
　Jonathan 118
　Joseph............. 10, 39, 354
　Nathan 108, 357
　Joshua.......... 21, 251, 301
　Nicklus................... 242
　Stephen.................. 202
Woodard, see Woodward
Woodbridge, Enoch............. 326
　Ruggles.................... 50
　William.................... 196
Woodburn, John........... 10, 287
Woodbury, Conn. 343
Woodcock, Asahel........ 117, 357
　Elkanah.................. 357
Woodford.................. 9, 63
Woodstock................. 7, 12
　county convention at... 102–3, 104–5
　roads and/or bridges .. 86, 177, 306,
　　　　　　　　380–81
Woodward (Woodard)
　Amos.................... 349
　Araunah 278
　Beza 42, 44
　Ebenezer.................. 242
　Elisha................... 361
　Joseph............... 281, 285
　Thomas................... 357
　Timothy 92

Woodworth, William 37
   William, Jr. 37
Woolf, William 294
Worcester, Benjamin.............39
Worrin, *see* Warren
Worshburn, *see* Washburn
Wright (Right, Wrieght, Write)
   Abel........................387
   Asaph 373
   Benjamin, Jr..................282
   Charles 54
   Ebenezer................197, 304
   John.......................387
   Jonathan............33, 158, 159
   Joseph 377
   Josiah......................54
   Peter 347
   Phinehas Rn 282

Wright (Right, Wrieght, Write) (*cont.*)
   Samuel......................243
   Silas........................356
   Simeon......................294
   Solomon 54, 206
Wylie, James...........198, 311, 312
Wyman (Wiman)
   Daniel.....................289
   William.....................218

Y

Yeaw, William.................208
Yewes, David...................98
Young (Yong)
   Ichabod.....................58
   John.......................151
   Thomas.....................273
Youngman, Peter...............202